D1476658

Appraising Residential Properties

Readers of this text may also be interested in the following publications from the Appraisal Institute:

- *The Appraisal of Real Estate,* twelfth edition
- *The Student Handbook to THE APPRAISAL OF REAL ESTATE*
- *The Dictionary of Real Estate Appraisal,* fourth edition
- *Using Residential Appraisal Report Forms: URAR 2005 (Form 1004) and Exterior Inspection (Form 2055)* by Mark R. Rattermann, MAI, SRA
- *Using the Small Residential Income Property Appraisal Report (Fannie Mae Form 1025/Freddie Mac Form 72)* by Mark R. Rattermann, MAI, SRA
- *Using the Individual Condominium Unit Appraisal Report Forms: Fannie Mae Form 1073 and Exterior-Only Form 1075* by Mark Rattermann, MAI, SRA
- *Appraising the Tough Ones: Creative Ways to Value Complex Residential Properties* by Frank E. Harrison, MAI, SRA
- *Market Analysis for Real Estate: Concepts and Applications in Valuation and Highest and Best Use* by Stephen F. Fanning, MAI
- *Scope of Work* by Stephanie Coleman, MAI, SRA

Appraisal Institute®

*Professionals Providing
Real Estate Solutions*

Appraising Residential Properties

FOURTH EDITION

Appraisal Institute • 550 West Van Buren • Chicago, IL 60607 • www.appraisalinstitute.org

Vice President, Development: Larisa Phillips
Director, Publications: Stephanie Shea-Joyce
Senior Technical Writer: Michael McKinley
Book Editor: Mark Boone
Supervisor, Book Design/Production: Michael Landis
Book Production Specialist: Sandra Williams

For Educational Purposes Only

The materials presented in this textbook represent the opinions and views of the developers. Although these materials may have been reviewed by members of the Appraisal Institute, the views and opinions expressed herein are not endorsed or approved by the Appraisal Institute as policy unless adopted by the Board of Directors pursuant to the By-laws of the Appraisal Institute. While substantial care has been taken to provide accurate and current data and information, the Appraisal Institute does not warrant the accuracy or timeliness of the data and information contained herein. Further, any principles and conclusions presented in this textbook are subject to court decisions and to local, state and federal laws and regulations and any revisions of such laws and regulations.

This textbook is sold for educational and informational purposes only with the understanding that the Appraisal Institute is not engaged in rendering legal, accounting or other professional advice or services. Nothing in these materials is to be construed as the offering of such advice or services. If expert advice or services are required, readers are responsible for obtaining such advice or services from appropriate professionals.

Nondiscrimination Policy

The Appraisal Institute advocates equal opportunity and nondiscrimination in the appraisal profession and conducts its activities in accordance with applicable federal, state, and local laws.

Library of Congress Cataloging-in-Publication Data

Appraising residential properties.–4th ed.
    p. cm.
Includes bibliographical references (p.) and index.
ISBN-13: 978-0-922154-92-0
    1. Real property–Valuation–United States. I. Appraisal Institute (U.S.)
HD1387.A685 2006
333.33'82–dc22

2006052005

Table of Contents

Foreword

Since the third edition of *Appraising Residential Properties* was published in 1999, the residential real estate market has climbed to unprecedented heights. Buoyed by historically low interest rates, sales volume and price levels have reached record peaks. At the same time, competition in the mortgage lending market has heated up with the entry of new players. The Internet, automated valuation models (AVMs), and other analytical tools used by lenders have reduced the length of time between loan qualification and closing, which has put pressure on residential appraisers to deliver opinions of value more quickly than ever.

To create this new edition of *Appraising Residential Properties,* the Appraisal Institute has looked back at the significant changes in the profession and forward to the opportunities that the future will present. The new textbook has been significantly updated to reflect recent changes in the Uniform Standards of Professional Appraisal Practice, the 2005 revisions to the residential appraisal report forms, and changes in the real estate market and appraisal practice.

The fourth edition includes new chapters on the use of statistics in real estate appraisal and residential appraisal specialties, new discussion of automated valuation models (AVMs), and a greater emphasis on the scope of work decision in the valuation process. The ANSI/NAHB standard for measuring the size of houses has been included in the text along with basic instructions on the use of financial calculators. Data sources have been updated and expanded and the discussions of residential design and construction have been reorganized and revised significantly.

The fourth edition of *Appraising Residential Properties* was revised and reorganized in light of the required core curriculum of the Appraiser Qualifications Board, which will be implemented in January 2008. Thus, it satisfies the needs of new appraisers with an eye to the future as well as established professionals who seek to expand their businesses. The profession's continued vitality depends on the enthusiasm and innovation of a new generation of appraisers combined with the experience of established practitioners. The fourth edition of *Appraising Residential Properties* reflects the contributions and interests of both groups.

Terry R. Dunkin, MAI, SRA
2007 President
Appraisal Institute

Acknowledgments

The development of the *Appraising Residential Properties,* fourth edition, would not have been possible without the participation of the following members of the textbook development team: Sandy Adomatis, SRA; Michael Christensen, SRA; Kathy Coon, SRA; Winfield Cooper, SRA; Larry Disney, SRA; Mark Freitag, SRA; Louis Garone, SRA; Diane Gilbert, MAI, SRA; Vickie Gill, SRA; Cheryl Kunzler, SRA; Frank Lucco, SRA; John Maggi, SRA; Karen Mann, SRA; Mark Rattermann, MAI, SRA; Sara Schwartzentraub, SRA; Alan Simmons, SRA; George Sparks, SRA; and the chair of the Publications Review Panel, Richard Marchitelli, MAI. In addition to reviewing chapters of the textbook, the members of the development team directed the revision efforts of the technical writer and content consultants. Margaret Hambleton, SRA; James Vernor, MAI; and Danny Wiley, SRA, also participated in early planning efforts related to the revision of the textbook.

Other reviewers of specific sections of the textbook included Michael W. Casey, past president of the American Society of Home Inspectors; Stephanie Coleman, MAI, SRA, director of screening of the Appraisal Institute; Rich Heyn, SRA; Mark R. Linné, MAI; and Kenneth M. Lusht, MAI, SRA.

In addition, the following were involved in the development of the content of the textbook: Jim Amorin, MAI, SRA—market area maps from Site To Do Business; Richard L. Borges, MAI, SRA—manufactured housing; Andrew Brorsen, MAI, SRA—houses on ranches and farms; John Cirincione, SRA—electronic data standards; Claudia Gaglione, Gaglione & Dolan—appraiser liability in property inspection; Richard E. Polton, MAI—affordable housing; Judith Reynolds, MAI—historic houses; and Marvin L. Wolverton, MAI—statistics in appraisal.

Also, FloodSource provided a flood map, MLS of Northern Illinois, Inc., provided screen shots of MLS database searches, and the National Association of Home Builders Research Center provided information on the national standard (ANSI Z765-2003) for measuring the size of single-family residential buildings. The staff of the Y.T. and Louise Lee Lum Library at the Appraisal Institute provided research assistance and the Starbucks at 550 W. Van Buren provided coffee.

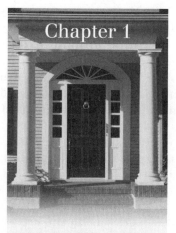

Chapter 1

Introduction to Residential Appraisal

Owning a home has always been an essential ingredient of the American Dream—part of the required trio of "food, clothing, and shelter." A home is the single largest financial investment most people will ever make, and the residential real estate appraiser plays an essential, but often unacknowledged, role in facilitating that investment.

Homebuyers have many reasons for investing in a home, which may be as diverse as the people making the purchases. Some people buy homes so that they can establish and raise a family. Others seek homes near work, shopping, and entertainment. Practically all purchasers have an interest in the financial benefits of owning a residence. Sometimes these benefits take the form of rental income, but more commonly they include tax benefits, the availability of home equity loans, and the anticipation of realizing a higher resale value when the property is sold.

Individual homeowners are not the only people to benefit from the purchase and ownership of residential property. The community as a whole and the national economy are also enriched. Many homeowners invest labor and capital to maintain and improve their properties. Property ownership often gives people a greater sense of community responsibility and civic attachment. In many areas citizens form groups to influence zoning boards and other political bodies for the protection and maintenance of their neighborhoods. Moreover, the purchase of a new home supports the

---

What is USPAP?

The purpose of the Uniform Standards of Professional Appraisal Practice (USPAP) is to promote and maintain a high level of public trust in appraisal practice by establishing requirements for appraisers. It is essential that appraisers develop and communicate their analyses, opinions, and conclusions to intended users of their services in a manner that is meaningful and not misleading.

Source: *Uniform Standards of Professional Appraisal Practice* (Washington, D.C.: The Appraisal Foundation, 2006).

construction industry and adds to the tax base of the local government. Because home ownership has such far-reaching consequences, government organizations often try to improve conditions in the housing market to stimulate the general economy.

If society is to have any stability, the rights to own and use real estate must be safeguarded. The successful management of this limited resource is an essential activity. Appraisers of real property evaluate the utility and desirability of property and develop opinions of its value for various reasons, including purchase and sale, financing, taxation, investment, and insurance. Residential appraisers consider the utility and value of residential properties, thereby helping to ensure that decisions made by buyers, sellers, government officials, insurers, investors, and others are based on well-informed, carefully reasoned judgments. In that way, professional appraisal practitioners help promote the stable and orderly development of a fundamental societal resource.

What Is an Appraisal?

Appraisal is the act or process of developing an opinion of value. A real property appraisal provides an answer to a client's specific question about the value of a real property interest. A significant point to keep in mind is that appraisers do not create or establish value because only market participants, through their interaction, establish value. Value is never a fact; it is always an opinion. An appraiser's opinion of value reflects what market participants believe to be the value of a property.

Appraisers base their opinions on research in the appropriate market, the collection and verification of pertinent data, and the application of appropriate analytical techniques. When these activities are combined with knowledge, experience, and professional judgment, they result in a solution to the client's problem. Furthermore, because the opinion offered by a professional real estate appraiser is unbiased and substantiated by relevant data and sound reasoning, it carries considerable weight.

The objective of a real property appraisal is to develop an opinion of the defined value of an interest in real estate. It is important to keep in mind that it is not the real estate itself (land and buildings) that has value; rather, it is the rights to that real estate that have value. An appraisal always begins with the identification of those rights.

According to the Uniform Standards of Professional Appraisal Practice, *value* is the monetary relationship between properties and those who buy, sell, or use those properties. In appraisal practice, the word "value" is always qualified. That is, the appraisal objective is to develop an opinion of *some type* of value–market value, use value, investment value, etc. An important step in the appraisal process is to identify *the type of value* to be developed.

The objective of most appraisal assignments is *market value*. There are many different definitions of market value, so it is important for the appraiser to clarify which definition is being used. (The concept of market value is discussed more fully in the next chapter.) Generally speaking, market value is the most probable price that knowledgeable parties would agree upon when acting without duress. Most residential appraisal work is devoted to developing opinions of the most likely selling price of residential real estate. This book, therefore, will focus on the background, data, and techniques needed to research and form sound judgments of the market value of residential properties.

It is important to keep in mind that an appraisal is not a report. This is a common misconception among appraisers' clients because the report usually is the only evidence they have of the appraisal. A report, however, is merely the means by which the opinion of value is communicated. The focus of an assignment, from the appraiser's viewpoint, is the agreement with the client to provide a specific service: an opinion of value, based on a stated definition, as of a specified date, prepared under a certain scope of work, to satisfy a specified intended use, for a specified intended user(s).

Why Are Appraisals Needed?

Each year buyers, sellers, lenders, builders, insurers, brokers, and government officials make real estate decisions involving billions of dollars, and these decisions depend on real estate appraisals. Informed investment or loan decisions based on competent real estate appraisals help prevent business failures.

It is extremely important that appraisers exercise objectivity. In many real estate decisions, one or both parties have a strong vested interest in a particular conclusion, such as a high or low value opinion. As an objective investigator, an appraiser must provide an unbiased opinion that does nothing more than reflect the interaction of market participants, regardless of the intended user or the intended use of the appraisal report.

The services of a professional real estate appraiser may be required in a variety of circumstances, such as the following:

- Decisions concerning market transactions
- Tax questions
- Legal claims
- Investment planning and counseling
- Other real estate-related matters

Market Transactions

To prepare for a market transaction in which property ownership is transferred, different parties may request separate appraisals to answer specific questions. Both the seller and the potential buyer are typically interested in the real property's market value. The buyer needs to know the property's market value to decide on an acceptable offering price, while the seller, or sales agent, may use the market value opinion to select a price at which to sell or list the property.

Most sales of residential properties involve financing, and the financial institution from which the buyer requests a loan needs certain information. Because the amount of the loan is usually based on a set loan-to-value ratio, the institution requires a market value opinion. Financial institutions may also be interested in long-term forecasts of neighborhood stability and conditions in the real estate market because the property will be pledged to them as security for a fairly long period of time. Potential insurers and underwriters of mortgage loans are interested in similar information.

Tax Questions

Tax assessors need estimates of real property value to calculate ad valorem taxes, which are based on property value. Property owners who wish to challenge their tax assessments may hire appraisers. To calculate gift and inheritance taxes on real estate, value estimates of the bequeathed property are required. Various income tax provisions require appraisals as supporting evidence. For example, estimates of historical values may be needed to establish capital gains taxes.

Legal Claims

When the government exercises the right of eminent domain and takes possession of private property, an appraisal is frequently required to help establish the amount of just compensation to be paid to the owner. Just compensation is generally based on the market value of the property taken, but additional compensation may be required by the law. When only a portion of the real estate is taken, market value estimates may be needed for the property as a whole and for the property that remains after the taking. Many state courts require a valuation of the part taken and an estimate of the severance damage or special benefits to the remainder. Appraisals may also be required for arbitration between adversaries, such as lawsuits over damage to real estate or the court division of property after a divorce.

Investment Planning and Counseling

An appraiser's expert opinion on real estate matters is often sought by investors, builders, and government officials. Investors in residential apartment buildings may seek advice on investment goals, alternatives, resources, constraints, and timing from appraisers. Individuals who invest in capital markets may need appraisal advice to decide whether to purchase real estate mortgages, bonds, or other types of securities.

Homeowners who are considering renovation work may be interested in an analysis of the costs and benefits involved. Homebuilders may consult appraisers on the feasibility of a project, its market value, or the marketability of specific design features in the local area. Zoning boards, courts, and planners often need to consult appraisers about the probable effects of their proposed actions.

Other Uses of Appraisals

There are many other situations in which residential appraisals may be required. Financial institutions that are considering whether or not to foreclose on a property may be interested in the price the real estate might bring in a forced sale or auction. Lenders often require an appraisal for the removal of private mortgage insurance (PMI). Appraisals can facilitate corporate or company purchases of the homes of transferred employees.

Questions about insurance often necessitate an appraisal. A homeowner may want to know how much insurance to carry and which parts of the property are covered under the provisions of an insurance policy. The insurer may be interested in the value of the insured parts to decide how much to charge for the policy. Value estimates may be needed by the policyholder to support casualty loss claims, or an insurance adjuster may hire an appraiser to examine and evaluate the property damage and provide a basis for a negotiated settlement.

These cases do not represent all of the circumstances in which an appraisal may be requested, but they do suggest the broad scope of a professional appraiser's activities.

The Nature of Assignments

Completing an appraisal assignment involves three steps, which can be broadly stated as follows:

1. Identification of the problem to be solved
2. Identification of the scope of work necessary to solve the problem
3. Application of research and analysis necessary to produce a credible result

Identification of the Problem to Be Solved

The problem to be solved, or question to be answered, is identified by seven key parameters:

1. Who is the *client*?
2. Are there any other *intended users*?
3. What is the *intended use* of the assignment results?
4. What *type of value* is being sought?
5. As of what *effective date*?
6. What *property characteristics* are relevant to the assignment?
7. Are there any *assignment conditions* such as hypothetical conditions, extraordinary assumptions, or supplemental standards?

Once the appraiser has made these seven identifications, the appropriate scope of work to solve the problem can be determined.

Scope of Work

Scope of work is the type and extent of research and analyses in an assignment. In a residential appraisal assignment, some key scope of work considerations will be:

- To what degree will the property be inspected?
- What data sources will be researched? How far back in time should the research go?
- Which of the traditional approaches to value will be applied?

Depending on the intended use, some assignments will call for a more thorough investigation by the appraiser than other assignments. Some assignments will require the appraiser to visit the subject real estate and observe firsthand its physical condition and other characteristics. In other assignments the appraiser may be able to omit the property visit and base the appraisal on one or more extraordinary assumptions about the characteristics of the property that are relevant to the valuation problem. Some assignments call for the application of two, or even three, of the traditional approaches to value, while other assignments require no more than one approach. The scope of work decision is the most important decision an appraiser will make in the appraisal process because the application of the appropriate scope helps to ensure the assignment results are credible and appropriate for the intended use.

Research and Analysis

The appraisal process involves the gathering of relevant data and the analysis of that data to form a credible value opinion. If the type of value sought is market value, the property's *highest and best use* must first be determined. (See Chapter 11.) The property's highest and best use helps the appraiser delineate the market area for the subject property, the likely buyers for it, and the likely use to which they would put it. Highest and best use also helps the appraiser in the selection of competitive properties to be used in the comparable analysis.

The appraiser forms a value opinion by applying one or more of three traditional approaches to value:

- The sales comparison approach
- The cost approach
- The income capitalization approach

In single-unit residential appraising, the primary approach to value is usually the sales comparison approach. (This approach is the focus of Chapters 16, 17, and 18.) The cost approach might also provide a credible indication of value, depending on the age and condition of the improvements and the availability of reliable construction cost information. The income approach is generally applicable only when there is an active rental market for such properties in the subject's market area. In the appraisal of single-unit investment properties and two- to four-unit properties, the income capitalization approach may be the primary approach.

Communicating the Appraisal

The results of the assignment are communicated to the client in an *appraisal report.* An appraisal report may be written or verbal (oral). Either way, an appraisal report must contain specific elements, as providing the value conclusion only would be misleading. For example, among other information the report must include the type of value, the effective date of value, and any extraordinary assumptions or hypothetical conditions used in the analysis.

Oral reports are commonly used in legal work such as court testimony, hearings, arbitrations, or depositions. Oral reports may be used when the opinion of value is transmitted to the client verbally before the delivery of a written report. However, most appraisal reports are communicated in writing; that is, on paper or electronically. An appraisal report may be long or short, and it can be presented as a self-contained, summary, or restricted use report, depending on the informational needs of the client and any other intended users. (Descriptions of the various types of appraisal reports are provided in Chapter 21.)

Appraisal Consulting and Other Related Services

While the most common service provided by an appraiser is rendering an opinion of value, appraisers may take on other, related services as well. *Appraisal consulting* is defined as the act or process of developing an analysis, recommendation, or opinion to solve a problem, where an opinion of value is a component of the analysis leading to the assignment results. Appraisal consulting involves an appraisal as an interim step in developing a different sort of opinion. Examples include feasibility studies and highest and best use studies.

Real property consulting is defined as the act or process of developing an analysis, recommendation, or opinion to solve a problem, where an opinion of value is NOT a component of the analysis leading to the assignment results. Real property consulting is similar to appraisal consulting, but real property consulting does not involve an appraisal. Examples include market studies, supply and demand studies, and land utilization studies.

An appraiser *acting as an* appraiser cannot be compensated in a manner that is contingent on the results of the analysis. Also, an appraiser cannot be an advocate; that is, an appraiser cannot represent the cause or interest of another. An appraiser can be an advocate only for his or her own opinions because an appraiser is defined as one who provides valuation services competently and in a manner that is independent, impartial, and objective.

An appraiser is permitted to act in another capacity, however, i.e., *not* as an appraiser. Some real estate appraisers wear other hats. For example, some appraisers are also real estate brokers, loan officers, or attorneys. In such non-appraiser roles, advocacy and contingent fee arrangements are not only permitted, they are the norm. When acting in such another capacity, an appraiser must be certain to clarify his or her role. That is, the appraiser must actively disclose that, while he or she is an appraiser, he or she is not acting as an appraiser in providing that particular service. This topic is discussed further in Chapter 23.

Residential Appraiser Qualifications

Given the public's reliance on the opinions of appraisers and the broad scope of appraisal activities, appraisers must obviously possess personal integrity, diligence, and professionalism. In addition, there are specific skills, experience, and qualifications required of residential appraisers.

Licensing, Certification, and Designation

Until the late 1980s, most states did not require that individuals meet specific qualifications to perform appraisals. Since then, however, the need to have professional opinions prepared by knowledgeable, unbiased individuals has been recognized, and licensing or certification of appraisers is now mandatory under certain circumstances. Every state now has an appraiser regulatory law.

The Appraisal Institute encourages professionalism by awarding membership designations to appraisers who meet its requirements of experience, education, and ethical practice. By enforcing The Appraisal Foundation's Uniform Standards of Professional Appraisal Practice and its own Code of Professional Ethics and by sponsoring educational programs, the Appraisal Institute has worked to advance the status of professional real estate appraisers throughout the United States and to make the public aware of the high-quality work performed by designated appraisers. Continuing education is the cornerstone of professional development. Appraisers who pursue continuing education demonstrate their interest in maintaining their skills at a level far above the bare minimum required to satisfy state licensing requirements. Practitioners who complete a rigorous educational program and earn recognized professional designations find their employment and business prospects considerably enhanced. Professionalism helps regulate the industry and strongly encourages quality appraisal work.

Skills

An appraiser must possess strong communication, investigative, and analytical skills. Good communication skills are needed because appraisers must regularly seek essential information from diverse individuals, some of whom may be reluctant to provide it. Moreover, it is essential that appraisers be able to communicate their findings in an orderly, logical, and grammatically correct manner. Clear communication is a sign of clear thinking and sound, considered judgment. Written reports to clients must be clear and credible. Ambiguity and inconsistency are unacceptable.

Good appraisers are good detectives. They are naturally inquisitive and enjoy knowing where and how to obtain information. An appraiser must be sensitive to new trends and developments in the community and be aware of the countless ways in which data can be misleading. Appraisers must also be open-minded. Market value, which the appraiser seeks to estimate, is shaped by the needs, desires, and motivations of market participants, which may not conform to the appraiser's personal preferences.

Analytical skills are also important. Appraisers must know how to analyze the data they collect and draw logical conclusions. They should understand the reasoning behind the three approaches to value–the cost, sales comparison, and income capitalization approaches–and recognize that one approach may be more or less reliable than another in a particular situation. With good analytical skills, an appraiser can divide an assignment into a series of distinct tasks and provide much more efficient appraisal service.

Recent advances in the high-tech industry have found broad application in appraisal practice, so appraisers must keep up to date. In decades past, an appraiser armed with a clipboard, measuring tape, and slide rule was considered adequately equipped. Today, appraisers rely heavily on electronic devices ranging from hand-held financial calculators to laser measuring tools. The Internet and computerized databases have become essential for research purposes. Spreadsheet and other computer applications are commonly used for analysis. Savvy appraisers have learned to take advantage of recent advances in GIS (geographic information systems) and AVM (automated valuation model) technology. Appraisers need to be receptive to advances in technology in order to fully benefit from new applications.

Two attributes that are essential in appraisal practice are reasonableness and common sense. These characteristics, which are acquired through experience, help the appraiser gather and analyze data and draw sound, supportable conclusions. But ultimately, the most important characteristic for an appraiser to possess is the ability to remain independent, unbiased, and objective, often in the face of temptation or outright pressure to yield to the desires or suggestions of interested parties. The professional appraiser must remain a disinterested third party, which sometimes requires him or her to relate opinions and conclusions that interested parties do not wish to hear.

Experience

A knowledge of techniques and practical skills are important, but the ultimate test of an appraiser's ability comes on the job. Experience is essential in appraisal, and it is generally reflected in the salaries and fees an appraiser can earn. Learning the art of real estate appraisal takes time, but time alone is not enough. Appraisers will benefit from experience only if they constantly work at self-improvement through formal education such as the courses and seminars offered by the Appraisal Institute and other professional organizations.

Employment as a Residential Appraiser

To dedicated, qualified professionals, the field of residential appraisal can present stimulating challenges and rewarding opportunities. Each property presents unique problems, and each assignment challenges the appraiser to find creative, efficient solutions. The many appraisers who work in public and private institutions receive salaries commensurate with their experience, ability, and education. Those with effective business skills may choose to enter private practice, where they can enjoy the flexibility and remuneration that independence can often supply.

In addition to challenging work and monetary rewards, professional appraisers derive satisfaction from knowing that their services are important to the community. The public relies on real estate appraisers' opinions to make decisions concerning investment, land use and development, and critical legal matters. As a result, the integrity, responsibility, and sound judgment of professional appraisers can earn them the respect of the communities in which they practice.

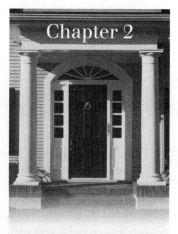

Chapter 2

Real Property
Ownership and Value

What is valued in an appraisal? Although appraisers investigate and analyze land and structures, these physical entities do not, strictly speaking, possess value or utility. Rather, it is the right to use property that has value. The various rights to use real estate are conveyed in a deed and corroborated by a title or contract. When the ownership of a parcel of real estate is transferred, these rights change hands. To highlight this distinction, property is divided into two legal categories: real estate and real property.

Real Estate

Real estate is the physical land and appurtenances attached to the land—i.e., structures. Real estate is the physical entity, which includes everything that is fixed and immobile. It encompasses all the natural attributes of the land as well as everything affixed to the land in a relatively permanent way by people.

The concept of real estate incorporates three important elements:

1. *Land* is the earth's surface, both land and water, and all its components. Land includes all natural resources in their original state—e.g., mineral deposits, timber, water, coal deposits, and soil.

2. *Improvements* are buildings or other relatively permanent structures or develop-

> **land.** The earth's surface, both land and water, and anything that is attached to it whether by the course of nature or human hands; all natural resources in their original state, e.g., mineral deposits, wildlife, timber, fish, water, coal deposits, soil.
>
> **improvements.** Buildings or other relatively permanent structures or developments located on, or attached to, land.

ments that are located on, or attached to, land. This category includes both improvements to the land such as access roads and utilities, which prepare the land for a subsequent use, and improvements on the land such as buildings and landscaping.

3. A *fixture* is an item that was once personal property—i.e., a movable possession that is not part of the real estate—but that has since been installed or attached to the land or the building in a rather permanent manner.

fixture. An article that was once personal property but has since been installed or attached to the land or building in a rather permanent manner so that it is regarded in law as part of the real estate.

It is not always apparent whether an item is truly a fixture, and thus part of the real property, or whether it should be considered personal property, and therefore not included in the real estate value opinion. An appraiser may need guidance to appreciate these legal distinctions, which are usually set forth in state law and may vary according to statute. Most courts use the following criteria to judge the status of an item:

1. The manner in which the item is affixed. Generally an item is considered personal property if it can be removed without causing serious injury to the real estate or to itself. (Note: There are exceptions to this rule.)

2. The character of the item and its adaptation to the real estate. Items that are specifically constructed for use in a particular building or installed to fulfill the purpose for which the building was erected are generally considered permanent parts of the building.

3. The intention of the party who attached the item. Frequently the terms of a lease reveal whether the item was meant to be permanent or whether it was to be removed at some time.[1] For example, an apartment or house lease may specify that items such as bookshelves and mini-blinds may be installed by the tenant and removed as personal property at the termination of the lease.

To ascertain the full extent of the physical entity being appraised, the various components of the property must be distinguished in an appraisal. The appraiser must determine the exact boundaries of the site, the nature of any improvements to and on the site, and the status of any improvements, including fixtures. Obviously, the inclusion or exclusion of an item from the appraiser's analysis can increase or decrease the total value opinion. If an appraiser is asked to include the value of certain items of personal property in the final value opinion, the effect of these inclusions must be precisely stated in the appraisal report.

---

1. Raymond J. Werner and Robert Kratovil, *Real Estate Law,* 10th ed. (Englewood Cliffs, N.J.: Prentice-Hall, Inc., 1993), 11–16.

Real Property

Real property refers to all interests, benefits, and rights inherent in the ownership of physical real estate. Understanding the concept of real property is necessary because the ownership of real estate consists of various interests, benefits, and rights that can be separated without dividing the physical real estate. Real property rights have been compared to a bundle of sticks in which each stick represents a separate, transferable right. The individual rights to real estate include the rights to occupy the real estate, to sell it, to lease it, to enter it, to give it away, to borrow against it, or to exercise more than one or none of these rights. This aspect of real property divisibility is reflected in the bundle of rights theory.

Because real property rights are divisible, larger or smaller bundles of rights can be created by selling or leasing all or part of the sticks in the bundle. These partial bundles of rights (known as *partial interests*) are contained in estates. An *estate* is the degree, nature, or extent of interest that a person has in property. Various possible estates are discussed below; each represents a different degree of real property ownership.

Bundle of Rights

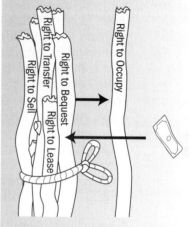

Fee Simple Estates

Most residential properties are held in fee simple. A fee simple estate is an absolute ownership unencumbered by any other interest or estate. The owner of a fee simple title possesses all the rights and benefits of the real estate subject only to the powers of government, which include taxation, eminent domain, escheat, and police power. The owner of a fee simple title possesses a complete bundle of rights.

Leased Fee Estates

When an owner enters into a lease agreement with a tenant, two less-than-complete estates are created: a leased fee estate and a leasehold estate. A leased fee estate is an ownership interest held by a landlord with the right of use and occupancy conveyed by lease to others; the rights of the lessor (the leased fee owner) and the leased fee are specified by contract terms contained within the lease. Specific lease terms vary, but a leased fee generally provides for rent to be paid by the lessee (the tenant) to the lessor (the landlord) under stipulated terms. Typically the lessor has the right of repossession at the termination of the lease, default provisions, and the rights to sell, mortgage, or bequeath the property during the lease period. When a lease is legally delivered,

leased fee interest. An ownership interest held by a landlord with the rights of use and occupancy conveyed by lease to others. The rights of the lessor (the leased fee owner) and the lessee are specified by contract terms contained within the lease.

leasehold interest. The interest held by the lessee (the tenant or renter) through a lease transferring the rights of use and occupancy for a stated term under certain conditions.

the lessor must surrender possession of the property to the lessee for the lease period and abide by the lease provisions.

Leasehold Estates

A leasehold estate is the right to use and occupy real estate for a stated term under certain conditions as conveyed by the lease. Under a lease, the tenant usually acquires the rights to possess the property for the lease period, to sublease the property, and to improve the property under restrictions specified in the lease. In return the tenant must pay rent, surrender possession of the property at the termination of the lease, and abide by the lease provisions established with the lessor.

In states such as Hawaii, residences have long been built on leased land.[2] Leases may be for as long as 99 years or for 50 years or less. To protect the mortgage, some leases provide that the interest of the fee owner is subordinate to the interest of the mortgagee or lender. However, most leases give the mortgagee the right to take over the land rent payments if the mortgagor defaults. Usually the mortgagee also has the right to find a new mortgagor to continue the lease payments. When the lease expires, the improvements become the property of the landowner, who may extend the lease after modifying it to reflect current market conditions.

Estates Encumbered by Mortgages

Property owners can limit or restrict their real property interest in exchange for a mortgage loan. The owner is obligated to repay the loan according to a certain schedule and to pledge the real estate as security. The value of an owner's interest minus the debt, or mortgage, is called *equity*. The lender's interest consists of the right to repayment plus the right to foreclose on the loan if the owner defaults; the lender can legally force a sale of the property to recover all or part of the money owed.

equity. The net value of the property obtained by subtracting from its total value all liens or other charges against it; the value of an owner's interest in property in excess of all claims and liens.

easement. An interest in real property that conveys use, but not ownership, of a portion of an owner's property. Access or right-of-way easements may be acquired by private parties or public utilities. Governments dedicate conservation, open space, and preservation easements.

Estates Subject to Easement

Granting or selling an easement can also create a less-than-complete estate. An *easement* is an interest that conveys use, but not ownership, of a portion of a real property. In other words, someone is allowed to perform a specific action on another person's property;

---

2. To reduce the social and economic evils of concentrated land ownership, the Hawaii legislature adopted the Land Reform Act of 1967. In a 1983 decision, the Court of Appeals for the Ninth Circuit found the reform act unconstitutional. This ruling was reversed the following year when the Supreme Court upheld the ruling that the state of Hawaii had indeed met the public use requirement in exercising its power of eminent domain. See Jerome G. Rose, "From the Courts: Supreme Court Upholds Redistribution of Ownership of Hawaii Land," *Real Estate Law Journal* (Winter 1985), 263-269.

for example, a city diverts a road through privately owned land. A right-of-way allows the owner of the dominant estate (the easement holder) access rights across the servient estate (the property subject to the easement), and the owner of the servient estate (the property owner) is not permitted to restrict access. Often easements are attached to the land and continue to burden the servient estate even when the property is sold; these easements are called *appurtenant easements*. A utility easement that permits power lines to run along one side of a property is an appurtenant easement. Information on the burdens and benefits of easements can be found in title reports.

Identifying Property Rights

Fee simple estates, leased fee and leasehold estates, mortgages, and easements represent only a few of the many ways in which property rights may be divided. Just as various components of the physical real estate must be separated for appraisal purposes, property rights can be divided into ownership interests like corporate shareholder interests or parnerships or into financial interests such as equity or debt. Therefore, an appraiser must identify precisely which property rights are being included in a valuation. The value conclusions reached in appraising the same parcel of real estate will differ depending on whether the fee simple estate or some other estate is being valued.

Condominiums

Condominium ownership is a form of fee ownership of separate units or portions of multiunit buildings that provides for formal filing and recording of a title to a divided interest in real property. A condominium owner holds title to an individual unit in a multiunit property and has an undivided interest in common areas of the property. The owner of a condominium is the sole proprietor of the three-dimensional space within the outer walls, roof or ceiling, and floors of the individual unit. He or she can lease, sell, mortgage, or refinance this unit separately from the other units in the property. In addition, the owner, together with the owners of the other units, has an undivided interest in common areas such as the site on which the building stands, the public portions of the building (e.g., entryways, corridors, elevators), the building foundation, the outer walls, the parking areas, and all driveways and recreational facilities.

The condominium deed must contain an exact horizontal and vertical description of the location of the condominium unit. The boundaries of the common areas and the individual units are shown on the plot plan, or plat, and the architectural plans, which must be publicly recorded in many states.

Condominium owners usually form an association to manage the real estate in accordance with adopted bylaws. A typical condominium or homeowners' association is governed by a board of directors elected by the individual owners. It operates under a set of bylaws that is recorded in the master deed and complies with state laws concerning condominiums. Usually a majority of the owners must vote to change the bylaws and all of the owners must agree to change the master deed. Management and maintenance expenses are generally divided on a pro rata basis and levied as a monthly, quarterly, or annual fee.

Condominiums can be new units or existing units that have been converted to condominium ownership. They may be units in high rises, townhouses, small groups of party-wall units, or freestanding units. (Techniques used in the valuation of condominiums, cooperatives, timeshare properties, and PUD units are discussed in Chapter 23.)

Cooperatives

Cooperative ownership is a form of ownership in which each owner of stock in a cooperative apartment building or housing corporation pays a proportionate share of operating expenses and debt service on the underlying mortgage, which is paid by the corporation. A cooperative, or co-op, is created when a stock corporation is organized to issue an authorized number of shares of stock at a specified par value. The corporation takes title to an apartment building and prices the various units. The price per unit determines the number of shares that a tenant, who is a shareholder in the cooperative apartment corporation, must purchase to acquire a proprietary lease. Under the lease the tenant-shareholder must pay a monthly maintenance fee, which may be adjusted later by the corporation's board of directors. The fee covers the costs of management, operations, and maintenance of public areas. Shareholders use their shares in the corporation to vote on the election of directors, which gives them some control over property conditions.

Timeshare Properties

Timesharing is the sale of limited ownership interests in residential property: single units, apartments, or hotel rooms. The timeshare purchaser receives a deed that conveys title to the unit for a specific part of the year. Timesharing generally applies to resort and vacation housing. Under this arrangement, one property is purchased by several owners, each of whom has the right to use the property for a predetermined period of time. For example, 10 timeshare owners may buy a house at a ski resort. The owners share the cost of the property equally, and each has the right to use the property for two weeks during the ski season and three weeks at another time. The remaining two weeks are for property maintenance.

Planned Unit Developments (PUDs)

A planned unit development (PUD) is a type of land development in which buildings are clustered or set on lots that are typically smaller than usual. Large, open, park-like areas and recreational facilities are included within the development. In exchange for the right to build on smaller lots, the developer agrees to set aside some vacant land to be used by the community or a homeowners' association. Streets, landscaping, and public facilities can be designed in PUDs with greater flexibility than is possible in conventional neighborhoods.

The individual single-family residences in a PUD are owned in fee simple or as condominiums with joint ownership of open areas; in some areas local law requires that open areas be deeded to the city. Driveways, parking areas, and recreational facilities may also be jointly owned by the residents. An undivided interest in these common areas runs with the title to each property. Consequently, these areas must be included in a visual inventory of the site when individual properties are appraised.

Contracts, Leases, and Deeds

The legal documents that appraisers commonly consult in determining the ownership interest under scrutiny in an appraisal assignment include real estate sales contracts, lease documents, and deeds. Under the current Uniform Standards of Professional Appraisal Practice, it is good practice to obtain and review the real estate documents if the appraisal is for a current sale.

Contracts

Contracts are voluntary agreements between legally competent parties to perform (or not perform) a legal act for a stated legal consideration. The five elements of a valid contract are

1. Consent (no undue duress, menace, or misrepresentation)
2. Offer and acceptance (i.e., a "meeting of the minds")
3. Legally competent parties (in essence, buyers and sellers who know what they are doing)
4. Consideration (regardless of whether the consideration is deemed adequate)
5. Legal purpose (i.e., not an illegal act)

If a contract is not valid, it may be a void contract–having no legal force or binding effect, usually because one of the elements of a valid contract is missing–or a voidable contract–technically valid but with at least one party having the option of legally voiding the contract.

Appraisers may need to consult various types of contracts when researching sales and lease transactions. A real estate sale contract serves multiple purposes. It is the receipt of the buyer's earnest money that accompanies the purchase offer and it becomes the legally binding agreement for the sale when signed by both parties. Also, the contract may specify the sale price, any sales or financing concessions, a contract date and potential closing date, the legal description of the land, the title and form of deed to be conveyed, and other information of interest to appraisers.

An option contract is an agreement that confers the right to buy, which may or may not be exercised within a certain time frame. A common example is a lease contract that gives the lessee the option to buy the property.

A land contract (or *contract for deed* or *installment sale contract*) may be used when financing is tight or a buyer's credit may be inadequate for traditional financing. The most significant difference between a land contract and a more traditional real estate sale contract is that the deed is not delivered to the purchaser until the final payment of the land contract is made. The purchaser has all the rights of occupancy that go with normal ownership, but the seller is protected because foreclosure is easier than under a mortgage.

Leases

A lease is a type of contract transferring one of the fundamental ownership rights–the right of occupancy–from the lessor (landlord) to the lessee (tenant). Leases create the partial interests in real property discussed earlier–leased fee and leasehold interests. A lease contract will specify a lease term, a rental rate, and who pays which expenses.

Deeds

The terms *title* and *deed* are related concepts. Title is, in essence, proof of ownership of real property in whatever form that evidence of ownership may take. A deed is the written document that helps establish title to real property. Appraisers review deeds for the same reason they analyze sale contracts–a deed is a record of important information about the real estate. The elements of a deed include

- Identification of grantor and grantee
- Legally competent grantor
- Words of conveyance
- Financial consideration
- Execution through a written document
- Delivery by the grantor and acceptance by the grantee

Title to real property can be transferred voluntarily through sale or gift or involuntarily through the operation of law such as eminent domain or foreclosure. When property ownership is transferred without the use of a traditional sale contract–in a foreclosure proceeding, for example–some form of deed will still be granted. In a foreclosure, often a bargain and sale deed is used.

Types of Leases

- Escalator lease
- Flat rental lease
- Graduated rental lease
- Gross-up lease
- Index lease
- Percentage lease
- Revaluation lease
- Sandwich lease/sublease

Types of Deeds

- General warranty deed
- Special warranty deed
- Bargain and sale deed
- Quitclaim deed

Limitations on Property Use

Individuals who own estates in real property are limited in their use of the property only by the legal property rights they possess, by the physical characteristics of the real estate, and by economic feasibility. This fact has considerable significance in real estate appraisal because value is created by the expectation of benefits that can accrue from ownership rights. Because various factors limit the potential uses and benefits that an estate can provide, the estate's value is limited as well. Thus an appraiser must carefully study the legal limitations, physical limitations, and economic limitations to which a parcel of real estate is subject. If any of these limitations change, the highest and best use and the value of the parcel may change as a result.

Legal Limitations

Legal limitations effectively restrict the ways in which property can be used. In the United States, public laws governing the use and development of land give the property owner the fullest possible freedom consistent with the rights accorded to others. However, the government reserves certain powers over property use, which take precedence over the rights of individuals who hold title to property. Subject to constitutional and statutory requirements, the government can, at any time, exercise four powers for the public benefit. All property ownership is limited by these four powers of government:

1. Taxation
2. Eminent domain
3. Escheat
4. Police power

Taxation is the right of government to raise revenue through assessments on valuable goods, products, and rights. Under *eminent domain*, the government can take private property for public use upon the payment of just compensation to the owner. *Escheat* gives the state titular ownership of a property when its owner dies without a will or any ascertainable heirs. *Police power* is the right of government under which property is regulated to protect public safety, health, morals, and general welfare.

Under the power of taxation, state and local governments can tax the owners of real property at any level so long as the taxes are imposed fairly.[3] Property taxes in different jurisdictions vary, and high taxes can limit or discourage many kinds of land use and development.

The power of eminent domain can be exercised by agencies acting under government authority such as housing departments and public utilities. Under this power, the agency can take private property and use it for public

taxation. The right of government to raise revenue through assessments on valuable goods, products, and rights.

eminent domain. The right of government to take private property for public use upon the payment of just compensation. The Fifth Amendment of the U.S. Constitution, also known as the takings clause, guarantees payment of just compensation upon appropriation of private property.

escheat. The right of government that gives the state titular ownership of a property when its owner dies without a will or any ascertainable heirs.

police power. The right of government through which property is regulated to protect public safety, health, morals, and general welfare.

just compensation. In condemnation, the amount of loss for which a property owner is compensated when his or her property is taken; should put the owner in as good a position pecuniarily as he or she would be if the property had not been taken; generally held to be market value, but courts have refused to rule that it is always equivalent to market value.

---

3. Under the U.S. Constitution, the federal government is prohibited from taxing real property directly.

purposes upon payment of just compensation to the owner. The private use of property can also be restricted by eminent domain. For example, a utility can acquire an easement in a property for an underground electrical line or a sewer and water line.

The government's police power is the most direct, comprehensive, and frequently invoked legal limitation on property use. Through this police power, the government has the right to enforce zoning ordinances, sanitary regulations, rent controls, historic preservation acts, utility requirements, and building, housing, plumbing, and electrical codes and regulations. These controls can affect almost every detail of property use, from permitted land uses to the size of windows and doors; even the type of finish can be regulated. Often the codes also specify what action is to be taken if a building does not conform to the ordinance requirements. It is essential that appraisers be familiar with all zoning ordinances and other regulations in effect in the area.

In addition to government restrictions on property, private voluntary and involuntary legal limitations exist. Private voluntary limitations include deed restrictions, lease agreements, CC&Rs (conditions, covenants, and restrictions), mortgage notes with provisions that limit property use, and party wall agreements, which grant owners of adjoining properties the common right to use a wall erected on the boundary line between them. Private involuntary limitations include easements, rights of way, and encroachments.

Private legal limitations can restrict the use or manner of development and even the way in which ownership can be conveyed. The purchaser of an encumbered property may be obligated to use the property subject to restrictions. Thus, there are many legal restrictions created by private agreement or imposed by government that affect the potential uses of real estate.

Physical Limitations

The land's physical characteristics and the laws of nature dictate that many conceivable uses of real estate are difficult or impossible to achieve. Obviously, a 120-ft.-by-150-ft. mansion cannot be built on a 100-ft.-by-120-ft. tract of land. Furthermore, it is not practical to build houses, raise crops, or construct office buildings in many places on the surface of the earth.

Historically, land with irregular topography, earthquake fault areas, wetlands, floodplains, areas with the potential for landslides, and excessively cold or hot areas have limited utility for residential users, although some people may be willing to endure a certain amount of discomfort or risk. In fact, in recent years, the greatest population growth in the United States has occurred in the coastal areas that are most at risk from natural disasters such as flooding and hurricanes.

People often migrate to these areas because of the amenities associated with living near a body of water and by the favorable climatic conditions. Physical factors affect the engineering and design of structures as well. Due to climatic conditions, building design in an area may be limited to a narrow range of building types.

The physical characteristics of real estate and the environment are influenced not only by natural conditions but also by man-made conditions. Proximity to roads and highways and access to shopping centers, workplaces, and recreational facilities can affect how a given parcel of real estate is used.

The laws of nature do not change, but the effects of natural conditions on specific locations can be mitigated. The limits of physical possibility are constantly being pushed back through technological advancements. For this reason, appraisers must keep abreast of changing physical conditions in the area as well as developments in science and technology, particularly construction techniques and building design. All these factors can affect the range of possible uses to which real estate may be put.

Economic Limitations

Although a use may be legally permissible and physically possible, it may not be economically practical for an owner to consider. The market strongly discourages uses that are not economically feasible. Conversely, uses that are economically productive or beneficial are encouraged by the market so long as they are legally permissible. (Chapter 3 examines economic conditions that affect property use decisions.)

Changing economic forces and constraints can alter the balance between the legal and physical limitations on property use. If economic pressures are strong enough, existing physical and legal limitations can be overcome or modified. For example, zoning ordinances can be changed if a large constituency will benefit from their revision. Similarly, significant physical limitations can be overcome if demand is sufficient or technological advances are available to correct them. Often these funds *will* be spent if there is a likelihood that greater benefits or income can be secured from the projected use of the real estate.

Limitations Combined

Together legal, physical, and economic limitations shape the ways in which real estate can be used. Legal restrictions limit the rights of individuals to use property in specific ways. Physical limitations can make certain uses impossible or difficult. The economic limitations created by market forces also have a strong impact on property use. To study how real estate can be used productively, real estate appraiser-analysts examine these limitations and their effect on the benefits the real property is expected to produce.

The Concept of Value

As mentioned previously, *value* can be broadly defined as the monetary worth of goods or services to people. However, this definition is not sufficiently precise for appraisal purposes because *monetary worth* may have different meanings to various people involved in real estate activities. The concept of value may have one meaning to a buyer or seller and another to a lender, owner, investor, insurance adjustor, or tax collector. These different interpretations can be attributed to the fact that different individuals tend to focus on distinct aspects of real estate–i.e., different benefits, interests, or possible uses. Consider the following examples:

- Buyers and sellers consider the monetary worth (market value) of a residential property in terms of the prices of other, nearby properties that are similar in quality and utility.
- Lenders may consider the price a property would bring in a forced sale (liquidation value), rather than the prices obtained for comparable properties under typical market conditions.
- Investors with unusual investment criteria may find that a particular property is ideally suited to their needs. For these investors, the monetary worth (investment value) of the real estate may be higher or lower than the value of a similar property to other buyers and sellers.

A property may provide its owner with certain valuable benefits and income that could not be realized by another owner. The monetary worth of the real estate to that owner might then be different than its worth to typical buyers and sellers of similar property. If the property were sold on the open market, the price obtained could be different from its investment value or use value.

Opinions of value may vary depending on the investor's perspective. In defining the appraisal problem, therefore, the appraiser *must* specify the precise type of value to be estimated–e.g., market value, use value, assessed value, or some other type of specified value. The value concept selected must be precisely defined at the beginning of the valuation process.

Market Value

The concept of market value is of paramount importance to business and real estate communities. Vast sums of debt and equity capital are committed each year to real estate investments and mortgage loans based on estimates of market value. Individuals involved in real estate taxation, litigation, and legislation also have an ongoing, active concern with market value issues. In virtually every aspect of the real estate industry and its regulation at local, state, and federal levels, market value considerations are of vital importance.

For these reasons, the definition of market value used by appraisers and their clients must be clearly understood and communicated.

The various definitions of market value reveal the different beliefs and assumptions about the marketplace and the nature of value among practitioners. Although market value is a simple concept–i.e., an objective value created by the collective behavior patterns of the market–in practice, the specifics of the assignment (i.e., scope of work) dictate which definition of *market value* is appropriate.

Despite differing schools of thought, it is generally agreed that market value results from collective value judgments, not from isolated opinions. A market value opinion must be based on objective observation of the collective actions of the marketplace. The standard of measurement must be cash, so increases or decreases in market value caused by financing and other terms are measured against an all-cash value.

A good market value definition should incorporate the concepts that are most widely agreed upon–e.g., willing, able, and knowledgeable buyers and sellers who act prudently–and give the appraiser a choice among

1. All cash
2. Terms equivalent to cash
3. Other precisely revealed terms

Differences from the all-cash market value must still be quantified in terms of cash.

Certain sections of the definition of market value used by the Federal National Mortgage Association (Fannie Mae), the Federal Home Loan Mortgage Corporation (Freddie Mac), the Department of Veterans Affairs (VA), and many other federal financial institutions are revisited in Fannie Mae's Single-Family Selling Guide as follows:

> The asterisked section of the definition provides consistent interpretation for the appraiser. Specifically, we want to emphasize that the phrases "... those costs that are normally paid by sellers as a result of tradition or law in a market area; these costs are readily identifiable since the seller pays these costs in virtually all sales transactions ..." refer to all of the sellers in a specific market area. No distinction is made between a specific group of sellers, builders, developers, or individuals in the resale market–they all are considered to be individual sellers in the market. To illustrate: When a property seller is paying part of the purchaser's settlement or closing costs–or is paying for an interest-rate buydown or other below-market financing–but virtually all of the other sellers in the market are not doing the same as a result of law or tradition, the appraiser would need to make an adjustment even if there are other groups of sellers–such as builders–who also are offering concessionary financing.
>
> The appraiser can adjust a comparable property that has special or creative financing or sales concessions by comparing it to other properties that had financing terms offered by a third-party institutional lender–as long as that lender is not already involved in the subject property or transaction. The appraiser should use his or her judgment in establishing the dollar amount for any adjustment to ensure that it approximates the market's reaction to the financing or concession at the time of the sale.[4]

---

4. *Fannie Mae Single-Family Selling Guide,* Part XI: Property and Appraisal Guidelines, Chapter 2: Appraisal (or Property Inspection) Documentation (06/30/02), 205: Definition of Market Value (06/30/02).

market value.

1. The major focus of most real property appraisal assignments. Both economic and legal definitions of market value have been developed and refined. Continual refinement is essential to the growth of the appraisal profession.

2. The most widely accepted components of market value are incorporated in the following definition:

   The most probable price, as of a specified date, in cash, or in terms equivalent to cash, or in other precisely revealed terms, for which the specified property rights should sell after reasonable exposure in a competitive market under all conditions requisite to a fair sale, with the buyer and seller each acting prudently, knowledgeably, and for self-interest, and assuming that neither is under undue duress.

3. Market value is defined in the Uniform Standards of Professional Appraisal Practice (USPAP) as follows:

   A type of value, stated as an opinion, that presumes the transfer of a property (i.e., a right of ownership or a bundle of such rights), as of a certain date, under specific conditions set forth in the definition of the term identified by the appraiser as applicable in an appraisal. (USPAP, 2006 ed.)

   USPAP also requires that certain items be included in every appraisal report. Among these items, the following are directly related to the definition of market value:

   1. Identification of the specific property rights to be appraised.
   2. Statement of the effective date of the value opinion.
   3. Specification as to whether cash, terms equivalent to cash, or other precisely described financing terms are assumed as the basis of the appraisal.
   4. If the appraisal is conditioned upon financing or other terms, specification as to whether the financing or terms are at, below or above market interest rates and/or contain unusual conditions or incentives. The terms of above- or below-market interest rates and/or other special incentives must be clearly set forth; their contribution to, or negative influence on, value must be described and estimated; and the market data supporting the opinion of value must be described and explained.

4. The following definition of *market value* (as cited on the Uniform Residential Appraisal Report form) is used by agencies that regulate federally insured financial institutions in the United States:

   The most probable price which a property should bring in a competitive and open market under all conditions requisite to a fair sale, the buyer and seller, each acting prudently, knowledgeably and assuming the price is not affected by undue stimulus. Implicit in this definition is the consummation of a sale as of a specified date and the passing of title from seller to buyer under conditions whereby:

   1. Buyer and seller are typically motivated;
   2. Both parties are well informed or well advised, and each acting in what he considers his own best interest;
   3. A reasonable time is allowed for exposure in the open market;
   4. Payment is made in terms of cash in U.S. dollars or in terms of financial arrangements comparable thereto; and
   5. The price represents the normal consideration for the property sold unaffected by special or creative financing or sales concessions* granted by anyone associated with the sale.

5. In 1993, the Appraisal Institute Special Task Force on Value Definitions put forward the following definition of *market value:*

   The most probable price which a specified interest in real property is likely to bring under all of the following conditions:

   1. Consummation of a sale occurs as of a specified date.
   2. An open and competitive market exists for the property interest appraised.
   3. The buyer and seller are each acting prudently and knowledgeably.
   4. The price is not affected by undue stimulus.
   5. The buyer and seller are typically motivated.
   6. Both parties are acting in what they consider their best interest.
   7. Marketing efforts were adequate and a reasonable time was allowed for exposure in the open market.
   8. Payment was made in cash in U.S. dollars or in terms of financial arrangements comparable thereto.
   9. The price represents the normal consideration for the property sold, unaffected by special or creative financing or sales concessions granted by anyone associated with the sale.

   This definition can also be modified to provide for valuation with specified financing terms.

* Adjustments to the comparables must be made for special or creative financing or sales concessions. No adjustments are necessary for those costs which are normally paid by sellers as a result of tradition or law in a market area; these costs are readily identifiable since the seller pays these costs in virtually all sales transactions. Special or creative financing adjustments can be made to the comparable property by comparisons to financing terms offered by a third-party institutional lender that is not already involved in the property or transaction. Any adjustment should not be calculated on a mechanical dollar for dollar cost of the financing or concession but the dollar amount of any adjustment should approximate the market's reaction to the financing or concessions based on the appraiser's judgment.

Persons performing appraisal services that may be subject to litigation are cautioned to seek the exact definition of market value applicable in the jurisdiction where the services are being performed. For further discussion of this important term, see *The Appraisal of Real Estate,* 12th ed. (Chicago: Appraisal Institute, 2001), 21-24.

Source: *The Dictionary of Real Estate Appraisal,* 4th ed. Chicago: Appraisal Institute, 2002. (Updated)

HUD also provides protocols for handling sales and financing concessions in Appendix D of HUD Handbook 4150.2:

- Report the type of financing such as conventional, FHA or VA, etc.
- Report the type and amount of sales concession for each comparable sale listed. If no concessions exist, the appraiser must note "none."
- The appraiser is required to make market-based adjustments to the comparable sales for any sales or financing concessions that may have affected the sales price.
- The adjustment for such affected comparable sales must reflect the difference between the sales price with the sales concessions and what the property would have sold for without the concessions.

The goal of adjusting financing concessions is to achieve cash-equivalent prices.

In some litigation matters, appraisers must use the precise definition of market value that is applied in the jurisdiction in which the services are being performed. Because government and regulatory agencies define or interpret market value from time to time, individuals performing appraisal services for these agencies or for institutions subject to their control should use the applicable market value definition.

Other Types of Value

Along with an increased emphasis on market value, the realities of today's real estate market frequently require that other kinds of value be considered. These other values include use value and assessed value. Anticipated sale price is a related value concept.

Use Value

Use value is the value of a specific property for a specific use. This value concept is based on the productivity of an economic good. Use value refers to the value that the real estate contributes to the enterprise of which it is a part, without regard to highest and best use or the monetary amount that might be realized upon its sale. Use value may vary with the management of the property and external conditions such as changes in the business environment. For many real properties, use value and market value will differ.

When the property being appraised is of a type that is not commonly sold or rented, it may be difficult to determine whether an opinion of market value or use value is appropriate. Limited-market properties can present special problems for appraisers.

Many limited-market properties are improved with structures that have unique physical designs, special construction materials, or layouts that severely restrict the property's

use value. In real estate appraisal, the value a specific property has for a specific use; may be the highest and best use of the property or some other use specified as a condition of the appraisal; may be used where legislation has been enacted to preserve farmland, timberland, or other open space land on urban fringes.

utility. Generally they are only suitable for the use for which they were built. Consequently, such properties are often called *special-purpose* or *special-design properties.* Homes that have been adapted to other uses or homes designed for the physically disabled are examples of special-purpose or special-design properties. In some locales, places of worship and schools may be limited-market properties.

In certain circumstances, limited-market properties may be appraised at their use value based on their current use. In other circumstances, they are appraised at market value based on the most likely alternative use. Because there is a relatively small market for these properties and lengthy market exposure is often required to find a buyer, evidence to support a market value estimate may be sparse. Nonetheless, if a market exists, the appraiser must search diligently for all available evidence of market value. If a property's current use is so specialized that there is no demonstrable market for the property but the use is viable and likely to continue, the appraiser may render an opinion of use value.

A use value opinion should not be confused with a market value opinion. If no market can be found or if data are not available, the appraiser cannot conclude a market value and should say so in the report. However, for legal purposes it is sometimes necessary to estimate market value even though no market can be found. In these cases, the appraiser must comply with the legal requirement but will have to reach an opinion of market value by other means, relying on judgment rather than direct market evidence.

Assessed Value

Assessed value is applied in ad valorem taxation and is established by the municipal authority legally charged with this responsibility. Assessment schedules may not conform to market value, but they usually relate to a market value base.

Anticipated Sales Price

Anticipated sales price is defined by the Employee Relocation Council as

> The price at which a property is anticipated to sell in a competitive and open market, assuming an arm's-length transaction whereby:
>
> 1. The analysis reflects the property "as is" and is based on its present use as a residential dwelling.
> 2. Both buyer and seller are typically motivated; both parties are well-informed or well-advised and acting in what they consider their best interests.
> 3. Payment is made in cash or its equivalent.
> 4. A reasonable marketing period, not to exceed 120 days and commencing on the date of appraisal (inspection), is allowed for exposure in the open market. The analysis assumes an adequate effort to market the subject property.

5. Forecasting is applied to reflect the anticipated trend of market conditions and prices during the subject property's prospective marketing period.[5]

Insurable Value

Insurable value is the value used by insurance companies as the basis for insurance and reflects the replacement cost of physical items that are subject to loss from hazards. Insurable value is that portion of the value of an asset or asset group that is acknowledged or recognized under the provisions of an applicable loss insurance policy, often considered to be replacement or reproduction cost plus allowances for debris removal or demolition less deterioration and noninsurable items.[6]

5. *The Relocation Appraisal Guide* (Washington, D.C.: Employee Relocation Council, 2001) as quoted on the Employee Relocation Council Summary Appraisal Report form (2003).

6. *Marshall Valuation Service,* Glossary, s.v., insurable value.

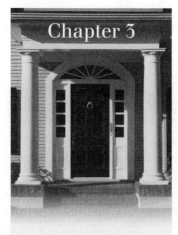

Chapter 3

Principles of Real Estate Economics

Every residential appraiser should be familiar with the fundamental principles of real estate economics. These concepts originate in basic economic theory and have been refined and made practical by real estate appraisers. Although economic principles provide a conceptual base, real estate appraisal is concerned with more than just theoretical matters. Every objective, professional appraisal must be supported by a solid understanding of the economic principles that govern how value is created and how it changes in the real estate market. To conduct professional appraisals, practitioners must recognize how economic principles operate in particular valuation situations. These fundamental ideas resurface throughout the remaining chapters of this book.

The principles and concepts of real estate economics may be organized into three broad categories:

1. General economic principles, which can be observed in a wide variety of markets
2. Characteristics unique to real estate markets
3. Principles relating to the agents of production, which create real estate and the benefits that accrue from its use

General Economic Theory

The general principles of economic theory are the laws and concepts that characterize the actions of buyers and sellers (i.e., the market) who exchange various types of goods and services. These fundamental ideas apply to real estate markets and to related markets that directly or indirectly influence property values by impacting the consumer's purchasing power or expendable income. Fundamental concerns applicable to real estate are

1. The principle of supply and demand
2. The concept of competition
3. The principle of substitution
4. The principle of anticipation (i.e., property resale or reversion)
5. The definition of a market

Supply and Demand

The law of supply and demand is the most fundamental of all economic principles. This principle applies to the prices of all goods and services that are bought and sold in competitive markets. As applied to real property, this law states that the price of real property varies directly, but not necessarily proportionately, with demand and inversely, but not necessarily proportionately, with supply. It affirms that, all else being equal, the market will usually pay less for an item when it is available for sale in greater quantity, and the market will usually pay more for the item when less of it is available. Similarly, when the number of items that purchasers demand increases, the prices paid for these items can be expected to rise, provided that the supply remains constant; if demand decreases, prices can be expected to fall.

In residential markets, increases in supply may result from new construction, conversion from other uses, or the actions of many owners who decide to sell at a given time, such as when there is a severe downturn in the economy. Decreases in supply usually result from demolition, conversion to other uses, slow or limited construction of new residences as a result of limited land or the cost of construction financing, and the actions of owners who decide to abstain from selling their property. Changes in demand typically occur more rapidly than changes in supply, so demand is the more critical price determinant. (Analysis of supply and demand is a basic component of the market analysis process, which is presented in detail in Chapter 10.)

Figures 3.1 and 3.2 illustrate the operation of supply and demand in real estate markets. Supply is represented by the various numbers of a type of real estate available for sale or lease at various prices. As the upward-sloping supply curve in Figure 3.1 suggests, suppliers are usually more willing to increase production when prices are higher. Similarly, demand is reflected in the numbers of a type of real estate demanded at various prices for purchase or

supply and demand. In economic theory, the principle that states that the price of a commodity, good, or service varies directly, but not necessarily proportionately, with demand, and inversely, but not necessarily proportionately, with supply. In a real estate appraisal context, the principle of supply and demand states that the price of real property varies directly, but not necessarily proportionately, with demand and inversely, but not necessarily proportionately, with supply.

rent. The demand curve in the figure slopes downward because more is demanded at lower prices. The point where these curves intersect is the price at which a given property will most probably be sold.

Figure 3.2 shows how real estate markets react when demand shifts. In this example demand has decreased, so the whole curve moves to the left. If supply remains constant, the curves intersect at a different point, and the price at which the property will most probably be sold drops.

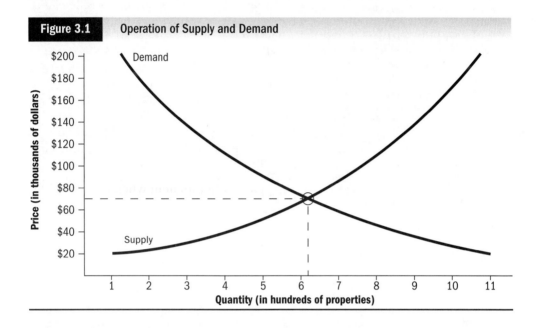

Figure 3.1 Operation of Supply and Demand

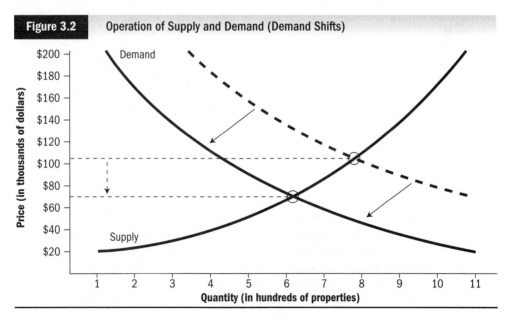

Figure 3.2 Operation of Supply and Demand (Demand Shifts)

Four economic factors must be present to create value:

1. Desire
2. Utility
3. Scarcity
4. Effective purchasing power

The interaction of these factors is reflected in the principle of supply and demand.

Desire is a purchaser's wish for an item to satisfy an actual need or an individual want beyond essential life-support needs. Desire is limited by effective purchasing power.

Utility is the ability of an item to satisfy a human want, need, or desire. It varies with the wants and needs of different individuals. Sometimes improving the usefulness and quality of an item can increase the demand for it. However, changes in utility can only go so far toward augmenting demand.

Scarcity is the present or anticipated supply of an item relative to the demand for that item. The availability of an item must be somewhat limited for needs or wants to be perceived. If an item is abundant, its existence will be taken for granted. Air is the classic example of a necessary item that is typically so abundant that it has no definable economic value.

The final factor of value is effective purchasing power, the ability and willingness of people to pay for the goods or services that they desire. Individuals must have purchasing power to translate their desires into demand. Desire coupled with purchasing power is sometimes called *effective demand*. Often the effective demand for an expensive item diminishes when income levels fall or the cost of financing to acquire the item rises. Changes in purchasing power have a pronounced effect on real estate markets because real estate transactions involve large sums of money.

Competition

Supply and demand exert pressure on prices through competition. An auction is a familiar example of competition among buyers. Most markets are not like auctions, however, because sellers must also compete. When demand is weak compared with supply, competition between sellers can become especially intense. The quality and utility of the item may be improved, and special incentives may be offered to attract the limited number of buyers. In many cases, prices must also be reduced.

Competing sellers hope to make a profit by obtaining prices that are somewhat greater than their expenses for acquiring or producing the item. When strong demand for an item emerges, the first sellers frequently do make sizable profits. Soon, however, other sellers join the competition, which drives prices down. Sometimes so many suppliers join the market that competition is very intense and prices fall below the cost of production, which undermines profits for everyone. In this situation, some sellers go bankrupt and others refrain from any further production or acquisition until all the oversupplied items have been absorbed and demand can resume at higher prices—hence, excess competition can be ruinous.

In the long run, balance is restored in the market, at least in theory. When demand is not strong enough to raise prices, nor weak enough to lower prices, prices stabilize and the forces of supply and demand are in equilibrium. At the point of equilibrium, prices are generally fairly close to the costs required to produce the item and to compensate developers with an acceptable margin of profit, called *entrepreneurial incentive* or *profit.*

Substitution

Substitution is another principle that has broad significance in all economic activities. The principle of *substitution* affirms that when several similar or commensurate commodities, goods, or services are available, the one with the lowest price will attract the greatest demand and the widest distribution. Because competition underlies this principle, the prices at which similar items are sold in a

> **substitution.** The appraisal principle that states that when several similar or commensurate commodities, goods, or services are available, the one with the lowest price will attract the greatest demand and widest distribution. This is the primary principle upon which the cost and sales comparison approaches are based.

market tend to grow increasingly uniform. Sellers who face a shrinking demand for their products are soon forced to lower their prices to prevailing levels if they are to sell at all. Sellers who experience the most intense demand for their products due to their lower prices may raise prices to established levels to reap greater profits.

When the items that different sellers are offering are physically similar, like oranges at a fruit market, it is easy to see how the principle of substitution operates. But substitution works equally well when the characteristics of items of similar utility are more abstract. For example, investors may perceive bond issues, mortgage loans, and other long-term capital instruments to be more or less interchangeable for their purposes. These investments all involve similar levels of risk, tie up money for approximately the same amount of time, and produce similar yields. As a result, these investments directly compete with one another for investors' funds.

Because investments compete for investment capital, conditions in the mortgage market closely follow conditions in financial markets, and the mortgage market is sensitive to developments that affect investment in other financial markets. Appraisers must perceive these market relationships to understand changes in price levels in the residential market. The amount and terms of mortgage money available at any given moment strongly affect the demand for housing.

The principle of substitution is also basic to the three approaches to value in the valuation process. (The valuation process is covered more fully in Chapter 5, and the individual approaches to value are discussed in Chapters 13 through 19.) In the cost approach, a value indication is produced by adding the cost of producing a substitute residence to the value of the land. The reasoning behind this approach is that no one will spend more money for a property than it would cost to buy similar land and erect a similar structure without undue delay. In the sales comparison approach, the market value of a residence is estimated by examining the prices at which comparable residences have recently been sold. In the income capitalization approach, market value is based on the economic benefits that a property offers, which are indicated by market-derived rates of return.

Anticipation

The expectation of future benefits creates value. The concept of *anticipation* affirms that value is created by the expectation of benefits to be derived in the future. According to this concept, the value of a property in the market at a given time is the present value of all the future benefits that people perceive the property will yield.

This understanding of the source of value applies to all types of property, even residential properties in which the expected benefits take the form of home ownership, occupancy, and tax benefits such as deductions on federal income taxes for state and local property taxes and the interest paid on mortgages. The appraiser applies the concept of anticipation most directly, however, to property that generates a rental income. The future benefits of owning these properties take the form of an income stream and a reversion (i.e., the lump-sum benefit that an investor receives or expects to receive at the termination of an investment).

In light of anticipation, appraisers recognize that the present value of future benefits reflects the time value of money. More money or benefits in the future is equal to less money or fewer benefits today.

Markets

anticipation. The perception that value is created by the expectation of benefits to be derived in the future.

market.
1. A set of arrangements in which many buyers and sellers are brought together through the price mechanism.
2. A gathering of people for the buying and selling of things; by extension, the people gathered for this purpose.

Supply and demand, competition, substitution, and anticipation are all demonstrated in the operation of markets. A market is a set of arrangements in which buyers and sellers are brought together through the price mechanism. A stock exchange, for example, is a market established in a convenient location where buyers come to obtain the goods or services offered by sellers. However, the product does not always have to be brought to market, as the real estate industry demonstrates. Real estate markets qualify as markets because buyers and sellers interact, compete, and cause identifiable changes in real estate prices.

Each market has its own unique characteristics, which depend on the arrangements that buyers and sellers have developed and the patterns of activity that have evolved. Perhaps the most important feature that identifies a specific market is the degree of direct competition among the different items sold in it. When the competition is direct, the activities are considered to be taking place in the same market. The distance between individual properties is not as significant as their substitutability.

Real estate markets have many characteristics that set them apart from other markets. Five different real estate markets can be identified in terms of typical users and property types. These markets define the basic land use types analyzed in highest and best use:

- Residential markets
- Commercial markets
- Industrial markets
- Agricultural markets
- Special-purpose markets

Each of these markets can be further divided into smaller markets (known as *submarkets*), in which buyers seek and sellers offer properties with specific features, locations, and prices. When the characteristics of the properties are very similar, the result is direct competition among the buyers who represent demand and the sellers who represent supply. Increased similarity makes price relationships closer and the market more focused. Identifying and analyzing submarkets within a larger market is called *market segmentation.*

market segmentation. The process by which submarkets within a larger market are identified and analyzed.

Neighborhoods, Districts, and Market Areas

A neighborhood is defined by certain characteristics that differentiate it from other neighborhoods and adjacent areas. Often neighborhood residents have common social characteristics such as age, income, and lifestyle. Many neighborhoods are identified by landmarks and defined boundaries; properties may have similar architectural styles or a particular blend of styles. A neighborhood can also be characterized by the mix of amenities and services that appeal to the people who choose to live there.

These features are not constant or uniform in all neighborhoods. They usually change over time and in different ways in each particular case. The character of a neighborhood is continually evolving in response to changing social, economic, governmental, and environmental (including physical and geographical) conditions. The life of a neighborhood frequently follows a cyclical pattern and is affected by many factors, including its age, its position within the larger community, and the appeal of competitive neighborhoods.

The idea of a neighborhood is familiar to most people, but appraisers use the term in a specific sense. For appraisal purposes, a *neighborhood* is an area of complementary land uses. One essential aspect of this definition is the concept that the various land uses function as a unit. Most residential neighborhoods contain a variety of land uses. Different areas are improved with detached single-family dwellings, apartment buildings, and amenities and services such as parks, places of worship, cinemas, schools, and businesses. All of these elements tend to function together in a neighborhood, and the state of each element can often strongly affect the state of the whole neighborhood. As the principle of balance suggests, failing businesses, poorly maintained residential blocks, an inappropriate mix of land uses, and other detrimental conditions that affect segments of a neighborhood can directly reduce the appeal of neighborhood properties. These conditions often signal a pattern of change in a neighborhood, which may affect the value of all properties within its boundaries.

A *district* is a type of neighborhood that is characterized by homogeneous land use. Districts are commonly composed of apartments or of commercial, industrial, or agricultural properties. In large cities, an apartment district usually covers an extensive area; in smaller cities, an apartment district may be limited in size. The apartment buildings in a district may be multistory or single-story, high-rise or row, garden or townhouse. Individual units may be rented or privately owned as cooperatives or condominiums.

The concepts of neighborhood and district overlap, but a necessary distinction must be made. The term *neighborhood* suggests a variety or balance of complementary land uses, while the term *district* refers to an area where one type of use predominates. Sometimes a neighborhood is composed of various districts. The *market area* is the area in which properties effectively compete with the subject property in the minds of probable, potential purchasers and users.[1] The residential market area usually includes much of the subject neighborhood. Occasionally, however, only a segment of the neighborhood may be in the market area. The market area can also extend beyond the neighborhood when other neighborhoods compete with the subject neighborhood in the minds of potential purchasers. Often these other neighborhoods are near the subject neighborhood or located a similar distance away from a major employment center. Rural properties belong to a market area that is far more extensive than the market areas for urban or suburban properties. A market area is defined by the type of property, the type of transaction (e.g.,

neighborhood. A group of complementary land uses; a congruous grouping of inhabitants, buildings, or business enterprises.

district. A type of market area characterized by homogeneous land use, e.g., apartment, commercial, industrial, agricultural.

market area. The geographic or locational delineation of the market for a specific category of real estate, i.e., the area in which alternative, similar properties effectively compete with the subject property in the minds of probable, potential purchasers and users.

---

1. In 1997, the term *neighborhood* was changed to *market area* in Rule 1-3(a) of the Uniform Standards of Professional Appraisal Practice.

rental or sale), the geographic area in which competition exists, and the homogeneity of properties within its boundaries.

Characteristics of Real Estate Markets

Real estate markets share some general characteristics with markets of all kinds, but other features make them unique. These features can best be illustrated by comparing real estate markets with a perfect, hypothetical market in which supply and demand operate smoothly, freely, and efficiently. As Table 3.1 clearly shows, real estate markets are not efficient. In fact, many economists believe that real estate markets are among the least efficient markets in existence.

Table 3.1	Comparison of Efficient Markets and Real Estate Markets
Efficient Markets	**Real Estate Markets**
Goods and services are essentially homogeneous items that are readily substituted.	No two parcels of real estate have identical characteristics and so the price of one parcel cannot be directly inferred from the price of another.
Because the quality of goods and services tends to be fairly uniform, prices are relatively low and stable.	Prices are not low. Most transactions involve a mortgage loan, which allows financing considerations to have an effect on price. Purchasing power is also very sensitive to demographics, wage levels, employment figures, etc.
A large number of market participants creates a competitive, free market, and none of these participants has a large enough share of the market to have a direct and measurable influence on price.	There are usually only a few buyers and sellers interested in a particular type of property at one time, in one price range, and in one location. An individual buyer or seller can influence price through exertion of control on supply and/or demand.
Self-regulating markets require few government restrictions.	Federal, state, county, and local regulations govern the ownership and transfer of real estate. The demand for specific uses of real estate is often legally limited through zoning. The Federal Reserve System manipulates the market by controlling the supply of credit.
Supply and demand are never far out of balance. The market returns to equilibrium quickly through the effects of competition.	Supply and demand tend toward equilibrium, but this point is seldom achieved. The supply of real estate for a specific use does not adjust to market demand quickly, and demand can change while new supply is being developed.
Buyers and sellers are knowledgeable and fully informed about market conditions, the behavior of other market participants, past market activity, product quality, and product substitutability.	Market participants are not always well informed and are seldom experienced in the market.
Market information is readily available.	Information is not readily available.
Buyers and sellers are brought together by an organized market mechanism. Sellers can easily enter the market in response to demand.	Buyers and sellers are not brought together formally.
Goods are easily transported from place to place.	Real estate is immovable. Demand in one place can not be met by supply in another.
External economic conditions can have an effect on price.	Externalities have a very significant effect on value.

With the advent of databases such as multiple listing services, real estate markets have become more efficient. At the same time, increased expendable income, aggressive lending, and increased mobility have made real estate markets more volatile.

Four Forces That Influence Value

Appraisers must understand the forces that influence value. As discussed in Chapter 2, legal, physical, and economic restrictions limit the use of real property. They can also increase, sustain, or diminish property values by affecting the supply of or demand for properties of a specific type in a particular area at any given time. Appraisers consider four broad, dynamic forces that influence value:

1. Social trends and standards
2. Economic conditions
3. Governmental rules and regulations
4. Environmental conditions

The interaction of these forces affects the value of every parcel of real estate available in the market so these forces are all studied as part of a full analysis of any market for real property. Market analysis is discussed in more detail in Chapter 9.

Social Trends and Standards

A change in demographics, such as an influx of population into or a migration out of an area, directly alters the demand for properties in that area. Changes in birth and death rates, marriage and divorce rates, population age, and household formation can also influence the characteristics of demand for real estate. Different types of consumers have different neighborhood and building preferences, and their favor or disfavor is reflected in the prices consumers will pay for property.

Economic Conditions

The purchasing power of a population limits its capability of acquiring real estate and directly influences demand. Purchasing power is determined by economic conditions such as employment and wage levels, industrial contraction or expansion, the community's economic base, price levels, and the cost and availability of credit. On the supply side, influential economic conditions include the stock of available vacant and improved properties, new properties under construction or in the planning stage, occupancy rates, the rent and price patterns of existing properties, and construction costs.

Governmental Rules and Regulations

The legal climate at a particular time in a specific place can impede the normal operation of supply and demand. The government's readiness or reluctance to provide necessary facilities and services helps shape land-use patterns and, therefore, affects property values in certain locations. Significant government activities may include

- Public services such as fire and police protection, utilities, refuse collection, and transportation networks
- Local zoning, building, and health codes, which may support or obstruct specific land uses
- National, state, and local fiscal policies
- Special legislation that influences general property values—e.g., rent control laws, statutory redemption laws, restrictions on forms of ownership such as condominiums and timeshare arrangements, homestead exemption laws, environmental legislation regulating new development, and laws that affect the types of loans, loan terms, and investment powers of mortgage lending institutions

Environmental Conditions

Natural barriers to future development include rivers, mountains, lakes, and oceans. Man-made features such as federal and state highways, railroads, airports, and navigable waterways also influence the potential use and value of real estate. Climatic conditions such as snowfall, rainfall, temperature, humidity, topography, and soil conditions are other important environmental influences. The natural character and desirability of a property's surrounding area or neighborhood are environmental factors that can exert a substantial influence on property values.

Also, access to public transportation, schools, stores, service establishments, parks, recreational areas, cultural facilities, places of worship, sources of employment, and product markets all have a very strong effect on a property's marketability in the eyes of potential buyers. The use of land can be changed if it is economical to do so, but the location of land is fixed. The location of property is therefore a critical consideration.

The four forces that affect property value are not mutually exclusive; often they are interrelated. For example, political forces such as the actions of the federal government stimulate the housing market, so they must also be considered economic forces. Classification of these forces is useful in considering the variety of value influences that exist and how they interact to affect supply and demand in real estate markets.

Four Forces in the Local Residential Market

An appraiser is typically most interested in the market area for the subject property. Within this geographic area or political jurisdiction, alternative, similar properties effectively compete with the subject property in the minds of probable, potential purchasers and users. Outside this area, zoning regulations may differ, locations may not appeal to the same buyers, builders may not incur the same costs, and other value influences will have different effects. Thus the market area is the geographic area in which value-influencing forces have similar effects on competing properties and market participants.

Because the location of real estate is fixed, the area in which buyers and sellers compete directly is often small and can be delineated geographically. People with a certain level of income and demographic characteristics—e.g., age, number of young children—often shop for residences in particular neighborhoods. These buyers compete most directly with other buyers who have the same income level and preferences. Similarly, home sellers usually face the most direct competition from neighbors who have similar properties for sale. Less direct competition may come from sellers of comparable properties in competitive neighborhoods some distance away.

In another context, many of the costs of residential development in an area are determined by competition in local construction and financial markets and by municipal development policy and regulation. Early in the valuation process, the appraiser must specify the submarket to which the subject property most likely appeals by identifying the area in which the four forces affect value in a similar manner. Recent sales considered comparable and other indications of value drawn from within the market area generally have the greatest reliability for valuation purposes.

Changes, Trends, and Cycles

Most of the changes that affect supply and demand in real estate markets are not random. An appraiser must understand why the market is changing because this knowledge may affect the outcome of the appraisal assignment. Changes that are pervasive or relate to many other changes that are occurring are called *trends*. A trend is a series of related changes brought about by a chain of causes and effects. Trends reflect the momentum of the market and develop in recognizable patterns. An appraiser can analyze these patterns to make forecasts.

For example, the increase in energy costs in the 1970s produced a major trend that affected the general economy and had a pronounced impact on real estate. Some of the consequences of this trend were recessions in regions of the country economically reliant on cheap, plentiful sources of energy (such as Texas and the aging centers of heavy industry in the Midwest and Northeast), high inflation and interest rates throughout the nation, and increased demand for smaller, energy-efficient housing.

Many important trends that affect real estate prices occur in cycles. Frequently real estate values follow the larger business cycle, and fluctuations in value are related to the rise and fall of the gross domestic product. Another influential cycle is the neighborhood life cycle of growth, stability, decline, and revitalization. This cycle is usually much longer than the business cycle.

Seasonal cycles also affect real estate values. In many areas of the country, for example, construction slows down during the winter, thus decreasing supply. In some areas, people prefer to sell their homes when the landscaping is most attractive, usually in late spring or summer. Many leases turn over on an annual basis. Neighborhoods near large universities may have rent cycles tied to segments of the school year.

Neighborhood Life Cycles
Most neighborhoods go through a natural cycle of changes, which affects their character, their desirability, and the value of real estate located there. Neighborhoods go through periods of
1. Growth
2. Stability
3. Decline
4. Revitalization

Growth
A neighborhood begins its life when buildings are constructed on vacant, newly cleared land or when properties are converted from a different use. This development may create a new community or it may expand an existing community to accommodate new demand for real estate. Neighborhoods often begin their growth during periods of local economic expansion. When employment prospects are good and interest rates are relatively low, developers are motivated to construct new units.

A neighborhood's growth period may be short-lived or it may last several years. Growth may continue as long as the neighborhood is perceived as a good value. Growth may stop when the demand for new housing diminishes as a result of shifts in buyer preferences or when the supply of housing is restrained by high construction or financing costs. If the neighborhood is successfully developed, new construction will attract new inhabitants. As the neighborhood gains public recognition and favor, demand is sustained. As long as vacant land is plentiful, land prices will usually remain low in comparison to improved property prices. In a successful development, prices for both vacant land and improved properties usually increase as growth continues.

Because neighborhood growth frequently coincides with expansion in the local and regional economy, funding for public works to support the development often increases. Public works are usually not profitable on a small scale. For example, a sewer trunk line, which may open thousands of acres for development, is generally not extended in small sections. Public restrictions on development often accompany public funding. In many cases, further development must conform to detailed land-use plans drawn up by local government and municipal agencies.

During the growth of a neighborhood, activity is generally vigorous. As a result, the buildings constructed during this period tend to be relatively similar in appearance, reflecting the building practices and market preferences of a particular time. The economic history of a city can often be discerned by studying the dominant architectural styles of its neighborhoods.

Stability

Neighborhood growth ends when it is no longer profitable to build, when other neighborhoods become better values, or when the neighborhood is fully developed. The neighborhood then enters a relatively stable period. A period of stability can also occur after a period of revitalization, when it is no longer profitable to convert properties from one use to another or to renovate them. In the stable phase, changes do not usually stop completely but they proceed at a slower pace. New construction may continue on a limited basis once demand increases or financing terms improve.

Neighborhood stability is characterized by the absence of marked growth or decline. The neighborhood settles into a comfortable pattern of activity. The demand for both new and existing units is generally balanced with the supply. Many residents remain, so property turnovers are relatively low. Real estate values stabilize and may even appreciate, depending on the neighborhood's popularity and the strength of demand. Zoning codes are enforced and there is strong economic and social pressure for dwellings to conform to neighborhood and legal standards. The boundaries of the neighborhood are usually clearly demarcated.

This period of stability may last for some time. Buildings are aging but residents have enough income to meet their maintenance costs, so deterioration is not substantial. Neighborhoods have no established life expectancy, so decline is not imminent in all older neighborhoods.

Decline

A period of decline begins when a neighborhood can no longer compete with comparable neighborhoods. Maintenance costs may become too high due to the age of the dwellings or, more likely, because the location, style, and utility of residences have lost their appeal.

During this period, properties may fail to attract buyers.[2] "For sale" signs appear more frequently and turnovers increase. Neither new nor older residents have enough money to maintain the buildings adequately. Because residents cannot support the community businesses and services that were formerly in demand, building maintenance declines, vacancies increase, and businesses change hands. During a period of decline, building codes and zoning regulations may not be enforced. The boundaries of the neighborhood become less distinct and the number of rental units often increases in comparison with owner-occupied units.

---

2. At one time lenders were accused of contributing to discrimination against minorities by unfairly penalizing neighborhoods because of the low incomes and racial backgrounds of their residents; this practice is known as *redlining*. The integration of neighborhoods was mistakenly thought to signal the beginning of a decline in their life cycles. Some banks refused to make mortgage loans in certain inner-city areas due to their high default rates, rather than basing their decisions on individual investment risks. This practice was held to be unlawful by the courts and by federal agencies that have regulatory authority over lending institutions.

   For more information, see *www.hud.gov/offices/fheo* and *www.fairlending.org*.

Revitalization

Neighborhood decline ends when the dominant land use changes or a period of renewal begins. The decline in values ceases and a new balance is struck. Deteriorated buildings are torn down, other buildings are converted to more intensive uses, and the neighborhood is ready to begin its cycle of change once more.

gentrification. A neighborhood phenomenon in which middle- and upper-income persons purchase neighborhood properties and renovate or rehabilitate them.

When revitalization occurs, it is usually the result of changing preferences and community patterns. For example, economic growth in the larger community may increase the demand for housing in the neighborhood. Organized community efforts such as redevelopment programs and historic renovation may contribute significantly to revitalization; revitalization can also begin spontaneously, without planning or formal municipal assistance.

In a process that has become known as *gentrification,* middle- and upper-income people purchase properties in urban neighborhoods to renovate or rehabilitate them, thereby revitalizing the neighborhood. These properties may have been of marginal quality and reflected residential or other uses. Often apartment buildings are upgraded, converted to condominiums or cooperatives, and removed from the rental stock. Sometimes obsolete office buildings and former industrial sites are converted into residential uses. This type of activity can change the orientation of the entire neighborhood.

Gentrification appears to stem from the preponderance of single people and small families in metropolitan areas who want to live in proximity to urban activities. As a consequence of gentrification, poorer residents who cannot afford the high rents and rising prices are displaced. These lower-income groups may have moved into the older city neighborhoods when others found them unappealing and unattractive. The scarcity of federal funds for low-income housing has compounded the plight of those groups.

A period of revitalization, like a period of decline, is often marked by increased change and a greater disparity between property values in different parts of the neighborhood. Revitalization usually proceeds block by block. Once the effort gathers momentum, more remodeling is undertaken by residents who foresee a substantial increase in property values. The changes that accompany revitalization are usually noticeably different from the changes brought about by decline. Neighborhood revitalization usually fosters an atmosphere of hope as large numbers of tradesmen and homeowners work to repair or remodel neighborhood properties.

The four stages described reflect how neighborhoods and districts evolve, but they should not be taken as rigid guides to market trends. Changes do not necessarily follow in sequence. Decline may proceed at a barely perceptible rate. At any time, major changes can occur to interrupt the order of the neighborhood life cycle. An external influence such as a new highway that changes traffic patterns can bring about decline or revitalization. A neighborhood that is in a stage of growth may decline suddenly rather than stabilize. An area that is developing as a residential neighborhood may, due to a sudden external change, begin to grow as a commercial district. Appraisers can only reach conclusions about the stage of a neighborhood and the likely trend in its property values after they have performed a market analysis. Discussions with local residents, merchants, brokers, bankers, appraisers, municipal planners, zoning officials, and other knowledgeable persons can contribute greatly to an appraiser's understanding of neighborhood development.

Siting Factors and Economic Base Analysis

siting factor. The origin of settlement in a city, which generally influences subsequent land use and growth patterns.

economic base analysis. A survey of the industries and businesses that generate employment and income in a community as well as the rate of population growth and levels of income, both of which are functions of employment. Economic base analysis is used to forecast the level and composition of future economic activity. Specifically, the relationship between basic employment (which brings income into a community) and nonbasic employment (which provides services for workers in the basic employment sector) is studied to predict population, income, or other variables that affect real estate values or land utilization.

The forces that affect property values can often be best understood by studying how a specific community has evolved in shape and character. How do the various neighborhoods in a city affect one another? Does the subject neighborhood lie in the path of an expanding, wealthier community, or are residents moving to locations that offer access to workplaces on less congested routes? An appraiser notes the community's siting factor–i.e., the reason the site was originally chosen for settlement–as well as the reasons for subsequent growth, patterns of change, and factors likely to encourage, direct, or restrict future development. This information can help the appraiser complete the analysis of market conditions in the city and region and begin to focus on market conditions in the specific neighborhood–i.e., the formal process of market analysis.

Historically, people settle in locations because of their particular advantages:

- Defensible terrain
- Access to water
- Location on trade routes or at intersections where goods could be profitably traded
- Availability of economic resources such as arable or mineral-rich land
- Proximity to political centers

Many of these considerations influenced the sites selected for early American communities and affect the places that new communities are developed today.

In addition to the original siting factor, an appraiser is interested in what makes an area a desirable or undesirable place to live now. The economic health and stability of the region or community is particularly important. The economic soundness of an area is formally studied in an economic base analysis. An economic base analysis examines which local businesses and industries draw purchasing power into the area and which serve the local population. Such an analysis also assesses the diversity of the economy in the area and its ability to weather cyclical fluctuations.

If an area's economic base is concentrated on a single industry, the area may be susceptible to resource depletion, competition from imitation products produced elsewhere, or technological developments that supplant the need for its products. Similarly, areas that cannot weather cyclical economic fluctuations will present greater risks to lenders, who will be forced to raise rates, which will then discourage growth and demand in the area. In contrast, areas that have a diversity of basic industries and occupations tend to fare better over the long term.

Sometimes an appraiser must consult specialists with expert information on the region's economic base, particularly if a long-term study of supply and demand or a marketability study is needed. For most residential appraisals, however, a detailed, formal analysis of the area's economic base is not required. Nonetheless, appraisers should be sensitive to changes in the economic climate of a region, especially changes that may not have been anticipated by market participants. The sudden arrival or departure of a major employer, for example, can have a substantial effect on the demand for housing in an area.

Important technological, economic, and political developments also influence the shape and character of American communities. With an understanding of these factors, an appraiser can develop a useful perspective on ongoing trends that affect many cities and regions in the United States.

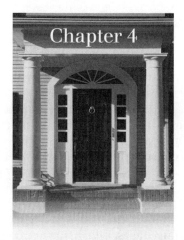

Chapter 4

Residential Real Estate Financing

The market for residential property is strongly influenced by trends in mortgage financing and their effects on the supply and demand of real estate. Almost all purchases of one- to four-family homes involve some form of financing because few households have the financial wherewithal to pay in cash. For example, a single-family home at the current national average price of around $235,000 is a significant investment for a household with annual income of around $45,000, the current U.S. average. The availability of funds and the terms at which those funds are available have a significant effect on offering prices, selling prices, and ultimately the affordability of housing.

Mortgage loans compete with other investments (e.g., stocks, bonds, more liquid investments) for available money in the capital markets, and lenders compete with one another to make home loans. Mortgage brokers are playing an increasingly important role in the mortgage process, giving homebuyers more options for obtaining loans than consumers have ever had before. Within the lending community, the competition for prospective loans and the desire to fill the pipeline can stretch the limits of underwriting criteria into risky areas, and this can lead to illegal practices such as predatory lending and mortgage fraud.

To make a reasonable forecast of the market, appraisers must thoroughly research the types of financing currently available and analyze historical trends. This chapter focuses on sources of mortgage money, factors that influence the mortgage market, the typical and atypical financing plans found in the marketplace, and how all these interactions may affect residential appraisers.

Sources of Mortgage Money

Funds for financing the purchase of a single-family residence can come from either primary or secondary sources. Primary sources are institutions that assemble money deposited by savers or investors and lend it directly to borrowers. Individuals who make mortgage loans are also included in this category. Institutions that are secondary financing sources do not raise money or make mortgage loans directly. These institutions facilitate financing opportunities by buying and selling existing mortgages, which increases the efficiency of the lending market.

Primary Sources

Mortgage pools and trusts, banks, and mortgage companies provide funds for most home purchases. Life insurance companies invest some money, but they tend to be interested in multifamily residences and other types of income-producing property. Table 4.1 shows the percentage of mortgage debt held by various primary sources.

Banks and other savings institutions act as financial intermediaries. When other investments offer better interest rates, depositors withdraw their money and invest elsewhere. This is called disintermediation, and it affects the availability of mortgage funds. In the 1970s and 1980s, disintermediation reduced the funds available for home financing more than once. The operations of the secondary mortgage market can help offset these shortages.

disintermediation. The transfer of money from low interest-bearing accounts to higher interest-bearing accounts.

Secondary Mortgage Market

The development of the secondary mortgage market has greatly facilitated the financing of real estate over the past few decades. At one time, many lending institutions made home loans and held them until maturity. Now they sell packages of mortgage loans to investors in the secondary

Table 4.1	Distribution of Mortgage Funds for One- to Four-Family Homes
Loan Source	**% of Loans**
Savings institutions	10.6%
Mortgage pools or trusts (GNMA, FHLMC, FNMA, private mortgage conduits)	56.9%
Commercial banks	19.3%
Federal agencies and other agencies	2.8%
Mortgage companies, REITs, pension funds, finance companies, and others	10.4%
Life insurance companies	<0.1%
Total	100.0%

These figures are based on statistics compiled by the Federal Reserve. *Federal Reserve Bulletin* (July 2006): Table 1.54.

Figure 4.1	The Flow of Funds

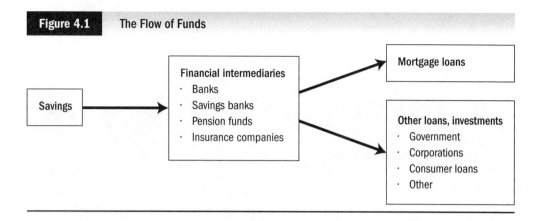

mortgage market and free additional funds for further home financing. Private investors and institutions purchase home mortgages as do governmental and quasi-governmental agencies such as Fannie Mae, Freddie Mac, and Ginnie Mae. Because governmental and monetary authorities believe that home buying and home building can improve a depressed economy, the secondary mortgage market is often used to stimulate housing activity.

Fannie Mae

Fannie Mae (formerly known as the Federal National Mortgage Association) is an independent government agency with lines of credit to the Federal Reserve System. Fannie Mae has a major influence on the secondary mortgage market. Its principal purpose is to purchase mortgages from the primary mortgage market, which increases the liquidity of primary lenders. Fannie Mae then resells packages of these pooled mortgages to investors at a discount. Two important activities of the association are the over-the-counter program, in which Fannie Mae posts the prices it will pay for the immediate delivery of mortgages, and the free market system commitment auction, in which FHA, VA, and conventional mortgages are sold in separate, simultaneous auctions.

Freddie Mac

Freddie Mac (formerly known as the Federal Home Loan Mortgage Corporation) is a government-sponsored enterprise overseen by HUD and the Office of Federal Housing Enterprise Oversight. Freddie Mac was created in 1970 to

secondary mortgage market. A market created by government and private agencies for the purchase and sale of existing mortgages; provides greater liquidity for mortgages. Fannie Mae, Freddie Mac, and Ginnie Mae are the principal operators in the secondary mortgage market.

Fannie Mae. Federal National Mortgage Association (FNMA). A private, shareholder-owned company, which was created by Congress in 1938 as a part of the Federal Housing Administration but became a private company in 1968, that purchases mortgages from banks, trust companies, mortgage companies, savings and loan associations, and insurance companies to help distribute funds for home mortgages.

Freddie Mac. Federal Home Loan Mortgage Corporation (FHLMC). A shareholder-owned corporation, created by Congressional charter in 1970, that facilitates secondary residential mortgages sponsored by the Veterans Administration and the Federal Housing Administration as well as residential mortgages that are not government protected. Freddie Mac buys residential mortgages and funds them in the capital markets in one of two ways: using mortgage-backed securities or a variety of debt instruments.

increase the availability of mortgage funds and generate greater flexibility for mortgage investors. Freddie Mac helps expand and distribute capital for mortgage purposes by conducting both purchase and sales programs.

In its purchase programs, Freddie Mac buys single-family and condominium mortgages from approved financial institutions. This gives the institutions greater liquidity in times of credit stringency so they can continue making mortgage funds available for housing. While Fannie Mae programs include insured and guaranteed mortgages, most Freddie Mac activity is in the conventional mortgage field. In its sales programs, Freddie Mac sells its mortgage inventories, thus acquiring funds from organizations that have excess capital. These funds are used to purchase mortgages from organizations with shortages. Because Freddie Mac's operations are conducted nationally, they help make mortgage capital available in all regions of the country.

Government National Mortgage Association

The Government National Mortgage Association (Ginnie Mae) is a federally owned-and-financed corporation under the Department of Housing and Urban Development. Ginnie Mae is the third major player in the secondary mortgage market. Its operations also make mortgage capital available to housing markets. Fannie Mae is an independent agency, but Ginnie Mae is a government organization that gets financial support from the U.S. Department of the Treasury. Ginnie Mae has special assistance programs that facilitate making mortgage loans that could not be made without its support. The organization also manages and liquidates certain mortgages acquired by the government, but its most important role in the secondary mortgage market is in the Mortgage-Backed Securities Program.

Ginnie Mae is authorized to guarantee the timely payment of principal and interest on long-term securities that are backed by pools of insured or guaranteed mortgages. The most popular security is called a pass-through certificate because it is based on mortgage payments that are passed on to the holder of the security. In the Mortgage-Backed Securities Program, mortgage originators pool loans in groups of $1 million or more, issue covering securities, and obtain a Ginnie Mae guarantee. Through this program, investors who do not have the capacity to make mortgages can still be involved in home finance markets. Ginnie Mae securities make excellent investments, so these securities are traded extensively.

Ginnie Mae. Government National Mortgage Association (GNMA). A federally owned and financed corporation under the Department of Housing and Urban Development that subsidizes mortgages through its secondary mortgage market operations and issues mortgage-backed, federally insured securities.

The development of collateralized mortgage obligations (CMOs) as a major investment banking activity is due in part to Ginnie Mae guarantee arrangements. These investment instruments are attractive because the debt is usually secured by Ginnie Mae certificates covering pools of residential mortgages. Because of Ginnie Mae's participation, these bonds receive high-quality risk ratings. Ginnie Mae guarantees also allow these bonds to be sold at low interest rates. As CMOs have proliferated, some have been secured using Fannie Mae, Freddie Mac, and even conventional institutional mortgages as collateral. The CMO vehicle has provided great liquidity for the mortgage industry and has helped monetize the mortgage element in real estate investment.

Private Sector Transactions

Although most secondary mortgage market activity is generated by Fannie Mae, Freddie Mac, and Ginnie Mae, many private sector transactions also take place. Banks and insurance companies that make mortgages often sell loan portfolios, or participations, to private or institutional investors. Real estate investment trusts (REITs) also purchase mortgages from institutions, which gives the sellers the liquidity they need to continue their lending programs.

pass-through security. Security, representing pooled debt obligations repackaged as shares, that passes income from debtors through an intermediary to investors. In real estate financing, the most common type of pass-through is a mortgage-backed certificate, usually government-guaranteed, in which the principal and interest payments of home owners pass from the originating bank or savings and loan through a government agency or investment bank to investors, net of service charges.

collateralized mortgage obligations (CMOs). Bonds issued and sold in capital markets on debt collateralized by pools of Ginnie Mae, Fannie Mae, Freddie Mac, and conventional institutional mortgages. CMOs are an important source of liquidity for the mortgage industry.

private mortgage insurance (PMI). Insurance provided by a private mortgage lender to protect against loss caused by a borrower's default on a residential or commercial mortgage loan.

The development and growth of *private mortgage insurance* programs has facilitated private activity in the secondary mortgage market. In the residential market, private programs have been successful in insuring mortgage loan increments that exceed legal ratios. This has encouraged private secondary mortgage market operations, which could not occur without insurance.

Influences on the Mortgage Market

The availability of mortgage financing in the United States is influenced by many organizations and by developments at various levels. The decisions of the Federal Reserve are of great importance because they affect the amount of credit available throughout the nation. The activities of the Treasury Department, which reflect the economic policy of the federal government, also influence mortgage rates. For example, changes in the yield rate on 10-year Treasury bonds have a direct impact on the money available for investment in real estate and thereby on the mortgage rates offered by lenders (see Figure 4.2). Competition in international financial markets and fluctuations in the business cycle can also have pronounced effects. These forces combine to create the economic climate within which the secondary mortgage market operates. In turn the secondary mortgage market influences the availability of funds in the primary mortgage market.

Figure 4.2   Treasury Bonds and Home Loans

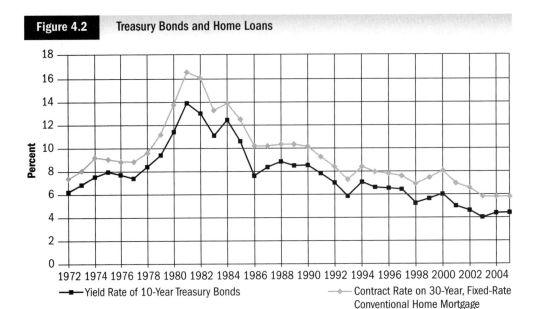

Source: Federal Reserve <www.federalreserve.gov/releases/H15/data.htm>

Primary lenders are subject to other constraints in addition to those imposed by secondary mortgage market conditions. To measure the risk associated with a mortgage loan, primary lenders must consider the economic health of the region, the community, and the market area as well as the location of the specific property, the property type and characteristics, and the income level and credit rating of the potential buyers. Lenders adjust the terms of financing by raising interest rates, charging points, or using other devices to reflect the risks they associate with the loan.

Mortgage loan underwriters frequently call on appraisers for the unbiased value estimates they need to assess loan risk. In addition to analyzing the borrower's credit, underwriters consider the collateral, analyzing the property based on the appraisal and judging the property's acceptability as security for the loan being sought. Market analysis is critical to the underwriter's determinations. Properties in market areas characterized by instability or declining values usually are not eligible for maximum financing. Furthermore, a property that is rated in poor or fair condition, that currently has a nonconforming use, that suffers from a serious functional problem or proximity to a nuisance, or that lacks an active pool of comparable sales can decrease the borrower's eligibility or increase the required down payment.

The Federal Reserve System

The policies of the Federal Reserve System have the most significant influence on the terms and availability of mortgage financing. Through its actions, the Federal Reserve regulates the supply of credit available throughout the national economy. To a limited extent, the Federal Reserve can even influence the timing and severity of the major economic shifts that create business and real estate cycles. Throughout the 1990s and continuing on today, the chairman of the Federal Reserve has become a very powerful figure who is able to influence financial markets through announcements that are carefully observed by market participants.

The Federal Reserve System is composed of 12 regional banks, which serve the 12 Federal Reserve regional districts, and numerous member banks, which include all nationally chartered commercial banks and many state-chartered banks. The Federal Reserve can act independently to further national economic goals. "The function of the Federal Reserve System is to foster a flow of credit and money that will facilitate orderly economic growth, a stable dollar, and long-run balance in our international payments. Its original purposes, as expressed by the founders, were to give the country a lasting currency, to provide facilities for discounting commercial paper, and to improve the supervision of banking."[1] As the economy changed, broader objectives were outlined, namely "to help counteract inflationary and deflationary movements, and to share in creating conditions favorable to a high level of employment, a stable dollar, growth of the country, and a rising level of consumption."

Credit Regulation Devices

The Federal Reserve uses three devices to regulate the supply of money and credit:

1. The reserve requirement
2. The federal discount rate
3. The Federal Open Market Committee (FOMC)

The reserve requirement establishes the amount of deposit liabilities that member banks must keep in reserve accounts. These funds cannot be made available for business loans. The Federal Reserve can expand or contract the supply of available credit by changing its reserve requirement, which alters the amount of money banks can lend.

The federal discount rate is the rate of interest at which member banks can borrow funds from the Federal Reserve. This borrowing privilege gives member banks an important advantage over other banks in times of great demand. The Federal Reserve can encourage or discourage borrowing by raising or lowering the interest rate charged. When borrowing is discouraged by the Federal Reserve, banks have fewer funds available for loan programs.

The third credit regulation device, the Federal Open Market Committee, is the most potent of the Federal Reserve's tools and the most commonly used. To increase the supply of credit, the FOMC writes

---

1. *The Federal Reserve System: Purposes and Functions* (Washington, D.C.: The Federal Reserve Board, 1985). Available online at <www.federalreserve.gov/pf/pf.htm>.

Federal Reserve System. The central banking system of the United States, which was created in 1913 to manage money and credit and to promote orderly growth of the economy. The Federal Reserve System operates independently of Congress and the president. The Federal Reserve regulates the money supply, determines the legal reserve of member banks, oversees the mint, effects transfers of funds, promotes and facilitates the clearance and collection of checks, examines member banks, and serves other functions; consists of 12 Federal Reserve Banks, their 24 branches, and national and state banks that are members of the system. All national banks are stockholding members of the Federal Reserve Bank of their district; membership is optional for state banks and trust companies.

reserve requirement. A requirement of the Federal Reserve System that member banks keep part of their deposit liabilities frozen in reserve accounts.

federal discount rate. The interest rate charged by the Federal Reserve for funds borrowed by member banks.

Federal Open Market Committee (FOMC). A committee composed of the Federal Reserve's Board of Governors, the president of the New York Federal Reserve Bank, and four district reserve bank presidents; buys and sells government securities in the open market to regulate the money supply and interest rates. As the Federal Reserve System's most important policy-making group, the FOMC creates policy for the system's purchase and sale of government and other securities in the open market.

Federal Reserve checks and buys U.S. government securities from securities dealers who deposit the checks with their banks. This increases balances in the reserve accounts of these banks and permits them to make more loans. To restrict credit, the FOMC sells securities to dealers who pay with their checks, which reduces their banks' reserve account balances. Thus business loans and economic growth are discouraged.

U.S. Department of the Treasury

The U.S. Department of the Treasury implements the fiscal policies of the United States government and exerts a substantial influence on credit and mortgage markets. The Treasury Department helps manage the government's finances by raising funds and paying bills. To raise funds, the Treasury Department prints currency, collects taxes, and borrows money. Bills are paid when Congress appropriates funds for various national projects. The Treasury Department does not have a day-to-day regulative influence on money markets like the Federal Reserve, but it does have a sizable impact. When the government borrows heavily to meet its deficit payments, less money is usually available to the private sector. When the government prints money to meet its obligations, it weakens the buying power of the dollar and contributes to inflation.

Financial Trends

Restricted credit can have a severe impact on activities that require borrowed funds, including property purchases, home construction, refinancing, renovation, and home equity lending. When the Federal Reserve pursues a tight monetary policy and interest rates rise, the market for real estate can go into a steep decline. (See Figure 4.3.) In 1981 and 1982 the prime rate, which is the interest rate that banks charge their best customers, rose to 21.5%. Mortgage loans are usually about two percentage points higher than the prime. Consequently, during these years very few home loans were made. Mortgage funds were scarce because lenders were reluctant to lend for long terms without knowing how high money costs might run. As a result, variable-rate mortgages were introduced and for a time they dominated the market. Rollover mortgages, periodic adjustable-rate mortgages, and other renewable mortgages were

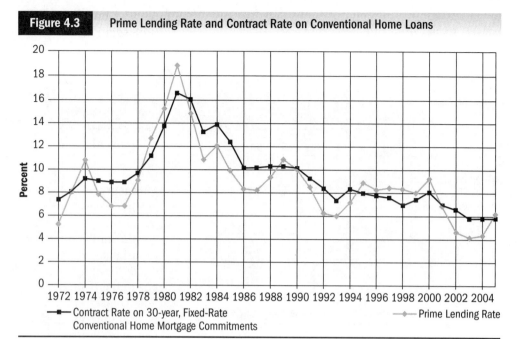

Figure 4.3   Prime Lending Rate and Contract Rate on Conventional Home Loans

Legend:
— ■ — Contract Rate on 30-year, Fixed-Rate Conventional Home Mortgage Commitments
— ◆ — Prime Lending Rate

Source: Federal Reserve <www.federalreserve.gov/releases/H15/data.htm>

common. Still many buyers kept away from the market entirely due to high rates and unfamiliar financing arrangements.

To bring people back into the real estate market, many sellers offered nonmarket financing terms geared to the buyers' ability to pay. Builders arranged to buy down institutional mortgage charges by making initial lump-sum payments for buyers, thereby selling off existing housing stock and increasing the pace of development.

The experience of the market in the early 1980s demonstrates how sensitive the mortgage market is to conditions in the money market. In the mid-1980s, a less restrictive climate returned to the money market. With inflation tamed, the Federal Reserve was able to relax its credit policy. Interest rates fell and more funds became available. The mortgage market was quick to respond. Variable-rate mortgages became less popular, and long-term, fixed-rate, fully amortizing first mortgages once again became the dominant form of financing for most single-family residences. The precipitous decline in interest rates during the early 1990s helped stabilize financing for real estate and increase the volume and velocity of real estate market activity, contributing to rapid home price appreciation across the country. In the 2000s, interest rates hit 40-year lows, spurring home purchases, refinancing, construction, renovation, and home equity borrowing (see Figures 4.4 and 4.5). At the same time, home ownership levels surged as renters took advantage of the low rate environment to become homeowners. The pace of home sales and mortgage originations only declined after the Federal Reserve began to raise interest rates slowly.

Figure 4.4 Mortgage Originations (New Purchases and Refinancing)

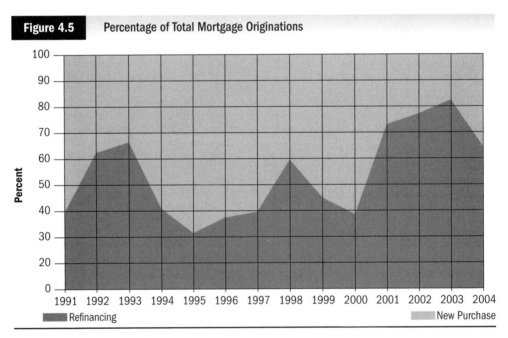

Figure 4.5 Percentage of Total Mortgage Originations

Loan Risk and Points

Institutions and individuals who lend money analyze the risks associated with a residential loan in the same way they would consider any other investment. The security of real estate provides an added incentive for many institutions and individuals to make mortgage loans. Real estate is typically considered excellent collateral because it is fixed in location and likely to remain useful for a long period. Its utility and therefore its value are protected by a wide range of public services and governmental organizations. However, certain risks are involved in making mortgage loans. Delinquencies and foreclosures can be costly, and at some point the loan may be greater than the price the real estate would bring in a forced sale. These risks could result in losses for the financial institution.

To analyze the relationship between financing and real estate values, an appraiser must consider the mortgage lending system and the specific risks involved. The interest rate that is quoted for a mortgage loan represents the cost of the money. This annual rate of return reflects the risks of the specific investment given the property type, the market area and region where the property is located, and the credit rating of the borrower. The rates for residential real estate mortgages, however, also depend on the cost of money in capital markets. Homebuyers must compete with other groups for funds. When the supply of money available in capital markets is substantially reduced, the housing market is one of the first areas to suffer.

To compete in the market, lenders have traditionally found it necessary to charge points or use a discount rate. For example, a lender making a $100,000 loan at the going rate of 7% may feel that conditions in financial markets warrant some adjustment of the loan. The lender may ask the borrower to pay points for the right to borrow the money. One point equals 1% of the loan amount. If four points are required on a $100,000 loan, the buyer would pay $4,000. Alternatively, the lender might adjust the loan by applying a discount rate. If the loan is discounted at 3%, the amount of money actually advanced at the time of closing is 3% less than the original $100,000. Thus the borrower pays 7% interest on $100,000, even though only $97,000 was loaned. The discount increases the yield to the lender; it can compensate for higher risk or make the mortgage yield meet the yields obtainable on other investments.

As the tools necessary for sophisticated financial analysis have become more affordable and more powerful, the discipline of risk management has evolved in all industries. In real estate lending, the growth of the secondary markets and the transparency of transactions have fostered the implementation of a wide range of risk management tools and techniques including portfolio management, loan

discount rate. An interest rate used to convert future payments or receipts into present value. The discount rate may or may not be the same as the internal rate of return (*IRR*) or yield rate, depending on how it is extracted from the market and/or used in the analysis.

pooling, syndications, loan participation, mortgage-backed securities, and derivatives.[2]

Traditionally a lender's annual internal rating of the risk associated with a loan ranged from classifications like "acceptable" to "loss" with a handful of descriptive rankings in between. The first Basel Accord in 1988 initiated an international effort to link regulatory capital requirements to investment risk. As a result, large banking institutions began developing more robust systems for measuring and managing risk in their loan portfolios. Current risk classification systems are numerically based and data are updated more frequently, allowing for deeper, more timely statistical analysis by lenders. These systems can incorporate data from Standards and Poors, Fitch, and other ratings agencies as well.

A measure of the risk inherent in a home loan takes into account the creditworthiness of the borrower as well as the marketability of the real property. In the lending process, a credit check is ordered well before the appraisal because of the importance of the borrower's FICO (Fair Isaac & Co.) score as an indicator of risk. Lenders generally pick one score from the three rating agencies (Experian, Trans Union, and Equifax), the middle score of the three, or a "merged" score. On the collateral side, automated valuation models (AVMs) and other valuation methods have emerged as analogous tools to increase the speed and accuracy of risk analysis.

Use of AVMs by Lenders

The current generation of automated valuation models grew out of the computer-assisted mass appraisal techniques pioneered by the property assessment community, which had access to the large amounts of property data needed for meaningful and accurate statistical analysis. (See Chapter 22 for a discussion of the mechanics and use of statistical applications in residential real estate appraisal.[3]) In the lending community, AVMs are currently being used for quality control, quality analysis, audits, refinance, portfolio marketing, pre-qualification, bond insurance, fraud detection, private mortgage insurance (PMI), loss mitigation, real estate owned (REO) management, home equity, and loan servicing. A variety of products are emerging such as appraiser-assisted valuation models (AAVMs), insured AVMs, and AVM + Inspection. Modeling application are also being tied to geographic information systems (GIS), aerial mapping, and global positioning systems (GPS). As real estate professionals work to refine data standards, increase data accuracy, and revise models, appraisers continue to wrestle with the fundamental technology, the market shift, and ultimately how appraiser will compete in the evolving marketplace.

Some appraisers fear that the use of AVMs will obviate the need for the services of appraisers in all mortgage transactions except for

---

2. Richard W. Gilmore, "Banking and Risk Management for the Appraiser: An Appraiser's View," Paper presented at the 23rd Pan-Pacific Congress, San Francisco, September 19, 2006.

3. See also "Advisory Opinion 18: Use of an Automated Valuation Model (AVM)," *Uniform Standards of Professional Practice* (Washington, D.C.: The Appraisal Foundation, annual publication).

special-use situations. Some functions once performed by in-house appraisers at lending institutions–e.g., analyzing individual properties within a portfolio–or by fee appraisers–e.g., drive-by appraisals for low-risk mortgages–are likely to be automated, resulting in fewer traditional assignments for residential appraisers who have not diversified.

The growing practice of AVM cascading allows lenders to survey the results of multiple value models for increased accuracy, but the practice has been criticized as an opportunity for lenders to select the highest value estimate from the various models, i.e., "value shopping."

Mortgage Fraud and Appraisal Fraud

The volume of mortgage originations has risen with home prices and so has the opportunity for mortgage fraud such as property flipping. Property flipping involves the acquisition of a property in poor condition and a subsequent sale, usually in a short time after only superficial cosmetic improvements, to a poorly informed buyer. The perpetrators of the fraud may use an inflated appraisal to secure a loan for the sale of the property that is being flipped. According to the Federal Bureau of Investigation, more sophisticated criminals are now using identity theft–of appraisers as well as borrowers or sellers–and straw borrowers, shell companies, and industry insiders to falsify mortgage documents.

Client pressure on appraisers and value inflation are the respective cause and effect of most appraisal fraud, i.e., the client, usually someone involved in making a mortgage loan, intimidates or coerces an appraiser, who delivers a higher value opinion than the unbiased market value opinion called for in the professional standards. Figures from agencies that monitor the situation vary, but appraisal fraud is believed to be present in a significant percentage of mortgage fraud cases.[4]

Financing Plans

Traditional Loans

The most common kind of financing available to homebuyers is the fully amortizing, fixed-rate, mortgage loan. A commonly used fully amortizing loan is contracted to be repaid with equal, periodic payments, usually on a monthly basis, which provide the lending institution with both a return of the investment through the recovery of principal over the term of the loan and a return on the investment in the form of interest. With a fixed-rate loan, the interest rate does not vary but remains at the same percentage over the life of the loan. The mortgage payments are structured so that the payments in the first years are mostly interest and the payments made in later years reduce the principal (see Figure 4.6). This repayment schedule allows for level periodic payments and gradual equity buildup over the term of the loan.

---

4. See also Claire Nicolay, "Mortgage Fraud: Confronting the Threat, Protecting the Profession," *Valuation Insights & Perspectives* (First Quarter 2006): 4-5, 7; and Steven R. Smith, "Predatory Lending, Mortgage Fraud, and Client Pressures," *The Appraisal Journal* (April 2002): 200-213.

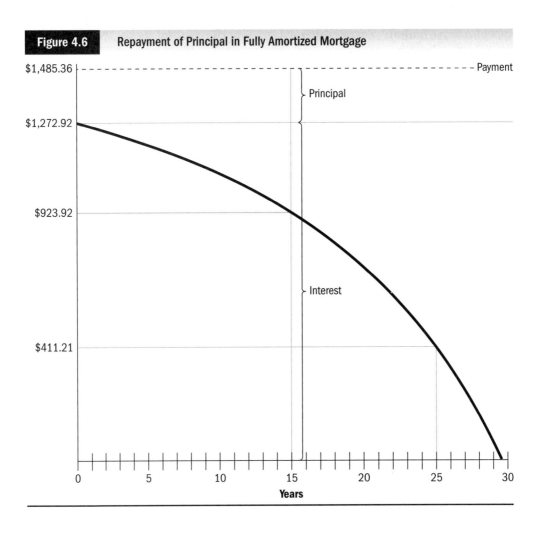

Figure 4.6   Repayment of Principal in Fully Amortized Mortgage

By the end of the term, the loan is fully amortized—i.e., the principal and the interest are entirely paid.

A variable-rate mortgage has an interest rate that rises or falls according to a specified schedule or, more commonly, follows the movements of a standard or index to which the interest rate is tied. Variable-rate mortgages protect the lender because their interest rates rise when interest rates in the general money market rise. When rates are rising, the yield, or rate of return, from a fixed-rate mortgage investment may not be competitive with the yields available from other real estate investments or securities.

A mortgage with a balloon payment is a financial obligation in which the monthly installment mainly repays the interest on the loan, usually set at a fixed rate for a short term. The balance on the principal of a balloon mortgage becomes due when the obligation matures and is paid with the final installment as a lump sum, or "balloon." Balloon mortgages are often used for first and second mortgages in which the monthly payments only partially amortize the principal balance over the duration of the loan.

A "first" mortgage loan is the one with the oldest date of recording or the first priority lien. The date of record of a second mortgage is more recent than the first mortgage and therefore the second mortgage has an inferior priority lien. If a first mortgage is paid off and the second mortgage is not, the second mortgage becomes the first mortgage. It is possible for a first mortgage lender to subordinate its loan to the second mortgage lender thus exchanging positions.

Normally traditional mortgages cannot be obtained for the full purchase price of a property without special arrangements or insurance. Most institutional lenders are subject to state laws and federal regulations that prescribe maximum loan-to-value ratios between the amount of the mortgage loan and the value of the security pledged. Many lending institutions require a buyer to make a cash down payment of at least 20% of the sale price, but it is common for lenders to go higher with mortgage insurance or other loan programs. Most loans are for a specified term, usually 15 to 30 years (40-year loans are found in some markets). If the mortgagor (borrower) defaults on the loan, the mortgagee (lender) can foreclose–i.e., take legal action to force a sale and recover all or part of the loan amount.

Mortgages are either conventional, guaranteed, or insured. The typical first mortgage is a conventional mortgage that is not guaranteed or insured by any institution. Some mortgages are guaranteed or insured by a governmental agency such as the Federal Housing Administration (FHA) or the Department of Veterans Affairs (VA) or by a private company. Since the 1930s the FHA has been insuring loans, principally but not solely to people with limited financial means. The VA, which is the largest source of guaranteed mortgages, provides a similar service to veterans. FHA and VA mortgages tend to have lower interest rates, longer terms, and higher loan-to-value ratios than conventional loans. The VA maintains a fee panel of appraisers across the country. FHA dropped its panel of

balloon mortgage. A mortgage that is not fully amortized at maturity, and thus requires a lump sum, or balloon, payment of the outstanding balance.

Parties Involved in the Underwriting Process

From a borrower's pre-qualification application to the signing of the mortgage documents at the closing, more than a dozen people may be involved in a typical mortgage transaction in some professional capacity. The buyer and seller may each engage real estate brokers and lawyers as representatives in the sale contract negotiations. The buyer may hire a home inspector. In addition, the buyer may employ a mortgage broker or mortgage banker to seek out a loan. (Increasingly real estate brokers do double duty as mortgage loan officers, expanding the services they have traditionally provided to their clients.) The lender hires an appraiser, and the appraiser's report may be examined by an in-house review appraiser to ensure that the value opinion is credible.

Depending on the type of loan, other participants in the underwriting process can include

· A private mortgage insurance (PMI) company
· Loan officer
· Processor
· Closing agent
· Insurance agent
· Underwriter
· Surveyor
· Environmental professional

Even in a relatively straightforward refinancing transaction, a mortgage broker or mortgage banker and all the lender's support staff will be involved to some degree in the transaction.

appraisers and has shifted to approving FHA appraisers but allowing them to be selected by the lender, unlike the VA. Fannie Mae and Freddie Mac require the lender to approve and select the appraiser. However, they hold the lender responsible for the appraisal process.

A type of insured loan is offered by private mortgage insurance companies that cover conventional mortgages. These companies insure the risk to lenders who advance 10% or 15% more than the amount traditionally loaned on a conventional mortgage. If an 80% loan-to-value mortgage is standard, a private mortgage company can provide insurance for an additional 10% or 15%, which increases the loan-to-value ratio to 90% or 95%.

The legal restrictions and requirements that apply to mortgages vary from state to state. These requirements provide homeowners with protection and encouragement and also address the lender's risk. The interests of both parties must be balanced, as can be clearly seen in the foreclosure laws of various states. A state with foreclosure legislation that is extremely favorable to the borrower may attract few funds from outside the state. States that provide more protection for the lender by requiring short periods for foreclosure tend to attract more funds from around the country.

Subordinate Mortgages

In addition to a first mortgage, second or additional mortgages can be used to facilitate the purchase of a home. Such junior mortgages are subordinate to the rights of the first mortgagee, the primary lender. A junior mortgage may be required when the buyer is unable to arrange for adequate financing through a single mortgage. Because the first mortgagee has lien priority, a second position lender can incur a substantial loss if the borrower defaults. Interest rates on junior mortgages reflect this increased risk to the lender. They can, however, provide additional funds to the borrower and facilitate a purchase that might not be possible otherwise.

A mortgage is the traditional means of financing the purchase of a house, but in some states the same end is accomplished with different legal arrangements. In some western states, deeds of trust are used instead of mortgages. Money is borrowed in the same manner as it is with a mortgage loan, but a third party, the trustee, holds title to the property. When a borrower has met all of the financial obligations, title is conveyed to the borrower.

Creative Financing

When interest rates are high, the monthly payments on typical loans can be higher than most consumers can afford to pay. Faced with a shrinking market for their properties, sellers may entice buyers by adjusting prices. Sellers who are reluctant to lower their prices can sometimes appeal to buyers by offering alternative or creative financing. These plans may call for monthly payments that are lower than those required with typical financing. In some of these arrangements, the seller provides the financing rather than a lending institution. In others, both the seller and a lending institution play a role.

Besides high interest rates, there are other reasons for using alternative financing arrangements such as mortgage assumptions and installment sale contracts. When mortgages do not prohibit assumptions or require lender approval, easier credit requirements may make creative financing attractive to buyers. Sellers who provide financing may have less stringent credit requirements than lending institutions. Furthermore, loan assumptions and contract sales generally close faster and are less costly.

The arrangements described below are some of the most common of the many creative financing instruments that came into existence in the early 1980s.[5] Appraisers should be familiar with all creative financing plans and be aware of those that were typical of market practices at the time of sale and those that were not. For example, in the mid-1980s in markets such as Texas and Louisiana, some homebuilders were buying 30-year fixed rate interest loans with 3 points and the lender was charging 18 to 20 loan discount points. This resulted in artificially inflated sale prices, making it difficult for appraisers to arrive at cash equivalent market values.

assumption of mortgage. A purchase of mortgaged property in which the buyer accepts liability for existing debt. The seller remains liable to the lender unless the lender agrees to release the seller.

seller financing. Funding for an acquisition provided by the owner of real estate, who takes back a secured note; usually used when the buyer has insufficient funds for a down payment or cannot otherwise qualify for a traditional mortgage loan from a lending institution. The buyer typically takes full title to the property when the loan is fully repaid. If the buyer defaults on the loan, the seller can repossess the property.

installment sale. A sale in which the proceeds are to be received in more than one payment.

buydown. A lump-sum payment to the lender that reduces the interest payments of the borrower. The cost of the buydown is usually reflected in the price paid and can be expressed as a percentage of the principal.

Mortgage Assumption

In a mortgage assumption a buyer takes over the remaining payments on a loan originally made to the seller. If the loan carries a rate of interest that is lower than current rates, the buyer may be willing to pay a higher price for the property to obtain the favorable financing terms. The interest rate, monthly payment, and maturity of the mortgage can remain the same when the loan is assumed. Mortgages guaranteed by the VA or insured by FHA are assumable only with lender approval.

Not all mortgages can be assumed. Some contain due-on-sale clauses stipulating that the outstanding loan balance will become due when the mortgaged property is sold or transferred. In some mortgage contracts, any assumption requires approval of the buyer and can cause a change in the interest rate.

---

5. See Terrence M. Clauretie and Stacy G. Sirmans, *Real Estate Finance: Theory and Practice*, 5th ed. (Mason, Ohio: Thomson Higher Education, 2006), Chapter 6: Alternative Mortgage Instruments and Chapter 7: Financing and Property Values; and William B. Brueggeman and Jeffrey D. Fisher, *Real Estate Finance & Investments*, 12th ed. (New York: McGraw-Hill/Irwin, 2005), Chapter 6: Adjustable Rate and Variable Payment Mortgages.

Seller Loan

A seller may be willing to finance all or part of the purchase price of a property. If the buyer receives title to the property and the seller places a mortgage against the property, such loans are typically called purchase-money mortgages. A buyer may be willing to pay a higher price for a property to obtain favorable, below-market financing terms from the seller.

Installment Sale Contract

Under an installment sale contract, a seller allows a buyer to purchase property by making periodic payments. The title does not pass from the seller to the buyer until the buyer has satisfied the contract by paying all or a specified portion of the purchase price. Quite often the terms of a sale contract are different from those available for a first mortgage. An installment sale contract may have a shorter term, specify a balloon payment, or provide for a higher loan-to-value ratio. Interest rates may be higher or lower than those available through conventional means. If the terms are favorable, a buyer may be willing to pay a higher price for a property purchased in this manner. State laws regarding contract of sale have become more stringent over the last few years, and a lender or seller initiating this financing vehicle must be careful.

Buydown Plan

In a buydown plan, a homeseller usually advances a lump-sum payment to the lender to reduce, or buy down, the interest payments of the borrower. (A buyer can also buy down a mortgage.) The buydown period may range from one year to the entire term of the mortgage. Builders sometimes buy down interest rates on loans to increase sales activity in new subdivisions. Buying down the interest rate is very similar to paying points up front to supplement the lender's yield. Buying down a mortgage or paying lender points allows a lender to loan money at a lower rate because the upfront money increases the overall yield. Appraisers are typically concerned with points paid by the seller on behalf of the borrower in the comparable sale transactions.

Reverse Mortgage

Homeowners who are at least 62 years old can tap into their home equity during their retirement years through a reverse mortgage. This financing tool was created in the 1980s to provide seniors who are "cash poor" but "house rich" with a source of income, allowing them to stay in the homes they own free and clear for the rest of their lives. (In some states, reverse mortgages have only become available more recently.) This arrangement reverses the normal lending process, with the homeowner receiving payments from the lender for the length of the loan, which can last as long as the borrowers live in the property.

The total amount of the loan and any fees and interest that have accrued are not repaid until the property is sold after the borrowers have left the house. The lender relies on the anticipated value of the home as the eventual source for repayment. Factors beyond the market value of the property influence the value of a reverse mortgage, including the age (but not the income or credit rating) of the occupant of the house, current interest rates, the characteristics of the various reverse mortgage programs, and forecasts of the anticipated sale price of the home.

Trends in Financing Plans

Trends in the mortgage markets affect the types of financing plans readily available. Low interest rates have reduced the demand for creative financing and increased the demand for refinancing loans as well as home equity loans and other financing options that allow homeowners to borrow against their equity. No money down loan programs bring new homeowners into the market, and low rates encourage refinancing of higher rate or adjustable rate loans. Increasing interest rates cool off the property markets, which in turn increases the complexity of the financing plans being offered and often reduces the volume of mortgage originations and the number of traditional residential appraisal assignments.

The volume of business for residential appraisers who focus on market value appraisals for underwriting purposes will be greatly affected by the state of the primary and secondary mortgage markets. The ability of mortgage brokers to shop around for the best mortgage rate and terms on behalf of a borrower and for consumers to perform similar searches online increase the competition among lenders. As that competition intensifies, lenders who want to deliver loan products more efficiently will want the appraisal component of the financing process to be cheaper and faster. Appraisers should be aware of how trends in the money market influence their business prospects and how the financing plans in use at the time of an appraisal affect the various analyses that make up the valuation process.

> **reverse annuity mortgage (RAM).** A type of mortgage designed for retirees and other fixed-income homeowners who owe little or nothing on their homes; typically permits owners to use some or all of the equity in their homes as supplemental income while retaining ownership. These owners are borrowing against the value of their homes on a monthly basis; the longer they borrow, the less equity they retain. The loan becomes due on a specific date or when a certain event occurs, e.g., the sale of the property or death of the borrower. Also called reverse mortgage or home equity conversion mortgage.

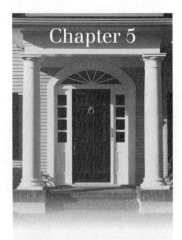

Chapter 5

The Valuation Process

The valuation process is a systematic procedure developed to produce well-researched, credible opinions of real property value. The process consists of a series of steps, beginning with the identification of the valuation problem and the way in which the valuation problem can be solved. To solve the problem, the process proceeds through the collection of pertinent data, the selection and application of appropriate analytical approaches, the reconciliation of value indications, and the final opinion of value. The valuation process concludes when the value conclusion is reported to the client. The steps in the process and the methods of analysis can be adapted to address any appraisal situation. Although the valuation process is designed primarily for market value appraisals, it provides a general framework within which most valuation assignments are conducted.

The valuation process consists of eight basic steps, which are illustrated in Figure 5.1. Each phase of the process will be briefly discussed in this chapter, and more detailed discussion of specific steps will be presented in subsequent chapters.

> **the valuation process.** A systematic procedure employed to provide the answer to a client's question about the value of real property.

Step 1. Identification of the Problem

A precise understanding between the appraiser and the client eliminates ambiguity about the nature of the client's problem to be solved and alerts the appraiser to the amount and nature of the data that will be needed to solve the problem. The identification of the appraisal problem has six specific components:

1. Identify the client and intended users.
2. Identify the intended use of the appraiser's opinions and conclusions.
3. Identify the purpose of the assignment, including the type and definition of the value to be developed.
4. Identify the effective date of the appraiser's opinions and conclusions.
5. Identify the characteristics of the property that are relevant to the purpose and intended use of the appraisal.
6. Identify any assignment conditions, which may include extraordinary assumptions and hypothetical conditions.

Figure 5.1	The Valuation Process

Identification of the Problem

Step 1	Identify client and intended users	Identify the intended use	Identify the purpose of the assignment	Identify the effective date of the opinion	Identify the relevant characteristics of the property	Assignment conditions	
						Extraordinary assumptions	Hypothetical conditions

Step 2	**Scope of Work Determination**

Data Collection and Property Description

Step 3	Market Area Data	Subject Property Data	Comparable Property Data
	General characteristics of region, city, and neighborhood	Subject characteristics of land use and improvements, personal property, business assets, etc.	Sales, listings, offerings, vacancies, cost and depreciation, income and expenses, capitalization rates, etc.

Data Analysis

Step 4	Market Analysis	Highest and Best Use Analysis
	Demand studies Supply studies Marketability studies	Site as though vacant Ideal improvement Property as improved

Step 5	**Site Value Opinion**

Application of the Approaches to Value

Step 6	Cost	Sales Comparison	Income Capitalization

Step 7	**Reconciliation of Value Indications and Final Opinion of Value**

Step 8	**Report of Defined Value**

Identify the Client and Intended Users

Appraisals may be used in many different ways by various clients:

- Lenders may want to know how much money to lend to a home buyer.
- Buyers and sellers may want a value estimate to analyze offers to buy or sell.
- Courts may use value estimates as a basis for just compensation in eminent domain proceedings.

Anyone who receives a copy of the appraisal report is not necessarily an intended user of the report and the appraiser's conclusions and opinions. In fact, the client helps the appraiser identify who the other intended users are, but the appraiser must make the decision as to who the audience for the appraisal report is based on the expressed needs of the client and the nature of the assignment. In other words, the client approaches the appraiser about the assignment, but the appraiser determines who is the intended user of the opinions and conclusions expressed in the appraisal report. The appraiser is responsible for ensuring that the appraisal report contains sufficient information so that the intended users can understand it properly.

Identify the Intended Use

An appraiser can often avoid misdirected effort and other problems by agreeing with the client in advance on the intended use of the appraisal, in essence, why the client and intended users need the service. The intended use of an appraisal is the key element in identifying the appraisal problem and the extent of the research and analysis necessary to solve the problem. Any changes in the intended use of the appraiser's conclusions and opinions during the performance of the valuation process is likely to require a new determination of the scope of work.

Some possible intended uses may relate to

- Financing
- Litigation
- Condemnation
- Divorce settlement
- Buy/sell decision
- Tax reporting
- Portfolio evaluation
- Arbitration
- Partnership value
- Estate value
- Charitable donation

Identify the Purpose of the Assignment (Type and Definition of Value Opinion)

Many types of value may be estimated in appraisals such as market value, investment value, use value, or assessed value. Each of these types of value has a separate definition, and special techniques may be required to estimate the particular type of value sought. Therefore, it is essential to specify the type of value being reported. If developing an opinion of market value is the purpose of an appraisal assignment, the clients or the courts may request that the appraiser use a specific legal or economic definition of *market value*. The Uniform Standards of Professional Appraisal Practice require an appraiser to identify the type of value being estimated and provide a definition.

Once the type of value to be estimated has been identified, the appraiser can select the most appropriate valuation techniques and determine the data to be collected. Including the definition of value in the report also communicates the objective of the appraisal to the intended user of the report.

Identify the Effective Date of the Value Opinion

A specific date of value is essential because the factors that influence value change constantly. Abrupt changes in business and real estate markets affect property values. Even without dramatic market shifts, values are subject to gradual change. For example, the physical condition of a property may change. Therefore, a value opinion must be reported as of a particular date, though that date is not necessarily the date the appraisal report is delivered to the intended user. Identifying a specific date allows an appraiser to isolate and quantify all the factors that influence value as of that date.

Most appraisals require current estimates of value, and the client and the appraiser usually agree on the time frame in advance. The date of inspection is often used as the effective date of the value opinion if no other date is specified. However, retrospective and prospective appraisals are not uncommon.[1] An appraisal for inheritance tax purposes usually requires a value opinion as of the date of the testator's death. To make insurance adjustments, insurers may require a value opinion as of the date of casualty. Appraisals used in lawsuits frequently require a value opinion as of a date set by the court. In eminent domain proceedings, for example, value is estimated as of the date when the petition to condemn was filed or as of some other date stipulated by statute or the court. Similarly, appraisals for divorce litigation require value opinions as of a specified date, e.g., the date of filing or dissolution. Some appraisals prepared for mortgage financing require value opinions as of a prospective or future date, e.g., when a house being appraised from blueprints and specifications will be completed.

---

1. Appraisers should check with their clients as to the specific date of value required. For lending purposes, Fannie Mae will not accept appraisals of prospective value that are based on adjustments for anticipated market conditions.

Identify the Relevant Characteristics of the Property

To identify the relevant characteristics of the real property that must be analyzed in a specific appraisal assignment, an appraiser answers the questions, "What is the subject property?" and "What is its nature?"

Location and Physical, Legal, and Economic Attributes

In every appraisal, the real estate to be valued must be precisely identified. A street address is often acceptable, but a complete legal description may be preferred. Legal descriptions are derived from land surveys and maintained in public records under state and local law. They may be found in deeds, abstracts of title, mortgages, and other public documents.

Land may be described using various systems of identification:

1. The metes and bounds system
2. The rectangular or government survey system
3. The lot and block system

Appraisers should be familiar with the types of legal description that are most prevalent in their area of practice. (The three common systems of land description are discussed in detail in Chapter 7.)

The improvements are described and analyzed later in the valuation process, but some appraisers mention the property type within the identification of the problem. This is a matter of choice and custom. The identification of the real estate should leave no doubt as to the location and physical, legal, and economic attributes that influence the value of the real property being appraised.

Real Property Interest to Be Valued

In addition to identifying the real estate, the appraiser must precisely define the ownership rights that will be valued in the assignment. Because real property is defined as the rights of ownership, it is important to specify the particular rights to be valued in an appraisal.

In most areas of the country, the most typical residential appraisal assignments are performed to estimate the value of the rights of absolute ownership–i.e., the fee simple interest. Occasionally, appraisals to estimate the value of other rights are requested. Fractional rights such as easements, encroachments, and subsurface mineral rights may have to be valued separately. Appraisers may also be asked to estimate the value of partial interests created by the severance or division of ownership rights. Liens and other limitations on ownership should be identified in the identification of the appraisal problem.

Personal Property, Trade Fixtures, or Intangible Items

Any items of personal property, trade fixtures, or intangible items that will be accounted for in the value opinion must be identified. For example, in an appraisal assignment involving a house being sold with the furniture (i.e., personal property), the appraiser must make sure the client knows whether the value of the furniture will be included in the value opinion being developed.

Known Restrictions

If known restrictions limit the use of the subject property, those restrictions must be identified in the definition of the appraisal problem. The most common restrictions on land use include

- Encumbrances
- Leases
- Reservations
- Covenants
- Contracts
- Declarations
- Special assessments
- Ordinances

Fractional Interest, Physical Segment, or Partial Holding

When the purpose of an appraisal assignment is to value an interest that is less than the fee simple interest in the real estate, the Uniform Standards of Professional Appraisal Practice do not require the appraiser to value the whole. The scope of work for an appraisal assignment involving a fractional interest may be less extensive than an assignment involving the whole fee simple estate with the value of the whole then allocated into its component parts.

Identify Any Assignment Conditions

To complete the identification of the problem, all limitations and assumptions affecting the development of an opinion of value must be identified. The appraiser does not choose to apply limiting conditions or assumptions to an assignment. Rather, the nature of the problem to be solved drives the necessary assignment conditions. Regardless of the nature of the assignment, though, the assignment conditions cannot be so restrictive that the results of the appraisal assignment are no longer credible or become biased.

Limiting conditions might specify that no court testimony or attendance in court will be required unless separate arrangements are made, that no engineering survey has been made by the appraiser, or that data on the size and area of the property have been obtained from sources believed to be reliable. The Uniform Residential Appraisal Report (URAR) form, which is used in assignments for federal agencies and most financial institutions, contains an expanded limiting condition clarifying that the appraiser is not an expert in the field of environmental hazards and the appraisal report is not to be considered an environmental assessment of the property. This limiting condition acknowledges that the appraiser is responsible for noting in the appraisal report any adverse conditions (such as, but not limited to, hazardous wastes and toxic substances) that were observed during the inspection of the property or that became apparent during the normal research involved in performing the appraisal.

In addition to any common limiting conditions and assumptions, certain extraordinary assumptions or hypothetical conditions may be necessary. Whether or not it is appropriate to use such extraordinary assumptions or hypothetical conditions in an appraisal depends on the intended use and the nature of the appraisal problem. Also, any supplemental standards or jurisdictional exceptions—i.e., assignment conditions relating to law or public policy—must be identified at the outset of the appraisal assignment.

Hypothetical conditions, extraordinary assumptions, supplemental standards, and jurisdictional exceptions will all affect the intended use of an appraiser's opinions and conclusions. It is essential that the intended users and the appraiser clearly understand any assignment conditions.

Extraordinary Assumptions

If certain relevant property information is unknown, the appraiser may need to base the appraisal on one or more extraordinary assumptions about uncertain information. Extraordinary assumptions presume information to be factual when it may not be. If found to be false, this assumption could alter the appraiser's opinions or conclusions. For example, to develop an opinion of prospective value in the appraisal of proposed construction, the appraiser may have to assume that the improvements will be completed on some future date. Even though it is not possible to know whether the construction will, in fact, be complete then, it is possible for the appraisal to be based on the extraordinary assumption that the property will be completed as of that future date. Another common example of the use of an extraordinary assumption is the appraisal of a property suspected of having environmental contamination. The property could be appraised as if it were not contaminated even though it is not known for sure whether that is the case.

Hypothetical Conditions

In contrast to an extraordinary assumption, a hypothetical condition takes into account what is known to be contrary to what exists, but the hypothetical condition is asserted by the appraiser for the purposes of analysis. Using the same example of proposed construction, the hypothetical condition that the improvements were already completed could be used in the

extraordinary assumption. An assumption, directly related to a specific assignment, which, if found to be false, could alter the appraiser's opinions or conclusions. Extraordinary assumptions presume as fact otherwise uncertain information about physical, legal, or economic characteristics of the subject property; or about conditions external to the property such as market conditions or trends; or about the integrity of data used in an analysis. An extraordinary assumption may be used in an assignment only if:
- It is required to properly develop credible opinions and conclusions;
- The appraiser has a reasonable basis for the extraordinary assumption;
- Use of the extraordinary assumption results in a credible analysis; and
- The appraiser complies with the disclosure requirements set forth in USPAP for extraordinary assumptions.

hypothetical condition. That which is contrary to what exists but is supposed for the purpose of analysis. Hypothetical conditions assume conditions contrary to known facts about physical, legal, or economic characteristics of the subject property; or about conditions external to the property, such as market conditions or trends; or about the integrity of data used in an analysis. A hypothetical condition may be used in an assignment only if:
- Use of the hypothetical condition is clearly required for legal purposes, for purposes of reasonable analysis, or for purposes of comparison;
- Use of the hypothetical condition results in a credible analysis; and
- The appraiser complies with the disclosure requirements set forth in USPAP for hypothetical conditions.

appraisal as of a current effective date. In other words, even though the improvements are obviously not complete at the current time, the appraisal could be performed under the hypothetical condition that they were. Again, a common application of a hypothetical condition is an appraisal of a property affected by environmental contamination. The hypothetical condition that the property was not contaminated–even though there is known contamination present–could be used to appraise the property.

Supplemental Standards

When residential appraisers perform valuation services for government-sponsored enterprises such as Fannie Mae and Freddie Mac, those entities may have appraisal-related requirements that affect the process of developing or reporting a value opinion. These restrictions, known as *supplemental standards,* are in addition to the requirements imposed by the Uniform Standards of Professional Appraisal Practice. Only government agencies, government-sponsored enterprises, and other public agencies can set public policy that creates supplemental standards to USPAP. Some contractual matters between an appraiser and the client that add assignment requirements beyond what USPAP dictates would not be considered supplemental standards because those additional requirements are not related to public policy.

Jurisdictional Exceptions

If a law or public policy creates an assignment condition that contradicts a portion of the Uniform Standards of Professional Appraisal Practice, the public policy may supersede the affected portion–but only that portion–of USPAP. These rare deviations from USPAP are known as *jurisdictional exceptions.* Whereas supplemental standards effectively add to USPAP, jurisdictional exceptions subtract from USPAP.

Step 2. Scope of Work Determination

The term *scope of work* refers to the extent of the process in which data are collected and analyzed. An analysis of the nature and significance of the appraisal problem helps the appraiser determine how much and what types of data are needed and which valuation techniques must be applied to fulfill the assignment's obligations. Under current professional standards, appraisers have the flexibility to provide a broad range of valuation-related services by precisely determining the scope of work of an assignment. However, with that flexibility comes the responsibility to develop credible appraisal conclusions and clearly communicate those conclusions to the intended user of the appraisal. According to the Uniform Standards of Professional Appraisal Practice, in all appraisal assignments, the appraiser is responsible for

1. Identifying the problem to be solved
2. Determining and performing the scope of work necessary to develop credible assignment results

3. Disclosing the scope of work in the appraisal report

A thorough, clear statement of the scope of work of the assignment eliminates confusion between the appraiser and the client and serves to protect both from false interpretation or misunderstanding upon completion of the assignment.

A work plan of the steps required to complete the assignment is useful in determining the scope of work because it allows the appraiser to create a schedule for data collection. Each task is allocated a certain amount of time and a place in the sequence. Then a person is selected to complete each task—e.g., the appraiser, someone on the appraiser's staff, or an outside specialist. While not required for smaller assignments, detailed work plans are essential in long, complex assignments. A clear understanding of the scope of work represented by a detailed work plan can help prevent errors and omissions and may make data collection more productive. A work plan can also be useful when the client and appraiser negotiate the appraiser's fee.

Often, a tour of the neighborhood is necessary to familiarize the appraiser with the task ahead. Any special conditions that may require additional research can be noted. A preliminary investigation may not be necessary if the appraiser has had considerable experience with the neighborhood and the property type.

A useful work plan includes a list of all the general and specific data needed. Information on value influences in the area and the neighborhood (the resource base for market analysis and highest and best use analysis) should be listed along with data on the subject and comparable properties (the information used in the application of the approaches to value). If information from soil experts, engineers, legal specialists, or other professionals will be required, this should be noted.

The main procedures to be performed and the types of data needed should be indicated on a flowchart in the order in which they will be used. The responsibility for completing each task should be properly delegated and noted on the chart. This is particularly helpful when learning the process, working on an unfamiliar type of property or market area, or working on a complex assignment.

Step 3. Data Collection and Property Description

After the preliminary analysis, the appraiser is ready to begin collecting pertinent data. The amount and type of data required will vary with the type of property being appraised, the value being estimated, the presentation of the report, and the intended use of the value conclusion.

Many appraisal assignments require information on market transactions of similar vacant and improved real estate, cost and depreciation estimates, and income, expense, and gross rent multiplier data. Data fall into three categories:

1. *General data* about conditions in the nation, region, city, and neighborhood that affect value
2. *Specific data* about the site, the improvements, and comparable properties
3. *Competitive supply and demand data* that relate to the competitive position of the property in its past, current, or anticipated market

The accuracy of all data obtained should be verified by cross-checking different sources and inspecting the subject property. Within each of the three categories of data, a distinction can be made between primary and secondary data and how that type of data was collected and verified. Data confirmed or verified directly by the appraiser (i.e., primary data) will be considered more credible by the user of the appraisal report than third-party data collected from secondary sources like multiple listing services that are assumed to be correct (i.e., secondary data).

General Data

The collection of general data usually involves all or many of the following steps:

1. Compile information on how social, economic, governmental, and environmental forces interact and affect real estate values on national, regional, and local levels. Appraisers need this information to develop an understanding of how these four forces influence the value and use of the subject property.
2. Study the neighborhood, identifying its boundaries and major characteristics. Neighborhood inspection may be performed during the preliminary survey. Because many of the forces that influence value affect most properties in a neighborhood in the same way, identifying neighborhood boundaries is an important step toward selecting relevant market data. When necessary, neighborhood inspection helps to begin the process of market area delineation in cases where the neighborhood and market area are not the same.
3. Identify the stage in the life cycle of the neighborhood. Neighborhoods typically go through a cycle of changes—i.e., growth, stability, decline, and revitalization—which affect property values. Without an understanding of the market forces behind these changes, the appraiser cannot effectively identify the highest and best use of a property.
4. Conduct additional research into the local market. Although some changes that affect values in a neighborhood are immediately discernible, others may require time-consuming study. In particular, appraisers should focus on factors that pertain to the long-term prospects of the area. Neighborhood zoning ordinances, municipal development projects, locally available financing terms, and plans for transportation networks can provide useful indications of how

neighborhood values have been evolving. This information may enable an appraiser to forecast future trends.

5. Rate the quality of the neighborhood. Appraisers must try to identify and understand the amenities and shortcomings that make a neighborhood more or less attractive to market participants. This critical step in data collection will allow the appraiser to determine the locational advantages or disadvantages of the subject and comparable properties.

Specific Data

Specific data are collected for the subject property and each proposed comparable, which is the basis for property productivity analysis, the final step of the market analysis process. First the appraiser inspects the subject property's site and improvements. Site data include information on the size, shape, and location of the lot, the orientation of the building(s), the topography, available utilities and site improvements, and the property's compatibility with surrounding land uses. The improvements are described in terms of their style, design, and layout as well as their structural and mechanical components. The appraiser rates each component for its quality, condition, functional utility, energy efficiency, and market appeal. Comparable properties are usually analyzed in less detail than the subject, but all factors that affect their values and establish their comparability (i.e., the elements of comparison) must be analyzed fully and accurately.

Specific data also include information on seller concessions and financial arrangements that could affect the selling prices of the comparables. The history of ownership and use of the subject property should be investigated to establish whether toxic wastes or hazardous materials may be present on the property. The recent listing and sales history of the subject property is carefully analyzed to gain insight into the subject's acceptance in the marketplace.

If sales comparison is the primary approach, the data collected must be sufficient to allow the appraiser to recognize and adjust for differences between the subject and similar properties. When the cost approach is emphasized, the subject property description must be detailed enough to support a valid estimate of the costs of reproducing or replacing the improvements with a comparable structure and to indicate an accurate measure of depreciation. If the income capitalization approach is applicable to the subject property, the appraiser is obligated to investigate comparable rental properties to derive gross rent multipliers, expenses, and market rents. The appraiser must also determine the degree of comparability between the subject and competitive properties to ensure that their sources of income are the same.

Competitive Supply and Demand Data

Competitive supply and demand data relate to the competitive position of the property in its present and future market. Supply data include inventories of existing and proposed competitive properties as well as vacancy and absorption rates. Demand data include population, income, employment, and survey data pertaining to potential property users. From these data an estimate of future demand for the present use or for prospective uses of the property is developed in the market analysis process. The neighborhood analysis section of the Uniform Residential Appraisal Report (URAR) form calls for a description of market conditions in the subject neighborhood.

Step 4. Data Analysis

Appraisal assignments involving the development of an opinion of market value require analysis of the market trends affecting the real estate as well as the highest and best use of the real estate. Often market and neighborhood analysis serves as the basis of highest and best use analysis.

Market and Neighborhood Analysis

Market analysis is defined as the study of real estate market conditions for a specific type of property, and it is the basis on which highest and best use analysis rests. A description of prevalent market conditions helps the reader of an appraisal report understand the motivations of participants in the market for the subject property. An economically depressed region exhibits a certain pattern of real estate transactions, while a region with a growing population and an expanding economic base exhibits another. Broad market conditions provide the background for local and neighborhood market influences that have direct bearing on the value of the subject property.

Even the simplest valuation assignments must be based on a solid understanding of prevalent market conditions. Market analysis serves two important functions. First, it provides a background against which local developments are considered. For example, property values may rise because an area is becoming more economically attractive than the areas that surround it. To develop an understanding of the conditions in the subject area and surrounding areas, an appraiser interviews market participants and relates their perceptions to statistical data. Second, a knowledge of the broad changes that affect supply and demand gives an appraiser an indication of how values change over time. Changes in residential real estate values do not relate only to the subject property's neighborhood. The supply of and demand for housing are affected by broader trends and cycles as well. Recognizing that these broader changes cause values to shift over time, appraisers carefully scrutinize long-term regional price trends.

The data and conclusions generated by market analysis are essential components in other portions of the valuation process. Market analysis identifies the most probable

market analysis.
1. The identification and study of the market for a particular economic good or service.
2. A study of market conditions for a specific type of property. (USPAP, 2002 ed.)

alternatives uses for a particular site, provides data on timing so the alternatives can be tested for financial feasibility, and provides support for the assessment of risk and probability that further focuses the final selection of the highest and best use of the subject property within its local market.

In addition, market analysis yields information needed for each of the three traditional approaches to value. In the cost approach, market analysis provides the basis for making an adjustment to market value for the depreciation affecting the subject property, i.e., measuring physical deterioration and functional and external obsolescence. In the income capitalization approach, rents, expenses, and multipliers are determined by the market forces of supply and demand. In the sales comparison approach, the conclusions of market analysis are used to delineate the market and thereby identify comparable properties, to identify potential buyers and their criteria for purchases, and to determine a market conditions adjustment.

The extent of market and neighborhood analysis and the level of detail appropriate for a particular assignment depend upon the appraisal problem under examination. For standard residential appraisal assignments, the neighborhood analysis process is often a straightforward description of the state of the local market at a particular time. When appraisers are doing business in a generally stable market on a daily basis, they should have all the necessary demographic and economic information to document market conditions on file. When the assignment is more complex—e.g., an analysis of the feasibility of a subdivision development—a more detailed market analysis will be required. No matter what the level of complexity, the logic of the market analysis must be communicated to the reader through the appraisal report.

Highest and Best Use Analysis

Highest and best use analysis is essential to the valuation process. The highest and best use of both the site as though vacant and the property as improved must meet four criteria. The highest and best use must be

1. Legally permissible
2. Physically possible
3. Financially feasible
4. Maximally productive

These criteria are usually considered sequentially. For example, a use may be financially feasible, but this is irrelevant if it is legally prohibited or physically impossible.

Highest and best use analysis is performed in two steps. First the site is analyzed as though vacant and available for development. This process serves two important functions—identification of comparables and site value estimation. The highest and best use of all comparable property sites should be similar to that of the subject property. Ana-

highest and best use. The reasonably probable and legal use of vacant land or an improved property, which is physically possible, appropriately supported, financially feasible, and that results in the highest value. The four criteria the highest and best use must meet are legal permissibility, physical possibility, financial feasibility, and maximum productivity.

lyzing the highest and best use of the site as though vacant also helps the appraiser develop an opinion of site value.

In this first analysis, the potential uses of the vacant land are analyzed with respect to the four criteria. Each use is tested to see whether it is legally permissible, physically possible, and financially feasible. Uses that do not pass the initial tests are eliminated from further consideration. The uses that remain are analyzed and the one that is maximally productive is selected as the highest and best use of the site as though vacant.

The highest and best use of a site may be to remain vacant or it may be to develop the site. If development is contemplated, the appraiser seeks to determine what type of building or other improvement should be constructed and when. The highest and best use conclusion for a site should be as specific as the marketplace indicates.

In the second step of the analysis, the highest and best use of the property as improved is examined. This process also serves two functions. The appraiser confirms that each comparable improved property has a highest and best use similar to that of the subject property and therefore would serve as a reasonable substitute property. The analysis also helps the appraiser determine whether the improvements should be demolished, renovated, or retained in their present condition. Identification of the existing property's most productive use is crucial to this determination.

In this second analysis, the same four criteria are applied to the existing improvements. Of the legal uses that are physically possible and financially feasible, the one that is maximally productive is the highest and best use of the property as improved. In analyzing the highest and best use of improved properties, appraisers must consider any rehabilitation or modernization that is consistent with market preferences. For example, the highest and best use of a residence should reflect any rehabilitation required to provide the amenities that are standard in the given market.

In residential appraisal, analyzing the highest and best use of a property is often a simple process that is clearly supported by the surrounding development and economic conditions. But the conclusions reached at this point of the valuation process have significant influence over subsequent analyses—e.g., as a basis for depreciation analysis in the cost approach, as support for the selection of improved property sales and for which adjustments to make or not to make in the sales comparison approach, and as a basis for the selection of rents and multipliers in the income capitalization approach.

Step 5. Site Value Opinion

In many market value appraisal assignments, separate opinions of site value are required. For example, site value opinions are necessary in the development of the cost approach, to test site amenity adjustments in the sales comparison approach, and to test comparability through the land-to-value ratios of the subject and comparable properties. Some appraisals are performed to estimate site value only. Ad valorem tax assessments in some areas require separate indications of site value, and a site value opinion is essential to highest and best use analysis.

The most reliable method for estimating site value is the sales comparison approach. Sales of similar vacant parcels are researched, analyzed, compared, and adjusted to provide a value indication for the land being appraised. When sufficient data are not available for sales comparison, however, procedures such as allocation and extraction can be used to value land.

Step 6. Application of the Approaches to Value

Once pertinent data have been collected, the appraiser is ready to apply one or more of the three approaches to value. Each approach will result in at least one indication of value. The appropriateness of a given approach depends on the nature of the valuation problem and the amount of reliable data available. For example, the sales comparison approach is most applicable when sufficient data can be collected on recent sales of comparable properties. If a property has many special features or no comparable properties have been sold recently, the sales comparison approach may not be very reliable. If a property is newer and exhibits little depreciation, the appraiser might place greater emphasis on the cost approach. If the property being appraised appeals to an active rental market, the income capitalization approach should be given serious consideration. All applicable approaches should be used whenever possible.

All three approaches rely on market data and on the principle of substitution, which holds that the price or rent that a property is likely to command will closely reflect the prices or rents obtainable for similar properties in the same market. The cost of constructing a similar structure, minus depreciation, can be added to site value to produce one value indication, while sales of comparable properties can be analyzed to produce another. Studying the value of properties that have similar gross incomes provides a third method for deriving a value indication. Because all three approaches are based on an understanding of how buyers and sellers interact, they should yield similar value conclusions.

Cost Approach

The cost approach is based on the premise that property value is indicated by the current cost to construct a new improvement minus depreciation plus the value of the site. The cost approach is applied in the following steps:

1. Estimate the value of the site as though vacant and available to be developed to its highest and best use.
2. Estimate the direct (hard) and indirect (soft) costs of the improvements as of the effective appraisal date.
3. Estimate an appropriate entrepreneurial incentive or profit from analysis of the market.
4. Add estimated direct costs, indirect costs, and the entrepreneurial incentive or profit to arrive at the total cost of the improvements.
5. Estimate the amount of depreciation resulting from any of the three major categories: physical deterioration, functional obsolescence, and external obsolescence.
6. Deduct the estimated depreciation from the total costs of the improvements to derive an estimate of their depreciated cost.
7. Estimate the contributory value of any site improvements that have not already been considered. (Site improvements are often appraised at their contributory value, i.e., directly on a depreciated-cost basis.)
8. Add the site value to the total depreciated cost of all improvements to arrive at the indicated value of the property.

cost approach. A set of procedures through which a value indication is derived for the fee simple interest in a property by estimating the current cost to construct a reproduction of (or replacement for) the existing structure, including an entrepreneurial incentive, deducting depreciation from the total cost, and adding the estimated land value. Adjustments may then be made to the indicated fee simple value of the subject property to reflect the value of the property interest being appraised.

The cost approach is most reliable when the property improvements are new or nearly new and they are the highest and best use of the site. If the utility and condition of the property are close to ideal, depreciation will be minimal. Because depreciation can be difficult to estimate, the cost approach is less reliable and less convincing when it is used to value older properties. When an improvement has special construction features or sales considered comparable are unavailable, the cost approach is especially useful.

Sales Comparison Approach

The sales comparison approach is used to value most residential properties because it is direct and easy to understand. When properly applied, this approach is usually the most reliable and the most persuasive. To apply the sales comparison approach, the appraiser considers the prices of similar properties that have recently been sold. These prices can indicate the value of the subject property once they are adjusted to reflect any differences between the subject and the comparables. The procedural steps are

1. Identify and research comparable properties that have been sold recently, and ascertain the price, property rights conveyed, financing terms, conditions of sale (buyer and seller motivations), and market conditions (time) involved in each transaction. Verify the accuracy of this information.

2. Examine each sale considered comparable to determine how it differs from the subject property and how these differences affect its value. The elements of comparison include
   - Real property rights conveyed
   - Financing terms
   - Conditions of sale
   - Expenditures made immediately after purchase
   - Market conditions
   - Location
   - Physical characteristics (size, construction quality, condition of improvements)
   - Economic characteristics (e.g., rent, expenses, gross rent multipliers)
   - Use (zoning)
   - Non-realty components of value

3. Adjust the sale or unit price of each comparable for observed differences between the subject and the comparables. Compare the comparable to the subject. If the comparable is inferior to the subject, adjust the price of the comparable upward; if the comparable is superior to the subject, a downward adjustment is made to the price of the comparable. In all cases the comparable sales are adjusted to reflect the characteristics in the subject property. This process simulates what each comparable would have sold for had it been similar to the subject.

4. Reconcile the results of these comparisons into a single value indication or range of values.

sales comparison approach. A set of procedures in which a value indication is derived by comparing the property being appraised to similar properties that have been sold recently, then applying appropriate units of comparison and making adjustments to the sale prices of the comparables based on the elements of comparison. The sales comparison approach may be used to value improved properties, vacant land, or land being considered as though vacant; it is the most common and preferred method of land valuation when an adequate supply of comparable sales are available.

comparables. A shortened term for similar property sales, rentals, or operating expenses used for comparison in the valuation process; also called *comps*.

elements of comparison. The characteristics or attributes of properties and transactions that cause the prices of real estate to vary.

Income Capitalization Approach

As a general term, *capitalization* refers to the conversion of an income stream into an indication of value. In the income capitalization approach, property value is measured in relation to the anticipated future benefits that can be derived from property ownership (the principle of anticipation). When the property being appraised competes in an active rental market, the appraiser can derive an indication of value by converting the anticipated future benefits into a present value through capitalization. The capitalization technique applied depends on the income characteristics of the subject property and the data available for analysis.

The income capitalization approach is not applicable in many segments of the residential market. However, some small multifamily dwellings and a certain segment of the single-unit residential market are bought as investments for their return potential (monthly rent and reversion), To apply the income capitalization approach in valuing residential properties, a gross rent multiplier (*GRM*) is applied to an estimate of market rent. The steps are

1. Identify and research competitive rental properties that have been sold recently. Divide the sale price of each by its gross monthly market rent at the time of sale to obtain its *GRM*.

2. Estimate the monthly market rent that the subject property should command in light of present and anticipated rent levels and the property's market appeal.

3. Multiply the subject property's monthly market rent by a *GRM* selected from the *GRMs* of competing properties to obtain an indication of the value of the subject property.

To derive reliable *GRMs*, the appraiser must analyze truly comparable properties that have very similar ratios of operating expenses to gross rent, are unfurnished, and have rental rate at or very near market norms.

Step 7. Reconciliation of Value Indications and Final Value Opinion

The last analytical phase in the valuation process is the reconciliation of the various value indications into a final value conclusion. Obviously, the application of more than one approach will result in more than one value indication. Even if only one approach is applied, a range of values may be derived that needs to be refined into a single figure.

To perform reconciliation, an appraiser reviews each stage of the valuation process and tests the reasonableness of each conclusion reached. The appraiser asks

• Which data seem to be the most reliable?

• Which approach should be given the greatest weight in light of the purpose of the assignment and the information available?

• Finally, and perhaps most importantly, do the results make sense?

These questions must be asked and answered throughout the valuation process, but final reconciliation is the appraiser's last opportunity to perform such a review.

Each valuation approach serves as a check on the other approaches used. A wide variation among the value estimates derived often suggests that one approach is not as applicable as the others or that valuation procedures have not been properly applied. Unrealistic conclusions must be closely scrutinized. Once the appraiser is satisfied that the general range of value indications is justified, each indication is weighted according to its appropriateness and reliability. Finally, the appraiser selects a single value opinion or a range of value opinions based on the market data and on informed judgment.

> **reconciliation.** The last phase of any valuation assignment in which two or more value indications derived from market data are resolved into a final value opinion, which may be either a final range of value or a single point estimate.

Step 8. Report of Defined Value

An appraisal is not complete until the conclusion and the reasoning behind it have been communicated to the client, usually in a written report. In addition to the final opinion of value, a written report should include all the pertinent data considered and all the methods of analysis used in the appraisal.

The appraisal report is a tangible expression of the appraiser's service, so its organization, presentation, and overall appearance are important. By signing a report, the appraiser accepts responsibility for its contents. Appraisal reports prepared by members or affiliates of the Appraisal Institute must meet certain requirements.[2]

Appraisals may be communicated orally or in writing. Examples of written reports include self-contained reports, summary reports, and restricted use reports.

A self-contained report is the most comprehensive method for communicating the results of an appraisal to a client. This type of report is used when complete, detailed documentation is needed. A self-contained appraisal report presents the pertinent evidence and the logic employed to reach the final value opinion in a manner that is simple and convincing. Self-contained reports are usually organized to follow the major steps in the valuation process.

Sometimes a client requests that a summary report be prepared. A summary report must meet extensive reporting requirements, but the level of detail presented is substantially

> **self-contained appraisal report.** A written appraisal report prepared under Standards Rule 2-2(a) of the Uniform Standards of Professional Appraisal Practice (USPAP, 2002 ed.), which sets forth the data considered, the appraisal procedures followed, and the reasoning employed in the appraisal, addressing each item in the depth and detail required by its significance to the appraisal and providing sufficient information so that the client and the users of the report will understand the appraisal and not be misled or confused.

---

2. See the Standards Rules relating to Standard 2 of the Uniform Standards of Professional Appraisal Practice for the specific requirements that apply to reports of value opinions (appraisals) performed by Appraisal Institute members and affiliates.

reduced. Form reports, which are often used in appraising residential properties, may be restricted use reports, though most of the residential industry recognizes them as summary reports.

The majority of residential appraisals for lending purposes are summary reports prepared on standardized forms. Form reports are preprinted documents that appraisers complete as they proceed through the valuation process. These standardized forms allow users of appraisal reports to compare and consider many appraisals quickly and to discern immediately whether all the required information has been supplied. Form reports are commonly used by lending institutions, government agencies, and employee transfer companies, which must process large numbers of appraisals.

Restricted use reports include many of the items in the definition of the problem in abbreviated form, a brief statement of how the appraisal was conducted, and the value conclusion. A restricted use report must contain a prominent use restriction to ensure that the client understands the limited utility of such a report.

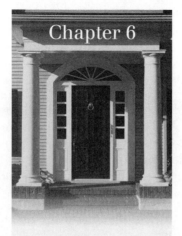

Chapter 6

Beginning the Appraisal

An appraisal starts when a representative of a financial institution, employee of a relocation company, homebuyer, seller, representative of an estate, lawyer, or some other party contacts the appraiser with a value-related question about real property. The appraiser and the client discuss the appraisal problem and the scope of work required to complete the assignment. If the client does not know what is involved in the completion of the assignment, the discussion takes the form of client education. The client may not understand what professional services the appraiser can and cannot provide, while the appraiser may not have the requisite knowledge or experience to competently complete the assignment.[1] A clear understanding of the problem to be solved and the role of the appraiser are essential at the onset of the appraiser's work.

A contract between the appraiser and the client precedes even the first step of the valuation problem, i.e., identifying the appraisal problem. The appraiser and client will usually agree on a fee, timeline, format for delivery of the appraiser's opinions and conclusions, and

---

1. Most residential assignments are not beyond the abilities of professionally trained, experienced appraisers, but in some cases special expertise may be required. In these instances the Uniform Standards of Professional Appraisal Practice (USPAP) require that the appraiser immediately disclose the lack of knowledge or experience to the client and take all steps necessary or appropriate to complete the appraisal competently. The Competency Rule states

    Prior to accepting an assignment or entering into an agreement to perform any assignment, an appraiser must properly identify the problem to be addressed and have the knowledge and experience to complete the assignment competently; or alternatively, must:

    1. disclose the lack of knowledge and/or experience to the client before accepting the assignment;

    2. take all steps necessary or appropriate to complete the assignment competently; and

    3. describe the lack of knowledge and/or experience and the steps taken to complete the assignment competently in the report.

other issues before the appraiser has completed a formal study of the scope of work necessary to solve the appraisal problem. In fact, only four or five of the major elements involved in the identification of the appraisal problem are likely to be well established when the appraiser agrees to begin the assignment:

- The intended use of the appraisal
- The type and definition of value
- The effective date of the value opinion
- The location of the property
- Perhaps the identification of the property rights to be valued as one of the relevant characteristics of the property

Limiting conditions and assumptions are often not revealed until after the property inspection.

Two fundamental characteristics of the subject property–the identification of the real estate and the property rights conveyed–must be investigated before the collection of other market data begins. At this early stage, the appraiser may have only a street address to identify the property, not a legal description. Similarly, the property rights may have been named by the client–e.g., fee simple, leased fee estate, fee subject to a mortgage–but the specific character of these rights and any limitations imposed by private restrictions and the four powers of government have not yet been established.

The initial discussions between the appraiser and the client about the appraisal problem and the negotiation of a contract for the assignment set the stage for the appraiser's determination of the scope of work, in particular the extent of data collection, confirmation, and reporting required. The scope of work serves as a blueprint for the assignment and the steps to be taken to solve the appraisal problem.

Work Schedule and Preliminary Strategy

Once the appraiser has a general definition of the appraisal problem and a preliminary description of the property to be appraised, a schedule for data collection can be developed. Experienced appraisers who are familiar with the market and the type of property being appraised can review the necessary steps mentally, but appraisers with less experience and those performing complex assignments should list the kinds of data needed and draw up a schedule for the collection effort. Written schedules are particularly helpful if the services of additional staff or outside professionals will be needed to perform property inspections, collect and confirm market data, or perform other tasks that influence the eventual value opinion. (A sample assignment plan is shown in Figure 6.1.) Tasks that involve the greatest amount of time should be scheduled first so that they are completed in time.

Appraisers who delegate tasks that are part of the valuation process should recognize that they are personally responsible for all work con-

Figure 6.1	Sample Assignment Plan

Assignment Plan

Client: _____

    Address: _____ Phone: _____

Intended User(s): _____

Intended Use: _____

Type of Value: _____

Effective Date: _____

Characteristics: _____

    Address: _____

    Legal: _____

    Interest: _____ Type: _____

    Size: _____ Age: _____

    Lot Size: _____

    Description: _____

Owner's Name: _____ Phone # _____

Extraordinary Assumptions: _____

Hypothetical Conditions: _____

Scope of Work: _____

    Inspection: _____

    Identify Property:

	❏ Inspection	❏ Appraisal
	❏ Assessor's records	❏ Data bank
	❏ Owner	❏ Buyer
	❏ Agent	❏ State data
	❏ County records	

    Physical Factors: _____

    Economic Factors: _____

    Analysis: Type:

	❏ H & B U	❏ Market
	❏ Sales	❏ Cost
	❏ Income	

    Extent: _____

Type of Report:

	❏ Self-Contained	❏ Summary
	❏ Restricted Use	

Date of Completion: _____ Fee: _____

Source: Stephanie Coleman, *Scope of Work* (Chicago: Appraisal Institute, 2006), 48.

ducted on their behalf or in their name. To ensure that clients, the public, and third parties are not misled, the Uniform Standards of Professional Appraisal Practice require, when applicable, that the appraiser certify in the report that no one provided significant professional assistance to the person signing the report. If there are exceptions, the name of each individual who provided significant professional assistance must be stated along with a clear explanation of what tasks the assistant performed.

The appraisal strategy described in this chapter is just that–a strategy. It is not a specific procedure to be applied in every circumstance, but a description of the steps followed to collect data in the majority of residential appraisals. Appraisal clients have different needs, and properties have different governmental, social, economic, and environmental characteristics that influence value. In various markets, different types of information will be more or less reliable. Moreover, all appraisers have developed their own methods for researching and compiling data.

Appraisers are contractually bound to fulfill the services agreed upon with their clients. They also have an obligation to the public, to third parties using the appraisal report, to the appraisal profession, and to themselves to perform appraisal services in accordance with high ethical and professional standards through licensing laws and the Uniform Standards of Professional Appraisal Practice. Keeping these differences in mind, the data collection steps presented in this chapter are those usually undertaken at the beginning of the valuation process.

Data Collection

Data collection involves several tasks, which may be grouped into two general steps:

1. The appraiser reviews legal, tax, and assessment information on the subject property and prepares for the field inspection by gathering the necessary tools and equipment. Using the information gathered before the field inspection, the appraiser notes the legal description of the property and all public and private restrictions that limit property use.

2. The appraiser then makes a field inspection of the site and improvements. In describing the subject property, the appraiser observes how site characteristics combine to shape the highest and best use of the site and notes any problems or special advantages that may affect site value. The description of the improvements focuses on the quality and condition of the improvements.

Initial Research

The appraiser needs to collect reliable data on the subject property from informed sources within a brief period of time. The most knowledgeable source is usually the property owner, who may also be the occupant or, in the case of rental property, the property manager. Sales agents and brokers often have detailed information on property characteristics. A representative of a financial institution that holds the property mortgage may also be a good source. Often an appraiser with good communication skills can secure the cooperation of these important individuals.

Several kinds of information can be obtained from the owner or agent by asking questions about the sale and listing history of the subject property:

- When was the property last sold?
- If the sale occurred within the past three years, what was the reason for the sale?

- What was the sale price and what type of financing was involved?
- What was the prior listing history?
- Is there a current or recent listing, option, or agreement of sale?
- If there is a current agreement of sale, what is the price and what are the terms?

The appraiser should acquire all necessary documentation (such as contracts and amendments) to verify this essential data.

Knowing the subject property's sale and listing history is vital in an appraisal. The statements and actions of actual buyers and sellers of the property may be more indicative of the property's value than the patterns revealed by the sales of other properties, even the most comparable ones. Indeed, the Uniform Standards of Professional Appraisal Practice and secondary market participants require that this type of information be considered if it is available in the normal course of business. Information on current or recent listings, offers, or agreements of sale can suggest a probable range of value within which the appraiser's final value conclusion may fall. Usually, in a market performing under normal conditions, a sale is consummated at a price that is lower than the seller's asking price but higher than the buyer's initial offering price.

The appraiser asks a second set of questions to obtain a preliminary description of the subject:

- What is the style or design of the dwelling?
- How many dwelling units (e.g., accessory units, two- to four-family) are involved?
- How many stories does it have and how many bedrooms and bathrooms?
- How old is it and have there been any additions to or remodeling of the original structure? Were building permits obtained?
- Does the site have any amenities that impact value (e.g., view, size, topography)?
- Does the owner or agent have a legal description or a recent survey of the property?
- Are there any additional improvements on the site such as a pool, guest house, or barn?

The answers provided by the owner or agent help the appraiser form a general picture of the property to be appraised. This preliminary description will help the appraiser select comparable properties for analysis.

The appraiser will also want to determine if non-realty items of property should be considered. If the appraiser has agreed to consider items of personal property as part of the opinion of value, they must be identified. The question of personal property is relevant if the appraisal has been requested for a sales transaction. The appraiser may also ask the owner about non-realty items during the property inspection. The inclusion of personal property may affect the value conclusion and therefore must be specified in the appraisal report. In appraisals needed for lending purposes, appraisers are often specifically requested to omit personal property. However, if personal property is to be included, its treatment should conform to the requirements of the Uniform Standards of Professional Appraisal Practice.

After the sale and listing history and preliminary description have been established, the appraiser makes an appointment to inspect the property. Appraisers should be very courteous to homeowners and maintain good relations with brokers and agents because these individuals can be important sources of vital data now and in the future. The information obtained from these interested parties must be verified by checking with other sources and inspecting the property. An examination of public records and an on-site inspection of the subject property provide data that are essential to property analysis.

Field Inspection

The appraiser observes the physical characteristics of the site and the improvements to describe the principal features and any additional advantages or disadvantages the market is likely to consider. The appraiser then forms an opinion of how the site can best be used, given its legal and physical limitations and its relationship to its surroundings. Assuming the site is put to its highest and best use, the appraiser considers how the physical characteristics of the site and the present condition of the existing site improvements add to or detract from property value. Value influences are examined in light of neighborhood and local market preferences.

The appraiser describes the improvements by noting the size, style, design, and layout of all buildings. The appraiser rates the construction quality and maintenance condition of each building, describing the structural components, materials, and mechanical systems as well as the quality and condition of each component. Any special problems are noted. The appraiser considers how the building elements observed combine with the site's characteristics to shape the highest and best use of the property as improved. Any problems or deficiencies in the present condition of the improvements that might prevent the property from realizing its highest and best use must be described.

What is an improvement?

Homeowners may confuse the term *improvement* with a renovation, remodeling, or upgrade of existing structures. To real estate professionals, *improvements* are buildings or other relatively permanent structures or developments that are located on, or attached to, land. This category includes both improvements to the land such as access and utilities, which prepare the land for a subsequent use, and improvements on the land such as buildings and landscaping.

field inspection. Inspection of the physical characteristics of a site to describe its principal features and gather data that could be used in later analyses.

Property Inspection and Home Inspection

Property inspection is an integral part of the analysis of the site and improvements in most appraisals, but the "inspection" performed by an appraiser should not be confused with the services rendered by professional home inspectors, engineers, or other technical specialists. Advisory Opinion 2 of the Uniform Standards of Professional Appraisal Practice states, "An inspection conducted by an appraiser is usually not the equivalent of an inspection by an inspection professional (e.g., a structural engineer, a licensed home inspector . . .)." In a typical residential appraisal, the purpose of an appraiser's property inspection is to gather information on the relevant property characteristics for the analysis of value, not to identify structural defects and needed repairs. In contrast, the purpose of an inspection by a professional home inspector is not related to valuation issues. In fact, the standards of professional practice of the American Society of Home Inspectors include general limitations that exempt ASHI members from determining the market value or marketability of property. Likewise, HUD explains explicitly to homebuyers that, "The home inspector does not estimate the value of the house."[2]

Clearly, an inspection of a house as part of an appraisal and an inspection by a home inspector include similar activities–visual observation of the site and structure and an effort to identify major defects. The similarities are reinforced when appraisers use the language of home inspectors to describe their actions. They may say, "I need to set up a time to inspect your house." as opposed to "I would like to walk through your residence to observe conditions that relate to valuation issues." Although the means used by appraisers and home inspectors may be similar, the ends of their respective property inspection processes are distinctly different. The appraiser is interested in how the condition and quality of the property compare to other properties in the market area at the time of the appraisal. In contrast, the home inspector focuses on the existing condition of the property as it relates to current and future component and the performance of mechanical systems. In other words, an appraisal is performed for the lender while a home inspection is performed for a homebuyer.

A homeowner's confusion about the purpose of the appraiser's inspection is understandable because the homeowner's only meeting with the appraiser is typically during the appraiser's walk-through of the site and improvements. An uninformed homeowner may even think that the appraiser's inspection is the complete extent of the work involved in an appraisal because the homeowner is unlikely to see the appraisal report. In contrast, the client and intended users of an

> **What does *property inspection* mean?**
>
> In this text, the term *property inspection* is used in a general sense to denote visual observation of the site and improvements.

---

2. From *For Your Protection, Get a Home Inspection* brochure available online at <www.pueblo.gsa.gov/cic_text/housing/inspection/home.htm>.

appraisal must not be confused, so the extent of the analysis of the site and improvements (including the inspection process) should be clearly disclosed in the appraisal report.

The appraiser determines the extent of the property inspection necessary while making the scope of work decision. Some assignments require an exterior-only inspection (i.e., a drive-by), in which the appraiser relies on other sources to describe the property's physical characteristics. The Uniform Residential Appraisal Report form includes the certification, "I performed a complete visual inspection of the interior and exterior areas of the subject property." Fannie Mae's Selling Guide adds: "We expect that appraisals based on an interior and exterior inspection will include a complete visual inspection of the accessible areas of the property. *The appraiser is not responsible for hidden or unapparent conditions.*" (emphasis added) The Selling Guide also states:

> The appraiser must consider all factors that have an impact on value and marketability in the development of the appraisal report. The appraiser is expected to consider and describe the overall quality and condition of the property and identify items that require immediate repair as well as items where maintenance may have been deferred, which may or may not require immediate repair. The appraiser must address any needed repairs or any physical, functional, or external inadequacies in the "comments" section of the appraisal.

Inspection Tools and Equipment

Before making an actual field inspection, the appraiser gathers all the tools and equipment necessary for this phase of the assignment. The appraiser will probably want to collect information on the subject site, the subject improvement, and potential comparables all in one trip, so careful planning is needed. Most appraisal offices have many of the useful tools listed in Figure 6.2 on hand.

The affordability and ease of digital photography and portable computing improves continually, and advancements in technology affect typical appraisal practices in the field and in the office. For example, appraisers who use digital cameras no longer have to wait for film to be developed, which increases their efficiency. However, lending institutions and other clients expect that increased efficiency to result in quicker turnaround times for appraisals. Likewise, wireless technology allows for data to be transmitted directly from the field. Appraisers will need to keep up with emerging technologies and decide for themselves which new tools work best in their markets and in their practices.[3]

When building blueprints or plans are available, they can help the appraiser identify the structural and mechanical details of an improvement. Plans and blueprints may also be used to verify the dimensions

---

3. See the Appraisal Institute's Tech Forum at<www.appraisalinstitute.org/resources/aiforum.asp> for more information and discussion of state-of-the-art appraisal tools.

Figure 6.2	The Appraiser's Tools

Measuring equipment	50- or 100-ft. fiberglass wind-up tape measure
	12- to 20-ft. tape measure that can be worn on a belt
	Measuring wheel for exterior measurement
	Sonic or laser measuring tool
	Carpenter's folding rule
	Bevel or adjustable angle tool for measuring angles
	Ladder
Drawing equipment*	Straight edge, architect's scale, engineer's scale, and graph paper for transferring measurements onto scale drawings
	Template and protractor for drawing curved lines and angles
Photographic equipment	Digital camera with zoom lens, ample memory, and extra batteries or a 35mm camera with regular, wide-angle, and telephoto lenses
	Camera phone or disposable camera, as a backup
	Flash attachment for interior photography
Maps and plats	GPS device to identify land boundaries in watery, wooded, and mountainous areas
	Maps that can be downloaded or scanned:
	· Street and highway maps
	· Address maps
	· Municipal maps
	· Plat books
	· Census maps
	· Soil maps
	· Topographical maps
	· Floodplain maps
	· Zoning maps
	· Traffic count maps
	· Survey plats
	· Subdivision maps
Calculators	Inexpensive pocket calculator
	Financial calculator for more complex calculations
Dictation equipment	Tape recorder or digital recorder that is portable, compact, and compatible with transcription equipment in the office
Portable computers	Laptops with wireless communication capability to access MLS, mapping software, and deed plot software for plotting lengthy and complex legal descriptions, calculating area, and producing final drawings
	Tablet computer with "autoCAD lite" drawing software
	Personal digital assistant (PDA)
Carrying equipment	Briefcase (for the most professional appearance) or portfolio, catalog case, or file folder
	Clipboard for taking notes
	Toolbox with flashlight (and extra batteries), and level (or a marble) to check surfaces
Miscellaneous office supplies	Hiking boots or waterproof boots and raincoat or work clothes for inspecting rough terrain
	Binoculars for visual inspection of the roof and other inaccessible areas
	Inspection and standard appraisal forms or checklists

* Used less frequently as computer drawing programs have become more affordable and user-friendly.

of a building, but the appraiser cannot rely on plans for calculating size. The appraiser must measure the improvements during the field inspection because the plans may not have been followed accurately or, more likely, alterations and additions may have been made after the plans were prepared.

Appraisers often use a checklist during the field inspection to ensure that no important items are overlooked. They adapt the list of items included on standard form reports or develop their own checklists.

Describing and Rating the Site and Improvements

With the data requirements in mind and the necessary equipment and materials at hand, the appraiser is ready to begin the inspection of the improvements. In each step of the inspection, the appraiser performs two tasks:

1. The appraiser describes and classifies the building element being studied.
2. The appraiser then rates the element.

Each physical component must be rated for quality and for condition to determine its effective age (i.e., the age indicated by the condition and utility of the structure, which is determined by the appraiser's analysis of the market) as opposed to its actual age (i.e., the number of years that have elapsed since building construction was completed). The rating process is called a quality and condition survey. Layouts and designs are also considered in terms of their functional utility. The appraiser determines how the functional utility of the building relates to its construction quality and maintenance.

In the context of a building description, quality refers to the character of construction and the materials used in the original work. The physical deterioration of the improvements is not considered in rating their quality. When well-chosen materials are applied in a suitable manner with sound construction techniques and good workmanship, quality results. The Marshall & Swift *Residential Cost Handbook* provides six quality ratings–low, fair, average, good, very good, and excellent–and indicates separate costs for each category.

A structure may have a functional layout and attractive design but be constructed with inferior materials and poor workmanship. These deficiencies increase maintenance and utility costs and affect the marketability of the property adversely. On the other hand, a building can be too well constructed–i.e., its cost is not justified by its utility. Most purchasers will not want to pay the excess costs even though they may be recaptured through reduced maintenance expenses.

An excess in the capacity or quality of a structural component, as determined by mar-

quality and condition survey. An analysis of the quality and condition of building components that distinguishes among deferred maintenance items (those in need of immediate repair), short-lived items (those that must be repaired or replaced in the future), and items that are expected to last for the remaining economic life of the building.

ket standards, is called a *superadequacy*. For example, a single-unit house with a four-car garage would have a superadequacy if the houses in the market generally have one- or two-car garages. Superadequacies should be considered in the quality survey, as should the related concept of overimprovement. An overimprovement is an improvement that does not represent the maximally productive use of the site on which it is placed because it is too large or costly and cannot develop the highest possible site value. For example, a house with a brick-paved driveway would be an overimprovement in a neighborhood where all other driveways are gravel.

Conversely, a deficiency is an inadequacy in a structural component, as determined by market standards. An older house with a kitchen area that is not wide enough to accommodate the modern appliances typical for the market area would suffer from a deficiency. An improvement that is inadequate to develop the highest and best use of its site is an underimprovement. Underimprovements are usually structures of lesser cost, quality, and size than typical properties in the neighborhood. For example, a three-bedroom house with a one-car garage in a neighborhood where garages generally accommodate two cars would be an underimprovement. In an area with a hot, humid climate, a lack of central air-conditioning could be considered an underimprovement, particularly in a market in which that feature is viewed as standard equipment.

superadequacy. An excess in the capacity or quality of a structure or structural component; determined by market standards.

deficiency. An inadequacy in a structure or one of its components; determined by market standards.

overimprovement. An improvement that does not represent the most profitable use for the site on which it is placed because it is too large or costly and cannot develop the highest possible land value; may be temporary or permanent. Can be considered a superadequacy and measured accordingly in estimating depreciation.

underimprovement. An improvement that is inadequate to develop the highest and best use of its site; usually a structure that is of lesser cost, quality, and size than typical neighborhood properties.

Zoning and Building Codes

The appraiser should be thoroughly familiar with all zoning regulations, building codes, housing codes, and private restrictions that are applicable to the subject property. This information is needed to determine whether existing or potential property uses conform to local codes. The design and construction of buildings are regulated by building, plumbing, electrical, and mechanical codes and may be limited by deed restrictions as well.

During the field inspection the appraiser should look for current uses that do not conform to legal requirements and consider how these uses might affect the property's value. If, for example, a garage has been converted into living area without a building permit, it may now require upgrading to meet building code standards or may even constitute an illegal use. A building that does not comply with local codes probably has less value than a similar building that does. Making a building conform to the standards set forth in the code may produce additional expenses for its owners and limit the future use of the improvements.

The identification of superadequacies and deficiencies occurs within the context of the market. A property with an apparent functional problem—say, a three-bedroom house with a single bathroom—would not suffer from a deficiency or superadequacy if the property conforms to the characteristics of competitive properties. The market must recognize a difference for overimprovements or underimprovements to affect value, so the appraiser must be able to make meaningful comparisons between the subject property improvements and comparable properties in describing the improvements.

In the description of the improvements, the condition of an improvement refers to the extent of physical deterioration in the property. Overall wear and tear and the level of maintenance dictate a building's condition. The appraiser generally distinguishes between items that must be repaired immediately and those that may be repaired or replaced at a later time.

Functional utility is the ability of a property or building to be useful and to perform the function for which it is intended, according to current market preferences and standards. The term also refers to the efficiency of a building's use in terms of architectural style, design and layout, traffic patterns, room size and type, and energy efficiency. A building may have functional utility but an undistinguished architectural style, while another building may have an admired style but little utility. Form and function should work together to create successful architecture. The appraiser considers the functional utility of a building in relation to its construction quality and condition.

functional utility. The ability of a property or building to be useful and to perform the function for which it is intended according to current market tastes and standards; the efficiency of a building's use in terms of architectural style, design and layout, traffic patterns, and the size and type of rooms.

Liability and the Appraiser's Property Inspection

In the past, appraisers seldom faced the threat of litigation. That is no longer the case. Potential liability arising from the inspection of the property being appraised must always be considered by residential appraisers. It is important that appraisers remain mindful of the borrower or purchaser who might review a report at a later date looking for a basis for a lawsuit. The report should be written so as to persuade the purchaser that such efforts would not be successful. Expressly stating that the appraisal is not a home inspection is a good place to start.

According to the records of Liability Insurance Administrators (LIA), which manages the Real Estate Appraisers Professional Liability Insurance Program endorsed by the Appraisal Institute, the most common claim made against residential appraisers is the claim made by a borrower that the appraiser failed to discover and disclose some defective condition in the subject property. Typically, this claim is presented within months of the borrower taking possession of the property. Some claims taken from LIA files include the following:

- In Pennsylvania, the borrowers' two young children began experiencing respiratory problems shortly after moving into their new home. The owners finally traced a mildew odor to one of the bathrooms. After pulling off the wallpaper, they discovered what they later learned was a toxic form of mold. A mold abatement specialist advised them to leave the home immediately. A lawsuit was filed against the sellers, the real estate agents, and the appraiser.

- In Alabama, buyers moved into their new home only to discover that the sellers had left behind boxes, cartons, and bags in the attic. Several months later, the buyers finally got around to cleaning out this debris left behind by the previous owners. While they were doing so, they discovered what looked like evidence of prior fire damage in the form of partially charred beams and eaves. They called in a contractor who told them the damage needed to be repaired immediately or their roof could collapse. A lawsuit was filed against the sellers, the real estate agents, and the appraiser.

- In California, a woman was excited about the purchase of her first home. Within days of moving in, she was startled when she saw sparks flying out of an electrical outlet in the laundry room. She called the home warranty company, which sent out an electrician. He advised that the home's wiring was in poor condition. It looked like new wiring was mixed in with old wiring and all the work had been poorly done. He was concerned about the potential fire hazard this posed and recommended that she get some estimates to have the entire home rewired. This purchase was a "For Sale by Owner" situation. The home was sold "as is" and the buyer did not use the services of a real estate agent, nor did she hire a home inspector. She did file a lawsuit against the sellers and the appraiser.

In each of these examples, the appraiser was sued for negligently failing to discover and disclose the defective condition that was later found in the property. It is true that most residential appraisal reports contain limiting conditions. Each of the reports prepared in connection with these examples contained a limiting condition with language similar to the following:

> The appraiser has noted in this appraisal report any adverse conditions (such as needed repairs, deterioration, the presence of hazardous wastes, toxic substances, etc.) observed during the inspection of the subject property or that he or she became aware of during the research involved in performing this appraisal. Unless otherwise stated in this appraisal report, the appraiser has no knowledge of any hidden or unapparent physical deficiencies or adverse conditions of the property (such as, but not limited to, needed repairs, deterioration, the presence of hazardous wastes, toxic substances, adverse environmental conditions, etc.) that would make the property less valuable, and has assumed that there are no such conditions and makes no guarantees or warranties, expressed or implied. The appraiser will not be responsible for any such conditions that do exist or for engineering or testing that might be required to discover whether such conditions exist. Because the appraiser is not an expert in the field of environmental hazards, this appraisal report must not be considered as an environmental assessment of the property. (Uniform Residential Appraisal Report Form, Fannie Mae Form 1004, March 2005)

The presence of a similar limiting condition in each appraisal report in the previous examples did not prevent the appraiser from being named in the lawsuit.

The language of the limiting condition noted above already says that "the appraiser is not aware of any hidden or unapparent physical deficiencies or adverse conditions," but that might not be enough. In the scope of work section of the report, the appraiser might consider adding some additional, explanatory language indicating that the appraisal report is *not* a home inspection report and that it should not be relied upon to disclose hidden or unapparent conditions of the property. If this type of language were included, it would be difficult for the borrower to claim that he or she was relying on the appraisal report for that purpose.

Certain states have decided, in published opinions, that the appraiser owes no duty to a borrower to disclose hidden defects. The Minnesota Supreme Court ruled that the appraiser owes no duty of care to a purchaser and that the purchaser cannot rely on the appraisal as a warranty of the value or condition of the home (*Baker v. Surman,* 1985). Similarly, New Jersey's appellate court ruled that the appraiser was not liable to the purchaser after the purchaser found numerous defective conditions in the property (*Zielinski v. Professional Appraisal Associates,* 1999). The Alabama Supreme Court specifically found that there is no duty of care that runs from the appraiser, hired by the lender to appraise the subject house, to the purchaser of the property to determine the condition of the property and to report any defects to the purchaser (*Brushwitz v. Ezell,* 2001).

Other states have found the opposite to be the case. In Washington, the Supreme Court found that the appraiser does owe a duty to the purchaser to disclose defective conditions in the property. In this case, the problem was with a roof that needed repairs. Despite finding a duty, the court still ruled in favor of the appraiser. It was determined that the purchaser had known something of the roof problem before signing the purchase contract and that he had taken the cost of repair into account when making his offer. The court decided that the purchaser did not rely on the appraisal (*Schaaf v. Highfield,* 1995).

All of these cases were decided before the newest Fannie Mae appraisal forms became effective in 2005. Certification 23, found in those new forms, reads as follows:

> The borrower, another lender at the request of the borrower, the mortgagee or its successors and assigns, mortgage insurers, government sponsored enterprises, and other secondary market participants may rely on this appraisal report as part of the mortgage finance transaction that involves any one or more of these parties. (Uniform Residential Appraisal Report Form, Fannie Mae Form 1004, March 2005)

It remains to be seen whether or not the inclusion of this language in the appraiser's certifications will affect how the courts rule in the future when determining the appraiser's duty to a purchaser.

If a court is unwilling to dismiss a lawsuit based on the finding that there is a duty owed by the appraiser to the purchaser, the purchaser would still have to successfully argue that he or she reasonably relied on the appraisal to disclose the condition at issue. In most transactions, purchasers sign a contract that legally obligates them to buy the property before the appraisal report has even been ordered. Although the purchase contract might contain an appraisal "contingency," that would usually apply to the opinion of value stated in the report, not to any information about the condition of the property or about needed repairs.

When an appraiser is sued by a purchaser, the appraiser often has to defend against an allegation that he or she never actually conducted an inspection of the interior of the property. The claim indicates that had the appraiser truly inspected the property, he or she would have seen the defect and mentioned it in the report. The fact that the defect was not disclosed leads to the conclusion that the home was not inspected.

Typically the appraisal report shows only exterior photos taken of the property. These photos sometimes strengthen the purchaser's suspicion that no interior inspection was done. For this reason, interior photos can be helpful to an appraiser who has to defend against such allegations. Whether or not the interior photos are included with the report is a decision left to the appraiser and the client. However, even if they are not included in the report, such photos can be helpful to the appraiser's defense should aspects of the interior inspection later be called into question. For example, interior photos prove the appraiser was actually inside the home. They may also serve to refresh the appraiser's memory about the property in question. Interior photos are also helpful in that they depict the condition of the property as of the date of the appraiser's visual inspection.

Liability Insurance Administrators has claims files full of examples in which the presence of interior photos helped to get the appraiser out of a lawsuit much faster than he or she would have if no photos had been available. Examples include the following:

- In California, purchasers sued the seller/builder and the appraiser for failing to disclose defective conditions that the purchasers had discovered in their new home. According to the complaint, several weeks after the buyers moved into the newly constructed property, a number of their kitchen cabinets fell from the walls causing damage to the walls, counters, floors, and appliances as well as to the contents of the cabinets. The appraiser was dismissed from the case after showing a photograph of the kitchen in which the cabinets were firmly affixed to the walls. Nothing in the photo indicated that the cabinets were likely to fall or that they had been installed incorrectly. This appraiser always takes interior photos of kitchens and baths, and he was glad he had done so in this case.

- In West Virginia, an appraiser noted some water stains on the ceiling of the dining room in a home. The real estate agent explained that the stains were the result of a prior roof leak that had been repaired. The seller had hired a licensed contractor to do the work, and the purchaser had been provided with the receipts and guarantee information. The appraiser noted the agent's comments in the report, but he also snapped a photo so he could refresh his own recollection if he were to be questioned about the stains.

Although the roof had been repaired, it seems the entire problem had not been remedied. Unbeknownst to all, moisture in the attic caused mold to appear months later. The appraiser was shocked when he was notified that he had been sued by the purchasers. He explained that he knew nothing about the mold and that all he had seen during his inspection were the water stains. When the appraiser looked through the workfile, he found the photograph he had taken that showed the water stains. It was not until the photo was produced that he was dismissed from the case. Counsel for the real estate agent then asked if they could use the photograph to show how the ceiling looked to their client prior to the purchase.

- In Georgia, an appraiser noted that the property he was appraising had a crawl space. He conducted his normal "head and shoulders" inspection and noted nothing out of the ordinary. He also took a photograph for his file. More than a year later, the appraiser received a demand letter from an attorney for the purchasers. Months after moving into the home, there was a heavy rainfall and a significant amount of water was found in the crawl space. The homeowners were advised that failing to correct the problem could jeopardize the stability of their home's foundation. In addition to exterior grading and drainage work, they were advised to install a sump pump. The homeowners' attorney claimed the water was in the crawl space for months, most likely at the time of the appraiser's inspection. Since the appraiser failed to bring this problem to anyone's attention, it was demanded that he agree to pay for all necessary repairs. The appraiser provided a photo of the clean, dry crawl space and explained that this was how the crawl space looked at the time of the appraisal. No lawsuit was ever filed–at least nothing that named the appraiser as a party.

Identifying Comparables

Selecting properties that are truly comparable to the subject property is essential to all three valuation approaches. (Chapter 16 provides a detailed description of the requirements a comparable must satisfy.) For a property to be considered comparable, it should include features similar to the subject property and be competitive with it. In other words, the comparable property should appeal to many of the same people who would consider purchasing the subject property. It should be located within the subject property's market area and ideally would have been sold recently.

Comparable properties provide data that can be applied in each of the three approaches to value. To gather data for the sales comparison approach, the appraiser identifies improved properties that have been sold recently and are comparable to (i.e., would serve as purchase alternatives for) the subject property. To apply the cost approach the appraiser needs data on unimproved property, or vacant sites, that have been sold recently and are comparable to the subject site. The analysis of comparable site sales will indicate site value, to which depreciated improvement costs are added to provide an indication of the value of the total property. The income capitalization approach usually requires data on comparable or competitive rental properties. These properties must be identified to determine market rents and sale prices and to derive gross rent multipliers. Market rent–the rent that the subject rental property should command in the open market–is multiplied by an appropriate gross rent multiplier to generate a value indication. Thus, the appraiser must identify comparable improved sales, vacant sites, and rental properties.

In addition, appraisers collect descriptive information on the characteristics of each comparable property, asking questions such as

- What are the size and shape of the lot?
- Does the property have a favorable or an unfavorable location in the neighborhood?
- What is the composition of the soil?
- Are there any special topographical features on the site?
- How old are the structures and of what type are they?
- Does the property have any special feature such as a remodeled basement, a desirable view, or atypical upgrades or finishes?
- Are there any problems with the property (such as structural defects, a dysfunctional floor plan, or dated decor)?

Appraisers rarely have the opportunity to inspect the interiors of comparable properties. Generally, appraisers will only be familiar with the interiors of comparables if they have already appraised them. Much of the appraiser's information must be obtained from parties to the transactions or from real estate agents and other appraisers who work in the same market area. It is wise to collect as much data as possible and then contact knowledgeable parties for further information or clarification.

Data Sources

The appraiser needs market experience, skill, and judgment to locate possible comparables. Sources of information on a particular type of property in a given area may be many or few. The appraiser is obligated to collect all the information required and make sure that the information ultimately used is reliable and indicative of the subject property and its market. Data can be verified by consulting and cross-checking several sources.

Multiple Listing Services

A multiple listing service (MLS) can be extremely useful to real estate appraisers. These services are usually sponsored by local boards of Realtors or individual brokers. Information on listings received by participating brokers and completed sales transactions is collected in the MLS and made available by subscription, often to members only. Current listing and sales information is often available by computer and can be accessed via the Internet. Subscribers to the MLS can enter the description of a property and specified parameters and receive a print-out of similar properties. (See Figure 6.3.) Listings and sales data may also be published in a book with an index of recently sold properties.

Property descriptions in the MLS may specify house size and type, the number and type of rooms, the year built, and the lot size. Information on zoning, taxes, the school district, and utilities may also be cited. While room size is often cited, gross living area, if reported, is typically not measured to a specific standard and is often taken directly from public record sources. The sale price of each property is indicated and sometimes the financing and seller concessions are specified. The broker's name is listed and often a photograph of the house is included. Much of this information is collected from property owners and agents, but the information is only as reliable as its source. Often property owners do not know the precise area of the plot in square feet or the exact date of construction. Nevertheless, an MLS can be extremely useful as an initial source of information.

Title Insurance Companies

Title insurance protects property owners from the possibility that their title will be contested. To do this, title insurance companies obtain copies of many public records relating to the real estate, including assessment records and a detailed history of past sales of the property. Title companies issue title reports, which summarize their findings. Many title companies will research sales in an area for an appraiser. Generally a fee is charged, but if the research is limited their services may be free. Title companies can be an extremely valuable source of information for identifying comparables.

Transfer Records

Most jurisdictions have a public office or depository for deeds where transactions are documented and made public. This process, known as *constructive notice*, ensures that interested individuals can research and, when necessary, contest deed transfers. Most county recorder's offices keep index books to deeds and mortgages so that the book and page on which the deed is recorded can be located. Some county offices, often in larger metropolitan areas, have developed searchable computer databases that allow for electronic access of public records.

Deeds contain important information on potentially comparable properties, including a legal description of the real estate and the date the deed was recorded. A deed also lists the names and addresses of people who can be contacted to verify the transaction. The names of the buyer, the seller, and the title company; mailing addresses for the buyer, the buyer's attorney, and the broker; a lender loan number; and the buyer's new tax billing address may all be found in a deed.

Figure 6.3 Sample Data Sheets from MLS

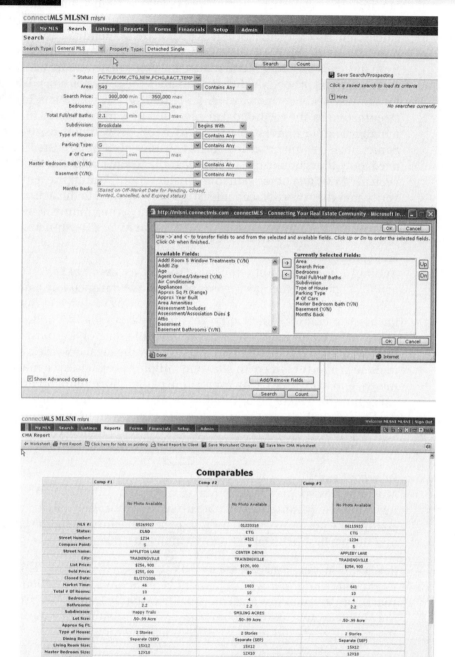

Courtesy of MLS of Northern Illinois, Inc. (www.mlsni.com)

Some deeds indicate the cash consideration–i.e., the actual price at which the property was transferred. Others have a stamp that indicates the transfer tax paid, from which the cash consideration can be calculated. However, these figures do not always reflect the actual sale price. Some purchasers deduct the estimated value of personal property from the true consideration to reduce the amount of transfer tax paid. If these personal property values are inflated, the recorded consideration for the real property may be less than the true consideration. In other circumstances, the recorded consideration may be overstated to obtain a higher loan or understated to justify a low property tax assessment. Some states require that the legal consideration be reported on the deed, but other "nondisclosure" states will accept a minimal recording such as "$1.00 and other valuable consideration." The appraiser should verify that the recorded consideration corresponds to the actual price paid for the property. If there is a discrepancy, the circumstances that account for the recorded consideration should be determined.

Tax Records
Another important public record is the tax assessment roll, which is usually kept with other tax records at the municipal or county assessor's office. All privately owned property in the county or district is listed on the assessment roll, which indicates the taxpayer's mailing address, the assessed value of the property, and often the date of the most recent transfer of ownership. Other records kept by the local tax assessor may include property cards with land and building sketches, area measurements, and sale prices. However, some of the information on property cards may be dated and unreliable. In many states, tax information is now computerized, and some assessors offices can provide online access to public property tax records. Tax assessment data can be useful for the preliminary identification of comparables.

Published News
Most city newspapers feature real estate news. Although some of this news may be incomplete or inaccurate, the appraiser may be able to confirm the details of transactions by contacting the negotiating brokers and the parties involved, who are usually listed.

Realtors, Appraisers, Managers, and Bankers
Real estate and financial professionals often have information about real estate transactions and can provide valuable leads. These sources may be definitive, but if the information obtained is third-party data, the appraiser should try to verify it independently.

Internet Sources
The growth of the Internet as a repository of information and a medium of commerce has made a wealth of information available to appraisers. Most national residential real estate brokerage firms have online listing services designed for homebuyers and sellers, and appraisers can

find useful information at these sites as well. The federal government has facilitated the dissemination of census and economic data via the Internet. Also, state and local governments have begun to make many public records available online, increasing accessibility to the data held by those governmental bodies. In some cases, this greater access to public record data helps lower the cost and amount of time spent by appraisers on the phone or visiting municipal records offices.

Internet search engines are useful tools for finding local sources for the information that appraisers need, and e-mail is useful for communicating with those sources. Figure 6.4 lists several Web sites that are useful starting points in the data collection process. Just like other forms of secondary data, information from the Internet needs to be cross-checked and verified with independent sources.

The Appraiser's Files

Whenever possible, appraisers should accumulate information on properties offered for sale. They can request that their names be added to the mailing lists of banks, brokers, and other individuals who sell property. Classified ads can provide information on asking prices, which may indicate the strength or weakness of the local market for a particular type of property and the trend of activity in the area. Offers to purchase are also useful and may be obtained from brokers or managers. Generally, listings are higher than eventual transaction prices and offers are somewhat lower.

Figure 6.4	Internet Resources for Residential Appraisers

Government Sites
www.bls.gov
www.census.gov
www.fedstats.gov
www.hud.gov
www.asc.gov
State licensing board Web sites
Municipality and county Web sites

Cost Service Information
www.marshallswift.com

Demographic and Economic Information
Federal, state, county, and municipal Web sites

Mortgage and Loan Information
www.allregs.com
www.bankrate.com
www.efanniemae.com

Residential Real Estate Industry Information
NETRonline.com
www.realtor.com

Professional Associations
www.ansi.org
www.appraisalfoundation.org
www.appraisalinstitute.org
www.appraisers.org
www.boma.org
www.ccim.com
www.irem.org
www.mbaa.org
www.nahb.com
www.nmhc.org
www.realtor.org
www.uli.org

For an updated list, see www.appraisalinstitute.org/publications/books/resources/residential/

Data Standards

In the mortgage industry, advances such as credit scoring and automated credit decision-making tools have accelerated mortgage transactions, and new developments such as electronic mortgages (eMortgages) are beginning to come to market. As in any e-commerce application, these innovations depend on the efficient, rapid, and error-free transmission of data between trading parties. Indeed, data standards can be seen as the lubricant for the engine of e-commerce.

Standards efforts fall into several categories. "Horizontal efforts" are generally designed to reduce complexity across a technology that touches on multiple areas, e.g., the work of the World Wide Web Consortium (W3C) in establishing and maintaining standards for the Web. "Vertical efforts," on the other hand, are focused on developing interoperability within the context of a single industry.

The operations of the mortgage industry are not limited to a small group of professionals working in narrowly defined roles. Instead, the mortgage industry operates in numerous areas that are represented by their own sets of stakeholders. This increases complexity and can present problems. For example, appraisers have different business processes and information systems than mortgage bankers. Yet, an appraiser's valuation determination must be integrated into the credit process. In a manual system, this is easily accomplished. The inherent inefficiency of manual processes, however, has led the mortgage industry to become very automated and the flow of data must be streamlined. Individual firms can create dedicated electronic interfaces with their trading partners but this solution is not scalable. As the number of interfaces grows, so too does complexity and cost. Data standards are one way to reduce the expense and burden of maintaining the infrastructure.

In the context of vertical standards efforts, data standards at their core represent an agreement between individual firms—often, competitors—to use a common format for data interchange. This agreement does not threaten any competitive advantage held by these firms. Rather, competitiveness is enhanced by reducing unnecessary complexity in an area common to all firms, allowing innovators to concentrate on their core competencies.

No Common Data Standard

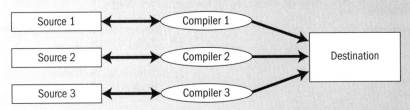

With Common XML Data Standard

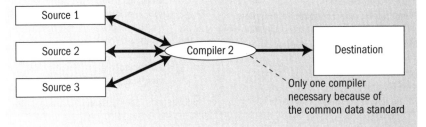

In 1994 a coalition of real estate organizations, including the Mortgage Bankers Association (MBA), Fannie Mae, Freddie Mac, and the Appraisal Institute, formulated standards for electronic data interchange (EDI), which has greatly influenced appraisal practice. In 1999, the MBA chartered MISMO, the Mortgage Industry Standards Maintenance Organization, to continue the data standardization effort by developing XML-based data standards for the mortgage industry. XML (eXtensible Markup Language) has become the universal language for data on the Internet and it is becoming the primary medium for business interchange because XML describes information in a way that can be understood by someone without any programming experience.

Federal agencies, including secondary mortgage market agencies such as Fannie Mae and Freddie Mac, have implemented electronic commerce and data standardization measures. For residential transactions, the REPI (Real Estate Property Information) Workgroup of MISMO is responsible for mapping the XML data definitions to the appraisal forms used by Fannie Mae and Freddie Mac. Although the data tags are mapped to the appraisal forms, the process is centered on the data stream, not the form. Users will have the ability to share real estate property data and appraisals from diverse resources.

Adobe's Portable Document Format (PDF) has already been widely adopted—as a de facto standard—throughout the mortgage banking system. PDF files are regularly used for many mortgage documents. The format's accuracy and fidelity—both for viewing and printing—make it a logical format of choice for both fully electronic and hybrid paper/electronic documents such as appraisal reports.

As real estate markets become more data rich, and as the data are increasingly standardized, the ability to predict future performance and accurately gauge present performance will be demanded by the clients that valuation professionals serve. Having this strong data foundation will permit appraisers to leverage modeling tools in GIS and business geography. In turn, this will transform the nature of real estate information and decision making. With data standardization, enabling tools can be used to enhance the speed and accuracy of real estate data transmission and permit the transformation of raw data into relevant knowledge.

References and Resources

www.adobe.com/standards

www.adobe.com/financial/mortgage_automation.html

www.mismo.org

www.opengeospatial.org

"AI, MISMO Unite to Develop Common Data Standards for Valuation, Mortgage Industries," *Valuation Insights & Perspectives* (Third Quarter 2005): 24–25.

Phil Britt, "MISMO and XML: Keeping Up with the Mortgage Industry," *Valuation Insights & Perspectives* (Second Quarter 2004): 18–20, 58.

John Cirincione, Daniel Szparaga, and Grant Ian Thrall, "XML-Based Data Standards Being Developed for the Mortgage Industry May Significantly Impact the GIS Community," *Geospatial Solutions* (June 2005): 37–40.

Donald R. Epley, "Data Management and Continual Verification for Accurate Appraisal Reports," *The Appraisal Journal* (Winter 2006): 62–76.

John W. Ross, "The Appraisal Institute's Continued Forays into Setting Technology Standards [Viewpoint]," *Valuation Insights & Perspectives* (Second Quarter 2004): 22–23.

W. Lee Minnerly, *Electronic Data Interchange (EDI) and the Appraisal Office.* (Chicago: Appraisal Institute, 1995).

Gilbert H. Castle III, ed. *GIS in Real Estate: Integrating, Analyzing, and Presenting Locational Information.* (Chicago: Appraisal Institute, 1998).

Data Verification

Sale prices, listing prices, options, offers, rejections, financing terms, seller concessions, and rental rates may be listed in multiple listing services. The transfer tax stamped on a deed may also indicate the sale price, but this information must be used with caution. Title companies also supply this type of data. In all cases, however, it is best to verify information with the parties involved in the transaction—i.e., the buyer, the seller, the sales agent or broker, attorneys for both parties, or the mortgage lender. Not only are these sources often more reliable, but these individuals can answer important questions about the conditions of the sale such as

- What were the specific financing terms?
- Did the seller participate in the financing? If so, how much financing did the seller provide and was the sale price influenced?
- Were any of the parties to the transaction under duress?
- Was any personal property included in the transaction?
- How long was the property on the market and did it receive enough exposure?
- Were the buyer and seller related or unusually motivated?
- Was the sale atypical for any other reasons?

The conditions of the sale can affect the property price and therefore its reliability as an indication of market value. In most cases, only an individual involved in the sale can supply this type of information. The names and addresses of the parties involved in a transaction can be found in title records, abstracts, and public records—particularly the property deed.

While questionable or unverifiable sales are typically excluded from further consideration, sometimes they are the only sales available. In these cases, the appraiser must fully disclose their use and any limitations on the reliability of the results.

The Uniform Standards of Professional Appraisal Practice require appraisers to collect, verify, and analyze all information necessary for credible assignment results. Verification is as integral to understanding a market as the data-gathering process itself. Advisory Opinion 22 highlights the importance of verification to the appraiser's understanding of the market, the subject property, competitive properties, and any conditions of sale affecting the sales data:

> An appraiser is expected to be at least as knowledgeable as the typical market participant is about the market for the type of property to be appraised. By completing research and verification steps while performing the assignment, the appraiser is expected to become as knowledgeable about the subject property and its comparables as the typical market participants.

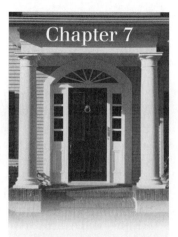

Chapter 7

Site Description

Appraisers describe and analyze the site of the subject property for a variety of reasons. First and foremost, the site description in the appraisal report clearly identifies the parcel to be appraised for the client. Information gathered in the site analysis is also used throughout the valuation process, for example:

- In the selection of comparable properties
- As the basis of the analysis of the highest and best use of the site as though vacant
- For the development of a separate opinion of site value, when required in the cost approach or by other assignment conditions

The site's market appeal, utility, and highest and best use will influence site value as well as the market value of the property as a whole. The analysis of those influences is the focus of the site description.

Descriptive data include site dimensions, area, zoning, location, topography, utilities, site improvements, present use, and highest and best use. In site analysis, appraisers consider the conformity of site size in relation to zoning and land use statutes as well as whether the location of site improvements is legal and conforms to existing zoning and building setback requirements. Zoning changes are often made after improvements are built, creating legal but nonconforming improvements. These distinctions are important for users of appraisal services and should be noted in the appraisal report and considered in highest and best use analysis.

In the selection of comparable properties, location should be the first consideration. Then, comparable properties should be identified as similar in size and other physical characteristics. In most cases the sites of comparable properties will have the same or a similar highest and best use as the site of the subject property. Transitional properties may pose special problems.

Site description and analysis provide much of the data needed to form a separate estimate of land or site value. This separate estimate is needed for the cost approach and provides the basis for any site adjustment required in the sales comparison approach. A separate land or site value estimate may also be required when the appraisal is being prepared for casualty loss estimates, local tax assessments, or eminent domain proceedings. (Site valuation techniques are described in detail in Chapter 12.)

Site analysis gives the appraiser an understanding of how the property is currently being used. The desirability of the property as a whole is affected by the general relationship between the building and the site and by the pattern of zones into which the improved site is divided. Typical land-to-building ratios indicate economic utility and should be considered in measuring property productivity. Maintenance and landscaping can also affect property value. Site analysis combined with the analysis of the improvements indicates how the property as a whole can be used most productively in its improved state and what effect its present condition has on the total property value.

Most importantly, site analysis provides the basis for determining the highest and best use of the site as though vacant. An appraiser who has studied the neighborhood and the local market will be able to judge how the physical and legal characteristics of the site interact with its surroundings to shape its maximum economic potential, i.e., highest and best use, which is the key to estimating the market value of the property.

If the tract being appraised is unimproved, vacant land, then detailed data on various characteristics may have to be collected as part of the site analysis. Often developers want highest and best use or feasibility studies performed before they prepare land for a particular use. These studies examine the quality of the soil and the cost of bringing utilities to the site, among other considerations. Appraisers may need to seek assistance from an engineer or other professional in these situations. When the property is already improved and the highest and best use is not for redevelopment of the site, the appraiser may assume that the soil is suitable and the site is physically usable, but these assumptions and their effects must be clearly stated in the appraisal report.

Legal, Tax, and Assessment Information

One reason to review legal information on the property is to identify the precise area to be valued in the appraisal. Often the appraisal assignment will be to value the fee simple interest in a detached, single-unit dwelling with access from a public street. The site is the area identified in the legal description of the real estate. The appraiser should verify that the legal description corresponds to the property being appraised. Sometimes other areas must be investigated as well. For example, if a right of way across an adjoining property runs with the title, this property should be examined to verify the ease of access.

The appraiser should review the deed or abstract of title to the property, which specifies the property rights conveyed and any limitations on these rights. The records of the county tax assessor or tax collector provide information on the property's assessed value, annual tax burden, and any special assessments.

Legal Descriptions of Real Estate

A legal description of real estate describes a parcel of land (which may be called a lot, plot, or tract) in such a way that it cannot be confused with any other parcel. Legal descriptions of real estate are based on precise surveys and are maintained as public records in accordance with local and state laws. They may be found in the deed filed in the public recorder's office or in the copy held by the owner. Because legal descriptions of real estate are the most accurate, they are the form of identification required in most appraisals.[1]

There are three principal systems for the legal description of land:

1. The metes and bounds system
2. The rectangular or government survey system
3. The lot and block system

Combinations of these systems are used throughout the United States.

Metes and Bounds System

The metes and bounds system is the oldest form of real estate identification currently in use, dating back centuries to when a buyer and seller would pace around the property, note boundary markers, and make property measurements. In the metes and bounds system, a point of beginning (POB) is established and related to a survey benchmark, and then the boundaries of the tract are described by proceeding from the POB for certain distances and along certain courses until the boundary line is "closed" by returning to the exact POB.

metes and bounds system. A system for the legal description of land that refers to the parcel's boundaries, which are formed by the point of beginning (POB) and all intermediate points (bounds) and the courses or angular direction of each point (metes).

rectangular (government) survey system. A land survey system used in Florida, Alabama, Mississippi, and all states north of the Ohio River or west of the Mississippi River except Texas; divides land into townships approximately six miles square, each normally containing 36 one-square-mile sections of 640 acres, except when adjusted for the curvature of the earth.

lot and block system. A system for the legal description of land that refers to parcels' lot and block numbers, which appear on recorded maps and plats of subdivided land; may also be used for assessment maps.

---

1. Note that it is possible for long-held legal descriptions to no longer "close" when satellite imagery and electronic measuring techniques are used.

While the metes and bounds system can be quite accurate, particularly for irregularly shaped parcels, the resulting description can be extremely long and cumbersome to employ, with increased chances of typographical errors. Most states still use this system today, often as a supplement to or in combination with other systems of legal description.

Figure 7.1 is an example of a metes and bounds description of a parcel of land.

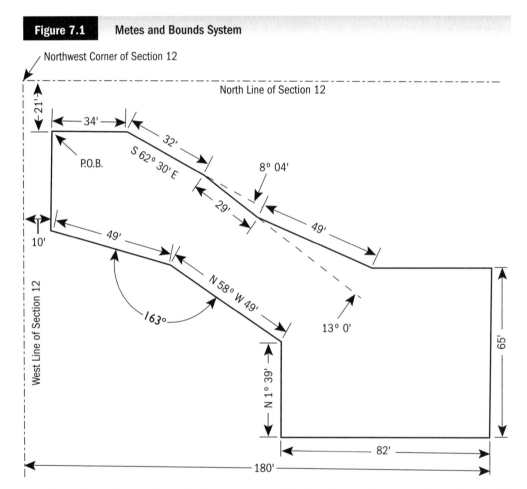

| Figure 7.1 | Metes and Bounds System |

Description of Tract: Commencing at the Northwest corner of Section 12 thence South along the section line 21 feet; thence East 10 feet for a place of beginning, thence continuing East 34 feet; thence South 62 degrees, 30 minutes East 32 feet; thence Southeasterly along a line forming an angle of 8 degrees, 04 minutes to the right with a prolongation of the last described course 29 feet; thence South 13 degrees, 0 minutes to the left with a prolongation of the last described line a distance of 49 feet; thence East to a parallel with the West line of said Section and 180 feet distant therefrom; thence South on the last described line a distance of 65 feet; thence due West a distance of 82 feet; thence North 1 degree West 39 feet; thence North 58 degrees West a distance of 49 feet; thence Northwesterly along a line forming an angle of 163 degrees as measured from right to left with the last described line a distance of 49 feet; thence North to the place of beginning.

Rectangular or Government Survey System

In 1785 the federal government passed a land ordinance establishing the rectangular survey system, also known as the government survey system, which would become the principal method of legal description used for most land west of the Ohio and Mississippi Rivers, as well as in Alabama, Florida, and Mississippi. The system was established to facilitate the rapid sale of land the government had acquired through purchases and treaties.

In the rectangular survey system, a tract of land is identified by the portion of a map grid to which it corresponds. East-west baselines and north-south meridians intersect at initial reference points established by the Commissioner of the U.S. General Land Office. Range lines and township lines are drawn parallel to meridians and baselines respectively at six-mile intervals, forming a grid of six-mile squares, which identify individual townships. These lines are adjusted for the curvature of the earth every 24 miles. Townships are further divided into 36 one-square-mile sections, with sections numbered in a back-and-forth, or serpentine manner, as shown in Figure 7.2. Sections, in turn, can be divided into increasingly smaller fractions. Figures 7.2 and 7.3 illustrate applications of the rectangular survey system.

Lot and Block System

The lot and block system identifies small parcels through subdivision maps submitted by real estate developers. Lot and block lines are recorded on a map with each lot and block labeled with a letter or number. When that map becomes public record, each lot in the development can be precisely identified by its lot and block number.

The short and easily understood lot and block descriptions are used for many routine transactions, and lot and block maps identified by subdivision name or number can be found by searching map records in the public recorder's office. A complete legal description states the lot number, block number, subdivision name or number, and either the location of the subdivision within the survey system or the volume and page number of the map record. Figure 7.4 is an example of a lot and block land description.

Some government authorities use a variation of the lot and block system to identify property for taxation purposes. Parcels are grouped together in blocks. Although a tax parcel cannot be used as a legal description for property conveyance in most jurisdictions, some appraisal report forms provide space for recording the tax parcel number of the subject property.

Property Rights Conveyed

Identification of the property rights to be appraised begins with specification of the legal estate to be valued–i.e., the fee simple interest or a partial interest. The Uniform Standards of Professional Appraisal Practice require that the real property rights appraised be clearly identified because of the value impact of separating one or more rights from the bundle of rights that make up fee simple ownership.

Figure 7.2   Government Survey System

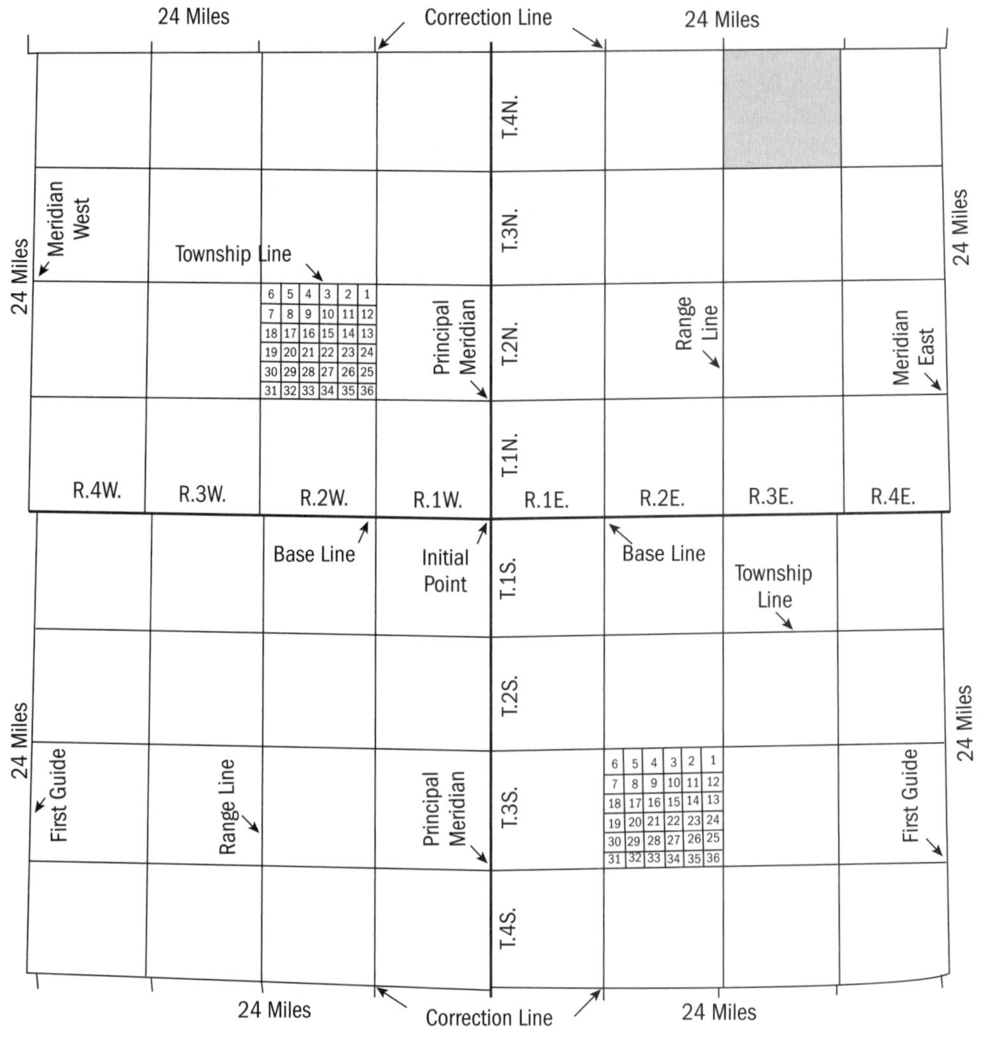

Description of the shaded township: Township 4 North. Range 3 East (T.4N., R.3E.). The township is four township rows north of the baseline and three range lines east of the principal meridian. (The township is located in northern California, so the baseline and principal meridian may be further identified as Mt. Diablo Base and Meridian.)

Source: John S. Hoag, *Fundamentals of Land Measurement* (Chicago: Chicago Title and Insurance Company, 1976), 8. Reprinted through the courtesy of Chicago Title Insurance Company.

Figure 7.3   Division of a Section of Land

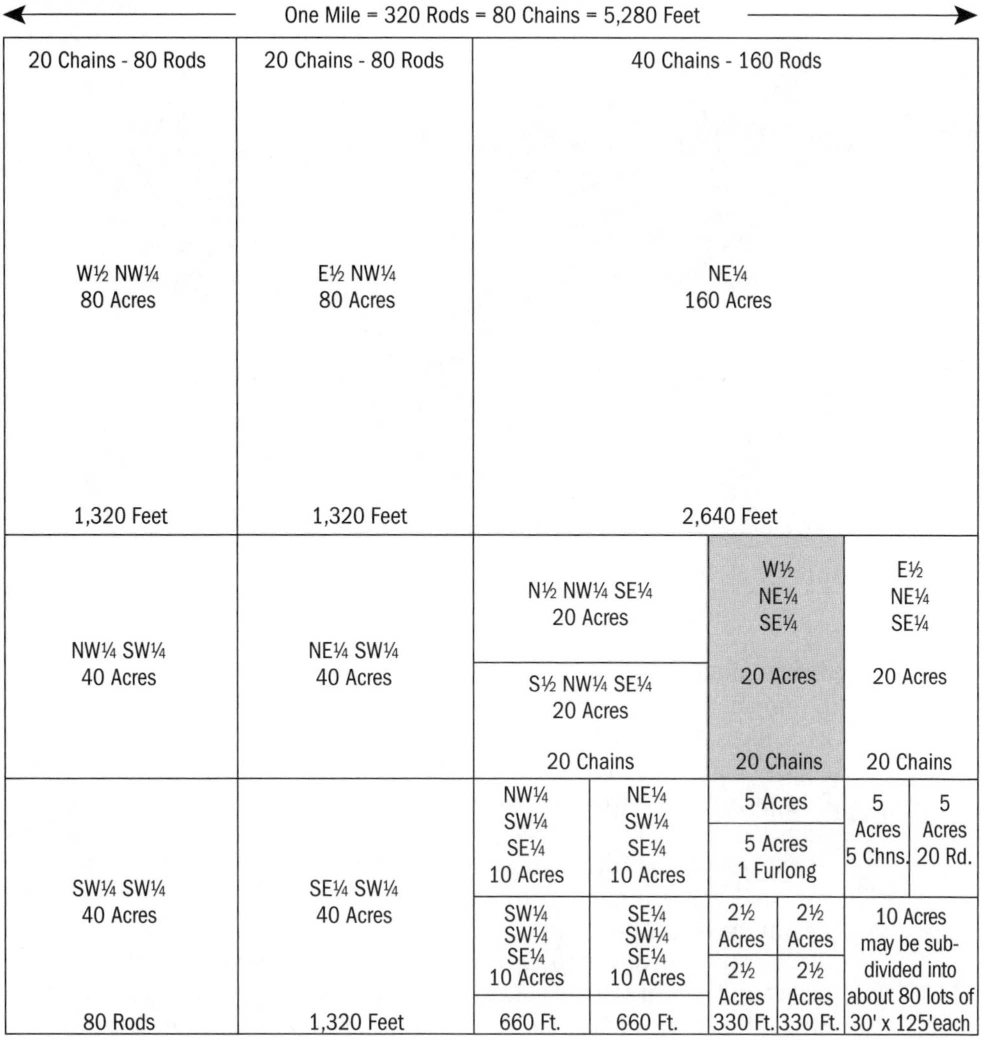

One Mile = 320 Rods = 80 Chains = 5,280 Feet

20 Chains - 80 Rods	20 Chains - 80 Rods	40 Chains - 160 Rods		
W½ NW¼ 80 Acres	E½ NW¼ 80 Acres	NE¼ 160 Acres		
1,320 Feet	1,320 Feet	2,640 Feet		

| NW¼ SW¼
40 Acres | NE¼ SW¼
40 Acres | N½ NW¼ SE¼
20 Acres

S½ NW¼ SE¼
20 Acres

20 Chains | W½
NE¼
SE¼

20 Acres

20 Chains | E½
NE¼
SE¼

20 Acres

20 Chains |

SW¼ SW¼ 40 Acres	SE¼ SW¼ 40 Acres	NW¼ SW¼ SE¼ 10 Acres	NE¼ SW¼ SE¼ 10 Acres	5 Acres 5 Acres 1 Furlong	5 Acres 5 Chns.	5 Acres 20 Rd.
		SW¼ SW¼ SE¼ 10 Acres	SE¼ SW¼ SE¼ 10 Acres	2½ Acres 2½ Acres	2½ Acres 2½ Acres	10 Acres may be sub- divided into about 80 lots of
80 Rods	1,320 Feet	660 Ft.	660 Ft.	330 Ft.	330 Ft.	30' x 125'each

Figure 7.4	Lot and Block System

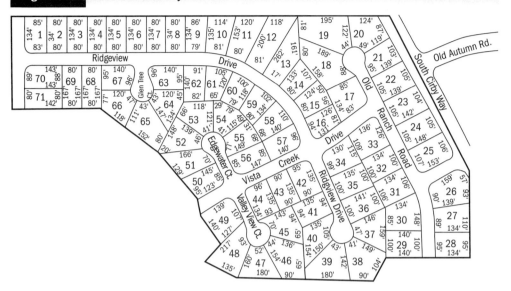

Woodridge Unit #1. Owner: Sunrise Properties, Sacramento, Calif.; engineer: Morton & Pitalo, Sacramento, Calif.

Public Limitations

Zoning ordinances and a variety of building, plumbing, fire, and electrical codes are among the many public limitations that restrict property rights. These restrictions are imposed under police power (one of the four powers of government), which gives the government the right to regulate land use and development for the public's benefit. Zoning laws may originate at the city or county level, but they are often subject to regional, state, and federal control.

Generally land is zoned to allow a specific type of use–e.g., residential, agricultural, commercial, industrial, or special-purpose. Along with the type of use, a maximum intensity of use may be indicated. Special zoning ordinances are imposed in zones subject to floods, earthquakes, and other natural disasters. Zoning laws may also restrict property development in environmentally sensitive areas and historic preservation districts.

Zoning ordinances and building, plumbing, and electrical codes may specify building height; front, side, and rear yard requirements; density of use; building setback; construction materials; and the architectural detailing of improvements. Housing codes establish what constitutes a legal dwelling, and these regulations may also influence room sizes; floor plans; heating, plumbing, sanitary, and electrical systems; and many other details. In short, zoning ordinances and other legal codes derived from the planning and zoning functions of police power can regulate almost any aspect of property use.

Zoning regulations frequently specify the action to be taken if a property does not conform to a particular ordinance. This information is significant in appraisals because a property that does not conform to legal requirements usually may not be replaced if it suffers major damage. Often a property owner wants to retain a nonconforming use when the existing property is worth more than the ideal improvement allowed by the zoning regulations, but many zoning codes allow a nonconforming use to continue only if the property suffers less than a certain percentage of damage. Thus if the nonconforming property sustains substantial damage, it may incur an additional value penalty in comparison with conforming properties. (Chapter 11 examines the subject of nonconforming use in more detail.)

Data Sources

Property rights are identified in property deeds and abstracts of title. A copy of a deed can be found in the public records office or obtained from the property owner. Information on the police power limitations applicable in an area can be requested from local zoning offices and county or municipal planning offices. Maps are used to show areas where specific requirements apply and books describe the corresponding laws in detail. Many appraisers acquire copies of the maps and regulations in effect in the areas where they work.

Zoning laws are not static. They can and do change in response to strong community and economic pressures. Consequently, an appraiser should be aware not only of the ordinances that are currently in effect but also of the possibility that these regulations will change. In transitional areas, market participants will take the probability of zoning changes into account and may consider alternative uses of a property beyond those that the existing zoning would suggest. However, an appraiser who relies on the likelihood of such a zoning change in a valuation must collect documentary evidence to support this belief, which can normally be obtained from local planning or zoning boards. Consideration of the probability of a zoning change may affect the scope of work of the appraisal analysis by requiring additional extraordinary assumptions or hypothetical conditions.

Private Agreements and Restrictions

Private agreements can also limit the rights to use property. In certain parts of the country–e.g., Houston, Texas, and much of Alaska–private deed restrictions are preferred to zoning laws as a means of regulating property use. In addition to private agreements, restrictions arising from eminent domain proceedings limit property use.

Easements and Rights of Way

Easements and rights of way are rights extended to nonowners of property usually for specific purposes. For example, easements or rights of way may be granted to neighbors. They may also be acquired by the government upon payment of just compensation. Through eminent domain proceedings, government agencies can acquire the right to install electrical transmission lines, underground sewers, and tunnels or to allow for flowage, aviation routes, roads, walkways, and open space. These restrictions generally run with the land and continue to encumber the property even if it is sold. An easement or right of way across a neighboring property that benefits the subject property constitutes an enhancement, not a limitation, on the property rights of the subject.

Other Deed Restrictions

Other restrictions on use may be described in property deeds. Developers frequently impose such restrictions as part of the initial sales agreement to protect the value of all the properties in the development. For example, a sales agreement may include a clause that prohibits the outside storage of boats or recreational vehicles on a site. In general, conditions, covenants, and restrictions (commonly known as *CC&Rs*) are written into deeds or leases to specify permissible uses in a neighborhood and thereby stabilize property values. Property characteristics that can be controlled through CC&Rs include

- Lot size
- Setback
- Placement of buildings
- Number and size of improvements
- Architecture
- Cost of improvements

Party Wall Agreements

A party wall agreement may be needed when improvements are erected so that a common wall is used by owners of abutting properties. Party wall agreements are not necessarily recorded in writing.

Riparian and Littoral Rights

Riparian and littoral rights are concerned with the use of water or a shore by an owner whose land borders a stream, river, lake, ocean, or other body of water. Riparian rights may include the right to construct piers, boathouses, and other improvements over the water or to use the water for fishing and recreational purposes. Littoral rights pertain to the use and enjoyment of the shoreline, and they safeguard the owner against artificial interference that might change the position of the shoreline.

Data Sources

Title reports and abstracts of title may contain some information about restrictions on property rights, but they do not always go into detail. A copy of the property deed or other conveyance should be obtained from the county recorder so that all limitations imposed on the property can be thoroughly identified.

Tax Status

Like public and private restrictions, taxes constitute a legal limitation on property rights. The burden of taxation can also influence the highest and best use of property and its market value. In certain school districts, for example, taxes may be disproportionately high. High taxes may discourage buyers who have no school-age children from purchasing a home there. Because taxes can affect property values, comparing the tax burdens of the subject property and each proposed comparable property can reveal important clues about their differences. If taxes are found to influence the values of comparable properties differently, the appraiser can allow for the difference in the adjustment process.

The tax burden of a property is calculated from three variables:

1. The *assessed value* of the property
2. The *tax rate* applied in the particular jurisdiction
3. Local (e.g., township or county) and state *multipliers*

The property's assessed value may be of interest to mortgage lenders.

A property's assessed value, or assessment, is the value of the property according to the tax rolls. Taxes are assessed in relation to this value, hence the term *ad valorem* (according to value) *taxation.* Tax rolls often show the assessed value of the property as a whole as well as an allocation of value between the land and the improvements. In some areas different tax rates are applied to the assessed values of these two property components.

Assessed value usually bears some relation to market value, but the assessed value of a property often differs from its market value for several reasons. First, assessed value may be based on a percentage of market value—e.g., 80% rather than 100% of market value. This percentage is called an *assessment ratio.* Second, properties are assessed in many communities at infrequent intervals. Consequently, unless a property has been revalued recently, its assessed value may not reflect a realistic relationship to market value. Likewise, areas with caps on property tax increases may have extreme variances because the assessed value is recalculated on the sale of a property. Third, assessors rarely have access to precise data regarding the subject or comparable properties. Appraisers do sometimes use assessment data such as land-to-improvement value ratios to derive market value conclusions, but only when there is little other evidence available and then only with extreme caution.

The tax rate is the ratio between the taxes levied and the assessed value. Tax rates may be expressed in dollars owed per $1,000 of value, which is called the *mill rate* (one mill = 0.001), or in dollars owed per $100 of value (1% = 0.01). Thus the tax burden of a property can be calculated by multiplying the tax rate by the property's assessed value. Consider the following examples:

Assessed value	$50,000	Assessed value	$100,000
Mill rate	25 (0.025 × $50,000)	Tax rate	4.0% (0.04 × $100,000)
Taxes	$1,250	Taxes	$4,000

This system is sometimes confusing and makes it difficult to compare the taxes in one community with the taxes in another. Very different assessment ratios and mill rates can produce the same tax burden, depending on their combined influence. Appraisers must recognize this to compare the tax status of different properties correctly.

Special Assessments

Special assessments may be levied by a district taxing authority for a finite period of time to pay for public improvements such as sewers, street paving, and sidewalks. Usually the tax assessment is based on the benefits that the property will derive from the improvement, not the cost of providing the improvement to a specific property. Thus if two lots are assumed to derive a similar value enhancement from the installation of a sewer line, they will probably be subject to the same special assessment even if the installation costs for one property are higher than the costs for the other. Special assessments cannot be deducted from the property owners' income tax.

Special service areas are contiguous areas within counties or municipalities that are provided with special public improvements. These improvements are paid for by levying a tax on all properties within the area for a designated period. Generally, this special tax levy is added to regular property taxes for a specified period of time and can be deducted from the property owners' income tax. Appraisers must identify special service areas and analyze how special tax levies affect property values. If the tax bill on a particular property seems abnormally high compared with the taxes on competitive properties, the appraiser should investigate the cause.

Data Sources

An appraiser may consider future zoning laws, but future trends in property taxes must be investigated along with current assessments. A short history of tax assessments and tax rates can help an appraiser form a conclusion about the probable trend in property taxation. Discussions with tax officials can give the appraiser a sense of the probability of revaluation, the likely direction of future assessments, and the possible imposition of a cap or limit on real estate taxation.

Physical Characteristics

An appraiser observes the physical characteristics of the site to describe its principal features and any additional advantages or disadvantages the market is likely to consider. The appraiser then forms an opinion of how the site can best be used, given its legal and physical limitations and its relationship to its surroundings. Assuming the site is put to its highest and best use, the appraiser considers how the physical characteristics of the site and the present condition of the existing site improvements add to or detract from property value. Value influences are examined in light of neighborhood and local market preferences.

Many physical characteristics of a site are considered in the site description, including

- Size and shape
- Topography, soil, and drainage
- Location, access, and environmental influences
- On-site and off-site utilities

Size and Shape

To describe the size and shape of a site, an appraiser notes the site dimensions, including frontage, width, and depth. The appraiser plots the site's shape to calculate its area. Dimensions are usually expressed in feet and tenths of feet for easy calculation. Area is usually expressed in square feet or sometimes in acres. The appraiser also considers whether assemblage, the combination of two or more sites, is desirable and whether excess or surplus land is present.

Dimensions

The site's width is the distance between the side lines of the lot. When the shape of a lot is irregular, the average width is often used. Many communities prescribe a minimum width for detached, one-unit residential lots. Another important measurement is the width at the building line. Many zoning regulations specify a minimum width at this line so the site can be used to construct a particular type of improvement.

Frontage refers to the length of a site where it abuts a thoroughfare or accessway. Minimum frontage is often specified by zoning requirements. In the valuation of residential lots, front footage is sometimes used as a unit of comparison, most often in the case of waterfront properties, but the importance of frontage varies from one location to another. Consequently, care must be exercised in using this unit of comparison for residential lots. Frontage in excess of the standard amount considered acceptable in the neighborhood may not add proportionate value to the value of the lot.

Most residential neighborhoods have a standard lot depth. Lots that have less depth generally sell for less and lots with excess depth for more, but the premium or penalty is rarely proportionate to the dimensions involved. In many communities, a zoning ordinance specifies the minimum depth for detached,

average width. Average measure of distance between the side lines of a lot; used when the shape of a lot is irregular.

width at the building line. Distance between the side lines of a plot measured at the building line, i.e., the line established by ordinance or statute that delimits an area up to the street line wherein no structure is permitted.

front footage. The distance between the side lines of a plot measured along the property line that abuts a road, waterway, railroad, or other facility.

one-unit residential lots. The minimum depth for attached, one-unit residential lots varies, but these lots usually need not be as deep as detached, one-unit residential lots. Residential building sites are often sold on a per-building-lot basis, if there is minimal variance in shape and size, with the market making no distinction for variances in size and shape.

The size and shape of a site affect the uses to which it can be put and therefore its value. For instance, an odd-shaped parcel may be appropriate for a dwelling but inappropriate for commercial or industrial use. Zoning, neighborhood standards, and community development goals all have an impact on how sites of various sizes and shapes may be used. Given a particular use, the appraiser can determine how the size and shape of a site affect its value by analyzing sales data on parcels of various sizes and shapes. If the subject property has a characteristic that is unusual for the neighborhood, this should be noted and discussed.

An appraiser considers not only the overall dimensions of the site, but also how different parts of the site can be developed. A regularly shaped parcel may have a swamp, stream, or cliff within its borders that limits its utility. All such features should be described and their effects on value carefully considered.

Size

The size or area of a parcel is determined by its linear dimensions and by its shape. An appraiser can consider both of these variables by drawing a scale figure of the site, dividing the drawing into standard geometric figures, and calculating the area of each figure.

Specialized computers and software programs are also available for computing the areas of both the site and the improvements. A geographic information system (GIS) can automate the process of computing areas. Although computer assistance is available, appraisers should still be familiar with the geometric formulas for calculating areas, which are used to compute site size and to measure improvement characteristics. Some basic formulas are described and illustrated in Figure 7.5.

Plottage, Excess Land, and Surplus Land

In analyzing how site size affects site value, the appraiser must also consider plottage, excess land, and surplus land. Plottage is an increment of value that results when two or more sites can be assembled or combined to produce greater utility and value. A parcel has plottage value when its highest and best use is realized by combining it with one or more other parcels under a single ownership or control. If the parcels have a greater unit value together than they did separately, plottage value results. Analysis of neighboring land uses and values will indicate whether the property being appraised has plottage value.

plottage. The increment of value created when two or more sites are combined to produce greater utility.

Figure 7.5 **Basic Formulas for Calculating Area**

A **square** is a four-sided figure with sides of equal length that meet at right angles—i.e., angles of 90 degrees. The area of a square is the length of one side squared.

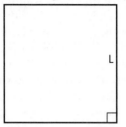

Area = Length × Length $A = L \times L$

The **rectangle** is a four-sided figure with sides that meet to form right angles. Parallel sides of a rectangle are of equal length. The area of a rectangle is its length times its width.

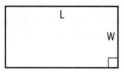

Area = Length × Width $A = L \times W$

A **triangle** is a three-sided figure. The height of a triangle is measured by drawing a line from one of its corners to the side facing it, called the base, to intersect the base at a right angle. The area of a triangle is its height times its base divided by two.

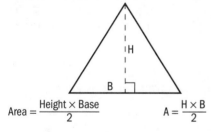

$$\text{Area} = \frac{\text{Height} \times \text{Base}}{2} \qquad A = \frac{H \times B}{2}$$

A **trapezoid** is a four-sided figure with two parallel sides and two sides that are not parallel. The angles that join the sides in a trapezoid are not usually right angles. The area of a trapezoid is the sum of the lengths of its parallel sides, multiplied by the height, and divided by two.

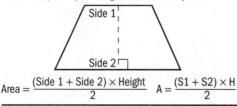

$$\text{Area} = \frac{(\text{Side 1} + \text{Side 2}) \times \text{Height}}{2} \qquad A = \frac{(S1 + S2) \times H}{2}$$

A **circle** is a curving figure in which all points along the curve are of an equal distance from one central point. This distance is called the circle's radius. A diameter is a line that passes through the center of the circle and divides it in half; it is always twice as long as the radius. The area of a circle is 3.1416 (π) times the radius squared.

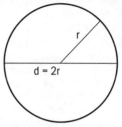

Area = 3.1416 (π) × Radius²

A **slice of a circle** is a pie-shaped area bounded by two radius lines and an arc of the circle. As the angle between the radius lines grows larger, a broader arc and larger area of the circle are sliced out. A circle has 360 degrees, so to calculate the area of a slice, divide the angle by 360 and multiply by the area of the circle.

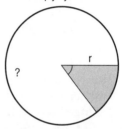

$$\text{Area} = \frac{\text{Angle subtended}}{360°} \times \text{Area of the circle}$$

To measure the area of a **fragment of a circle,** compute the larger area of the slice that corresponds to its arc and then subtract the excess triangular area. The area of the slice is calculated as described above. The area of the triangle can be found by measuring the base and height and applying the standard triangle formula, i.e., base × height/2.

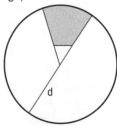

Area = Area of corresponding slice – Area of triangular shape

excess land. In regard to an improved site, the land not needed to serve or support the existing improvement. In regard to a vacant site or a site considered as though vacant, the land not needed to accommodate the site's primary highest and best use. Such land may be separated from the larger site and have its own highest and best use, or it may allow for future expansion of the existing or anticipated improvement.

surplus land. Land not necessary to support the highest and best use of the existing improvement but, because of physical limitations, building placement, or neighborhood norms, cannot be sold off separately. Such land may or may not contribute positively to value and may or may not accommodate future expansion of an existing or anticipated improvement.

Excess land, defined earlier as an unused portion of a site that can have a different highest and best use than the existing improvements, differs from plottage in that excess land need not be combined with another parcel to add value. In any given market, the land and improvements that form an economic unit reflect a typical ratio. If an improved property has excess land, this land may not add a proportionate amount of value to the value of the property. Depending on its size, configuration, access, and location, the excess land may be considered separately from the land that supports the improvements. If the excess land is independently marketable or has value for a future use, its market value as vacant land constitutes an addition to the estimated value of the property.

Like excess land, surplus land is not necessary for the use of the existing improvements, but surplus land does not have a different highest and best use nor can it be separated from the rest of the land. A house on a double lot situated so that the improvements are appropriately placed within the boundaries of one lot would probably have excess land. (See Figure 7.6.) On the other hand, if the improvements straddled the two lots or the lots did not meet the minimum site size dictated by zoning requirements, the additional land would most likely be considered surplus land, which gives the owner fewer use options than excess land, and thus usually has less contributory value to the property as a whole. (Analyzing the highest and best use of excess land and surplus land is discussed further in Chapter 12.)

Topography, Drainage, and Soil
To evaluate the topography of a site, an appraiser examines

- Land contours
- Grades
- Natural drainage
- Drainage systems
- Soil conditions
- General physical utility

Land Contours
All variations in elevation should be described. Sites with extreme topographical conditions tend to have lower values because of increased building costs. Steep slopes are more susceptible to landslides and may increase construction costs or preclude construction altogether. In some

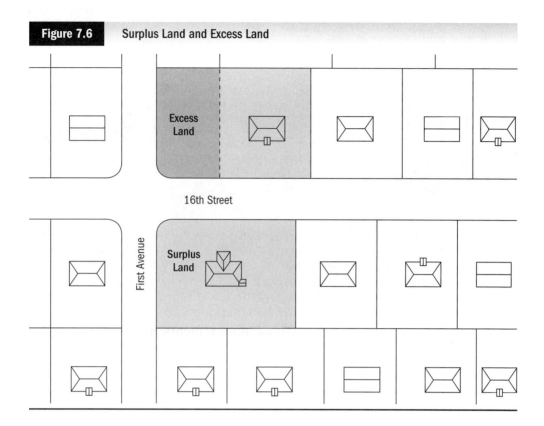

Figure 7.6   Surplus Land and Excess Land

16th Street

First Avenue

Excess Land

Surplus Land

cases, however, the disadvantages of a high elevation may be offset by an excellent view.

An ideal residential lot has a slope that rises slightly from the street to the improvement and then gently falls off. What is desirable in one neighborhood, however, is not necessarily desirable in another. A lot that is higher or lower than the level of the abutting street may create additional costs for owners due to poor drainage, erosion, or diminished accessibility. If the site is unimproved, these features can limit the usefulness of the site for development.

topography. The relief features or surface configurations of an area, e.g., hills, valleys, slopes, lakes, rivers. Surface gradations are classified as compound slope, gently sloping land, hilly land, hogwallows, hummocks, rolling land, steep land, undulating land, and very steep land.

drainage. A system of drains (e.g., tiles, pipes, conduits) designed to remove surface or subsurface water or waste water and sewage.

Drainage

Drainage depends on natural topography and the ability of the soil to absorb water. Natural drainage may be a problem if the site is downstream from properties that have a right to direct excess flows onto it. Some system must be provided to drain the site of surface water and groundwater. Storm sewers should be present in the water disposal area. In some cases, a simple swale may efficiently channel the water from the surface of the lot to the street or into natural drainage, or a system of tiles can be used to remove surface and subsurface water from some sites. When the site is located in a designated flood hazard area, the appraiser must consider whether any of the topographical features of the site increase or decrease its susceptibility to flooding in comparison with other neighborhood properties.

The appraiser should be particularly concerned with how the site's drainage characteristics may affect the improvements. A house with a basement must have drains to carry the water out from under the basement and prevent leaks from developing. If a house is built on a slope, special precautions must be taken to keep the runoff water away from the sides of the house.

Soil Conditions

The character of the subsoil can have a substantial effect on the usefulness of a site and the cost of preparing it for building. Subsoil quality can also affect where improvements can be constructed on the site and influence building design. If bedrock must be blasted or the soil is unstable, the cost of improving the site will increase. Similarly, extra expenses may be incurred for building foundation walls or sinking piles if a site must be filled in. Percolation, permeability, and the absorption capacity of the soil must be considered to assess the site's suitability for septic and storm water systems.

In many areas the fertility of the surface soil of a site can affect the lawn and landscaping surrounding the property, which are important to the site's marketability. The appraiser notes whether the soil appears to be suitable for cultivation and typical of the surrounding neighborhood. When appraising a new subdivision, an appraiser determines whether or not the natural surface soil, the topsoil, will need to be replaced after construction with better soil. If the topsoil is naturally sandy or rocky, it may need to be replaced.

Frequently subsoil conditions are known to local builders and developers. An appraiser may ask that an engineer trained in soil mechanics be retained to test the qualities of the soil for construction, but an expensive soil study is not necessarily needed as part of the appraisal. If the soil-bearing capacity is in doubt, however, the appraiser should inform the client of the need for a soil study. If soil tests are not made, the appraiser must describe the assumptions made concerning soil characteristics in the limiting conditions and assumptions section of the report.

Location, Access, and Environmental Influences

The study of location includes analysis of

- Linkages, i.e., the time-distance relationship between the site and supporting facilities
- The type and orientation of the lot within the existing street pattern
- Access to the site
- Street improvements

- Environmental nuisances and hazards
- Climate and view

For residential property, locational characteristics are often the largest contributors to value, so the comparability of properties may be significantly affected by differences in view, proximity to environmental nuisances and hazards, and other features.

Transportation

The highest and best use of the site and therefore its value are strongly affected by the site's location in relation to transportation routes. Lots that are far away from major transportation routes or accessible only from narrow streets may be less appealing. Lots with easy access to schools, workplaces, and recreational facilities often have greater appeal to residential users. Both vehicular and pedestrian access should be considered.

The quality of highways and the density of traffic during rush hours are also important considerations in the study of transportation. The availability, proximity, and quality of public transportation systems are also significant, particularly if many neighborhood residents commute. An appraiser is especially interested in any aspects of the

Drawing a Plot Plan

If the location of the improvements on the site is critical, a plot plan may be drawn that shows the boundaries of the lot and the location of improvements. The plot plan can also be created using appropriate computer software and inputting the proper measurements. In addition to the house and the garage or carport, the plot plan may show sidewalks, driveways, patios, and pools. Any relevant rights of way, easements, or encroachments may also be indicated on the plan.

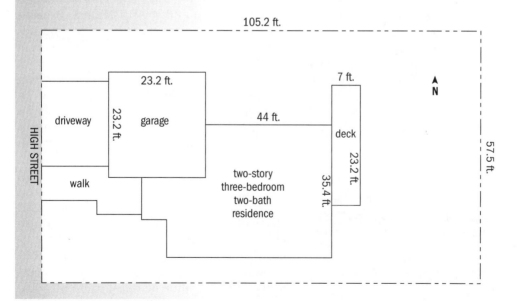

site that make it different from other neighborhood sites and from comparable properties.

Lot Type and Orientation

Some common types of lots are

- Interior
- Corner
- Cul-de-sac
- Flag

Interior lots have frontage on only one street. The main access to the lot is usually from that street, although a rear alley may also provide access. Interior lots are often the most regular in shape, particularly if the neighborhood is designed in a grid format. The appraiser should note the distance and direction to the nearest intersection(s) from interior and cul-de-sac lots.

If the highest and best use of the site is for residential use, a corner location may have both advantages and disadvantages. A corner site can have an automobile entrance on the side street, thus reducing driveway areas. This can be especially advantageous in areas where interior lots have little frontage. Corner lots may also allow greater flexibility in the building layout and provide more light and air than interior lots. However, corner lots may also have disadvantages such as less privacy, less security, and greater susceptibility to traffic hazards and nuisances. Corner lots may have two building setback lines, one from each street, which reduces the area on which improvements can be built. For this reason, corner lots are generally larger than interior lots. Corner sites may also be subject to higher special assessments because they have more sidewalk area and street frontage. Because corner sites have both advantages and disadvantages in the market, an appraiser must assess the impact of such a location, called corner influence, by studying market data.

Cul-de-sac lots are located at the end of dead-end streets where circular turn-around areas are common. These lots are generally tapered, have very little frontage, and are somewhat irregular in shape. Parking may be more difficult on cul-de-sac lots, but there can be compensatory advantages. Cul-de-sac lots may have bigger backyards and less street traffic, so they may be particularly desirable to families with children.

corner influence. The effect on value produced by a property's location at or near the intersection of two streets; the increment of value or loss in value resulting from this location or proximity.

A flag lot is a rear lot with a long narrow access. The lot and access route resemble the shape of a flag on a pole. Flag lots have greater privacy, but a residence built on such a lot may be difficult to find and have poor access. Views of surrounding rear yards on adjacent properties may often be inferior.

Figure 7.7   Types of Lots

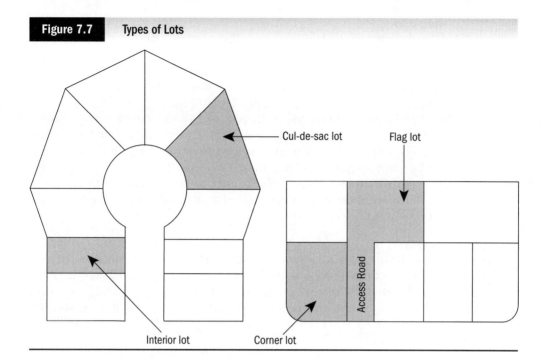

Cul-de-sac lot   Flag lot

Access Road

Interior lot   Corner lot

Access to the Site

Access to the site is closely related to lot type. Access may be provided by a public street or alley, a private road or driveway, or a right of way across an abutting property. When access depends on a private road, the appraiser should find out who maintains the road and whether the lending institutions serving the neighborhood write mortgages for houses without a public street address.

The ease of entry to the lot by car is also noted. The grade of the driveway should provide reasonably convenient access. Lots with driveways that slope up to the street are often less desirable than lots with driveways that are level or slope down. It is dangerous to back into traffic or enter traffic when oncoming cars cannot be seen well. The market often penalizes a site for access problems.

Street Improvements

The quality and condition of abutting streets and street improvements also affect the value of a site. A description of street improvements includes information on the width of the street or alley, the type of paving, and the condition. The direction of traffic and the number of lanes are also important, as are the quality and condition of gutters and storm sewers, curbs, streetlights, sidewalks, trees and plantings, and bicycle lanes. In some areas lenders may require additional information if the property frontage is on a private road.

Nuisances

Convenient service facilities contribute to the value of a site, but they can detract from site value if they are too close. Hospitals, firehouses, gas stations, public schools, stores, restaurants, and medical offices are desirable if they are nearby but not immediately adjacent to the property. The presence of industrial plants, large commercial or office buildings, noisy highways, utility poles and high-tension wires, motels and hotels, and vacant houses in a residential neighborhood generally has a negative effect on nearby property values. Uses that do not mix well or do not conform to neighborhood standards and properties that are poorly maintained or produce odors, noises, and pests can decrease the value of residential properties and may suggest an alternative highest and best use for the site.

Hazards

Heavy traffic is the most common hazard in residential neighborhoods. The market often recognizes this problem, and properties located on heavily traveled streets are penalized for their proximity to noise, fumes, congestion, and accidents. Within the same neighborhood, lots bordering streets with different volumes of traffic can have substantially different values. Families with small children are particularly concerned about traffic hazards. Speed controls, speed bumps, and well-maintained sidewalks to schools and play areas can reduce traffic hazards. Conversely, speed bumps and similar controls may hurt property values in areas with predominantly older residents, where easy access for emergency vehicles is a concern.

The potential for floods, landslides, and earthquakes must be considered as well as the hazards presented by ravines, bodies of water, fault lines, unstable soils, subsurface mines, gasoline storage tanks, toxic wastes, and railroads. If possible hazards are observed in the neighborhood, the appraiser should investigate what measures have been taken to protect the subject property from danger.

In some areas, radon gas percolates up through the soil and infiltrates homes. Current construction techniques can exacerbate a potential radon problem. Cracks in concrete slabs can allow radon gas to enter a basement or home, and "tight" buildings cause it to be trapped inside. To prevent this problem, construction and repair techniques have been developed that promote air exchange and allow the radon gas to disperse.

Flood hazards are especially important in appraisals because in many parts of the country lenders cannot issue a mortgage in a flood hazard area unless the mortgagor purchases flood insurance. If an appraiser learns that the site being appraised is in an identified flood hazard area, the appraiser should investigate the availability and cost of flood insurance. The potential for flooding of the subject property and comparable sites must be discussed in the appraisal report.

Local government offices often maintain flood maps and officials may know whether or not a site is in a flood zone. It is wise to obtain copies of local flood maps for regular office use. (Figure 7.8 is an example of a county flood map.) These maps identify different kinds of flood zones such as areas of 100-year flooding or areas of 100- to 500-year shallow flooding. Maps may be available electronically from a local government office and are also available from the Federal Emergency Management

Figure 7.8 Flood Map

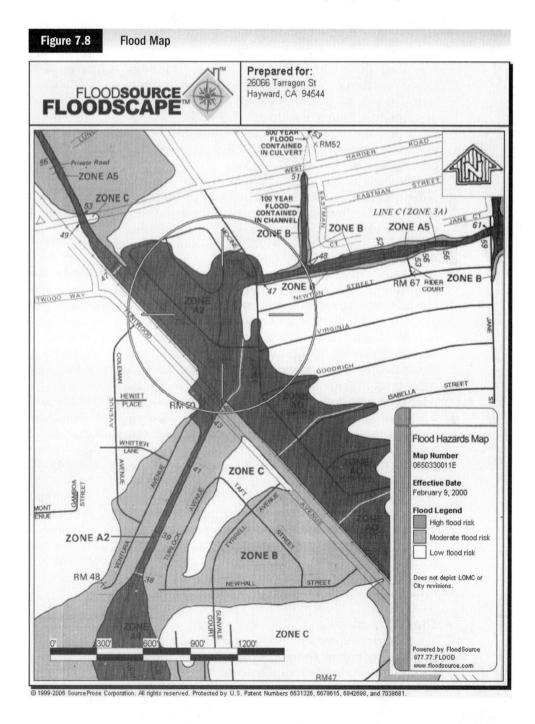

Agency (FEMA). Most clients require that the appraiser cite the FEMA panel number in the appraisal report. The presence of velocity zones, which denote wave action, may also be noteworthy, especially in areas prone to hurricanes and other storm surges.

Climate

Most climatic conditions affect the subject property and comparable properties in the same way, so general climatic conditions are usually described along with community and neighborhood characteristics. However, a particular site may benefit or suffer from a special climatic characteristic such as high winds. If so, this must be noted in the site description. Climatic conditions may suggest the best orientation for building improvements. If the position of the site relative to the street precludes a building orientation that suits climatic conditions, a value penalty may result.

The significance of climate and its effect on property value may differ depending on the highest and best use of the site. The appraiser must consider how climatic considerations and other environmental influences affect the highest and best use of the site.

View

The view from a property can substantially affect its value. Lots in the same neighborhood that are similar in all respects except their locations and orientation often have different values attributable to the difference in view. Views of water, golf courses, mountains, or valleys are most popular. A commanding view of the surrounding landscape can sometimes compensate for adverse topographic or climatic characteristics. For example, coastal properties in Florida are in flood zones but often carry a value premium over properties further inland. Conversely, a poor view can produce a value penalty. An appraiser should also consider the likelihood of the property's view being obstructed in the near future. The allowable or proposed uses of a large vacant tract abutting a residential development may not have an immediately apparent influence on the view and therefore the value of homes in the subdivision. If the proposed uses are not investigated, however, the residents of the existing homes may find themselves looking at a shopping center or an apartment building in a few years, which would likely be considered a value penalty. In an urban environment, the view of a skyline or the sunlight provided by a southern exposure may be a prime selling point for units in a high-rise condominium, but the development of a taller building across the street may eliminate the view and plunge the existing units into shadow.

Site Improvements

The description and analysis of the site include an inspection of all site improvements. Generally, improvements included in site value (commonly called *improvements to the site*) are treated in the site description, while all others (known as *improvements on the site*) are described with the building improvements. Appraisers should follow the practices common in the market area to avoid misleading the client or other readers of the appraisal report. The final opinion of value of the property as a whole should not be affected by how various improvements are classified in the analysis. In calculating depreciation for income tax purposes, however, improvements that are part of the site are usually not considered depreciable. Various examples of improvements to and on a site are listed in Figure 7.9.

Figure 7.9	Site Improvements		
Improvements to the Site	**Improvements on the Site**		
· Clearing	· Sidewalks	· Courtyards
· Grading	· Landscaping	· Swimming pools
· Drainage	· Septic systems	· Fences
· Public and private utility installation	· Wells	· Walls
· Site access routes	· Driveways	· Lights
· Curbs	· Parking areas	· Poles

On-Site and Off-Site Utilities

An appraiser notes the utilities present on the site and those that are available nearby. Essential utilities in many residential markets include

- Water
- Electricity
- Natural or propane gas
- Telephone and data lines for Internet connections
- Sewerage
- Trash collection
- Cable television

If the utilities on the site are inadequate, the availability and cost of obtaining utility service must be considered. Both highest and best use and site value may be strongly affected by the availability of utilities. Likewise, competitive properties may not be usable as comparables if adjustments for difference in public and private utilities cannot be supported by market evidence.

Water

A residential site must have an adequate supply of acceptable water. Water may be obtained from a municipal or private company or from a well. The FHA Minimum Property Standards require that a public water supply should be used if one is available. Some residents obtain water directly from rivers, streams, or lakes or from rainwater collected and stored in tanks on the roof. These houses are not considered satisfactory by FHA standards because they do not have a consistent, adequate supply of safe water.

When water is supplied by a public or publicly regulated company, the appraiser usually checks its availability on the site and determines if the water pressure is sufficient. When water is supplied by an unregulated company, the appraiser must report this fact and investigate the dependability of the water supply. Shallow or artesian wells should be capable of sustaining a flow of five gallons per minute. The water should meet the bacterial and chemical purification requirements set by local health authorities.

When appraising vacant land that is not linked to a public water supply, an appraiser may try to determine the likelihood of finding an adequate water supply for the site by checking the wells dug on surrounding properties. In rural areas, it is often customary for property owners to share water wells.

Sewage Disposal

Connection to a municipal sewage system is usually desirable, but many areas have no sewer system. If no public sewers exist, a percolation test may be required to determine whether the soil on the site can absorb the runoff from a septic system, or if some other private sewage disposal system such as a lagoon is required. If a percolation test is not made, this fact should be reported in the appraisal report.

Garbage Collection

Some sites do not have garbage collection service because they are located on private roads or in rural areas. If these services must be purchased separately, a value penalty may result depending on the expectations of market participants in the area. In the absence of public disposal systems, owners may resort to using private dump sites, which create many problems.

Easements

An easement is an interest in real property that conveys use, but not ownership, of property owned by another. One common type of easement is an easement for utilities. Easements tend to limit the uses to which a site can be put and the types of improvements that can be built on it. During the field inspection the appraiser checks the site for any observable evidence of easements. Easements are almost always identified when title or record data are researched, but some easements may not be recorded. The appraiser should also investigate compliance with private restrictions and any potential infringements.

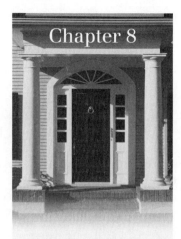

Chapter 8

Description of the Improvements: Design

A description of the subject improvements can help an appraiser select suitable comparable properties from a preliminary list of potential comparables. In the sales comparison approach, the appraiser uses the description of the subject improvements to make adjustments for differences between the subject and each of the comparable properties. The description of the improvements also provides the data needed to estimate reproduction or replacement cost and depreciation in the cost approach and operating and maintenance expenses in the income capitalization approach. Thus, the quality of the appraiser's observation of the building and the clarity of the description directly affect the reliability of all three approaches to value.

Steps in the Description of the Improvements

There is no set sequence of steps in the description of the improvements that can be used for all appraisals. Different types of properties and varying appraisal styles may require that different procedures be used to inspect improvements. The steps described here are presented in a sequence common to many appraisals.

The appraiser usually begins by observing the general placement of the improvements on the subject site and considering the effects of their location. The exterior is observed in detail, starting with the foundation, framing, exterior covering, and roof of the residence. (These structural components are discussed in the next chapter.) The building features and the materials used are noted, and each feature is rated for quality of construction, condition, and market appeal. The appraiser measures the exterior dimensions of the main improvement and draws a scale diagram of the improvement on a sheet of graph paper, tablet computer, or drawing device. Photographs of the exterior of the improvements are taken, the architectural style of the main improvement is identified, and the compatibility of the residence with its use and environment is considered.

The interior of the residence is observed next. The appraiser notes the number and type of rooms and considers the functional utility of the layout. The quality of workmanship and the materials used in the interior finish are observed. Potential problems are carefully studied, and their cause and cost of repair are evaluated. Photographs of the interior of the improvement are often taken as workfile documentation of observable deterioration and to help the appraiser recall specific condition issues.

During the observation of the interior, the appraiser also notes the condition and quality of the mechanical systems–heating, cooling, electrical, plumbing, hot water, and waste disposal. (Mechanical systems and equipment are described in the next chapter.) Air-conditioning, insulation, and energy efficiency are considered in the analysis and any built-in equipment is noted. An appraiser should report any obvious evidence of potential problems such as leaks and, if the scope of work requires it, recommend an inspection by a professional.

Appraisers also inspect site improvements such as porches, patios, decks, and balconies as well as wall attachments, stairs, roof attachments, special rooms, basements, and attic areas. Also, the appraiser measures the garage and any outbuildings and rates them for construction quality, condition, and market appeal.

Orientation and Placement of Improvements on the Site

As mentioned previously, an appraiser observes the location and orientation of the improvements on the site at the outset of the property observation. In examining the improvements, the appraiser notes how the residence is situated in relation to the sun and how it is adapted to the benefits or constraints of the site location.

During the summer, the sun rises in the northeast, travels in a high arc, and sets in the northwest. During the winter, it rises in the southeast, travels in a low arc, and sets in the southwest. A well-designed house takes advantage of the movement of the sun with a southward orientation and small or few windows to prevent air leakage. A large roof overhang shades the house in the summer months when the sun is high. In the winter when the sun is low, the warmth of the sun can enter the windows of the house. Outbuildings, trees, and vegetation that are appropriately placed can shelter the main improvement from the sun, wind, and noise. The placement of improvements on the site, orientation toward the sun, and similar issues may impact value in some markets but may be minor (or negligible) value influences in others.

Measuring Size

Determining the size of a house is sometimes a formidable task. Methods and techniques for calculating building size vary regionally and according to property type. Local practices may reflect biases that significantly affect value opinions. Appraisers must be familiar with the measurement techniques used in their areas as well as those used elsewhere in the market. The NAHB Research Center developed a consensus standard through the American National Standards Institute accreditation process that establishes a uniform method for determining the finished area for attached and detached one-unit housing. This measurement standard is recognized by many federal agencies. (The standard document, ANSI Z765-2003, is reprinted in Appendix B.)

Because FHA, VA, Fannie Mae, and Freddie Mac are major players in the mortgage market, the standards those agencies use are applicable in most appraisals. Whatever measurement standards and practices are applicable to a specific appraisal problem, an appraiser must be consistent in the use, interpretation, and reporting of building measurements within each assignment. Failure to do so can adversely affect the quality of the appraisal report.

The most common building measurement applied to one-unit residences is gross living area. The dimensions of a building can be ascertained from plans, but these dimensions should be checked against the actual building measurements. The area of attached porches, detached garages, and minor improvements is calculated separately.

Gross living area is defined as the total area of finished, above-grade residential space. It is calculated by measuring the area within the outside perimeter of a house and includes finished and habitable, above-grade living area only. Finished basement or attic areas are not included in total gross living area.

The gross living area of a rectangular house is measured by attaching the end of the tape measure to one exterior corner of the residence, measuring the distance to the next corner, and then repeating this pro-

---

Below-Grade and Above-Grade Living Space

Gross living area, as defined by Fannie Mae, is calculated for all residential properties (except condominiums and cooperatives) using the exterior building dimensions of each floor. Garages and basements are excluded. Fannie Mae considers a level to be below grade if any portion of it is below grade, regardless of the quality of its finish or the window area of any room. Therefore, a walk-out basement with finished rooms would not be included in gross living area.

The agency does recognize that below-grade rooms not included in gross living area may contribute substantially to the value of a property, particularly when the quality of the finish is high. In completing the URAR form, the appraiser reports such areas on the line provided for "basement and finished areas below grade," which appears in the sales comparison analysis adjustment grid.

The ability of a residential property to meet Fannie Mae criteria for a mortgage can affect its marketability. That is, if the amount of the government-sponsored mortgage funds available for houses with a certain gross living area does not match the market levels for competitive properties in the market, the property may suffer a diminution in value attributable to living area that is considered below grade by Fannie Mae but above grade by the market in general.

For further discussion of problems encountered in measuring gross living area, see Cliff L. Cryer, "How Big Is This House?" *The Real Estate Appraiser* (April 1992): 21-26.

cess until all exterior walls have been covered. After noting the measurements on a rough diagram of the house, the appraiser checks to see whether the measurements of parallel sides of the structure are equivalent. This procedure is known as *squaring the house.* The total front building measurements should equal the total rear measurements, and the total left-side measurements should equal the total right-side measurements. Minor discrepancies may suggest that the corners of the structure are not perfect right angles, while greater discrepancies may be attributable to errors in measuring or to rounding inconsistencies.

If the house has attachments or an irregular shape, the appraiser sketches the shape of the house and measures each side. Once all the measurements have been verified, the appraiser divides the figure drawn into smaller geometric units, calculates the area of each, and adds the areas together. (Formulas for calculating the area of various geometric shapes were presented in Chapter 7.) Areas not normally considered part of the gross living area, such as attached garages and entryways, must be excluded from the calculations. Computer programs are available for calculating areas, but the appraiser must still square the house to obtain the measurements.

Measuring the subject property and calculating the square footage is the appraiser's responsibility. Assignment conditions may prevent the appraiser from gaining access to the property. In this instance, an appraiser may find it necessary to consult an alternative source that the appraiser believes to be credible. An appraiser should never accept an estimate of the subject's gross living area from a third-party source without attempting to verify the information. The appraiser should provide the sources of the information and clearly disclose any discrepancies (e.g., two different sources reporting different square footages).

The square footages of comparable properties are often obtained from tax records, real estate agents, builders, or other appraisers. The appraiser must always document the source of this information.

For proposed construction or a house still under construction, an appraiser may need to rely on the builder plans because there is no physical structure to measure. However, once the dwelling is completed, the appraiser must measure and calculate the square footage during the final inspection process. Failure to verify the actual measurements could result in a value based on the builder's size even though the property actually built was not the same size.

The method applied to calculate property size must also be determined. If an unverified statement of property size is used in a value analysis, the resulting opinion could be erroneous. Different description practices in local and regional markets further complicate the situation. For example, a comparison of condominiums based on square footage may produce inaccurate results if the size of the subject property is expressed in terms of net living area, which is measured along interior walls, and all the market data are expressed in terms of gross salable area.

Sketch of the House

A sketch or floor plan of the residence and its garage or carport showing the location of doors, windows, and interior walls is sometimes included as part of an appraisal report. Many appraisers take pride in their ability to draw professional diagrams, but detailed drawings are not required for most residential appraisals. Simple, neat sketches of the exterior drawn to approximate scale are usually requested by lenders. These sketches may indicate the placement of interior walls and should show the same dimensions used to calculate the gross living area.

Photography

Photographs are an important part of an appraisal report. Photographs that are out of focus or badly developed are not acceptable. Digital photographs are acceptable, and on some occasions professional photographs taken with a 35mm camera are required. Color digital photographs have become a standard part of appraisal reports.

There is no general rule as to what property features should be photographed. At a minimum, appraisal reports should include

- Photographs of the front and rear of the house, showing the sides as well
- Photographs of any major site improvements
- A street scene, including any external (off-site) conditions that create obsolescence (e.g., roadway ramps, adjacent commercial use, dangerous conditions)

Additional photographs may be needed depending on client requirements. If the assignment warrants the additional documentation, photographs of construction details and the interior of the house should also be included.

Architectural Styles

In the description of the improvements, the appraiser identifies the architectural style of the main improvement and considers its effect on property value, based on its conformity and compatibility within the market area. A wide variety of building forms and ornamentation may be identified. An appraiser uses the system of description or identification prevalent in the specific market area so that the client and other users of the appraisal report will understand the style identified.

Architectural Compatibility

One important factor affecting the desirability of a particular architectural style is its conformity or compatibility with the standards

> **architectural style.** The character of a building's form and ornamentation.
>
> **compatibility.** The concept that a building is in harmony with its uses and its environment.

of the market. Compatibility indicates that a building is in harmony with its use or uses and its environment. This harmony applies to the form, materials, and scale of the structure. Styles of different periods frequently clash. A cubistic dwelling would not harmonize with eighteenth-century colonial buildings. A monumental or ostentatious building is out of place in a modest setting. Market value is frequently diminished by incompatibility of design.

There are several types of incompatibility. The various elements of a structure can be incompatible with one another. Alternatively, a structure can be incompatible with its site or location in the neighborhood. Compatibility is influenced by a variety of factors, including

- Zoning
- Construction and maintenance costs
- Land value
- The physical features of sites
- Architectural trends
- Technology

Sometimes these influences impose conformity.

The materials used in a structure should be in harmony with one another and with the building's architectural style. A building designed to be built of a particular material will not necessarily be effective if it is constructed of another material. An architectural design should not combine distracting features or building materials that vary excessively.

Architectural design and building materials should be well integrated and in harmony with the site. A frame building in a wooded, hilly area will probably harmonize with its setting more than a brick building. A frame residence located in a neighborhood of brick homes usually suffers a value penalty.

Perhaps most important, the architectural style of a building should be in harmony with the styles of neighborhood structures and with market standards. Often the predominant uses and building styles in an area can be readily observed; however, the trend of development may be more difficult to discern. An architectural style that appears atypical may actually indicate a future trend.

The impact of a nonconforming building design should be carefully considered. A somewhat unusual design that is attractive and generally in harmony with other buildings in the area may command a higher price than its more typical neighbors. A house with an incongruous design, however, will probably sell at a price below the general market level. If it does not, it may have special features that compensate for its lack of conformity.

Evaluating the value effect of a nonconforming design may require appraisal judgment. There may be sufficient demand for a detached dwelling in a neighborhood of row houses to mitigate any value penalty resulting from incompatibility. Sometimes functional utility may override design as a primary market requirement. If the general proportions and scale of an atypical building are in harmony with its surroundings and the structure has functional utility, the unusual design may not impose a value penalty. In any case, the positive and negative effects of a building's nonconformity should be carefully considered because appraisers have a responsibility to reflect market preferences in their analyses.

Trends in Architectural Styles

Neighborhood properties that conform to the standards of the local market generally have the highest value in relation to construction costs. Although there is room in a free market economy for individual expression, commonly shared tastes characterize most of the real estate market. These preferences form the standards of the market, but market standards do change over time.

Market tastes and standards are influenced by both the desire to preserve tradition and the desire for change, variety, and efficiency. Architectural trends respond to the desire to preserve tradition by incorporating elements of past architectural styles, while new elements of architectural design are developed in response to the desire for change.

When an architectural style becomes extreme, tastes may shift back to past styles. Extremely ornate ornamentation is often replaced with simple forms. A reactive shift provides contrast to the dominant architectural style that precedes it. Changing tastes produce avant garde or experimental building styles, which are ultimately tested in the market. An experimental style eventually is abandoned or becomes accepted. Design elements discarded in a reactive swing are not lost forever, however. Old forms may disappear for a time and later reappear in a modified form. Figure 8.1 illustrates some common architectural styles.

Changes in architectural style often correspond to the economic life cycles of buildings. Major revisions in architectural styles typically occur at the end of a building life cycle, or about every 30 to 50 years. For example, after roughly 40 years as the predominant residential architectural style in the U.S. during the suburban housing boom of 1945–1985, "Minimal traditional" architecture gave way to exteriors with more detail.

Newly constructed buildings, which may or may not be designed by professional architects, tend to have broad market appeal. When a building is no longer new, however, it will be compared with other buildings in terms of the quality and functionality of its architectural style. Form (e.g., linear, centralized, clustered) and structure are the most basic components of architectural style (e.g., Queen Anne, Italianate, Minimal traditional). They define the possible uses and modifications of a building, and their influence on value increases as time goes by.

Various architectural styles are found in different parts of the country. These style differences can largely be attributed to the availability of natural materials such as wood, stone, and clay and to differences in climate. Changes in building technology have made styles more uniform in recent years and have changed the way buildings are designed and constructed.

Figure 8.1 Common Architectural Styles

Cape Cod

Colonial

Georgian

Tudor

Victorian

Mission

Bungalow

Row House

California Ranch

Contemporary

Postmodern

The development of the Franklin stove, for example, modified the layout of rooms in residences because fireplaces were no longer needed to provide heat. The introduction of household appliances in the early twentieth century eliminated the need for root cellars, pantries, and large laundry rooms, reducing the number of rooms in homes and changing room arrangements.

The prevalent use of central heating and air-conditioning in the mid-twentieth century has resulted in the standardization of architectural styles throughout the country. Regional building styles that were developed to use local building materials and meet the demands of climate have been almost obliterated. The thick, mud masonry walls and small windows of Southwestern architecture were well-suited to the hot, dry weather of the region. Overhanging roofs were used on homes in the rainy Northwest so that windows could be opened for ventilation without admitting the rain. The saltbox houses of New England were windowless and steep-roofed on one side to provide protection against the harsh north wind.

With the development of central heating and air-conditioning, many of these differences in regional styles became unnecessary. Beginning in the mid-1970s, however, energy considerations became more important, and builders began once again to incorporate structural defenses against climate into new construction. Energy consciousness has prompted climate-compatible designs to resurface. Energy-saving features such as insulated window frames and energy-producing features such as solar roof panels are considerations in estimating market value because consumers become increasingly interested in conservation when energy markets become more volatile and the costs of heating and cooling a home increase.

Despite the general disappearance of functional differences between housing styles in different climatic regions, market preferences may still vary between residents of different neighborhoods. Appraisers must recognize not only the typical architectural styles, housing types, and amenities in a community but also the current desirability of those characteristics within different submarkets and how the trends are likely to change over time.

No Accounting for Taste

In analyzing the effect of architectural style on value, an appraiser's personal taste is immaterial. Instead, an appraiser must be able to determine the market's current preferences for particular styles and types of housing.

Types of Houses

To describe the architectural style of a residence and evaluate its conformity or compatibility with market tastes and standards, appraisers should be familiar with the advantages and disadvantages of various types of houses. Common house designs include one-story, one and one-half story, two-story, bi-level, and split-level houses.

One-Story House

The entire living area in this type of house is on ground level. One-story houses have proven to be acceptable in the resale market. They generally have a simple design that can be adapted to any type of topography.

one-story house. A dwelling with the entire living area on a single level, such as a ranch, rambler, or bungalow.

one and one-half story house. A dwelling based on the design of a single-story cottage with additional bedrooms and bathrooms or unfinished storage space on a second floor; called a Cape Cod in some areas.

two-story house. A dwelling with two levels where the lower level is at ground level, differentiating it from a bi-level house.

bi-level house. A house built on two levels, with the lower level partially below ground level. In different parts of the country, bi-level may denote a two-story dwelling, a raised ranch, or a split-foyer dwelling.

split-level house. A house with living areas on two or more levels with one level positioned approximately midway between the other levels.

Because most of the exterior is accessible, a one-story house is easier to maintain and attachments can be made at ground level. The absence of stairs is appealing to many purchasers.

A one-story house has disadvantages too. All the living area is on one level, so noise spreads throughout the house. In some communities, a single-story design is associated with tract developments, which may have limited appeal. Furthermore, without sufficient screening or proper site placement, a one-story house may lack privacy.

One and One-Half Story House

A one and one-half story house, which is called a Cape Cod in some areas, usually has its main rooms and one bedroom and bathroom on the ground floor. Other bedrooms and bathrooms may be located on the smaller second floor, or the entire second floor may be unfinished and used for storage.

| Figure 8.2 | One-Story House |

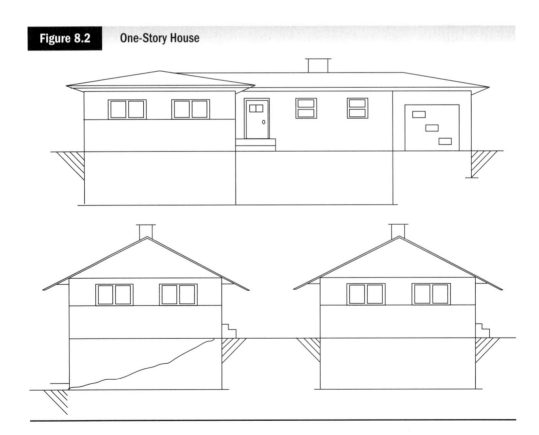

One advantage of a one and one-half story house is its compactness. This type of house is less expensive to heat than a one-story residence with the same square foot area. A one and one-half story house also has visual appeal. Houses with dormers can be especially attractive. During the 1950s and 1960s, many of these homes were built and sold with only the first floor finished. The second floor was often completed later to provide extra living space for an expanding family. These houses provide a practical advantage to growing families with limited means.

The design of many one and one-half story houses has certain disadvantages. The stairway to the second floor in such a house is often narrow and steep. These stairs take up little room on the ground floor, but they make it very difficult to move furniture upstairs. Often space is wasted in a one and one-half story house because only a portion of the second floor has enough ceiling height to be used as living area. The space under the eaves is usually a storage area. The rooms are small in many one and one-half story homes, and there are rarely more than two bedrooms on the ground floor. A house without dormers may have

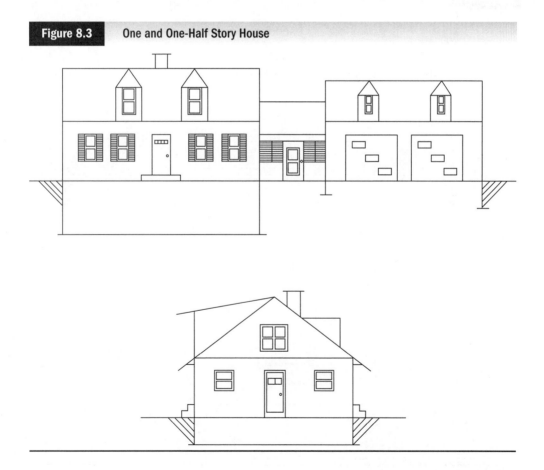

Figure 8.3   One and One-Half Story House

lighting and ventilation problems, and the upper level may lack temperature control and insulation. It can be quite expensive to finish this type of house, particularly if electricity, plumbing, and other services have to be extended to the upper level after construction.

Two-Story House

Two-story houses may be built in many architectural styles. In most two-story homes, the main rooms and sometimes a guest bedroom and bathroom are located on the ground floor; other bedrooms and bathrooms are on the upper floor.

The main advantage of a two-story house is that living and working areas are separated from private areas. Many buyers prefer these houses because they suggest the gracious living style of the American past. A two-story house can be built on a smaller lot than a one-story house with the same amount of living area. Foundation and roof costs are lower for the same total floor area.

Figure 8.4	Two-Story House

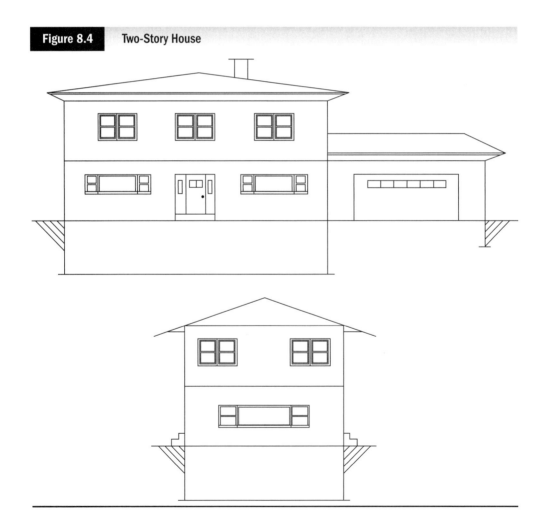

Disadvantages of a two-story design include the problems posed by the stairway that connects the ground level to the private areas. The space under the stairway can be used for closets and storage areas so that space is not wasted, but rooms on the second level have no direct access to the exterior. This can be hazardous in the event of a fire or emergency. Furthermore, a two-story design is not easily adapted for expansion upward or outward.

Bi-Level House

A bi-level may also be known as a *raised ranch* or *split-foyer house*.[1] Most of the living area in a bi-level house is on the upper level. The lower level may serve as an extra family room, recreation room, or spare bedroom. A bi-level house usually rests on a concrete slab with foundation walls that rise four feet or less above ground level. The remaining one and one-half stories are built over the foundation walls.

This type of house provides additional living area at the lowest cost. In some markets, the lower level is not regarded as a basement but as part of the gross living area. Both levels lend themselves to a variety of

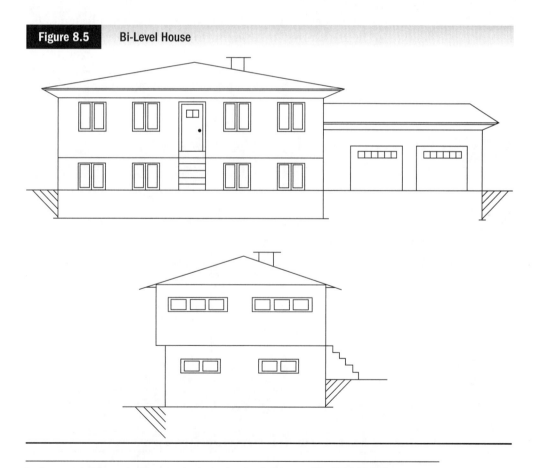

Figure 8.5   Bi-Level House

---

1.   In some parts of the country, *bi-level* may also denote a two-story dwelling or a split-level (tri-level) dwelling.

attachments. Part of the lower level can be converted into a garage or finished after the upper level is completed. The lower level may have windows to provide light and ventilation and doors to allow for exterior access and more convenient traffic patterns.

The main disadvantage of a bi-level design is that the lower level is sometimes cold and damp and may require special heating and insulation. Heat rises from the lower level through the split entryway and warms the upper level. Heating costs can be high if the house is poorly designed.

The ductwork in a bi-level house is hard to install because the foundation level is a functional living area, not a basement or crawl space. All traffic between the two levels must go by way of the interior stairs, which are usually located in the center of the house.

Because of its design limitations, the bi-level house poses challenges for architects. In a poorly designed bi-level house, the division of interior zones may be clumsy or the exterior may be visually unappealing, particularly in areas where lots are level. Bi-level houses may be more visually appealing on a site with a slope.

Split-Level House

Split-level houses include tri-levels and quad-levels with basements. This type of house allows its residents to live on several levels. Two levels are normally finished prior to occupancy. A split-level house consists of a two-story portion, which is constructed like a bi-level, and a one-story portion. The two-story portion is built over a slab or a partial basement; the one-story portion sits on a slab or above a base-

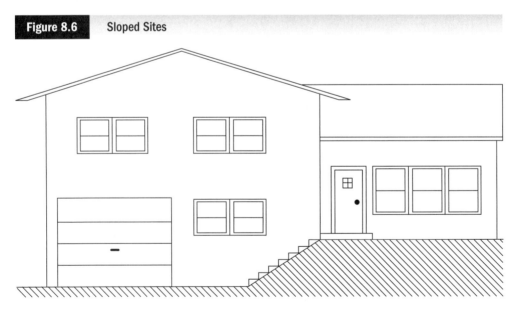

Figure 8.6	Sloped Sites

A split-level (or bi-level) design is a practical solution to the challenges provided by a sloped site.

Figure 8.7   Split-Level House

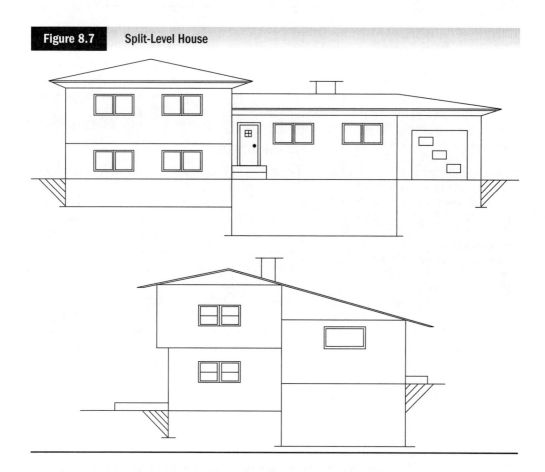

ment or crawl space. The design of the structure can be described as side-to-side, front-to-back, or back-to-front, referring to the relative placement of the one-story and two-story sections.

The upper level of a split-level house, which is separated from the middle level by a half flight of stairs, is reserved for bedrooms and bathrooms. The middle level, which is separated from the upper and lower levels by half flights of stairs, contains a living room, a dining area, a kitchen, and a laundry area. The lower level has additional living areas such as a family room, a recreation room, a den, or extra bedrooms. The lower level usually provides access to the garage.

A split-level home provides additional living area at a very low cost. In most parts of the country, the lower level is considered part of the gross living area, not a basement. The design lends itself to irregular topography, and both the middle and lower levels can accommodate exterior attachments. All the zones within the residence are well set off from one another, yet easily accessible. The traffic pattern is efficient. The lower level provides convenient access to the garage and can be finished after the middle and upper levels are complete. The design can accommodate an overhanging upper level, if desired.

A split-level house may have the same heating and insulation problems as a bi-level house. Because heat rises, the upper levels tend to be warmer than the lower level. The architectural limitations of the bi-level are also found in the split-level design, although split-levels have more versatility. Like bi-level houses, split-level houses may have less visual appeal if the topography of the site is flat.

House Zones

As part of the property observation process, an appraiser examines the interior layout of the house. A house can be divided into three zones and various circulation areas. The private-sleeping zone contains the bedrooms; the family, master, and private bathrooms; and the dressing rooms. The living-social zone consists of the living room, the dining room, the family or recreation room, the den, and any enclosed porches. The working-service zone consists of the kitchen, the laundry, the pantry, and other work areas. Corridors, stairways, and entrances are considered circulation areas. Figure 8.8 shows the zone divisions in a well-designed house.

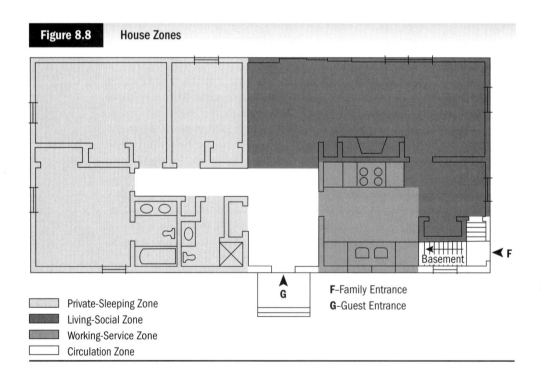

Figure 8.8   House Zones

F-Family Entrance
G-Guest Entrance

☐ Private-Sleeping Zone
■ Living-Social Zone
▨ Working-Service Zone
☐ Circulation Zone

The three zones within a home should be separated from one another so that activities in one zone do not interfere with those in another. The private-sleeping zone should be insulated from the noise of the other two zones by closets, hallways, or other rooms. Occupants should be able to move from bedrooms to bathrooms in the private zone without being seen from the other areas of the house.

The working-service zone is the nerve center of the house where most household chores are performed. Someone working in the kitchen should be able to monitor the guest and family entrances as well as activities in the private zone, the porch, the patio, and the backyard via the circulation areas.

The guest entrance should lead into the center of the house. This entrance should be near a guest closet and the guest lavatory. Ideally the entrance will lead directly to the living-social zone and be separated from the private-sleeping area by a noise and visibility barrier. Hard flooring is needed in the guest entrance to withstand mud and dirt tracked in from the outside.

The family entrance should lead into the kitchen from the garage, carport, or breezeway or from a circulation area such as a porch or deck. Traffic coming in this entrance should not have to pass through the work area in the kitchen. Residents should also be able to move from the family entrance through the service zone to the private-sleeping zone without going through the living-social zone.

A house with a basement may have a separate, outside entrance to the basement. The basement entrance should lead to stairs and hallways that have direct access to the private-sleeping zone, the living-social zone, and both the guest and family entrances. Circulation areas such as the main hallway, a bedroom hallway, stairways, and a rear or service hallway should provide access to the different house zones without passing through individual rooms. Circulation areas should be well-lit and contain closets and storage space in strategic locations.

Design Problems

Common design problems historically reported by homeowners in surveys conducted by the National Association of Home Builders include

- Front door opens directly into living room.
- No closet in front hall.
- No direct access from the front door to the kitchen, bathroom, or bedroom without passing through other rooms.
- Rear door does not lead directly into the kitchen and does not provide convenient access to the street, driveway, and garage.
- No comfortable eating area in or near the kitchen.
- No access to the basement from outside.

- No convenient access from the kitchen to the separate dining area.
- Stairways are located off a room, not off a hallway or foyer.
- Bedrooms or bathrooms are visible from the living room or foyer.
- Recreation or family room is poorly located and not visible from the kitchen.
- Walls between bedrooms are not soundproof.
- Outdoor living areas such as decks and patios are not accessible from the kitchen.

- A wide selection of exterior facades, styles, and interior plans
- Bonus space such as a third story, a walkout basement, or a guest casita (small pavilion resembling a loggia)
- An enhanced main bedroom suite
- Gathering zones and private zones
- Environmentally sensitive and responsible design, including the use of energy-efficient appliances, daylighting, alternative or recycled building materials, passive solar design, and native vegetation and xeriscaping (water-sensitive landscaping for arid and semi-arid areas)
- A focus on outdoor living, with multiple outdoor spaces and features (e.g., barbecue pits, pools, fountains, hot tubs, backyard fireplaces)
- Special areas for pets in laundry or mud rooms that feature outdoor access, automatic water fountains, and pet bathing areas
- Resort-like amenities

Source: Urban Land Institute, *Residential Development Handbook* (Washington, D.C.: ULI, 2004), 352.

Floor plans depend on the size and value of the individual residence and often vary from region to region.

Rooms in Residential Properties

In the field inspection of the interior of a house, an appraiser studies the specific dimensions and characteristics of the individual rooms in the structure and notes any problems with the building's design.

Living Rooms

Until the middle of the twentieth century, the living room was considered the center of a house. More recently, the status of the living room has changed. Many homeowners socialize, relax, and entertain in their family rooms, patios, and kitchens, rather than in living rooms. These other areas have expanded, and the size and importance of the living room have diminished.

The living room may be located in the front of the house or, if the view or access to outdoor areas is better, at the back or side of the house. Often the dining room is located at one end of the living room, usually adjacent to the kitchen. Ideally the living room should be located away from the traffic patterns to other rooms but easily accessible from the guest entrance.

Living rooms can be square, rectangular, or L-shaped. Square living rooms make furniture arrangement difficult and are the least desirable. Rectangular living rooms should be neither too narrow nor too wide. Living rooms combined with dining areas are usually L-shaped. A living room should have at least one wall with windows for a view and ventilation and another wall long enough for a couch and other furniture. Many homeowners complain that too many breaks in the walls of rooms for doorways, windows, and fireplaces make it difficult to arrange furniture comfortably. Sufficient outlets should be available for lamps and appliances. Traffic should not have to pass through the conversation circle in the living room.

Kitchens

The kitchen serves more functions than any other room, often acting as the focal point in the layout of the service and entertaining areas of a home. It is often the most important and by far the most expensive room in the house. More than 120 miles are walked each year in the average kitchen during the preparation of just two meals a day; a well-designed kitchen can eliminate 40 miles from this route.

The best location for the kitchen depends on many factors, including the lifestyle of the household and the size of the family. The kitchen should have access to the dining area and to the front or rear entrance. If outdoor areas are used for meals, the kitchen should also have access to them. If the house has a family room, the kitchen should be visible from this room and allow convenient access to it. The kitchen is ordinarily close to but separated from the dining area, but a large kitchen is often combined with an informal dining area.

Kitchens should be well ventilated and well lit. The window area should be no less than 10% of the floor area and a window over the sink is ideal. In addition to the work areas, cabinets, storage space, appliances, and built-in equipment are needed. A kitchen may also accommodate a family activity center, a dining area, a laundry area, a trash storage area, or a pantry.

All kitchens with more than one counter have a work triangle as an essential design feature. Most kitchen layouts are based on the three points of the work triangle:

1. The sink/food preparation area
2. The refrigerator
3. The cooking area

In a well-designed kitchen, the cumulative length of the legs of the triangle is no less than 12 feet and no more than 23 feet.

The sink area is the place where food is prepared, dishes are washed, and garbage is disposed of. This accounts for 40% to 45% of kitchen activity. Appliances in the sink area may include a dishwasher, a trash compactor, and a garbage disposal. Single-basin sinks are generally adequate and are common in new construction when dishwashers are installed. Double-basin sinks are better suited to washing dishes by hand. The space beneath the sink is used to store cleaning products and utensils.

The sink area should be lit by a window above the sink and overhead lighting. Wall cabinets are useful nearby and the dishwasher should be no more than 4 feet away. The sink should be approximately 4 to 6 feet from the cooking area and 4 to 7 feet from the refrigerator.

Usually perishable foods are stored in a combination refrigerator and freezer. The refrigerator is ideally located next to 36 to 42 inches of uninterrupted counter space, which is known as a landing area. The refrigerator should be near the food preparation area and close to a spigot that supplies water if it has an icemaker. It should also be convenient for unloading groceries. For energy efficiency, the refrigerator should not be located so close to the oven and range that it is affected by the heat put out in the cooking area.

The cooking area in a kitchen combines a range/cookstove with a conventional oven. Most homes now have microwave ovens as well. Counters on each side of the stove should be made of a heatproof material. Gas or electricity powers the cooking appliances. The cooking area should never be near a window. Curtains can catch fire, reaching across a range to get to the window is dangerous, and cleaning above the range can be difficult. All cabinets should be at least 30 inches above the range. A ventilator or fan over the range is desirable to remove smoke and cooking fumes. Many fire-related injuries and accidents occur in the cooking area, so a fire extinguisher should be close at hand.

As cooking practices change so do kitchen layouts and appliances. Today many people cook on barbecues and outdoor grills or with microwaves, woks, and other appliances, which are personal property rather than realty. Layout is often more important than sheer size. Kitchens may be U-shaped or L-shaped with one counter or two. Larger kitchens may have an island in the center. Figure 8.9 illustrates several common kitchen layouts.

In a U-shaped kitchen, cabinets and counters are located along three walls. This design requires the most space, but it is considered to be the most efficient. The work triangle is compact so it is easily separated from traffic patterns through the kitchen. The sink is at the base of the U and the refrigerator and cooking area face each other on the arms of the U. The counter space is continuous and storage space is ample.

Some U-shaped kitchens have certain disadvantages. Too compact a triangle cramps the work area, while too open a triangle necessitates too much walking.

The L-shaped kitchen has counters and work areas arranged in two perpendicular, adjacent lines. The sink is usually centered on the long side of the L, with the refrigerator at the end of this counter; the cooking area is on the other side of the L. This design is best for small kitchens. It also works well for large kitchens because the work triangle is separated from traffic and the rest of the kitchen can be used for other purposes. This configuration is popular because it can accommodate various arrangements. Its major disadvantages are the placement of appliances, the potential for wasted space, and the distance between the work centers at the ends of the L.

A two-counter kitchen, which is also known as a *corridor* or *Pullman kitchen*, has cabinets and work areas on two opposite walls. The work triangle also serves as a passageway for traffic through the kitchen. The sink and cooking area are on one side across from the refrigerator. There should be at least 4 feet between the two counters so that cabinets and appliances can be opened.

A one-counter kitchen, which is also known as a *strip kitchen* or *galley*, has all the work areas aligned along one wall. This design does not create a work triangle, but it suits scaled-down appliances and works well when kitchen space is limited to less than 12 feet along the

Figure 8.9   Typical Kitchen Designs

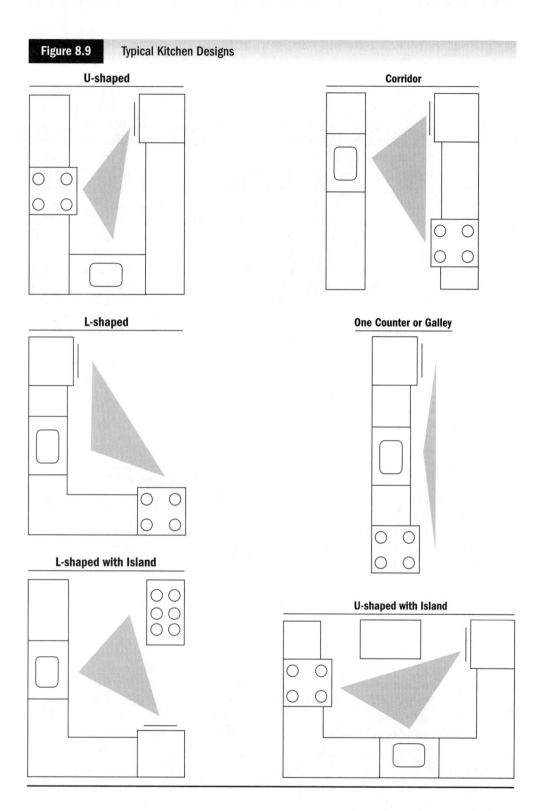

U-shaped

Corridor

L-shaped

One Counter or Galley

L-shaped with Island

U-shaped with Island

wall. The sink should be centrally located, with the refrigerator and the range at opposite ends of the wall. One-counter kitchens are most often found in apartments and small condominiums.

Island kitchens may be U-shaped or L-shaped. One-counter kitchens may have an island in the center—usually for the sink or the cooking area. Because the island reduces the area of the work triangle, islands are usually used in larger kitchens. In large kitchens the island may also set off an informal eating area.

Some kitchens have additional areas located outside the work triangle. A separate food preparation area, for example, may require counter space, extra electrical outlets, and storage for cooking utensils. A work desk or personal computer area may be included in a kitchen if space permits. This area may include a desk, a personal computer, a telephone, a calendar, and other home management tools.

Some kitchens have special work surfaces for baking and extra storage for baking supplies and utensils. Homeowners who entertain frequently may have kitchens with wet bars and storage areas for bottles and glasses. A serving or buffet counter in a pass-through area between the kitchen and dining room can facilitate informal meals. A barbecue inside the kitchen may be handy for special types of cooking, but this equipment must be located near an exhaust fan or hood. Unusual kitchen features may constitute overimprovements, depending on the standards of the market.

Common Kitchen Problems

- Insufficient base cabinet storage
- Insufficient wall cabinet storage
- "Dead space" in corners
- Insufficient counter space
- No counter beside the refrigerator
- Not enough window area
- Poorly placed doors that waste wall space
- Traffic through the work triangle, which can be dangerous
- Too little counter space on either side of the sink
- No counter beside the range
- Insufficient space in front of cabinets
- Too great a distance between the sink, range, and refrigerator
- A range located under a window

Top New Trends in Kitchens

- Induction cooking
- Independent storage control options in refrigerator/freezer compartments
- Drawer-style appliances that feature refrigeration, warming, and even microwave capability
- Alternatives to stainless steel appliance finishes
- High-tech, interactive appliances
- Compact appliances designed for islands or butler's pantries
- Steam cooking options for ovens
- Built-in coffeemakers and instant hot water dispensers, built-in beverage centers
- Euro-style cabinetry featuring clean lines and unconventional shapes
- New options in interior shelving for cabinets
- Alternative countertop finishes
- Designer-linked product lines

Source: National Kitchen and Bath Association in *Professional Builder* (Jan. 1, 2006)

Dining Areas

Most houses built before the 1950s had separate dining rooms. Many newer houses have dining areas that are part of another room—e.g., eat-in kitchens, breakfast nooks, and living room–dining room combinations are common. Most homebuyers prefer a house with a family room and an eat-in kitchen to one with a formal dining room and no family room.

The dining room is part of the living-social zone of a house. It should be directly accessible to the kitchen but separate from it. Forty-two inches of space is needed behind each chair, and the area should accommodate a table that seats six persons. Extra room is needed to store dishes, silver, and glassware, and artificial light is usually provided by a chandelier.

Dining Area Floor Plan Problems	
· Stairs that open into the dining area	· No partition between the kitchen and dining areas
· Inadequate outlets, switches, lighting, and ventilation	· Traffic passing through the dining area
	· Insufficient space for furniture arrangement

Bedrooms

The number of bedrooms in a house is an important design consideration. The standard may be indicated by neighborhood analysis. Three- and four-bedroom houses have wide acceptance in the market. Houses with five or more bedrooms may represent an overimprovement in many areas. They usually appeal only to large families. Of course, luxury homes may have more than five bedrooms.

Privacy is important, so bedrooms should be located in the most secluded parts of the house. They should be accessible from a central hallway, which connects to the other zones of the house. Bedrooms should be insulated from the noise produced in other zones of the house and from the street noise outside. Placing closets along bedroom walls can minimize the transmission of sound from adjacent rooms.

The largest bedroom is usually the master bedroom, which often has access to a master bathroom. Other bedrooms may be used for children and guests. Extra bedrooms may be converted into dens, studies, home offices, or family rooms.

Some bedrooms have additional space for clothes storage and dressing areas. Because cross ventilation is important, corner bedrooms are preferred, although the prevalence of central air-conditioning has diminished the need for windows on multiple walls. Bedrooms should have adequate natural and artificial light. For safety, each bedroom should have a window that provides exterior access and be equipped with or near to smoke and fire detectors.

The number of bedrooms is one of the prime criteria in the selection of comparable homes. A lack of properties with a similar number

- Insufficient room to arrange furniture
- Not located near a hallway or bathroom*
- Serves as a passageway to basement, attic, or another room
- Not adequately separated from other house zones
- No soundproofing
- Insufficient closet space
- Lack of lighting in bedroom or closet

*Note that a living-social area not located near a bathroom is commonly called a den or study, not a bedroom.

of bedrooms in the subject property's market area may indicate an under- or overimprovement in the subject property.

Bathrooms

Bathrooms are the smallest rooms in the house and they often seem to be the least adequate. Like kitchens, they are expensive to construct and finish. Each residence should have at least one full-size bathroom. In many markets houses with only one bathroom are obsolete. Nationwide, the percentage of homes built with 1½ bathrooms or less dropped from 41% in 1975 to 4% in 2005, and over the same period the percentage of homes built with three or more bathrooms increased from only 5% in 1975 to 26% in 2005. Neighborhood or market area analysis will indicate the standard for the area, which is a critical consideration in the comparability of competitive properties.

A bathroom may be identified as the family bathroom, a powder room, or a master bath. The terminology used to describe bathrooms and lavatories varies in different parts of the country. In most areas a full-size bathroom consists of a room with a toilet or water closet, a washbasin or sink, and a tub. A three-quarter bathroom has a toilet, a wash basin, and a stall shower. A half-bath or two-thirds bath, which is also known as a *lavatory, lavette,* or *powder room,* has a toilet and a washbasin. The number of fixtures present and the sufficiency of the plumbing should be noted.

There should be at least one bathroom on each floor of a multilevel residence. The best location for bathrooms is determined by the plumbing and the room layout. The family bathroom and the master bath are part of the sleeping-private zone. The powder room is usually part of the living-social zone. Entry to the bathroom should be private, and walls shared by bathrooms and other rooms should be soundproofed.

Bathrooms require the most heat and the best ventilation of any of the rooms in the house. A window may not be necessary. Interior bathrooms without windows are cheaper and generally acceptable in the market. Ventilation can be provided by a vent to the outside or a fan that starts automatically when the light is turned on.

Family or Recreation Rooms

The concept of a family room evolved in America after World War II. A family room is the area set aside for recreation and relaxation away from the more formal living room. The first family rooms were finished basements or attics. Later, enclosed porches and extra bedrooms were converted into family rooms. Today, a family room may be used as a den, a study, a guest room, a nursery, a library, a TV room, a game room, or for all of the preceding uses at once. Flexibility of use is a key feature.

Ideally a family room is near the kitchen, but it may be located wherever space is available. If possible, it should be toward the rear of the house to provide access to the outside. There is no standard layout for a family room. A badly designed family room may have poor access to the kitchen and the outside, insufficient heat, too few electrical outlets, or too many walls and doors that do not allow for suitable furniture arrangement.

Great rooms are larger and less formal than the dining rooms, living rooms, and kitchen areas that they supersede. A great room is generally used for the functions formerly served by the living room and dining room. Smaller, formal living and dining rooms may still be present in a house with a great room, but the latter is likely to be where busy residents eat their meals while they relax, socialize, or do other things like watch television, work on a computer, or sit and chat. The demographic and cultural shift to a more informal, less structured lifestyle requires more flexible living space. The ceiling height of a great room can be up to double the height of other rooms in a house, generally to provide a dramatic open space.

The popularity of dedicated media rooms and home theaters has shifted with the evolution of the technology. Flat screen televisions and wireless connections to stereo and computer equipment require less space and hardware than high-end entertainment centers once did, allowing for more flexibility in deciding where to watch a movie or to mount audio speakers. Rather than limiting the location of a large-screen television to a room with adequate space for the accompanying cabinetry, a flat screen television can be hung on most walls (e.g., in a bedroom), with the audio and video equipment housed in a separate area, usually the basement, and controlled via a wireless remote control.

Laundry Areas

The laundry area and kitchen make up the working-service zone of the house. The location of the laundry room is a matter of convenience. Several locations are acceptable in the market. The laundry area can be on the same level as the living area or on another level. Ideally the laundry area should be a separate room that is accessible to the kitchen and the exterior of the house. Laundry facilities may be located in a closet or pantry, an enclosed porch, a mudroom, a breezeway, an attached garage, a detached garage connected to the house by a breezeway, a bedroom/bathroom area, or a basement. A laundry room in the finished portion of the house is ideally located in or near the areas where laundry is gathered for washing and returned for storage (e.g., near the main bedroom). The main consideration is the location of the plumbing fixtures needed for the washing machine. There should also be ventilation for the dryer and room to fold clothes. Laundry rooms are not usually included in the room count.

Home Offices

The decreasing cost of communications and information technology has made working from home (i.e., telecommuting) an option for office workers and their employers. Dedicated workspace in the home has increasingly become a part of the design of new residential construction, often in the form of a "bonus room" with an unidentified function in the original house plan. In an existing home, that space may have to be carved out of the current floor plan by converting an unused bedroom or living room. Unless the demand for home offices in a neighborhood is particularly high, however, the cost of a home office remodeling project is not yet likely to be fully reflected in the market value of the home.[2] The telecommuting trend and accompanying demand for home offices are driven by economic phenomena such as outsourcing and lifestyle trends which are, in turn, influenced by demographic changes.

The modern home office is usually not as elaborate as the shelf-lined library once found in a traditional, high-end home, nor is it simply a filing cabinet and computer desk hidden in a guest bedroom or a corner of the basement. The space reserved for office work within a residence should have adequate data connections for phone and fax lines and high-speed Internet access along with storage space for files and standard office equipment (e.g., computer, fax machine, and other equipment). The quality of finish and furnishings is likely to match the overall preferences of the market segment.

---

2. In 2005, a home office remodeling project contributed less than 75% of its cost on average to the property resale price, according to *Rebuilding* magazine's annual "Cost vs. Value Report."

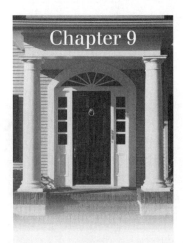

Chapter 9

Description of the
Improvements: Construction

This chapter extends the discussion of building description begun in the previous chapter, focusing on the individual components of building construction (e.g., roofing materials and types of windows and doors) rather than the qualities of the building components after they are incorporated into a structure (e.g., the number of stories of a house or the layout of rooms). This chapter also illustrates potential functional and physical problems that are associated with specific building materials and construction techniques.

There is no prescribed method for describing the construction of dwellings, but it is often useful to deal with the building components in the sequence in which they were constructed. This practice allows an appraiser to note indications of problems that may have arisen at each stage of construction. An appraiser might use the format outlined in Figure 9.1 to describe the construction and condition of residential improvements as the individual elements are added during the construction process. Alternatively, an appraiser might concentrate on the building components listed on one of the standard form reports. For example, an appraiser might organize an examination of building improvements based on the "improvements" section of the Uniform Residential Appraisal Report as shown in Figure 9.2. (For more information on the descriptive data collected on form reports, see Chapter 21.) Using a systematic format in the field inspection can help the appraiser avoid omitting any significant items.

Figure 9.1   Components of Residential Construction

I. Exterior
   A. Substructure
      1. Clearing and stake out
      2. Test boring
      3. Excavation and WDO (wood-destroying organism) treatment
      4. Footings
      5. Foundation walls
         a. Slab on ground
         b. Crawl space
         c. Basement
         d. Pier and beam
      6. Grading
   B. Superstructure
      1. Framing
      2. Exterior covering and trim
         a. Exterior walls
         b. Exterior doors
         c. Windows, storm windows, and screens
         d. Roof covering and drain system
         e. Chimneys, stacks, and vents
   C. Insulation and ventilation
II. Interior
   A. Floor covering(s)
   B. Walls and ceiling
   C. Doors
   D. Stairs
   E. Molding and baseboards
   F. Painting, decorating, and finishing
   G. Cabinets
   H. Fireplaces
III. Equipment and mechanical systems
   A. Plumbing system
      1. Piping
      2. Fixtures
   B. Hot water
   C. Heating system
      1. Forced air
      2. Hot water
      3. Steam
      4. Unit heating
      5. Fuels
         a. Coal
         b. Fuel oil
         c. Natural gas
         d. Electricity
         e. Solar energy
   D. Air-conditioning and ventilation system
   E. Electrical system
   F. Miscellaneous systems and equipment (e.g., appliances)
IV. Attachments, garages, and outbuildings

Figure 9.2	Improvements Section of the URAR

General Description	Foundation	Exterior Description materials/condition	Interior materials/condition
Units ☐ One ☐ One with Accessory Unit	☐ Concrete Slab ☐ Crawl Space	Foundation Walls	Floors
# of Stories	☐ Full Basement ☐ Partial Basement	Exterior Walls	Walls
Type ☐ Det. ☐ Att. ☐ S-Det./End Unit	Basement Area sq. ft.	Roof Surface	Trim/Finish
☐ Existing ☐ Proposed ☐ Under Const.	Basement Finish %	Gutters & Downspouts	Bath Floor
Design (Style)	☐ Outside Entry/Exit ☐ Sump Pump	Window Type	Bath Wainscot
Year Built	Evidence of ☐ Infestation	Storm Sash/Insulated	Car Storage ☐ None
Effective Age (Yrs)	☐ Dampness ☐ Settlement	Screens	☐ Driveway # of Cars
Attic ☐ None	Heating ☐ FWA ☐ HWBB ☐ Radiant	Amenities ☐ Woodstove(s) #	Driveway Surface
☐ Drop Stair ☐ Stairs	☐ Other Fuel	☐ Fireplace(s) # ☐ Fence	☐ Garage # of Cars
☐ Floor ☐ Scuttle	Cooling ☐ Central Air Conditioning	☐ Patio/Deck ☐ Porch	☐ Carport # of Cars
☐ Finished ☐ Heated	☐ Individual ☐ Other	☐ Pool ☐ Other	☐ Att. ☐ Det. ☐ Built-in
Appliances ☐Refrigerator ☐Range/Oven ☐Dishwasher ☐Disposal ☐Microwave ☐Washer/Dryer ☐Other (describe)			
Finished area **above** grade contains: Rooms Bedrooms Bath(s) Square Feet of Gross Living Area Above Grade			
Additional features (special energy efficient items, etc.)			
Describe the condition of the property (including needed repairs, deterioration, renovations, remodeling, etc.).			
Are there any physical deficiencies or adverse conditions that affect the livability, soundness, or structural integrity of the property? ☐ Yes ☐ No If Yes, describe			
Does the property generally conform to the neighborhood (functional utility, style, condition, use, construction, etc.)? ☐ Yes ☐ No If No, describe			

(left vertical label: I M P R O V E M E N T S)

Inspection of Construction Components

As discussed in Chapter 6, the property inspection conducted by an appraiser has more in common with the homebuyer's walk-through than with the activities of a professional home inspector. The appraiser looks for evidence of value-influencing features of the subject property and compares the quality and condition of the existing improvements to market norms. Obvious deficiencies and needed repairs should be noted in the description of improvements because those issues may have to be accounted for as damage in the cost approach calculations and in the selection of comparables in the sales comparison and income capitalization approaches.

Substructure Inspection

The substructure is the most difficult portion of a home's structure for an appraiser to inspect because most of the components are underground and not readily accessible. When possible, an appraiser should look for evidence of bulges or cracks in foundation walls, which may cause leakage, and for holes, crumbling, or poor interior surfaces, which may indicate that the concrete was not poured properly. Evidence of mineral sediment on basement walls could indicate that walls or window wells leak or that the basement has flooded in the past. Mineral powder stains on the floor may indicate cracked floors or clogged basement drains, and a musty odor or other evidence of mildew suggests leakage or inadequate ventilation.

Superstructure Inspection

Sometimes an appraiser can easily identify structural problems in older homes such as

- Exterior walls that bulge
- Girders, roof ridge lines, or rafters that sag
- Window sills that are not level
- Windows or doors that stick (because of defective framing, poor carpentry, or settling) or that have wracked frames
- Ponding on a low-slope roof

Sometimes the services of a professional consultant may be needed to confirm the existence of major problems, such as structural failure, lack of roof integrity, or environmental hazards.

Visible cracks in walls do not necessarily indicate problems with framing. All houses settle, and most houses develop some ceiling and wall cracks. (Large cracks resulting from the failure of the foundation due to a soil problem such as a sinkhole would require the opinion of a professional engineer.) More compelling evidence of defective framing includes large cracks on the outside of the house between the chimney and the exterior wall or multiple cracks running outward from the upper corners of window and door frames. Roofing that was installed improperly or is too heavy to be supported by the existing roof structure (i.e., joists, beams, and trusses) can cause cracks as well.

An experienced, knowledgeable appraiser may be able to detect structural problems in a new house by studying blueprints. Some observable problems in new houses can include

- Floor joists that are oversized and cost more than they contribute to value
- Floor joists that are undersized and may later cause the floors to be bouncy or buckle and sag
- Subflooring made of older materials that are costlier, noisier, and less water-resistant than newer materials
- Partitions that are improperly sized or improperly placed
- Use of solid masonry, rather than wood frame or frame and veneer, except where the use of masonry conforms to the market
- Walls that are not wide enough to support their intended load or to accommodate sufficient insulation

Building Materials Inspection

General construction details can be described on a room-by-room basis, but if the features do not vary significantly from room to room, they can be described for the house as a whole. Evidence of functional problems and other important, observable physical qualities of building materials should be noted.

Equipment and Mechanical Systems Inspection

The scope of work of the appraisal assignment will suggest how detailed the description of equipment and mechanical systems should be. In typical assignments, appraisers do not test equipment to make sure it is in good working order. Regardless of the intensity of the inspection of the improvements, however, clear evidence of functional problems such as corroded water pipes that are clearly visible in the basement should be reported.

Substructure

To prepare a site for construction of the substructure, the land is first cleared and staked out, test borings are drilled to examine the condition of the soils, and the site is excavated to accommodate footings, the foundation floor, and underground utility lines. Once the basic elements of the substructure have been installed and the site has been graded, construction of the above-ground improvements can begin. All the above-grade improvements of a building rest on the solid base of the substructure. Typically a house will be constructed over a basement or a crawl space or on a concrete slab directly on the ground. The characteristics of each of the three types of foundations are outlined in Table 9.1.

Footings support a house's foundation and prevent excessive settlement or movement of the structure. Generally made of concrete poured into clean trenches or wood forms, footings can be arranged in several ways depending upon their function. Building codes and environmental conditions dictate the size and depth of footings required to support an intended load.

The foundation walls of a house, which are usually below grade or ground level, form an enclosure for basements and crawl spaces, and they support walls, floors, and other structural loads (see Figure 9.3). The least expensive and most popular types of foundations are made of poured concrete walls or concrete-and-cinder-block walls that rest on concrete footings. Foundations in older structures may be made of cut stone or stone and brick, which are more costly materials and require more skill to install. Treated timber is sometimes used, but these foundation walls do not meet building codes in certain areas.

Columns and posts of various materials provide the central support for the building's beams and superstructure. Older buildings can have wood posts, masonry posts, or wood beams, while many newer structures are built with steel columns and I-beams. In a pier-and-beam foundation, piers (posts) resting on footings support beams or girders, which in turn support the superstructure. Many building codes prohibit the use of pier-and-beam

substructure. A building's entire foundational structure, which is below grade, or ground, and provides a support base or footings on which the superstructure rests.

footings. The supporting parts of a foundation that prevent excessive settlement or movement by distributing building loads directly to the soil.

slab. Any broad, flat, relatively thin piece of wood, stone, or other solid material; often used to describe a floor or foundation of concrete, either on the ground or supported above it.

Table 9.1   Comparison of Foundation Types

Type of Foundation	Structural Characteristics	Functional Advantages	Functional Disadvantages
Slab	Slab-on-ground foundations are either permanent foundations built on footings or floating foundations used on unstable soil or in areas with poor drainage. Floating slab-on-ground foundations are also called *mat or raft foundations or monolithic slabs.* They are made of concrete slabs heavily reinforced with steel so that the entire foundation acts as a unit to help prevent major cracking.	A slab-on-ground foundation is the most economical type of foundation and eliminates the need for first-floor framing. It is also suitable for mass production in tract or prefabricated housing and in areas with a high ground water table, where basements are unsuitable.	Without heating coils, slab-on-ground foundations can be cold. In extremely cold regions of the country, they may be regarded as underimprovements. Furthermore, the mechanical systems in buildings with slab-on-ground foundations must be placed in the walls, the attic, or in separate rooms. Flooding can also be a problem if there are no drain tiles around the perimeter of the foundation, if the floor has an inadequate pitch, or if the finish grade of the site does not slope from the slab.
Crawl space	Footings support foundation walls, columns, and other framing members built over a crawl space. The floor of the crawl space may be sand, gravel, concrete, or undisturbed soil. **Use of space:** A crawl space can provide storage space for a home's mechanical systems and ductwork. **Access to space:** Interior or exterior hatches provide access to a crawl space.	If a crawl space foundation is used, the building's systems need not be put on the ground floor. Ductwork can be run below the floor framing, which reduces costs. In a crawl space foundation, the ground floor is elevated above the exterior ground line and foundation walls are shorter, so costs are lower.	Crawl spaces may be damp or hold standing water, and inspection of physical problems in crawl spaces can be difficult. Modern crawlspaces may be covered with plastic sheeting to help prevent vapor transmission or they may even be air-conditioned in humid climates to prevent condensation.
Basement	Basements are similar to crawl spaces, but they are usually seven to eight feet deep. The basement floor is constructed like a slab. **Use of space:** An unfinished basement provides storage space like a crawl space. A finished basement can also provide extra living area, if effectively waterproofed and ventilated. Basements can also be used for recreation and laundry rooms. **Access to space:** A basement may have an interior stairway to the living area as well as exterior access, i.e., a walkout basement.	Basements provide extra living area at a minimum cost.	Basements are more costly than crawl spaces and are not required in many warmer climates. A basement in the Deep South or the West might well constitute an overimprovement; the cost of this feature will probably not be recaptured when the property is resold.

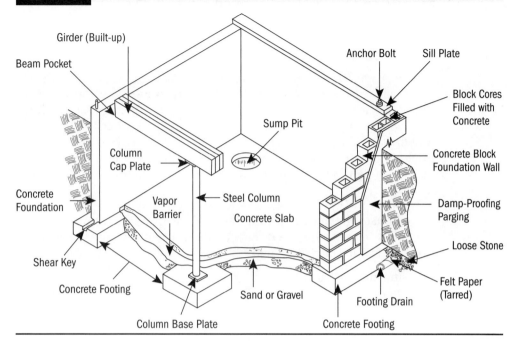

Table 9.2   Comparison of Types of Footings

Type of Footing	Construction Characteristics	Functional Characteristics
Wall footing	Concrete grade beam running around the perimeter of the site, resting on undisturbed earth below the frost line, and extending out from both sides of the foundation walls it supports. (The drain tile, a specially designed pipe laid outside the wall footings, drains ground water to a storm sewer, dry well, or sump.)	Distributes the load of the walls over the subgrade.
Column footing or spread footing	Generally square slabs of concrete, though if an extra load is to be supported the concrete may be reinforced with steel rods or mesh.	Supports vertical columns and posts in the superstructure as well as fireplaces, furnaces, and chimneys.
Stepped footing	Standard concrete footings connected at different heights.	Supports structures on lots that slope.
Spread footing or extended footing	Concrete slabs extending out further than normal from beneath the foundation walls they support.	Supports structures on lots where the soil has poor load-bearing capacity.

foundations in conventional homes. Nevertheless, pier-and-beam foundations are often used for resort houses and for outbuildings and porches because this type of construction is relatively inexpensive.

Superstructure

The term *superstructure* refers to the frame of the building and all elements of the exterior structure. The structural frame is the load-bearing skeleton of a building. Floors and ceilings, exterior and interior walls, and the roof are all attached to the frame, which can be constructed out of wood, masonry, or layers of both materials. Alternative framing materials such as foam-core panels, light-gauge steel framing, and welded-wire sandwich panels may become more attractive when wood prices rise.

Framing

Most houses in the United States are built with wood framing, including many homes with brick veneer siding. The most common types of wooden frame construction are

- Platform construction
- Balloon framing
- Plank-and-beam framing

When platform construction is used, one story of a dwelling is constructed at a time so that the ceiling of each completed level serves as the platform for the next. Studs are cut at the ceiling height of the first story, horizontal plates are laid on top of these studs, and more studs are cut for the second story. With this method of construction, walls and partitions can be preassembled and tilted up into position. Also, special framing can be used for doors and windows.

Although it is less common today than platform construction, balloon framing was often used in the past to construct multistory buildings with brick, stone, or stucco veneer. The long studs running from the top of the foundation wall to the roof line, which distinguish balloon framing from platform construction, provide more stability in upper floors. In balloon-frame construction, the entire wall frame acts a single unit; in contrast, one single-story unit of platform construction sits on top of another independent unit and can slide from side to side in extreme conditions. Named for its lightness, balloon framing is rarely used today because the long studs needed are expensive and the framing method has poor fire resistance.

superstructure. The portion of a building that is above grade.

framing. A system of joining structural members that provides lateral, longitudinal, transverse, and vertical support for a building.

platform construction. A type of construction in which one story of a structure is constructed at a time and each story serves as a platform for the next. Studs, which are the vertical framing members, are cut at the ceiling height of the first story, then horizontal plates are laid on top, and more studs are cut for the second story.

balloon frame. In construction, a type of framing in which the studs extend from the foundation sill plate to the roof. The second floor is supported by a horizontal ribbon or ledger board and joists that are nailed to the studs.

plank-and-beam framing. A type of construction in which heavier structural members are spaced farther apart than in other framing systems and supporting posts, roof beams, and the roof deck are left exposed as part of the interior decor.

Figure 9.4   **Platform Construction**

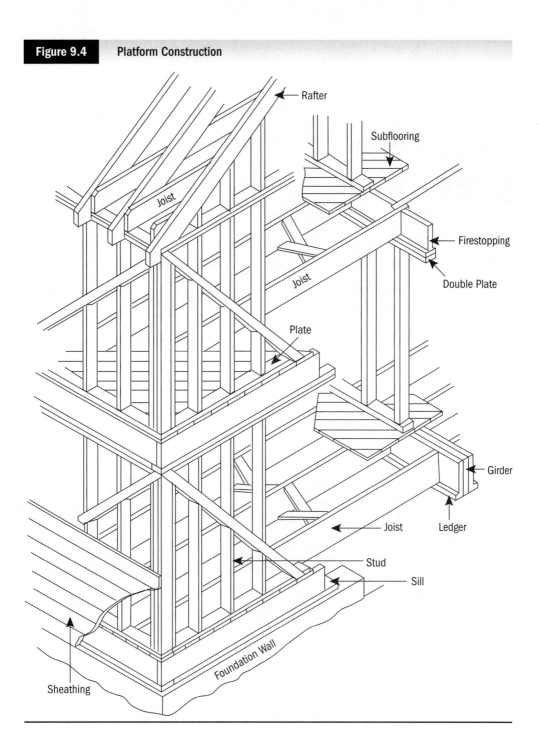

Originally used in colonial-era houses and barns, plank-and-beam framing regained popularity in the mid-1970s when architects began to incorporate exposed-beam ceilings into house designs. The framing members used in plank-and-beam framing are much larger and heavier and are spaced farther apart than those used in other framing systems. The wood beams can be up to eight feet apart and are supported on posts and exterior walls.

Figure 9.5   Plank-and-Beam Framing

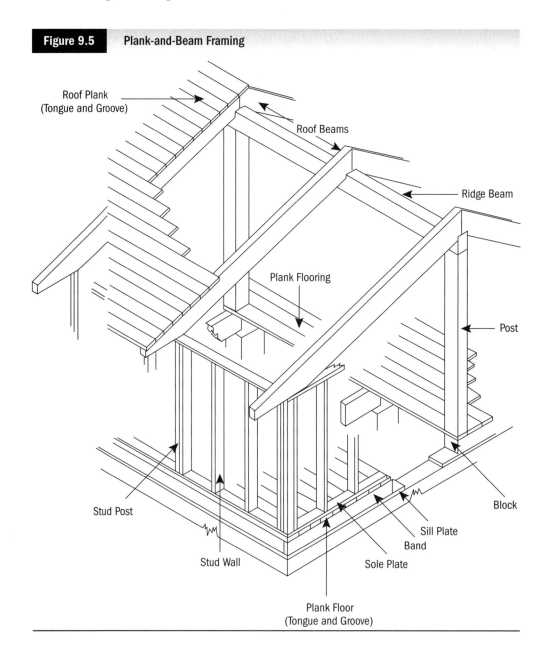

The use of light steel in house frames is growing for a variety of reasons, primarily because the price of steel is less volatile than the price of wood and because steel framing systems can be more efficiently assembled by properly trained contractors than wood-frame structures. In coastal areas prone to hurricanes and in hot climates, steel framing is more common because it has better wind and termite resistance. Another perceived advantage is the natural fire resistance of steel structural members; steel does not provide fuel for fire to spread. It is common to see homes with wood structural framing and steel-studded interior non-bearing walls. Homes framed entirely of steel are relatively uncommon.

Some modern buildings are constructed with solid masonry exterior walls, which act as part of the structural framing system. These walls are often two layers (wythes) thick or have a face layer backed by masonry of another material with the two layers joined by metal wall ties or masonry headers. Other buildings are constructed with hollow masonry walls filled with insulation material and interior framing of steel beams or reinforced concrete. Because of their greater weight, masonry walls require larger footings than wood-frame walls.

Roof Construction

A roof frame must be able to support its own weight as well as that of finish materials. It must also be able to withstand the forces applied by snow, ice, seismic activity, wind, and rain, which will vary by region. Different types of roofs require different types of framing, which can usually be inspected from inside a house's attic. Low-slope roofs (sometimes called flat roofs) require horizontal joists supported by the building's exterior walls and interior load-bearing elements. Angled roofs (such as gable, gambrel, and shed roofs) employ rafters that slope up from the joists at the desired pitch of the roof. As an alternative to a traditional roof frame of joists and rafters, triangular trusses can be used for additional support. Because trusses do not require interior, load-bearing walls, they increase flexibility in building design. Trusses are generally engineered prefabricated components and should not be field-modified.

Building Materials

After the framing of a structure is complete, construction of the building's skin can begin. This includes the exterior walls, doors and windows, and the roof covering. Once the exterior surfaces of the house have been covered, finish work on the interior walls, ceilings, floors, and trim can begin.

Exterior Wall Surfaces

The most visible portion of a house's skin, the exterior wall siding, is attached to a layer of wall sheathing made of wood, plywood, insulated board, or gypsum. The sheathing is nailed directly to the studs

Figure 9.6 Types of Roofs

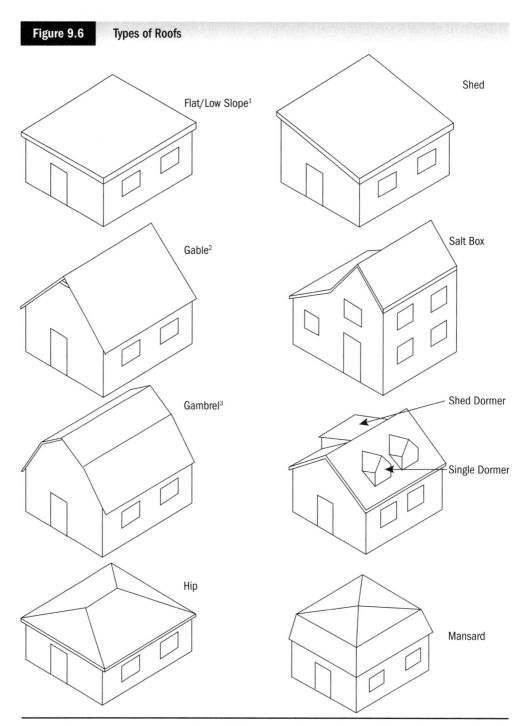

Flat/Low Slope[1]

Shed

Gable[2]

Salt Box

Gambrel[3]

Shed Dormer

Single Dormer

Hip

Mansard

1. Used in industrial and commercial buildings, but less often in houses.
2. The common, sloped roof with the planes of the roof forming a triangle with the ceiling.
3. Popular for barns and for Cape Ann and Dutch colonial houses. (Cape Ann is a variant of Cape Cod architecture and is distinguished by its roof. Whereas Cape Cod homes are gable-roofed, Cape Ann homes are gambrel-roofed.)

and may require additional bracing in the corners. Sheathing materials naturally provide some insulation, and roll-out material made of felt paper or house wrap is applied over the sheathing to provide waterproofing. Flashing is strip metal of tin or copper nailed to the top and bottom of the sheathing where it meets the foundation and roof. Flashing is applied wherever dissimilar materials meet or wall penetrations exist because there is an increased risk of leakage.

The finish material on the exterior of the walls comes in various patterns and materials. Exterior walls of solid brick, stone, or concrete block do not require additional siding but may have siding for design or aesthetic reasons.

Roof Covering

Like exterior walls, the roof of a home comprises a layer of finish material over layers of sheathing and sheathing paper with flashing at areas prone to leakage. The exterior roof covering prevents moisture from entering the building, and the metal flashing adds further protection where roof slopes intersect and wherever projections extend through the roof.

Sheathing may be made of wood boards, oriented strand board or plywood panels, or sheet material. In most parts of the United States, the sheathing is covered with composition asphalt shingles, which are available in various weights and styles. Other common roof coverings are shingles or shakes made of wood (usually cedar), slate, metal, and tile. Flat roofs are often covered with a final coat of hot asphalt or roofing compound applied directly to the sheathing paper for waterproofing. A layer of light-colored gravel or stone is applied on top to reflect sunlight. Other roofs may be constructed of fiberglass, corrugated metal or standing-seam metal panels, or clay, plastic, rubber, or metal tile.

Most roof coverings must be replaced several times during a building's life. An appraiser must consider the overall condition of the roof to estimate its remaining useful life. Most conventional residential roofing materials are designed for a service life of approximately 20 years.

Doors

The quality of a dwelling's doors generally corresponds to the overall quality of construction. Exterior doors are typically made of solid wood, metal, fiberglass, or glass, while interior

---

Horizontal Siding Patterns

- Bevels or clapboards made of wood, particle board, aluminum, vinyl, hardboard (i.e., concrete and fiber), steel, or other materials.
- Tongue-and-groove lap boards
- Natural wood surface of a log cabin's timber frame
- Shiplap/Dolly Varden siding (i.e., beveled wood siding that is rabbeted along the bottom edge)

Other Types of Siding

- Wood, leftover asbestos or asbestos-cement, or asphalt shingles (wood or wood-composite siding must be stained, sealed, or painted.)
- Stucco siding—traditional, single-coat, or synthetic stucco/Exterior Insulating and Finish System (EIFS)
- Masonry veneer
- Panels, glass block, glazed tile, plastic, or other materials

Types of Doors

- Panel doors
- Flush doors
- Combination doors
- Batten doors
- Dutch doors
- Sliding glass doors
- Bifold doors
- French doors
- Bypass doors
- Pocket doors

doors are generally hollow-core wood or composition doors. Older houses may have solid wood interior doors. Hollow exterior doors usually indicate poor-quality construction and such components may be deficiencies in the property.

Windows

Like doors, windows give an appraiser an indication of the overall construction quality of a house. Windows have a major impact on a structure's energy efficiency so proper installation is increasingly important. Historically window frames have been made from wood, which is easy to work with and has good insulating properties, though plastic, aluminum, and steel frames are also popular. Most modern homes will be equipped with solid vinyl or vinyl-clad windows.

An appraiser must be able to identify window type, material, and manufacture as well as energy-saving features, such as low-emissivity (low-e) insulated glass, multiple glazing, and storm sashes. Smaller windows and windows placed high off the floor are more energy-efficient and increase security. Larger windows enhance view amenities, but this advantage should be balanced against the higher cost of proper installation and any reduced structural resistance to wind loads (e.g., wind storms).

Floor Coverings

The material used to cover a house's floors can vary widely, depending largely on budget and on the function of various rooms within the house. In living areas, expensive hardwood floors were once standard in many areas, while soft woods are more common today in low-cost houses. Ceramic tile is popular for bathrooms and other potentially wet areas such as kitchens and laundry rooms. Less expensive floor coverings commonly found in kitchens, laundry, baths, foyers, and mud rooms (i.e., wet areas) include rolled linoleum or no-wax vinyl flooring.

To install wall-to-wall carpeting, strips of wood are attached directly to the subflooring or to a suitable underlayment material with special adhesives. Carpeting can be installed over subflooring with the necessary padding. Ceramic tile in bathrooms can be laid in a bed of plaster or attached with a special adhesive to the subflooring. The different types of kitchen flooring are all attached with adhesives.

Concrete slabs can be stained, painted, or covered with other materials. Terrazzo flooring is made of colored marble chips mixed into cement that is ground to a smooth surface after it is laid. In certain special areas, such as hearths, mud rooms, and entry halls, a material with an irregular surface, such as slate, brick, or stone, can be used as flooring to avoid slipperiness when wet. A properly installed and well-maintained floor covering can help protect the foundation from water-related problems in areas commonly exposed to water.

subfloor. A floor that is laid on top of the floor joists and underneath the finish floor.

Figure 9.7   Types of Windows

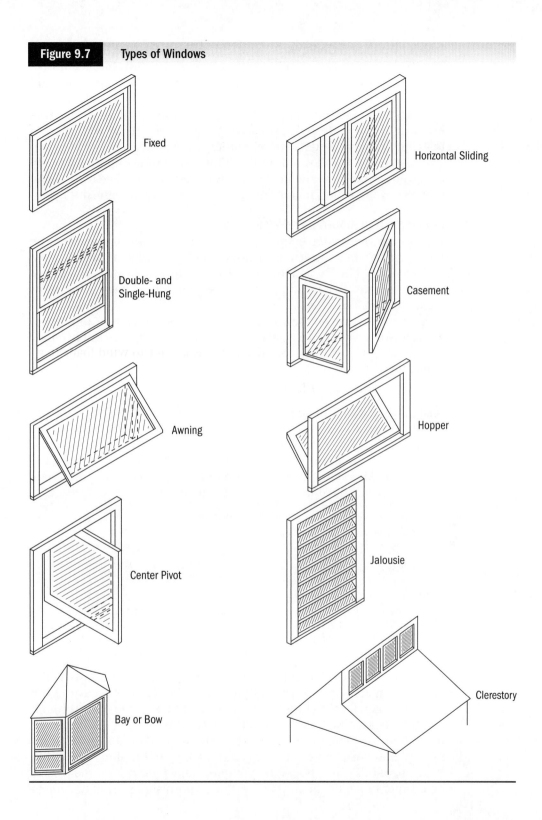

Fixed

Horizontal Sliding

Double- and Single-Hung

Casement

Awning

Hopper

Center Pivot

Jalousie

Bay or Bow

Clerestory

Interior Walls and Ceilings

The finishes of walls and ceilings should provide a durable, decorative cover that is waterproof in areas subject to moisture like bathrooms and basements. Today, most interior walls are made of wood studs covered with drywall material. Plaster is used less frequently than it once was because of the material's expense, the need for skilled workmen to install it properly, and its susceptibility to cracking.

Gypsum board and wood composition materials are applied directly onto studs or masonry, while ceramic wall tiles are installed in the same manner as floor tiles, using cement plaster or special adhesives.

Moldings, Baseboards, and Wainscoting

Various interior design elements that can be built into a house include moldings, niches, and trim around doors, windows, baseboards, and ceilings. The thicker the wood and more intricate the pattern, the more expensive moldings are. Plastic moldings have become an inexpensive alternative.

A different finish on the lower half of a wall is known as wainscoting. A chair rail, designed to protect the wall from being marred by chair backs, can serve as the upper cap of the wainscot.

Insulation and Ventilation

Insulation helps homeowners economize on fuel and provides comfort in both warm and cold climates. It also reduces noise and impedes the spread of fire. Newer homes are generally more energy efficient than similar older buildings, though the heavy building materials used before the 1940s provided some insulation. Special insulating materials can usually be added to older homes to increase energy efficiency.

Insulating Materials

Type of Insulation	Location in Home
Loose-fill	Structural cavities (e.g., attic, in hollow walls)
Flexible (batt or blanket)	Where loose-fill insulation is impractical or where attached foil or paper facing is desired as a vapor barrier
Rigid	Often as part of walls
Reflective	Same as rigid insulation except air space is needed for foil to reflect radiated heat
Foamed-in-place	In wall cavities as well as around pipes, ductwork, furnaces, water heaters, etc.

The R value of insulation materials is a quantitative measure of the ability of insulation to resist the flow of heat. The R value measures the British thermal units (Btus) that are transmitted in one hour through one thickness of the insulation. The higher the R value, the better the insulation. Local building codes establish standard minimum R values for a region based on the climate and the type of building. Atypically thick insulation in a house (sometimes called *superinsulation*) may be a superadequacy in certain markets. Appraisers should be able to judge if the combination of insulation, ventilation, and heating and air-conditioning systems meets local standards.

Ventilation (usually with fans or holes) is needed to reduce heat in enclosed spaces such as attics and spaces behind walls and to prevent condensation of water in enclosed spaces. Moisture is the great enemy of building materials, particularly wood; prolonged exposure to moisture promotes rot, mold,[1] and decay. Ventilation holes should be covered with screens to keep out vermin.

The measures a homeowner takes to insulate and ventilate a house should complement the capacity of the building's heating and air-conditioning systems to maintain a comfortable living environment within the structure. The capacity of a fully modernized heating system can be diminished if a house is poorly insulated, allowing heat to escape. On the other hand, in some cases superadequate insulation can trap harmful, naturally occurring gases such as radon within a house.[2]

> **R value.** A standard for measuring the ability of an insulation material to resist the flow of heat. R value is derived by measuring the British thermal units (Btus) transmitted in one hour through the thickness of the insulation. The higher the R value, the more effective the insulation.

Figure 9.8	Ventilation

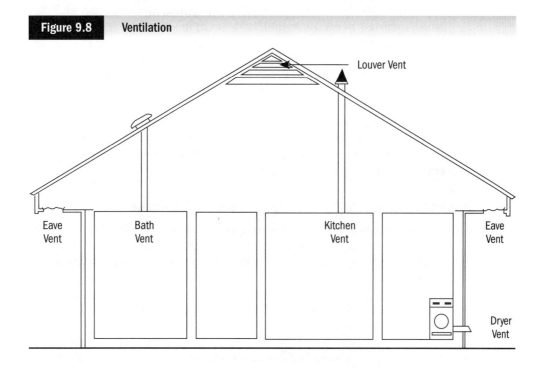

Eave Vent

Bath Vent

Kitchen Vent

Eave Vent

Louver Vent

Dryer Vent

---

1. In addition to moisture, mold needs an adequate temperature and some sort of organic material to grow. See Michael V. Sanders, "Mold: What Appraisers Should Know," *Valuation Insights & Perspectives* (Third Quarter 2005): 42–43.

2. Radon is a colorless and odorless radioactive gas linked to lung cancer. Cracks in foundations and basement walls and dirt crawlspaces are the most likely ways for radon to enter a living area. The only way to detect the presence of radon is to test for it, which is beyond the scope of the inspection in most or all appraisals. For more information on radon, see *A Citizen's Guide to Radon* (Washington, D.C.: U.S. Environmental Protection Agency, revised September 2005).

asbestos-containing materials (ACMs). Any material or product containing more than 1% asbestos.

Exposure to certain insulating materials can cause health hazards for building occupants. Appraisers should be able to recognize the possible presence of asbestos and urea-formaldehyde foam insulation and know what their reporting responsibilities are in a particular assignment.

Asbestos is a nonflammable, natural mineral substance that separates into fibers. Asbestos-containing materials (ACMs) were widely used in structures built between 1945 and 1978 as thermal and acoustical insulation, or for fireproofing and soundproofing. Other ACMs were used in siding and roofing shingles. Asbestos fibers pose a threat to human health when they are distributed in the air. The potential of any ACM to release fibers depends on its degree of friability—i.e., how easily it is crumbled or pulverized—and if it found in a location where it will be disturbed. Dry, sprayed-on thermal insulation over structural steel is highly friable. Densely packed, nonfibrous ACMs such as vinyl asbestos floor covering and pipe insulation are not considered friable under normal conditions. Nevertheless, these materials will become friable if they are broken, sawed, or drilled.

In April 1982 the Consumer Product Safety Commission (CPSC) banned the use of urea-formaldehyde foam insulation in residences and schools. The ban resulted from the commission's investigation of the effects of formaldehyde gas, which can be released from the insulation at very high levels, especially immediately after installation. The ban took effect in August 1982 and was lifted in April 1983 by a federal court of appeals, which held that the health risks had not been proven. The ban was not retroactive, so it did not affect the approximately 500,000 homes built between around 1970 and 1982 that already had urea-formaldehyde foam insulation, but use of the material in residential construction has diminished greatly.

Protection Against Decay and Insect Damage

All wood is susceptible to decay and insect damage. Wood decays when it is continually exposed to moisture and water, which enable destructive organisms to propagate on or beneath its surface. The most common of these organisms are aerobic fungi, which thrive in a warm environment when moisture and oxygen combine with a cellulose material. Sapwood from all wood species is prone to decay; heartwood may have low to very high susceptibility to decay depending on its species.

Insects damage wood more rapidly and more visibly than fungi. Several species of insects damage wood, but subterranean, dampwood, and drywood termites are by far the most destructive. Subterranean termites are very adaptable and found throughout the United States. They live in colonies in moist soil and infest both damp and dry wood. Dampwood and drywood termites are only found in certain geographic areas. Drywood termites establish colonies in wood and are extremely difficult to eradicate.

Appraisers and Hazardous Substances

Most appraisers do not have specialized knowledge of hazardous substances, nor are they typically expected to be experts in the detection and remediation of environmental contamination. The role and responsibility of the appraiser in detecting or measuring environmental substances affecting a property are addressed in Guide Note 6 to the Standards of Professional Appraisal Practice of the Appraisal Institute. The guide note takes its direction from the Competency Rule of the Uniform Standards of Professional Appraisal Practice, which requires that the appraiser either

· Properly identify the problem to be addressed and have the knowledge and experience to complete the assignment competently

or

· Disclose the appraiser's lack of knowledge and/or experience to the client before accepting the assignment, take all steps necessary or appropriate to complete the assignment competently, and describe the lack of knowledge and/or experience and the steps taken to complete the assignment competently in the report

If no hazardous substances are known or suspected to be present, an appraiser can proceed with an appraisal with a standard disclaimer or limiting condition stating that the opinion of market value was developed with the assumption that hazardous substances do not exist. The Uniform Residential Appraisal Report form includes such a statement:

> The appraiser has noted in this appraisal report any adverse conditions (such as needed repairs, deterioration, the presence of hazardous wastes, toxic substances, etc.) observed during the inspection of the subject property or that he or she became aware of during the research involved in performing this appraisal. Unless otherwise stated in this appraisal report, the appraiser has no knowledge of any hidden or unapparent physical deficiencies or adverse conditions of the property (such as, but not limited to, needed repairs, deterioration, the presence of hazardous wastes, toxic substances, adverse environmental conditions, etc.) that would make the property less valuable, and has assumed that there are no such conditions and makes no guarantees or warranties, expressed or implied. The appraiser will not be responsible for any such conditions that do exist or for any engineering or testing that might be required to discover whether such conditions exist. Because the appraiser is not an expert in the field of environmental hazards, this appraisal report must not be considered as an environmental assessment of the property.

A similar statement regarding adverse conditions affecting value appears in the Appraiser's Certification portion on the next page of the URAR form.

If hazardous substances are suspected, the appraisal may be completed with the extraordinary assumption that there are no hazardous substances affecting the property's value. If hazardous substances are known to be present on the subject property, the appraiser and client may agree that it would be useful to complete the assignment under the hypothetical condition that the contamination is not present. In most cases in which hazardous substances are known to be present, the appraiser and client will need to consult with an environmental professional.

The presence of asbestos-containing materials, radon, mold, or other environmental contaminants is generally perceived as a detriment to value. The market tends to penalize contaminated properties more when the nature of a suspected contaminant's effect is first brought to light and captures headlines. Over time, as the dangers associated with substances like radon and mold are better understood and the effectiveness of remediation efforts improves, the severity of the influence of those substances on value tends to decrease.

For further investigation, see Richard J. Roddewig, ed. *Valuing Contaminated Properties: An Appraisal Institute Anthology* (Chicago: Appraisal Institute, 2002) and the "Environment and the Appraiser" column, which appears periodically in *The Appraisal Journal*.

Protecting Improvements from Decay and Insect Damage

· The ground can be sloped away from the building foundation to provide good drainage.
· Vapor barriers may be installed on the interior sides of exposed walls.
· The soil in crawl spaces can be covered with polyethylene.
· Flashing should be maintained.
· Gutters, downspouts, and splash blocks can be used to carry water away from the foundation walls.
· Poured concrete foundation walls may be laid.
· Masonry foundations can be capped with concrete.
· Wood and soil can be treated with pesticides.
· Buildings can be constructed of dry, naturally durable woods.
· Metal termite shields may be installed.
· Regular maintenance inspections can be conducted.

Equipment and Mechanical Systems

A house's mechanical systems must be in good working order for the building to provide adequate shelter and comfort for its inhabitants and for the property to realize its full market value. A house may contain many different types of mechanical systems and equipment, but the three essential systems in a modern residence are

1. Plumbing
2. Heating and air-conditioning
3. Electrical system

Plumbing

The plumbing system consists of piping, which is mostly covered or hidden, and fixtures and equipment, which are visible. The appraiser should report signs of defects or needed repairs in the plumbing system.

Much of the cost of a plumbing system is spent on piping. The quality of the materials used, the way the pipes are installed, and the ease with which they can be serviced are significant factors in considering the durability of piping and the cost of maintenance. A high-quality piping system can last for the life of the structure. However, many homes have pipes that will not last.

Types of Piping

Material	Use
Copper, galvanized steel, or brass	Water pipes
Cast iron	Waste lines
Plastic (PB, PE, PVC, CPVC)	Waste (PVC, ABS), vent, and water lines (PB, CPVC for hot water lines; PB, PE, PVC, CPVC for cold water lines)
Lead	Waste water pipes only
Black steel	Fuel gas

Good-quality bathroom fixtures are made of cast iron covered with acid-resistant vitreous enamel. Fiberglass and other materials are also used. Kitchen sinks may be made of stainless steel, enameled steel, or cast iron that is covered with acid-resistant enamel or solid surface countertops. Some homes have specialized plumbing fixtures such as laundry tubs and wet bars.

Hot Water System

A typical hot water system receives its heat from a boiler or a self-standing water heater powered by electricity, gas, or oil. The size of the hot water tank needed in a residence is determined by the number of inhabitants and their water-using habits as well as the recovery rate of the unit. Newer technology has been developed allowing smaller units to heat water more quickly and efficiently. These are often called *tankless* or *point-of-use water heaters*. Some homes have solar heating components for the hot water supply.

Types of Plumbing Fixtures

Bathrooms	Lavatories or washbasins
	Bathtubs
	Showers
	Toilets or water closets
	Bidets
	Urinals
Kitchens	Single or double sinks installed in countertops or cabinetry
	Garbage disposals
	Dishwashers
	Instant hot water units
Fittings	Faucets
	Spigots
	Drains
	Shower heads
	Spray hoses
	Escutcheons

Figure 9.9   Plumbing

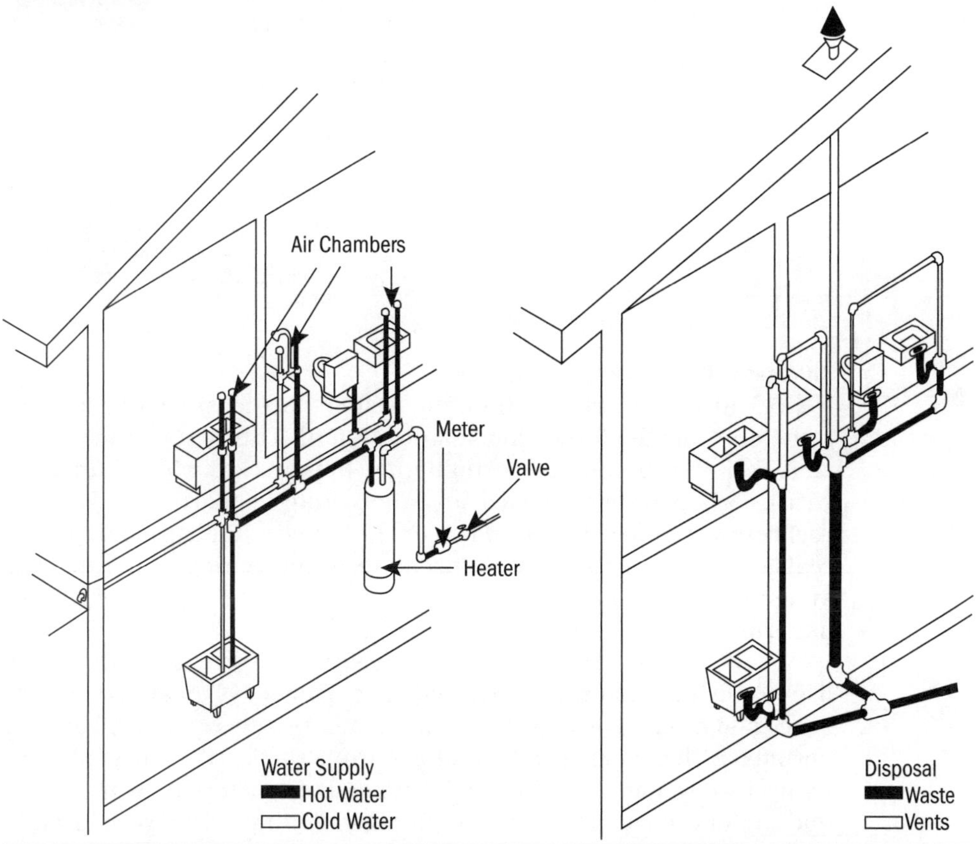

Air Chambers

Meter

Valve

Heater

Water Supply
■■■ Hot Water
☐ Cold Water

Disposal
■■■ Waste
☐ Vents

Heating Systems

Most common heating systems are classified as

- Forced air heating
- Hot water heating
- Steam heating
- Unit heating

The amount of heat a system can produce is rated in British thermal units. The Btu requirement for a heating plant depends on the cubic content, exposure, design, and insulation level of the structure to be heated as well as local market considerations.

Types of Heating Systems

Transmission Medium	Fuel	Fixtures/Equipment
Forced air	Natural gas, fuel oil, coal, or electricity	Furnace or heat pump, air ducts (Thermostats, filters, humidifiers, air cleaners, and air purification devices are common equipment.)
Hot water	Natural gas, fuel oil, coal, or electricity	Cast-iron or steel boiler, pump/circulator, piping, radiators or radiant piping in floors or ceilings
Steam	Natural gas, fuel oil, or coal	Boiler, piping, radiators (Many states require licenses for certain classes of steam boilers. Appraisers must be familiar with boiler license laws.)
Unit	Electricity, natural gas	Wall heater, baseboard units, heating units installed in air-conditioning ducts. (Electric radiant heaters can be installed in floors or ceilings with individual room thermostats.)

Differences Between Heating Systems

Nearly all central air-conditioning systems are designed to use the same ducts as the forced air heating system. This is not always possible, however, because air-conditioning requires larger ducts. In these cases, add-on systems ducted separately from heat are used. Heating registers are generally placed low on the walls, while air-conditioning registers should be placed higher up or in the ceiling. Older heating systems relied on gravity and had large ducts and simple distribution patterns for circulation.

A new technology called *high velocity mini-duct air distribution* uses a ring of narrow ducts around the perimeter of an attic or crawl-space and a series of small, two-inch tubular ducts radiating from the perimeter. Heated air can be pumped from above, while cool air will naturally circulate down through the small diameter ductwork. Mini-duct systems do not require extensive installation of ductwork in walls and floors, so they can be a cost-effective alternative to retrofitting an older home with traditional HVAC ductwork.

Figure 9.10   Heating Systems

Extended Plenum System

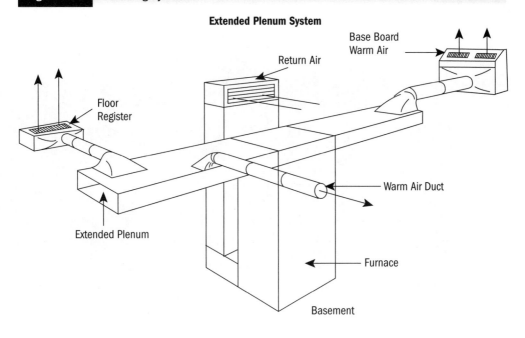

Perimeter Loop Warm Air System

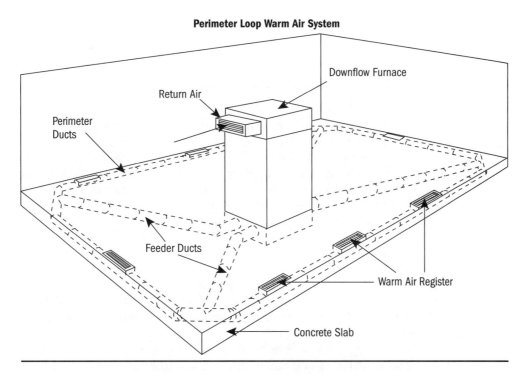

Figure 9.10 Heating Systems *(continued)*

Gravity Hot Air System

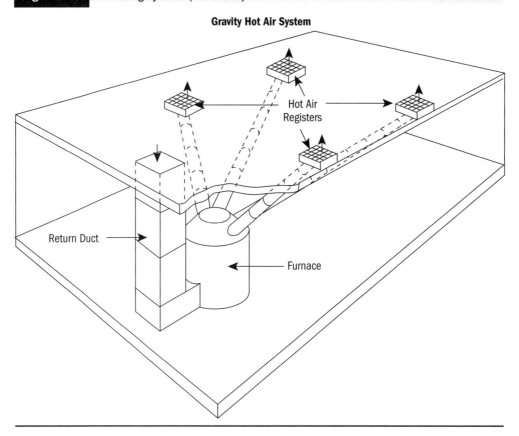

A distinction is made between radiant hot water heating and conventional convection heating. In a conventional system, room air is warmed as it passes over the heated metal of a radiator and is then circulated in an area of colder air—i.e., through convection. Radiant heating depends on heat being transferred directly from heating elements into the air and objects in the room, and it is produced by narrow hot water pipes that are embedded in floors, walls, or ceilings.

A steam system uses radiators to transfer heat into rooms and objects by radiation and convection. The common, cast-iron radiator successfully accomplishes this dual process. Steam heating systems are generally only found in older homes. Zone control is now widely used to meet various heating needs in different parts of a building. The amount of heat available for distribution is controlled by separate temperature controls.

Unit or location-specific heating systems may make use of radiant floors, walls, or ceilings with electric panels or cables under the surface or infrared units. An electrical resistance system is the least expensive system to install because it does not require a furnace, furnace room, ducting, flue, or plumbing. However, it does require much more electrical service than would otherwise be needed and a great deal of wiring to each unit in the building. Electrical wall heaters are common in bathrooms, and electric baseboard heaters are common in homes built in the 1970s. Other location-specific heaters include gas wall or floor furnaces and unit heaters.

The automatic regulation of a heating system contributes to its operating efficiency. A multiple-zone system with separate thermostats is more efficient than a single-zone system with one thermostat. Complex systems provide individual temperature controls for each room. Programmable thermostats can also adjust the temperature according to a schedule, automatically cooling the house while the occupants are out (at work or school) and then heating the house to a comfortable temperature when the occupants are scheduled to return.

Houses built before central air-conditioning systems were common often relied on the whole house plenum concept–i.e., heating and cooling traveled throughout the whole house via free air movement. Doors raised an inch or so above the floor and transom windows above doors allow air to move in and out of a room even with the door closed. Replacement flooring in an older house that eliminates the gaps underneath doors can cause temperature disparities between rooms and hallways because the original airflow is disrupted. The placement of a thermostat in a room that is colder or warmer than other areas in the house because of the impeded airflow can exacerbate the problem.

Fuels for Heating Systems

In certain areas and for certain types of buildings, a particular type of fuel may be more desirable than another. The heating systems of many buildings, however, do not use the most economical fuel. For example, during the natural gas shortage in the middle and late 1970s, a moratorium was declared on the use of natural gas, and buildings constructed then were equipped with heating systems that use other fuels. In a given area for a specific use, different fuels have significant advantages and disadvantages, which may occasionally change as the supply of and demand for different fuels change.

Characteristics of Various Fuel Types

- The burning of certain types of *coal* creates environmental problems.
- In spite of their high cost, *fuel oil* and *propane* remains popular because they are easy to transport and store. Many fuel oil tanks are found underground, which could have negative environmental ramifications.
- *Natural gas* is convenient because it is continuously delivered by pipelines, eliminating the need for storage tanks. In many parts of the country, gas is the most economical fuel.
- *Electric heat* is costly, except in a few areas with low-cost power.
- *Solar heating* systems, other alternative energy systems, and energy-efficient items are found in some houses. Residential appraisals reported on Fannie Mae/Freddie Mac forms must include a separate description and value estimate for these features.

Air-Conditioning and Ventilation System

In the past ducts, fans, and windows were used to reduce heat and to provide fresh air in most buildings. Ducts and fans are still used in many buildings. In certain parts of the western United States, where humidity remains low even during periods of high heat, some buildings are cooled with a simple system that blows air across wet excelsior or another water-absorbing material. Package units that apply this procedure are still manufactured for residential and commercial use. They consume less power and are less expensive than conventional air-conditioning but they are less efficient at cooling. These units are often called swamp coolers, but the correct name is evaporative cooler.

Air-conditioners range from small, portable units to units that provide tons of cooling capacity. The capacity of an air-conditioning unit is rated in tons of refrigeration. One ton of refrigeration equals 12,000 Btu per hour. An engineer's expertise is often necessary to determine whether a home has too much or too little air-conditioning for the climate. If an engineer is consulted, the appraisal report should disclose the assistance provided by the engineer and contain data to support the conclusion.

Electrical System

A well-designed electrical system should provide sufficient electrical service to power all the electrical equipment in the building. Sometimes a single electrical service supplies power to more than one building. Wall switches, receptacles, and lighting fixtures are also part of the electrical system.

Many houses have a single-phase, three-wire system that provides at least 120/240 volts and 100 amperes of electricity. Thirty-ampere systems are now obsolete and residences with 60 amperes of service normally sell for less than similar homes with greater electrical service. Service of 150, 200, 300, or 400 amperes is needed to power modern electrical appliances and air-conditioning so most newer homes will have service of at least 200 amperes.

Attachments, Garages, and Outbuildings

Certain building improvements are not included in the calculation of gross living area, yet those amenities can certainly add to the attractiveness and livability of a residence and thereby increase the market value of the property. In some parts of the country, homeowners expect that a typical house in their neighborhood would include a two-car garage. The absence of such a feature would affect the price a potential buyer would be willing to pay for such a property. An understanding of market standards is essential for judging the importance of ancillary improvements such as attachments, garages, and outbuildings.

Porches can be open (no screening), screened, or enclosed. A primary distinguishing feature of a porch is a permanent roof covering. A porch should not be confused with a patio, and appraisers should be consistent in their terminology. Terms such as *veranda* and *lanai* are sometimes used by builders and owners in certain locales to describe a porch. An appraiser should stick to the simple, basic description of a porch, i.e., a covered area with a floor that may have partial walls and may be screened. In contrast, a patio may be only a floor (a concrete

Types of Ancillary Improvements

Ground attachments	Porches
	Patios
	Decks
	Breezeways
Wall attachments	Balconies
	Exterior stairwells
	Window wells
	Oriel windows
	Bay windows
	Window attachments such as awnings and shutters
Roof attachments	Cupolas
	Skylights
	Dormers
	Antennas
	Weather vanes
	Turrets
Vehicle storage	Garages
	Carports
Outbuildings	Greenhouses
	Garden sheds
	Carriage houses
	Barns
	Cabanas
	Boat houses
	Docks
	Recreational facilities
	Storage buildings

slab without a foundation, brick, flagstone, or other surface). Patios may be screened (similar to screening over a pool) but they are still open to the elements. There is a significant difference in the function and utility of a porch (i.e., a covered area) and a patio. Decks are usually made of wood and supported on footings, and they can be located at ground level or raised above the ground. Decks can have functionality similar to either porches or patios, depending on whether they have a roof.

Appraisers should be able to judge whether the addition of amenities such as oriel and bay windows or skylights and dormers contribute more to value than their cost. On the other hand, attachments that add individual character such as weather vanes and turrets should not make a property incompatible with community standards. Such nonessential improvements are more common in high-priced residential markets.

In addition to vehicle storage, garages can provide space for workshops, laundry rooms, and general storage. The measurement of space in an attached garage can be complicated by the fact that the garage shares walls with living space, but the area of the living space should include the wall that divides the living area from the garage. The dividing wall should never be included in the calculation of the garage area.

Detached garages have been less popular in certain areas of the country, although a covered breezeway between the garage and house alleviates some of the inconvenience of a detached garage. However, a trend in new construction toward houses with detached garages and access from alleyways has been noted in some areas. These "new urbanism" developments replicate the character of mixed-use organic growth.

Some nonessential improvements such as various types of outbuildings may not have been constructed at the same time as the main structure. Appraisers should pay attention to differences in the quality of construction of different building components. Also, amenities such as cupolas, turrets, and balconies require special construction skills, which may be scarce or cost more in certain markets.

Site Improvements and Special Features

Site improvements not included in the site valuation can be considered part of the building improvements. In form reports, some of these items are covered in the site section while others are dealt with in the description of improvements. A distinction is made between improvements to a site such as grading, drainage, and utility installation, and improvements on a site.

Landscaping modifies the natural site to achieve a functional or decorative effect. Landscaping often improves the overall appearance of a property and enhances its value, but the desirability of plants is a matter of individual taste. The more elaborate the garden, the more care it will require. The value enhancement produced by good landscaping depends on the character and standards of the neighborhood.

Some trees and shrubs are considered part of the raw land, not site improvements. An appraiser considers the maturity, health, and overall appearance of trees and notes any risk of damage that might result from dead trees or branches falling on or striking the residence in a storm. Trees and shrubs are planted for practical as well as aesthetic reasons. Deciduous trees are best placed on the western side of a property, where they will provide shade from the hot afternoon sun in the summer but allow the sun's warmth to shine through in the winter. Conifers planted on the northern side of a house can act as windbreaks.

Lighting and sprinkler systems can contribute to the residents' enjoyment of an outdoor area. Special yard improvements such as statuary, barbecues, planters, fountains, and birdbaths tend to give a residence an individual character. However, if these improvements seem to be in poor taste given the standards of the neighborhood, they may discourage buyers and affect property value adversely.

Walls and fences of stone, wood, or metal often form barriers around the perimeter of a lot. The cost and condition of walls and fences can vary greatly, and the structures provide varying degrees of privacy, decoration, and security. Appraisers should recognize that the walls and fences of the subject property may encroach on abutting properties and vice versa.

Improvements *on* a Site

· Landscaping
· Walls and fences
· Walks
· Driveways and parking areas
· Pools and ponds
· Water garden
· Waterfront improvements
· Recreational facilities

Walks provide access from the streets and from driveway and parking areas to the entrances of the house. Walks can be made of concrete, brick, stone, or patio blocks. They should provide convenient access and not become muddy when it rains.

Driveways and parking areas provide access from the street to the garage. They may be made of a variety of materials including gravel, stone, concrete, bricks, pavers, asphalt, or earth. The slope of a driveway should facilitate access, and both driveways and parking areas should be pitched to drain water away from the improvements or special engineered drainage should be provided. Parking areas must allow adequate space for a driver to turn around.

Pools may be heated or unheated and vary in size and quality. Pool construction, depth, equipment, and maintenance requirements will influence the value contributed by a pool. Since most above-ground pools are easy to move, they are usually considered personal property. All pools should be equipped with some form of child safety barrier system. The contributory value of a swimming pool varies considerably by geographic region and in specific neighborhoods. The comparables within the subject's market will reflect the probable value of a pool.

Any ponds and lakes near or on the property may be shallow or deep. Their shoreline features, construction, erosion, accretion, stocking, and manner of use should be considered. An appraiser should also note where water enters and leaves ponds and lakes and examine the potential for flooding.

Waterfront improvements include breakwaters, seawalls, piers, boat hoists, and beaches. An appraiser notes the condition, quality, and usefulness of these improvements and considers any riparian or littoral rights.

Recreational areas include terraces, tennis courts, bridle paths, golf courses, whirlpool baths, and even heliports and airplane hangars. These amenities should always be considered in light of the probable market for the subject property.

In addition to certain site improvements, appraisers must describe certain special features of the interior of a house such as built-in features, appliances, and fireplaces. Most cabinets installed before the 1940s were made of wood and custom built at the construction site, but today factory-made wood or metal cabinets are also used. Cabinets must be installed level and plumb to operate properly. They should be screwed, not nailed, to the wall studs, and the screws should go through to the framing members.

Like cabinetry, kitchen appliances such as dishwashers, trash compactors, garbage disposals, and some refrigerators are typically built in and therefore must be accounted for in the property description. Appraisers should note whether the design of kitchen appliances is consistent with the layout and whether there is any physical deterioration.

Most fireplaces do not provide a building's primary source of heat. Because of their design, many fireplaces have little heating power.

Some devices can be installed to make fireplaces better sources of heat such as ducts surrounding the firebox that return hot air into the room rather than let it escape through the chimney.

A typical fireplace has a single opening with a damper and a hearth. More complex designs feature two, three, four, or more openings. Prefabricated fireplaces or woodstoves and flues are often installed in buildings constructed without fireplaces. These fireplaces must be listed by Underwriters Laboratories, Inc. and installed according to the manufacturer's instructions, or they can be potential fire hazards. To be safe, a fireplace should be supported by noncombustible material and equipped with a noncombustible hearth that extends at least 16 inches in front of the opening and at least 8 inches on each side. Any unlisted wood or fireplace stoves may be a fire hazard.

Overall Condition of the Residence

A complete building description includes a quality and condition survey of the main improvements. To describe their condition, an appraiser classifies building components as

1. Items requiring immediate repair (often called *deferred maintenance*)
2. Items for which maintenance may be required over the economic life of the building but which it is not feasible to replace as of the date of the appraisal (often called *short-lived items*)
3. Items that are expected to last for the full economic life of the building (often called *long-lived items*)

Items Requiring Immediate Repair

Some homes are exceptionally well maintained, but almost all will contain items in need of repair on the date of the appraisal. Repairing these normal maintenance items (commonly called *deferred maintenance items*) should add as much or more value to the property than the cost of repair. When the cost approach to value is applied, these are considered items of curable physical deterioration. The appraiser's repair list should include items that constitute a fire or safety hazard. Many clients request that these items be listed separately in the report. Sometimes the appraiser is asked to estimate the cost of each repair, which is called cost to cure.

Common home repairs include

- Touching up exterior paint
- Doing minor carpentry on stairs, molding, trim, floors, and porches

short-lived item. A building component with an expected remaining economic life that is shorter than the remaining economic life of the entire structure.

long-lived item. A building component with an expected remaining economic life that is the same as the remaining economic life of the entire structure.

deferred maintenance. Curable, physical deterioration that should be corrected immediately, although work has not commenced; denotes the need for immediate expenditures, but does not necessarily suggest inadequate maintenance in the past.

cost to cure. The cost to restore an item of deferred maintenance to new or reasonably new condition.

- Redecorating interior rooms
- Fixing leaks and noisy plumbing
- Loosening stuck doors and windows
- Repairing holes in screens and replacing broken windows or other glass
- Rehanging loose gutters and leaders
- Replacing missing roof shingles and tiles
- Fixing cracks in pavements
- Doing minor electrical repairs
- Replacing rotted floorboards
- Exterminating vermin
- Fixing cracked or loose bathroom and kitchen tiles
- Repairing septic systems
- Eliminating fire hazards

Short-Lived Items

The economic life of a building is the period over which the improvements contribute to property value. Short-lived items will usually have to be repaired at some time prior to the end of the economic life of the building. The remaining economic life of a building component is the estimated period during which the component will contribute to property value. If the remaining economic life of the component is shorter than the remaining economic life of the structure as a whole, the component is known as a *short-lived item.*

Short-lived items include

- Interior paint and wallpaper
- Exterior paint
- Floor finishes
- Shades, screens, and blinds (often considered personal property)
- Waterproofing and weatherstripping
- Gutters and leaders
- Roof covering and flashing
- Water heater
- Furnace
- Air-conditioning equipment
- Carpeting
- Kitchen appliances (considered short-lived components only if built-in)
- Sump pump
- Water softener system (often this component is rented)
- Washers and dryers (often considered personal property)
- Ventilating fans

Although a building's paint, roof, and wallpaper may show signs of wear and tear, they may not be ready for replacement on the date of the appraisal. The appraiser must determine whether repairing or replacing the item will add more value to the property than it will cost. If, for example, a house has an exterior paint job that is three years old and exterior paint normally lasts five years, the paint has suffered some depreciation. Repainting the house on the date of the appraisal, however, would probably not add enough value to the property to justify its cost.

An appraiser also considers whether repairing an item is necessary to preserve other components. For example, a roof cover must be replaced because if it is not, the economic life of the other components will be reduced.

The appraiser notes whether the condition of short-lived items is better or worse than the overall condition of the residence.

Long-Lived Items

The final step in the quality and condition survey is a description of items that are not expected to require repair or replacement during the economic life of the building. A building component with an expected remaining economic life that is the same as the remaining economic life of the entire structure is a long-lived item. Repair may not be required because the components have been built to last and have been well maintained. However, the long-lived items in a building are rarely in exactly the same condition. The appraiser should focus on those items that are not in the same condition as the rest of the building.

Long-lived items include

- Foundation
- Hot and cold water pipes
- Plumbing fixtures (may also be considered functional components)
- Electric service connection (may also be considered a functional component)
- Electric wiring
- Electric switches and outlets
- Electric fixtures
- Ducts and radiators

Sometimes defective long-lived items are not considered in need of repair because the cost of replacement or repair is greater than the amount these items contribute to the value of the property. A serious crack in a foundation wall, for example, may be considered incurable physical deterioration. Incurable depreciation that results from problems in the original design of a residence is considered incurable functional obsolescence.

The Description of Improvements in the Appraisal Report

To be able to describe the improvements in any detail, appraisers must have a working knowledge of the construction process and a good understanding of which building components and features contribute significantly to value in the subject property's market area. All homes need to be heated and cooled, but the quality and condition of a house's air-conditioning system in one area (say, Arizona) may be much more significant in a homebuyer's eyes than in another area (like Minnesota). The appraiser communicates the market's preferences to the client through the appraisal report.

The level of detail reported in the description of improvements depends on the scope of work of the appraisal assignment. For a drive-by appraisal, an appraiser will not inspect the interior of the residence and consequently will not be able to judge the quality and condition of interior finishes, equipment, and other improvements. The scope of work of such an assignment precludes a detailed analysis of the design and construction of the house. An assignment to value a residence with evidence of structural damage will require much closer scrutiny of the construction, perhaps even consultation with a structural engineer or other professional. Again, the scope of work of the assignment determines the extent of the inspection of the property and the description of the improvements.

The information collected by the appraiser during the investigation of the site and improvements of the subject property helps the appraiser delineate the market area of competitive properties and select comparable sales, make adjustments for physical characteristics in the sales comparison approach, develop a reproduction or replacement cost estimate, and ultimately support the appraiser's opinion of value. In the appraisal report, the appraiser communicates to the client which property characteristics are important in the ensuing analyses of the valuation process, i.e., market analysis, highest and best use analysis, and the application of the approaches to value.

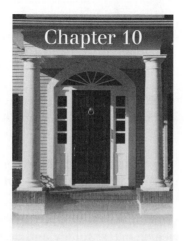

Chapter 10

Neighborhood and Market Area Analysis

The object of study in most appraisal assignments is market value, which is derived from market data and reflects the interaction of supply and demand in a particular market area. Different levels of market analysis are required depending on the purpose of the appraisal assignment. To conduct a *market study*, the general market conditions that affect a specific area or a particular property type must be studied. A careful investigation of historical and potential levels of supply and demand may be needed. Similarly, to perform a *marketability study*, an appraiser investigates how a particular property or class of properties will be absorbed, sold, or leased under current or anticipated market conditions. Marketability studies are often requested by developers and entrepreneurs who need to know the risks associated with subdivision, condominium, or retail projects. For many standard residential appraisal assignments (e.g., for mortgage underwriting purposes), the *neighborhood analysis* required to complete the neighborhood section of a form report is a relatively straightforward process.

Appraisers regularly update their files to include new data on the area in which they usually work. Considerable background research on the local and neighborhood market

market study. A macroeconomic analysis that examines the general market conditions of supply, demand, and pricing or the demographics of demand for a specific area or property type. A market study may also include analyses of construction and absorption trends.

marketability study.
1. A process that investigates how a particular piece of property will be absorbed, sold, or leased under current or anticipated market conditions; includes a market study or analysis of the general class of property being studied.
2. A microeconomic study that examines the marketability of a given property or class of properties, usually focusing on the market segment(s) in which the property is likely to generate demand. Marketability studies are useful in determining a specific highest and best use, testing development proposals, and projecting an appropriate tenant mix.

is conducted in advance, and then additional data are collected as part of the specific assignment. Typically, an appraiser draws upon information available in office files and makes additional inquiries to supplement and update these data. He or she completes the research for the assignment by examining the characteristics of the specific subject neighborhood and, in some cases, the larger market area during the field inspection.

In-house research, supplemental investigation, and field inspection are undertaken to answer interrelated questions concerning the following:

- The basic characteristics of the residential real estate market, including price levels, price changes, supply and demand relationships, and market activity patterns. For example, in considering supply and demand issues, the number of days properties are listed on the market and the inventory of listings, pending sales, and closed sales are important indicators.
- The features, locations, and possible alternative uses of both vacant and residential properties, which contribute to or detract from value in this market
- The boundaries and major characteristics of the neighborhood where the subject property is located
- The competitive advantages and disadvantages of the neighborhood in light of expected norms as well as the amenities, facilities, and appeal of comparable neighborhoods
- The present mix of land uses and the likely pattern and direction of future changes in land use

The conclusions drawn in market analysis are likely to affect all aspects of the appraiser's subsequent analyses. An understanding of the market area, market characteristics, neighborhood land uses, and anticipated changes is essential to every appraisal. This preliminary analysis affects the selection of appropriate market data, the determination of highest and best use, the adjustment of the sale prices of comparables, the estimation of depreciation, and the derivation of income and expense information.

Proper market analysis can ensure that the appraiser does not use inappropriate data or double-count—i.e., consider a value influence in more than one category and make two adjustments to a price for one value influence.

Neighborhoods and Market Areas

Appraisers make a distinction between the neighborhood in which a residence is located and the market area in which comparable properties will be found. The latter is formally defined as "the geographic or locational delineation of the market for a specific category of real estate, i.e., the area in which alternative, similar properties effectively compete with the subject property in the minds of probable, potential purchasers and users." In contrast, a neighborhood is defined more generally as "a group of complementary land uses." In other words, the neighborhood boundaries in which the subject property is located may contain residential properties that are not comparable to the subject as well as commercial properties that serve the residents of the neighborhood, whereas the boundaries of the market area for the subject will be defined first and foremost by the proximity of comparable properties. In some cases, the subject's neighborhood and market area may have concurrent boundaries, but in others the market area may contain several neighborhoods or portions of different neighborhoods.

Appraisers tend to focus on the value influences in the market area rather than the neighborhood. Analyzing the market area helps to provide a framework, or context, in which the opinion of property value is developed. The analysis identifies the area of influence and

How to Define the Boundaries of a Market Area

1. Examine the subject property. Market area analysis always starts with a thorough understanding of the subject property.
2. Examine the area's physical characteristics. Note the degree of similarity in land uses, structure types, architectural styles, and maintenance and upkeep, and using a map, identify where these characteristics change. Also, note any physical barriers such as major streets, railroad tracks, rivers, or other topographical features that correspond to possible changes in the market area.
3. Draw preliminary boundaries on the map.
4. Compare the preliminary boundaries to the available demographic data using geographical units like zip codes, census tracts, and block groups.

Courtesy of Site To Do Business Online (www.stdbonline.com)

establishes the potential limits within which the appraiser searches for data that can be used to apply the approaches to value. Market area analysis also helps the appraiser determine an area's stability and may indicate future land uses and value trends.

Market Area Value Influences

Changes that affect real estate values can originate at international, national, regional, municipal, community, and neighborhood levels. When a specific market area is being considered, the influences on local property values are most relevant.

In a market study, present conditions of supply and demand are investigated and the social, economic, governmental, and environmental forces that cause these conditions to change are analyzed. Trends and cycles at national and regional levels affect many types of real estate and often provide the standard against which local market fluctuations are measured. Therefore, an appraiser's analysis usually relates these broader trends to conditions in specific geographic areas. The markets studied are defined in terms of the location, type, size, age, condition, and price range of the properties considered. Table 10.1 identifies value influences and indicators at different geographic levels.

Ultimately, a specific market area is delineated. The most useful comparable data analyzed in an appraisal are drawn from the specific market area because it is within this area that alternative, similar properties effectively compete with the subject property.

In collecting data and inspecting the neighborhood, the appraiser attempts to identify major value influences, observe how they are changing, and relate these conclusions to the subject property and potentially comparable properties. Value influences, or forces that affect value (as presented in Chapter 3), are classified as

- Social
- Economic
- Governmental (which includes legal factors)
- Environmental (which includes physical and geographic factors)

Although these influences often overlap, it is helpful to consider each category separately.

Social Influences

Social influences on neighborhood property values include

- Population characteristics and trends
- The quality and reputation of the establishments that serve the neighborhood
- Community and neighborhood organizations
- The absence or extent of crime and litter

Table 10.1	Value Influences and Indicators by Area

Regional

- Regional price level indexes
- Interest rates
- Aggregate employment and unemployment statistics
- Housing starts, building permits issued, and dollar volume of construction
- State laws governing development, environmental protection, and low- and moderate-income housing

Community

- Local population
- Long-term and seasonal employment
- Income and wage rates
- Diversity of employment
- Interest rates
- Net household formation
- Household income
- Availability of mortgage money
- Competitiveness with other communities
- Adequacy of utilities and transportation systems
- Zoning, subdivision regulations, and building codes
- Days on market
- Nuisances and hazards
- Percent built up

Neighborhood

- Age
- Stage in life cycle
- Rates of construction and vacancy
- Market activity levels, absorption rate, turnover rate, volume of sales
- Motivations of buyers and sellers
- Property use before and after sale
- Presence of desired amenities
- Maintenance standards
- Economic profile of occupants
- Availability of mortgage money
- Days on market
- Nuisances and hazards
- Percent built up

Note that some value influences are felt directly at more than one level.

Population Characteristics

Population and demographics change as a result of natural growth or decline and movement into or out of an area. Although many factors influence an individual's decision to move, the most compelling impetus may be economic necessity.

People with sufficient economic means and opportunities tend to move to areas where they can live and work in security and comfort and where their children will have the best economic future. In the 1970s

Population Characteristics

· The current population
· The size and composition of households
· The population makeup
· Population density, which is usually important in areas dominated by high-rise residences
· The occupant employment profile
· The education, skill, and income levels of residents

Where to Find: Population Data

· The U.S. Census Bureau*
  <www.census.gov>
· American Community Survey
  <www.census.gov/acs/www/>
· Utility companies*
· Local chambers of commerce
· County offices
· School districts
· Visitors' bureaus
· State demographer databases

* If census figures are not up to date, the population of a neighborhood can be estimated by multiplying the number of electric or water meters in the area by the ratio of population to the number of meters that was calculated at the time of the last census.

the population trend in the United States was toward the Sun Belt states and away from the industrial states of the Northeast. Economic conditions in particular areas of the country altered this picture in the 1980s. The shift toward a service- and research-based economy revitalized regions such as the Boston area, but the decline in oil production and agriculture left regions such as Texas in an economic recession. By the 1990s the situation had changed once more. Employment levels began to decline in New England, which felt the full impact of the national economic slump. During the same period, diversification in Texas was creating a stronger employment base. Different regions of the country, certain areas within individual states, and even specific areas within a given metropolitan area have very different economic characteristics. This variation is more extreme today than it has been for most of the twentieth century. After 2000, the dot com downturn in Silicon Valley negatively impacted the San Francisco market, but repercussions from this event rippled across the country because investors in dot com companies covered the nation.

Birth and death rates, the age at which people start families, and the number of children in a typical family all affect population size over the long term. Marriage and divorce rates also influence the rate of new household formation. Furthermore, appraisers are interested not only in the numbers of units desired but also in the kinds of units desired. Specific population characteristics can explain differences in demand. Young families with children, single professionals, and older adults often have different preferences as to housing features and neighborhood amenities. These segments of the population also tend to have different levels of income, which allow them to make their preferences felt. Thus, the ages, number of children, gender, occupation, and income of residents are all likely to be relevant in a study of the market population.

Appraisers should identify and quantify the trends that the population characteristics suggest. For instance, if a neighborhood is becoming increasingly attractive to households with young children, residences with extra rooms and play areas may be in great demand. If middle- and upper-income professionals prefer city neighborhoods close to restaurants and cultural facilities, low-maintenance properties in particular neighborhoods may become especially desirable. Trends can be identified by observing absorption rates and price changes for different types of residences and neighborhoods over several years. Understanding the social forces behind these price changes can help the appraiser forecast a neighborhood's future. However, such forecasts must be based on factual evidence that is clearly stated in the appraisal report.

Quality of Services and Establishments

The appraiser should investigate how residents and potential buyers rate the quality of businesses and other establishments that serve the neighborhood, in comparison with the services provided in competitive neighborhoods.

- Do they think there are enough restaurants in the area?
- Is parking a problem?
- Are shopping facilities, medical facilities, and recreational areas adequate?
- How good are the neighborhood schools and places of worship?
- How do potential buyers feel about area establishments and the neighborhood's future?

Community and Neighborhood Associations

The presence of neighborhood and community groups can affect the stability of a neighborhood and the value of its residential property. Some neighborhood groups are legal entities formed by the original developers or by the homeowners themselves; they are concerned with maintaining common areas and providing certain services such as garbage disposal, snow removal, water supply, and police and fire protection. Voluntary associations such as block clubs and crime watch groups organize neighborhood crime protection efforts, lobby against undesirable rezoning or development, and sponsor revitalization projects, block parties, and street fairs. Community spirit can make a neighborhood more stable and may even reverse a trend toward declining property values.

Crime and Litter

When a neighborhood is reputed to have a high crime rate, some residents may move and potential residents may decide not to purchase homes there. Better street lighting, increased police protection, and effective neighborhood crime watch groups can improve a neighborhood's crime problem to some extent.

> **Where to Find: Crime Statistics**
>
> Local police departments usually have information on the number and types of crimes reported in an area, which are frequently available online.

The absence of litter and graffiti in public and private areas suggests that property owners care about their neighborhood. The presence of an unusual amount of litter or graffiti suggests neighborhood apathy and may indicate a change in the neighborhood's occupancy characteristics. The level of crime in the neighborhood and the presence of litter or graffiti should be stated in the neighborhood section of the appraisal report and must be factually supported.

Economic Influences

Economic influences center around the financial ability of neighborhood occupants to rent or own property, to maintain it, and to renovate or rehabilitate it when necessary. The overall physical condition of properties indicates the relative financial strength of area occupants and how this strength is translated into neighborhood upkeep. The economic characteristics of occupants may also reflect present conditions and future trends in real estate supply and demand.

Economic Profile of Residents

There is a direct relationship between the income and employment profile of neighborhood residents and price and rent levels. The type, stability, and location of employment all have a strong impact on the value of residential property because employment determines the ability of individuals to purchase or rent in a particular area. Income levels tend to establish a range of property values in a neighborhood.

The demand for housing can increase or decrease substantially due to a change in purchasing power, even if the size of the population remains the same. Overall shifts in the level of demand may occur when people have more money to spend on housing needs. The type of housing desired may also change.

Purchasing power depends on the disposable income–i.e., personal income that remains after taxes and other payments to government–that a household wants to allocate to housing expenditures. Employment, income, and savings levels as well as the average number of wage earners in a household should be considered. Tax levels indicate how much money is available to purchase goods and services of all kinds. The prices of other basic goods suggest how much money can be spent on housing. Housing expenditures include the price of residences, mortgage financing, property taxes, and maintenance costs.

Local business conditions must also be considered. Relevant data on local business activities include

- Retail sales levels
- Real estate transfers
- New housing starts

An appraiser may compile a wealth of information on local businesses, but these data are only useful if they can be used to relate recent or likely future changes in the economy to specific changes in the demand for a specific type of real estate. For example, upper-income housing in an area may respond to a factory closing differently than lower-income housing. Similarly, business fluctuations may not affect rent levels in the same way they affect the prices of single-family residences.

Types and Terms of Financing

The mortgage financing available may be the single most important factor considered in the study of demand. To assess how the income of a population affects its purchasing power, an appraiser considers the requirements of mortgage lenders who serve the market population in the area.

When primary sources have little credit available or the credit terms are too restrictive, the demand for housing contracts. High interest rates translate into high monthly payments. If mortgage payments exceed the portion of monthly household income that can be spent for housing, an increasing number of homeowners will default and others may be discouraged from entering the real estate market. Sellers may offer creative financing arrangements, which call for monthly payments that are lower than those required with typical financing but such financing can increase the long-term debt burden.

The availability and terms of mortgage financing are affected by economic decisions and changes on many levels. Appraisers should carefully track each influence and consider its effects. The Federal Reserve can increase or decrease the supply of credit available to its member banks, which will result in monetary expansion or contraction. The amount of credit that lenders can offer home-buyers also depends on how much money other individuals have deposited with them. The savings level, in turn, reflects national, regional, and local business conditions. The size of the national debt is another factor affecting credit availability. The U.S. Department of the Treasury strongly competes with private sources to obtain a share of the country's available credit. When the government borrows heavily to pay its bills, the credit supply may shrink and interest rates may rise.

Where to Find: Mortgage Information

Appraisers need broad knowledge of national and local developments to understand the full implications of specific market conditions in the immediate area.

· An appraiser may find printed data on current interest rates and the availability of financing in the survey updates of multiple listing services and title companies.

· Most local newspapers provide comprehensive listings of interest rates on everything from Treasury bills to mortgages.

· Local lending institutions can quote the rates on conventional, VA, and FHA loans and indicate how many points are charged.

· Local Realtors can supply information on the financing arrangements involved in their most recent transactions.

Property Price and Rent Levels

The price and rent levels of neighborhood properties usually demonstrate a high degree of conformity. The value of a subject property is strongly affected by the prices at which similar, nearby properties have been sold. Neighborhood prices and rents constitute the primary source of market data for appraisal analysis. Price and rent levels indicate the interaction of value influences. If price levels are changing, an appraiser should fully investigate what is causing this change.

Development, Construction, Conversion, and Vacant Land

Vacant land suitable for the construction of additional houses may exist within a neighborhood simply because the owners do not wish to sell or develop the land. However, the presence of vacant land may also indicate a lack of effective demand for improved properties or possibly suggest the likelihood of future construction activity.

If there are only a few vacant lots in a neighborhood, their development usually will not have a substantial impact on most other neighborhood properties. However, if these lots are specifically zoned for nonresidential use or variances are granted to permit nonresidential construction, the presence of an atypical use may have an adverse effect on existing residential properties. If a neighborhood has many vacant lots, the values of existing properties will be more significantly affected by the anticipated development of these lots. Similarly, if many nonresidential properties are likely to be converted to residential use, existing residential properties may be affected through a possible oversupply.

In performing market area analysis, an appraiser should obtain information about buildings under construction and proposed future development as well as the existing supply of properties. Supply increases that result from recent construction activity can be studied by analyzing new housing starts. The number, location, type of unit, and price or rent of the new units constructed should be considered. An appraiser can use data on housing starts supplemented with information on proposed construction activity and projected demand to form a picture of the relationship between supply and demand in the market and to decide whether an oversupply or undersupply is likely to be created by current construction. For example, an analysis of trends for the past several may show a balanced supply-demand relationship at present but project an oversupply in the future. The evidence of an oversupply or extended marketing time can suggest a potential for external obsolescence in the analysis of depreciation.

Where to Find: Housing Supply and Demand Data

- Data on the number of properties available for sale and lease can be obtained from multiple listing services and realty advertisements in newspapers. The number of properties available for sale should be compared to the number sold in the past six months to a year.

- Local and regional planning agencies and departments of development can provide data on projected expansion and authorized construction permits. Many local governmental agencies report building permits issued and sales transactions by specific areas or subdivisions on their Web sites.

- Other good sources for housing starts are publications of local and national home builders associations. Housing stock is usually a local matter but local situations may reflect national trends.

- Appraisers can obtain data on local vacancy and occupancy levels from chambers of commerce, builders' boards, and real estate management companies.

- For information on costs, appraisers should consult local builders and developers and refer to cost estimating services, which provide multipliers for adjusting national cost data to local conditions.

Extent of Occupant Ownership

Neighborhoods in which most residences are owner-occupied are often more stable and pose less investment risk to lenders than neighborhoods with many tenant-occupants. Owners generally maintain their properties better than tenants. When the ratio of owner-occupied to tenant-occupied residences in a neighborhood changes, decline or revitalization may be indicated.

Government Influences

Government and legal influences on property values include the laws, regulations, and taxes imposed on properties in the market area and the administration and enforcement activities associated with these constraints.

The appraiser gathers data on government influences in the subject market area to get a picture of how the situation in this market area compares with that of other, competitive market areas. Police power regulations, private restrictions, and taxes can restrict the rights of property ownership and influence property values. In market area analysis an appraiser tries to ascertain the following:

- How the benefits produced by local regulations stand in relation to the burdens they impose. The local situation is then compared with the situation in competitive market areas.
- How much government provisions and their enforcement add to or detract from the stability of the market area.
- How these provisions relate to the neighborhood or community master plan. The likelihood and effect of future changes in legislation are also assessed.

> **Important Factors Concerning Government**
>
> · Taxation and special assessments in relation to the services provided and in comparison with other market areas in the community
> · Public and private restrictions
> · Schools
> · The quality of fire and police protection and other public services
> · Government planning and development activity

Taxation and Special Assessments

Tax burdens can vary significantly, and variations in taxes may significantly influence the decisions of potential buyers. Divergent tax rates often affect market value. Local taxes may favor or discriminate against certain types of property. Community development programs may depend on tax revenues. The appraiser should

> **special assessment.** An assessment against real estate levied by a public authority to pay for public improvements, e.g., sidewalks, street improvements, sewers; also called betterment tax.

- Examine local assessed values and tax rates
- Compare the burdens created by various taxes
- Measure their effect on the values of different types of real estate

Special assessments are directly related to the additional services or advantages provided–e.g., for private beaches or extra fire protection. Properties subject to high special assessments may or may not be penalized. A special assessment lien may reduce the price of a house by approximately the amount of the lien.

Counties and cities may have the authority to impose optional taxes such as sales and earnings taxes on residents. When competing communities are subject to different sales and local earnings taxes, the relative desirability of the communities may be affected. These variations often have a more significant effect on the marketability of commercial and industrial real estate than ad valorem taxes do. Such variations can indirectly influence residential real estate values.

Public and Private Restrictions

Zoning regulations and building codes are important to the stability of a neighborhood. They provide legal protection against adverse influences, nuisances, and hazards. Some buyers seek out neighborhoods that have effective zoning laws, building codes, and housing and sanitary codes. The enforcement of these codes, regulations, and restrictions should be effective and equitable in comparison with enforcement in competitive neighborhoods. Figure 10.1 shows a zoning map.

Figure 10.1	Zoning Map

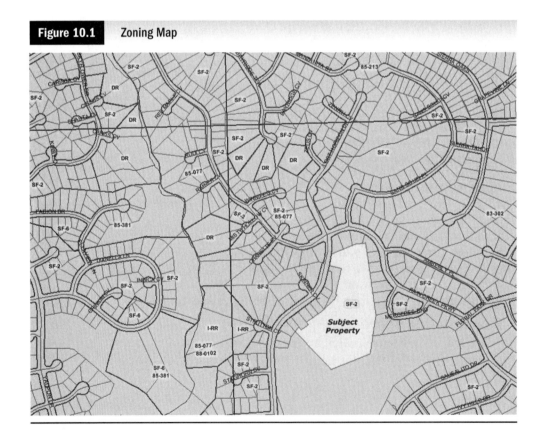

Changes in zoning may have positive or negative effects on the neighborhood as a whole, and changes can have different effects on individual properties in the neighborhood. For example, rezoning a corner site from residential to commercial use might have a negative effect on the neighborhood as a whole although it increases the value of that particular property. Appraisers must be sensitive to the ramifications of both real and proposed zoning changes. The probability of zoning changes in transitional areas should be explored through discussions with zoning officials. Anticipated zoning changes can affect the highest and best use, and hence the value, of the subject and potential comparable properties. Interim uses (i.e., temporary uses to which properties may be put until they are ready for their long-term highest and best uses) must also be considered.

When existing zoning and building regulations are not enforced, property values in a particular market area may decline. When zoning variances are obtained easily and without consideration of their effect on surrounding properties, the stability of the market area can be threatened and the value of neighboring properties may decrease. Zoning violations often include illegal signs, illegal uses, and conversion of properties to a density of use that is higher than the density permitted for surrounding properties.

Deed restrictions often protect properties from the negative impact of an incompatible use, either on the subject site or in some cases on adjoining properties. If these restrictions are not enforced, lower values may result. However, some deed restrictions written long ago may be obsolete or unenforceable. Generally, any deed restriction that is against the public interest cannot be upheld.

Schools

Many families choose a neighborhood for the quality of its schools because schools are of immediate concern to families with children. Because today's economy is oriented toward service and high technology industries that require well-trained workers, communities with good educational facilities and institutions of higher learning are increasingly favored by business and industry. The reputation and probable future of a neighborhood's schools is a basic consideration in the market analysis.

Fire and Police Protection

Government-provided services are vital to the maintenance and preservation of neighborhoods and communities. The decision of a potential homebuyer may be influenced by

- The type of fire-fighting service provided
- The size of the fire district
- The distance between the residence and the nearest firehouse
- The reputation of the local police force and its effectiveness in preventing crime

The strength and reputation of volunteer services are of particular importance in some semi-rural and nearly all rural communities.

Where to Find: Information on Planned Developments	**Planning and Development Activity**

Where to Find: Information on Planned Developments

· City and county building and planning commissions, as well as real estate boards and builders' organizations, can provide detailed information on existing and proposed units.

· Building permit information, which can usually be obtained from the planning, building, or zoning departments, indicates the types of housing being considered in the area and may give the appraiser an indication of expectations for a short-term forecast.

· Municipal and regional planning departments have information on existing and proposed subdivisions to supplement permit information.

· If the community being investigated is too small to have a planning department, the town clerk or the public works department may have this type of information.

· The Council of Governments (COG), which is composed of representatives from several municipal and county governments, is another source of information on supply and demand trends. These facilities vary in terms of staffing and funding. Transportation plans and land use records can be obtained from COGs, and some COGs also keep detailed housing information.

Planning and Development Activity

Planning for the future development of communities is an important task of government. Good planning can maintain the integrity and character of existing neighborhoods and provide ideas for the future use of undeveloped areas. Poor planning for recreational facilities, schools, and service areas may contribute to neighborhood disintegration. The requirements imposed on developers influence the type and quality of services available to homeowners and have a strong effect on the value of existing structures or the financial success of proposed developments. By protecting open space areas, the government can deter developers from modifying the environment to maximize the number of units built.

Development activity may be indicated by analyzing current market sales, absorption trends, expected returns, marketing problems, and future development plans. By comparing the number of lots being platted to the number of building permits issued, an appraiser can assess the relative oversupply or undersupply of subdivision lots and its impact on existing real estate.[1]

Larger communities have land-use planning facilities. Existing or proposed land-use plans can be consulted to learn of anticipated future development. Many states have statutes requiring that city governments control land use according to approved plans.

Environmental Influences (Including Physical and Geographic Factors)

Natural and man-made features that affect the market area and its location are considered environmental influences.

Siting Factors

The community siting factors are those things that prompted the community to develop in its specific location. Typically they include ease of access to major transportation hubs, ease of development resulting from physical or environmental characteristics, and climatic conditions.

---

1. The appraisal of subdivisions and feasibility studies for proposed subdivision developments are special topics that are covered more fully in Douglas D. Lovell and Robert S. Martin, *Subdivision Analysis* (Chicago: Appraisal Institute, 1993). A new publication on the appraisal of subdivisions will be released in 2007.

Location Within the Community

The changes occurring in a neighborhood are usually affected by changes in the larger area of influence. Therefore, a neighborhood may benefit or suffer because of its location within a market area. A neighborhood adjacent to a growing business district, for example, may benefit from nearby shopping and municipal services, but it may also suffer from increased congestion and other nuisances. The rapid growth of one market area or neighborhood may adversely affect a competitive market area or neighborhood. Areas located in the direction of growth may benefit, while other areas away from growth may suffer.

Transportation Systems and Linkages

Transportation systems provide the basis for expected linkages between the subject property and amenities, which have a strong influence on the desirability of specific neighborhoods. An appraiser should consider the destinations to which typical occupants commute as well as the distance, time, and quality of the transportation services available. If adequate facilities are not available, the neighborhood will be at a disadvantage compared with competing neighborhoods with better linkages. In studying location and transportation, an appraiser should consider both existing and proposed transportation facilities as well as all existing and planned facilities to which residents may be expected to commute.

For the occupants of single-unit residential neighborhoods, linkages to workplaces, schools, and shopping areas are usually the most important. Access to recreational facilities, houses of worship, restaurants, and stores are somewhat less important. A nearby shopping center can enhance property values in a neighborhood. Heavy, slow traffic on highways can reduce values in some areas, particularly if these highways are the primary linkages between the neighborhood and major centers of employment. Some linkages have special importance to certain groups of people. Proximity to schools may be a priority for people with children, while public transportation and services are important to the elderly.

Public transportation is crucial to people who do not own automobiles or prefer not to use them for commuting. Even in areas where most families own two or more cars, unstable energy costs, high automobile maintenance and insurance costs, and the convenience of public transportation make linkages an important consideration.

The transportation characteristics of the neighborhood usually apply to most properties in the neighborhood. However, the walking distance to and from public transportation can be an important vari-

---

Important Environmental Considerations

- Siting factors for both the community and the subject property
- The location of the market area within the community
- The transportation system and important linkages expected by the market
- Services, amenities, and recreational facilities
- The topography, soil, subsoil, climate, and view
- Patterns of land use and signs of change in land use patterns
- The age, size, style, condition, and appearance of residences and neighborhood facilities

linkage. Time and distance relationship between a particular use and supporting facilities, e.g., between residences and schools, shopping, and employment.

Figure 10.2   Linkages to Major Employers

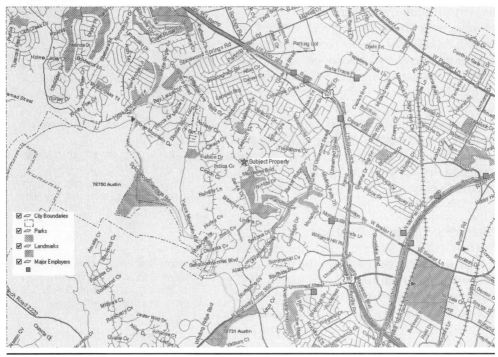

Courtesy of Site To Do Business Online (www.stdbonline.com)

able if residents are expected to use these facilities frequently. Urban apartment dwellers usually prefer to be within walking distance of public transportation. The territory through which commuters must pass is also important. People dislike walking through poorly lighted streets and rundown areas.

The street pattern of the neighborhood may have a significant bearing on the value of a property's location in the community and on transportation linkages. Contemporary neighborhoods are planned with curving streets, cul-de-sacs, and circular drives. These features take up valuable space and can increase land costs, but they do add privacy and reduce the traffic hazards often found in older neighborhoods with square-block street patterns. Streets should be laid out to make use of natural contours, wooded areas, and ponds. Traffic in residential areas should move slowly and easily. Ideally, expressways and boulevards should lie outside residential neighborhoods but offer convenient access to local streets.

Appraisers should also note the quality of street lighting, pavement, sidewalks, curbs, and gutters. Well-maintained streets and shade trees contribute to the overall desirability of a neighborhood. In congested areas, the availability of street parking can also influence property values.

Services, Amenities, and Recreational Facilities

Amenities and services can have a substantial impact on the desirability of a neighborhood, particularly in more affluent areas. The businesses, schools, cultural facilities, and houses of worship that serve the neighborhood affect its desirability. High-value neighborhoods provide recreational facilities such as parks, beaches, pools, tennis courts, country clubs, and libraries. These facilities can help a neighborhood attract new residents. Community homeowners' associations can keep a neighborhood in good condition by helping maintain recreational facilities and other amenities that increase the neighborhood's desirability. The presence, location, and accessibility of recreational facilities and services should be noted in the appraisal report.

Topography, Soil, Climate, and View

Topography and climatic conditions can have a positive or negative effect on neighborhood property values. The presence of a lake, river, bay, or hill often provides a scenic advantage. A hill may mean little in a mountainous region, but an elevated or wooded section in a predominantly flat area can enhance property values. A river, lake, or park may act as a buffer between a residential district and commercial or industrial areas and reinforce the neighborhood's identity.

Topographic and climatic features can also be disadvantageous. A river that floods penalizes the value of homes along its banks. Abrupt changes in elevation can make access difficult and construction more costly. The soil in an area may have poor bearing capacity, quality, absorption, or drainage characteristics, which typically raise the cost of development or, in extreme cases, may prevent development. Climate can also have a negative effect. Although a neighborhood usually shares the same climate as competitive neighborhoods, the subject neighborhood may suffer from special conditions such as increased wind, fog, or rain. Conversely, some neighborhoods may offer protection from the elements.

The desirability of certain types of topography depends on the kind of residential development that is present or contemplated. For expensive homes, large hillside or wooded sites are often desired. Tract developers, however, usually seek a level area or plateau, which is better suited to subdivision construction and can be developed less expensively. Generally, an area slightly higher than surrounding neighborhoods is preferred.

Patterns of Land Use and Signs of Change

In a stable neighborhood the mix of land uses is balanced and conforms to market standards. Each use has a clearly defined area and these areas are well buffered from one another. The neighborhood's boundaries are usually explicit and buildings generally conform to one another and to their immediate environment. Excessive homogeneity can detract from value, but a balanced mix is typical and desirable in the market area.

Neighborhood change is often signaled by

- A poor mix of land uses
- Considerable variation in construction, maintenance standards, and ownership status
- Indistinct boundaries

Values may be rising, falling, or about to shift. The neighborhood may be entering a stage of decline, revitalization, or conversion to another type of neighborhood.

To optimize property values, residential areas should be protected from the hazards and nuisances of nearby land uses. Excessive traffic and odors, smoke, dust, and noise from commercial and manufacturing enterprises limit a residential neighborhood's desirability, as does a location next to an airport, a nuclear power plant, or a toxic waste disposal site. Neighborhoods suffering from these conditions may have stable property values, particularly if the adverse conditions have been present for some time, but property prices and values in these neighborhoods are likely to be lower than values in similar or competitive neighborhoods that do not suffer from adverse influences.

Age, Size, Style, Condition, and Appearance of Residences

The character of a residential neighborhood is reflected by its "average" house. The structural and architectural quality, age, and condition of typical residences are physical characteristics that have a substantial effect on the desirability of a neighborhood. In stable neighborhoods, the average house suggests the type of improvement that constitutes the highest and best use of the subject site. An appraiser should also note the sizes and shapes of typical sites and typical land-to-building ratios in the neighborhood.

The condition of individual homes and their architectural compatibility influence the general appearance of a neighborhood. Well-kept yards, houses, and community areas reflect good maintenance. Landscaping, trees, open space, and the proper maintenance of vacant lots also make a neighborhood more desirable. Public and commercial establishments should present a neat, compatible appearance. Poorly maintained public areas, vacant stores, and the presence of graffiti on buildings detract from a neighborhood's desirability and often indicate a period of change.

Adequacy and Quality of Utilities

Gas, electricity, water, telephone, cable television service, and sanitary sewers are essential in municipal areas to meet contemporary standards of living. The availability of utilities affects the direction and timing of neighborhood growth and development. The absence of any of these services tends to decrease values in a neighborhood, and unusually high costs for these services also influence values. However, appraisers should compare competing neighborhoods prior to making this determination. A lack of utilities is not uncommon in many rural and unincorporated areas.

Procedures for Neighborhood/Market Analysis

In most residential appraisals, the subject property's neighborhood coincides with the market area. The extent of market analysis and the procedures applied depend on the property type and the purpose and intended use of the appraisal. For most common residential appraisal assignments, there are two major steps in analyzing value influences in a neighborhood:

1. Planning the analysis effort and collecting pertinent market information

2. Inspecting the neighborhood and, when necessary, conducting additional research to resolve questions raised by the field inspection

Planning the Analysis and Collecting Data
Essential Data

An appraiser begins to study the market area by determining what data are needed to solve the appraisal problem, where these data can be obtained, and how they can best be collected. The data required depend on the purpose of the assignment and the use to which the appraisal will be put. The purpose of most appraisal assignments is to reach a market value conclusion, so this discussion will focus on the data needed for these appraisals. In typical market value appraisals such as those used by mortgage lenders, market area analysis is performed to fulfill the following objectives:

- To reveal the market preferences and price patterns on which a market value opinion can be based. This understanding is developed by analyzing data on asking and sale prices and rent levels for properties of different ages with various features and by studying construction costs, supply and demand levels, anticipated changes in supply and demand, and market activity patterns.

- To reach a general conclusion concerning the highest and best use of the site as though vacant, which is required for site valuation. Many characteristics of the market area–e.g., zoning, tax assessments, accessibility, schools, and cultural facilities–contribute to the determination of the highest and best use of the site as though vacant.

- To consider which specific improvements within the general use category would constitute the highest and best use of the site as though vacant. Generally the ideal improvements for the subject property are suggested by the characteristics of other neighborhood property improvements.

- To determine the highest and best use of the property as improved, considering the structures already on the site as well as neighborhood and market standards.

- To define the primary area from which comparable properties will be selected. Several parts of the subject neighborhood or other neighborhoods may be acceptable for this purpose, but locations nearest the subject property and most similar in character are generally the best.

- To discern if and why different locations in the same market area or within competing neighborhoods have different values. This knowledge helps the appraiser adjust sales of properties considered comparable for locational differences within the market area.
- To consider the positive and negative value influence of the neighboring properties and nearby land uses.
- To identify various value influences in the market area and rate the neighborhood in comparison with other, competitive neighborhoods. This information will allow the appraiser to use comparables fromcompetitive neighborhoods if necessary and make the necessary adjustments for neighborhood location. It may also help the appraiser understand the neighborhood's most probable future.
- To learn about recent changes in the market area that may have affected values since the comparables were sold. This information provides a basis for making adjustments for market conditions, i.e., changes in value over time.
- To examine the long-term prospects of the market area to decide whether the subject property will qualify as security for a long-term loan. This objective is particularly important when the client is a lender or loan underwriter.

If the appraisal is to be used in a land use study or for site selection, a different emphasis may be required.

Once the appraiser has reviewed the objectives of the market area analysis, necessary data must be collected and analyzed to identify value influences. The picture the appraiser forms from this descriptive and numerical information will be tested and refined during the field inspection of the neighborhood. The condition of the improvements and the proximity of other uses will also become evident from the field inspection.

Collection Tools

In addition to a vehicle and a map of the area, the appraiser may need a form or checklist to facilitate the collection of data. Such a list may suggest important items that might otherwise be overlooked. If the appraisal is to be communicated in a form report, many appraisers use the form during the field inspection to make field notes.

Where to Find: Essential Data for Market Area Analysis

- Some information can be compiled from census tables, utility line maps, and MLS listings.
- Many counties have GIS mapping with various overlays available online at no charge, which can provide a great deal of information on road maintenance, utilities, environmental features, and utility services.
- Other data will be obtained from interviewing people familiar with the market area—buyers, sellers, brokers, property owners, and officials responsible for public services in the area.
- Data on standardized or statistically defined areas such as cities, counties, tax districts, and census tracts are available from municipal and county sources. However, the areas covered rarely conform to the neighborhood boundaries that the appraiser has identified. Thus during inspection of the neighborhood, corroborative research is often necessary to ascertain whether the general data collected are appropriate for the market area being studied.
- If an appraiser is unfamiliar with a given neighborhood, the field inspection is often the best place to start collecting data.

Form reports are requested by organizations, businesses, and federal agencies that wish to have the results of appraisals presented in a standardized format. The most widely used form is the Uniform Residential Appraisal Report (URAR). Fannie Mae and Freddie Mac require the URAR form for appraisals of properties with mortgages that these agencies may purchase, and the VA and HUD use the form for appraisals of properties with mortgages these departments guarantee or insure. Appraisal report forms include space to record many variables important to market area analysis. (See Figure 10.3.)

Figure 10.3   Neighborhood Section of the URAR

Note: Race and the racial composition of the neighborhood are not appraisal factors.

Neighborhood Characteristics			One-Unit Housing Trends				One-Unit Housing		Present Land Use %	
Location ☐ Urban	☐ Suburban	☐ Rural	Property Values ☐ Increasing	☐ Stable	☐ Declining		PRICE AGE		One-Unit	%
Built-Up ☐ Over 75%	☐ 25–75%	☐ Under 25%	Demand/Supply ☐ Shortage	☐ In Balance	☐ Over Supply		$ (000) (yrs)		2-4 Unit	%
Growth ☐ Rapid	☐ Stable	☐ Slow	Marketing Time ☐ Under 3 mths	☐ 3–6 mths	☐ Over 6 mths		Low		Multi-Family	%
Neighborhood Boundaries							High		Commercial	%
							Pred.		Other	%
Neighborhood Description										
Market Conditions (including support for the above conclusions)										

Although the checklists provided on forms like the URAR serve an important purpose, they should not limit the appraiser's analysis. There may be important value influences in the specific neighborhood that the form does not list. However, each form does have a space for comments, and any considerations not indicated on the checklist can be addressed there. Moreover, the comments must support the appraiser's conclusions pertaining to the market for the subject property. Many appraisals submitted on forms require further explanation or clarification, so the appraiser provides additional narrative material as attached sheets or addenda, which are considered part of the appraisal.

Neighborhood Inspection

The next stage in market area analysis is the visual inspection, which is conducted in several steps:

- Inspect the area's physical characteristics. The appraiser drives or walks around the subject area to develop a sense of place and observe the degree of similarity among land uses, types of structures, architectural styles, and maintenance levels in the area.
- Identify market area boundaries. On a map of the area, the appraiser notes points where the physical characteristics of the land and properties change perceptibly. A copy of this map should be included in the appraisal report. These points generally mark the limits of the market area. The appraiser also identifies any physical barriers

such as major streets, hills, rivers, and railroads that may define the market area's boundaries. Neighborhood occupants, business people, brokers, and community representatives may be questioned to get their opinions of how far the market area extends and what features characterize its different parts.

- Observe land uses and signs of change. The appraiser looks for signs of change in the market area and tries to assess the direction of change, its likely effect on the subject property, and recent changes that may have affected comparable properties. These trends may be noted on the map for future reference.
- Rate the neighborhood for quality. The appraiser should rate various aspects of the neighborhood in comparison with other neighborhoods that appeal to the same market population.

A neighborhood is never rated in absolute terms. Its quality is rated only in comparison with other neighborhoods. The rating suggests the neighborhood's appeal to market participants who are shopping for houses in that neighborhood and competitive neighborhoods.

Reporting Conclusions of the Market Area Analysis

In the appraisal report, an appraiser specifically describes all beneficial and detrimental conditions discovered in the market area analysis. Appraisers must be careful about the use of phrases like "pride of ownership" because they are vague and subjective and in some cases can be viewed as discriminatory. Instead, an appraiser should record precise, impartial observations made during a personal inspection of the neighborhood. Descriptive phrases such as "many broken windows," "tall weeds on site," "no litter present," or "well-kept lawns" convey meaningful information about the value-influencing factors at work in the market area.

The process of market area analysis should

- Delineate the market area boundaries, locate the subject property within the market area, and discuss the relationship between the subject and the observed features of the market area.
- Provide a background for estimating remaining economic life expectancy and effective age.
- Reach a conclusion, based on the data presented, concerning the probable future of the market area and how this future will influence the subject property and similar properties.

Generally, a comprehensive market area analysis will include investigation of the items listed in Figure 10.4, but the scope of work of the appraisal assignment dictates how extensively the research is conducted and how detailed the conclusions of market area analysis must be reported to the client.

Figure 10.4   Market Area Analysis Checklist

Boundaries defined and justified _____

Predominant and ancillary types of improvements _____

History/development, siting, and trends _____

Price range and rental rates _____

Typical age and condition of improvements _____

Neighborhood life cycle stage and trends _____

Percent built-up _____

Typical financing _____

Location and accessibility _____

Land usage and potential for change _____

Homogeneity of surrounding properties _____

Vacancy _____

Turnover in ownership _____

New construction activity _____

Utilities/adequacy _____

Nuisances and/or hazards _____

Support facilities and other expected linkages _____

Analysis/conclusions relative to property appraised _____

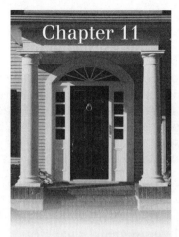

Highest and Best Use

Analyses of the city and region, the neighborhood and the local market, and the site and improvements all contribute data that can help determine the subject property's highest and best use. The appraiser studies this information and decides which legally permitted, physically possible, and financially feasible use of the property will be most productive.

The highest and best use of a property reflects the market's perception of its potential. As the basic principle of anticipation affirms, the potential future use of a property strongly influences its present value. Consequently, highest and best use analysis is an essential step in the valuation process.

This chapter focuses on the purpose of highest and best use analyses, the techniques employed to reach a highest and best use conclusion, and the relationship between highest and best use and the three approaches to value. Special appraisal situations that can complicate highest and best use analyses are also described.

Definition of Highest and Best Use

The current definition of *highest and best use* in appraisal usage is:

> The reasonably probable and legal use of vacant land or an improved property, which is physically possible, appropriately supported, financially feasible, and that results in the highest value. The four criteria the highest and best use must meet are legal permissibility, physical possibility, financial feasibility, and maximum productivity.

This definition indicates that two analyses of highest and best use may be undertaken in an appraisal. One analysis focuses on the *highest and best use of the site as though vacant* and available for development to its highest and best use, and the other is concerned with the *highest and best use of the property as improved.* These two analyses of highest and best use are distinct and serve different functions in the valuation process.

Highest and Best Use of the Site as Though Vacant

In analyzing the highest and best use of the site as though vacant, the site is considered as though it were vacant and ready for development. Even if there are improvements on the property, the property is considered as though it were vacant for the purposes of this analysis. The following questions must be answered:

- If the site is, or were, vacant, should it remain vacant or should it be improved and, if so, what type of improvement should be constructed on it?
- When should the improvement be built?

To conduct the analysis, an appraiser considers proposed uses of the site as though vacant, which may include agricultural, residential, commercial, industrial, or special-purpose uses (i.e., the five basic types of land use). First, each use is tested to see whether it is legally permitted, physically possible, and financially feasible. The test of financial feasibility is applied after the first two criteria are met. Uses that fail any of these three tests are eliminated from further consideration. Then, of the uses that remain, the one that is maximally productive is selected as the highest and best use of the site as though vacant.

As the range of possible uses is narrowed, the uses that remain must be scrutinized carefully. If the appraiser concludes that the site as though vacant should be improved, the client is so informed. At this point the client may want the appraiser to continue the analysis to determine the building characteristics that would create maximum productivity. If a residential use is the highest and best use of the site as though vacant, the appraiser should identify the specific characteristics of a residence that would be maximally productive.

- What would be the approximate size, or square foot area, and price of the residence?
- How many stories would it have?
- How many bedrooms and bathrooms would it contain?
- What would be the architectural design?
- What amenities or features would it have?

ideal improvement. The improvement that takes maximum advantage of the site's potential given market demand, conforms to current market standards and the character of the market area, and contains the most suitably priced components; the improvement that represents the highest and best use of the land as though vacant.

To form a clear understanding of the ideal improvement for the site as though vacant, the appraiser conceives of an improvement that would take maximum advantage of the site's potential and conform to the current standards of the market. Moreover, all components of the ideal improvement would be suitably priced. If this new improvement were to be the highest and best use of the site as though vacant, it presumably would have no physical deterioration or functional obsolescence. Thus, any difference in value between the existing improvement and the ideal improvement would be attributable to these forms of depreciation. The appraiser also must consider external obsolescence, which would affect the existing improvement and the new improvement equally.

In market valuations, analyzing the highest and best use of the site as though vacant and preparing a cost estimate of the ideal improvement serve a variety of purposes. The appraiser's determinations provide information that can be used in all three approaches to value.

In the cost approach, the site must be valued separately from the existing improvements. This requires a separate highest and best use analysis of the site. One technique used to value the site alone is analysis of the sale prices of potentially comparable vacant sites. These vacant parcels can only be truly comparable to the subject site if they have similar highest and best uses.

Existing improvements that do not develop the site to its highest and best use are usually worth less than their cost. A new building that is poorly designed may be worth less than its cost due to the functional obsolescence of its design. The improvement that constitutes the highest and best use is the one that adds the greatest value to the site.

In the sales comparison approach, highest and best use analysis serves as a test in the selection of comparables. The sites of potentially comparable properties should have the same or a similar highest and best use as though vacant as the site of the subject property. If they do not, the sale properties are not comparable.

A highest and best use study may be performed outside of an appraisal assignment. A client may be interested in a project's feasibility—i.e., the likelihood that the project will satisfy explicit objectives. Most feasibility studies are more detailed than highest and best use analyses conducted for market valuation purposes, but the two are closely related. If the purpose of the appraisal is to study feasibility, a more detailed analysis of alternative uses and market conditions is usually required.

highest and best use of land or a site as though vacant. Among all reasonable, alternative uses, the use that yields the highest present land value, after payments are made for labor, capital, and coordination. The use of a property based on the assumption that the parcel of land is vacant or can be made vacant by demolishing any improvements.

highest and best use of property as improved. The use that should be made of a property as it exists. An existing improvement should be renovated or retained as is so long as it continues to contribute to the total market value of the property, or until the return from a new improvement would more than offset the cost of demolishing the existing building and constructing a new one.

Highest and Best Use of the Property as Improved

To determine the highest and best use of the property as improved, an appraiser compares the existing improvements with the ideal improvement. The appraiser attempts to answer these questions:

- Given the existing improvements on the site, what use should be made of the property and when should this use be implemented?

- Are any changes such as modernization, repairs, remodeling, or renovation needed?
- Would these changes contribute more value to the property than they would cost?
- How should the existing or modified structure be used and by whom?
- Should it be owner-occupied, rented, or used for commercial purposes?

In many appraisal situations, the highest and best use of the property as improved will be the same as, or similar to, the highest and best use of the site as though vacant. The potential benefits that could accrue to the site as though vacant from constructing the ideal improvements can often be realized by the existing improvements if modest changes are made. This is particularly likely if the improvements are relatively new or suffer from only minimal deferred maintenance.

In some cases, however, the presence of improvements alters the property's potential to produce benefits. Consider, for example, a large, older residence in an area that has been rezoned for commercial use. If the site were vacant, it would most likely be developed with a commercial use. However, because the improvements currently on the site contribute to value, the property's highest and best use as improved could be continued use as a residential unit, not conversion to a commercial use permitted by zoning. In this case, the improvements contribute value to the property. Improvements can detract from the value of property if they contribute nothing and an expense must be incurred to demolish or remove them.

To analyze the highest and best use of the property as improved, the four tests are once again applied, with special attention paid to the features of the existing improvements that differ from those of the ideal improvement. Reasonable uses that are legally permitted, physically possible, and financially feasible are contemplated. Of the uses that meet these tests, the use that is maximally productive is selected as the highest and best use of the property as improved.

Alternative uses may involve minor renovations such as replacing radiators or touching up paint, or they may necessitate substantial improvements such as adding a bathroom or finishing a basement. An appraiser may conclude that the existing improvement should be completely razed and a new structure be built to take its place. In another situation, an appraiser might decide that no structural changes are necessary and determine that the most productive use would be realized by converting the building to an apartment or a non-residential use.

Analyzing the highest and best use of the property as improved helps the appraiser identify items of depreciation, which must be described in the cost approach. In the sales comparison approach, this highest and best use conclusion helps the appraiser recognize the existing and potential characteristics of the subject property that contribute to value in the market area. Comparable properties should have the same or a similar highest and best use as improved.

Concept of Consistent Use

It is critical that the two analyses of highest and best use not be confused in the course of an appraisal. A site value estimate, which is based on a conclusion of the site's highest and best use as though vacant, may not be added to a value estimate of an improvement based on the highest and best use of the property as improved. The concept of consistent use holds that land cannot be valued on the basis of one use while the improvements are valued on the basis of another. As long as the value of a property as improved is greater than the value of the site as unimproved, the highest and best use is the use of the property as improved.

> **consistent use.** The concept that land cannot be valued on the basis of one use while the improvements are valued on the basis of another. The concept of consistent use must be addressed when properties are devoted to temporary interim uses. Improvements that do not represent the land's highest and best use but have substantial remaining physical lives may have an interim use of temporary value, no value at all, or even negative value if substantial costs must be incurred for their removal.

Consider the appraisal of a residential property located on a commercial artery. The site is currently occupied by a dwelling that is in fairly good condition. Recently the site has been zoned for commercial use, which is the highest and best use of the site as though vacant. Under a commercial use, the site has a market value of $30,000.

The highest and best use of the property as improved is continued residential use subject to minor repairs. Nearby residential properties that are not attractive to commercial users but are otherwise comparable to the subject property have been selling for approximately $70,000. The site value of these properties is estimated to be $10,000, and the value of the comparable improvements is estimated to be $60,000.

An appraiser would violate the concept of consistent use by adding the $60,000 improvement value to the $30,000 site value to obtain a $90,000 total value indication for the subject property. The $60,000 indication of improvement value, which was derived from an analysis of sales of residential properties in a residential location, relies on an estimate based on a residential highest and best use of the property as improved, while the $30,000 indication of commercial site value in a commercial location is an estimate based on a commercial highest and best use of the site as though vacant. The two indications are not compatible, so they may not be added together.

An appraiser could properly estimate the value of the subject property by analyzing sales of commercially zoned residential properties located on the commercial artery with similar highest and best uses of the site as though vacant.

The Four Tests

To test for the highest and best use of a site as though vacant or a property as improved, an appraiser must consider all reasonable alternative uses. The highest and best use must meet four criteria:

1. Legal permissibility
2. Physical possibility
3. Financial feasibility
4. Maximum productivity

These four criteria are often considered in this sequence.[1] Each contemplated use is first tested to determine whether it is legally permissible. Next, uses that are legally permitted are examined to decide whether they are also physically possible. If the uses pass both the legal permissibility and physical possibility tests, the appraiser then considers whether the use is financially feasible–i.e., produces a return that is at least greater than the investment. Finally, considering the legally permitted and physically possible uses that are financially feasible, the appraiser measures the residual value of the land for each alternative use. The one that produces the highest land value is maximally productive.

Legal Permissibility
Site as Though Vacant

Each potential use must be tested for legal permissibility. Zoning ordinances, building codes, historic district controls, environmental regulations, and other public and private restrictions can all have an impact on the potential uses of land.

To determine whether a use is legally permissible, an appraiser must consider both present and anticipated zoning restrictions. If there is a reasonable probability that a change in zoning regulations could occur, an appraiser may consider a use that is not currently allowed under the existing regulations as the highest and best use. However, the appraiser is obligated to disclose all factors pertinent to this determination, including the time and expense involved in securing the zoning change and the risk that the change may not occur. (These hypothetical conditions must be fully disclosed in the appraisal report.) Zoning changes may affect the use density and yard and bulk regulations that control the size and location of buildings.

---

1.   It is not necessary to consider the first two tests in this order at all times. Physical possibility may be considered before legal permissibility. After the first two tests, however, the tests of financial feasibility and maximum productivity must be applied in this order.

Changes in zoning regulations can affect the highest and best use of land in another way. When regulations change, existing improvements may cease to conform to the current law. The current use will be permitted to continue, however, and this use may be more productive than the use allowed under the new zoning. In this case, the highest and best use of the property would be to maintain the legally nonconforming use of the existing improvements.

Building codes can prevent land from being developed to its highest and best use by imposing burdensome restrictions that increase the cost of construction. This is particularly true in metropolitan areas where different municipalities or jurisdictions have different building codes. Residential development trends in metropolitan areas are greatly influenced by off-site requirements specified in building codes. Less restrictive codes typically result in lower development costs and attract developers to an area, while more restrictive codes discourage development.

Increasing concern over the effects of land use has led to environmental regulations, which also must be considered in highest and best use analysis. Appraisers must consider regulations designed to protect clear air, clean water, wetlands, and historic areas and investigate the public's reaction to proposed projects. Opposition from local residents and community groups has stopped many real estate developments.

Property as Improved

Many legal considerations that affect the highest and best use of vacant land affect improved property as well. Major remodeling or renovation usually requires a building permit and must comply with the building codes currently in effect. Many communities use their control over permits, codes, and tax incentives to encourage renovation and discourage unwanted conversions. Legal restrictions can have a substantial effect on the highest and best use of property as improved. Commercial or income-producing uses of residences may be restricted by zoning laws or private agreements.

A trend away from demolition and toward preservation of existing structures became evident in the early 1980s. The preservationist trend has led to historic district zoning controls, which make demolition permits difficult or impossible to obtain in some areas. One effect of these controls has been to decrease significantly the number of instances in which the highest and best use of property is to demolish the existing improvements. Moreover, the special tax incentives that are sometimes available for maintaining older buildings may substantially enhance their value and thus influence their highest and best use.

Physical Possibility
Site as Though Vacant

Location has a substantial effect on highest and best use. Commercial and industrial uses frequently require convenient access to transportation networks and proximity to raw materials, labor pools, consumers, and distributors. Commercial enterprises must be located on thoroughfares or in other places accessible to potential customers. Residential uses generally require utility service and the amenities and environment provided by a neighborhood.

Analysis of the community and the neighborhood can provide important clues as to how the location of a site affects its highest and best use. Current patterns and anticipated trends must both be considered. Location is studied by investigating linkages, access, and the direction of community growth. An appraiser may ask:

- How is the site situated with respect to roads and utilities?
- Will the quality of the schools, the social amenities, and the reputation or prestige of the area attract residential users of a given income level?
- How convenient would the site be for other types of uses?
- How will the pattern of community growth affect the future potential of the site?

Size, shape, and topography can also affect the highest and best use of a site as though vacant. Agricultural and industrial uses may be precluded by the small size of certain parcels, particularly if nearby land is not available for plottage. An irregular shape, poor soil of subsoil conditions, or uneven terrain can restrict the range of possible uses for a site and may increase the costs of constructing improvements.

The highest and best use of a site may require combining it with another parcel for a use that requires a larger area (i.e., assemblage). The land would then have plottage value. An appraiser must consider the possibility that all or part of the land will be assembled with other parcels. If the highest and best use conclusion is predicated on the likelihood of an assemblage, this must be clearly stated in the appraisal report. Sometimes a site has excess land, which is land that may accommodate a separate highest and best use, or surplus land, which would not accommodate a separate highest and best use.[2] If there is excess land, only part of the site will be used for its primary purpose. The rest may have another highest and best use or may be held for future expansion of the anticipated improvement.

When the topography, subsoil, or topsoil conditions of a site make development dangerous or costly, its value is often adversely affected. In a given area the sites available for a particular use compete with one another. If it will cost more to grade or lay foundations on one site than on more typical sites, the site may not appeal to the same users and might have a different highest and best use. Alternatively, the highest and best use might remain the same, but the site could have a lower value.

Property as Improved

Physical and environmental conditions also shape the highest and best use of the property as improved. The size, design, and condition of the

---

2. The terms *excess land* and *surplus land* were defined in Chapter 7.

improvements limit the range of productive uses to which the property can be put. For example, additions can usually be made to one-story houses more easily than to two-story houses. The property's ability to accommodate the present use is often relevant to the highest and best use conclusion. Obviously the condition of the existing improvements and the number of deferred maintenance items and short-lived items requiring repair or replacement influence the feasibility and cost-effectiveness of various remodeling projects.

Financial Feasibility

After eliminating uses that do not meet the criteria of legal permissibility and physical possibility, the remaining uses must be tested for financial feasibility. If there is sufficient demand for the property, some market participant will be willing to translate that demand into value, either by buying or renting the property. A use is financially feasible if the income or value benefits that accrue from the use sufficiently exceed the expenses involved. If the benefits exceed the costs by only a marginal amount, a project may not be feasible. To estimate these benefits and costs, an appraiser must carefully examine the supply of and demand for the use in question.

Site as Though Vacant

The potential highest and best use of a site is usually its long-term land use or a use that is expected to remain on the site for the normal economic, or useful, life of the improvements. Most buildings are expected to last at least 25 years, and some may last more than 100 years. A building's value or income usually reflects a carefully considered and highly specific long-term use program. Homeowners may base their decisions to buy on the anticipation of tax advantages and property appreciation, but the benefits of owning residential property are usually the benefits of occupancy and the reversion upon resale–i.e., the lump-sum benefits the investor receives when the investment is terminated.

The benefits of owner occupancy are intangible and difficult to calculate, but a developer's anticipated return from the sale of houses in a proposed residential development can be measured. After an allowance is made for the absorption period–i.e., the time it takes to market the developed units successfully–these benefits must be sufficient to justify all construction and other expenses the developer of the vacant site will incur and provide an entrepreneurial profit. In this case, financial feasibility is determined by analyzing the anticipated return rather than an income stream.

Property as Improved

The feasibility of renovation or rehabilitation projects is often more difficult to calculate than the feasibility of construction on vacant sites because costs may be harder to estimate. Renovation estimates may be based on unit-in-place costs for new work plus an allowance for the normally higher costs of repair work. Rehabilitation estimates are frequently based on recent costs for the same or equivalent work on similar properties. Homeowners and property managers may keep records that include specific bids for renovation work such as exterior painting, roof repair, or exterior decorating.

The cost of repair work on existing improvements rarely equals the cost of similar work in new construction. Modernizing and remodeling work is usually more expensive for several reasons. Although the quantity of material used may be the same, more labor is involved in repair and the conditions are different. Altering a structure usually involves tearing out old work and performing smaller tasks under conditions that are not conducive to efficiency. If the contractor's estimate is a flat fee, it may be substantially higher than the cost of identical work in new construction because the contractor seeks protection against complications that may arise as the remodeling progresses. Unforeseen complications may necessitate the replacement of existing conduits, pipes, and structural load-bearing members.

The owner must pay the architect's fee, the cost of supervision, and the contractor's profit and loses the use of the house while the work is being done. The financial feasibility of renovation or rehabilitation is determined by analyzing whether the costs incurred will be recovered through a higher anticipated sale price or an increased income stream. This is the foundation of the test of "curability," which is analyzed in the application of the cost approach.

Maximum Productivity

Of the financially feasible uses, the use that produces the greatest residual land value is the long-term highest and best use. As mentioned previously, the primary benefits of owning many residential properties are the intangible benefit of owner occupancy and the anticipated reversion. Nevertheless, a measure of maximum productivity can be evaluated in the following situations:

- If the highest and best use of a vacant parcel of land is a single-family residence, the price of the site must reflect the greatest return on the developer's capital expenditure.
- To apply the test of maximum productivity to projected rental units, the project's ability to generate the highest anticipated income stream and reversion are compared to the developer's investment in the land.
- To test the maximum productivity of improved properties where the highest and best use requires renovation or rehabilitation, the most cost-effective means of modernization is analyzed.

Highest and Best Use Conclusion

Upon completion of the analysis, a conclusion as to the highest and best use of the property is required. With respect to the highest and best use of the site as though vacant, the conclusion may be to leave the land vacant or to improve it. With respect to the highest and best

Highest and Best Use Checklist

Analysis of Highest and Best Use as Vacant

Legal Use
- What is the current zoning (R-1, residential single-family, one unit per acre)?_____
- What does the zoning allow? (See ordinance for uses by right and special waiver.)_____
- Are there deed restrictions?_____ Is the location in a PUD with restrictions?_____
- What are the minimum lot sizes and setbacks?_____
- Is there a possibility of a change in zoning?_____ What is the time frame and cost?_____

Physically Possible
- Size _____
- Shape _____
- Access _____
- Utilities _____
- Flood plain _____
- Wetlands _____
- Special view _____
- Quality of roads _____
- Special nuisances or hazards (location next to gas station, etc.) _____
- Location _____
- Soil and subsoil conditions _____

Financially Feasible

Note: Make sure market area analysis sets the stage for following analysis.
- Discuss market activity levels in the defined neighborhood or marketing area, including days on the market, list-to-sale ratio, number of listings, number of properties sold, price range of new construction, and absorption rates.
_____
- Is financing available and on what terms?_____
- What are the income levels of buyers and are there ample buyers to necessitate a particular product?_____
_____
- Are builders building in this area and, if so, is the profit reasonable?_____
- What product does the market most demand that the legal aspects of this property would allow and the physical characteristics would accommodate?_____

Maximally Productive
- What would be the best type of product to build on this site (residential, commercial, industrial, etc.)?_____
- If required, what is the ideal improvement? (Provide the most acceptable size range, number of stories, quality, and architectural design of structure.) _____
- How many bathrooms, bedrooms, garages, carports, porches, pools, etc. would this market command? (The market area section of the report sets the stage for this analysis.)_____
- What quality and general price range would be most in demand? (The market area analysis sets the stage for this determination.) _____

Highest and Best Use as Improved

Consider the four tests above and how the current structure compares to the ideal improvement:
- Are there any changes required to the current structure to bring it to the highest and best use?_____
- Would the changes contribute more value to the property than they would cost? _____
- Discuss functional or external obsolescence and how they affect the property "as improved." _____
- Discuss the physical depreciation charged to the current structure and how it may affect the value and marketability of the property. _____
- Would the current improvement be most profitable as an owner-occupied property or tenant-occupied property?
_____

use of the property as improved, the conclusion may be to continue the use as developed or to change it through renovation, remodeling, demolition, or conversion.

Special Situations in Highest and Best Use Analysis

The steps described in this chapter constitute the basic procedure for testing highest and best use; they are used in many appraisal situations. However, in certain circumstances it may be difficult to determine highest and best use. Special situations in highest and best use include

- Interim uses
- Legally nonconforming uses
- Excess and surplus land

Many of these highest and best use problems are found in properties located in transitional neighborhoods.

Interim Uses

Often the highest and best use of a site as though vacant or of a property as improved may be expected to change in the foreseeable future. A tract of land may not be ready for development now, but urban growth patterns suggest that it will be suitable for development in several years. Similarly, improved urban property may not be renovated until the demand for renovated units is great enough to justify the expense. In neighborhoods that are in transition, the highest and best use for the near future of the site as though vacant or the property as improved may differ from the long-term highest and best use.

A short-term highest and best use is called an *interim use*. If the appraiser determines that an interim use is warranted until the long-term highest and best use of a property can be realized, the appraiser must carefully estimate the duration of the interim use, the financial risks and rewards associated with conversion to the long-term highest and best use, and the benefits or costs that the interim use will contribute to the value of the site or the improved property. An interim use can often last several years and in some cases may be indefinite.

interim use. The temporary use to which a site or improved property is put until it is ready to be put to its future highest and best use.

legally nonconforming use. A use that was lawfully established and maintained, but no longer conforms to the use regulations of the current zoning in the zone where it is located.

An interim use can affect the value of a site or an improved property positively or negatively. It may produce marginal benefits or income but not contribute nearly as much as the long-term highest and best use. The interim use would remain in place until the value realized from a change of use would more than offset the cost of acquisition, the cost of holding the property during construction or conversion, and the cost of holding the property during sale or lease-up.

Legally Nonconforming Uses

A legally nonconforming use is a use that was lawfully established and maintained but no longer conforms to the regulations of the zone in which it is located. A nonconforming use is usually created by the imposition of zoning or a change in zoning ordinances that occurs after the original construction of the improvements.

A change in zoning regulations may make an improvement inadequate for the highest and best use of the site. A single-family residence in an area that has been rezoned for commercial use would no longer represent the highest and best use of the site as though vacant. In this case, the legally nonconforming residential use would probably be maintained as an interim use until the existing improvement has depreciated sufficiently to make either conversion to a commercial use or razing the existing improvements for complete commercial redevelopment of the site feasible.

A zoning change can sometimes create a value premium for an improvement. A reduction in the permitted density or a change in development standards may make a nonconforming use more valuable. A country store, for example, might be located in an area that has been entirely rezoned for low-density residential use. Local zoning ordinances would permit the existing use to continue but prohibit any expansion or major alteration of the improvements.

Regulations concerning what may or must be done with a nonconforming use differ. Some jurisdictions require that nonconforming uses be phased out over a period of time. If a nonconforming use is discontinued or terminated because the improvements have been damaged by a storm or fire, for example, reestablishing the use may depend on the degree of damage incurred. Because laws vary in different jurisdictions, an appraiser must study the regulations that apply to the subject property and each comparable used in the appraisal and check enforcement records to determine how long the local government allows nonconforming uses to continue.

When a zoning change creates a value premium for a nonconforming improvement, continuation of the use often produces more benefits or income than would be possible if the improvement were new. In many nonconforming use situations, the property value estimate reflects the nonconforming use. Land value is estimated on the basis of the legally permissible use, assuming the land is vacant and its value is deducted from the total property value. The remaining value reflects the contribution of the existing improvements as well as any possible premium for the nonconforming use.

Legally nonconforming uses that correspond to the highest and best use of the property as improved are often easy to recognize. In some situations, however, determining whether an existing nonconforming use is the highest and best use of the site requires careful analysis of the incomes produced or values achieved by the nonconforming property and by alternative uses to which the property could be put if it were made to conform with existing regulations.

Because few sales of properties considered comparable exist for legally nonconforming properties, application of the sales comparison approach is difficult.

Excess and Surplus Land

Many large sites have more than one highest and best use. In some situations a vacant site or a site considered as though vacant may actually consist of two separate economic units. If the portion of the site allocated to one particular use is improved, complies with the zoning requirements, and is suited to the use of the improvement, the highest and best use of this part of the site would be as improved. The highest and best use of the other, unimproved portion of the site—i.e., the excess land—would be for development in conformity with zoning regulations.

In other situations, the unused portion of a site may not be separated and simply be surplus land. In other cases, depending on the location of the improvement(s), the site may not be suitable for two economic units, each with a separate highest and best use, creating surplus land, which may only be used for the future expansion of the existing improvement(s). Frequently, a site with surplus land is oversized compared with competitive sites. In these instances the value of the oversized site may be greater than that of competitive properties but may not be as great as that of a similar property with excess land.

The analysis of different approaches to value may have ramifications for property value. For example, consider a large residential site that could be divided into two full lots for development. Under the cost approach, land value is estimated as if the land were vacant and unimproved. Accordingly, the appraiser arrives at a $10,000 value indication for each lot with a site value of $20,000. However, at present a house straddles the lot lines. Under the sales comparison approach, the site value is estimated as improved and its value is included in overall property value. In applying the sales comparison approach, the appraiser realizes that because of its impaired functional utility—as a result of the misplacement of the improvements—an adjustment to the property value is appropriate. The appraiser reconsiders the indication of property value from the cost approach. Here too impaired functional utility penalizes the property's value and warrants the same adjustment. This adjustment usually takes the form of incurable functional obsolescence caused by the building's location on the lot.

Highest and Best Use in Neighborhoods in Transition

Some of the most difficult residential assignments are appraisals of properties located in areas that are undergoing transition. Transitional neighborhoods present major problems in highest and best use analysis and in the application of the three approaches to value. Many special highest and best use situations can be combined in neighborhoods in transition. Selecting between highest and best use alternatives in these neighborhoods is often difficult. Interim uses are common and zoning changes and violations are more likely to occur. Multiple uses and unusual uses also increase in frequency. Appraisers using the same valuation techniques and the same market data may arrive at different opinions when valuing properties in transitional neighborhoods.

> **multiple use.** A combination of compatible land uses in an area.
>
> **transition.** Changes in market area use, e.g., agricultural to residential, residential to commercial.

Neighborhood and market area analyses are especially critical when the use of the subject property may be about to change. An appraiser may ask

- What factors in the neighborhood or the larger community are causing the transition?
- Where have the most rapid changes been taking place?
- Where are changes likely to occur in the future?
- When will change start and come to an end?

The appraiser must carefully identify the different markets that may compete for use of the subject property.

- If an adjacent neighborhood is expanding, will it grow to encompass the subject property and the subject neighborhood?
- How strong is the demand for the new use and how will it be met by the anticipated supply?
- When will the effects of change be felt most acutely?
- If the subject neighborhood is declining, how and when will the subject be affected?
- Do potentially comparable properties offer the same prospects to their purchasers?
- Will the long-term highest and best use of the improvement be conversion to a more intensive use?
- If so, when might the change occur and how will the interim use contribute to value?

These are the kinds of considerations that must be investigated in appraising properties in transitional neighborhoods.

In new neighborhoods, conformity to surrounding property uses is generally a reliable indication of the highest and best use of the site as though vacant. In older neighborhoods and in transitional neighborhoods in particular, conformity does not reliably indicate the probable highest and best use of the site. For example, consider the highest and best use of a site as though vacant in a declining residential neighborhood of large, 70-year-old, two- and three-story houses that sell for $90,000 to $100,000. It would not be feasible to replace any of these houses with similar new improvements because the costs of constructing a large dwelling would probably greatly exceed its expected selling price. The highest and best use of the site might be to build a smaller house that is more compatible with the incomes of current area residents or to put the site to some alternative use.

In the past when the highest and best use of a property in a transitional neighborhood changed, the logical alternative was to raze the improvements and redevelop the site. However, in light of the current interest in preserving older structures, other alternatives should be investigated. Existing improvements can be remodeled, renovated, restored, rehabilitated, or even relocated in some cases. Tax incentives and local regulations may make one of these alternatives more probable, and more productive, than demolition.

Zoning changes frequently occur in transitional neighborhoods. When a neighborhood is declining, zoning regulations may not be enforced. As the neighborhood begins to stabilize, new ordinances are often put into effect. In growing neighborhoods there may be strong economic pressures to alter existing zoning ordinances. An appraiser investigates the probability and likely content of zoning changes and estimates their effect on the highest and best use of the site or improved property. These factors should be described in the appraisal report.

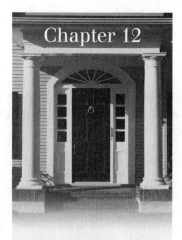

Chapter 12

Land and Site Valuation

Although the words *site* and *land* are sometimes used synonymously, these terms must be differentiated in the valuation process. A parcel of land is a portion of the earth's surface in its natural state, while a site is land that has been improved–e.g., cleared, graded, and provided with utilities, drainage, and access–to prepare it for its intended use. Consequently, a site often has more value than a parcel of raw land.

Land value and site value should never be confused in an appraisal. If sales of similar properties are used to estimate site value, the appraiser must make sure that these sales are also of sites, not raw land. If an indication of raw land value is used in the cost approach, the depreciated value of the improvements, which is added to the land value, must reflect the value contribution of clearing, grading, drainage, soil compaction, installation of utilities, and other on-site and off-site improvements that were not previously included in the land value component. Consistency must be maintained throughout the valuation process.

Land as a Source of Value

Land is said to *have* value, while improvements *contribute* to value. Land may be seen as the value base on which improvements are built. Improvements can constitute a penalty on land value when they contribute no value as an interim use and their demolition requires removal costs.

It is useful to distinguish between site improvements *to* a site and site improvements *on* a site. Improvements to a site are improvements such as clearing and grading that *transform* a parcel of land *into* a site.

They are included in the value of the site as though vacant. In contrast, site improvements on a site are improvements such as landscaping that *contribute additional value* to the site, and they are not included in the value of the site as though vacant.

Unlike improvements, land is not a *wasting asset* and therefore does not depreciate in the traditional sense. However, the value of land may change as a result of external conditions and market forces. Only improvements depreciate in value.

Commodities can be manufactured, but land is provided by nature and its supply is relatively fixed. Major changes in the earth's surface have occurred over the centuries, but the supply and quality of land do not change much over time. These natural events rarely affect the land appraisers are concerned with. There are, however, a few notable exceptions including changes in coastal areas and weather-related changes.

Land is affected by accretion or erosion along a shoreline, pollution from harmful wastes such as radon and other toxic materials, inundation by volcanic ash and lava flows, exhaustion by improper farming methods, and ecological imbalances that transform agricultural land into desert. Earthquakes and landslides also change the surface of the earth, and faults beneath the surface can create vast sinkholes. These occurrences are relatively rare.

Because land is generally fixed in supply and location, its value accrues entirely from its potential to serve an economically productive or beneficial use for people. A parcel of land may have utility as the site of a building, recreational facility, agricultural tract, or right of way for transportation routes. If land has utility for a specific use and there is demand for that use, the land has value to some category of users. Its value in the market depends on its relative attractiveness to prospective purchasers in comparison with other parcels.

Market Forces That Influence Land Values

The forces that affect land values are closely related to those that affect the values of improved properties. A thorough analysis of the market forces at work in a city, region, neighborhood, and market area should yield much information that is relevant to the land value estimate. Significant social, economic, governmental, and environmental influences on value should be considered in the analysis.

Trends in the value of land and of improved properties do differ. When overall values are appreciating, land values may increase more slowly than the values of improved properties, and the first developers in a popular area may reap unusually large profits. However, as competition increases and profits are cut, the observed rate of change in land values becomes more similar to the rate of change in the values of improved properties. When improvements are new, land values tend to equal the values of improved properties once all costs of construction and a normal entrepreneurial profit are deducted. When only a few lots remain in a popular location, the value of a parcel of land in that location sometimes increases beyond the level justified by its productivity. In this case, prospective owners or owner-occupants may pay higher land and construction costs than the broader real estate market would seem to warrant. Nevertheless, these occurrences are relatively rare. On the whole, the market tends toward equilibrium.

Land and Site Valuation in Residential Appraisal

When improved residential property is being appraised, a separate site valuation is needed to derive an indication of value by the cost approach. To arrive at a total property value indication using this approach, the value of the site must be added to the depreciated reproduction or replacement cost of the improvements. Site valuation is also needed to apply some techniques in the income capitalization approach. Some assignments that may require land valuation include appraisals for property taxation, insurance, and condemnation.

In the sales comparison approach, an understanding of how much value the site contributes to the overall value of the subject property can help an appraiser determine the suitability of the comparable properties selected for analysis. Generally, a comparable property should have a site-to-property value ratio that is similar to that of the subject property. If a potential comparable and the subject property have dissimilar site-to-property value ratios, their highest and best uses may differ as well.

Land is valued as though vacant, unimproved, and available for development to its highest and best use. Therefore, the land component of a property must be analyzed and valued separately. A developer needs to know the value of vacant or improved land to decide if a project is feasible. Landowners may want to know the value of their land to establish a sale price. Land and improvements are sometimes taxed at different rates, so separate valuations may be needed for tax assessment purposes.

Land and Site Valuation Techniques

The most common approach to estimate land or site value is sales comparison. If a sufficient number of vacant land comparables are not available, less direct valuation techniques can be employed. These alternative procedures include allocation, extraction, land residual, ground rent capitalization, and subdivision development analysis. The last three techniques are more commonly used in commercial land or site valuation.

> For the purposes of this discussion, the same techniques are applied in land valuation and site valuation.

Sales Comparison

Of the various techniques available for estimating land value, none is more persuasive than sales comparison. Sales of similar land parcels or sites are analyzed and compared and sale prices are adjusted to compensate for differences. The process results in an indication of value for the land parcel or site being appraised. Adjustments are derived from market data using paired data set analysis or other methods. The adjusted sale prices provide a value range conclusion that can be reconciled into an opinion of land or site value.

The sales comparison approach to value is discussed in detail in Chapter 16. The steps used in land or site valuation are summarized below:

1. Collect data on sales of similar land parcels or sites and information on listings and offers.
2. Analyze the data to determine the comparability of these land parcels or sites with the subject land parcel or site. Develop appropriate units of comparison and study each element of comparison.
3. Adjust the sale prices of the comparable land parcels or sites to reflect how they differ from the subject.
4. Reconcile these adjusted sale prices into a single value indication or range of value indications for the subject land parcel or site.

Collecting the Data

Data on land sales and ground leases are available from Internet-based data services, newspapers, records of deeds and assessments, other appraisers, and other sources. Interviews with buyers, sellers, lawyers, lenders, and real estate brokers and agents involved in the transactions can provide more direct information. An appraiser identifies the property rights, legal encumbrances, physical characteristics, and other site features involved in each sale of a potentially comparable property. Sales with special financing or sales affected by unusual motivation must be identified, analyzed, and included in an appraisal assignment with caution. For example, parcels that are purchased for assemblage may not provide good indications of market value because the value in use (to create a larger and more useful tract of land) may differ from value in exchange (market value).

In addition to recorded sales and signed contracts, an appraiser considers active listings of properties, offers to purchase, options, pending sales, and other incomplete or ongoing but not yet closed transactions. Offers are less reliable than signed contracts and recorded sales. An actual sale price is usually lower than the initial asking price but higher than the initial offer to buy. Negotiations may proceed through several stages. Offers may provide an indication of the limits on value for a subject property or neighborhood, but they are not conclusive and are inadmissible in some courts and not recognized by some users of appraisal services. They should still be identified and analyzed to provide support to other data included in the appraisal report.

USPAP and standard practice require appraisers to research the market history for the subject property. This can give an excellent indication of market value for the subject or it may be meaningless. The standards require that the appraiser research, analyze, and report a three-year sales history. Some appraisers consider this to be a part of the sales comparison approach, while others think it is independent. In either case, it is a standard part of the process and includes the analysis of land or sites.

Analyzing the Data for Comparability
To be comparable, a parcel of land or a site should be in the same market area as the subject or in a market area comparable to that of the subject–i.e., it should effectively compete with the subject property in the minds of potential buyers. Comparable transactions should be recent and the parcels of land or sites should be substantially similar to the subject in terms of the elements of comparison described below. Each comparable used should be analyzed.

Comparable parcels should have the same highest and best use as the subject parcel. The subject parcel is considered as though vacant in this analysis, even if improvements are located upon it. The highest and best use of the subject and the comparables is determined by carefully studying the supply and demand trends in the neighborhood and the market area. All current, anticipated, and potential development activity should be investigated as part of this analysis. (See Chapter 11 for a more detailed discussion of highest and best use.)

Units of Comparison and Elements of Comparison
The data collected on each property and transaction must be analyzed to ensure their comparability and consistency with other data. The units of comparison applied to the market data may include price or rent per acre, square foot, front foot, allowable dwelling unit, and lot.

An appraiser analyzes a sale using as many units of comparison as possible to determine whether any particular unit or units reveal a consistent pattern in the given market. It is sometimes possible to correlate the results obtained using two or more units of comparison to arrive at a land or site value estimate–e.g., dollars per acre, lot, unit, or square foot. If any inconsistency is observed in the data, the cause should be investigated.

The elements of comparison used to analyze sites or vacant parcels include:

- Property rights and limitations on use
- Financing terms
- Conditions of sale (motivation)
- Expenditures made immediately after purchase, such as costs for demolition, grading, installation of utilities, and repairs to correct a flooding problem
- Market conditions (time)
- Location
- Physical characteristics

- Available utilities
- Other characteristics such as zoning

As a general rule, the greater the dissimilarity between the subject and comparable, the less reliable the comparable will be for deriving a market value indication. When the sale price of a comparable property requires large adjustments for any element of comparison, the potential for distortion and error in the analysis generally increases. A comparable sale becomes less reliable as more adjustments are made. The adjusted sale price of the comparable property requiring the least adjustment should be given the most weight in sales comparison analysis.

Market conditions and location are often the most significant elements of comparison. If sale prices have been changing rapidly over the past several months and adequate data are available, the sale dates of the comparables should be as near as possible to the effective date of the appraisal. If an appraiser must choose between sales of properties close to the subject property that occurred several years ago and recent transactions in more distant locations, a decision based on logic must be made. In those circumstances, the character of the market may dictate the choice of comparables. For example, in a stable market, sales in more distant locations may be appropriate, while in a rapidly increasing or decreasing market, more recent sales will be the most indicative.

Size may be a less important element of comparison than sale date and location in many markets. Most property types have an optimal site size and extra space may not add value at the same rate as the space needed to facilitate the primary use. In other words, if the market requires a site with 0.5 acre and the subject has 0.75 acre, the extra 0.25 acre will have value, but be valued at a lesser rate per acre (or square foot) than the initial 0.5 acre. The additional land may be excess land, which can accommodate a separate highest and best use, or it may be surplus land that is not needed to support the existing improvements. Excess land may be sold separately in the market.

Because sales of sites with different sizes may have different unit prices, appraisers should either find comparable properties that are approximately the same size as the subject property or convert the sale prices to size-related unit prices such as price per square foot or price per acre. However, a per-unit comparison may not always be appropriate. If a comparable is considerably larger than the subject property, the law of diminishing returns may influence the land or site value, resulting in a lower price per unit of comparison than a smaller property in the same location might have.

Zoning is often a basic criterion in the selection and analysis of comparables. Sites that have the same zoning as the subject property are more appropriate comparables. If sufficient sales of sites in the same zoning category are not available, data from sites with similar zoning can be used after adjustments are made.

Adjusting Sale Prices to Reflect Differences

After comparable data are collected and categorized and comparable properties are examined and described, sales data can be assembled in an organized and logical manner. Sales data may be reported on a market data grid that provides a separate line item for each significant property characteristic. Adjustments for dissimilarities between the subject parcel and each comparable parcel are made to the sale price of each comparable to provide a value indication for the subject. The set of adjusted sale prices indicated by the comparable sales provides an indicated range of value.

Adjustments for elements of comparison can be derived from market data using various analytical techniques. The application of these techniques may produce quantitative adjustments or qualitative analyses. Quantitative adjustments are derived from

- Paired data analysis
- Statistical and graphic analysis
- Trend analysis
- Other methods, such as direct comparison, e.g., of costs of demolition or costs of environmental remediation (Note: Actual costs do not necessarily reflect market value differences)

Qualitative differences are studied using

- Relative comparison analysis
- Ranking analysis

To perform paired data analysis, the appraiser must be able to find comparable parcels that differ significantly from the subject in only one respect. The prices of these comparables are studied to determine how that one variable affects price. Scatter diagrams and other analytical tools can be used to study the effects of location and physical property characteristics. Often an adjustment for market conditions can be derived by studying the trend in sales of comparable properties over the past several years. This technique is known as *trend analysis.* Regardless of the procedure selected, an appraiser must collect and review sufficient data to make the analysis statistically meaningful and indicative of the market. Without a broad market sample, paired data analysis cannot provide reliable results, particularly when the data are contradictory.

Relative comparison analysis and ranking analysis are used to make qualitative judgments about the subject and comparable properties. In both, comparables are identified as

paired data analysis. A quantitative technique used to identify and measure adjustments to the sale prices or rents of comparable properties. To apply this technique, sales or rental data on nearly identical properties are analyzed to isolate a single characteristic's effect on value or rent.

trend analysis. A quantitative technique used to identify and measure adjustments to the sale prices of comparable properties; useful when sales data on highly comparable properties are lacking, but a broad database on properties with less similar characteristics is available. Market sensitivity is investigated by testing various factors that influence sale prices.

relative comparison analysis. A qualitative technique for analyzing comparable sales; used to determine whether the characteristics of a comparable property are inferior, superior, or equal to those of the subject property. Relative comparison analysis is similar to paired data analysis, but quantitative adjustments are not derived.

ranking analysis. A qualitative technique for analyzing comparable sales; a variant of relative comparison analysis in which comparable sales are ranked in descending or ascending order of desirability and each is analyzed to determine its position relative to the subject.

inferior, superior, or equal to the subject property. These techniques are similar to paired data set analysis, but in relative comparison and ranking analyses the differences between properties are not quantified.

Once an adjustment is derived for each difference, it can be applied to the prices of all the comparables that differ from the subject in that characteristic. Quantitative adjustments may be applied in dollars or percentages and are usually made in a particular order. Adjustments for property rights, financing, conditions of sale, and market conditions are generally applied before adjustments are made for location and physical characteristics. Similarly, quantitative adjustments are typically made before sale prices are reduced to per-unit prices. Reducing sale prices to per-unit prices based on size allows the appraiser to compare parcels of different dimensions and eliminates the need to adjust for differences in size.

Qualitative differences are generally considered after quantitative adjustments have been applied. Analysis of qualitative differences provides the basis for reconciliation. *If market data do not exist, quantitative adjustments are unsupportable and should not be made.* All adjustments made to comparables should be set forth in the appraisal report in a logical and understandable manner. (While there is no government-sponsored vacant site appraisal form, many appraisers use a narrative format, create their own adjustment grid for site valuation, or use the site section of a form such as the AI Reports Summary Appraisal Report–Residential, which is shown in Figure 12.1.)

Reconciling the Results

To reconcile the value indications derived from sales comparison, each step in the analysis is reviewed. The reliability of each data source, specific comparable, and analytical method is considered. The reasons for any differences among the sales data for properties considered comparable are investigated. The initial questions to be asked might include:

- How current are the data that support the use conclusion?
- Do they seem to conform to the pattern of growth in the neighborhood?

It is especially important to scrutinize the highest and best use conclusion on which the land or site value estimate is based. An appraiser should ask questions about

- The number of adjustments. The smaller the number of adjustments, the more comparable the property is.

Figure 12.1   Site Section of the AI Reports™ Summary Appraisal Report

Client:		Client File #:	
Subject Property:		Appraisal File #:	

SITE VALUATION

Site Valuation Methodology

☐ **Sales Comparison Approach:** A set of procedures in which a value indication is derived by comparing the property being appraised to similar properties that have been sold recently, then applying appropriate units of comparison and making adjustments to the sale prices of the comparables based on the elements of comparison. The sales comparison approach may be used to value improved properties, vacant land, or land being considered as though vacant; it is the most common and preferred method of land valuation when an adequate supply of comparable sales are available.

☐ **Market Extraction Method:** A method of estimating land value in which the depreciated cost of the improvements on the improved property is estimated and deducted from the total sale price to arrive at an estimated sale price for the land; most effective when the improvements contribute little to the total sale price of the property.

☐ **Alternative Method:** (Describe methodology and rationale)

Site Valuation

ITEM	SUBJECT	COMPARISON NO. 1	COMPARISON NO. 2	COMPARISON NO. 3
Address				
Proximity to Subject				
Sales Price		$	$	$
Price / _____		$	$	$
Data Source/ Verification				
Sale Date				
Location				
Site Size				
Site View				
Site Improvements				
Net Adjustment				
Indicated Value		$	$	$
Net Adjustment		%	%	%
Gross Adjustment		%	%	%

Site Valuation Comments:

Site Valuation Reconciliation:

Opinion of Site Value	$

- Gross and net adjustments. The total dollar amount of adjustments and the net dollar amount after applying all positive and negative adjustments are measures of comparability.
- The total amount of data. The overall reliability of the sales comparison approach generally improves as more data is analyzed.

Even minor differences in the zoning of neighborhoods or the regulations for subdivisions in which comparables are located may affect factors on which the highest and best use conclusion is based. Variations in zoning and highest and best use are qualitative differences that should be analyzed and reconciled.

Finally, a value indication is selected from the adjusted sale prices of the comparable parcels. The greatest weight is usually given to the sale or sales of comparables that are most similar to the subject, i.e., those that required the least adjustment.

Example
An appraiser is asked to estimate the value of a vacant building lot in the Pine Meadows subdivision. Several vacant lots in the subdivision have recently sold. Analysis of these sales and others in the market area indicates that values have been increasing by 5% per year and demand for vacant lots has been sustained. The appraiser verifies that each sale of a property considered comparable occurred with market financing and without unusual motivation. The sales are similar in all characteristics except those noted below:

Subject

Price	?
Size	18,000 sq. ft
Date of sale	Current
Site location	Near river

Sale 1

Price	$48,300
Size	16,000 sq. ft.
Date of sale	1 year ago
Site location	On hill

Sale 2

Price	$52,000
Size	18,000 sq. ft.
Date of sale	1 month ago
Site location	Near river

Sale 3

Price	$55,000
Size	22,000 sq. ft.
Date of sale	1 year ago
Site location	Near river

To convert each sale price into a price per square foot, the appraiser divides the sale price by the square footage. The sales information is then organized on a market data grid.

	Subject	Sale 1	Sale 2	Sale 3
Price	?	$48,300	$52,000	$55,000
Size (square feet)	18,000	16,000	18,000	22,000
Price per square foot	?	$3.02	$2.67	$2.50
Date	Current	1 year ago	1 month ago	1 year ago
Location	River	Hill	River	River

Next, the appraiser isolates the effect of different elements of comparison and makes the appropriate adjustments. Financing for all the sales is typical, so there is no need for a financing adjustment. The first adjustment will be for market conditions (time). Sales 1 and 3 occurred one year ago. An analysis of the change in market conditions indicates that they must be adjusted upward by 5%.

	Subject	Sale 1	Sale 2	Sale 3
Price	?	$48,300	$52,000	$55,000
Size (square feet)	18,000	16,000	18,000	22,000
Price per square foot	?	$3.02	$2.67	$2.50
Date	Current	1 year ago	1 month ago	1 year ago
Adjustment for market conditions		Sale 1: $48,300 × 1.05 = $50,715		Sale 3: $55,000 × 1.05 = $57,750
Location	River	Hill	River	River

Then the appraiser converts the adjusted sale prices into unit prices and derives an adjustment for location. Sale 1 differs from Sales 2 and 3 in location.

	Subject	Sale 1	Sale 2	Sale 3
Price	?	$48,300	$52,000	$55,000
Size (square feet)	18,000	16,000	18,000	22,000
Price per square foot	?	$3.02	$2.67	$2.50
Date	Current	1 year ago	1 month ago	1 year ago
Adjusted for market conditions		$50,715	$52,000	$57,750
Adjusted price per sq. ft.		$3.17	$2.67	$2.63
Location	River	Hill	River	River

The hill location is evidently superior. The difference in location is approximately $0.50 per square foot. Because Sale 1 is superior to the subject, it must be adjusted downward by $0.50.

	Subject	Sale 1	Sale 2	Sale 3
Price	?	$48,300	$52,000	$55,000
Size (square feet)	18,000	16,000	18,000	22,000
Price per square foot	?	$3.02	$2.67	$2.50
Date	Current	1 year ago	1 month ago	1 year ago
Adjustment for market conditions		$50,715	$52,000	$57,750
Adjusted price per sq. ft.		$3.17	$2.67	$2.63
Location	River	Hill	River	River
Adjustment for hill		$2.67	$2.67	$2.63

Now the results can be reconciled. The indicated value range is $2.63 to $2.67 per square foot. In this example, Sale 2 is given more weight, so the unit price is likely to be in the higher end of the range. However, any amount within the range would be a supportable conclusion. A value of $48,000 ($2.66 × 18,000) is indicated as the land value estimate for the subject property using the sales comparison procedure.

Applicability
Sales comparison analysis is generally the most reliable way to estimate land or site value. It is the easiest technique to apply and produces the most persuasive results. However, this procedure cannot be directly employed if sufficient data on recent sales of comparable land parcels or sites are not available. Furthermore, current conditions of supply and demand must be considered, or the value indication produced may reflect historical, not actual, market values.

Allocation
Allocation may be used when data on recent land sales are insufficient and sales comparison analysis cannot be supported. The allocation procedure is based on the belief that a normal or typical ratio of land or site value to property value can be found in competitive or similar properties in comparable neighborhoods–particularly if these neighborhoods are stable. Three steps are involved in allocation:

1. Identify the typical ratio between land or site value and improved property value in competitive neighborhoods. (An estimate of this ratio can be obtained from assessor's data, through market observation, or from builders of new homes.)
2. Find sales of improved properties in the subject neighborhood that are located on parcels of land comparable to the subject parcel.
3. Apply the allocation ratio to the sale prices of properties considered comparable to develop a value estimate for the subject parcel.

Example
For underwriting purposes, an appraiser is asked to allocate the value of an older residence to the land and building. For several years, no unimproved land sales have occurred in the neighborhood, so the appraiser must use a land valuation technique other than sales comparison.

The appraiser found vacant land sales in a competing neighborhood of the same market area in which the subject is located. She could have applied the sales comparison technique and adjusted for differences in the locations, but she determined that the allocation technique provided better evidence. To apply the technique she used the following sales of vacant land and improved properties in the nearby neighborhood.

> **allocation.** A method of estimating land value in which sales of improved properties are analyzed to establish a typical ratio of land value to total property value and this ratio is applied to the property being appraised or the comparable sale being analyzed.

Vacant Land Sales in Competing Neighborhood

	Sale 1	Sale 2	Sale 3	Sale 4
Sale price	$87,000	$75,200	$76,500	$90,500
Area (in square feet)	21,000	16,500	16,985	21,500
Price per square foot	$4.14	$4.56	$4.50	$4.21

These sales indicate that a larger site had a lower price per square foot, but overall the prices are fairly consistent. The appraiser then extracted a ratio of land value to property value within the comparable neighborhood by analyzing sales of improved properties in the comparable neighborhood. Based on the analysis of vacant land sales, a land price of $4.50 per square foot was applied to the sales of smaller improved properties (Sales 1 and 4), and a land price of $4.25 was applied to the sales of larger properties (Sales 2 and 3).

Sales of Improved Properties in Competing Neighborhood

	Sale 1	Sale 2	Sale 3	Sale 4
Sale price	$345,900	$389,000	$379,500	$349,500
Area (in square feet)	18,000	22,565	23,000	17,560
Price per square foot	$4.50	$4.25	$4.25	$4.50
Land value (V_L)	$81,000	$95,901	$97,750	$79,020
Ratio of land value to property value	23.42%	24.65%	25.76%	22.61%

Again, a fairly consistent pattern was found. The appraiser estimated a ratio of land value to property value of 24% and applied that ratio to sales of improved properties in the subject property's neighborhood.

Sales of Improved Properties in the Subject Neighborhood

	Sale 1	Sale 2	Sale 3	Sale 4
Sale price	$365,000	$385,000	$356,800	$359,000
Ratio of land value to property value	24%	24%	24%	24%
Indicated land value (V_L)	$87,600	$92,400	$85,632	$86,160

Based on the application of the allocation technique, the value of the subject property would fall in the range of $85,600 to $92,400. The appraiser could refine this range further by considering other amenities such as trees, location, lot size, and view.

Applicability

Allocation is usually applied to residential properties when data on improved property sales are available but data on sales of vacant lots are not. In densely developed urban areas, vacant land sales may be so rare that values cannot be estimated by direct comparison. Similarly, vacant sites may seldom be sold in remote rural areas. Allocation usually yields less conclusive results than direct sales comparison, but in some situations it may be the only method available.

The allocation ratio can only be used in a fairly stable market, and it is generally most reliable when the improvements are relatively new. As improvements age and depreciate, the ratio between land or site value and total property value tends to increase. However, depreciation may occur at different rates for different properties. As the years pass, the range of land-to-property value ratios for different properties may become increasingly broad and the ratios may become less reliable indicators of total property value. When the requirements for allocation cannot be met, the extraction procedure may be more useful.

It is imperative in this analysis that the subject and comparables have a similar highest and best use. For example, assume a residential property with commercial zoning sold for $189,000 but was purchased for and subsequently used as a residence. Based on commercial pricing, the site value has a market value of $155,000. The site-to-value ratio (82%) could not be applied to a property in which the site value was not based on commercial pricing.

Allocation ratios are often cited in tax assessment rolls, which show an assessed value for the land, which does not depreciate, and a separate assessed value for the depreciable improvements. Tax information can be used as a check on other data, but it is rarely used independently because it may not reflect all the considerations that affect market value. Mass appraisal data and information from developers of new residential subdivisions, when available, can be used in allocation. Quantitative techniques can also be applied to find patterns in these data.

Extraction

The extraction technique is similar to the allocation procedure in that land or site value is estimated by applying a land-to-property value ratio to the prices of comparable improved properties. To estimate land or site value by extraction, however, the appraiser deducts the contributory value of the improvements from the total sale price of each comparable. The extraction procedure is accomplished in three steps:

1. Identify recent sales of comparable improved properties. If necessary, adjust the sale prices for financing, market conditions, and conditions of sale and any other applicable elements of comparison.
2. For each comparable property, estimate the cost to replace all the improvements, including an entrepreneurial profit, and deduct an estimate of depreciation from this estimate of replacement cost. The

remainder is an indication of the depreciated value of the improvements.

3. Subtract the depreciated value of the improvements from each adjusted sale price.

The resulting value indications are then reconciled into an opinion of land or site value for the subject.

> **extraction.** A method of estimating land value in which the depreciated cost of the improvements on the improved property is estimated and deducted from the total sale price to arrive at an estimated sale price for the land; most effective when the improvements contribute little to the total sale price of the property.

Example

An appraiser is retained to estimate the site value of a vacant lot in a fully developed, older neighborhood. There have been no recent sales of vacant lots, but three improved properties on lots near the subject have been sold recently and these lots are identical to the subject in size.

Property 1 was sold for $174,500. The estimated replacement cost of the improvements is $120,000, and the appraiser estimates that the residence is 25% depreciated. Property 2 was sold for $169,000, and the appraiser estimates that the depreciated improvements contribute $85,500 (replacement cost of $95,000 less 10% depreciation) to property value. Property 3 was sold for $168,000. The total cost of the residence, including entrepreneurial profit, was $90,000, but the appraiser estimates that the improvements have depreciated by 15%.

The appraiser extracts the contribution of the improvements from the price of each sale as shown below:

Property 1

Price of improved comparable		$174,500
Less contribution of improvements		
Cost of improvements	$120,000	
Less depreciation (25% × $120,000)	- $30,000	
		- $90,000
Site value		$84,500

Property 2

Price of improved comparable		$169,000
Less contribution of depreciated improvements		
Cost of improvements	$95,000	
Less depreciation (10% × $95,000)	- $9,500	
		- $85,500
Site value		$83,500

Property 3

Price of improved comparable		$168,000
Less contribution of depreciated improvements		
Cost of improvements	$90,000	
Less depreciation (15% × $90,000)	- $13,500	
		- $76,500
Site value		$91,500

The range of indicated site values is $83,500 to $91,500. It is reasonable to estimate the value of the subject site within this range.

Applicability

Like allocation, extraction is usually less reliable than direct sales comparison. The results are most conclusive when improvements are new and suffer little depreciation. The extraction procedure can also be used to value parcels of land in some older neighborhoods where improvements are fairly heterogeneous. Extraction is frequently used to value parcels of land in rural areas because the contributory value of improvements is often small and relatively easy to identify. The technique is also used in more developed areas where the market is in transition to new, higher-value homes for the same reason. The extraction procedure can be used to check the results of sales comparison analysis.

When extraction is used to estimate land or site value, the appraiser must remember to include an estimate of entrepreneurial profit in the replacement cost of the improvements if that cost is not already included. (See Chapter 13 for an in-depth discussion of the estimation of entrepreneurial profit or incentive.) Entrepreneurial profit represents fair payment for the builder-developer's expertise and assumption of risk. The developer provides entrepreneurial coordination, a necessary agent of production distinct from capital, labor, and land. If an appraiser does not allow for an appropriate amount of entrepreneurial profit in the extraction procedure, the land or site value estimate will be unreasonably high.

To apply the extraction procedure, an appraiser must fully understand the techniques for estimating costs and depreciation that are discussed in Chapters 14 and 15. The consistency of highest and best use discussed in relation to the allocation technique also limits the applicability of extraction. If the sale prices of the subject or comparables properties used to extract depreciation are influenced by a commercial use that is inconsistent with the uses of other properties included in the analysis, the results may not accurately reflect the market value of the subject property used as a residence.

Income Capitalization Techniques

Estimating land or site value using an income capitalization technique requires information than can be difficult for an appraiser to obtain, such as reliable land and building capitalization rates. As a result, the three techniques described below are generally not used as primary valuation techniques except in special situations such as subdivision development analysis.

Land Residual Technique

When income-producing properties are being appraised, the income attributable to the land can sometimes be isolated and capitalized into an indication of land or site value. The land residual procedure is an application of direct capitalization. (Capitalization of income is covered more fully in Chapter 19.)

The procedure is applied as follows:

- Determine what improvements represent the highest and best use of the site.
- Calculate the stabilized, annual net operating income (*NOI*) to the property by estimating its market rent and deducting operating expenses.
- Derive a building capitalization rate and a land capitalization rate from market data.
- Estimate the income attributable to the building using the IRV formula—i.e., $\text{Income}_B = \text{Value}_B \times \text{Rate}_B$.
- Subtract the income attributable to the building from the property's net operating income. The remainder is the income attributable to the land. Capitalize this amount into an indication of land value using the formula $\text{Value}_L = \text{Income}_L / \text{Rate}_L$.

The land residual procedure is usually applied only to property that produces income. Consequently, this procedure is not often applied to residential properties, which usually are not income-producing. The land residual procedure is better suited to feasibility analyses of proposed properties or to test the feasibility of alternative uses of a site rather than to estimate site value in a market value appraisal of an existing residential property.

When this procedure is applied to land being developed as an income-producing property, a great deal of data must be collected:

- Building value must be known or accurately estimated.
- The stabilized, annual net operating income to the property must be known or estimated.
- Both building and land capitalization rates must be extracted from the market.

Because of its extensive data requirements, the land residual procedure cannot be practically applied in most residential land or site valuation assignments. Nevertheless, the land residual technique can serve as a check on sales comparison analysis, and it is useful when sales of comparable sites are unavailable.

Ground Rent Capitalization

When the owner of a parcel of land charges ground rent for the right to occupy and use the land, the ground rent capitalization procedure can be used to arrive at the value of the lessor's interest in the land—i.e., the leased fee interest. Market-derived capitalization rates are used to convert ground rent into value.

This procedure is useful when an analysis of comparable sales of leased land indicates a range of rents and capitalization rates. If the current rent corresponds to market rent, the indicated land or site value will be equivalent to the market value of the fee simple interest in the parcel of land. If the ground rent paid under the terms of the existing contract (lease) does not correspond to market rent, the ground rent must be adjusted for the difference in property rights to obtain an indication of the market value of the fee simple interest.

An alternative method of ground rent capitalization involves discounting the anticipated cash flows (rental income) over the holding period and the reversion or lump-sum benefit received upon termination of the investment.

Ground rent capitalization is not generally applicable to single-family residential properties unless the subject includes a long-term land lease. To apply ground rent capitalization, an appraiser must derive a capitalization rate from the market that reflects the relationship between land sales and land rents. However, if sales are available to support such a derivation, these sales can often be used to value the land directly with sales comparison.

Ground rent capitalization can be applied when ground rent is being charged for the use of land and the ground rent corresponds to the owner's leased fee interest in the parcel of land. This procedure may be used in areas such as Hawaii and parts of Maryland and California where residential development is more likely to be on leased land than in other states.

When ground rent is capitalized, differences in lease terms, escalation clauses, and option periods must be identified and accounted for. When the current ground rent does not correspond to market rent, a property rights adjustment must be applied to the ground rent to obtain a market value indication of the fee simple interest in the land.

The most significant problem with this analysis is the comparability of the real estate rights for the subject and the rights involved in the comparable sales. If the subject has a 95-year land lease and there is a home on the site, the landowner's interest is the leased fee interest and the homeowner's interest is the leasehold. When researching comparable sales, the same issues arise. Sometimes the length of the term or the amount of rent will affect this analysis. The buyer of a leased fee interest was most likely concerned only with the income from the investment because the new owner was not likely to have the right to occupy the land for many years (i.e., for the length of the remaining lease term). On the other hand, the buyer of a leasehold interest probably acquired the right to occupy the property immediately.

Subdivision Development Analysis

Land is subdivided in the normal course of residential real estate development. A land developer divides a large plot into smaller parcels and installs utilities, roads, drainage, and other improvements that are required by law. Sometimes the finished lots are sold to other developers at this point. More often, the same developer continues the process by constructing residences on the sites and selling off the finished properties. The developer calculates the development costs, sales expenses, carrying charges, and a reasonable anticipated profit to derive the net proceeds from the sale of the finished units. An appraiser can simulate the developer's reasoning to develop an opinion of land or site value using subdivision development analysis.

This land valuation technique is unlike the other income capitalization techniques of land valuation because it is a form of yield, not direct, capitalization. The technique consists of the following steps:

- Estimate the size and number of the subdivided lots that could be developed from the subject parcel.
- Estimate the value of the finished lots by sales comparison.
- Estimate the development costs, the development schedule, the anticipated selling period, and a reasonable entrepreneurial incentive for the developer.
- Subtract all development costs and the entrepreneurial incentive from the anticipated gross sales price each year to derive the net proceeds of sale after development is complete and the individual lots have been sold.
- Select a discount rate that reflects the risk and required return on the investment incurred during the anticipated development and selling period. Discount the net sales proceeds over this period to obtain the present value of the raw land. The discount rate is often a function of the cost of funds from the institution that will finance the project. Subdivision developments are risky investments, so the interest rates are usually higher than for most other investments.

Valuing lots in a subdivision is a common assignment for real estate appraisers, but subdivision development analysis is a complex procedure and can only be applied to tracts of land for which the highest and best use is subdivision development. In a typical appraisal, the estimate of land or site value is not likely to be based on such a detailed analysis. If the appraisal is being performed for a developer who is contemplating a land purchase and interested in the feasibility of subdivision development, the procedure is appropriate. The land or site value estimates produced with this procedure should always be checked against the prices of other, similar parcels of raw land for which subdivision development is the highest and best use. This tool can be applicable in markets in which there is a wide range in the number of lots that can be developed per acre. For example, in areas with steep terrain, only one unit per acre may be possible, but a mile away developers may be able to develop four units per acre. This technique recognizes that difference.

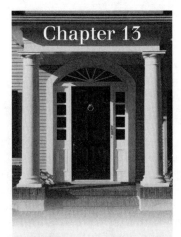

Chapter 13

The Cost Approach

The cost approach to estimating value is based on the reasoning that a purchaser will not normally pay more for a property than it would cost to purchase comparable land and have improvements of comparable utility constructed on that land without undue delay. To apply the cost approach an appraiser estimates the cost of reproducing or replacing the existing structure with a new building, deducts an appropriate amount for the loss in value caused by depreciation in the existing structure, and then adds the value of the depreciated improvements to an estimate of the value of the land.

The cost approach is applied in eight steps. An appraiser

1. Estimates the value of the site as though vacant and available to be developed to the highest and best use.
2. Estimates the direct (hard) and indirect (soft) costs of the improvements as of the effective appraisal date.
3. Estimates an appropriate entrepreneurial incentive or profit from analysis of the market.
4. Adds estimated direct costs, indirect costs, and the entrepreneurial incentive or profit to arrive at the total cost of the improvements.
5. Estimates the amount of depreciation in the structure and, if necessary, allocates it among the three major categories: physical deterioration, functional obsolescence, and external obsolescence.
6. Deducts the estimated depreciation from the total costs of the improvements to derive an estimate of their depreciated cost.

7. Estimates the contributory value of any site improvements that have not already been considered. (Site improvements are often appraised at their contributory value, i.e., directly on a depreciated-cost basis.)

8. Adds the site value to the total depreciated cost of all improvements to arrive at the indicated value of the property.

Relationship to Appraisal Principles

The cost approach is based on fundamental appraisal principles and reflects the thinking of those buyers and sellers in the residential real estate market who relate value to cost. Market participants typically judge the value of an existing structure by considering the prices and rents of comparable, existing buildings. They may also consider the costs of creating a new building with similar physical and functional utility. Therefore, the principle of substitution, which holds that value is indicated by the prices of similar items, suggests that the appraiser should study the costs of new structures as well as the prices of existing structures. Buyers and sellers are most likely to consider building costs when a building is relatively new and offers maximum physical and functional utility. When structures are older or possess less-than-optimal utility, market participants adjust their opinions of value accordingly. Buyers and sellers may also give considerable weight to a value estimate based on cost when the property has unique features and there are few recent sales of similar property for comparison.

The cost of construction affects, and is affected by, the interplay of supply and demand in the marketplace. Even if the cost approach is not emphasized in an appraisal, the trend in construction costs has a significant influence on property value and should be noted. The value of existing properties may increase or decrease, depending on the cost of creating competitive properties.

If total construction costs rise faster than the current prices of improved properties, the prospect of lower profits will reduce the incentive to develop new properties, and the supply of new units may contract. The lack of development should eventually push existing property prices upward because of less supply. Similarly, if construction costs fall faster than the prices of improved properties, new properties will be developed, and the prices of existing properties will fall because buyers will opt for new homes rather than higher-priced existing homes. Changes in construction costs may result from shifts in the prices of labor, materials, land, financing charges, contractor profits, architects fees, and many other factors. All of these costs are of concern to appraisers.

The cost of production and market value may be affected differently by externalities. Inflation may sometimes increase material and labor costs while not affecting market values; on the other hand, completion of a new sewer line may increase value but have no impact on cost. When improvements are new, their contribution to total property value tends to approximate the cost to construct them. Developers who build overly expensive residences or are careless about costs may quickly suffer losses and be forced to abandon their projects. They leave room for other developers who are more judicious in relating the costs of building improvements to the prices sustained by market demand. Often developers who find ways to lower their costs or build where property values are comparatively high are soon joined by a host of competitors. This principle of competition further alters the relationship between costs and property values. The process may take time, but ultimately the market moves toward balance, where the direct and indirect costs of a new building approximate the building's contribution to property value.

The cost approach is also supported by the principle of balance and the concept of highest and best use. The principle of balance indicates that in a given location there is an optimal combination of the agents of production that creates the greatest value and utility for the property. The combination of land and improvements in the existing property would be the optimal combination for that location. The optimal combination is the highest and best use of the site as though vacant, so a different use will result in a loss in value.

An existing structure and the site on which it is located may be out of balance in several ways. If a dwelling is an overimprovement, it may contribute value to the property but not nearly as much value as a similar structure would have on a more appropriate site or a site in a different location. In effect, the building cannot realize its full potential to produce benefits or income on its present site. Conversely, a building that is an underimprovement will not contribute as much value as an improvement that represents the highest and best use of the site. In this situation, the full potential of the site is not being realized by the improvement that exists on it. The combination of the site and the improvement is less than optimal.

Applicability

Because cost and market value are often most closely related when properties are new, the cost approach is particularly useful in deriving market value indications for new or relatively new construction. The approach is especially persuasive when land value is well-supported and when the improvements are new or suffer only minor depreciation and therefore represent a use that approximates the highest and best use of the land as though vacant.

The approach is widely used to estimate the market value of proposed construction and properties that are not frequently exchanged in the market. Buyers of these properties often measure the price they will pay for an existing building by the cost to build a replacement minus depreciation or by the cost to purchase an existing improvement and make any necessary modifications. Because comparable sales are not always available to analyze the market value of certain types of properties, current market indications of a building's depreciated cost or the cost to acquire and refurbish an existing building provide the best reflections of market thinking and thus of market value.

A number of factors limit the applicability of the cost approach. When improvements are older or are not the highest and best use of the land as though vacant, depreciation is more difficult to estimate. Furthermore, collecting and updating data on construction costs is a time-consuming task. As an alternative, an appraiser may rely on cost service manuals, but the data in these manuals do not always produce reliable results. When land sales are few, as in built-up urban areas, the land value estimate required in the cost approach may be difficult to support. Comparable properties may not provide sufficient relevant data, or the data from comparables may be too diverse to suggest an appropriate estimate of entrepreneurial profit. It may be difficult to apply the cost approach to special-design residences because the unique features of these properties make it extremely difficult to estimate functional and external obsolescence. It is always important to remember the goal in a market value appraisal is to develop an opinion of value. If no sales of such properties can be found, the question that should always be asked is, "Is there a market for this property?" The lack of sales may be an indication of the lack of a market. Any of these problems can seriously undermine the persuasiveness of the cost approach.

Despite these limitations, the cost approach is an essential valuation tool. It is especially significant when a lack of market activity limits the reliability of the sales comparison approach. When sales data on comparable improved properties *are* available, the cost approach can be used to test the value indication produced by sales comparison. The usefulness of the cost approach as a check on the sales comparison approach is particularly important because these two approaches may be the only means available to value a one-unit residence. The income capitalization approach is less frequently applied to one-unit residences.

Not only can the cost approach be used as an independent approach to market value, but information derived in the approach can also be applied in the other valuation approaches. If a feature of the subject property or a comparable property is deficient in comparison with market standards, the cost to cure the deficiency may serve as a basis for calculating an adjustment in the sales comparison approach. Adjustments for special-purpose property features, which incur extensive obsolescence, and for any new accessory buildings or site improvements, which are standard in the market and often contribute value equal to their cost, may be estimated in this way. However, because cost does not necessarily equal value, sales comparison adjustments are more reliable if supported with direct market evidence.

Depreciation estimates are extracted in the cost approach by comparing the existing structure with a newly constructed duplicate or replacement building. The subject property and the comparables used in the sales comparison approach generally suffer from various forms of depreciation, but the extent of physical deterioration and functional obsolescence varies among different properties. The adjustments made for property condition in the sales comparison approach should be related to depreciation estimates. To reconcile the value indications derived from the cost and sales comparison approaches, an appraiser often checks the depreciation estimates in the cost approach against the adjustments for property condition derived in the sales comparison approach.

The cost approach requires separate valuations of the land and the improvements, so it may be applied whenever land or the improvements must be valued separately. The segregation of land value from total property value is fundamental to certain methods of land valuation, including the extraction procedure and land residual technique of direct capitalization. The cost approach may also be used to calculate ad valorem property taxes, which require that property value be allocated between the land and the improvements.

Cost approach techniques can be especially useful when additions or renovations are being considered. The approach provides cost data that are essential to determine feasibility—i.e., whether the cost of the improvement can be recovered through an increase in the property's income stream or anticipated sale price. Cost approach data can help prevent the construction of overimprovements.

Components of the Cost Approach

Site Value

Usually the value of the land or site is estimated by sales comparison. Sales of vacant parcels considered comparable are analyzed, and the sale prices are adjusted to reflect differences between the sale properties considered comparable and the subject. The results are reconciled into an indication of land or site value. When sufficient data on recent sales of vacant parcels of land are not available, the allocation and extraction procedures can be applied to estimate land or site value. (These methods are described in detail in Chapter 12.)

When a land or site value indication is derived in the cost approach, it is essential that the principle of consistent use be observed. This principle prohibits an appraiser from valuing a parcel of land on the basis of one use and the improvements on the basis of another. In many residential valuations, the use of both the site and the improvements is obvious, and the highest and best use of the site as though vacant is often the same as the highest and best use of the property as improved. The existing improvements have utility but suffer depreciation.

Problems can arise when the property being appraised is located in a transitional neighborhood, where it is more difficult to determine the highest and best use of a site. An appraiser must be careful not to base a land or site value estimate on properties that only appear similar to the subject property or properties that are similar only as improved.

The comparable sites on which the value indication is based must have the same highest and best use as the subject property. A careful highest and best use analysis of the subject property and each comparable property is needed to make this determination.

Reproduction or Replacement Cost

The terms *reproduction cost* and *replacement cost* are not synonymous. They reflect two different ways of looking at a new structure to be built in place of the existing improvements. Application of the two concepts may produce two different cost estimates. An appraiser must select one of these concepts and use it consistently throughout the cost approach. The use of reproduction or replacement cost affects how depreciation is estimated.

reproduction cost. The estimated cost to construct, at current prices as of the effective date of the appraisal, an exact duplicate or replica of the building being appraised, using the same materials, construction standards, design, layout, and quality of workmanship and embodying all the deficiencies, superadequacies, and obsolescence of the subject building.

replacement cost. The estimated cost to construct, at current prices as of the effective appraisal date, a building with utility equivalent to the building being appraised, using modern materials and current standards, design, and layout.

Reproduction cost is the estimated cost to construct, at current prices, an exact duplicate or replica of the building being appraised using the same materials, construction standards, design, layout, and quality of workmanship and embodying all the deficiencies, superadequacies, and obsolescence of the subject building. To estimate the reproduction cost of a structure, an appraiser must ascertain the cost to construct a replica of the existing building using the same materials at their current prices. If the improvement contains superadequate features, the cost to reproduce these features is included in the reproduction cost estimate. An appraiser might estimate reproduction cost in valuing historic properties and newly constructed improvements.

Replacement cost is the estimated cost to construct, at current prices, a building with utility equivalent to the building being appraised, using modern materials and current standards, design, and layout. To estimate replacement cost, an appraiser calculates the cost to construct an equally desirable, substitute improvement. This improvement will not necessarily be constructed with similar materials or to the same specifications. Because materials readily available now would probably be substituted for the outdated or more costly materials used in the existing structure, the appraiser estimates the cost of construction with substitute materials. If the present structure contains a superadequacy such as high ceilings, the costs of producing this extra space in the existing building and all other costs resulting from the excessive ceiling height would be eliminated in the replacement cost estimate. Any inadequacies would also be eliminated in the replacement cost estimate.

The use of replacement cost frequently results in a building cost estimate that is considerably lower than an estimate based on reproduction cost. However, fewer deductions are usually made for obsolescence when replacement cost is used instead of reproduction cost. A replacement building has fewer items that are functionally obsolete than a reproduced building, so it suffers less depreciation. In using replacement cost, the appraiser must be careful to handle functional obsolescence appropriately.

Types of Costs

Regardless of whether reproduction or replacement cost is used, three types of costs are involved in the creation of an improvement and each must be reflected in the cost estimate. The three types of cost are

1. Direct costs
2. Indirect costs
3. Entrepreneurial profit or incentive

Direct costs, or *hard costs*, are expenditures for the labor and materials used in the construction of the improvement(s). The appraiser should be familiar with the types of labor and materials used in the subject property or an equivalent replacement property and with current costs in local construction markets. Direct costs can vary considerably, depending on the quality of the labor and materials involved, labor rates in the area, local building codes, and current conditions in the market—i.e., the supply of and demand for contractors' services. Even when the building specifications are the same, there may be a substantial difference between the bids submitted by different contractors. A contractor who is working at full capacity is often inclined to make a high bid, while one who is not so busy may submit a lower figure.

A building contractor's overhead and profit are treated as direct costs and usually included in the construction contract. These costs should not be confused with entrepreneurial, or developer's, profit or incentive, which is neither a direct nor an indirect cost. It is classified as entrepreneurial incentive or profit in a separate line item. If the contractor is also the developer, both types of profit may be combined in the building contract. Nevertheless, an appraiser must carefully distinguish between the two in cost calculations and in the appraisal report.

Indirect costs, or *soft costs*, are expenditures for items other than labor and materials. Indirect costs are usually calculated separately from direct costs. Many indirect costs are calculated as a percentage of direct costs. The percentage is converted into a dollar amount and then added to the direct costs. Some indirect costs such as professional fees are not related to the size and direct cost of the

> **direct costs.** Expenditures for the labor and materials used in the construction of improvements; also called *hard costs*.
>
> **indirect costs.** Expenditures or allowances for items other than labor and materials that are necessary for construction, but are not typically part of the construction contract. Indirect costs may include administrative costs; professional fees; financing costs and the interest paid on construction loans; taxes and the builder's or developer's all-risk insurance during construction; and marketing, sales, and lease-up costs incurred to achieve occupancy or sale. Also called *soft costs*.

improvements. These costs are expressed as lump-sum figures and added to the direct costs.

Direct Costs	Indirect Costs
Labor used to construct buildings	Architectural and engineering fees for plans, plan checks, surveys to establish building lines and grades, and environmental and building permits
Materials, products, and equipment	
Contractor's profit and overhead, including the cost of job supervision, workers' compensation, fire and liability insurance, and unemployment insurance	Appraisal, consulting, engineering, accounting, and legal fees
	The cost of permanent financing as well as interest on construction loans, interest on land costs, and processing fees or service charges
Performance bonds	
Use of equipment	
Security	
Contractor's shack, temporary fencing, and portable toilet (an OSHA requirement)	Builder's, or developer's, all-risk insurance and ad valorem taxes during construction
	Administrative expenses of the developer
Materials storage facilities	Cost of title changes
Power-line installation and utility costs	

Entrepreneurial incentive is a market-derived figure that represents the amount an entrepreneur (i.e., the developer) expects to receive in addition to direct and indirect costs as compensation for providing coordination and expertise and assuming risk. Entrepreneurial profit is the difference between the actual total cost of development and the market value of the property:

Market Value − Total Cost of Development = Entrepreneurial Profit (or Loss)

Entrepreneurial incentive may be considered a component of coordination, the fourth agent of production, which must be paid for along with expenditures for the other three agents of production—land, labor, and capital. Normally a development will not be undertaken without the expectation of an eventual profit.

The estimation of entrepreneurial incentive or profit may present problems for an appraiser for four reasons. First, some appraisers point out that the value associated with the amenities of a residence may be such that its sale price far exceeds the sum of the development costs (land, building, and marketing). These practitioners contend that it would be a mistake to attribute the entire difference between the sale price and total development cost to entrepreneurial profit. Thus, to ensure the reasonableness of the entrepreneurial incentive or profit estimate, an appraiser should carefully examine the source of any property value that is over and above the cost of development.

Second, some practitioners observe that in owner-occupied residential properties, entrepreneurial profit is often an intangible measure. Entrepreneurial profit is realized only when the property is first sold (even if the sale takes place several years after the property was built). Over time, entrepreneurial profit becomes obscured by the appreciation in property value.

Third, the way in which comparable properties have been developed affects the availability of data. The appraiser will usually find it possible to calculate entrepreneurial profit from actual cost comparables for speculatively built properties, especially residential properties such as condominium and multifamily developments. In a value estimate of a speculatively built property, entrepreneurial profit is a return to the developer for the skills employed and the risks incurred.[1] In large-scale residential developments, the issue is complicated by the fact that the developer's profit may not reflect the proportional contributions of the improved site and the improvements to overall property value. Developers of tract subdivisions often realize most of their profit on the value of the finished lots rather than the value of the houses built on those lots.

For properties that were custom-built, data on entrepreneurial profit may not be available because the property owner, who contracted the actual builders, was acting as the developer. The prices of upscale, custom-built properties often reflect the attractiveness of these amenity-laden properties as well as the high costs of the customized materials used. Thus, the breakdown of costs for custom-built residences may not be comparable to the breakdown for speculatively built properties, which further complicates the task of estimating a rate of entrepreneurial profit. Theoretically, however, the value of custom-built properties should also reflect an entrepreneurial incentive or profit.

Finally, the appraiser must scrutinize the cost data on which the value estimate is based to determine whether or not an allowance for entrepreneurial incentive or profit has already been made. If such research is not performed, it is possible that developer's profit could be double counted among the estimated costs. Data derived from sales of comparable sites often include an allowance for a profit to the land developer. Similarly, data extracted from sales of comparable properties may already include a profit to the developer. While cost estimating services quote direct costs (e.g., contractor's profit) and indirect costs (e.g., sales costs), they do not usually provide estimates of developer's profit.[2] Because different sources of data reflect costs in different ways, the appraiser should identify where developer's profit is considered in the estimate, i.e., whether it is an item already included in the replacement or reproduction cost plus land value, or if it is a stand-alone item added to replacement or reproduction cost plus land value.

entrepreneurial incentive. A market-derived figure that represents the amount an entrepreneur expects to receive for his or her contribution to a project and risk.

entrepreneurial profit. A market-derived figure that represents the amount an entrepreneur receives for his or her contribution to a project and for risk; the difference between the total cost of a property (cost of development) and its market value (property value after completion), which represents the entrepreneur's compensation for the risk and expertise associated with development.

entrepreneurial coordination. One of the four agents of production in economic theory (i.e., land, labor, capital, and entrepreneurial coordination).

---

1. The entrepreneurial profit is what was actually earned at the time of sale. This profit may differ from what the entrepreneur had anticipated (i.e., the incentive).

2. In actual practice, an additional estimate of entrepreneurial incentive or profit is not made in most estimates of the replacement or reproduction cost of existing residences based on cost service data.

An appraiser estimates entrepreneurial incentive or profit by analyzing development activity in the local market. Entrepreneurial profit may be expressed as a percentage of one of the following:

- Direct costs
- Direct and indirect costs
- Direct and indirect costs plus land value
- The value of the completed project

An appraiser follows the practice of the local market. Entrepreneurial profit is always estimated at the rates prevailing in the market as of the date of the value opinion.

Because the amount of entrepreneurial incentive varies considerably depending on economic conditions and the property type, a typical relationship between this cost and other costs may be difficult to establish. An appraiser may survey developers to establish the range of anticipated incentive and actual profit in the market. Often the appraiser will find that a developer keeps three targets in mind when estimating incentive:

1. What the developer wants to realize (maximum expectations in a best-case scenario)
2. What the developer must absolutely realize (minimum requirements in a worst-case scenario)
3. What the developer will accept and still stay motivated

To remain competitive, developers often vary their profit expectations according to the season and the condition of the market. If competition is strong but not ruinous in one submarket and cut-throat in another, construction costs and accompanying profit margins may vary considerably within the same market area. The appraiser should be able to confirm the amounts of entrepreneurial incentive or profit that are consistently found in the market. Although it may be difficult to estimate precisely, entrepreneurial incentive or profit is an essential development cost and should therefore be recognized in the cost approach.

Methods of Estimating Cost

To estimate replacement or reproduction cost in residential appraising, one of two methods is generally used:

- The comparative-unit method (which is the most commonly used)
- The unit-in-place method

To apply the comparative-unit method, an appraiser first derives an estimate of the cost per unit of area from the known costs of comparable new structures or from a recognized cost service. These unit costs are adjusted for the physical differences of the subject property and for time (or cost-trend) changes, and then the adjusted unit costs are applied to the dimensions of the subject.

In the unit-in-place method, costs for specific, individual construction components (e.g., the cost per linear foot of brick wall, the cost per hour for masonry work) are derived from market research or from cost service manuals. These unit-in-place costs are applied to the corresponding components of the subject property and are added together. If the unit-in-place method is applied using extremely detailed units, it can produce very reliable results.

A third technique, the quantity survey method, most closely simulates the procedure a contractor uses to develop a construction bid. It is rarely used in residential appraisal practice because of the excessive time and expense involved in the process. In the quantity survey method, the quantity and quality of all the materials used and all the labor required are estimated, and unit cost figures are applied to these estimates to arrive at a total cost estimate for materials and labor.

Appraisers should always check the results of the cost-estimating services with actual cost figures found in their markets. This ensures that the appraiser is measuring cost accurately.

The more commonly used cost-estimating methods are discussed in Chapter 14.

comparative-unit method. A method used to derive a cost estimate in terms of dollars per unit of area or volume based on known costs of similar structures that are adjusted for time and physical differences; usually applied to total building area.

unit-in-place method. A cost-estimating method in which total building cost is estimated by adding together the unit costs for the various building components as installed. Also called *segregated cost method*.

quantity survey method. A cost-estimating method in which the quantity and quality of all materials used and all categories of labor required are estimated and unit cost figures are applied to arrive at a total cost estimate for labor and materials.

Depreciation

The depreciation estimate is a critical element in the cost approach and is often quite difficult to develop. The procedures used to estimate depreciation include sales comparison techniques, the age-life method, and the breakdown method. (Chapter 15 covers depreciation in great detail.)

Depreciation is the amount by which the replacement or reproduction cost of a new structure must be adjusted to reflect the value of the existing structure. There are three main types of depreciation:

1. Physical deterioration
2. Functional obsolescence
3. External obsolescence

Existing, older structures usually suffer some physical deterioration. Normal wear and tear reduces the value of a building over time. Some forms of physical deterioration are economically feasible to cure, while others are incurable insofar as it would be impractical or uneconomic to correct them.

Many existing buildings suffer from design problems such as a poor floor plan, inadequate mechanical equipment, or excessively high ceilings. These forms of functional obsolescence can also reduce the value of a building. Using replacement cost instead of reproduction cost may eliminate some forms of functional obsolescence, but it usually cannot eliminate them all. Some forms of functional obsolescence are curable, while others are incurable. Curable forms of functional obsolescence may include deficiencies requiring additions, substitution, or modernization, or certain superadequacies, though superadequacies in structural components or materials are rarely curable.

If an existing structure is located on land that is inappropriate for that type of development, a further value penalty must be deducted for either functional or external obsolescence. In general, external obsolescence results from conditions outside the property. This negative factor is further identified as either external or economic. Examples of external factors may include

- Change in nearby land uses
- Proximity to incompatible land uses
- Detrimental factors such a traffic noise
- Frequency of flooding

Economic factors may include

- Mistaken forecasts of market demand
- A downswing in regional or national economic conditions
- Imbalance of supply and demand
- Property tax rates
- High interest rates

depreciation. In appraising, a loss in property value from any cause; the difference between the cost of an improvement on the effective date of the appraisal and the market value of the improvement on the same date.

physical deterioration. An element of depreciation; loss in value caused by wear, tear, age, and use.

functional obsolescence. An element of depreciation resulting from deficiencies or superadequacies in the structure.

external obsolescence. An element of depreciation; a defect, usually incurable, caused by negative influences outside a site and generally incurable on the part of the owner, landlord, or tenant.

Many other factors may be identified for a specific property or in each market or submarket. External obsolescence is almost always considered economically incurable. However, the obsolescence may be temporary.

All three types of depreciation must be carefully estimated, added together, and deducted from the cost new of the improvements to arrive at the depreciated cost of the existing structure.

Site Improvements and Accessory Buildings

Once cost and depreciation figures for the main improvement are calculated, site improvements must be examined. The value of garages and accessory buildings as well as paving, landscaping, fences and walls, patios, swimming pools, and other site improvements are estimated either by the amount they contribute to the property or by the depreciated cost of these items. If the land value estimate is based on raw land, the appraiser must also estimate expenses for clearing and grading the site, installing utilities, and preparing the site for development.

Final Value Indication

Normally the last step in the cost approach is accomplished by adding the depreciated costs of the improvements to the value of the site. The depreciated costs of all the structures on the property are combined to obtain the value contribution of the improvements. This sum is then added to the land or site value estimate to obtain a total property value indication by the cost approach.

This value indication will be the value of the fee simple interest in the subject property. If the property rights being valued reflect a different ownership interest, the indicated fee simple value must be adjusted to reflect the interest being appraised.

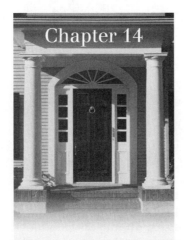

Chapter 14

Cost-Estimating Methods

A reliable and persuasive estimate of the cost to construct the subject improvements is the cornerstone of the cost approach. Whether a cost estimate is prepared by an appraiser familiar with construction plans and building specifications, materials, and techniques or with the assistance of a professional cost estimator, the appraiser is responsible for the result.

Appraisers must be aware of the cost basis–i.e., reproduction cost or replacement cost–represented by cost service data and make consistent comparisons to market-extracted cost data. Also, if cost service data and calculations are used, appraisers must make sure their measurements of the building area and perimeter and other appropriate measures are consistent with those used by the cost service.

Cost Data Sources

Data for estimating the current cost of improvements are published by cost-estimating services such as Marshall and Swift, F. W. Dodge Corporation, and R. S. Means Cost Estimating Service. Computer-assisted cost-estimating services can improve mathematical accuracy and efficiency in preparing a reproduction or replacement cost report.

The cost manuals published by these services usually show direct unit costs, but an appraiser must conduct research to find which costs are most applicable to the appraisal problem. Depending on the source of the data, quoted construction costs may include other necessary expenses.

cost service. Vendor of construction data used in the cost approach.

Cost manuals almost always include indirect costs such as legal fees, escrow fees, interest on construction loans; financing fees; appraisal fees; carrying charges; leasing, sales, and marketing costs; and property taxes. However, discounts or bonuses paid for financing may not be included. Familiarity with the cost service information used by appraisers is necessary to accurately estimate the cost to apply to a subject property.

Often the data furnished by national cost services do not include the costs associated with site improvements. These may include the costs of demolishing existing improvements, paving roads, installing storm drains, grading, and compacting soil as well as the fees and assessments for utility hookup.

Estimates of entrepreneurial incentive or profit are rarely, if ever, provided by cost services. Appraisers estimate these costs separately and add them to the reproduction or replacement costs derived from published cost data, if appropriate. An appraiser will need to interview developers to estimate entrepreneurial incentive. Developers have three levels of incentive. One is the price they would like to receive for their risk. The second is what would make them continue with the project. The last is the amount that they must have to do the project. The appraiser must be sure which level of incentive the developer is quoting. Interviewing local contractors and developers also provides an appraiser with additional support for the cost source information included in an appraisal assignment.

Entrepreneurial profit can be extracted from developers' final costs. The appraiser should keep a file of actual final costs to estimate a percentage of profit for the entrepreneur after all other costs have been paid. This is a simple mathematical calculation:

market value − total development cost = entrepreneurial profit (or loss).

Benchmark Buildings

The unit costs shown in cost-estimating manuals normally are given for a base, or benchmark, building of a certain size. Additions to or deductions from these unit costs are made if the actual area or volume of the subject building differs from the area or volume of the benchmark building. If the subject is larger than the benchmark building, the unit costs will generally be lower. If the subject building is smaller, the unit costs will probably be higher.

Most buildings vary somewhat in size, design, and quality of construction, so the benchmark building used in the manual is rarely identical to the building being appraised. Variations in roof design, building shape, and types of mechanical equipment can substantially affect unit costs. Some published manuals indicate what adjustments should be made for such differences. Costs for materials and labor are different in different parts of the country, and they often vary considerably from one construction market to another. Many cost manuals provide specific city and regional multipliers so that benchmark building costs can be adjusted to reflect these variations. Ultimately, however, the best way for an appraiser to derive costs and cost adjustments is to research the local market.

Cost-Index Trending

Cost services often provide cost indexes, which can be used to translate a known historical cost into a current cost estimate. Cost-index trending is useful when the comparative-unit method is applied to buildings that were constructed several years prior to the appraisal.

cost index trending. Cost-estimating technique used to convert historical data from cost manuals or electronic databases into a current cost estimate.

Base years and regional multipliers are identified in the manuals. Base year construction costs are based on an actual investigation of costs. Construction costs for subsequent years are calculated by multiplying these base year costs by a multiplier or index. To estimate the current costs of a building constructed several years earlier, an appraiser divides the current cost index by the index as of the date of construction and applies this ratio to the known historical costs. The procedure can be expressed with the following formula:

$$\frac{\text{current cost index}}{\text{index as of construction date}} \times \text{historical cost} = \text{current cost}$$

For example, consider a one-unit home that cost $175,000 to build in 1995. The cost index in July 1995, when the house was completed, was 315.4. The cost index as of the date of appraisal is 342.25, which yields the following calculations for current cost:

$$(342.25/315.4) \times \$175,000 = \$189,897$$
$$= \$189,900 \text{ (rounded)}$$

Certain problems can arise when an appraiser uses cost-index trending to estimate current reproduction or replacement cost. The accuracy of the figures on which the indexes are based cannot always be ascertained, especially when the cost manual being used does not indicate which components are included–e.g., only direct costs and some indirect costs. Furthermore, historical costs may not be typical or normal for the time period, and the construction methods used in the base years may differ from those in use on the date of the appraisal. Appraisers who use cost-index trending should recognize that recent costs are more reliable than older costs adjusted with an index. Although cost-index trending may be used to confirm a cost estimate, it is generally not an accurate substitute for a first-hand analysis of cost trends.

Cost-Estimating Methods

The appraisal techniques most commonly used to estimate the costs of an existing or proposed building include

- The comparative-unit method
- The unit-in-place method
- The quantity survey method

The available techniques vary in their complexity. The time and effort required to apply them and their relevance to the problem at hand is determined by the required scope of the assignment.

Comparative-Unit Method

The comparative-unit method is the simplest cost-estimating technique and usually the easiest to apply. This is the technique used in most typical residential appraisals.

To apply the comparative-unit method, an appraiser estimates the replacement or reproduction cost of the subject building by comparing it with recently constructed, similar buildings for which cost data are available. Unit costs are derived from the market (i.e., comparable buildings) and applied to the building characteristics of the subject building. Adjustments are made for physical differences and for time (or cost-trend) changes, if necessary. Indirect costs and entrepreneurial incentive or profit may be included in the unit costs or they may be computed separately. Variations exist, but the comparative-unit method is typically applied in seven steps. An appraiser

1. Identifies several sales of recently constructed buildings that are similar to the subject building.
2. Subtracts land value from the sale price of each comparable to obtain the replacement or reproduction cost of the improvements. Replacement or reproduction cost includes all direct and indirect costs as well as entrepreneurial incentive or profit.
3. Adjusts the replacement or reproduction cost of the improvements on the comparable properties to reflect how they differ from the subject. Adjustments are made for physical differences such as size, shape, quality of construction, finish, and built-in equipment (fixtures). In the cost approach, adjustments are based on the cost of the item. In the sales comparison approach, adjustments are based on the item's contributory value.
4. Divides the adjusted replacement or reproduction cost of the improvements on each comparable property by the unit of comparison, usually area or square foot, to arrive at the cost per unit of area.
5. Studies the trend in costs between the time the comparable properties were constructed and the date of the appraisal. The unit costs of the comparables are then adjusted to reflect cost differences over time.

6. Relates unit costs to property size and interpolates to estimate the appropriate replacement or reproduction cost. Generally unit costs decline as property size increases (i.e., the law of diminishing returns).

7. Applies the adjusted unit cost of the comparables to measurements of the subject building to obtain the current reproduction or replacement cost estimate of the main improvement.

Example

The subject property is a two-story residence built three years ago. The quality of construction is average for similar, mass-produced homes in the area. The house has a concrete block foundation, wood siding, fiberglass composition shingle roofing, ½-in. interior drywall, and a good- to average-quality finish. It has 3 bedrooms, 2½ baths, a full basement, and a roof dormer. The house does not have a fireplace. The mechanical equipment consists of combination forced-air heating and air-conditioning, and typical built-in appliances. The appraiser's measurements show that the structure contains 1,648 square feet of gross living area.

After inspecting comparable properties that were constructed and sold within the past three years, the appraiser decides to place the greatest emphasis on a single, similar property that has features typical of the subject neighborhood.[1] This comparable residence has 1,596 square feet of gross living area and was built and sold three years ago. It is located in the subject neighborhood and is similar to the subject, except that it has a foundation of poured concrete instead of concrete block and brick exterior walls instead of wood siding. This house does not have a roof dormer but it does have a fireplace.

The sale price of the comparable, including entrepreneurial incentive or profit, was $276,000. By means of sales comparison, site value on the date of construction is estimated at $52,000. The appraiser calculates the cost of the comparable dwelling as follows:

Sale price	$276,000
Less site value	− 52,000
Equals cost of comparable improvements	$224,000

This estimate is consistent with the costs listed in the construction contract and seems reasonable for the area.

Next the appraiser derives adjustments for differences between the comparable and the subject using information obtained from local contractors and building suppliers. These adjustments are applied to the cost of the comparable, and the adjusted cost is converted into a comparative unit cost. Another adjustment is made to reflect changes in cost over the past three years. Finally, the adjusted unit cost is ap-

---

1. This example is only an illustration. Data on the other comparables and the reconciliation of cost estimates are not included.

plied to the dimensions of the subject building. The calculations are shown below.

Cost of comparable improvements three years ago	$224,000
Adjustments	
Brick siding	– 26,000
Poured concrete foundation	– 3,500
Fireplace	– 5,000
Roof dormer	+ 2,400
Equals adjusted historical cost of comparable improvements	$191,900
Divided by gross living area of comparable (1,596 sq. ft.)	÷ 1,596
Equals adjusted historical unit cost	$120.24
Multiplied by time adjustment for cost-trend changes (119%*)	× 119%
Equals adjusted current unit cost	$143.08
Times gross living area of subject (1,648 sq. ft.)	× 1,648
Equals estimate of current reproduction cost of subject	$235,796

*   Based on the percentage increase in the cost-estimating service used by the appraiser.

Using the comparative-unit method, the appraiser estimates the cost of the subject residence to be $236,000 (rounded).

Sales comparison was used to derive a unit cost figure in the example, but this figure can also be developed using data from a recognized cost service. Cost data sources are discussed later in this chapter, but it should be noted that cost manuals usually do not include entrepreneurial incentive or profit. The appraiser must completely familiarize himself or herself with the methodology used in each cost service he or she uses to prevent the use of inaccurate cost estimates in any appraisal assignment.

Experienced appraisers recognize that the unit costs of structures typically decrease with size. Larger buildings do not necessarily cost proportionately more than smaller ones. Doors and windows can make construction more expensive, but usually the number of doors and windows in any one residence is limited. Plumbing, heating units, and kitchen equipment are major expenses, but the cost of these items is fairly stable in similarly sized homes. Equipment costs do not necessarily increase with the size of the building.[2]

Structures that are not designed in a conventional shape tend to have higher unit costs due to differences in design, engineering, skilled labor, and additional building materials. Figure 14.1 shows how the shape of a structure can affect its costs.

Applicability

The apparent simplicity of the comparative-unit method can be misleading. To develop dependable unit cost figures, an appraiser must carefully compare the subject building with similar or standard structures for which actual costs are known. Inaccuracies may result

---

2.   Appraisers should note that the ratio of equipment costs to the cost of the basic building shell has been rising steadily over the years. Additional equipment tends to increase building costs and depreciate more rapidly than the rest of the structure.

Figure 14.1   Costs and Building Shapes

Costs are higher for the structure with the longer perimeter.

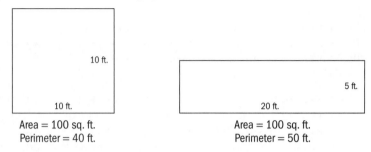

Area = 100 sq. ft.
Perimeter = 40 ft.

Area = 100 sq. ft.
Perimeter = 50 ft.

Higher costs are incurred for the larger perimeter and for the skilled labor needed to construct angles and irregular shapes.

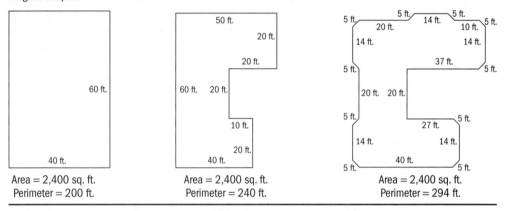

Area = 2,400 sq. ft.
Perimeter = 200 ft.

Area = 2,400 sq. ft.
Perimeter = 240 ft.

Area = 2,400 sq. ft.
Perimeter = 294 ft.

if the appraiser selects dissimilar buildings to compare or uses a unit cost that is not appropriate to the building being appraised. Nevertheless, proper application of the comparative-unit method can provide an appraiser with a reasonably accurate estimate of reproduction or replacement cost.

To apply the method correctly, an appraiser must assemble, analyze, and catalog data on actual building costs. Construction contracts for buildings similar to the subject are primary sources of cost data. Discussions with local contractors can supplement this information. Many appraisers maintain comprehensive files on the current costs for completed structures. These costs may be classified according to types of residences. Appraisers should also follow cost trends in local and competitive markets so that they can adjust costs for market conditions and location if necessary. Unit costs can be derived from cost data services, but costs vary in different markets and a first-hand analysis of the market can often produce data that are more reliable.

Unit-in-Place Method

The unit-in-place, or segregated cost, method allows an appraiser to estimate costs in greater detail. The appraiser derives unit costs for individual structural components and applies them to the components found in the subject property. The unit-in-place method can be applied to all the improvements on the property or separately to the main improvements and any accessory improvements.

The unit-in-place method has six steps. An appraiser

1. Collects data on current direct costs for various building components. Data can be obtained from an analysis of recent construction contracts, surveys of builders and contractors, and recognized cost services. Information on indirect costs and typical entrepreneurial incentive or profit are also collected.

2. Measures the components of the subject building, studies plans, and determines the number of units of each component that were required to construct the building. Excavating costs are typically expressed in dollars per cubic yard. Foundation costs may be reported in dollars per linear foot of perimeter or per cubic yard of concrete. Floor construction costs are expressed in dollars per square foot. The basic unit for roofing, called a *square*, is 100 square feet of surface area. Interior partitions may be reduced to dollars per linear foot. Costs for other items such as mechanical equipment are expressed in trade units such as cost per ton of air-conditioning or other selected units.

3. Applies the unit costs for each component to the number of units of the component found in the subject.

4. Estimates contractor's overhead and profit. If these items are already included in the unit costs, which is often the case, this step is omitted.

5. Estimates any indirect costs not included in the unit costs and adds them to the direct costs.

6. Estimates entrepreneurial incentive or profit and adds this amount to the direct costs and indirect costs to arrive at a replacement or reproduction cost estimate.

Example

Table 14.1 is an example of how unit-in-place costs may be applied for a one-story house.

Applicability

The unit-in-place method breaks down the cost of a building into its components. Such a cost estimate is useful for recording the quality of construction components and computing the cost of their reproduction or replacement. However, assembling the basic costs of the equipment, material, and labor used in the structure and combining these costs into a final cost estimate may require specialized knowledge. When fully

Table 14.1 — Unit-in-Place Costs

Component	Quantity	Cost	Extended Cost
Basic cost	1,442	$55.28	79,713.76
Roofing	1,442	$0.77	1,110.34
Energy	–	–	–
Foundation/hillside	1,442	$1.67	2,408.14
Seismic	1,442	$1.97	2,840.74
Subfloor	1,442	$1.98	2,855.16
Floor insulation	1,442	$0.86	1,240.12
Floor cover			
Hardwood flooring	1,000	$7.31	7,310.00
Ceramic tile	442	$8.61	3,805.62
Plaster interior	–	–	–
Heating/cooling	1,442	$1.90	2,739.80
Plumbing fixtures—Total 7 Base 8	-1	$820.00	-820.00
Plumbing rough-ins—Total 0 Base 1	-1	$320.00	-320.00
Dormers	–	–	–
Fireplaces	1	$2,650.00	2,650.00
Built-in appliances—appliance allowance		$2,300.00	2,300.00
Subtotal—adjusted residence cost			**107,833.68**
Basement	1,442	$12.84	18,515.28
Porches, decks, breezeways, etc.	200	$23.11	4,622.00
Balconies	–	–	–
Exterior stairways	–	–	–
Subtotal—residence cost			**130,970.96**
Garages/Carports	700	$19.26	13,482.00
Subtotal—all building improvements			**144,452.96**
Multipliers—current cost (1.06) × local (1.12) × other (1.00)		×	1.1872
Additional components	–	–	–
Total replacement cost			**171,494.55**
			rounded to 171,500.00

developed, however, the unit-in-place method substitutes for a complete quantity survey and can provide an accurate estimate of reproduction or replacement cost with considerably less effort.

Quantity Survey Method

The quantity survey method, which is the most comprehensive method of estimating building costs, simulates how a contractor develops a bid. To complete a quantity survey, an appraiser must prepare a detailed inventory of all the materials and equipment needed to build a house. The cost of each item as of the date of the appraisal is estimated along with the number of hours of labor needed to install each item at current rates. Finally, estimates of the contractor's overhead and profit, indirect costs, and the developer's profit are added to the cost of labor and materials.

The quantity survey method is similar to the unit-in-place method, but costs are identified in much greater detail. For example, the kitchen cabinets and plumbing in a structure might be broken down as follows in a quantity survey:

	Material			Labor			
	Units	Price	Total	Hours	Rate	Total	Total Cost
Cabinet work: base-finished w/ formica top	16	$44.00	$704.00	14	$14.60	$204.40	$908.40
Plumbing: 60-gal. hot water heater	1	$590.00	$590.00	8	$31.50	$252.00	$842.00

Example

Appraisers often summarize the details of a contractor's or cost estimator's cost breakdown in their appraisal reports. Figure 14.2 example presents a building description that might appear in an appraisal report. Table 14.2 then illustrates the applicaiton of the quantity survey method breaking down the costs of various building components. In an actual appraisal report, the improvement description and the cost estimation would be found in separate parts of the report. A complete quantity survey would contain more detailed information.

Figure 14.2 Building Description

General Description

The single-unit, one-story, ranch-style residence has seven rooms (living room, family room, dining room, kitchen, and three bedrooms), two full baths, and a full, unfinished basement. It has a two-car, attached garage but no porches. The gross living area is 1,442 square feet.

General Construction

The house has concrete footings and foundation walls. The exterior walls and roof covering are of cedar shingles. The wood, double-hung windows have combination aluminum storm windows and screens. The gutters and downspouts are aluminum, and batt insulation is used. The structure has wood platform framing, plywood subfloors, and oak floors. The kitchen has vinyl flooring and the bathrooms have ceramic tile wainscoting.

Construction Quality

The house is of average quality throughout and meets FHA minimum standards.

Mechanical Systems

Plumbing:	Copper water pipes and cast-iron waste pipes connected to municipal services in street. Electric, 60-gal., domestic hot water heater. One double, stainless steel kitchen sink. Each bathroom has a standard toilet, sink, and tub with a shower. Built-in laundry tub in basement and washer/dryer hook-up.
Heating:	Oil-fired, hot water furnace, two circulators, baseboard radiators.
Electrical:	200-ampere service, 16 circuits protected with circuit breakers, BX cable, adequate outlets and features.

Built-in appliances: Gas oven and range with hood and exhaust fan in kitchen.

Table 14.2	Summary of Quantity Survey	

Component	Cost
Survey and engineering	$2,500
Plans and plan checking	$2,500
Site preparation	$4,500
Excavation	$2,500
Footings and foundation	$7,300
Basement	$10,200
Framing	$10,000
Interior walls and ceilings	$6,000
Exterior siding	$5,500
Roof covering and flashing	$5,500
Insulation	$2,300
Fireplaces and chimneys	$2,500
Leaders and gutters	$2,000
Exterior and interior stairs	$2,500
Doors, windows, and shutters	$5,700
Storm windows, doors, and screens	$1,200
Main floor covering	$2,200
Kitchen flooring	$800
Bathroom and lavatory floors	$900
Hardware	$1,100
Water supply	$1,900
Water disposal	$1,500
Heating	$5,500
Cooling	$2,500
Domestic hot water	$1,500
Piping	$5,000
Plumbing fixtures	$4,400
Kitchen cabinets and counters	$3,200
Built-in appliances	$2,700
Shower doors	$700
Bathroom accessories	$600
Vanities, medicine cabinets, and counters	$1,000
Electric service	$2,500
Electric wires and outlets	$2,500
Lighting fixtures	$1,000
Painting and decorating	$3,500
Porches (none)	—
Patios	$700
Finish grading	$1,000
Landscaping	$2,200
Garages and carports	$7,500
Clean up	$600
Interest, taxes, and insurance	$2,500
Contractor's overhead and temporary facilities	$5,500
Professional services, permits, and licenses	$1,000
Selling expenses and carrying costs	$4,500
Contractor's profits	$3,500
Direct and indirect costs	$146,700
Plus entrepreneurial incentive (10%)*	$14,670
Total reproduction cost	$161,370

* It may not always be appropriate to consider entrepreneurial incentive at this point.

Applicability

The quantity survey method is the most comprehensive and precise way to estimate building costs, but it is also the most costly and time-consuming. It provides more detail than is normally required in an appraisal. When a complete building cost breakdown is needed, the services of a trained cost estimator should be obtained.

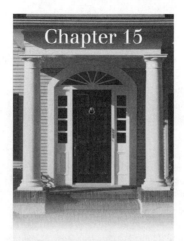

Chapter 15

Estimating Depreciation

In the cost approach a property value indication is derived by estimating the replacement or reproduction cost of the improvements, which comprises direct costs, indirect costs, and entrepreneurial incentive or profit. Depreciation is then subtracted from the replacement or reproduction cost estimate, and land or site value is added to the depreciated cost estimate. In this approach, cost is considered to be an indicator of the value of the improvements as if new. Because existing improvements usually contribute less value than their reproduction or replacement cost, an appraiser often must make an adjustment to reflect the loss in value that the existing structure has incurred since its construction. This deduction is the amount of depreciation the improvements have incurred.

Depreciation is the difference between the reproduction or replacement cost of an improvement and its market value as of the date of the appraisal. Three major factors may cause a building to lose value, or depreciate, over time:

1. Physical deterioration
2. Functional obsolescence
3. External obsolescence

These three types of depreciation can be broken down into more discrete components as illustrated in Figure 15.1. This model accounts for all elements of the total depreciation estimate. If a particular element is not a form of physical deterioration, it *must* be some form of obsolescence; elements of total depreciation that do not qualify as physical deterioration or functional obsolescence *must* be a form of external obsolescence.

Figure 15.1   Types of Depreciation

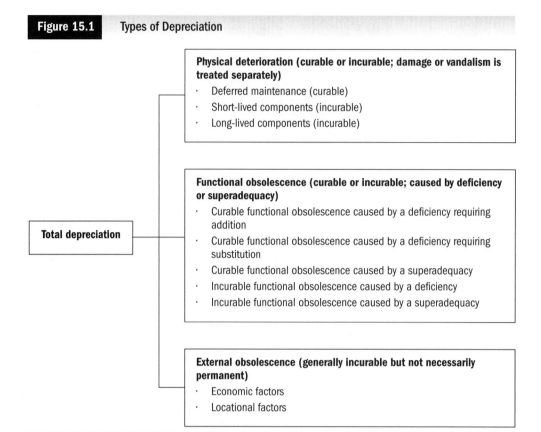

As a building ages, it is subject to wear and tear from regular use and the impact of the elements, reducing the value of the building over its life through physical deterioration. Careful maintenance may slow down this process, while neglect or improper maintenance may accelerate it.

All physical components of a structure fall into one of the three forms of physical deterioration:

1. Deferred maintenance
2. Deterioration of short-lived components
3. Deterioration of long-lived components

Damage or vandalism to a building (which is usually a curable and temporary influence on property value) is treated separately from physical deterioration because it is not included in the cost new of a project under development. Neither additional costs incurred to remediate damage on a construction site (e.g., graffiti that has to be sandblasted) nor damage to existing housing (e.g., a burglar rips the door off the jamb and a carpenter has to replace the door) are considered among the components of depreciation. By curing damage or vandalism, the life of the damaged building component is neither renewed nor prolonged; it is simply restored to its condition prior to the damage.

A building may also suffer from functional obsolescence due to some flaw in the site, structure, material, or design that diminishes its function, utility, and value. As the term *obsolescence* suggests, this type of value loss is often caused by the obsolete features of older properties, including buildings that are still in good repair. For example, older windows that do not provide sufficient insulation may cause functional obsolescence. Even a newly constructed building can have functional obsolescence due to a deficient feature such as a poor floor plan, unique traffic pattern, lack of privacy for bedrooms or baths, inadequate kitchen design, too small baths, excessively large or small rooms, or an overall lack of appeal due to the design of the dwelling. Problems like these are very specific to the market. A very small kitchen may be a large problem in one market but not a problem at all in another. A second kitchen in the basement may be a superadequacy in most markets but not in a weekend lakefront house.

The five forms of functional obsolescence are

1. Curable functional obsolescence caused by a deficiency requiring addition of a new item
2. Curable functional obsolescence caused by a deficiency requiring substitution of an existing item
3. Curable functional obsolescence caused by a superadequacy that is economically feasible to cure
4. Incurable functional obsolescence caused by a deficiency
5. Incurable functional obsolescence caused by a superadequacy

deficiency requiring additions. Functional obsolescence resulting from the lack of something that other properties in the market have.

deficiency requiring substitution or modernization. Functional obsolescence resulting from the presence of something in the subject property that is substandard compared to other properties on the market or that is defective and thereby prevents some other component or system in the property from working properly.

The only ways to offset functional obsolescence are to cure it or to hope that market standards change.

To test whether or not functional obsolescence is present, an appraiser decides whether the structure or its design conforms to current market standards. The quality of construction, materials, or design of a building may be inferior to current market standards (i.e., typical improvements) for the neighborhood. In this case, any savings realized from the lower construction costs will probably result in a disproportionately greater loss in the price obtainable for the property. If the structure and its design surpass market standards (superadequacies), the additional utility provided may not justify the additional cost. In either case, functional obsolescence must be deducted from the replacement or reproduction cost of the structure to reflect its diminished utility in comparison to market standards.

In contrast to functional obsolescence, external obsolescence is caused by a factor *outside* the subject, including economic factors such as oversupply in the market or expensive financing, or locational factors such as proximity to a nuisance or poor access to transportation routes. Interest rates that are rising quickly, for example, may cause current construction costs to outpace building values. Similarly, overbuilding in certain markets may create a surplus of space and depress rents and values. Although external obsolescence is generally incurable, it is not always permanent; for instance, market conditions such as overbuilding or high interest rates can change over time, eventually removing the influence of external obsolescence on a particular property. Unlike the other types of depreciation, which affect the improvements only, external obsolescence may affect both the site and improvements, and therefore the influence of the externality on value may have to be allocated between the site and the improvements.

A loss in value also results when a neighborhood changes and an improvement that was formerly well suited to its location is no longer appropriate. In this situation the site may or may not lose value; it may be more valuable as the site of a more intensive use. Although the existing improvements may be well designed and well maintained, if they are not what the market currently demands at that location they cannot contribute value commensurate with their cost. Such use of property in transitional situations is called an *interim use.* An example of an interim use may be a residential dwelling on a commercial site that is not yet ready to be developed with a new commercial structure. The interim use would be for continued use as a residence.

In some cases external or economic changes can restore the appropriateness of the location for the existing improvements. Often, however, land value or entrepreneurial incentive or profit will increase when such a change occurs, not the value contribution of the building. The contribution of a building to property value rarely rises above its cost. One exception to this general rule might be a residence of historical significance, which contributes more value than the cost of a new structure.

All three causes of depreciation–physical deterioration, functional obsolescence, and external obsolescence–reduce the value of an existing structure in comparison with its replacement or reproduction cost. An appraiser calculates the amount of depreciation in a structure by applying one of three techniques either independently or in conjunction with one another:

1. The market extraction method
2. The age-life method
3. The breakdown method

Depreciation is deducted from the reproduction or replacement cost of the existing improvements to estimate their contribution to the total value of the property.

Age and Life of Residences

The appraisal concept of depreciation is closely related to economic life, useful life, remaining economic life, remaining useful life, actual age, and effective age. Many techniques for estimating depreciation make use of these terms.

Economic Life and Useful Life

Economic life is the period of time over which improvements contribute to property value. A building's economic life begins when construction is complete and ends when the building no longer contributes any value to the property above land value. This period is shorter than the building's useful life, which is the total period over which a structure may reasonably be expected to perform the function for which it was designed. If buildings are adequately maintained, they may remain on the land long after they cease to contribute economically to property value. After the end of their economic lives, buildings may be renovated, rehabilitated, or remodeled, or they may be demolished and replaced with more suitable structures.

To estimate a building's economic life, an appraiser studies the typical economic life expectancy of recently sold structures similar to the subject in the market area. (See the discussion of the market extraction technique later in this chapter.) In other words, the quality of construction and functional utility of the existing residence are considered in the estimate of economic life. The present condition of the subject property is reflected in estimates of remaining economic life and effective age.

Long-lived building components have a useful life at least as long as the building's economic life expectancy, while short-lived components will probably wear out and need to be replaced before the building has reached the end of its economic life. Structural components of a building, like the foundation, framing, and underground piping, are typical long-lived components. The roof covering, floor finishes, HVAC components, and interior decorating of a building are examples of short-lived components. The distinction between short-lived and long-lived components becomes significant in the application of the breakdown method.

> **economic life.** The period over which improvements to real property contribute to property value.
>
> **useful life.** The period of time over which a structure may reasonably be expected to perform the function for which it was designed.

Although the economic life expectancy of a structure is difficult to predict, it is shaped by a number of factors, including:

- Physical considerations—i.e., the rate at which the physical components of the residence wear out, given the quality of construction, the use of the property, maintenance standards, and the climate of the region.

- Functional considerations—i.e., the rate at which building technology, tastes in architecture, and family size and composition change. These factors can make a residence obsolete or they can also remove obsolescence.

- External, economic considerations, especially long-term influences such as the stage in the neighborhood's life cycle.

Many of these considerations may become significant 20, 50, or even 100 years in the future, so they are obviously difficult to forecast with any accuracy. Nevertheless, market study and analysis of historical and geographical trends may provide important information. The economic viability of an improvement is a function of the location. If a property has good upside potential, owners will invest money to maintain it. If not, the maintenance will not be done and the total economic life will be shortened. Economic life expectancy is not a "one size fits all" number.

Remaining Economic Life and Remaining Useful Life

Remaining economic life is the estimated period over which existing improvements continue to contribute to property value. This concept refers to the economic life that remains in the existing structure. It begins on the effective date of the appraisal or some other specified date and extends until the end of the building's economic life. A building's remaining economic life is always less than or equal to, never more than, its total economic life.

remaining economic life. The estimated period during which improvements will continue to contribute to property value; an estimate of the number of years remaining in the economic life of the structure or structural components as of the date of the appraisal; used in the age-life method of estimating depreciation.

remaining useful life. The estimated period during which improvements will continue to contribute to property value; an estimate of the number of years remaining in the useful life of the structure or structural components as of the date of the appraisal; used in the breakdown method of estimating depreciation.

actual age. The number of years that have elapsed since contsruction of an improvement was completed; also called *historical* or *chronological age.*

effective age. The age of property that is based on the amount of observed deterioration and obsolescence it has sustained, which may be different from its chronological age.

Remaining useful life is the estimated period from the actual age of a component to the total useful life expectancy. Just as useful life is usually longer than economic life, the remaining useful life of a long-lived component is equal to or, typically, greater than its remaining economic life.

Actual Age and Effective Age

Actual age, which is sometimes called *historical age* or *chronological age*, is the number of years that have elapsed since building construction was completed. The prices of newly completed buildings are compared with the prices of similar, older structures to establish a correlation between actual age and the value of residences.

Effective age is the age indicated by the condition and utility of the structure. It is determined by an appraiser's judgment and is not market-derived. Similar buildings do not necessarily depreciate at the same rate. The maintenance standards of owners or occu-

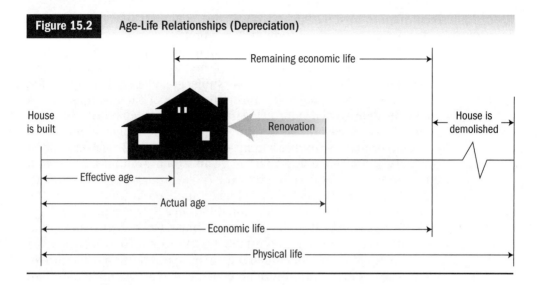

Figure 15.2 Age-Life Relationships (Depreciation)

pants can influence the pace of building deterioration. If a building is better maintained than others in the market area, its effective age will be less than its actual age. If a building is poorly maintained, its effective age may be greater. If a building has received typical maintenance, its effective age and actual age could be the same. Effective age is related to remaining economic life. The total economic life of similar structures minus the effective age of the subject building equals the remaining economic life of the subject. The total economic life of structures is not the same in every market and not the same at various stages of the life cycle of an improvement. Appraisers cannot extract this rate once and use it in other markets for different properties.

Methods of Estimating Depreciation

The three principal methods for estimating depreciation are

1. The market extraction method
2. The age-life method, along with its two variations
3. The breakdown method

The market extraction and age-life methods are used primarily to estimate the total depreciation of property, while the breakdown method can be used to allocate value loss to the individual components of depreciation.

Each of these methods is acceptable so long as it reflects the manner in which informed, prudent buyers would react to the condition of the structure being appraised and the appraiser applies the method consistently, logically, and cautiously. The methods are summarized and demonstrated in the following sections and their applicability and limitations are discussed in detail. These methods may be used in combination to solve specific problems or to test the reasonableness of the estimates derived from each method.

To apply the market extraction method, an appraiser develops a depreciation estimate by studying sales of comparable properties that have depreciated to the same extent as the subject residence. The land value at the time of sale is subtracted from the price of each comparable to obtain the depreciated value of the improvement. When the depreciated value of the improvements is subtracted from the replacement cost of the comparable, the result is a lump sum, dollar estimate of depreciation reflecting all forms of depreciation.[1] This dollar amount is converted into a percentage by dividing it by the replacement cost. The percentage of lump sum depreciation is then annualized by dividing it by the actual age or, if there is a significant difference between the actual age and effective age, by the effective age estimate. Once a range of annual percentages of depreciation is established, the appraiser reconciles the range and applies the concluded rate to the age of the subject improvement. The result is a lump sum percentage of depreciation that is then applied to the replacement cost of the subject. This rate can also be used in developing a total economic life expectancy.

In the age-life method, an appraiser estimates the total economic life of the existing improvements as well as its effective age based on an analysis of sales of similar structures. The ratio of effective age to total economic life is considered to be the extent to which the building has depreciated. This ratio is directly applied to the replacement or reproduction cost of the structure to arrive at a lump sum depreciation amount including all forms of depreciation, which is then deducted from the cost figure.

One variation of the age-life method distinguishes between curable and incurable items of depreciation, and another variation takes into account external obsolescence. In the first variation, the appraiser first estimates the cost to fix all curable items—i.e., items that can be repaired or replaced at a cost that is equal to or less than the amount of value that the item contributes to the total property. This amount is deducted from the replacement or reproduction cost of the structure to arrive at a figure adjusted for curable depreciation. Then the appraiser estimates the effective age and total economic life of the structure, assuming the curable items have been repaired, and applies the ratio of effective age to total economic life to the depreciated replacement or reproduction cost. The sum for incurable depreciation is then deducted from the depreciated cost.

In the second variation of the age-life method, the appraiser first determines if other properties in the market have incurred the same external obsolescence as the subject. If so, the appraiser can use the total economic life extracted from those sales considered comparable in the age-life ratio. If not, the appraiser must estimate depreciation

---

1. An appraiser may also use this lump sum estimate of depreciation to test the reasonableness of the depreciation estimate derived using the breakdown method.

exclusive of external obsolescence using a market-extracted economic life expectancy in the age-life ratio and then estimate external obsolescence using techniques from the breakdown method. The sum of estimated depreciation from the age-life method and estimated external obsolescence using the breakdown method would yield an estimate of total depreciation.

The breakdown method is a more detailed, expanded set of techniques for estimating depreciation. Separate estimates are derived for items of

- Curable physical deterioration
- Incurable physical deterioration
- Curable functional obsolescence
- Incurable functional obsolescence
- External obsolescence

Each category of depreciation is estimated by a specific method applicable to that form of depreciation. The sum of depreciation for all items is then subtracted from the replacement or reproduction cost of the improvements. The procedures in the breakdown method can also be used to allocate a lump sum estimate of depreciation determined by other methods into its components.

Regardless of the method applied, the appraiser must ensure that the final estimate of depreciation reflects the loss in value from all causes, and that no cause of depreciation has been considered more than once. Double charges for depreciation may produce overly low value indications in the cost approach. The first variation of the age-life method and the breakdown method provide an estimate of the cost to cure curable items of depreciation, which should be recognized in the application of the other approaches to value. This is typically done in the sales comparison approach and the income capitalization approach by deducting the cost to cure at the conclusion of each approach.

Reproduction and Replacement Cost Bases

An appraiser must estimate depreciation using the same basis from which costs were calculated—either reproduction or replacement cost. A reproduction is a virtual replica of the existing structure, employing the same design and similar building materials. A replacement is a structure of comparable utility constructed with the design and materials that are currently used in the building market. A reproduction may contain more items of functional obsolescence than a replacement structure does. These items might include high ceilings, a lack of adequate electrical outlets and plumbing facilities, and the use of expensive, outdated building materials and techniques. Obsolete items usually cost more in the current market and do not produce a proportionate increase in utility and value. An amount must be deducted from reproduction cost for these items of functional obsolescence.

The use of replacement cost usually eliminates the need to measure some, but not all, forms of functional obsolescence. Replacement structures usually cost less than reproductions because they are constructed with materials and techniques that are more readily available and less expensive in today's market. Thus a replacement cost figure is usually lower and may provide a better indication of the existing structure's contribution to value. A replacement structure typically does not suffer functional obsolescence resulting from superadequacies, but if functional problems are found in the existing structure, an additional amount must be deducted from the replacement cost. Estimating replacement cost generally simplifies the procedure for measuring depreciation in superadequate construction components. Examples of functional obsolescence are structural defects in an existing residence or excessively thick foundations. Such obsolescence would be corrected in a replacement building.

To avoid errors in measuring depreciation, an appraiser must be consistent and clearly understand the purpose of this step in the cost approach. Depreciation is estimated and deducted to adjust the cost to create a new reproduction or replacement improvement to reflect the value contribution of the existing improvement. Even a newly constructed improvement may not contribute as much value as it costs. Although it has no physical deterioration, a reproduction or replacement structure may suffer from external obsolescence and functional obsolescence. Any feature that creates a loss in value from the cost standard must be accounted for as an item of depreciation.

Market Extraction Method

Market extraction is the most direct means of estimating depreciation if a sufficient amount of sales data is available to support the appraiser's conclusion. The method is used primarily to extract total depreciation, to establish total economic life expectancy, and to estimate external

Figure 15.3	Differences Between Reproduction Cost and Replacement Cost
Reproduction Cost	**Replacement Cost**
A reproduction replicates the existing structure (i.e., form).	A replacement structure mimics the utility of the existing structure (i.e., function).
A reproduction employs the same design and similar building materials as the existing structure (past).	A replacement employs the design and materials currently used in the building market (present).
A reproduction is more likely to contain items of functional obsolescence.	A replacement structure is less likely to have items of functional obsolescence, particularly superadequacies.
Reproduction cost is usually higher because some outdated materials and techniques may be hard to come by in the current market.	Replacement cost is usually lower and may better represent the existing structure's contribution to value.

obsolescence. There are eight steps in the market extraction method. An appraiser

1. Identifies at least two sales of improved properties similar in location that appear to have approximately the same amount of depreciation as the subject property.
2. Makes appropriate adjustments to the comparables sales for certain factors, including property rights conveyed, financing, and conditions of sale. If an appraiser can quantify curable depreciation for items of deferred maintenance or functional obsolescence, this estimate should be applied to the sale price as an adjustment. (Depreciation extracted in this way will exclude curable items.)
3. Subtracts the land value at the time of sale from the sale price of each comparable property to obtain the depreciated cost of the improvements.
4. Estimates the replacement cost of the improvements on each comparable property at the time of sale. Reproduction cost can be used, but it must be applied in the same way.
5. Subtracts the depreciated cost of each improvement from the cost of the improvements to obtain a lump sum estimate of depreciation in dollars.
6. Converts the dollar estimates of depreciation into percentages by dividing each depreciation estimate by the replacement cost.
7. Annualizes the percentages of lump sum depreciation by dividing each total percentage of depreciation by the actual age estimate or, if there is a significant difference between the actual age and the effective age, by the effective age estimate.
8. Reconciles the range of annual percentage rates derived and applies an approximate depreciation rate to the cost of the subject improvements.

In an optional step of this procedure, the appraiser can calculate the total economic life expectancy of the subject using the reciprocal of the average annual rate of depreciation for the comparables as indicated in the market on the date of sale.[2]

> **market extraction method.** A method of estimating depreciation in which a range of estimates of the lump sum percentage of depreciation of comparables is reconciled into a rate that is applied to the age of the subject to obtain a lump sum percentage of depreciation.

Example

The subject property is a 12-year-old frame structure with an effective age of 12 years. The subject property contains 1,496 square feet of gross living area and is situated on a site that is valued at $26,000. The replacement cost of this residence is $80.21 per square foot of gross living area.

---

2. As is explained in an extended footnote to the age-life method (footnote 4 on page 296), with older residential properties it may be easier for the appraiser to find support for the total economic life expectancy. Data on total economic life may be used to arrive at an average annual rate of depreciation for the property and, thereby, to establish the overall percentage the property is depreciated.

The appraiser has found three sales of neighborhood properties similar to the subject property. All of the sales were fee simple, arm's-length, cash-equivalent sales and did not require immediate repairs. Property 1 was sold recently for $112,500. The appraiser estimates that the site is worth $26,000, and the replacement cost of the improvements is $117,500. The property's actual age, 15 years, corresponds to its effective age.

Property 2 was sold recently for $128,800. The appraiser estimates that the site is worth $24,000 and the replacement cost of the improvements is $116,000. The property's actual age is 8 years, which is the same as its effective age.

Property 3 was sold recently for $130,000. The appraiser estimates the site is worth $29,000 and the replacement cost of the improvements is $145,500. The property's actual age, which is equal to its effective age, is 20 years.

To estimate the average annual rate of depreciation in the subject property, the appraiser compares the three sales.

	Property 1	Property 2	Property 3
Sale price	$112,500	$128,800	$130,000
Less site value	− 26,000	− 24,000	− 29,000
Depreciated value of improvements	$86,500	$104,800	$101,000
Cost of improvements at date of sale	$117,500	$116,000	$145,500
Less depreciated value of improvements	− 86,500	− 104,800	− 101,000
Depreciation amount	$31,000	$11,200	$44,500
Percentage depreciation ($ dep./cost)	26.38%	9.66%	30.58%
Age of improvements	15	8	20
Average annual depreciation (%)	1.76%	1.21%	1.53%
100% / average annual depreciation	56.8182	82.6446	65.3595
Indicated total economic life	57.00	83.00	65.00

Because the age of the subject property (12 years) is approximately midway between the ages of Sale 1 (15 years) and Sale 2 (8 years), the average of these two annual depreciation rates (1.50% per year) becomes a reconciled rate for the subject property. The total economic life expectancy of the subject property would be approximately 67 years (1/0.0150).

With these figures the value of the subject property is estimated as follows:

Replacement cost	
1,496 sq. ft. @ $80.21	(rounded) $120,000
Less depreciation	
12 years @ 1.50% × $120,000	− 21,600
Depreciated cost of improvements	$98,400
Plus site value	+ 26,000
Total property value indication	$124,400
	(rounded) $124,500

Applicability

When sales data are plentiful, market extraction usually provides a reliable, persuasive estimate of depreciation; it is the most defensible of the depreciation tools because it is measured directly from the market. If sales are truly comparable, then the land sales or site valuation method used for the subject property would apply to the comparables, the source of the estimate of replacement cost that applies to the subject would also apply to the comparables, and the use of actual age would eliminate the need to "guess" the effective age of comparables that were not actually inspected by the appraiser. Many appraisers use this method to measure depreciation in all property types, including nonresidential property. By using matched data sets, different types of depreciation can be measured using the extracted annual depreciation rates. Most significantly, market extraction is the only method by which meaningful data can be extracted to support the total economic life expectancy of the property as of the date of property sale. Total economic life expectancy is calculated as the reciprocal of the average annual rate of depreciation.[3] The total economic life expectancy will be different from market to market and with different ages of improvements.

Despite the many advantages of market extraction, the properties compared must be similar to the subject and they must suffer from similar amounts and types of depreciation. When the properties compared differ in design, quality, or construction, it is difficult to ascertain whether differences in value are attributable to differences in those components or to a difference in depreciation. The method is also difficult to apply when the type or extent of depreciation varies greatly among the properties. If the sales analyzed were affected by special financing or unusual motivation, the problem is further complicated. The accuracy of the method depends heavily on the accuracy of the land value and replacement cost estimates of the comparable properties. If the sales are located in districts, market areas, or neighborhoods that are not comparable, the method may not be appropriate. In the market extraction method, all types of depreciation are considered in a lump sum; they are not broken down into various types.

In spite of its limitations, market extraction provides extremely reliable and convincing conclusions and may be used to check the results obtained by applying other methods.

Age-Life Method

Like market extraction, the age-life method assumes that depreciation occurs in a straight-line pattern. The age-life method identifies the rate at which buildings similar to the subject depreciate and then uses this rate, along with the effective age of the subject, to derive an

---

3. Using the reciprocal of the average annual rate of depreciation to calculate the total economic life expectancy of a property rests on the premise that depreciation occurs in a straight-line pattern. When the appraiser attempts to develop an estimate of total economic life expectancy on the basis of an annual rate, the straight-line assumption may have to be reconsidered in terms of its applicability to the subject and comparable properties. Because straight-line depreciation may not be the typical pattern, conclusions must be consistent with market data. Market support is more important than mathematical precision.

age-life method. A method of estimating depreciation in which the ratio between the effective age of a building and its total economic life is applied to the current cost of the improvements to obtain a lump sum deduction; also known as the *economic age-life method.*

estimate of depreciation. Although it is not always as accurate as other techniques, the age-life method is the simplest way to estimate depreciation. The method is applied in three steps. An appraiser

1. Conducts research to identify the total economic life of similar structures in the market area and estimates the effective age of the subject building. (The effective age may be the same as the actual age if the building has received typical maintenance.)
2. Divides the effective age of the subject by the anticipated total economic life of similar structures. The resulting ratio is then applied to the subject's reproduction or replacement cost to estimate lump sum depreciation.[4]
3. Subtracts the estimate of depreciation from the replacement or reproduction cost to arrive at the contribution of the improvements to property value.

Example

The subject property is located in a neighborhood that was developed during a land boom 20 years ago. Most of the properties nearby are similar to the subject in size and architectural style. These buildings appear to be maintained adequately. Through use of the market extraction method, the appraiser concludes that the typical economic life for properties in this market is 75 years. The subject has been especially well maintained, however, and the appraiser concludes that it has an effective age of only 8 years. The replacement cost is estimated at $248,000, and the site value is estimated at $90,600.

The appraiser estimates depreciation with the following calculations:

$$\text{Depreciation ratio} = \frac{8 \text{ years (effective age)}}{75 \text{ years (total economic life)}} = 0.107, \text{ or } 10.7\%$$

10.7% × $248,000 (replacement cost)	$26,536
Estimated depreciation	(rounded) $26,500
Replacement cost	$248,000
Less depreciation	− 26,500
Value contribution of the improvements	$221,500
Plus site value	+ 90,600
Total property value indication	$312,100

---

4. The estimate of the effective age of older residential properties depends largely on the appraiser's judgment. The appraiser may find it easier to derive support for the effective age estimate by first estimating the property's total economic life expectancy. Multiplying the total economic life expectancy by the percentage amount of depreciation derived from market extraction will indicate an estimate of the effective age.

A situation in which a property's total economic life expectancy might be estimated can be found in older residential neighborhoods where no change in highest and best use is imminent. At some point in the life of an older property, a decision must be made as to whether the existing building should be completely renovated or whether it should be razed and the site redeveloped. In either case, the building will probably have reached the end of its total economic life expectancy. (Examples of major renovation include the complete replacement of mechanical systems, the remodeling of all interior rooms, and the modernization of most building components.)

Applicability

The age-life method is usually the simplest way to estimate depreciation, working best for newer properties, and it is the most commonly used method. It does have certain limitations, though. First, because the percentage of depreciation is represented by the ratio of effective age to total economic life, this method assumes that every building depreciates on a straight-line basis over the course of its economic life. In other words, a house that has twice the effective age of another is presumed to suffer from twice as much depreciation. The method is flawed because depreciation does not always occur on a straight-line basis and therefore the estimate is not easy to "fine tune" using this method. In some markets buildings tend to depreciate more rapidly as they approach the end of their economic lives, while in other markets a different pattern may be observed. The straight-line pattern of depreciation is only an approximation, although it is usually a sufficiently accurate one.

Second, the age-life method does not divide depreciation into subcategories such as curable or incurable physical deterioration, curable or incurable functional obsolescence, and external obsolescence. Therefore, the method may not recognize differences in depreciation among residences as well as techniques that categorize different types of depreciation, and other steps may be required to break a lump sum estimate of depreciation into its various forms. In neighborhoods and market areas where residences suffer different types and amounts of depreciation, the age-life method may be difficult to justify.

Third, the age-life method does not recognize the difference between short-lived and long-lived items of physical deterioration. Because a single figure is used to reflect depreciation in the structure as a whole, varying amounts of depreciation in short-lived items are not directly reflected in the age-life ratio. For example, a building as a whole may be estimated to be 20% depreciated except for the roof which, unlike other roofs in the neighborhood, is estimated to be 90% depreciated. In this situation the breakdown method would allow an appraiser to make a more refined analysis.

Finally, one component of the age-life ratio's denominator (the total economic life expectancy of typical, similar structures) is the remaining economic life, which refers to a future period of time. Any forecast of future events calls for judgment, so the estimates of effective age and economic life may be difficult to justify. To minimize this problem, economic life estimates should be based on objective data to the greatest extent possible. Useful information can be obtained in several ways. Historical studies may shed light on the actual lives of similar structures, or the appraiser can sound out lenders, brokers, buyers, and sellers on how much longer they anticipate neighborhood structures similar to the subject will be economically useful.

Because depreciation is assumed to occur on a straight-line basis, a market-derived estimate of economic life can be obtained by identifying the annual rate of depreciation for similar structures and dividing this figure into 100%. The formula follows:

$$\text{Economic life} = \frac{100\%}{\text{annual \% depreciation}}$$

Market-derived information can help support the depreciation estimates used in the age-life method. This tool is misused in some cases because the rates of depreciation found in the market will not be the same for properties in different price ranges and market areas. Appraisers should be careful about using this tool and especially using total economic life estimates from one market and applying them to others.

Variation 1—Known Curable Items

The first variation of the age-life method provides greater accuracy by dividing depreciation into curable and incurable components. A form of depreciation is curable if, as of the date of the appraisal, the cost to cure the defect is equal to or less than the value that would be added by doing so. Otherwise, it is incurable. When an item is considered incurable it does not mean that the problem cannot physically be solved; it only means that it cannot be solved economically—i.e., the cure is simply not worth its cost.

This procedure is applied in five steps. An appraiser

1. Estimates the cost to cure all items of curable depreciation.
2. Deducts the cost to cure these items from the replacement or reproduction cost.
3. Estimates the effective age and remaining economic life of the structure as cured. Curing a major item can sometimes decrease the effective age of the building, prolong its remaining economic life, or both.
4. Applies the ratio between the adjusted effective age and the total economic life of the structure to the remainder of the replacement or reproduction cost to obtain the amount of incurable depreciation found in the building.
5. Deducts the incurable depreciation from the remainder of the replacement or reproduction cost to arrive at the improvement's contribution to property value.

Example. A house with a current replacement cost of $145,000 and a site value of $52,000 was built 18 years ago. The appraiser estimates that it now has an effective age of 15 years and a 45-year remaining economic life expectancy. Total curable physical deterioration and functional obsolescence in the structure amounts to $15,000. The appraiser estimates that by curing these items effective age could be reduced to 5 years and the remaining economic life expectancy could be extended to 55 years.[5] To estimate lump sum depreciation using this variation of the age-life method, the appraiser performs these calculations.

---

5. It is difficult to find market support for changes in effective age and remaining economic life expectancy estimates.

Replacement cost	$145,000
Less physical and functional curable items	– 15,000
Depreciated replacement cost	$130,000
Depreciated cost basis	
Remaining economic life	55 years
Effective age	5 years
Ratio applied to cost less physical and functional curable items (5/60)8.33%	
Less incurable items ($130,000 × 0.0833)	– 10,833
Total depreciated value of improvements	$119,167
Plus site value	+ 52,000
Total property value indication	$171,167
	(rounded) $171,000

Applicability. In this procedure, curable items of depreciation are cured at the outset, before estimating the incurable depreciation. This is helpful for a number of reasons. Most importantly, this procedure closely approximates the reasoning of an informed buyer contemplating a purchase. Beyond a certain point, a buyer may not consider age and life estimates especially relevant to a purchase decision and the significance of the cost approach may be diminished. A buyer frequently wants to know how much the residence will be worth after all problems that can be economically cured have been attended to. Most astute purchasers do not simply consider the property in its present, depreciated state; they are also concerned with its potential after any repairs have been made. This refinement of the age-life method addresses these concerns, which are not considered in the simpler procedure.

By curing the curable items the appraiser brings the property in line with existing market standards as far as possible. If the addition or repair of an item is considered so necessary that the market is prepared to award a value increase equal to or greater than its cost, the feature to be added or repaired usually conforms to market standards. For the appraiser, this variation of the age-life method can enhance the accuracy of the depreciation estimate in three ways:

1. The amount of depreciation to be deducted for curable items can usually be established with some certainty. Typically it is simply the current cost to cure. Once identified, the amount to be deducted for it is known.

2. When curable items are cured, the proportion of the estimate that depends on the judgmental age-life technique is smaller. The age-life ratio is applied only to items of incurable depreciation, so the potential for error is decreased.

3. When a building is cured of curable defects, incurable defects can usually be assessed more accurately. A partially cured building conforms more closely to market standards, so there may be more similar structures from which to derive an appropriate estimate of effective age and remaining economic life.

Limitations. A limitation of this procedure is that, like the simpler, unmodified age-life method, it does not divide incurable depreciation into physical, functional, and external subcategories or distinguish between short-lived and long-lived items. It assumes depreciation in incurable items occurs on a straight-line basis. Moreover, the estimates of effective age and remaining economic life still require judgment on the part of the appraiser. However, because these problems influence only the incurable portion of the depreciation estimate, their adverse effects are decreased. The same issue with the total economic life estimate exists in this calculation. The total economic life needs to be supported by market evidence.

Variation 2—Known External Obsolescence
The second variation of the age-life method can increase the accuracy of the depreciation estimate when external obsolescence is present in the subject property but not in comparable properties.

If sales of properties suffering from the same external obsolescence as the subject are available, then the total economic life extracted from those sales considered comparable can be used in the age-life method. If such sales do not exist, then the appraiser estimates depreciation exclusive of external obsolescence using the age-life method and adds an estimate of external obsolescence derived using techniques from the breakdown method, which is described later in this chapter.

Example. Overbuilding in the subject market has caused sale prices of one-unit homes to drop by 10% within the last year, according to the appraiser's observations of the market's history. Site value has not been affected by this market downturn. The replacement cost of the 10-year-old home being appraised is $120,000. With few sales of properties considered comparable in the market in the last year, the appraiser must consult records of older sales, dating from before the dip in prices. These data reveal a market-extracted total economic life expectancy of 50 years, which yields an estimate of depreciation excluding external obsolescence of 20% (10/50).

Using the age-life method, the depreciation estimate for the subject property is $24,000 ($120,000 × 0.20), and the estimate of the effect of external obsolescence is $12,000 ($120,000 × 0.10). The total depreciation then is calculated to be $36,000, with $24,000 allocated to all causes except external obsolescence and $12,000 to external obsolescence. Because the external obsolescence in this case was caused by oversupply in the market, once those additional homes are absorbed by the market, the effect of the external obsolescence will probably disappear.

Applicability. Like the first variation of the age-life method, this second variation allocates a portion of the total depreciation estimate to an individual component, in this case external obsolescence. Just as home buyers often want to know the value of a property after curable items have been repaired, those buyers are also concerned with the influence of external market forces on a potential purchase.

Limitations. The limitations of this procedure are similar to those of the less-complicated market extraction and age-life methods. The technique assumes depreciation in incurable items occurs on a straight-line basis. Also, the estimate of effective age requires judgment on the part of the appraiser and the remaining economic life still requires support. Because these problems affect only the depreciation estimate exclusive of external obsolescence, though, their adverse influences on the total depreciation estimate are decreased.

Breakdown Method

The breakdown method is the most comprehensive and detailed way to measure depreciation, though in actual practice the complete, formal breakdown method is rarely used because of the time and expense involved in collecting and analyzing the necessary data. The market extraction and age-life methods both yield a lump sum estimate of total depreciation, whereas the breakdown method is used to allocate, or "break down," the lump sum estimates into the individual depreciation components. The process of allocating depreciation is particularly important in the appraisal of residential properties because most form reports require that depreciation be allocated into its physical, functional, and external components.

> **breakdown method.** A method of estimating depreciation in which the total loss in the value of a property is estimated by analyzing and measuring each cause of depreciation (physical, functional, and external) separately.

Applying the Breakdown Method

The appraiser uses five basic techniques to estimate different types of depreciation in the various stages of the breakdown method:

1. Estimation of cost to cure, which measures curable physical deterioration and curable functional obsolescence
2. Application of an age-life ratio, which measures curable and incurable physical deterioration for both long- and short-lived components
3. Application of the functional obsolescence procedure, which measures all types of functional obsolescence
4. Paired data analysis, which can measure incurable functional obsolescence caused by a deficiency and also external obsolescence
5. Capitalization of rent loss, which can measure the same forms of depreciation as paired data analysis

Using the breakdown method, the appraiser can approach the estimation of individual components of total depreciation from opposite ends of the sequence of calculations:

- Given an estimate of total depreciation from the market extraction or age-life methods, the appraiser can work from the top down, allocating the total amount among the various components of depreciation.

- If an estimate of total depreciation cannot be derived from the market extraction or age-life methods, the appraiser can generate that figure from the bottom up, estimating each individual component of value, which when added together yield the total depreciation estimate.

These calculations are illustrated in Figure 15.4.

Because the complete breakdown method is rarely used in residential appraisal practice, detailed discussion of the various techniques for estimating each component of depreciation has been omitted here in favor of examples of the more common applications of those techniques. *The Appraisal of Real Estate* covers the breakdown method in great detail, and readers interested in further study of the subject should refer to that text.

Curable Physical Deterioration

The first step in the breakdown method is to estimate items of curable physical deterioration, also known as deferred maintenance. Items such as cosmetic repairs, touch-up painting, carpentry, plumbing, and electrical repairs fall into this category. Real estate agents have long recognized that most minor repairs add value that equals or exceeds their cost, so they encourage home owners to make these repairs before a house is offered for sale.

Items of curable physical deterioration are items in need of repair on the date of the appraisal, whether they are going to be repaired or not. The amount of depreciation to be allocated for these items is simply the cost to cure them. Often an appraisal client will request that these curable items be listed in the appraisal report along with an estimate of the cost to cure, which is the cost to restore an item of deferred maintenance to new or reasonably new condition.[6]

Cost-to-cure estimates should be based on actual contractors' bids or on the amounts indicated in contracts for similar work in recently completed properties. National cost services cannot be used to provide reliable estimates of the cost of repair and maintenance work because the cost for such work usually depends on the specific problems found in the house.

As an example, during a house inspection an appraiser notes the need to repaint the interior at a cost of $900 and refinish the interior floor at a cost of $800. Curable physical deterioration is estimated as the total cost to cure these items:

Interior painting	$900
Plus interior floor finish	+ 800
Total curable physical deterioration	$1,700

Functional Obsolescence (Excess Cost to Cure)

Functional obsolescence may be evident in the original design of the residence, or changes in market standards may have made some aspect of the structure, its design, or its components obsolete.

---

6. If damage or vandalism is severe enough, it becomes curable physical deterioration and is treated accordingly. The measure of damage is the cost to cure.

Figure 15.4 Breakdown Method Calculations

1. Top Down

Total depreciation estimate (from market extraction or age-life method)		$10,000
− Damage (vandalism)		− 500
= Depreciation (exclusive of damage)		9,500
Curable physical deterioration		
Deferred maintenance	1,500	
Incurable physical deterioration		
Short-lived components	2,000	
+ Long-lived components	+ 500	
− Physical deterioration		− $4,000
= Total functional obsolescence		$5,500
Curable functional obsolescence		
Curable functional obsolescence caused by deficiency requiring addition	2,500	
Curable functional obsolescence caused by deficiency requiring substitution	0	
Curable functional obsolescence caused by superadequacy	0	
Incurable functional obsolescence		
Incurable functional obsolescence caused by deficiency	1,000	
+ Incurable functional obsolescence caused by superadequacy	+ 0	
− Functional obsolescence		− $3,500
= External obsolescence		$2,000

2. Bottom Up

Curable physical deterioration		
Deferred maintenance	$1,500	
Incurable physical deterioration		
Short-lived components	2,000	
+ Long-lived components	+ 500	
Physical deterioration		$4,000
Curable functional obsolescence		
Curable functional obsolescence caused by deficiency requiring addition	2,500	
Curable functional obsolescence caused by deficiency requiring substitution	0	
Curable functional obsolescence caused by superadequacy	0	
Incurable functional obsolescence		
Incurable functional obsolescence caused by deficiency	1,000	
+ Incurable functional obsolescence caused by superadequacy	+ 0	
+ Functional obsolescence		+ $3,500
= Depreciation (exclusive of external obsolescence)		$7,500
+ External obsolescence (from paired data analysis or income capitalization)		+ $2,000
= Total depreciation estimate		$9,500
+ Damage (vandalism)		+ 500
= Total deduction from reproduction or replacement cost		$10,000

There are two major tests of curability for an item of functional obsolescence:

- If spending the money to cure the item will result in a value increment equal to or greater than the expenditure, then the item is normally considered curable.
- Also, if spending the money to cure the item will not result in a value increment equal to or greater than the expenditure, but will allow existing items to maintain their value, then the item is still considered curable.

When it is possible and reasonable to cure an item but there is no economic advantage to curing it, then the item is considered incurable.

All forms of functional obsolescence, whether curable or incurable or whether caused by a deficiency or by a superadequacy, can be estimated using the procedure illustrated in Figure 15.5. The use of the functional obsolescence procedure ensures that none of the components of this type of depreciation will be treated more than once and no charges will be incurred for an item already dealt with, e.g., elements already depreciated under physical deterioration.

The functional obsolescence procedure involves five steps:

1. *The cost of the existing item is identified.* This cost is derived from the replacement or reproduction cost estimate. Naturally, for items of curable functional obsolescence caused by a deficiency requiring an addition, there will be no cost to enter on this line.
2. *Any depreciation that has already been charged for the item is deducted.* In nearly all instances, any depreciation already charged for the item will be physical deterioration. As in Step 1, there will be no depreciation charged for items that do not currently exist, such as a deficiency requiring an addition.
3. *If curable, all costs associated with curing the item are added, e.g., the cost of installing a new item, the cost of removing the old item, and net salvage value.* The appraiser will have to calculate the cost to cure when testing an item for curability.

or

   If incurable, the value of the loss attributable to the obsolescence is added. The value of the loss can be obtained either through capitalization of rent loss or through paired data analysis. Again, this value will have to be calculated when testing for curability.
4. *A deduction for the cost of the item as though installed new on the date of the value estimate is entered, if appropriate.*
5. *The total of all previous entries yields the depreciation for functional obsolescence.*

When functional obsolescence takes the form of a deficiency requiring an addition, a component that is currently desired in the market such as an additional powder room (i.e., a half bath) is not present in the exist-

Figure 15.5	The Functional Obsolescence Procedure	
Step 1.	Cost of existing item	$xxx,xxx
Step 2.	Less depreciation previously charged	– $xxx,xxx
Step 3.	Plus cost to cure (all curable costs)	+ $xxx,xxx
	or	or
	Plus value of the loss (incurable items)	+ $xxx,xxx
Step 4.	Less cost if installed new	– $xxx,xxx
Step 5.	Equals depreciation for functional obsolescence	$xxx,xxx

ing structure. Expenditures for the addition would not be included in the reproduction or replacement cost. The deficiency might be curable, but an additional cost is required to bring the building up to market standards. The cost to install an item in an existing building is almost always greater than the cost to install the same item in new construction. Depreciation must be allocated for the extra expense the owner of the subject building must now incur, reflecting a cost that will not be realized as value. Curable functional obsolescence is measured as the difference between the cost of adding the component now, when the structure is complete, and the cost if the component were included in the structure as if built new on the date of the value opinion. This is commonly referred to as the *excess cost to cure*.

functional obsolescence procedure. A sequence of calculations that can be used to estimate all forms of functional obsolescence caused by a deficiency or a superadequacy, whether the obsolescence is curable or incurable.

excess cost to cure. The difference between the cost of adding the component when the structure is complete and the cost if the component were included in the structure as built on the date of the value opinion.

As an example, consider a two-story residence being appraised that has no half bathroom on the first floor, a feature that is standard in the market for this type of property. A half bathroom can be installed for $1,800, but it would have cost only $1,200 if it had been installed on the date of the value opinion as part of new construction. The curable functional obsolescence due to this deficiency is measured as the amount by which the cost of creating the addition exceeds the normal cost of the item installed new during construction, calculated as follows:

Cost of existing item	$0
Less depreciation previously charged	– 0
Plus cost to cure (all curable costs)	+ 1,800
or	
Plus value of the loss (incurable items)	
Less cost if installed new	– 1,200
Equals depreciation for functional obsolescence	$600

In other words, it will take $1,800 spent after construction to accomplish the same amount of utility as $1,200 spent during construction, both measured as of the date of appraisal.

External Obsolescence

External obsolescence is a loss in value due to influences outside the property. It is usually incurable, but it is not always permanent. A homeowner or landlord cannot cure an environmental problem such as a deteriorating neighborhood or an economic recession that creates a sluggish market. Outside forces, however, may change the detrimental factor.

External obsolescence generally results in a loss in the value contribution of the improvements, but the external factor causing the obsolescence may also lessen the value of the site. It may be caused by neighborhood decline, changes in market conditions, or the property's proximity to a detrimental influence such as an airport, railroad, landfill, commercial district, or other sort of nuisance. When market data are studied to estimate external obsolescence, it is important to isolate the effects of changes in land value from the effects of changes in the value of the improvements. In some situations, external losses may be attributed entirely to the site; in other situations, they may be attributed entirely to the improvements.[7] Often the external losses can be allocated between the site and improvements. This is an important step if the external obsolescence is already reflected in the site value estimate. A building-to-property-value ratio, derived through market analysis, may be used to allocate the value loss attributable to the building.

The two primary methods of measuring external obsolescence are

- Paired data analysis
- Capitalization of rent loss

In appraisals of one-unit residences, external obsolescence is usually estimated by paired data analysis. Sales of properties that are subject to the negative external influence are compared with sales of properties that are not. Not only must the effects of land value differences be isolated, but the effects of differences in the physical deterioration and functional obsolescence of the comparable structures must also be studied. Many of the problems that limit the usefulness of the paired data method in estimating total depreciation create difficulties in this portion of the breakdown method as well.

As an example, a one-unit residence located on a noisy street is being appraised. The appraiser finds two very similar comparable properties that were recently sold. One is adjacent to the subject and the other is farther away from the noisy street. The adjacent property was sold for $189,000, while the other sale was sold for $192,000. Using paired data analysis, the appraiser estimates external obsolescence as follows:

$$\$192,000 - \$189,000 = \$3,000$$

The land-to-improvement ratio is 1 to 4. Therefore, 20% ($\frac{1}{5}$) of the external obsolescence would be applicable to the land, and the remaining

---

7. External obsolescence would be attributable entirely to the land in a situation in which the cost to construct a particular home is identical on two subdivision lots, but one adjoins an expressway and sells for less than the other located away from the expressway. External obsolescence would be attributable entirely to the improvement in the case of a home in a transitional neighborhood where land use is changing from residential to commercial use.

80% (⅘) would apply to the improvements. The amount applicable to the improvements is $2,400 ($3,000 × 0.80). External losses are often, but not always, allocated based on land-to-building ratios. Some appraisers contend that losses initially apply to the land and only when they are more severe will they affect the improvement value.

Applicability

As the most detailed method of estimating depreciation, the breakdown method requires large amounts of data–often more than are available to an appraiser without having accumulated files over long periods of time. In addition, spending time identifying and quantifying each item of depreciation may not be an efficient use of the appraiser's workday.

Depreciation is estimated differently according to the type and cause of loss in value, and those types and causes overlap, complicating the application of the breakdown method. For example, older structures may be affected by a number of different forms of deterioration and obsolescence. Also, distinguishing the difference between deficiencies and superadequacies and between functional and external obsolescence can be difficult.

In situations where the market allocation and age-life methods of estimating depreciation cannot be applied, the breakdown method can be used to estimate all the various items of depreciation, with the sum of the individual components giving a total depreciation estimate.

Combined Methods

Different methods of estimating depreciation can be combined to solve specific problems, or the results of one method can be used to test the results of another. For example, if external obsolescence cannot be accurately estimated through paired data analysis or capitalization of an income loss, a lump sum indication of total depreciation can be derived through market extraction. Then an indication of depreciation from all causes other than external obsolescence can be derived with the breakdown method, and this figure can be subtracted from the estimate of total depreciation to derive an estimate of external obsolescence.

Market extraction can also be used to derive or verify an estimate of the annual overall rate of depreciation, which is the basis of the economic life estimate (economic life = 100% / annual rate of depreciation). The overall percentage of depreciation in each comparable is obtained by dividing its sale price minus the current site value and value contribution of the site improvements by its replacement or reproduction cost. This overall percentage is divided by the actual age of the comparable or, if there is a significant difference between the actual age and the effective age, by the effective age, to estimate the annual percentage of depreciation. Conversely, the total economic life expectancy is derived from data obtained in market extraction. The amount of depreciation in a comparable is divided by the replacement or reproduction cost of the comparable. The resulting percentage is divided by the age of the comparable to obtain the average annual rate of depreciation, the inverse of which is the total economic life expectancy.

Example

The subject is a 25-year-old home that has a replacement cost of $175,000. The total useful life expectancy in this market is estimated to be 75 years. There is no noted external obsolescence in this market and a site value of $40,000 is well supported. The estimated contribution of the site improvements is $10,000. Assume that property rights conveyed and site improvements are similar for all the comparable properties and that there were no financing, sales concessions, or immediate repairs affecting the sale prices. Data on three sales of similar properties are shown below.

	Sale A	Sale B	Sale C
Sale price	$210,000	$150,000	$125,000
Site value	$51,000	$37,500	$45,000
Replacement cost	$204,500	$216,350	$121,000
Actual age	20 years	30 years	25 years

The subject residence has a broken door, which must be replaced at a cost of $500. Data on the short-lived building components of the subject property follow:

Short-Lived Item	Actual Age	Useful Life	Cost to Replace
Roof cover	10 years	15 years	$9,000
Paint	New	5 years	$4,000
HVAC	5 years	20 years	$8,000
Floor finish	5 years	10 years	$6,000

The first step is to extract the average annual depreciation rate from the sales data provided.

	Sale A	Sale B	Sale C
Sale price	$210,000	$150,000	$125,000
Less site value	− 51,000	− 37,500	− 45,000
Depreciated cost of improvements	$159,000	$112,500	$80,000
Replacement cost	$250,000	$206,800	$137,000
Less depreciated cost of improvements	− 159,000	− 112,500	− 80,000
Total depreciation	$91,000	$94,300	$57,000
% of replacement cost	36.40%	45.60%	41.60%
Average annual rate of depreciation	1.82%	1.52%	1.66%
Total economic life expectancy	55 years	66 years	60 years

The second step is to reconcile the range of total economic life expectancy estimates into an appropriate estimate for the subject property. The resulting indications of depreciation applicable to the subject may be affected by the overall level of maintenance and location of the comparables. Because the overall goal of the extraction of depreciation is to apply a correct amount of depreciation to the subject, an appraiser can use the depreciation per year rate or, if the subject is very similar to these comparables, use a reconciled percentage within the indicated range (36.4%–45.6%). The indicated overall depreciation includes all forms of depreciation (physical, functional, and external) and would include different rates of depreciation for short-lived and long-lived items.

If the subject property has a functional problem that does not exist in the comparables, an additional adjustment would be necessary. If the comparables had a locational problem and the subject did not, an additional adjustment would need to be applied. These are aggregate numbers, and all forms of depreciation, if they exist, are included in the depreciation estimates.

The Sales Comparison Approach

The sales comparison approach is the most direct and reliable valuation approach in many appraisal situations. The basic steps involved in the sales comparison approach are as follows:

- The appraiser finds recent sales, listings, and/or pending offers (if available) for properties that are comparable to the subject property.
- The appraiser verifies that the data obtained are accurate.
- The appraiser selects relevant units of comparison to analyze each sale.
- The appraiser compares sales of comparable properties to the subject property in terms of various elements of comparison and adjusts the sale prices of the comparable properties to reflect how they differ from the subject property.
- The appraiser reconciles the various value indications derived into a single value indication or a range of values.

Strengths of the Approach

The sales comparison approach is a tool appraisers apply in many situations with a variety of quantitative and sometimes qualitative techniques. The approach derives its usefulness and analytic power from several factors:

- Its direct applicability to the principle of substitution
- Its simplicity

- Its use of observable market data
- Its wide applicability

Also, the sales comparison approach is a direct application of the principle of substitution, which holds that when similar or commensurate objects or commodities are available for sale, the one with the lowest price will attract the greatest demand and the widest distribution. The price at which an item will most likely sell in a market is closely related to the prices at which similar items in the same market are selling or have sold. The sales comparison approach is firmly based on this principle. Properties similar to the subject are found and their sale prices are adjusted to account for differences between the comparables and the subject. These adjusted sale prices serve as the basis for a value opinion.

The sales comparison approach is generally easy to apply. Furthermore, clients find the approach persuasive because the reasoning is easy to follow. A simple method based on reliable data and sound reasoning often results in extremely reliable conclusions.

In the sales comparison approach, an appraiser focuses on the property characteristics that make a difference in the market. The appraiser obtains from the market quantifiable data that indicate the differences in prices caused by differences in building features, site size, location, and other property characteristics. Adjustments for differences are based directly on the observed preferences of market participants.

The market data on which sales comparisons are based lend themselves to various types of quantitative analysis. Paired data analysis, scatter diagrams, and other analytical tools can be used to isolate the effect of specific variables on market prices. Statistical sampling can be used in the selection of comparables. By selecting some comparables that may be slightly superior to the subject and others that may be slightly inferior, an appraiser can develop a good sense of the value range for the subject property. Tabulated or graphed historical data on sales of similar property can be used to identify trends and discern changes in the market.

All three valuation approaches make use of sales comparison to some degree. The cost approach requires that land or site value be estimated separately, and this is often accomplished by analyzing the prices of comparable vacant land or land considered as though vacant. The cost of buildings and depreciation may also be estimated by sales comparison. In the income capitalization approach, the rent that the subject property is likely to produce is estimated by analyzing the rents of comparable properties, and capitalization rates and gross income multipliers are also derived from sales. Thus, sales comparison techniques have broad application in the valuation process.

Limitations of the Approach

The sales comparison approach has some important limitations. A conclusion derived from sales considered comparable is only as reliable as the data that support it. If the only recent sales are of properties that differ substantially from the subject, the prices of these properties will be subject to major adjustments and the reliability of the conclusion may be questionable. Properties with unique or special features often cannot be valued with sales comparison analysis. When the approach is applied in markets with few recent sales, the appraiser must proceed with extreme caution and pay careful attention to all factors that could affect current market conditions. The results of sales comparison reflect historical rather than current market conditions because market changes that have occurred since the sale dates of the comparables are not always readily discernible.

Comparables as Competitive Properties

For valuation purposes a property used as a comparable should be competitive with the subject property. Each potential comparable property should be similar to the subject in important features and be located in the same area or in a similar market area, i.e., one that is both comparable and competitive. Properties that do not appeal to the same market population should not be considered competitive, even if they are comparable to the subject in other ways. In ideal circumstances, comparable properties used in the sales comparison approach would compete directly with the subject property in the same market area, but sometimes data on sales of local comparables are unavailable. In that case transactions involving properties in other comparable, but not directly competitive, neighborhoods or locations may be used in the analysis.

What features must be similar for properties and neighborhoods to be considered comparable? Individual property features are important if the market population regards them as significant. Property characteristics established during the neighborhood analysis are used as a basis for the elements of comparison. An appraiser learns about the significance of property characteristics by observing variations and correlations in the sale prices of properties with different locations, sizes, designs, taxes, and other characteristics. Further insights into the comparability of neighborhoods can be gained by identifying the income levels, ages, and family sizes of prospective buyers. A careful highest and best use study can help identify which elements of comparison are important in the market.

There is no set rule as to distances between subject and comparable properties. The size of market areas can vary considerably depending on the size of the city, commuting times, the availability of public transportation, and property types. If there are many similar houses or neighborhoods that purchasers regard as more or less equal, the market area can be quite extensive. In other situations a market area may be quite small. Again, it is best to select comparable properties from the immediate neighborhood of the subject, but if sales data are not available, sales from the same market area or an altogether different, yet still comparable, market area may be acceptable.

Research and Selection of Sales of Properties Considered Comparable

To investigate and select comparable properties, an appraiser

- Researches and identifies potentially comparable properties
- Inspects the subject property, the neighborhood, and each potential comparable (to the extent allowed by the scope of work)
- Analyzes the highest and best use of each potential comparable to test its comparability with the subject
- Verifies data and eliminates sales that are not arm's-length transactions if an accurate adjustment for atypical conditions of sale cannot be calculated
- Analyzes differences between the subject property and each potential comparable and selects the best comparables available for use in the sales comparison approach

The process begins with the identification of potential comparables and concludes with the selection of the actual comparables to be used in the appraisal. Although the steps are not always followed in the order indicated, each task must be performed at some point in the valuation process. When the appraiser concludes that the differences between the subject property and a given comparable are not too great, the transaction may be used in sales comparison analysis.

Identification of Comparable Properties

Procedures for identifying comparable properties were discussed at length in Chapter 6. In brief, an appraiser first collects general information on the subject property that can be used to help identify comparables. Usually data on the property location, house type, building size, number of stories, number of bedrooms and bathrooms, and site size are sufficient, but additional detail can be helpful. Next, the appraiser tries to generate a list of properties in the subject neighborhood and competitive neighborhoods that meet this general description. Information may be obtained from office files, multiple listing services (MLS), public records, news publications, title companies, and knowledgeable individuals such as other appraisers, brokers, and bankers. An appraiser is primarily interested in comparable properties that have been sold recently. Contracts, offers, refusals, and listing prices of competitive properties may provide additional insights into the character of the local market.

How many comparables should be identified? An appraiser must have an adequate number of sales to establish a firm basis for the value conclusion. If the quality of the data collected is questionable, a larger pool of comparable properties should be considered. Increasing the number of comparables used adds time and expense, but a larger sample can produce more reliable results by adding better data to the pool.

The appraiser collects important data on each comparable transaction and records the legal, physical, and locational characteristics of the property as of the date of sale. The following items of information are generally needed:

Transactional Characteristics

Sale price

Financing terms

Date of sale

Names of parties (or others who can verify data)

Motivations of parties

Sales concessions

Legal, Physical, and Locational Characteristics

Legal description of the real estate

Real property rights conveyed

Location and neighborhood

Site size, shape, and location

Assessments

Public and private restrictions

Building type and size

Total number of rooms and number of bedrooms and bathrooms

Age of building

Physical condition

Functional utility

Size and type of garage

Non-realty components of value

Expenditures made immediately after purchase

Market conditions

Personal property included in sale

Field Inspection

After the neighborhood and the subject property have been inspected, the appraiser can usually eliminate several potentially comparable properties from consideration. Some of these properties may be located outside the boundaries of the subject neighborhood or competitive neighborhoods, which have now been more precisely identified. Other properties may no longer qualify as comparables because inspection of the subject has revealed that they are dissimilar.

Each remaining potential comparable must then be inspected. Generally, comparable properties are inspected from the outside because most property owners are reluctant to allow strangers into their homes. Moreover, a complete inspection of each comparable might be outside the scope of work determined by the appraiser. Information on construction features may be obtained from MLS data and tax assessment records and from building permits and blueprints kept on file at county and municipal offices. Photographs are commonly taken of each comparable for inclusion in the appraisal report.

Highest and Best Use Analysis

Each potential comparable should be analyzed to determine the highest and best use of the land as though vacant and the property as improved. When the sales comparison approach is used to value a residence, a detailed analysis of the highest and best use of the comparables is often unnecessary. However, the appraiser's analysis must be sufficient to establish that the properties are indeed comparable. Highest and best use analysis is particularly important in transitional neighborhoods.

The appraiser must also consider the markets to which the potentially comparable properties appeal. Does the land considered as though vacant have any special appeal for commercial users? Is the location of the improved site suitable for a nonresidential use? In some areas a residence located on a corner site or a busy street could accommodate an office. If this property is a potential comparable and the subject property is located on an interior site or secondary street, the highest and best use of the improved subject and the potential comparable may well differ. The highest and best use of the subject property and a potential comparable must be the same or similar for *both* the site as though vacant and the property as improved. Otherwise, the comparable should be eliminated from further consideration.

Verification of Data

Data on sales of properties considered comparable can be obtained by interviewing one of the parties to the transaction. Although the buyers and sellers were most actively and directly involved in the transaction, appraisers must recognize that those market participants are not disinterested parties. If necessary, information provided by interested parties can be corroborated through other sources. Statements of fact can be verified by real estate agents, closing agencies, lending institutions, property managers, and lawyers involved in the sale. Owners and tenants of neighboring properties can sometimes provide important clues about the reasons for the sale. In verifying data, an appraiser must recognize that some sources of information may be more reliable than others and always ensure the confidentiality of the parties consulted.

The appraiser seeks answers to the following questions:

- What was the sale price and what were the terms of the financing?
- Were any concessions or incentives other than financing involved in the sale?
- Were items of personal property included?
- Exactly when was the closing price established?
- Are the parties to the transaction related?

Sales used as comparables should be arm's-length transactions made in the open market by unrelated parties under no duress.

Analysis of Comparables: Elements of Comparison

Individual properties and the transactions in which they are exchanged may differ in many ways. From an appraiser's point of view, the important differences are those that affect the value of the property and the price obtained for it. These differences, which are called *elements of comparison*, include

1. Real property rights conveyed
2. Financing terms
3. Conditions of sale
4. Expenditures made immediately after purchase
5. Market conditions
6. Location
7. Physical characteristics
8. Economic characteristics
9. Use/zoning
10. Non-realty components of value

Other differences may be relevant in certain markets.

By studying properties for sale and actual sale transactions in the market area, an appraiser learns how much effect on value each different element of comparison produces. The comparables are analyzed in light of these differences, and their sale prices are adjusted to reflect the value of the subject. When the differences are minor, the adjusted sale prices of comparable properties provide a persuasive indication of value. When differences are more substantial, greater adjustments are required and the results are less reliable.

Differences between a sale and the subject property can be addressed either by the application of quantitative adjustments, expressed as dollar or percentage amounts, or by the use of qualitative analysis, where differences are addressed by relative comparisons, not specified adjustments. (Examples of the application of quantitative adjustments and qualitative analysis are provided in Chapter 18.) Quantitative adjustments are applied to the sale price of the sold comparable and sometimes to the list price of competing listings. These adjustments are usually made in a particular order. Adjustments for property rights, financing, conditions of sale, expenditures made immediately after purchase, and market conditions are applied before adjustments for location, physical characteristics, and other differences.[1] The first five quantitative adjustments are typically made before the sale prices are reduced to unit prices. Reducing sale prices to unit prices based on size allows the appraiser to compare houses with different dimensions and may eliminate the need to make an adjustment for differences in size.

Analysis of qualitative differences provides the basis for reconciliation. Qualitative differences are generally taken into consideration after the application of quantitative adjustments. Qualitative differences may be analyzed by means of an array in which the appraiser ranks

---

1. The sequence in which adjustments are applied is determined by the market data and the appraiser's analysis of those data. The sequence presented in this chapter and in Chapter 18 is provided for purposes of illustration. While this is a typical sequence for applying quantitative adjustments, it is not the only sequence in which such adjustments can be made.

the comparables as more or less similar to the subject. This ranking is used to determine which comparable or comparables are the most reliable indicators of the subject's value.

Real Property Rights Conveyed

At the outset an appraiser identifies the real property interest to be valued. For single-unit residential properties, this is generally the fee simple estate. If the valuation assignment involves an unencumbered fee simple property, the appraiser should ascertain that the legal estate of each comparable is identical to that of the subject. Income-producing real estate may be subject to existing leases, which may create a leased fee or leasehold interest. In some markets, residential properties are built on leased land. There usually are long-term leases that must be considered in the analysis of those properties. The property rights are divided by these leases into leased fee and leasehold interests.

Financing Terms

Financing terms can affect the price at which a property is sold. Sellers sometimes offer buyers a special inducement to purchase their property in the form of creative financing instruments. In these cases the final sale price reflects the value of both the financing inducement and the property. The value of financing reflects personal property, not real property. Therefore, the sale price of the comparable must be adjusted before it can be used as an indication of market value.

Financing plans can vary significantly. Special financing terms include seller-paid points, FHA insurance, VA guarantees, second mortgages, and buydown plans. These financing plans appear in the market when interest rates are high, and they become less popular when rates fall. Sellers, lenders, and others use financing instruments to sustain demand for real estate at current price levels.

Various techniques can be used to measure how financing considerations affect price. Two such techniques are paired data analysis and the calculation of cash equivalency with discounting procedures. Financing considerations are important, and Chapter 17 is devoted to this topic. Note that a financing adjustment is only required when the sale of a comparable was transacted with unusual financing terms. The existence of special financing terms offered with the subject property does not in itself require adjustment. The value opinion is not determined by the terms offered by the seller, but by the prior actions of buyers and sellers in the market (comparable sales).

Conditions of Sale

Unusual conditions of sale can also cause a comparable property to sell at a price that does not reflect its value. The motivations of the buyer and the seller are important conditions of sale. For example, a buyer who owns an adjoining site may be prepared to pay a price for the property that is higher than its market value. If a financial, business, or family relationship exists between the parties, the sale may not be an arm's-length transaction. One family member may sell property to another at a reduced price, or an individual might pay a higher-than-market price to acquire a property built or formerly owned by an ancestor.

Any special pressure, duress, or undue stimulus on a buyer or seller that does not affect typical market participants may produce an atypical price in that transaction. For example, the price paid for a property in a liquidation sale would probably not reflect its market value.

Market exposure is another important condition of sale. To qualify as an open-market transaction, the property should have received adequate exposure in the market. In many markets this means that a sign was posted in front of the house, or an advertisement was placed in a local publication, and that the comparable property was exposed for sale for approximately the normal marketing time for similar properties. Bids and acceptable prices usually stabilize around market value within the normal marketing period. Some appraisal assignments may call for an indication of value based on a quick sale, a liquidation sale, or a transaction consummated within a specific number of days.

When a property sells much more quickly than expected, it may suggest that the buyer was unusually motivated or that the seller was poorly informed. When a property is on the market for an unusually long time, it may be because the seller was holding out for a certain price or a certain buyer or because the property has problems that the market recognizes. Whatever the reason, the transaction is probably less reliable as a comparable and should be investigated further or eliminated from consideration.

No transaction is perfect. Appraisers must occasionally use sales data that do not precisely reflect open-market, arm's-length transactions. An appraiser should carefully judge each situation to determine how much the variance affects the price of the comparable. If the transaction is substantially different from the norm, the sales data should not be used regardless of how similar the subject and comparable may be in other ways. Only modest differences can be accounted for with an adjustment for conditions of sale.

Expenditures Made Immediately After Purchase

To arrive at a sale price, a knowledgeable buyer considers expenditures that will be necessary to maximize the potential of a newly acquired property. Such expenditures include the cost to demolish and remove obsolete improvements, the cost associated with an application for rezoning, and the cost to remediate environmental contamination. Consider the sale of a residential property improved with a small, obsolete house in an area of newly developed manor-style homes. The negotiated sale price was $100,000. The buyer had the improvements removed, at cost of $10,000, in anticipation of developing the site with a single-family home similar to the surrounding homes. In the analysis of sales of sites in the area, the price of this sale would most accurately be reflected as $110,000. The adjustment of $10,000, for expenditures made immediately after purchase, represents the true cost of acquiring the site.

Market Conditions

Market conditions generally change over time. The date of the appraisal is a specific point in time, so sales transacted before this point must be examined and adjusted to reflect any changes that may have occurred in the interim. Otherwise, the sale prices of the comparables will reflect the market conditions as of the date when they were sold, not the current value of similar real estate. Changes in market conditions are usually measured as a percentage relative to previous price levels.

Market conditions can change for various reasons, but two of the most important considerations are inflation or deflation and changes in supply and demand. Inflation and deflation generally can be observed throughout the regional economy. The rate of change in price levels is often easy to estimate. Tracking changes in supply and demand requires more research. Overbuilding is one common cause of an increase in supply, and the unexpected departure of a major employer can cause demand to fall suddenly. (Changes in supply and demand are discussed in Chapters 3 and 10.)

The best indications of changes in market conditions are provided by the prices of properties that have been sold and resold several times. Because different types of properties are affected differently by changing market conditions, these properties should be similar to the subject property. If several property resales can be collected, they will provide an adequate database.

The market conditions adjustment is sometimes referred to as a *time* adjustment. It should be emphasized, however, that it is not time that necessitates this adjustment, but shifts in the market. If considerable time has elapsed but market conditions have not changed, no adjustment is required.

Location

Adjustments for location are often difficult to make. The adjustment and the reasoning behind it should be carefully supported in the appraisal report. Generally the largest adjustments for location are required when the comparable properties are not located in the subject neighborhood or market area. Adjustments might also be required for properties located in the same neighborhood that are subject to different influences. The character of the immediate neighborhood, traffic density, view, and siting are all significant factors in making adjustments for location.

Every location has its advantages and disadvantages. The desirability of a location is judged in comparison with alternative locations. An appraiser investigates the effects of location by considering how the prices of physically similar properties in various locations differ. Adjustments for location are generally calculated as percentage adjustments. If some difference related to location has already been considered in the opinion of site value, the appraiser should be careful not to overstate the size of the locational adjustment. Like all adjustments, the goal is to replicate market behavior, in other words, determine how much more or less the typical buyer would pay for this attribute. If a buyer would not pay more or less for the feature, no adjustment is needed.

Physical Characteristics

A comparable may differ from the subject property in many physical characteristics, including building size, architectural style, functional utility, building materials, construction quality, age and condition of improvements, and site size. Overall attractiveness and special amenities can introduce other variables. Sometimes separate adjustments are required to reflect each major difference in physical characteristics.

Adjustments for the physical differences between the subject and other improved properties usually cannot be made simply by adding or subtracting the difference in the reproduction or replacement cost of the varying components. Unless the subject and comparable improvements are both new, the cost of a component does not usually reflect its contribution to value accurately. The effect on value produced by a physical difference must be estimated through careful analysis of the market. To perform this analysis, an appraiser collects information on how variables such as age, size, and condition affect the prices of similar real estate in the local market.

Economic Characteristics

This element of comparison is usually applied to income-producing properties. For residential properties with a demonstrable rental market, income-producing characteristics such as tenant mix, the length of lease terms, lease conditions, operating expenses, the management history of the property, and similar factors are significant in the valuation process.

An adjustment for an economic characteristic should not be made if the property attribute that affects income is already reflected in another element of comparison. If a comparable home is in a neighborhood with a lower property tax rate, the comparable's lower expenses could be considered an economic characteristic warranting an adjustment, but the lower tax rate probably translates into higher property values and will already be reflected in the adjustment for location. Also, the economic characteristics of a property that affect value must be distinguished from differences in real property rights conveyed and from changes in market conditions.

Use/Zoning

In general, potential comparables will be discarded if their highest and best use is not the same as that of the subject property. When sales transactions considered comparable are scarce though, the use of comparable properties with a different current use or highest and best use may be warranted; in these situations an adjustment for differences in use is necessary.

Zoning is one of the primary determinants of the highest and best use of vacant land because it serves as the test of legal permissibility.

When comparable properties with similar zoning are scarce, parcels with slightly different zoning but the same highest and best use as the subject property may be used as comparables, and an adjustment may not be necessary if the highest and best use is the same. An adjustment may be made to take into account differences in utility.

Non-realty Components of Value

Personalty, business value, or other non-realty items that influence either the sale prices of the comparables or the ownership interest in the subject property should be analyzed separately from the real property. The economic characteristics of non-realty components of value–e.g., economic life, associated investment risks, rate of return criteria, and collateral security–differ from those of the realty in most cases.

Properties such as timeshare condominiums, which have high expense ratios attributable to business operation, typically include a significant business value component. Where the business operation is essential to the use of the real property, the value of the non-realty component must be analyzed and reported.

Market Data Grids

One important analytical tool used in the sales comparison approach is the market data grid. An appraiser may sketch a grid during the field inspection to record data quickly or fill in the spaces on a preprinted table. Market data grids can take many forms, but usually each comparable is identified in the top row of the grid (see Figure 16.1). The sale prices of the comparables are entered in the next row, and the gross living area and unit price of each comparable are shown in the following rows. The elements of comparison are listed on the left side of the grid.

The blank spaces across from each element of comparison are filled in with information that indicates the difference or similarity between the subject and each comparable property. The differences in value resulting from these variances are also noted once the amounts have been established by market analysis. Amounts of differences, or adjustments, may be expressed in dollars or percentages. Whenever adjustments are made, they should be applied in a particular sequence, which is discussed in Chapter 18. The market data grid shown in Figure 16.1 calls for dollar adjustments to reflect value differences.

Market data grids are extremely useful in the analysis of comparables. They show at a glance which comparables are most similar to the subject and should therefore be accorded the most weight in reconciling the results. With a market data grid an appraiser can quickly locate pairs of comparables that are similar in all but one element of comparison. These paired data can be analyzed to pinpoint how much value the market ascribes to a particular property characteristic.

market data grid. A tabular representation of market data organized into useful, measurable categories.

Uniform Residential Appraisal Report

File #

There are	comparable properties currently offered for sale in the subject neighborhood ranging in price from $			to $	
There are	comparable sales in the subject neighborhood within the past twelve months ranging in sale price from $			to $	

FEATURE	SUBJECT	COMPARABLE SALE # 1		COMPARABLE SALE # 2		COMPARABLE SALE # 3	
Address							
Proximity to Subject							
Sale Price	$		$		$		$
Sale Price/Gross Liv. Area	$ sq. ft.	$ sq. ft.		$ sq. ft.		$ sq. ft.	
Data Source(s)							
Verification Source(s)							
VALUE ADJUSTMENTS	DESCRIPTION	DESCRIPTION	+(-) $ Adjustment	DESCRIPTION	+(-) $ Adjustment	DESCRIPTION	+(-) $ Adjustment
Sale or Financing Concessions							
Date of Sale/Time							
Location							
Leasehold/Fee Simple							
Site							
View							
Design (Style)							
Quality of Construction							
Actual Age							
Condition							
Above Grade Room Count	Total Bdrms. Baths	Total Bdrms. Baths		Total Bdrms. Baths		Total Bdrms. Baths	
Gross Living Area	sq. ft.	sq. ft.		sq. ft.		sq. ft.	
Basement & Finished Rooms Below Grade							
Functional Utility							
Heating/Cooling							
Energy Efficient Items							
Garage/Carport							
Porch/Patio/Deck							
Net Adjustment (Total)		☐ + ☐ -	$	☐ + ☐ -	$	☐ + ☐ -	$
Adjusted Sale Price of Comparables		Net Adj. % Gross Adj. %	$	Net Adj. % Gross Adj. %	$	Net Adj. % Gross Adj. %	$

(Vertical label on left side: SALES COMPARISON APPROACH)

I ☐ did ☐ did not research the sale or transfer history of the subject property and comparable sales. If not, explain

My research ☐ did ☐ did not reveal any prior sales or transfers of the subject property for the three years prior to the effective date of this appraisal.

Data source(s)

My research ☐ did ☐ did not reveal any prior sales or transfers of the comparable sales for the year prior to the date of sale of the comparable sale.

Data source(s)

Report the results of the research and analysis of the prior sale or transfer history of the subject property and comparable sales (report additional prior sales on page 3).

ITEM	SUBJECT	COMPARABLE SALE # 1	COMPARABLE SALE # 2	COMPARABLE SALE # 3
Date of Prior Sale/Transfer				
Price of Prior Sale/Transfer				
Data Source(s)				
Effective Date of Data Source(s)				

Analysis of prior sale or transfer history of the subject property and comparable sales

Summary of Sales Comparison Approach

Indicated Value by Sales Comparison Approach $

The total difference in value between the subject property and each comparable can also be calculated from the market data grid. The price of each comparable is adjusted for value differences ascribed to the elements of comparison. The resulting figures indicate a range of values for the subject property by the sales comparison approach.

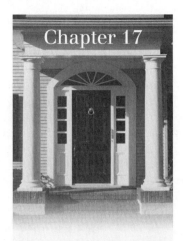

Chapter 17

Cash Equivalency

The definition of market value most commonly used in residential appraisals (i.e., the definition listed on the Fannie Mae/Freddie Mac residential appraisal report forms) assumes that "the price represents the normal consideration for the property sold unaffected by special or creative financing or sales concessions granted by anyone associated with the sale." While the definition implies that the value listed on the appraisal report has expenses of sale similar to a cash sale, not all comparables will have these cash terms. Therefore, it may be necessary to exclude some sales or adjust for any increase in price caused by such unusual terms.

Appraisals undertaken to estimate market value require a financing adjustment if special financing has influenced the sale price of a comparable property. The various techniques used to estimate adjustments for special financing include

- Analysis of market-derived paired data
- Simple arithmetic for estimating the value of seller-paid points and considerations other than cash
- Cash equivalency calculations that involve discounting

Whenever a property sells with atypical financing, the financing plan may have influenced the sale price. Most creative financing plans are inducements offered by the seller that allow the buyer to make periodic payments that are lower than those required with market financing, allow the seller to pay various up-front cost for the borrower, or, in some cases, allow the seller to give the buyers the down payment money. The value

cash equivalency analysis. The procedure in which the sale prices of comparable properties sold with atypical financing are adjusted to reflect typical market terms.

of financing represents personal property, not real property. If comparable sales with unusual financing are to be used in sales comparison, the value of the financing incentive must be distinguished from the value of the real property. The price of the comparable must be adjusted to reflect the amount of cash the seller would have received if no special financing agreement had been made or no extra "buyers financing expenses" had been assumed by the seller.

An understanding of "normal consideration" is critical in determining whether the financing arranged for a sale considered comparable involves any special advantages or disadvantages. Whether financing represents "normal consideration" may be established by analyzing six factors. (See Figure 17.1.) Financing terms are continually subject to change, so the appraiser is advised to check the local market.

Figure 17.1	Significant Factors in Residential Financing
1. Loan-to-value ratio	Typically loan-to-value ratios range from 70% to 80%, but they may run as high as 100%. Sometimes just obtaining a higher LTV ratio will cause a buyer to pay more for a specific property.
2. Interest rate	Comparing the current market interest rates available to the most qualified buyers with the terms obtained by the buyer of the comparable property may show some buyer advantage. For many years a favorite tool in the residential market was to have the seller take back a mortgage at below-market rates.
3. Amortization period	In some markets a longer amortization period may be an incentive to buy a particular property; long-term mortgages or interest-only loans are available in most markets, however, which makes this option less important.
4. Term of the balloon	Most mortgages that provide for a balloon payment have terms of three to seven years, but some may extend up to 10 years. In some markets, this may be an incentive to buy a particular property, but it usually is not.
5. Number of points	In most markets, typical financing will not include any seller-paid points. Since paying points up front is a way of increasing a lender's yield, this is a common tool in some markets to allow buyers to qualify for a loan with a lower interest rate than they would otherwise be able to afford.
6. Frequency of payments	Conventionally payments are made on a monthly basis, but a mortgage may be paid quarterly, semiannually, or annually. This is not usually a source of favorable terms in most markets.

Nonmarket financing plans can be translated into terms that represent the cash paid to the seller as of the date of sale. This is called *rendering the terms cash equivalent.*[1] Cash equivalency is estimated in several ways. The effect of special financing can be measured by analyzing market-derived paired data or the amount can be calculated with simple arithmetic or the use of discounting techniques. Calculated adjustments for special financing are often somewhat higher

---

1. See Guide Note 2 to the Appraisal Institute's Standards of Professional Appraisal Practice, "Cash Equivalency in Valuations."

than market-derived adjustments because appraisers fail to estimate the holding period correctly. Appraisers should only use a calculated adjustment when they are confident that the adjustment accurately reflects market thinking.

Comparison of Sales Transactions

Adjustments for cash equivalency derived by comparing recent sales transactions are generally the most reliable. These adjustments can be estimated from paired data analysis. To apply this technique an appraiser finds pairs of sales considered comparable that are essentially similar except for the inclusion of special terms in one of the comparables. The effect of financing is indicated by the difference between the prices of the paired sales. Similarly, if a newspaper advertisement quotes a sale price for a new home and indicates that the developer is offering a $5,000 or 5% discount for an all-cash purchase, the appraiser has a solid basis for estimating the effect of the financing arrangement on the price of the house.

The problem with deriving these adjustments is obtaining sufficient sales data to isolate the influence. Often an appraiser will not find sufficient comparables to conduct a reliable paired data analysis. One or two sets of matched data may not constitute an adequate sample. However, even a limited sample can be useful if the reasonableness of the adjustment derived from paired data analysis is tested against the results of other cash equivalency techniques. In purchases transacted with atypical financing, one of the parties involved may have had special motivations to complete the sale. When paired data analysis is used to derive an adjustment, the price difference between comparables may reflect both a financing inducement and special motivation. Consequently, financing and conditions of sale may be combined into a single adjustment. Sales considered comparable that do not reflect arm's-length transactions should only be used with extreme caution.

Adjusting for Seller-Paid Points

An adjustment for seller-paid points is one cash equivalency adjustment that is relatively easy to calculate. The seller-paid points are applied to the mortgage amount and the result is deducted from the total price.[2] For example, consider a comparable property that was sold for $130,000. The buyer made a $30,000 cash down payment and financed the balance of the sale price with a $100,000 FHA-insured mortgage. The seller paid the lender three points, which is 3% of the mortgage amount of $100,000, or $3,000. The cash equivalent price of the comparable is therefore $127,000 ($130,000 × 0.03 = $3,000 and $130,000 − $3,000 = $127,000). This cash equivalent price is then used as the basis for further sales comparison adjustments. This adjustment

---

2. At one time, the VA and FHA required the seller to pay the points that apply to mortgages underwritten by these agencies. This requirement has been discontinued.

is based on the logic that a seller who has to pay these extra costs will just add the cost to the sale price. While the amount may not seem significant in this case, seller-paid points can equal up to 10% of the sale price in some markets.

Appraisers who work for agencies such as the FHA or VA must use procedures that are consistent with agency regulations.

Adjusting for Considerations Other Than Cash

In a property sale, the seller and buyer may agree on a price that includes items of real or personal property. To determine the cash equivalency of the sale price in this situation, the appraiser focuses on the cash amount that the seller received for the items traded.

For example, an appraiser is analyzing a complicated sale in which the seller reportedly sold the property for $86,000. The sale was financed with a 10% cash down payment, and the buyer assumed the existing mortgage balance of $50,000 at current market rates. The seller also received a trade property from the buyer. The seller believed that this property was worth $15,000 but was only able to sell it for $10,000. The seller also received a new car with a sticker price of $17,500.

To estimate the cash equivalent value of the sale, the appraiser totals the following figures:

Cash down payment	$8,600
Mortgage balance	50,000
Trade property	10,000
Car	+ 17,500
Cash equivalent sale price	$86,100

Discounting Cash Flows

Many techniques for deriving cash equivalency adjustments involve discounting cash flows. Lenders and investors commonly discount cash flows to estimate what a future stream of payments is worth at present. They use discounting procedures and financial function tables to make these calculations. Appraisers can apply the same principles to convert future payments into the present value of a financing plan when the pattern of the anticipated payments is known. Such cash equivalent adjustments should only be used with extreme caution, however. They should be checked against more reliable adjustments derived directly from sales data, if such data are available.

A stream of income expected in the future is not currently worth the sum of all the anticipated payments to be received. Normally, money that is invested today is expected to earn interest and produce more money in the future. This is why a future income stream must be *discounted.* A discount factor is applied to the income stream to obtain its present value.

For example, the upper half of Table 17.1 shows the effects of compound interest on a single cash flow today of $1,000 earning 5% interest per year for 10 years. The lower half of the table shows the value "today" of a

Table 17.1 — Time Value of Money

Compound Interest Over Time

Year	Begin. Bal.		Add Interest		End Bal.
1	$1,000.00	×	105%	=	$1,050.00
2	$1,050.00	×	105%	=	$1,102.50
3	$1,102.50	×	105%	=	$1,157.63
4	$1,157.63	×	105%	=	$1,215.51
5	$1,215.51	×	105%	=	$1,276.28
6	$1,276.28	×	105%	=	$1,340.10
7	$1,340.10	×	105%	=	$1,407.10
8	$1,407.10	×	105%	=	$1,477.46
9	$1,477.46	×	105%	=	$1,551.33
10	$1,551.33	×	105%	=	$1,628.89

Discounting for Time

Year	Begin. Bal.		Discount Rate		End Bal.
10	$1,628.89	÷	105%	=	$1,551.33
9	$1,551.33	÷	105%	=	$1,477.46
8	$1,477.46	÷	105%	=	$1,407.10
7	$1,407.10	÷	105%	=	$1,340.10
6	$1,340.10	÷	105%	=	$1,276.28
5	$1,276.28	÷	105%	=	$1,215.51
4	$1,215.51	÷	105%	=	$1,157.63
3	$1,157.63	÷	105%	=	$1,102.50
2	$1,102.50	÷	105%	=	$1,050.00
1	$1,050.00	÷	105%	=	$1,000.00

Present value is the value of a future payment or series of future payments discounted to the current date. The present value of a series of payments depends on the size of the payments, the schedule of payments, and the interest rate that applies to each portion of the schedule. When these variables are known, present value can be estimated using an appropriate financial function table, a financial function calculator, or a computer program.

Present value of $1 is a compound interest factor that indicates how much $1 due in the future is worth today. A future amount due, such as a balloon payment, is multiplied by this factor to obtain its present value. When the payment amount and the interest rate are known, the present value factor can be found with an appropriate financial function table, a financial function calculator, or a computer program.

Present value of $1 per period is a compound interest factor that indicates how much $1 paid periodically is worth today. An amount payable periodically, such as a monthly mortgage payment, is multiplied by this factor to obtain its present value. When the payment amount and the interest rate are known, the present value factor can be found with a financial function table, a financial function calculator, or a computer program.

Mortgage constant (R_M) is a rate that reflects the relationship between annual debt service and the principal of the mortgage loan. It is used to convert annual debt service into mortgage loan value. The mortgage constant equals the annual debt service divided by the mortgage loan value. Using the debt service payment or the mortgage loan principal and the interest rate and term, the mortgage constant can be obtained with a direct-reduction loan factor table, a financial function calculator, or a computer.

cash flow of $1,628.89 that will be received in 10 years. Notice that $1,000 grows to $1,628.89 over 10 years, and $1,628.89 that will not be received for 10 years is worth $1,000 today.

Discounting Mortgages Made at a Below-Market Rate

Procedures for estimating the present value of a financing instrument vary, depending on what information is known about the financing plan and how future repayment is scheduled. When a mortgage loan at a below-market rate is assumed or the seller makes a mortgage loan at a below-market rate, the cash flow for the entire stated term of the mortgage can be discounted in three steps.

1. Determine the monthly payment. When the mortgage amount, the contract interest rate, and the term are known, the mortgage constant can be obtained from the appropriate table and the monthly payment can be calculated.

2. Determine the present value of the monthly payments over the stated term at the market interest rate by applying a present value of $1 per period factor. The result is the market value of the mortgage.

3. Add the down payment to the value of the mortgage. This sum is the cash equivalent sale price.

Example

A comparable single-family residence was sold for $110,000 with a down payment of $25,000 and an $85,000 mortgage from the seller for a 20-year term. The seller charged 10% interest when market rates were 13%. The cash equivalent sale price can be calculated as follows:

Monthly payment on $85,000 for 20 years @ 10%

$85,000 × 0.00965 (direct-reduction loan factor

[mortgage constant, R_M]) = $820.25

Present value of $820.25 for 20 years @ market rate of 13%

(monthly conversion frequency) = $820.25 × 85.3551

(PV of $1 per period) = $70,012.52

Cash equivalent value of mortgage (rounded)	$70,000
Plus down payment	+ 25,000
Sale price adjusted for financing	$95,000

The calculations above assume the buyers believe they will hold this mortgage loan for 20 years and that the favorable interest rate would have benefits for that period of time. If the holding period is shorter than 20 years or the buyers believe interest rates will not be this high for that length of time, this long holding period is overstated, and the adjustment would be also.

Figure 17.2	Financial Calculator Keystrokes	
	Keystroke	**Output**
110,000 − 25,000 =	85,000 PV	85,000.00
Set the term	20 g n	240.00
Set the interest rate	10 g i	0.83
Set the balloon payment	0 FV	0.00
Solve for payment	PMT	-820.27
Change I to market rate	13 g i	1.08
Solve for PV of mortgage	PV	70,014.12
Add back in downpayment	25,000 +	95,014.12

Discounting Mortgage Assumptions, Seller Loans, and Balloon Mortgages

A slightly more complicated, but probably more realistic, calculation can be used to estimate the cash equivalency of mortgage assumptions and seller loans. Many mortgage loans are not held for the entire mortgage term but are repaid early. A more elaborate calculation is used to reflect this fact. Financing plans that involve balloon payments may also be adjusted using this technique. A balloon mortgage is not fully amortized at maturity, so a lump-sum, or balloon, payment of the outstanding balance is required.

To estimate cash equivalency when a balloon mortgage is used, present value is determined separately for two distinct phases of the loan repayment schedule:

- The period during which scheduled payments are being made
- The point at which the balance is recovered in a balloon, or lump-sum, payment

The following procedure is recommended:

1. Determine the monthly payment.
2. Estimate the probable life expectancy of the loan. This can be either the actual term of the mortgage stated in the loan document or the average mortgage life of loans on the type of property in question.
3. Discount the monthly payments over the probable life expectancy of the loan by applying a present value of $1 per period factor at the market interest rate.
4. Discount the projected loan balance at the due date of the balloon or at the end of the average mortgage life by applying a present value of $1 factor at the market interest rate.
5. Add together the present value of the monthly payments (from Step 3), the present value of the projected balance (from Step 4), and the down payment amount. The resulting sum is the cash equivalent sale price of the property.

Example

The procedure for balloon mortgages is demonstrated using the same data presented in the previous example:

Monthly payment: $820.25

Average mortgage life for similar property (from lenders): 7 years

Present value of $820.25 per month for 7 years at market rate of 13% (monthly conversion frequency)

$$\$820.25 \times 54.9693 \ (PV \text{ of } \$1 \text{ per period}) = \$45,090 \text{ (rounded)}$$

Present value of future mortgage balance

Number of years remaining: $20 - 7 = 13$

PV of $820.25 per month @ 10% contract rate for 13 years (monthly conversion frequency)

$$\$820.25 \times 87.1195 \ (PV \text{ of } \$1 \text{ per period}) = \$71,460 \text{ (rounded)}$$

Future balance payment converted to present value

PV of $1 factor for 7 years @ 13% market rate
(monthly conversion frequency)

$$\$71,460 \times 0.4045 \ (PV \text{ of } \$1) = \$28,906 \text{ (rounded)}$$

$45,090 (*PV* of mortgage paid in 7 years) + $28,906 (*PV* of balance)

Cash equivalent value of the mortgage	$73,996
Plus down payment	+ 25,000
Adjusted sale price of comparable	$98,996
	or $99,000 (rounded)

This second procedure requires more calculations, but it more accurately reflects the accounting method used by lending institutions.

Figure 17.3	Financial Calculator Keystrokes

	Keystroke	Output
110,000 − 25,000 =	85,000 PV	85,000.00
Set the term	20 g n	240.00
Set the interest rate	10 g i	0.83
Set the balloon payment	0 FV	0.00
Solve for payment	PMT	-820.27
Change *n* to holding period	7 g n	84.00
Solve for balloon	FV	-71,461.41
Change to market rate	13 g i	1.08
Solve for PV of mortrage	PV	73,995.67
Add back in down payment	25,000 +	98,995.67

Discounting procedures for estimating cash equivalency can provide mathematical solutions for a wide range of financing problems. However, appraisers should only use these calculations when they are confident that they reflect market behavior accurately. Calculated adjustments are often somewhat larger than market-derived adjustments, especially if the holding period used in the calculation is longer than the market is recognizing. Adjustments derived by comparing recent sales transactions are more reliable than adjustments based on discounting procedures alone.

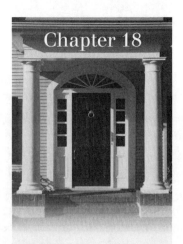

Chapter 18

Application of the Sales Comparison Approach

After all potentially comparable properties have been identified and inspected, and the transaction data have been verified, the appraiser selects the comparables that will actually be used in the appraisal. The comparable properties may be quite similar to the subject property, but they can never be exactly identical to it. Therefore, the prices of the comparables must be adjusted to reflect their significant differences from the subject.

The appraiser first identifies the effect on value produced by each difference. This is accomplished through analysis of market data. Paired data analysis may facilitate this task. Next, the appraiser applies dollar or percentage adjustments to the price of each comparable. Adjustments are usually made in a particular sequence. As the sequence of adjustments proceeds, the price of each comparable is reshaped until it ultimately approximates a current, open-market sale price that corresponds to the value of the subject property. Qualitative analysis then considers the influence of the elements of comparison that resist precise mathematical adjustment, which sets the stage for reconciliation. (Quantitative adjustments and qualitative analysis complement each other and are often used in combination.) The adjusted prices of the comparables are reconciled to provide a final indication of the value of the subject property by the sales comparison approach.

Purpose of Adjustment

A sales comparison adjustment is made to account (in dollars or a percentage) for a specific difference between the subject property and a comparable property. As the comparable is made more like the subject, its price is brought closer to the subject's unknown value.

- If the comparable is *superior* to the subject, a *downward* adjustment must be applied to the price of the comparable.
- If the comparable is *inferior* to the subject, the price of the comparable must be adjusted *upward* to reflect the difference.

Because only the price of the comparable is known, only it can be adjusted. The unknown value of the subject is suggested by the price of the comparable once it has been adjusted for all differences from the subject.

Units of Comparison

Units of comparison are the components into which a property may be divided for purposes of comparison. Because only like units can be compared, each sale price is stated in the same units of comparison.

units of comparison. The components into which a property may be divided for purposes of comparison, e.g., price per square foot, front foot, cubic foot, room, bed, seat, apartment unit.

All units must be appropriate to the appraisal problem. When unit prices related to size are used, adjustments for differences in size may be unnecessary. Single-unit residential properties are usually compared on the basis of gross price but they can be analyzed based on a price per square foot of living area. Apartment properties are often analyzed on the basis of price per apartment and price per room. Price per square foot of gross building area or leasable building area may also be used for some two- to four-unit properties.

Many properties can be analyzed with several different units of comparison, so an appraiser should determine which unit or units are the most appropriate and reliable. The units of comparison selected can have a significant bearing on the reconciliation of value indications in the sales comparison approach. Adjustments can be made either to the total sale price of the comparable property or to a unit price such as price per square foot of gross living area.

Units of comparison can help an appraiser decide whether a potentially comparable property is in fact comparable to the subject property. For example, if an appraiser finds that one potentially comparable property sold for $150 per square foot of gross living area while most other properties similar to the subject sold for about $133 per square foot of gross living area, the discrepancy would suggest that there is something different about the more expensive property. The reasons for the discrepancy should be investigated, and if the potential comparable is not truly comparable, it must be eliminated from further consideration. In this example, the unit of comparison applied was price per square foot of gross living area. It is quite possible that the comparable with the higher price per square foot above grade has a basement. For example, Comparable B has a basement and Comparable A does not.

Item	Comparable A	Comparable B
Sale price	$200,000	$225,000
Gross living area	1,500	1,500
Price per square foot (GLA)	$133.33	$150.00
Basement	No	Yes

Scatter Diagrams

A scatter diagram is an analytical instrument that can be used to help organize data and set up a market data grid. Scatter diagrams used in sales comparison typically list a unit of comparison along one coordinate axis and the unit price on the other. The coordinates of each comparable are plotted on the graph. Table 18.1 lists the sale prices, gross living areas, and prices per square foot of gross living area for nine comparable properties. These data are portrayed on the scatter diagram in Figure 18.1.

An appraiser could analyze this scatter diagram to derive an estimate of the unit price of the subject property. A line or curve that

Table 18.1	Tabular Representation of Data								
	Sale A	Sale B	Sale C	Sale D	Sale E	Sale F	Sale G	Sale H	Sale I
Price	$84,000	$72,000	$96,000	$92,000	$89,000	$83,000	$79,000	$81,000	$85,000
Gross living area in sq. ft.	2,150	1,800	2,700	2,500	2,400	2,100	1,900	2,060	2,300
Price/gross living area	$39.00	$40.00	$35.60	$36.80	$37.10	$39.50	$41.60	$39.30	$37.00

Note. Figures are rounded

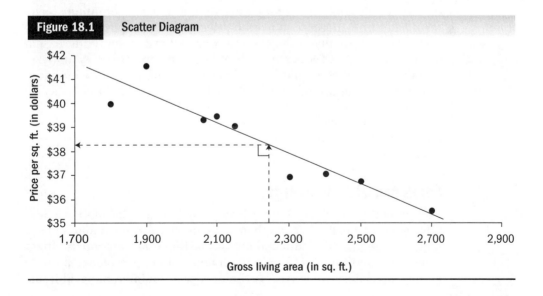

Figure 18.1 Scatter Diagram

corresponds to the central tendency of the scatter pattern is plotted. Then the position of the subject property along this line or curve is located by drawing a perpendicular line from the gross living area of the subject on the horizontal axis of the graph to the point where it intersects the curve. A perpendicular line drawn from this point to the vertical axis will indicate the unit price of the subject property.

The sales properties' comparability with the subject is also depicted in the diagram. This analytical tool allows an appraiser to distinguish readily between closely comparable properties and those that are less comparable. However, the points in a scatter diagram do not always fall into a roughly linear pattern. When no line approximating a central tendency is suggested by the graph, the scatter diagram technique is unreliable.

Dollar and Percentage Adjustments

Quantitative adjustments may be applied to the prices of comparables in two ways. The dollar amount of the difference can be calculated and added to or subtracted from the total price or unit price of the comparable. Adjustments derived from paired data analysis are often entered on a market data grid as dollar adjustments. Alternatively, the relationship between the subject and a comparable property can be expressed in terms of a percentage of value. When percentage adjustments are employed, the price of the comparable is adjusted to reflect a percentage of increase or decrease in value.

The adjustments required for certain elements of comparison, in particular for market conditions and location, are frequently derived in percentages. Sales data may indicate that market conditions have resulted in a 5% increase in overall prices during the past year or that prices for a particular category of property have recently increased 0.5% per month (or 6% per year). Similarly, an appraiser may analyze market data and conclude that properties in one location command prices that are approximately 10% higher than similar properties in another location.

Whether they are expressed in dollars or percentages, all adjustments should be derived from the sale price of the comparable property if possible.

Sequence of Adjustments

Once quantitative adjustments are derived, they must be applied to the price of the comparable. In applying both percentage and dollar adjustments, the sequence of adjustments may be important, especially when sales data are limited. Depending on application, percentage adjustments may not be transitive—i.e. their order is not interchangeable, as

Table 18.2	Subtotaling Percentage Adjustments			
	Column 1			**Column 2**
Sale price	$125,000	Sale price		$125,000
Adjustment 1	+ 10%	Adjustment 1		10%
Subtotal	$137,500			
Adjustment 2	– 10%	Adjustment 2		(10%)
Subtotal	$123,750			
Adjustment 3	+ 5%	Adjustment 3		5%
Subtotal	$129,938			
Adjustment 4	– 5%	Adjustment 4		(5%)
Result	$123,441	Cumulative adjustment		0%
		Result		$125,000

shown in Table 18.2. Column 1 was subtotaled after each percentage adjustment, but Column 2 was just summed. The results are different because of the method used to apply these percentage adjustments.

Whenever percentage adjustments are added to or subtracted from an intermediate price in the adjustment process, the sequence should be carefully considered. If the percentages are not subtotaled after each adjustment, the order of adjustment does not affect the result. This sequence is determined by the market data and the appraiser's analysis of those data. For purposes of illustration, the following sequence of dollar adjustments is provided:

1. Property rights conveyed
2. Financing (cash equivalency)
3. Conditions of sale (motivation)
4. Expenditures made immediately after purchase
5. Market conditions (time)

After applying these five adjustments, additional adjustments may be made for

6. Location
7. Physical characteristics
8. Economic characteristics
9. Use
10. Non-realty components of value[1]

The sequence of adjustments is illustrated in Table 18.3.

sequence of adjustments. The order in which quantitative adjustments are applied to the sale prices of comparable properties. The sequence of adjustments is determined by the market and through analysis of the data. Percentage adjustments must be applied in a specific sequence whenever they are added and subtracted—i.e., real property rights conveyed, financing (cash equivalency), conditions of sale (motivation), market conditions (time), and physical characteristics.

---

1. The sequence illustrated in this chapter is based on a sequence first presented by Halbert C. Smith in *Real Estate Appraisal* (Columbus, Ohio: Grid, Inc., 1976). While it is a typical sequence for applying quantitative adjustments, it is not the only sequence in which such adjustments may be made.

	Subject	**Sale 1**		**Sale 2**		**Sale 3**		**Sale 4**		**Sale 5**	
Table 18.3		Market Data Grid Adjustments Applied on a Gross Dollar Basis									
Sale price	?	$201,000		$200,500		$205,000		$195,000		$205,500	
		Descr.	**Adj.**	**Descr.**	**Adj.**	**Descr.**	**Adj.**	**Descr.**	**Adj.**	**Descr.**	**Adj.**
Real property rights conveyed	Fee simple	Fee simple (same)	0	Fee simple (same)	0	Fee simple (same)	0	Fee simple (same)	0	Fee simple (same)	0
Financing	Conv.	Seller (superior)	-3,500	Conv. (similar)	0	Seller (superior)	-3,500	Seller (superior)	-3,500	Conv. (similar)	0
Conditions of sale	Arm's-length	Arm's-length (same)	0	Arm's-length (same)	0	Arm's-length (same)	0	Arm's-length (same)	0	Arm's-length (same)	0
Adjusted price*		$197,500		$200,500		$201,500		$191,500		$205,500	
Expenditures made immediately after purchase	None	None (same)	0	None (same)	0	None (same)	0	None (same)	0	None (same)	0
Date of sale	Current	1 year ago (inferior)	+5,000	Current (similar)	0	Current (similar)	0	1 year ago (inferior)	+5,000	Current (similar)	0
Adjusted price†		$202,500		$200,500		$201,500		$196,500		$205,500	
Location	Average	Good (superior)	-6,000	Average (similar)	0	Average (similar)	0	Average (similar)	0	Average (similar)	0
Garage	2-car	1-car (inferior)	+4,000	2-car (similar)	0	1-car (inferior)	+4,000	1-car (inferior)	+4,000	2-car (similar)	0
Pool	No	No (similar)	0	No (similar)	0	Yes (superior)	-5,000	No (similar)	0	Yes (superior)	-5,000
Use	Single-unit residence	Same (similar)	0	Same (similar)	0	Same (similar)	0	Same (similar)	0	Same (similar)	0
Economic characteristics	None	None (similar)	0	None (similar)	0	None (similar)	0	None (similar)	0	None (similar)	0
Non-realty components	None	None (similar)	0	None (similar)	0	None (similar)	0	None (similar)	0	None (similar)	0
Net adjustment‡		-2,000		0		-1,000		+4,000		-5,000	
Final adjusted sale price		$200,500		$200,500		$200,500		$200,500		$200,500	
For reconciliation purposes											
Gross adjustment§		$18,500		0		$12,500		$12,500		$5,000	
Total adjustment as percentage of sale price		9.20%		0.00%		6.10%		6.41%		2.43%	

* Sale price adjusted for financing

† Sale price further adjusted for market conditions

‡ Difference between positive and negative adjustments made for location, garage, and the absence or presence of a pool

§ Total positive and negative adjustments applied to each comparable

Market Data Grid

Data on the subject property and comparable properties may be organized and analyzed on a market data grid. Each important difference between the subject and the comparable properties that can affect value is considered an element of comparison. Each element is assigned a row on the grid and the total prices or unit prices of the comparables are adjusted to reflect the value of these differences.

Market data grids can be extremely useful. They identify which comparables have the fewest differences from the subject and should be accorded the most weight in reconciliation. Market data grids also facilitate the totaling of adjustments to calculate the value differences between the subject property and each comparable.

Table 18.3 is a sample market data grid that reflects typical elements of comparison and the proper sequence of adjustments. The sample grid has a separate line for each applicable element of comparison. When the subject and a comparable are similar in regard to a given element of comparison, no adjustment is required for that element. In this market data grid, adjustments are applied on a gross dollar basis.

Quantitative Adjustments

Sales of comparable properties are analyzed so an appraiser can judge how property differences affect price and identify whether and how much individual elements of comparison must be adjusted. Any recent sale of the subject property should also be analyzed to see whether it falls within the range reflected by the sales considered comparable. Several methods can be used to study market data to determine quantitative adjustments, including paired data analysis and units of comparison.

Paired Data Analysis

Through paired data analysis an appraiser can derive the amount of value attributable to a difference in an element of comparison directly from the market data. When two sales considered comparable are very similar in all but one characteristic, the appraiser may be able to conclude that the difference in this single characteristic accounts for the difference in their prices.

For example, assume that a property is sold twice within a short period of time and no changes have occurred in the property or the neighborhood during this period. An adjustment for market conditions may be derived from the prices of the two transactions. Similarly, if two very similar properties located in different neighborhoods are sold within a limited period, an adjustment for location can be calculated from their sale prices. After adjustments are made for market conditions and location, the effects of other variables on price should be isolated, if possible. In practice, it is often difficult for an appraiser to identify several matched data sets from the sales of comparable or similar properties. Listings and offers to buy can also be used for this analysis, but they provide less reliable results.

Usually the number of available comparables is limited and an appraiser rarely finds pairs that directly indicate the effect of each element of comparison. Many pairs of comparables on the market data grid differ from one another in more than one element, so it can be difficult to isolate the effects of each individual variation. Often a more complicated procedure must be applied to obtain the necessary information. To apply this procedure the appraiser makes a series of paired data identifications and repeated adjustments directly on the market data grid. Each step in this procedure is demonstrated in the following example.

Step 1
On a market data grid, the appraiser notes the significant differences between each comparable property and the subject property in the appropriate spaces. If a comparable is identical to the subject in a given respect, "same" is indicated on the grid.

Table 18.4

	Subject	Sale 1		Sale 2		Sale 3		Sale 4		Sale 5		Sale 6	
Sale price	?	$105,000		$101,000		$96,000		$109,800		$103,000		$103,800	
Condition	Good	Good	Same	Poor		Poor		Good	Same	Good	Same	Poor	
Site shape	Irreg.	Reg.		Reg.		Irreg.	Same	Irreg.	Same	Reg.		Irreg.	Same
Garage	1-car	2-car		1-car	Same	1-car	Same	2-car		1-car	Same	2-car	
View	Yes	No		Yes	Same	No		Yes	Same	No		Yes	Same
Access	Poor	Poor	Same	Poor	Same	Poor	Same	Good		Poor	Same	Good	

Note: Throughout this example it will be assumed that the sale prices of the comparables have already been adjusted for property rights, financing, market conditions, conditions of sale, and location.

Step 2
The appraiser finds a pair of comparables that differ from one another in only one respect. In this case, Sales 4 and 6 are paired because they differ only in the condition of the improvements.

Table 18.5

	Subject	Sale 1		Sale 2		Sale 3		Sale 4		Sale 5		Sale 6	
Sale price	?	$105,000		$101,000		$96,000		$109,800		$103,000		$103,800	
Condition	Good	Good	Same	Poor		Poor		**Good**	**Same**	Good	Same	**Poor**	
Site shape	Irreg.	Reg.		Reg.		Irreg.	Same	**Irreg.**	**Same**	Reg.		**Irreg.**	**Same**
Garage	1-car	2-car		1-car	Same	1-car	Same	**2-car**		1-car	Same	**2-car**	
View	Yes	No		Yes	Same	No		**Yes**	**Same**	No		**Yes**	**Same**
Access	Poor	Poor	Same	Poor	Same	Poor	Same	**Good**		Poor	Same	**Good**	

Step 3

Using paired data analysis, the appraiser determines whether the presence of the feature in question is an advantage or a disadvantage and how much value the market ascribes to it.

Next, the direction of the adjustment must be determined. If the comparable is inferior to the subject, an upward adjustment is called for. If the comparable is superior to the subject, a downward adjustment is needed. If the comparable is equal to the subject in this respect, no adjustment is made. The goal of the analysis is to find what the price of the comparable would be if the comparable were more like the subject.

An adjustment amount is entered on the grid *only* when the comparable differs from the subject. In this example, the good condition of the improvements in Sale 4 is an advantage valued at $6,000.

Table 18.6

	Subject	Sale 1		Sale 2		Sale 3		Sale 4		Sale 5		Sale 6	
Sale price	?	$105,000		$101,000		$96,000		$109,800		$103,000		$103,800	
Condition	Good	Good	Same	Poor	+$6,000	Poor	+$6,000	Good	Same	Good	Same	Poor	+$6,000
Site shape	Irreg.	Reg.		Reg.		Irreg.	Same	Irreg.	Same	Reg.		Irreg.	Same
Garage	1-car	2-car		1-car	Same	1-car	Same	2-car		1-car	Same	2-car	
View	Yes	No		Yes	Same	No		Yes	Same	No		Yes	Same
Access	Poor	Poor	Same	Poor	Same	Poor	Same	Good		Poor	Same	Good	

Step 4

The price of each comparable that differs from the subject is adjusted by the amount indicated. After all necessary adjustments are made, the impact of a single difference will have been identified in the market data grid. Once one variable has been eliminated, other pairs of comparables that are identical in all but one characteristic can be identified by repeating Steps 2, 3, and 4.

Table 18.7

	Subject	Sale 1		Sale 2		Sale 3		Sale 4		Sale 5		Sale 6	
Sale price	?	$105,000		$101,000		$96,000		$109,800		$103,000		$103,800	
Condition				+ 6,000		+ 6,000						+ 6,000	
Adjusted price				$107,000		$102,000						$109,800	
Site shape	Irreg.	Reg.		Reg.		Irreg.	Same	Irreg.	Same	Reg.		Irreg.	Same
Garage	1-car	2-car		1-car	Same	1-car	Same	2-car		1-car	Same	2-car	
View	Yes	No		Yes	Same	No		Yes	Same	No		Yes	Same
Access	Poor	Poor	Same	Poor	Same	Poor	Same	Good		Poor	Same	Good	

Step 5

Steps 2, 3, and 4 are repeated until the values of all differences in the elements of comparison have been found. The adjusted figures are the prices the comparable properties would have sold for if they had resembled the subject property more closely. These figures provide the basis for deriving a value indication for the subject property using paired data analysis.

In this example the adjusted prices of the comparables are identical. In practice, the adjusted prices will not coincide when two sets of paired data yield different adjustments for the same element of comparison, or when other techniques are applied to produce different adjustments. In practice, the adjusted prices of comparable properties are almost never identical but they should converge toward a single number. Remember, when appraisers use paired data analysis, they are explaining the difference in price caused by the difference in the properties. This means the goal of the process is to bring the adjusted prices closer to each other. Closing the gap between the indicated values is not only good appraisal practice, it is the essence of paired data analysis.

Table 18.8

	Subject	Sale 1	Sale 2	Sale 3	Sale 4	Sale 5	Sale 6
Price	?	$105,000	$101,000	$96,000	$109,800	$103,000	$103,800
Condition			+ 6,000	+ 6,000			+ 6,000
Adjusted price			$107,000	$102,000			$109,800
Site shape		- 1,000	- 1,000			- 1,000	
Adjusted price		$104,000	$106,000			$102,000	
Garage		- 2,000			- 2,000		- 2,000
Adjusted price		$102,000			$107,800		$107,800
View		+ 4,000		+ 4,000		+ 4,000	
Adjusted price		$106,000		$106,000		$106,000	
Access					- 1,800		- 1,800
Adjusted price					$106,000		$106,000
Comp. prices after adjustment		$106,000	$106,000	$106,000	$106,000	$106,000	$106,000

Limitations of Paired Data Analyses

This brief discussion of paired data analysis may seem to suggest that identifying the effects of property differences from market data is a straightforward procedure that can produce accurate, complete mathematical results in all appraisals. Such an impression would be misleading. Appraisers develop an opinion of market value by applying their judgment to the analysis and interpretation of data. Paired data analysis is a tool that an appraiser can apply to market data in some circumstances. When used in conjunction with other analytical tools, this type of analysis supports and guides the appraiser's judgment, but it does not take its place.[2]

Perfect sets of comparables that vary in a single, identifiable respect are rarely found. Because properties that are sufficiently similar to the subject are usually limited in number, the decision to apply paired data analysis in a given situation is a matter of judgment. Often the sampling size may not be large enough to provide a solid statistical foundation for the appraiser's conclusions.

Nevertheless, paired data procedures are important valuation tools that appraisers should use whenever possible. Identifying matched data sets and isolating the effects of variables is a practical methodology for studying market data, even if a comprehensive paired data analysis cannot be performed. When only a narrow sample of market data is available, which would not lend itself to statistical analysis, paired data analysis can be used to test the results of other analytical procedures.

Units of Comparison

Units of comparison can also be used to identify the effects of variations in property characteristics. Units of comparison play various roles in different parts of the valuation process, but they are especially significant in the analysis of comparables, where they can be applied to derive adjustments on a per-unit basis.

Although properties can be divided into many different component parts, only a few units of comparison are commonly used in residential valuations. One property is generally compared with another in terms of the total property price, the price per square foot of gross living area, the price per room, or the price per living unit. Parcels of land may be compared in terms of total price, price per acre, price per lot, price per square foot, or price per front foot.

With units of comparison an appraiser can make adjustments for size differences between the subject and comparable properties. After adjustments are made for financing, conditions of sale, market conditions, and location, an appraiser may need to isolate the amount of value difference attributable to size. The appraiser can use a scatter diagram, plotting the square footage of gross living area on one axis and the price per square foot on the other. The results may then be reconciled to derive the amount of the size adjustment.

Adjustments may be applied on a unit sale price basis as the market data grid in Table 18.9 illustrates. Units of comparison may also facilitate paired data analysis. They can help isolate the effects of differences

---

2. For example, an appraiser may find three properties that are alike in all characteristics except that House A has a garage and Houses B and C do not. The difference in price between House A and House B is $2,000. Yet House C, which has no garage, is sold for the same price as House A, which has a garage.

    Another appraiser may find two comparable houses, priced at $150,000 and $152,000, which differ in four features. House Y does not have a garage. House Z does not have a backyard fence. House Y is painted white. House Z is painted blue. House Y is 17 years old. House Z is 15 years old. It may be virtually impossible to determine how much each of the four variables has contributed to the $2,000 price differential.

and resolve problems. Units of comparison are applied to paired data analysis in four steps:

1. Select a relevant unit of comparison such as price per square foot of gross living area.
2. Divide the sale price of each comparable by the number of units in that comparable. If, for example, the price of the comparable is $64,000 and its gross living area is 1,600 square feet, the calculation would be

$$\$104,000/1,600 \text{ sq. ft.} = \$65 \text{ per sq. ft.}$$

The derivation of a unit price helps reveal relationships and facilitates analysis of paired data and scatter diagrams.

3. Analyze paired data making adjustments to the unit sale price of the comparable rather than the total sale price.
4. After all adjustments have been made, multiply the adjusted unit sale price of each comparable by the number of units of comparison in the subject to obtain a value indication for the subject property.

Other Quantitative Adjustment Techniques

In addition to paired data analysis, an appraiser may use several other techniques to arrive at quantitative adjustments in the sales comparison approach–e.g., judgment, cost and depreciated cost data, rental and land value data, depreciation rates, regression analysis, and ranking analysis.

In some situations where paired data analysis is not conclusive, the appraiser may apply judgment to resolve the problem. For example, assume that House A has a two-car garage, brick siding, and a fenced yard and sold for $120,000. House B has a one-car garage, vinyl siding, and an unfenced yard and sold for $116,000. Based on an understanding of buyers' preferences in the market, the appraiser knows that the two-car garage is the most appealing feature of House A and accounts for the $4,000 price differential.

Cost and depreciated cost data may be used in making adjustments, especially data on the costs of upgrading existing homes and installing amenities in subdivision houses under construction. Buyers of new homes usually purchase a basic model and select various upgrade features to be installed during construction. Such features include garages, decks, basements, and air-conditioning systems. Interviews with contractors, construction experts, buyers, sellers, and brokers can provide an appraiser with information on the costs of such features. In appraising older houses, the appraiser may arrive at the value contribution of an amenity by adjusting its current cost downward, i.e., depreciating the current cost for the age of the house.

The difference in rent attributable to a difference between otherwise similar income-producing properties can be capitalized to derive an indication of the difference in the values of the properties. For example, the difference in the rent charged for two duplexes, one with a garage and the other without, can be multiplied by the appropriate gross rent

Table 18.9   Market Data Grid Adjustments Applied on a Unit Price Basis

	Subject	Sale 1		Sale 2		Sale 3		Sale 4		Sale 5		Sale 6	
Sale price		$99,000		$100,050		$96,100		$104,000		$99,200		$105,000	
Gross living area in sq. ft.	1,425	1,650		1,450		1,550		1,600		1,600		1,500	
Unit price		$60		$69		$62		$65		$62		$70	
Real property rights conveyed	Fee simple	Fee simple	0	Fee simple	0	Fee simple	0	Fee simple	0	Fee simple	0	Fee simple	0
Financing	Conv.	Conv.	0	Special	-2	Conv.	0	Conv.	0	Conv.	0	Conv.	0
Conditions of sale	Arm's-length	Arm's-length	0	Arm's-length	0	Arm's-length	0	Arm's-length	0	Arm's-length	0	Arm's-length	0
Adjusted price*		$60		$67		$62		$65		$62		$70	
Expenditures made immediately after purchase	None	None	0	None	0	None	0	None	0	None	0	None	0
Date of sale	Current	Current	0	6 mos.	+$3	Current	0	Current	0	6 mos.	+$3	Current	0
Adjusted price†		$60		$70		$62		$65		$65		$70	
Location	Average	Fair	+$5	Average	0	Fair	+$5	Fair	+$5	Average	0	Average	0
Garage	2-car	1-car	+$2	2-car	0	2-car	0	2-car	0	1-car	+$2	2-car	0
Quality of construction	Average	Fair	+$3	Average	0	Fair	+$3	Average	0	Fair	+$3	Average	0
Net adjustments‡		+$10		0		+$8		+$5		+$5		0	
Final adjusted sale price		$70		$70		$70		$70		$70		$70	
For reconciliation purposes:													
Gross adjustments§		$10		$5		$8		$5		$8		0	
Total adjustment as percentage of sale price		16.67%		7.25%		12.90%		7.69%		12.90%		0.00%	

*   Unit sale price adjusted for financing
†   Unit sale price further adjusted for market conditions
‡   Total adjustments for location, garage size, and quality of construction
§   Total positive and negative adjustments applied to each comparable

multiplier to derive the amount of the adjustment for a garage. (See the discussion of the income capitalization approach in Chapter 19.)

Rental data can also be used in another way. In markets where current sales data are not available because few sales have been transacted recently, an appraiser may calculate an adjustment for market conditions by analyzing changes in rents since the last sales occurred. For example, if rents have increased from $750 to $770 since the last sales were transacted, the appraiser may conclude that a market adjustment of 2.6% (20/750) is warranted.

Data on the rate of depreciation may also be used to derive an adjustment for the age of the property and condition of the improvement (physical characteristics). For example, using market-extracted depreciation (as discussed in Chapter 15), the appraiser is able to establish a 2% average annual rate of depreciation for properties in the subject market. Thus a 12-year-old subject property is assumed to be 24% depreciated, while a 15-year-old comparable is 30% depreciated. In this situation an upward adjustment of 6% to the sale price of the comparable, less land value, would seem to be appropriate. In most analyses, if the property includes other components such as garages, basements, porches, and other improvements, the percentage adjustment would have to be applied to the cost of the main structure only.

Differences in land values may also reflect the size of an adjustment for locational differences (i.e., immediate neighborhood, traffic density, view, frontage, and siting). After the appraiser estimates the land value of each comparable at the time of its sale, direct comparison of these values should shed light on the amount of an adjustment for location.

Regression analysis can be used to isolate and test the significance of specific value determinants. Regression analysis reveals apparent relationships between the values of different variables and their tendency to vary regularly with one another. Due to the ever-increasing power and affordability of personal computers, as well as practitioners' increasing comfort with what was once considered an esoteric statistical method, more real estate professionals are using regression analysis as an analytical tool in both appraisal practice and related real estate research. Data of sufficient quantity and quality are now available, as are the hardware and software needed to apply statistical methods to a relatively wide range of valuation assignments. (Regression analysis and other forms of statistical analysis are discussed in more detail in Chapter 22.)

> **regression analysis.** A method that examines the relationship between one or more independent variables and a dependent variable by plotting points on a graph and through statistical analysis; used to identify and weight analytical factors and to make forecasts.

Qualitative Analysis

Qualitative analysis can be undertaken after quantitative adjustments have been made. The analysis of qualitative differences generally forms the basis for reconciliation by revealing which comparables are the more reliable indicators of the value of the subject. The process of qualitative analysis takes into account the inefficiencies of real estate markets and the difficulty of making precise measurements of the differences between comparable properties and the subject. Techniques for studying qualitative differences among properties include relative comparison analysis and ranking analysis.

Relative Comparison Analysis

Relative comparison analysis is the study of the relationships indicated by market data without recourse to quantification. Appraisers often use this technique because it makes allowance for the imprecision and imperfections that are characteristic of real estate markets. In relative comparison analysis, the adjustments for differences among various elements of comparison are expressed in qualitative terms. The appraiser determines whether, on an overall basis, the comparable is inferior, superior, or equal to the subject property.

As an example, consider a 1,500-sq.-ft. single-unit home in average condition with 3 bedrooms, 2 bathrooms, and a 2-car garage. The location and view of the subject property are considered average for the market. The fee simple interest is being appraised for an arm's-length sale of the property with conventional financing terms.

The first comparable property, a 1,600-sq.-ft. home in average condition and of average-quality construction, was sold recently for $174,800. The property is considered to have better access to transportation routes and a better view than the subject. The price per square foot of Sale 1 is $109.25.

The second comparable, a 1,550-sq.-ft. home in fair condition and of poor-quality construction, was sold six months previously for $157,500. Sale 2, which has a view and location similar in quality to the subject, had a price per square foot of $101.61.

Sale 3, a 1,450-sq.-ft. single-unit property in fair condition and of poor-quality construction, sold three months previously for $150,000, which gives a price per square foot of $103.45. The location of the comparable property is considered inferior to the subject, but the view afforded by the less-accessible site is considered superior.

The fourth comparable property is a 1,400-sq.-ft. home in good condition and of average-quality construction. Nine months previously, the property sold for $147,000, for a price per square foot of $105. The location and view elements of comparison of Sale 4 are considered similar in quality to those of the subject.

The final comparable, a 1,550-sq.-ft. property in good condition and of average-quality construction, sold for $161,550 recently. The location of Sale 5 is considered similar to that of the subject, although the view that location affords is considered inferior. Sale 5 had a price per square foot of $104.23.

All the comparable properties have 3 bedrooms, 2 bathrooms, and 2-car garages, and all were sold in arm's-length transactions with conventional market financing. Furthermore, no adjustments needed to be made for real property rights conveyed or expenditures made immediately after purchase. In addition, the market for one-unit homes had been stable for the past 18 months, with negligible fluctuation in price.

The data used in the relative comparison analysis process are summarized in Table 18.10.

Table 18.10 **Market Data Grid for Relative Comparison Analysis**

	Subject	Sale 1		Sale 2		Sale 3		Sale 4		Sale 5	
Sale price	?	$174,800		$157,500		$150,000		$147,000		$161,550	
Size in square feet	1,500	1,600		1,550		1,450		1,400		1,550	
Price per square foot	?	$109.25		$101.61		$103.45		$105		$104.23	
Real property rights conveyed	Fee simple	Fee simple		Fee simple		Fee simple		Fee simple		Fee simple	
Financing	Conventional	Conventional		Conventional		Conventional		Conventional		Conventional	
Conditions of sale	Arm's-length	Arm's-length		Arm's-length		Arm's-length		Arm's-length		Arm's-length	
Expenditures made immediately after purchase	None	None		None		None		None		None	
Date of sale	Current	Current		6 months ago		3 months ago		9 months ago		Current	
Location (access)	Average	Good	Superior	Average	Similar	Poor	Inferior	Average	Similar	Average	Similar
Quality of construction	Average	Average	Similar	Poor	Inferior	Poor	Inferior	Average	Similar	Average	Similar
View	Average	Good	Superior	Average	Similar	Good	Superior	Average	Similar	Poor	Inferior
Condition of improvements	Average	Average	Similar	Fair	Inferior	Fair	Inferior	Good	Superior	Average	Similar
Overall comparability			Superior		Inferior		Inferior		Superior		Inferior

Assuming that all of the elements of comparison contribute equally to value, Sales 1 and 4 are superior to the subject property, and Sales 2, 3, and 5 are inferior. To determine a *bracket* for the value of the subject property, the comparables are arranged in order relative to their comparability:

Superior	Sale 1	$109.25
Superior	Sale 4	$105.00
	Subject	
Inferior	Sale 5	$104.23
Inferior	Sale 3	$103.45
Inferior	Sale 2	$101.61

The unit price of the subject property should be greater than that of the highest comparable of inferior quality and less than that of the lowest comparable of superior quality. In this example, the value of the subject property should fall within the range of $104.23–$105.

If the comparables are all superior or all inferior, only a lower or upper boundary can be set, and no range of possible values for the subject can be defined. If the available comparable market data do not bracket the subject property, other analytical techniques, such as the use of quantitative adjustments, should be considered. If the elements of comparison do not contribute equally to value in the market, the above analysis is not valid. To use this tool, the appraiser may have to ignore some of the elements of comparison of less significance to the typical buyer.

Ranking analysis can be employed to deepen the understanding of the influence on value of the various qualitative factors.

Ranking Analysis

Ranking analysis is generally used in conjunction with relative comparison analysis. Comparable properties are arrayed either in descending or ascending order according to their degree of similarity or dissimilarity to the subject property.

Ranking the comparables in the previous example generates the following data:

	Sale 1	Sale 2	Sale 3	Sale 4	Sale 5
Location (access)	Superior	Similar	Inferior	Similar	Similar
Quality of construction	Similar	Inferior	Inferior	Similar	Similar
View	Superior	Similar	Superior	Similar	Inferior
Condition of improvements	Similar	Inferior	Inferior	Superior	Similar
Overall comparability	Superior	Inferior	Inferior	Superior	Inferior

In this format, where the number of qualitative differences can be counted easily, the appraiser can see that Sales 4 and 5, with only one qualitative difference apiece, are the most similar to the subject property.

When combined with the application of quantitative adjustments, relative comparison and ranking analysis form the basis for reconciliation in the sales comparison approach.

Reconciliation

The final step in the sales comparison approach is the reconciliation of data. In this phase of the valuation process, the appraiser reviews the quality of the data and analyzes the appropriateness of the methodology applied, asking questions like:

- How reliable were the sources that supplied data on each sale considered comparable?
- Did the field inspection corroborate the factual data obtained from secondary sources?
- Was all information obtained from the parties to the sale verified?

To begin the process of reconciliation, an appraiser asks, "What could possibly be wrong with the data I have collected?"

After the legal, transactional, physical, and locational data on each sale considered comparable have been reviewed, the appraiser analyzes the data sources and the procedures used to derive adjustments, asking the following questions:

- What sales information was used?
- Was the sample large enough?
- If listings and offers were used as well as sales, how reliable are these data?
- How similar to the subject are the properties used in the database?
- How old are the data and do they conform to current market patterns?
- If they do not, why not?

The analytical procedures used to derive adjustments are also investigated by asking the following questions:

- Was paired data analysis used?
- If so, how well matched were the paired sales?
- Were scatter diagrams drawn?
- Which of the procedures applied is most reliable, given the constraints of the data?

All relevant analytical procedures should be applied to the data so the results of each analysis can be tested against the results of the others. If these results vary widely, the appraiser should find out why; if the results are similar, they must be reconciled. The greatest weight is given to the most reliable procedure.

Each adjustment must be fully understood before it is applied. Often appraisers erroneously reward or penalize a comparable twice for the same difference. If both quantitative adjustments and qualitative analysis are employed, adjustments must be applied consistently for each element of comparison—i.e., qualitative analysis of a particular element of comparison should not be performed on some comparables while quantitative adjustments are applied to other comparables for the same element of comparison. Certain differences between properties may represent mixed blessings. For example, a property may suffer from special tax assessments but benefit from the additional services that these taxes support. It is inconsistent to penalize a property for an obvious disadvantage without considering a compensating advantage, which may be less obvious.

Once all the prices of the comparables have been adjusted, a range of prices is indicated for the value of the subject property. These different prices must be reconciled. Assuming a current date of valuation, greater reliance is generally placed on comparables that were sold most recently and those that are most similar to the subject property. Comparables that require few adjustments are considered more reliable. Near the bottom of the Table 18.9 there is a line labeled "For reconciliation purposes." It is common appraisal practice for the appraiser to indicate the total adjustment to the sale price of each comparable and the total adjustment as a percentage of the price. This figure can help the appraiser assess each sale's comparability and aid in reconciliation.

Because the market is not perfect, many appraisers arrive at a range of values for the subject property in the reconciliation phase of the sales comparison approach. Often a single value opinion can be obtained only after all three approaches are completed. An appraisal is more credible if the indications of value derived in the other approaches fall into the range suggested by the sales comparison approach.

In the example used in the discussion of qualitative analysis, the unit price of the subject was estimated to be within the range generated in the relative comparison analysis—$104.23 to $105. Ranking analysis showed that Sales 4 and 5 had the fewest number of qualitative differences from the subject property, but Sale 5 could reasonably considered the most comparable because a deficiency in the view amenity would probably have less of an impact on value than the superior quality of the improvements in Sale 4. Considering the results of the qualitative analysis, the final unit price of the subject property should be weighted toward the price of Sale 5 within the range, yielding an estimate of $104.50 per sq. ft. This figure then produces a total value indication of $156,750 for the 1,500-sq.-ft. subject property.

Sample Application

The following appraisal problem illustrates the application of quantitative adjustment techniques, qualitative analysis, and an appropriate sequence of adjustments in the sales comparison approach. The problem solution is presented as it might appear in an appraisal report.

The subject property is improved with a 25-year-old single-unit residence on a single lot. It has the original kitchen, a one-car garage, and no air-conditioning. It contains 1,100 square feet of gross living area. The construction quality of the structure is average, and the site enjoys a lake view considered an amenity by the market.

Comparable A is a current cash sale of a property that was sold for $91,500. The house is on a double lot and has a modern kitchen, a one-car garage, and no air-conditioning. The 25-year-old property contains 1,100 square feet of gross living area. The structure is of average construction quality, but the site does not have the view amenity of the subject.

Comparable B was sold a year ago for $73,800 with market financing. The 25-year-old house is on a single lot and has an old kitchen, a one-car garage, and no air-conditioning. It contains 1,150 square feet of gross living area. The house features a similar view of the lake as the subject, and the construction quality of the structure is good.

Comparable C is a current cash sale of a property that was sold for $82,000. The 27-year-old house is on a single lot and has an old kitchen, a two-car garage, and central air-conditioning. It contains 1,300 square feet of gross living area. The structure is only of fair construction quality, and the site does not enjoy the same view of the lake as the subject. The property had also been sold two years ago for $74,550.

Comparable D is a current sale of a property that was sold for $80,000 with a 90% FHA loan requiring the seller to pay three points. The improvement is a 29-year-old house on a single lot with a view of the lake and has an old kitchen, a one-car garage, and central air-conditioning. It contains 1,200 square feet of gross living area. The construction quality of the structure is average.

Additional market data include these facts:

- Sites in this area are worth $10,000. The extra lot in Sale A could easily be sold for this amount. The house is situated on one lot, and the other is unimproved.

- The cost to modernize a kitchen in the subject neighborhood averages $7,500. However, the appraiser's study of subsequent sales of homes with modern kitchens indicates that the market is willing to pay $10,000 more for a home with a modern kitchen.
- Central air-conditioning is currently available in a new development of similar homes at a cost of $1,500. Many purchasers elect to have central air-conditioning installed as an upgrade feature. Although some homes in the subject neighborhood have central air-conditioning, an insufficiency of data rules out the use of paired data analysis to derive an adjustment for this feature.
- The average depreciation rate for homes in the subject's neighborhood is approximately 33.33%.

The first step toward solving the appraisal problem is to array the data by identifying both typical elements of comparison and those that are apparent from the problem statement. Such an array will help the appraiser determine which adjustments will not have to be made.

Analysis of the array (Table 18.11) indicates that three characteristics—property rights conveyed, conditions of sale, and expenditures made immediately after purchase—are similar for all the sales and for the subject property. Since these features are the same for all properties, they cannot account for differences in value and therefore may be eliminated from the adjustment grid. Many of the required adjustments can be derived from information given in the problem statement.

The financing adjustment for Sale D is calculated by multiplying the amount of the mortgage, $72,000 (90% of a sale price of $80,000), by 0.03 (i.e., the three points). Thus, the price of Sale D is adjusted downward by $2,160 and the cash equivalent price becomes $77,840.

The adjustment to Sale B for market conditions is derived by analyzing the sale price and resale price of Sale C, which sold two years

Table 18.11	Market Data Grid: Elements of Comparison				
	Subject	**Sale A**	**Sale B**	**Sale C**	**Sale D**
Property rights	Fee simple	Fee simple	Fee simple	Fee simple	Fee simple
Financing	Market	Cash	Market	Cash	3 points
Conditions of sale	Arm's-length	Arm's-length	Arm's-length	Arm's-length	Arm's-length
Expenditure made immediately after purchase	None	None	None	None	None
Date of sale	Current	Current	1 year ago	Current	Current
Improvement age	25 years	25 years	25 years	27 years	29 years
Lot	Single	Double	Single	Single	Single
Kitchen	Old	Modern	Old	Old	Old
Garage	1-car	1-car	1-car	2-car	1-car
Air-conditioning	No	No	No	Yes	Yes
View amenity	Lake	None	Lake	None	Lake
Construction quality	Average	Average	Good	Fair	Average
Size (GLA)	1,200 sq. ft.	1,100 sq. ft.	1,150 sq. ft.	1,300 sq. ft.	1,200 sq. ft.

prior to the current sale for $74,550. The total change over the two-year period was approximately 5% per year. Since Sale B sold one year ago, it is adjusted upward by 5%, or $3,690. After the adjustment for market conditions, the sale price of Sale B becomes $77,490.

The adjustment for the double lot in Sale A is $10,000, derived from the market data provided.

The adjustment for the modern kitchen in Sale A is $10,000, also derived from the market data. In this instance the adjustment is based on the contributory value of the modern kitchen, not the cost of modernization.

The contributory value of the central air-conditioning in Sales C and D is estimated to be $1,000. The cost of this feature in new construction is $1,500. Properties in the subject neighborhood are depreciated by approximately 33.33%. Since property components suffer similar depreciation, an air-conditioning system installed in a home in the subject neighborhood would reflect the overall depreciation of the property. Thus, the basis of the adjustment is the depreciated cost of the air-conditioning.

After all these adjustments have been estimated, a market data grid (Table 18.12) can be used to help derive the remaining adjustment for the difference in garage size.

Table 18.12	Market Data Grid: Quantitative Adjustments								
	Subject	Sale A		Sale B		Sale C		Sale D	
Sale price	?		$91,500		$73,800		$82,000		$80,000
Financing	Market	Cash	0	Market	0	Cash	0	3 points	-2,160
Cash equivalent price			$91,500		$73,800		$82,000		$77,840
Date of sale	Current	Current	0	1 year ago	+3,690	Current	0	Current	0
Current cash equivalent price			$91,500		$77,490		$82,000		$77,840
Lot	Single	Double	-10,000	Single	0	Single	0	Single	0
Kitchen	Old	Modern	-10,000	Old	0	Old	0	Old	0
Air-conditioning	No	No	0	No	0	Yes	-1,000	Yes	-1,000
Improvement age	25 years	25 years	0	25 years	0	27 years	?	29 years	?
Garage	1-car	1-car	0	1-car	0	2-car	?	1-car	0
View amenity	Lake	None	?	Lake	0	None	?	Lake	0
Construction quality	Average	Average	0	Good	?	Fair	?	Average	0

Adjustments for the last four elements of comparison listed in the Table 18.12 cannot be determined from the available market data, though they should contribute to differences in value. The value influence of those elements of comparison will be addressed later in qualitative analysis. At this point, the quantitative adjustments are applied to generate adjusted sale prices in Table 18.13.

Table 18.13 Market Data Grid

	Subject	Sale A		Sale B		Sale C		Sale D	
Sale price	?		$91,500		$73,800		$82,000		$80,000
Financing	Market	Cash	0	Market	0	Cash	0	3 points	-2,160
Cash equivalent price			$91,500		$73,800		$82,000		$77,840
Date of sale	Current	Current	0	1 year ago	+3,690	Current	0	Current	0
Current cash equivalent price			$91,500		$77,490		$82,000		$77,840
Lot	Single	Double	-10,000	Single	0	Single	0	Single	0
Kitchen	Old	Modern	-10,000	Old	0	Old	0	Old	0
Air conditioning	No	No	0	No	0	Yes	-1,000	Yes	--1,000
Net adjustments (for kitchen, air-conditioning, and lot)			-20,000		0		-1,000		-1,000
Adjusted sale price			$71,500		$77,490		$81,000		$76,840

In this example, the range of value opinions is still somewhat broad. Qualitative analysis can be based on unit prices, which are derived by dividing the adjusted sale price of each comparable by the amount of gross living area. Reducing sale prices to a size-related unit price usually reduces the necessity of making any type of size adjustment.

Newer homes generally sell for more than older homes. Comparables C and D, which are older than the subject, are probably inferior to the subject, while Comparables A and B are similar.

An adjustment for a larger garage cannot be isolated from an analysis of the available market data, but the extra space of the garage of Comparable C should add to the value of that property in comparison to the subject.

The view of the lake is desirable in this market and should increase property value. Comparables B and D share a similar view as the subject, but Comparables A and C do not and therefore are probably slightly inferior to the subject.

The construction quality of the subject property is average, which is similar to the quality of the structure of Comparables A and D. The construction quality of Comparable B is considered good, though, which is superior to the subject, and the quality of construction of Comparable C is only fair, which is inferior to the subject.

Qualitative analysis of all the attributes of the comparable properties that cannot be quantified is shown in Table 18.14. The data are then arrayed in descending order in Table 18.15, bracketing the subject property according to the indicated prices per square foot of the comparables. The ranking analysis also shows the overall comparability of the the individual comparable to the subject property.

Comparable A is the comparable most similar to the subject property with respect to gross living area, while Comparable D had the fewest number of qualitative differences. The unit price of Comparable A serves as the lower bound of the bracket derived from qualitative analysis. The range can be reconciled at $66.00 per square foot and this unit price can be used to derive a value indication for the subject. The value of the subject property can therefore be estimated at $72,600 (1,100 sq. ft. × $66 per sq. ft.).

Table 18.14 Market Data Grid for Qualitative Analysis

	Subject	Sale A		Sale B		Sale C		Sale D	
Adjusted sale price	?	$71,500		$77,490		$81,000		$76,840	
Gross living area	1,100 sq. ft.	1,100 sq. ft.		1,150 sq. ft.		1,300 sq. ft.		1,200 sq. ft.	
Unit price	?	$65.00		$67.38		$62.31		$64.03	
Improvement age	25 years	25 years	Similar	25 years	Similar	27 years	Inferior	29 years	Inferior
Garage	1-car	1-car	Similar	1-car	Similar	2-car	Superior	1-car	Similar
View amenity	Lake	None	Inferior	Lake	Similar	None	Inferior	Lake	Similar
Construction quality	Average	Average	Similar	Good	Superior	Fair	Inferior	Average	Similar
Overall comparability			Inferior		Superior		Inferior		Inferior

Table 18.15 Ranking Analysis

Comparable	Price per square foot	Overall Comparability
B	$67.38	Superior
Subject		
A	$65.00	Inferior
D	$64.03	Inferior
C	$62.31	Inferior

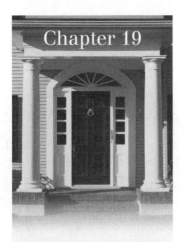

Chapter 19

The Income Capitalization Approach

In the valuation of residential property, the income capitalization approach is only applicable to properties for which an active rental market exists and where buyers consider the income from the property as a reason to purchase. In most markets, to apply this approach, an appraiser estimates the gross monthly income a property is expected to generate and capitalizes this income into a value indication using a gross rent multiplier (*GRM*). In some markets, a more sophisticated analysis of net income will be performed by some buyers, but in most residential markets the *GRM* analysis is most common.

The income capitalization approach is based on the assumption that the value of a rental property is directly related to its ability to produce income. The approach reflects the appraisal concept of anticipation, which affirms that value is created by the expectation of benefits to be derived in the future. Capitalization is the process of converting periodic and reversionary income into a lump-sum indication of value. In this common capitalization procedure, a multiplier (ratio) is applied to the anticipated income of a property to derive an indication of its value.

Different property types are valued with different income capitalization methods. The method and procedure selected should correspond closely to the market's perception of the relationship between income and value for the property being appraised. Only income capitalization with a gross rent multiplier is discussed here. This is usually the most appropriate procedure for valuing single-unit residences. A similar procedure can be applied to two- to four-unit buildings. Generally, the rental income of

capitalization. The conversion of income into value.

these properties is analyzed by applying additional units of comparison such as monthly rent per square foot of gross living area, per room, and per unit.[1] Appraisals of larger income-producing residential properties usually call for more advanced capitalization techniques and procedures, which are beyond the scope of this text.[2]

Outline of the Approach

To obtain a value indication for the subject property using the income capitalization approach with a *GRM*, an appraiser

1. Derives a *GRM* from market data. To do this, the appraiser finds recent sales of similar properties that were rented at the time of or immediately after the sale, divides the sale price of each property by its monthly rental income expectation, and reconciles the results.
2. Estimates the monthly market rent the subject property should command. This estimate can be based on
   - The actual rents of competitive properties that have been adjusted for the advantageous or disadvantageous features of the subject.
   - The current rental rates obtained by the owner of the subject property. These could be less than or more than the market rent, but so could the comparable rentals mentioned above. The actual rents for the subject are often a good indication of the market rent.
   - The current asking rental rates for competing properties. These comparable "for rent" properties will not give conclusive evidence of what the market will pay, but they will usually indicate a ceiling for the subject rents after adjustment.
3. Multiplies the estimated monthly market rent for the subject by the estimated *GRM* to obtain a value indication for the subject property.

Applicability

The income capitalization approach is most applicable to properties for which reliable sales and rental data exist and for which buyers will consider the income as a criteria for purchase. Residential properties that can produce income but are more typically owner-occupied may be valued with this approach if data are available. Assume, for example, that due to unfavorable economic conditions home purchases have declined. As a result, 20 units in a 200-site residential subdivision intended for owner occupancy have to be rented out instead. Some of these rental units are eventually sold to owners or investors. In this case, meaningful comparative data can be derived for application of the income capital-

---

1. A refinement of this simple capitalization procedure is applied to two- to four-unit buildings. The procedure employs an *effective gross rent multiplier*, which is the ratio between the value or sale price of a property and its *effective gross rent*—i.e., gross monthly rental income minus vacancy and collection loss.
2. For a complete discussion of appraisal techniques used in the valuation of all types of multifamily properties, see *The Valuation of Apartment Properties* by Arlen C. Mills and Anthony Reynolds (Chicago: Appraisal Institute, 1999).

ization approach, but it will usually be less reliable since the typical buyer's main criteria for purchase is not the rental income.

An active rental market for the subject property must exist to ensure a sufficient quantity of sales and rental data. The quality of the data is also important. The properties from which the gross rent multiplier is derived should be competitive with the subject property and similar to it in terms of market appeal, size, occupancy levels, lease characteristics, and expense ratios. The market rent estimated for the subject property should also be based on data from properties that are sufficiently comparable. It is fairly important to maintain an "apples to apples" comparison when using this technique.

The applicability of the income capitalization approach may be limited by legal and economic restrictions on property use. If, for example, the owner-occupant of a property is considering converting it to a rental use, zoning regulations must be investigated to determine if the contemplated use is legally permissible. Assuming the use is permitted, the costs and benefits of conversion must also be weighed.

The prevalence of rent control programs in some metropolitan areas affects the reliability of market rent data and the *GRMs* derived. Rent controls make future rental income less certain, but most rent control ordinances allow for some growth in rents, and increased operating expenses can often be passed on to tenants. If rents are prevented from keeping pace with operating expenses, property owners may try to further reduce operating expenses or to divest themselves of the property through sale or condominium conversion. Therefore, rent controls can represent a value penalty. To determine the impact of rent controls on property values in a given area, an appraiser might compare income-producing properties subject to rent controls with similar properties that are not.[3]

Gross Rent Multiplier

Derivation of a *GRM* from Market Data

The first step in the income capitalization approach is the derivation of a gross rent multiplier (*GRM*) from market data. An appraiser begins by gathering recent sales of properties that are competitive with the subject and similar to it in terms of lease, expense, and income characteristics. The price of each property is divided by the monthly rent from all units in the property as of the date of sale. The resulting *GRM* indications are then reconciled into a single figure. Differences in the properties are usually reflected in their rents, so *GRMs* are never adjusted.

3. Harold A. Davidson, "The Impact of Rent Control on Apartment Investment," *The Appraisal Journal* (October 1978); Robert J. Strachota and Howard E. Shenehon, "Market Rent vs. Replacement Rent: Is Rent Control the Solution?" *The Appraisal Journal* (January 1983); G. Donald Jud, John D. Benjamin, and G. Stacy Sirmans, "What Do We Know about Apartments and Their Markets?" *Journal of Real Estate Research*, vol. 11, no. 3 (1996); John Cicero, "The Appraisal of Occupied Cooperative Apartments in New York City," *The Appraisal Journal* (July 2002): 318-324; and M.H. Stiegler, "Rent Restrictions Not Considered for Low Income Housing Valuation," *The Appraisal Journal* (January 2002): 4.

A *GRM* reflects a typical ratio between the value or sale price of a property and its gross rent, which is the gross monthly rental income at the time of sale before expenses or vacancy and collection losses are deducted. When this ratio is applied to the subject property's market rent, it will provide a reliable value indication if the properties from which it was derived are truly comparable. The division of utility expenses between tenants and the landlord must be similar. The properties analyzed must also have similar expense-to-income ratios and lease terms.

The rental properties from which the *GRM* is derived need not be identical to the subject, but they should be competitive with it. They should be located in the same market area as the subject property or a similar market area and appeal to tenants of approximately the same income levels and household sizes. Four-bedroom houses are usually not in direct competition with two-bedroom houses. Sales should be fairly recent, especially if the market appears to be changing. In some areas a *GRM* derived from data that are more than six months old may prove unreliable; in others a *GRM* derived from two-year-old data may still be valid.

At this point in the income capitalization approach, the appraiser is concerned with the relationship between property value and rent. Thus, a competitive property that has a slightly higher rent than the subject because of its larger size or additional amenities can still be used to derive a *GRM*, provided the competitive property has a correspondingly higher value. The ratio between property value and income usually changes more slowly than either value or income. The comparability of market data becomes even more critical in the second step of the income capitalization approach when the appraiser analyzes the current rents of the most similar properties to estimate the rent that the subject property can command.

Expense Characteristics

The ratio between the operating expenses that the landlord incurs and the rent the building can command must be similar for the subject and all sale properties used in the analysis. Two houses that are equally desirable dwellings in the eyes of tenants may have different expense-to-income ratios. From a landlord's point of view, these properties will be regarded quite differently. It may be less economically productive to own and operate one building than to own and operate the other. A building that requires extraordinary maintenance or has higher taxes without higher rental income is obviously worth less. When such variations are found in the market data, the reliability of the *GRM* is diminished.

The typical operating expenses of rental properties can be divided into two categories:

1. Fixed expenses such as taxes and insurance charges that must be paid regardless of the level of occupancy.

2. Variable expenses that are determined by the level of occupancy. These include charges for routine cleaning, repair, and maintenance; for interior and exterior painting, garbage removal, and pest control; for electricity and other utilities paid by the landlord; and for other expense items.

An appraiser studies fixed and variable expenses by analyzing operating statements for the subject property and similar properties or by reviewing published statistics. This investigation is part of the rent survey and data collection effort.

Lease Provisions

The lease provisions applicable to the sale properties should be similar to those of the subject property. Because leases specify the obligations of the landlord and the tenant, differences in leases can influence the expenses the landlord must pay or the rent the property can attract. Thus unusual lease provisions may distort the relationship between income and value in a property. A lease that is especially favorable to the tenant, for example, may attract a higher-than-normal rent, although the value of the property is not proportionately higher. For example, some landlords will include furniture or some utilities with the lease, creating a much higher rental rate and much higher expenses. Some landlords offer property with weekly payment schedules or short-term leases to bring in higher rents. In some markets, it is common for landlords to divide the monthly rents by four to get a weekly rent. This practice increases the income substantially because there are 4.33 weeks in each month, not 4.0.

> **lease provisions.** Characteristics of a lease that specify the obligations of the landlord and tenant, e.g., lease period, amount of security deposit, division of expenses between tenant and landlord, penalties for breaking lease or for late payment of rent, restrictions on tenant activities.

Important Lease Provisions That Often Vary in Residential Properties

- Lease period
- Amount of security deposit (Some landlords may not require a security deposit, while others may insist on one-half the monthly rent, a full month's rent, or more.)
- Division of expenses between tenant and landlord
- Penalty for breaking lease
- Penalty for late payment of rent
- Restrictions on tenant activities
- Conditions that constitute violation of the lease by the tenant
- Provisions for termination of the lease by the tenant or landlord
- Landlord's maintenance obligations
- Landlord's landscaping obligations
- Furniture included in the lease agreement
- Options to renew the lease
- Conditions under which the tenant may sublet

Adjusting the Comparable Sales

If the opinion of market value for the subject is based on commonly accepted definitions (found on the standard residential forms), the value is based on "arm's-length" and "cash equivalent" terms. This means the value opinion will be in compliance with the defined value. However, if the comparable sales are not arm's-length and cash equivalent sales, then the *GRM* could not be an indication of value based on those terms. This means it may be necessary, to maintain an apples-to-apples comparison, to adjust the sale prices of the comparable sales used to extract the *GRM* for conditions of sale and special financing terms.

It is also possible that adjustments for property rights and alterations or repairs made immediately after the sale will be needed before a *GRM* can be extracted. Comparables with significantly different rights in realty will be difficult to adjust for and most appraisers will ignore that data when possible. Sales with significant needed repairs at the time of sale may not appeal to the same buyers or, in some cases, the condition may even preclude renting the property. For example, in some markets where foreclosure is common, the properties may sell to investors but the condition of the properties may be so bad that they are not rentable at any price. This will preclude a meaningful *GRM* extraction.

Reconciling *GRMs*

After the market data are assembled and several indicated *GRMs* are derived, the appraiser reconciles the results and selects a *GRM* that is appropriate for the subject property. The greatest emphasis is placed on *GRMs* derived from properties that are most similar to the subject. Rent and property value generally move in tandem, so *GRM* ratios should remain fairly stable. It is quite possible for some items to be reflected both in the rental rate and the sale price, but other items may be reflected in the sale price only, not in the rental rate. For example, a tenant will usually pay more rent for a property with a new kitchen, and a landlord will also. However, a tenant that does not pay any maintenance expenses will probably not pay more for a property with a new roof, but a landlord surely will. Most property amenities will convert to rent and sale prices, but some will not. If the item is reflected in the rent and sale price, by adjusting *GRMs* an appraiser would consider these differences twice. Adjustments to the GRM extracted from comparables should only be made for the reasons stated above.[4]

Example

After gathering sales of similar properties and verifying their prices and rents, the appraiser arranges the market data in Table 19.1. The appraiser selects a gross rent multiplier of 110 because this is the multiplier derived from the properties that are most similar to the subject in terms of location, size, property features, and expense characteristics.

---

4. Mark R. Rattermann, "Considerations in Gross Rent Multiplier Analysis," *The Appraisal Journal* (Summer 2006): 226–231.

Table 19.1	Reconciling *GRMs*		
Sale	**Verified Sale Price**	**Verified Monthly Rent**	**Indicated Gross Rent Multiplier (*GRM*)**
1	$199,500	$1,865	107
2	$290,000	$2,636	110
3	$206,000	$1,900	108
4	$212,500	$1,900	112
5	$214,750	$1,925	112
6	$270,000	$2,432	111
7	$160,000	$1,467	109
8	$265,000	$2,410	110
9	$222,500	$2,025	110
10	$224,500	$2,025	111
11	$220,000	$2,000	110

Monthly Market Rent Estimate

To derive a market value indication, the *GRM* is multiplied by the subject property's market rent. Appraisers must distinguish between market rent and contract rent. Market rent is the rental income a property would most probably command in the open market as of the date of the appraisal. Contract rent is the actual rent specified in a lease or actually received on a month-to-month basis. Contract rent and market rent are often the same amount, but it is not uncommon to find large differences.

The rent that the subject property currently generates may differ from market rent for a number of reasons. At the time of the lease agreement, the landlord or tenant may have been poorly informed or acting under duress. Market conditions may have changed since the lease was signed, or for some reason the lease terms may be unusually favorable to the tenant or the landlord. Contract rent is often lower than market rent if the parties are related or if the tenant has agreed to work for the landlord in exchange for lower monthly payments. To maintain full occupancy, the landlord may keep rents slightly below market levels.

An appraiser estimates the market rent the subject property should command by studying the rents of the most comparable rental properties and adjusting these rents for differences

market rent. The most probable rent that a property should bring in a competitive and open market reflecting all conditions and restrictions of the specified lease agreement including term, rental adjustment and revaluation, permitted uses, use restrictions, and expense obligations; the lessee and lessor each acting prudently and knowledgeably, and assuming consummation of a lease contract as of a specified date and the passing of the leasehold from lessor to lessee under conditions whereby:

1. Lessee and lessor are typically motivated.
2. Both parties are well informed or well advised, and acting in what they consider their best interests.
3. A reasonable time is allowed for exposure in the open market.
4. The rent payment is made in terms of cash in United States dollars, and is expressed as an amount per time period consistent with the payment schedule of the lease contract.
5. The rental amount represents the normal consideration for the property leased unaffected by special fees or concessions granted by anyone associated with the transaction.

contract rent. The actual rental income specified in a lease.

in lease terms and provisions, if applicable.[5] The appraiser also examines the rent the subject is currently generating, studies the existing leases, and asks the tenant and the landlord whether they believe the lease terms and rent are fair. This investigation is supported by the appraiser's analysis of the rents of competitive rental properties in the subject neighborhood.

Adjusting Market Data

When differences among properties influence the amount of income that the properties can generate, adjustments must be made. These adjustments can be derived using paired data analysis or other techniques. Data are arranged on a market data grid, differences for properties that vary in only one feature are isolated, and adjustments are made. The example that follows illustrates this process. The market data grid that accompanies the example is presented for purposes of illustration; all the adjustments shown will not be required in every application. Percentage adjustments for differences are provided.

Rental income for single-unit residences is typically stated as a dollar amount per month. For two- to four-unit apartment properties, rental income is typically broken down into monthly rent per square foot of gross living area or monthly rent per unit. Monthly rent per square foot of gross living area is used in the example, so a separate adjustment for differences in size is not needed. Note that the lot sizes of the comparable properties also vary slightly. No adjustment is made for lot size because the difference is usually negligible.

Example

In analyzing the market for a subject property, an appraiser finds a number of closely comparable rental properties. These properties vary in terms of size, leasing dates, lease provisions (the payment of utilities), expense ratios, location, construction quality, room count, and lot size. The rent data are displayed in Table 19.2 and adjusted in the market data grid (Table 19.3). The market rent of the subject is estimated to be $0.60 per square foot of gross living area per month.

Elements of Comparison

In estimating the monthly market rent the subject should command, adjustments are made to the actual rents of comparable properties for

- Transactional variations, chiefly market conditions and lease provisions
- Characteristics that influence the amount of income the property can generate such as location, size, quality, condition, and amenities
- Variations in operating expenses

---

5. The data used to estimate the market rent that the subject should command may come from the same sale properties used to derive the *GRM* or from different sale properties.

Table 19.2	Adjustment of Rent Data				
	Subject	**Rental 1**	**Rental 2**	**Rental 3**	**Rental 4**
Monthly rent	?	$915	$1,100	$950	$1,100
Gross living area in sq. ft.	1,450	1,450	1,475	1,500	1,475
Date of lease	–	6 mos.	Current	Current	Current
Lease provisions					
Payment of utilities	Tenant	Tenant	Owner	Tenant	Owner
Expense ratio*	–	25%	30%	30%	30%
Location	–	Inferior	Similar	Superior	Similar
Construction	–	Similar	Similar	Similar	Superior
Room count	6/3/2	6/3/2	7/3/2	6/3/2	6/3/2
Basement	Finished	Finished	Finished	Finished	Finished
Garage	2-car	2-car	2-car	2-car	2-car
Lot size in sq. ft.	9,450	9,450	9,475	9,450	9,475

* Expense ratios are derived by dividing total operating expenses by rental income.

Table 19.3	Market Data Grid for Market Rent Analysis								
	Subject	**Rental 1**		**Rental 2**		**Rental 3**		**Rental 4**	
Monthly rent	?	$915		$1,100		$950		$1,100	
Gross living area in sq. ft.	1,450	1,450		1,475		1,500		1,475	
Rent per sq. ft. of gross living area	–	$0.63		$0.75		$0.63		$0.75	
		Descr.	**Adj.**	**Descr.**	**Adj.**	**Descr.**	**Adj.**	**Descr.**	**Adj.**
Market conditions and lease provisions									
Date of lease	–	6 mos.	-0.03 (5%)	Current	0	Current	0	Current	0
Lease provisions: Payment of utilities	Tenant	Tenant	0	Owner	-0.12 (0.75 – 0.63)	Tenant	0	Owner	-0.12 (0.75 - 0.63)
Operating expenses									
Expense ratio	–	25%	-0.03 (5%)	30%	0	30%	0	30%	0
Characteristics influencing income									
Location	–	Inferior	+0.03 (5%)	Similar	0	Superior	-0.03 (5%)	Similar	0
Construction	–	Similar	0	Similar	0	Similar	0	Superior	-0.075 (10%)
Room count	6	6 (similar)	0	7 (superior)	-0.03 (5%)	6 (similar)	0	6 (similar)	0
Net adjustment*			-0.03		-0.15		-0.03		-0.195
Adjusted rent per sq. ft. of gross living area			$0.60		$0.60		$0.60		$0.555

* Difference between all positive and negative adjustments applied to each comparable or total adjustments if only negative or positive adjustments have been applied to the comparable.

Market Conditions and Lease Provisions

Changing market conditions can alter property income over time. When this is the case, the rental data of the comparable properties must be adjusted to reflect changes in market conditions. A percentage adjustment for market conditions is derived by analyzing the trend in rentals of income-producing property over several years. If all the rental data are current, a separate adjustment for market conditions is not needed unless market conditions have changed appreciably.

At times a market conditions adjustment may be needed when the data are only a few months old. If the rental data analyzed reflect a seasonal peak or trough, the estimate of rent derived from these data may be distorted. Many markets experience seasonal fluctuations in supply and demand that may affect property rents, particularly in areas where most leases turn over once a year. An appraiser should adjust comparable rents for these seasonal fluctuations when estimating the typical monthly rental for the subject property over the course of an entire year.

Rents can only be truly comparable if lease provisions are similar. An adjustment must be made for any significant lease difference that affects the rent a property can command or the obligations and expenses of the landlord. Adjustments for lease provisions are common when a property owner pays for utilities and when off-street parking is provided as part of the lease agreement. A downward adjustment is made when the comparable's lease terms are more favorable to the tenant than those included with the subject property; upward adjustments are made for leases that are favorable to the owner. An appraiser would also consider the effect of a long-term lease at below-market levels.

A landlord's reputation for honoring lease terms and performing maintenance and repairs punctually may also influence the actual rent of a property. If the appraiser finds that a comparable property is generating a lower rent because the landlord has an unusually poor maintenance record, an upward adjustment of the comparable rent may be justified.

The amount of rent charged is an important provision of the lease. An overly high asking rent can discourage prospective tenants and reduce the property's occupancy rate. There is a correlation between rental rates and occupancy rates in most markets.

Property Characteristics That Influence Income

Many features influence the rent a property is able to command. Location is a primary consideration. Tenants usually prefer a secure, central location with a pleasant view, adequate light, and available parking. Access to public transportation, proximity to public and private services and entertainment, and good linkages with workplaces and commercial centers are advantages in most rental markets.

The size of the building area is another important factor in most markets. Size needs vary with typical household sizes, the income of tenants, and the sizes of competitive properties in the area. Adjustments for size differences are based on an analysis of the trend in rents per square foot of gross living area in the market region.

Operating Expenses

Adjustments for variations in leases and the characteristics that influence property income must be made before the market rent of the subject property can be estimated. Some further adjustment may be necessary if the subject property has an expense-to-income ratio that is especially high or low. Variations in this ratio can affect the value of properties even when the income they produce remains constant.

Data Collection and Rent Survey

An appraiser may have difficulty compiling all the rental data needed to complete the first two steps of the income capitalization approach. Experienced appraisers collect relevant information continuously and keep it on file for use in specific appraisal assignments. Newspaper advertisements are a good source of data for analyzing trends in rents. Asking rents and actual rents do not usually vary as much as asking prices and sale prices for similar property. Interviews with landlords, tenants, real estate brokers, property managers, and neighbors can also provide useful information. In addition to rents and sales, data on typical expenses for a variety of residential properties should be collected. The appraiser can file these data by date and property type in a database for future use.[6]

In performing an appraisal the appraiser may collect required market data by conducting a *rent survey*. The focus of a rent survey is the subject property. The appraiser notes the size and characteristics of the subject property and interviews the current tenant or tenants. The appraiser asks about the rent being paid, anticipated rent increases or decreases, the benefits and drawbacks of the property, whether the rent and lease provisions are fair, and whether the tenant plans to leave when the lease expires. The actual rent and lease provisions may not be supported in the current market, but these data provide a good starting point for the appraiser's investigation.

The appraiser then researches the properties from which the *GRM* and comparable rents are to be derived. A separate data collection checklist can be completed for each rental property to help organize the data and ensure that the appraiser has collected all the necessary information. The location of the property, the names of the tenant and the landlord, and a brief rental history can be recorded on the form along with the property size, condition, special features, and other pertinent data. This data can be stored in a computerized database for future use.

Neighbors and tenants can frequently supply valuable information on the desirability of a property. Rental data should be verified, if pos-

---

6. All the quantitative data an appraiser collects can be stored electronically in a database. The appraiser can then access and disseminate that information quickly.

sible, by interviewing both the tenant and the landlord. The appraiser determines the amount of rent that is actually being paid, not how much the landlord would like to obtain for the property.

Data are collected for each rental property separately and additional information is often needed. A brief sales history of the property and a schedule of expenses can be useful. Sometimes expenses are detailed in a published operating statement compiled by the property owner for tax purposes. Accounting methods vary, so figures obtained from operating statements should be examined critically.

Application of *GRM* to Monthly Market Rent

To arrive at the market value of a residence using the income capitalization approach, the monthly market rent of the residence is estimated and then multiplied by the *GRM* selected. If, for example, a *GRM* of 140 is selected based on market analysis, and the monthly market rent of the subject property is estimated to be $1,200, the property's market value would be estimated as follows:

Estimated monthly market rent of property being appraised	$1,200
Times gross rent multiplier	× 140
Indicated market value	$168,000

In some situations it may be necessary to calculate market rent on an annual basis. Assume that the property in question rents for $1,400 per month during the nine-month school year and $900 per month during the remaining three months. The annual property rent is $15,300 ([9 × $1,400] + [3 × $900]) and the average monthly rent is $15,300/12, or $1,275. When this rent is multiplied by the *GRM* of 140, the indicated value of the property can be calculated as follows:

Average monthly rent of property being appraised	$1,275
Times gross rent multiplier	×140
Indicated market value	$178,500

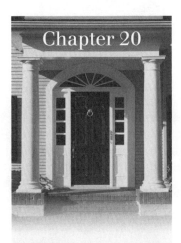

Chapter 20

Final Reconciliation

The last analytical step in the valuation process is the final reconciliation of value estimates. If more than one approach to value is developed, the indicated values must be reconciled to arrive at a final opinion of value. In some cases, the final opinion of value may be a range, but most often the final opinion will be a finite or point value conclusion.

In fact, reconciliation occurs throughout the valuation process. Sometimes different results are obtained from a single approach. In the cost approach, for example, estimates of depreciation may vary, depending on the method employed. In the sales comparison approach the adjusted sale prices of comparable properties can indicate different values; qualitative analysis may also have to be considered. In the income capitalization approach, rents and *GRMs* are reconciled. Some appraisers choose to reconcile these variations within the individual approaches only after the data associated with the other valuation approaches have been considered. In any case, all remaining differences in the value opinions derived must be reconciled at this stage in the valuation process.

Final reconciliation begins with a review of the entire appraisal. The purpose and intended use of the appraisal, the methods of data collection, and the analytical tools employed are reexamined in reconciliation. Each step of

Opinion versus Estimate

The definition of *appraisal* in the Uniform Standards of Professional Appraisal Practice was recently changed from *an estimate of value* to *an opinion of value*. In this textbook, *opinion* has been used where the term specifically describes the results of the valuation process. *Estimate* has been used for intermediate value conclusions within the valuation process and for more generic references.

The formal distinction between *estimates of value* and *opinions of value* has a further resonance since the introduction of automated valuation models (AVMs) into the residential appraisal arena. An AVM (and any other form of statistical modeling) can generate an estimate, whereas an opinion of value can only be developed by a person.

final value opinion. The range of values or the single dollar figure derived from the reconciliation of value indications and stated in the appraisal report.

the valuation process is tested for logic, consistency, and appropriateness. Mathematical errors are corrected and gaps in the data are filled in with further research. If the data are inadequate and additional data are not available, the effect of the incomplete data on the valuation conclusion is explained.

The results produced by each of the approaches to value are examined. The greatest emphasis is placed on the approach or approaches that are most applicable to the problem and make use of the most reliable and representative data. Finally, a single value indication or a range of values is developed. The value opinion should be rounded to reflect market norms and the appraiser's confidence in its accuracy. The value conclusion is presented to the client with the reasoning and documentation in the appraisal report.

The measures of central tendency (mean, median, and mode) may serve as useful tools in final reconciliation,[1] but the final value opinion does not simply represent the average of different value opinions. No mechanical formula is used to select one indication over the others; rather, the appraiser relies on the application of appraisal judgment and experience. The appraiser's judgment, experience, and proper application of appraisal techniques are critical in final reconciliation.

Review

To provide a basis for final reconciliation, an appraiser reviews the entire valuation process. The nature of this review and the need for it depend on the complexity of the assignment and the appraiser's confidence in the data and the analytical techniques applied. Even experienced appraisers review their valuations before submitting the conclusions to their clients to reduce the chances of error.

To perform a comprehensive review, the appraiser proceeds methodically through each step of the valuation process. Typically an appraiser considers whether

1. The appraisal is logical and the stated conclusion is appropriate to the purpose and intended use of the appraisal.
2. The data are accurate, adequate, and properly analyzed.
3. The data have been used in a consistent manner within each approach and are correlated from one approach to another.
4. The calculations are correct.

---

1. The measures of central tendency include the mean, the median, and the mode. The mean is the arithmetic average of the sum of the items in an array of data. The median represents the middle value in an array of an uneven number of items or the average of the two middle values in an array of an even number of items. The mode is the value appearing with the greatest frequency in an array. The average of the high-end value and the low-end value in a range of values is also a useful gauge. (See Chapter 22 for further information on statistical measures and applications.) The utility of these measures increases with the quantity of data analyzed. It is useful to apply measures of central tendency even when other reconciliation criteria are available.

5. The data and resulting opinion of value are reflective of the subject property and its market.

Logical Answer to the Client's Question

An appraisal is performed to provide an answer to a client's specific question, which the client will use to make some decision concerning the real estate in question. The appraiser must make sure that the solution provided is appropriate and is presented in a way that is meaningful and useful to the client.

Thus, the first question to ask is: Do the approaches and methods applied lead to meaningful conclusions that relate to the purpose, use, and scope of the appraisal? In most residential appraisals the purpose of the valuation will be to estimate market value, and the intended use of the appraisal will be to serve as a basis for a mortgage loan decision or a relocation purchase offer. The definition of value employed should be reviewed along with the assumptions and limiting conditions applicable to the appraisal to ensure that the value opinion derived satisfies all of the client's requirements as well as those of the appraisal profession. The extent of work carried out in collecting, confirming, and reporting data should correspond to the scope of the appraisal as described in the definition of the appraisal problem.

If a valuation is to be used in court, the value definition should be closely scrutinized. The definition used in a particular jurisdiction may contain subtleties that merit special attention. The value conclusion must be consistent with the property interests being appraised. The court may seek specific evidence regarding the amount a seller could obtain for a property in the open market or the amount a buyer would be willing to pay in the same market. A value indication reflecting the current highest and best use of the property may be sought, rather than one that considers other uses for which the property might be legally, physically, and economically suited. Various legal considerations may affect the character of the assignment and the appraiser's conclusions.

Accuracy and Adequacy of Data and Analysis

The data an appraiser collects must be factual. The data must support the conclusions drawn and provide a convincing representation of market patterns. Accuracy is enhanced if the appraiser is knowledgeable about the sources of the data and their relative reliability. Certain information cannot be taken too seriously. For example, market projections issued by local chambers of commerce can be inaccurate. Nevertheless, this type of information should be considered because it may supply important leads. Suspect information can be checked against data from independent sources. As a general rule, firsthand research is more persuasive than outdated, generalized information obtained from reference manuals.

Critical details pertaining to the subject and comparable properties and aspects of transactions that may have influenced sale prices must always be verified personally. The appraiser should interview one of the parties to the transaction, preferably the buyer or the seller, although attorneys, real estate agents, brokers, and lenders can also be contacted. Often documented evidence that is verified by one of these individuals is the most reliable and compelling form of data for appraisal purposes.

Appraisers should avoid using suspicious or questionable data. A property sale between related parties may not qualify as an arm's-length transaction and therefore the property should not be used as a comparable. The comparable sales selected must be truly representative of the market.

Using a reliable data source may not be enough. The appraiser must also be satisfied that the data accurately represent the thinking and behavior of market participants. To ensure that the data are representative, an appraiser attempts to locate and study a broad sample of comparable properties located in the neighborhood delineated for the subject property. A large base of general market data can also provide support for the valuation conclusion, even if these data are not derived from perfectly comparable properties. General information on market trends can be almost as revealing as specific sales of very similar properties. Therefore, it is very important that appraisers maintain good records on all kinds of real estate transactions.

To review the data collection effort, the appraiser first reexamines the purpose of the appraisal, the property interests being valued, and the assumptions and limiting conditions. Next the appraiser scrutinizes the neighborhood analysis. The comparables selected should all be located within the boundaries of the subject neighborhood or in similar, competitive neighborhoods within the overall market area.

By the reconciliation stage of the valuation, the appraiser has a broader picture of the market and can better judge whether the comparables are truly comparable. The observations made during the field inspection are also examined. Any changes in property boundaries, additions to the improvements since their original construction, and subsequent encroachments or easements should be carefully noted. Such changes can alter the appraiser's market value conclusion.

The accuracy and reliability of transactional data should be ascertained. Cost data are reviewed. Income and expense data must also be reexamined.

Consistency

An appraiser checks the consistency of the data and the reasoning applied in each valuation approach as well as the correlation between the approaches. Although the valuation approaches reflect different appraisal strategies, the data considered in the different approaches should be consistent.

To ensure consistency, the same highest and best use conclusion must be used throughout the appraisal. In the cost approach the appraiser

The appraiser should ask the following questions concerning:

Purpose of appraisal, property interest being valued, and assumptions and limiting conditions
- Given these parameters, was the data collection effort complete?
- Were city and regional data collected to provide a background for neighborhood analysis?
- If these data were collected, how reliable and current are they?
- Do market trends in real estate values support the adjustments for market conditions applied to the comparable properties?

Neighborhood analysis
- How were the neighborhood boundaries drawn?
- In light of what an appraiser has learned from the field inspection, should these boundaries be redrawn?
- If so, does this change affect the selection or reliability of the data used?

Comparability of comparables
- Do they provide the best indications of the value of the subject property in the market area?
- If they do not, what other evidence would be more persuasive?
- Would it be worthwhile to replace a comparable or include additional comparables?
- Have all available data on the subject property been used?
- If the subject property has been sold recently, has all information about that transaction been considered?
- How confident is the appraiser of the reasonableness of the adjustments made for property differences?

Observations during field inspection
- Does this information correspond to published information about the subject and comparable properties?
- Are the sketches and maps that were used accurate and up-to-date?

Accuracy and reliability of transactional data
- What sources were contacted for this information?
- How were the data verified—by the buyer, the seller, an attorney, or a lender?
- Is the information complete?
- Are sale prices, sales concessions, and special financing arrangements specified?
- Are any items of personal property included in the transactions listed?
- How were adjustments for special financing derived?
- Were the methods appropriate?

Cost data
- If a cost service was used, is the appraiser satisfied with the reliability of the cost estimates?
- Should these costs be confirmed by local contractors?
- Were costs for all the components of the subject property taken into account?
- Was a reasonable amount added for entrepreneurial profit?
- How reliable is the appraiser's estimate of land value?
- Are the estimates of various types of depreciation well supported?

Income and expense data
- Do the comparables have similar expense ratios and lease terms?
- Do the monthly rents of the comparables accurately reflect what the subject property can expect to command?
- Are these rent levels supported by the current market?
- Is the reconciliation of *GRMs* appropriate?

values the land or site as though vacant and the property as improved on the basis of the same use.

In reconciliation an appraiser checks to see that no item has been mistakenly counted twice in any portion of the appraisal. In the sales comparison approach, for example, adjustments should not be made twice for the same difference under two separate headings. Sometimes an adjustment for a difference in age is partially duplicated in an adjustment for physical condition. If these adjustments reflect the same difference, only one should be used.

In the cost approach an appraiser could mistakenly penalize a property twice by considering the same item of depreciation under two separate categories. If, for example, the functional obsolescence of a kitchen appliance is measured in terms of the cost to remove and replace it, additional depreciation cannot be charged for the deteriorated physical condition of the same appliance.

Review of Calculations

All mathematical calculations should be checked, preferably by someone other than the person who originally made them. Errors in arithmetic can lead to erroneous value indications and undermine the credibility of the entire appraisal. It is easy for people to overlook their own errors, so an independent check of numerical calculations is an important part of the appraiser's review.

Reconciliation Criteria

After the appraisal has been reviewed and the appropriateness of the value opinions derived in the various approaches has been determined, differences in the value opinions must be reconciled. There is no simple arithmetical or statistical procedure for reconciling value opinions. Rather, appraisers reach a final value conclusion or a range of conclusions by assessing their confidence in each estimate. The degree of confidence associated with a given opinion usually depends on the appropriateness of the valuation approach to the problem at hand and the quality and quantity of the data used.

Appropriateness

The criterion of appropriateness helps an appraiser decide how much weight to accord the value opinion derived from a particular approach. The appropriateness of a given approach is usually related to the type of property being appraised and the viability of the market. Market value reflects how the market perceives value, so the approach that most closely mirrors market perceptions usually produces the most credible results.

In many residential appraisals the sales comparison approach is accorded the greatest consideration. Sales comparison reflects the thinking of most buyers and sellers, who study and compare the prices of similar properties to find a reasonable price at which to buy or sell.

However, this approach may not be applicable in areas where sales are few or when the property being appraised has unique features.

In these situations, market participants may base their value decisions on cost factors. The cost approach is more appropriate when an improvement is newer and when it represents the highest and best use of the property. In these instances, depreciation is minimal. Cost analysis might also be important if typical purchasers interested in the property would plan on making substantial repairs or renovations.

In valuing older properties with a great deal of incurable depreciation, the cost approach tends to be less appropriate. Market participants, like real estate appraisers, have difficulty deciding how much depreciation the property has incurred.

When an active rental market exists and potential purchasers are interested in the property's ability to generate revenue, income capitalization may be the most reliable approach. The income capitalization approach is applicable when sufficient rental and sales data can be obtained. The income capitalization approach is typically not appropriate in market areas where investors are not active.

Each of the approaches must be viewed in light of the scope of work as described in the Uniform Standards of Professional Appraisal Practice. The first question to be asked is whether the approach is "applicable." If not, the appraiser simply notes its consideration and that it does not apply. If an approach does apply, the appraiser must then assess the "necessity" of the approach. If the approach is necessary to develop a credible value opinion, then it must be developed and included in the report. If it is not necessary, then it may be omitted but the omission must be addressed in the scope of work. In all cases, scope of work decisions need to be discussed with the client.

Quality of Data

The specific items of data used in an appraisal may reflect different degrees of accuracy. Therefore, an appraiser should consider the relative quality of the data used in each approach to weigh the reliability of the estimates derived. For example, are the cost data and depreciation estimates used in the cost approach as accurate as the adjustments made in the sales comparison approach or the market rent data and gross rent multipliers used in the income capitalization approach? An appraiser may have more confidence in the accuracy of the data used in one approach than the data used in another.

There are several ways to measure the quality of the data used in the sales comparison approach. If the adjustments made to the sale prices of properties considered comparable are too large or too numerous, then the margin of error is broad and accuracy is diminished. The need for many adjustments suggests that the comparable properties are not truly comparable. To judge the quality of the data, an appraiser may look at the number of adjustments made to each comparable. As the number of adjustments increases, the reliability of the value indication derived from that comparable decreases.

Another important measure is the size of the net adjustment as a percentage of the comparable's unadjusted sale price. The net adjustment to a comparable is calculated by adding the dollar amounts of all positive adjustments and deducting the sum of all negative adjustments. One problem with this test of comparability is that the appraiser cannot assume that positive and negative adjustments cancel each other out. A comparable with a net adjustment similar to that of other comparables may seem reasonable when, actually, either the positive or the negative adjustments have been incorrectly estimated. Also, a comparable may require a large degree of adjustment in a positive direction and an equally large amount of adjustment in a negative direction, generating a small net adjustment. In this case, the net adjustment may be small, but the sale may not be highly comparable to the subject. For these reasons appraisers also consider gross adjustments. The gross adjustment to a comparable is the sum of the amounts of all the adjustments made to the comparable's sale price, regardless of whether these adjustments are positive or negative. This sum is expressed as a percentage of the unadjusted sale price.

At times, however, the gross size of dollar adjustments may not be a good indicator of the quality of the comparable data either, particularly if few adjustments are needed. A single large adjustment may be more accurate and defensible than many smaller adjustments. For example, an appraiser may find abundant market evidence in a community to indicate the value added by a swimming pool, a garage, or an extra bedroom. An adjustment for the presence or absence of such a large item in a comparable might result in a gross adjustment that is larger than the gross adjustments made to other comparables. However, greater accuracy may be attributed to this adjustment because there is reliable market evidence to support it.

The tests described above are applied to check the reliability of each sale considered comparable as a basis for deriving a value indication for the subject property. These tests may also be used to reconcile different value opinions in the sales comparison approach and to determine the relative applicability of the approach.

The overall persuasiveness of the sales comparison approach is often enhanced by using a large number of sales considered comparable, but using a certain number of sales cannot guarantee a reasonable conclusion. The number of sales examined depends on the reliability of the sales and the client's requirements. Some clients insist on a minimum number of sales. The appropriateness of the valuation approach applied and the quality of the data employed determine the relevance of the value opinion derived from a given approach or sale considered comparable.

gross adjustment. The total adjustment to each comparable sale price calculated in absolute terms. All the adjustments, both positive and negative, are added together to determine the gross adjustment to a comparable sale price.

net adjustment. The difference between the total positive and negative adjustments made to a comparable sale price.

Quantity of Data

Although the data used in a given approach meet the criteria of appropriateness and quality, they may still be insufficient. When few reliable, recent sales are available but cost and depreciation data are abundant, increased emphasis may be given to the cost approach. Similarly, abundant data on one comparable may increase the appraiser's confidence in the value indication derived from this sale.

Of course, an appraiser will not be persuaded by the quantity of data alone. The data considered must be both relevant and accurate. When these data are interpreted by an experienced appraiser in a manner consistent with the purpose of the appraisal, a reliable value opinion will result. Sound appraisal conclusions rest on the application of reasoning and judgment.

Final Value Indication

After the various value opinions are weighed, the appraiser must reconcile them. The final value indication may be expressed as a point estimate, as a range of value, or as a value within a designated range.

A point estimate is the traditional way of expressing a value conclusion. The estimate of the subject property's value is stated as a single dollar amount--e.g., $150,000. A point estimate that reflects the appraiser's best opinion as to the approximate value of a property is required in many types of appraisals. Point estimates are requested for real estate tax purposes, just compensation estimates, and certain property transfer decisions. They are also used to calculate federal income tax depreciation deductions and to determine lease terms based on value. Lenders require point estimates because loan terms are based on loan-to-value (LTV) ratios. Clients may expect a point estimate even when they have not specifically requested one because this type of opinion has been customary in the past.

One problem associated with point estimates is that the presentation of a single figure may suggest greater precision than is warranted. Properly understood, a point estimate implies a range of value in which the property value most probably lies. The estimate on which a value indication is based is impartial, well-reasoned, and the very best a professional appraiser can provide in view of the evidence gathered and analyzed. Nevertheless, a point estimate is an opinion of the most likely dollar value of the interest being appraised subject to certain qualifying conditions. This opinion may, in fact, be too high or too low.

Occasionally an appraiser may have reason to avoid offering a "best" opinion and instead specify a range of value between two dollar figures. By reporting a range, the appraiser is indicating that the actual value is probably no lower than the low end of the range and no higher than the high end.

Stating a range of value can present serious problems, however. A wide range is of no use to a client, but a narrow range can be incorrectly interpreted as a guarantee that the price will fall between the extreme values. A client who is provided with a value range is likely to hold fast to whichever extreme suits his or her purposes.

Rounding

It is customary to round appraisal conclusions to reflect the lack of precision associated with them. Rounding may be based on rules of significant digits, but often a value conclusion is simply rounded to two or three digits.

Rounding should reflect how prices are expressed in the market. If market study reveals a pattern in pricing, the appraiser should round accordingly.

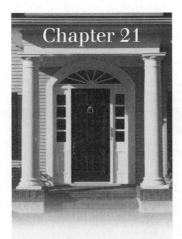

Chapter 21

The Appraisal Report

Like a well-crafted rhetorical argument, an appraisal report leads its reader from the definition of the appraisal problem through the appraiser's reasoning and relevant descriptive data to a specific value conclusion. The appraiser must present all facts, analysis, and conclusions clearly and succinctly. The length, type, and content of appraisal reports are based on the client's needs, regulatory requirements, the courts, the type of property being appraised, and the nature of the valuation problem.

Every appraisal report is prepared to answer a particular question and provide information needed by a client. Some common appraisal questions are

- What is the market value of the property?
- What is the highest and best use of the land as though vacant and the property as improved?
- What is the value of the part taken in condemnation and what is the damage or benefit to the remainder of the property as a result of the taking?

Reporting Requirements of the Uniform Standards of Professional Appraisal Practice

To ensure the quality of appraisal reports, The Appraisal Foundation has set minimum standards for the factual content, descriptive material, and scope of work. In addition, the appraiser is obligated to identify the type and definition of value, the intended use, and the intended users in all types of appraisal reports. Professional appraisal organizations, the individual states, and most government agencies have adopted these standards. To comply with the reporting requirements of the current Uniform Standards of Professional Appraisal Practice (USPAP) as promulgated by the Appraisal Standards Board of The Appraisal Foundation, an appraiser must communicate each analysis, opinion, and conclusion in a manner that is not misleading. Standards Rule 2-1 states:

> Each written or oral real property appraisal report must
>
> (a) clearly and accurately set forth the appraisal in a manner that will not be misleading;
>
> (b) contain sufficient information to enable the intended users of the appraisal to understand the report properly; and
>
> (c) clearly and accurately disclose all assumptions, extraordinary assumptions, hypothetical conditions, and limiting conditions used in the assignment.

Specific reporting requirements for written real property appraisal reports are set forth in Standards Rule 2-2. Standards Rule 2-3 states the required certification to be included with all written reports. Reporting requirements for oral reports are presented in Standards Rule 2-4.

Various types of reports can be identified by the reporting requirements applicable to them.[1]

Types of Reports

An appraisal report may be

1. Oral
2. Written

There are three types of written reports:

1. Self-contained
2. Summary
3. Restricted use

Usually a report is presented in the format dictated by the needs of the client. However, USPAP states that the ultimate format decision rests with the appraiser.

Oral Reports

An appraiser may make an oral report if the circumstances or the needs of the client do not permit or warrant a written report. Sometimes a client asks for the appraiser's opinion without detailed documentation. In this case, the appraiser must perform the analysis required and keep all the material, data, and working papers used to prepare the report in a file.[2]

---

1. See Standard 2 and Standards Rule 2-2 in the Uniform Standards of Professional Appraisal Practice (2006 edition).

2. See the Ethics Rule of the Uniform Standards of Professional Appraisal Practice for regulations governing record keeping, including the length of time an appraiser must retain a workfile.

Expert testimony is considered an oral report whether it is presented in deposition or in court. However, most oral reports are not made under oath; they are communicated to the client in person or by telephone. Today some appraisers transmit their reports to clients electronically, taking advantage of the capabilities of e-mail and EDI technology.

Each oral report should include a property identification and the facts, assumptions, conditions, and reasoning on which the value conclusion is based. Before communicating an oral report, the appraiser should file all notes and data relating to the assignment and prepare a complete memorandum of the appraisal analysis, conclusion, and opinion.

The Uniform Standards of Professional Appraisal Practice have specific reporting requirements for oral reports. Standards Rule 2-4 requires that oral reports address the substantive matters set forth for summary written reports. In cases where testimony is presented, a copy of the transcript or a summary of the testimony is acceptable as the file documentation.

> **oral report.** An unwritten appraisal report that includes a property description as well as all facts, assumptions, conditions, and reasoning on which the value conclusion is based. The reporting requirements for oral reports, which are the same as those applied to written reports, are set forth in the Standards Rules relating to Standard 2 of the Uniform Standards of Professional Appraisal Practice.
>
> **written appraisal report.** Any written communication of an appraisal, appraisal review, or appraisal consulting service that is transmitted to the client upon completion of an assignment.

Written Reports

According to Standards Rule 2-2, "Each written real property appraisal report must be prepared under one of the following three options and prominently state which option is used: Self-Contained Appraisal Report, Summary Appraisal Report, or Restricted Use Appraisal Report."

The appraiser may not be present when the report is reviewed or examined, so the report must be representative of the market and the appraiser's analysis. Regardless of the result, a good report will give the client a favorable impression of the appraiser's professional competence.

Self-Contained Report

A self-contained report usually requires the most thorough and time-consuming preparation. Within such reports appraisers have the opportunity to support and explain their opinions and conclusions and convince the readers of the soundness of the final value indication. This type of report answers the client's questions in writing and substantiates these answers with facts, reasoning, and conclusions. To be most useful to the client, the appraisal report must present adequate, pertinent supporting data and logical analysis that lead to the appraiser's conclusions.

A self-contained report describes all the facts and appraisal methods and techniques that have been applied in the valuation process to arrive at the value opinion or another conclusion. The report demonstrates the appraiser's ability to interpret relevant data, select appropriate valuation methods and techniques, and ultimately develop an opinion of a specifically defined value.

In preparing an appraisal report, descriptive material should be separated from analysis and interpretation. Typically factual and descriptive data are presented in the early sections of the report so that subsequent sections on data analysis and interpretation can refer to these facts and discuss how they contribute to the final value opinion. Unnecessary repetition is undesirable, but the presentation of data may depend on the nature and length of the report. Self-contained reports are usually organized to follow the steps in the valuation process.

Summary Report

As its name implies, a summary report summarizes the information reported and is therefore usually a shorter report. The basic difference between a self-contained report and a summary report is the level of detail provided. The information presented in a two-page section of a self-contained report might appear in two paragraphs in a summary report. Similarly, material presented in narrative form in a self-contained report might be presented in tabular form in a summary report.

The specific reporting requirements for a summary report do not differ greatly from the requirements for a self-contained report. Note, however, that the term *describe* as used in the requirements for a self-contained report is replaced with the term *summarize* in appropriate sections of the requirements for a summary report, indicating the more general level of detail required in the latter type of appraisal report.

Restricted Use Report

The third type of written report is the restricted use report. This type of report is less detailed and must include a use restriction that limits the client's reliance on and use of the report. In fact, the client must be noted as the only user of this type of report. The reporting requirements for this type of report are substantially different than those for either self-contained or summary reports.

The reporting requirements for the three types of written reports can be compared by scanning Table 21.1.

Highest and Best Use Statements in the Appraisal Report

All appraisal reports that use a market value definition should contain a statement that describes the appraiser's highest and best use conclusions. When the appraisal is performed as part of an analysis assignment to determine highest and best use, the analysis and conclusion of highest and best use are described in considerable detail and probable future incomes or returns are calculated. In most appraisal assignments, the highest and best use of the site should be reported along with a statement that the opinion was made under the theoretical presumption that the land was vacant and available for development.

Table 21.1 Comparison of Report Types

Self-Contained Appraisal Report	Summary Appraisal Report	Restricted Use Appraisal Report
i. State the identity of the client and any intended users, by name or type.	i. State the identity of the client and any intended users, by name or type.	i. State the identity of the client, by name or type; and state a prominent use restriction that limits use of the report to the client and warns that the appraiser's opinions and conclusions set forth in the report may not be understood properly without additional information in the appraiser's workfile.
ii. State the intended use of the appraisal.	ii. State the intended use of the appraisal.	ii. State the intended use of the appraisal.
iii. Describe information sufficient to identify the real estate involved in the appraisal, including the physical and economic property characteristics relevant to the assignment.	iii. Summarize information sufficient to identify the real estate involved in the appraisal, including the physical and economic property characteristics relevant to the assignment.	ii. State information sufficient to identify the real estate involved in the appraisal.
iv. State the real property interest appraised.	iv. State the real property interest appraised.	iv. State the real property interest appraised.
v. State the type and definition of value and cite the source of the definition.	v. State the type and definition and cite the source of the definition.	v. State the type of value and cite the source of its definition.
vi. State the effective date of the appraisal and the date of the report.	vi. State the effective date of the appraisal and the date of the report.	vi. State the effective date of the appraisal and the date of the report.
vii. Describe the scope of work used to develop the appraisal.	vii. Summarize the scope of work used to develop the appraisal.	vii. State the scope of work used to develop the appraisal.
viii. Describe the information analyzed, the appraisal methods and techniques employed, and the reasoning that supports the analyses, opinions, and conclusions; exclusion of the sales comparison approach, cost approach, or income approach must be explained.	viii. Summarize the information analyzed, the appraisal methods and techniques employed, and the reasoning that supports the analyses, opinions, and conclusions; exclusion of the sales comparison approach, cost approach, or income approach must be explained.	viii. State the appraisal methods and techniques employed, state the value opinion(s) and conclusion(s) reached, and reference the workfile; exclusion of the sales comparison approach, cost approach, or income approach must be explained.
ix. State the use of the real estate existing as of the date of value and the use of the real estate reflected in the appraisal; and, when an opinion of highest and best use was developed by the appraiser, describe the support and rationale for that opinion.	ix. State the use of the real estate existing as of the date of value and the use of the real estate reflected in the appraisal; and, when an opinion of highest and best use was developed by the appraiser, summarize the support and rationale for that opinion.	ix. State the use of the real estate existing as of the date of value and the use of the real estate reflected in the appraisal; and, when an opinion of highest and best use was developed by the appraiser, state that opinion.
x. Clearly and conspicuously: · state all extraordinary assumptions and hypothetical conditions; and · state that their use might have affected the assignment results.	x. Clearly and conspicuously: · state all extraordinary assumptions and hypothetical conditions; and · state that their use might have affected the assignment results.	x. Clearly and conspicuously: · state all extraordinary assumptions and hypothetical conditions; and · state that their use might have affected the assignment results.
xi. Include a signed certification in accordance with Standards Rule 2-3.	xi. Include a signed certification in accordance with Standards Rule 2-3.	xi. Include a signed certification in accordance with Standards Rule 2-3.

Note: No comment sections are included in this chart; the chart is prepared for discussion purposes only.

Source: Uniform Standards of Professional Appraisal Practice, 2006 edition.

Certification

In accordance with Standards Rule 2-3, all written reports must contain a certification similar in content to the following:

I certify that, to the best of my knowledge and belief:

- The statements of fact contained in this report are true and correct.
- The reported analyses, opinions, and conclusions are limited only by the reported assumptions and limiting conditions and are my personal, impartial, and unbiased professional analyses, opinions, and conclusions.
- I have no (or the specified) present or prospective interest in the property that is the subject of this report and no (or the specified) personal interest with respect to the parties involved.
- I have no bias with respect to the property that is the subject of this report or to the parties involved with this assignment.
- My engagement in this assignment was not contingent upon developing or reporting predetermined results.
- My compensation for completing this assignment is not contingent upon the development or reporting of a predetermined value or direction in value that favors the cause of the client, the amount of the value opinion, the attainment of a stipulated result, or the occurrence of a subsequent event directly related to the intended use of this appraisal.
- My analyses, opinions, and conclusions were developed, and this report has been prepared, in conformity with the Uniform Standards of Professional Appraisal Practice.
- I have (or have not) made a personal inspection of the property that is the subject of this report. (If more than one person signs this certification, the certification must clearly specify which individuals did and which individuals did not make a personal inspection of the appraised property.)
- No one provided significant real property appraisal assistance to the person signing this certification. (If there are exceptions, the name of each individual providing significant real property appraisal assistance must be stated.)

Standard Rule 2-2 states that the tasks performed by any individual providing appraisal assistance must also be summarized in the appraisal report.

Form Reports

In many appraisal situations, form reports meet the needs of financial institutions, insurance companies, and government agencies. In the secondary mortgage market created by government agencies and private organizations, form reports are required for the purchase and sale of most existing mortgages on residential properties. Because these clients review many appraisals, using a standard report form is efficient and convenient. When a form is used, those responsible for reviewing the appraisal know exactly where to find each category or item of data in the report. Specific primary lender criteria may call for something more than the information called for on a form report. By completing the form, however, an appraiser ensures that no item required by the secondary market has been overlooked. The Appraisal Institute's Guide Note 3 addresses the use of form reports for residential property. Each form report must comply with all reporting and certification requirements.

The method of valuation (i.e., scope of work) employed in an appraisal assignment and the resulting report is always determined by the nature of the specific appraisal problem. If a report form seems too rigid and does not provide for the inclusion of all the data that the appraiser believes to be pertinent, the relevant information and the appraiser's comments should be added as a supplement.

The appraiser should make sure that the completed report is consistent in its description of the property and provides all the data indicated by the categories listed. If the appraiser's determination of the highest and best use of the property does not conform to the use for which the form is appropriate, the form cannot be used. All data must be presented in a clear and comprehensible manner, and all form reports should include a proper certification and statement of limiting conditions.

The most widely used form report for residential appraisals is the Uniform Residential Appraisal Report (URAR) form, which is required by the Department of Housing and Urban Development (HUD), the Federal

---

Guide Note 3	The Use of Form Appraisal Reports for Residential Property

Introduction

Most residential appraisal assignments require a report on one of the approved forms used in the secondary mortgage market or by the employee-relocation industry.

Use of such forms does not lessen or change the appraiser's obligation to observe the requirements of the Standards of Professional Appraisal Practice. If a proposed appraisal assignment cannot be completed in accordance with the appraisal development and reporting requirements of USPAP and the Certification Standard and Code of Professional Ethics of the Appraisal Institute, the assignment must not be accepted.

Basis for Proper Evaluation

When using any form report, or signing a form report as a reviewer, it is the responsibility of the appraiser and the reviewer to ensure that the appropriate methods and techniques have been properly employed. Appropriate addenda must be added when additional information is required to complete the appraisal report in accordance with Standard 2 of USPAP.

Highest and best use appears on most forms merely as a box to be checked because the use of the form itself is a statement of highest and best use. Unless a detailed explanation is added to clarify, it is inappropriate to use a single-family dwelling report form if the appraiser concludes that the highest and best use of the property is a different use.

Summary of Standard Practices

1. Consider the intended use, purpose, definitions, assumptions, conditions, and limitations that are inherent in the form report used for a residential appraisal (S.R. 1-2 (a) through (h)).

2. Sign an appraisal report as a reviewer only when accepting full responsibility for the contents of the report (S.R. 2-3 and Standard 3).

3. Analyze and report any prior sales of the property being appraised within three years of the date of the appraisal (S.R. 1-5(b)(i), S.R. 2-2 9a) (ix), and 2-2(c)(ix)).

(Please Note: The purpose of the Guide Notes to the Standards of Professional Appraisal Practice is to provide Members with guidance as to how the requirements of the Standards may apply in specific situations.)

Housing Administration (FHA), the Department of Veterans Affairs (VA), the Farmers Home Administration (FmHA), Fannie Mae, and Freddie Mac for single-unit residential properties. Other forms used by government agencies are listed in Table 21.2.

The Employee Relocation Council (ERC) Residential Appraisal Report form was developed for use by members of the ERC, which is an independent organization that assists in the transfer of corporate employees. There are also other developer- or vendor-specific forms available. In all cases, it is the appraiser's responsibility to ensure that a specific form will accommodate a client's specific needs.

The URAR is specifically designed to be used for lending purposes. The Appraisal Institute has developed a series of form reports designed for use in appraisal assignments in which the client's needs may not be lending related. AI Reports™ are available from software vendors,

---

Table 21.2	Other Appraisal Forms and Their Uses	

Form	Name	Use
1004C	Manufactured Home Appraisal Report	A stand-alone (not an addendum) form used for manufactured home appraisals. This includes interior and exterior inspections of the improvements.
1004D	Appraisal Update and/or Completion Report	Designed to update a prior assignment within the USPAP requirements or to certify completion. Commonly used in new construction but can be used for stipulated repairs.
1025	Small Residential Income Property Appraisal Report	Designed for appraisals of two- to four-unit properties with interior and exterior inspections.
1073	Individual Condominium Unit Appraisal Report	Generally used for appraisals with interior and exterior inspections of individual condominium units. Not to be used for multiple units in the project.
1075	Exterior-Only Individual Condominium Unit Appraisal Report	Generally used for appraisals with exterior-only inspections of individual condominium units. Not to be used for multiple units in the project.
2000	One-Unit Residential Appraisal Field Review Report	Used for exterior-only reviews of single-unit homes including single-unit attached, detached, condominium, and cooperative units.
2000A	Two- to Four-Unit Residential Appraisal Field Review Report	Used for exterior-only reviews of two- to four-unit homes including attached, detached, and condominium units.
2055	Exterior-Only Inspection Residential Appraisal Report	Generally used for appraisals with exterior-only inspections of single-unit attached and detached homes. Commonly called the drive-by form.
2090	Individual Cooperative Interest Appraisal Report	Used for appraisals with interior and exterior inspections of single units in cooperative projects. Not found in all areas of the United States.
2095	Exterior-Only Inspection Individual Cooperative Interest Appraisal Report	Used for appraisals with exterior-only inspections of single units in cooperative projects.

Adapted from Mark Rattermann, *Using Residential Appraisal Report Forms: URAR 2005 (Form 1004) and Exterior Inspection (Form 2055)* (Chicago: Appraisal Institute, 2005), 2.

and guidelines for their completion can be downloaded from the Appraisal Institute Web site.

Uniform Residential Appraisal Report

Fannie Mae and Freddie Mac introduced the Uniform Residential Appraisal Report (URAR) form in 1986. This was the first time all major government agencies involved in mortgage activities agreed to use a common appraisal report form. A revised URAR form was released in June 1993, reflecting changes in industry standards and requirements over the intervening years as well as refinements of reporting standards. The newly updated form released in March 2005 is the result of changing market issues, which were not adequately addressed for the secondary mortage market and came to light in the aftermath of increasing values, property flipping, and escalating foreclosure rates in the early 2000s.

All appraisals for mortgages issued by Fannie Mae, Freddie Mac, HUD, VA, and FHA that may be sold in the secondary mortgage market must be communicated on the URAR form. This report form is designed for an appraisal of a one-unit property or a one-unit property with an accessory unit, including a unit in a planned unit development (PUD). The form is not designed to report an appraisal of a manufactured home or of a unit in a condominium or cooperative project.

A planned unit development is not a type of housing but, rather, a zoning alternative. PUD units may appear physically similar to condominium units, but the valuation of an individual PUD unit is now to be reported on the URAR Form 1004 only.

Individual Condominium Unit and Cooperative Interest Appraisal Report Forms

Fannie Mae Form 1073 is used for appraisals of individual condominium units with interior and exterior inspections. Form 1075 is used for appraisals of individual units with exterior-only inspections. Neither form should be used for multiple units in a project.

Freddie Mac/Fannie Mae Form 2090 is used for the appraisal of single units in cooperative projects with exterior and interior inspections. Form 2095 is used for the appraisal of single units in cooperative projects with exterior-only inspections.

All of these forms were revised in 2005 to be more consistent with the URAR form.

Small Residential Income Property Appraisal Report

The Small Residential Income Property Appraisal Report was also revised in 2005 to ensure conformity with the requirements of the Uniform Standards of Professional Appraisal Practice and to make the form consistent with the format of the URAR.

A small residential income property can be defined as a group of rental housing units, usually two to four, combined to create a multiple living space complex. This type of residential property shares many characteristics with apartment buildings; however, the owner of a small residential income property often occupies a unit within the complex whereas apartment properties are often professionally managed on behalf of an owner who does not live in the building. The fewer the number of units, the more ownership of a small residential income property takes on the character of an investment in a single-family home.

Employee Relocation Council Residential Appraisal Report

The Employee Relocation Council Residential Appraisal Report form is published by the ERC, a nonprofit membership organization founded in 1964. Its members include corporations, relocation service companies, brokers, and appraisers involved in the transfer of corporate employees.

The purpose of a relocation appraisal is to estimate the anticipated sale price of a relocating employee's primary residence, and the intended use of the appraisal is to assist an employer in facilitating the employee relocation process.

Filling Out Form Reports

The use of form reports requires special considerations, which are detailed in a series of Appraisal Institute publications, including

- *Using the Uniform Residential Appraisal Report Form: URAR 2005 (Form 1004) and Exterior Inspection (Form 2055)*
- *Using the Individual Condominium Unit Appraisal Report Forms: Fannie Mae Form 1073 and Exterior-Only Form 1075*
- *Using the Small Residential Income Property Appraisal Report: Form 1025/72*

These publications are updated more frequently than this textbook and therefore contain more timely information on the various forms, which change regularly.

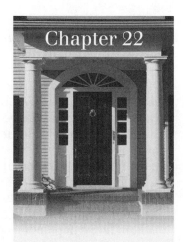

Statistics in Appraisal

An understanding of statistics is becoming increasingly important to residential appraisers as the single property appraisal mind-set and mass appraisal techniques merge. The traditional, single property appraiser adds value in this changing world by bridging the gaps between purely mathematical valuation models, local market conditions, and the physical real estate being analyzed. Appraisers can position themselves to maximize the value of their local market knowledge by acquiring a basic understanding of statistics. This has been acknowledged by the Appraisal Standards Board, which requires inclusion of a statistical training module in qualifying education beginning in 2008.

Statistics has been defined as the *science of data,* which "involves collecting, classifying, summarizing, organizing, analyzing, and interpreting numerical information."[1] Based on this definition, traditional appraisal methods have always been steeped in statistics. Although statistical analysis has been at the core of the valuation process, the tools necessary for more rigorous analysis and interpretation of numerical data are more available now than ever before, raising expectations for more "statistical" support for value conclusions. Therefore, residential appraisal is evolving toward a not-too-distant future where appraisers will be expected to have a more formal understanding of statistics, statistical models, and automated valuation modeling (AVM). With this in mind, a better description of the focus of this chapter would be the following definition of *statistics:* a summary measures that have been

---

1. James T. McClave, P. George Benson, and Terry Sincich, *Statistics for Business and Economics,* 9th ed. (Upper Saddle River, N.J.: Prentice Hall, 2005), 5.

descriptive statistics. A type of statistical application that uses summary measures, charts, and tables to describe a sample or population.

inferential statistics. A type of statistical application that involves the use of sample data to support opinions (i.e., inferences) concerning the population represented by the sample; can include estimates of actual but unknown population central tendency and dispersal, outcome predictions, and the underlying structure of cause-effect relationships.

population. All the items under consideration in a statistical analysis such as all of the detached, one-unit homes in a given market area.

parameter. A summary measure that describes a characteristic of a population (i.e., a *variable*).

sample. A subset of a population that has been selected for analysis.

computed from relatively little data, gathered by sampling a much larger collection of data called a population.[2]

Statistical applications are generally divided into two types—*descriptive statistics* and *inferential statistics.* The descriptive statistics category deals with the use of summary measures, charts, and tables to describe a sample or population. Inferential statistics involves the use of sample data to support opinions (i.e., inferences) concerning the population represented by the sample. Statistical inferences can include, among other things, estimates of actual but unknown population central tendency and dispersal, outcome predictions, and the underlying structure of cause-effect relationships.

While descriptive statistical tools such as tables, charts, and graphs are important and useful, they are not discussed in depth in this chapter. Much has been written about these tools and how they relate to appraisal, and this material is readily accessible in publications such as *The Appraisal Journal.*[3] Instead, this chapter concentrates on development of a basic understanding of the field of inferential statistics leading up to a discussion of simple and multiple linear regression. Because the field of statistics is a discipline unto itself, appraisers should consider the extent to which statistical methods will be used in their practices and determine the education and training they will need to master the necessary elements of statistics sufficient to provide credible appraisal services. This chapter can be viewed as an introductory lesson and first step along the path to statistical competence, which begins with precise definitions of fundamental statistical terminology.

Sample and Population, Inference and Description

A *population* consists of all of the items under consideration such as all of the detached, one-unit homes in a given market area. A *parameter* is a summary measure that describes a characteristic of a population (i.e., a *variable*). The mean size of all of the homes in a given market area is an example of a parameter. (Size is the variable and the population mean is the parameter.) In contrast, a *sample* is a subset of a population that has been selected for analysis. A *statistic* is a summary measure derived from sample data. The mean size of all of the houses in a sample

---

2. Heinz Kohler, *Statistics for Business and Economics* (Stamford, Conn.: Thomson, 2002), 4.

3. See, for example, a series of three articles by Bryan L. Goddard: "Graphics Improve the Analysis of Income Data," *The Appraisal Journal* (October 2000): 388–394; "The Power of Computer Graphics for Comparative Analysis," *The Appraisal Journal* (April 2000): 134–141; and "The Role of Graphic Analysis in Appraisals," *The Appraisal Journal* (October 1999): 429–435.

selected from detached, single-family homes in a given market area is an example of a statistic. Statistics are used to estimate parameters.

As stated earlier, *descriptive statistics* is concerned with data collection, presentation, and quantification. For example, descriptive statistics on a sample might include the sample size, the collection method, and the date and might numerically quantify the dispersion and central tendencies of the sample variables by reporting minimum and maximum values, range, quartiles, standard deviation, mean, median, or mode. Charts, graphs, and tables are elements of descriptive statistics, which also include histograms, pie charts, bar charts, line graphs, scatter plots, ordered arrays, relative frequency distributions, and percentage distributions. Descriptive statistical methods are applicable to population data as well as sample data.

Fundamentally, *inferential statistics* involves estimating a population parameter using sample data or reaching a conclusion concerning one or more populations based on sample data. For example, the National Association of Realtors (NAR) publishes monthly median home price statistics for various markets throughout the United States. Changes in the price level of the underlying population of homes are generally inferred from this sample statistic. The reliability and validity of this inference—how accurate the inference is—depend on a number of factors including sample size and how well the sample represents the population. A measure of accuracy is usually reported along with an inference, stating the degree of uncertainty associated with the inference. Uncertainty cannot, however, be quantified when the sample is a non-probability sample. Median home price statistics reported by NAR are derived from non-probability samples.[4] Therefore, the degree of uncertainty is not reported by NAR and cannot be calculated.

Measures of Central Tendency

Central tendency refers to a typical value that describes a sample or population variable. The three most frequently used measures of central tendency are the median, mean, and mode.

Median

The *median* is the middle value in an ordered array. The median is unaffected by extreme values in sample data, hence it is often reported when one or more extreme values distorts the ability of the mean to accurately depict central tendency. If there is an odd number of observations in a data set, then the median value is the $(n + 1) \div 2$ observation in an *ordered array* (data arranged numerically from lowest to highest or highest to lowest), where n represents sample size. If there is an even number of observations in a data set, then the median is the value halfway between the two middle observation values.

---

4. With a non-probability sample the probability of any given sample item being chosen from the underlying population is unknown. Examples of non-probability samples include convenience samples, intact groups, and self-selection.

median. The middle value in an ordered array of data arranged numerically from lowest to highest or highest to lowest

mean. The sum of the values of all observations on a variable divided by the sample size; also referred to as the *arithmetic mean, sample mean,* or *population mean.*

mode. The most frequently occurring observation in a sample data set.

Arithmetic Mean

The *arithmetic mean* is the most commonly reported measure of central tendency. It is often referred to as the *sample mean* or *population mean* or simply as the *mean.* The sample mean is represented by the symbol $\bar{x}$. Population mean is symbolized as the Greek letter μ. Sample mean is calculated by summing the values of all observations on a variable and dividing by the sample size (n). This is written mathematically as

$$\bar{x} = \frac{\sum\limits_{i=1}^{n} x_i}{n}$$

Since the arithmetic mean includes all observations on a variable, its calculation is affected by any extreme values, which may bias its depiction of central tendency. When this occurs the mean is not the best representation of central tendency.

The mean is very amenable to statistical inference when the population distribution is known or can be reliably approximated, or when the sample is adequately large. The *student's t distribution* is the most frequently used means of assessing the degree of uncertainty associated with statistical inferences based on the mean.

Geometric Mean

Central tendency for compound financial returns over time can be measured by the *geometric mean.* The geometric mean is mathematically calculated as

$$\bar{R} = [(1 + R_1) \times (1 + R_2) \times \ldots \times (1 + R_n)]^{1/n} - 1$$

where R_i is the rate of return in period i.

Mode

The *mode* is the most frequently occurring observation in a sample data set. It is not affected by extreme values, but it varies more from sample to sample. If more than one mode occurs, then the data are multimodal. For example, a data set with two modes is referred to as bimodal. Unlike the median and the mean, statistical tools are unavailable for making inferences on the mode.

Numerical Example

Table 22.1 shows an ordered array of a 36-item random sample of offering prices for lots in a large 1,500-lot residential subdivision. The data are used to illustrate the sample mean, median, and mode. The same data are used later to illustrate measures of dispersion and shape.

Since there is an even number of observations in the sample, the median is the arithmetic mean of the 18th and 19th ordered observations, which is $87,800. The most frequently occurring price is $90,000,

Table 22.1	Sample Data

$72,000
74,600
76,000
77,200
78,000
79,000
79,800
79,800
82,000
82,000
84,000
85,600
85,800
86,000
87,000
87,200
87,400
87,800
87,800
87,800
88,000
89,800
90,000
90,000
90,000
90,000
90,600
91,000
91,000
93,800
93,800
96,600
97,000
97,200
97,200
98,800

$$\Sigma_x = \overline{\$3,131,600}$$

$$\text{Simple Mean} = \bar{x} = \frac{\sum_{i=1}^{n} x_i}{n} = \frac{\$3,131,600}{36} = \$86,988.89$$

which occurs four times and is the mode. Since these data were randomly selected, these measures of central tendency can be used as estimators for the corresponding population parameters (population mean, population median, and population mode).

Measures of Dispersion

Dispersion measures indicate how much variation occurs for a given variable. These measures—standard deviation, variance, coefficient of variation, and range—are useful because they can be compared to the characteristics of a known distribution, such as the normal distribution, in order to determine whether a particular set of parametric inferential statistics can be used. They also facilitate comparison of two data sets to determine which is more variable.

Standard Deviation and Variance

These two measures of dispersion take into account how all of the data are distributed. Furthermore, the standard deviation lends itself to further statistical treatment allowing inferences to be drawn and statements to be made regarding the degree of uncertainty associated with an inference. For this reason the standard deviation is an often calculated and reported sample statistic. The sample standard deviation is denoted by the letter S and the population standard deviation is denoted by the Greek letter σ.

Calculations for these two standard deviations are

$$\sigma = \sqrt{\frac{\Sigma(x_i - \mu)^2}{N}}$$

and

$$S = \sqrt{\frac{\Sigma(x_i - \bar{x})^2}{n - 1}}$$

where N = population size and n = sample size. Variance is merely the square of the standard deviation. Sample variance equals S^2 and population variance equals σ^2. The sample standard deviation for the 36 lot prices in the sample is calculated in Table 22.2

When data are normally distributed, approximately 67% of the observations are expected to lie within the mean ± 1 standard deviation, 80% within the mean ± 1.28 standard deviations, and 95% within the mean ± 2 standard deviations. For this data set 23 observations (64%) lie within ±1 standard deviation of the mean, 26 observations (72%) lie within ±1.28 standard deviations of the mean, and 35 observations (97%) lie within ±2 standard deviations of the mean.

standard deviation. A statistical measure of the extent of absolute dispersion, variability, or scatter in a frequency distribution.

coefficient of variation. A measure of the relative chance for error in a forecast or estimate of the dependent variable; used for relative comparisons of dispersion among multiple sets of data.

Coefficient of Variation

The *coefficient of variation* (*CV*) is useful for relative comparisons of dispersion among

Table 22.2	Sample Standard Deviation		
Price (x_i)	Sample Mean ($\bar{x}$)	($x_i - \bar{x}$)	($x_i - \bar{x}$)^2
72,000	86,989	-14,989	224,666,790
74,600	86,989	-12,389	153,484,568
76,000	86,989	-10,989	120,755,679
77,200	86,989	-9,789	95,822,346
78,000	86,989	-8,989	80,800,123
79,000	86,989	-7,989	63,822,346
79,800	86,989	-7,189	51,680,123
79,800	86,989	-7,189	51,680,123
82,000	86,989	-4,989	24,889,012
82,000	86,989	-4,989	24,889,012
84,000	86,989	-2,989	8,933,457
85,600	86,989	-1,389	1,929,012
85,800	86,989	-1,189	1,413,457
85,800	86,989	-989	977,901
87,000	86,989	11	123
87,200	86,989	211	44,568
87,400	86,989	411	169,012
87,800	86,989	811	657,901
87,800	86,989	811	657,901
87,800	86,989	811	657,901
88,000	86,989	1,011	1,022,346
89,800	86,989	2,811	7,902,346
90,000	86,989	3,011	9,066,790
90,000	86,989	3,011	9,066,790
90,000	86,989	3,011	9,066,790
90,000	86,989	3,011	9,066,790
90,600	86,989	3,611	13,040,123
91,000	86,989	4,011	16,089,012
91,000	86,989	4,011	16,089,012
93,800	86,989	6,811	46,391,235
93,800	86,989	6,811	46,391,235
96,600	86,989	9,611	92,373,457
97,000	86,989	10,011	100,222,346
97,200	86,989	10,211	104,266,790
97,200	86,989	10,211	104,266,790
98,800	86,989	11,811	139,502,346

$$\Sigma(x_i - \bar{x})^2 = 1,631,755,556$$

$$S = \sqrt{\frac{\Sigma(x_i - \bar{x})^2}{n-1}} = \sqrt{\frac{1,631,755,556}{36-1}} = \$6,828$$

multiple sets of data because dispersion is standardized to each sample's mean. This is done by stating standard deviation as a percentage of the sample mean. The sample having the greatest coefficient of variation is the most dispersed.

$$CV = \frac{S}{\overline{X}} \times 100\%$$

For the chapter's illustrative data

$$CV = \frac{\$6,828}{\$86,989} \times 100\% = 7.85\%$$

Range

The *range* is a simple measure of the spread of the data. It is the difference between the largest observation and the smallest observation. When data are normally distributed, the range will be approximately equal to 6 standard deviations. The range for the illustrative data is $98,800 – $72,000, or $26,800. This range equates to 3.93 standard deviations.

Interquartile Range

Data can be divided into four quarters by the identification of quartiles. Quartile 1 (Q_1) is the midpoint between the lowest value and the median. Quartile 2 (Q_2) is the median, and Quartile 3 (Q_3) is the midpoint between the highest value and the median. For calculation purposes

$$Q_1 = \frac{n+1}{4} \text{ ordered observation}$$

and

$$Q_3 = \frac{3(n+1)}{4} \text{ ordered observation}$$

The following decision rules also apply:

- If the position point calculation is an integer, then the ordered observation occupying that position point is the quartile.
- If the position point is halfway between two integers, then the average of the next largest and next smallest ordered observation is the quartile.
- If the position point is neither an integer nor halfway between two integers, then the position point is rounded to the nearest integer and the corresponding ordered observation is the quartile.

For the illustrative data (36 observations) the position for Q_1 is 9.25 (37 ÷ 4) rounded down to the ninth ordered observation in accordance with the third decision rule above. Position 9 in the ordered array corresponds to $82,000, which is Q_1. The position for Q_2 is the median, which is $87,800. The position for Q_3 is 27.75 (111 ÷ 4) rounded up to the 28th ordered observation in accordance with the third decision rule above. Position 28 in the ordered array corresponds to $91,000.

The *interquartile range* is $Q_3 - Q_1$, or $91,000 – $82,000 = $9,000. When data are normally distributed, the interquartile range should be approximately equal to 1.33 standard deviations. In this illustration the interquartile range is 1.32 standard deviations ($9,000 ÷ $6,828). Quartiles are also useful for analyzing the shape of the data distribution, which will be illustrated in the next section.

Measures of Shape

Measures of shape are essential for determining how close to normal a data distribution is and the extent to which extreme values are distorting the difference between the median and the mean. The normal distribution, which is the basis for many statistical inferences, is symmetrical—hence its median and mean are equal.

One useful graphic illustration of shape is the box and whisker plot. It helps illustrate the extent of skewness, or lack thereof, in data. This plot is based on what is referred to as a *five number summary*. The summary is the lowest value, Q_1, the median, Q_3, and the highest value. The five number summary for the chapter's example data is $72,000, $82,000, $87,800, $91,000, and $98,800. The corresponding box and whisker plot, along with the sample mean, is shown below.

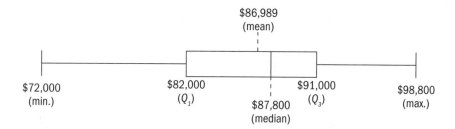

The box and whisker plot shows that the sample data are skewed to the left, both in terms of the interquartile range and in terms of the tails (i.e., $82,000 – $72,000 > $98,800 – $91,000). Another indication of skewness is the relationship between the median and the mean. When data are left-skewed, the mean will be less than the median. When the data are right-skewed, the mean will be greater than the median.

Skewness can also be captured through a graphic depiction of a frequency or percentage distribution. These graphic displays are called *histograms*. Figure 22.1 is a combination frequency and percentage distribution for the illustrative lot price data and the related percentage histogram.

The percentage histogram is derived from conversion of the numerical price data to categorical data (price category) reflecting counts and percentages within each category. If the data were symmetrical, then the distributions to the right and left of center would be mirror images. Instead the left side extends much further from the center (i.e., left skewness).

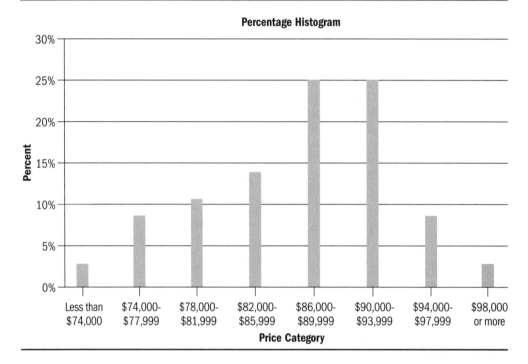

Figure 22.1	Frequency and Percentage Distribution with Percentage Histogram	
Price Category	**Frequency (Count)**	**Percentage of Total**
Less than $74,000	1	2.8%
$74,000 to $77,900	3	8.3%
$78,000 to $81,999	4	11.1%
$82,000 to $85,999	5	13.9%
$86,000 to $89,999	9	25.0%
$90,000 to $93,999	9	25.0%
$94,000 to $97,999	4	11.1%
$98,000 or more	1	2.8%

The statistical software packages Excel and SPSS provide more quantitative assessments of skewness within their descriptive statistics measures. Both rely on the same calculation of skewness, which is shown below.

$$Skewness = \frac{n}{(n-1)(n-2)} \; \Sigma \left(\frac{x_i - \bar{x}}{S} \right)^3$$

If a data distribution is symmetrical, the value in the parentheses is zero and skewness is zero. If it is left-skewed, the value in the parentheses is negative and skewness is negative. (If it is right-skewed, the value in the parentheses is positive and skewness is positive.) Skewness for the illustrative data is -0.303 based on this criterion, indicating left skewness as depicted in the box and whisker plot and the percentage histogram.

Appraising Residential Properties

Kurtosis

Kurtosis refers to the degree of "peakedness" in a data distribution. Curves with kurtosis of 3 are called *mesokurtic*. The normal distribution has kurtosis equal to 3. More peaked curves (*leptokurtic*) have values larger than 3 and less peaked curves (*platykurtic*) have values less than 3. The illustrative data is much less peaked than a normal distribution, which can be confirmed with Excel, Minitab, or SPSS descriptive statistics output.

Central Limit Theorem and Inference

Although the most popular and user friendly inference tests are based on the assumption that a sample has been derived from a normally distributed population (i.e., the so-called "bell curve" with skewness $= 0$ and kurtosis $= 3$), it is possible to make inferences concerning non-normally distributed populations if sample size is adequately large. The adequacy of sample size depends on the underlying population distribution. According to the central limit theorem, generally speaking—regardless of the shape of the underlying population distribution—the sampling distribution of a mean drawn from the population will be approximately normal with a sample size of at least 30. If the underlying population is fairly symmetrical (like the illustrative price data), the sampling distribution of the mean will be approximately normal with a sample size of at least 15. If the underlying population is normally distributed, then the sampling distribution of the mean is also normal, regardless of sample size.[5] The central limit theorem's importance is that it allows inferences to be drawn without knowing the actual distribution of the underlying population.[6] The price data sample consists of 36 observations, hence it can be used to make inferences about the mean of the underlying population price.

The chapter's illustrative price data have been drawn from a population with an unknown mean and standard deviation.[7] The sample data can be used to infer the underlying population mean because a probability sample (e.g., a simple random sample) was drawn. The sample mean ($\overline{x}$) is $86,989 and the sample standard deviation (*S*) is $6,828. A confidence interval is a statement about the degree of uncertainty asso-

---

5. See, for example, Levine, Krehbiel, and Berenson, *Business Statistics, A First Course,* 3rd ed. (Upper Saddle River, N.J.: Prentice Hall, 2003), 237–239.

6. Inferences on medians (versus inferences on means) derive from a discipline called *nonparametric statistics,* and they are useful for analyzing small samples when the underlying population distribution is unknown and the sample is so small that the central limit theorem cannot be relied upon to ensure approximate normality of the sampling distribution of the mean. Although nonparametric median tests are beyond the scope of this chapter, it is noted that a number of nonparametric tests are provided in many software packages, which are appropriate for making inferences about central tendency and distribution from a single sample and comparing the central tendencies of two or more small samples. For example, the SPSS software package includes several nonparametric single-sample analysis tools as well as independent-sample comparison tests and related-sample comparison tests. Because real property data often consist of small-sized samples, it is often useful to be able to apply a nonparametric test. Many introductory statistics textbooks include a chapter or two dealing with nonparametric statistics, providing a level of understanding sufficient for most real estate applications.

7. Population standard deviation is rarely known when making inferences about the true population mean. This is because μ must be known in order to calculate σ. Logically, if μ is known, then there is no need to infer it. However, in rare cases a population has been studied so many times that many estimates on *S* have been previously published, and they can be relied upon as estimators of σ rather than using *S* from a sample.

ciated with an inference, and *any inference should be accompanied with such a statement.* The confidence interval for the mean, when the population standard deviation is unknown, can be derived from the *student's t distribution* when the sample size is sufficient to invoke the central limit theorem or when the population is known to be normally distributed. Confidence intervals on μ (σ unknown) are based on the following:

$$\text{Confidence Interval} = \bar{x} \pm t_{n-1}\frac{S}{\sqrt{n}}$$

When $n = 36$, values of t_{35} are 1.6896 for a 90% confidence interval, 2.0301 for a 95% confidence interval, and 2.7238 for a 99% confidence interval. These t values can either be looked up in a statistical table or calculated using Excel. Excel, Minitab, and SPSS will calculate a confidence interval from a data set, given input on the level of confidence sought. The associated confidence intervals on the true population mean price for the lot price data are

90% Confidence	$85,066 \le \mu \le $88,912
95% Confidence	$84,679 \le \mu \le $89,299
99% Confidence	$83,889 \le \mu \le $90,089

With 90% confidence the degree of uncertainty is 10%. It falls to 5% and 1% as confidence rises, but the associated "cost" is a wider confidence interval. This level of uncertainty is referred to as "alpha" (α) in statistics.[8] Alpha is the probability of making a "Type I error"–i.e., inferring μ to be within a confidence interval when it is not. "Type II errors" are referred to as "beta" (β)–i.e., inferring μ to be outside of the confidence interval when it is actually within the interval.

central limit theorem. A theorem that holds that the sampling distribution of a mean drawn from a population will be approximately normal if the sample size is at least 30.

confidence interval. A measure of about the degree of uncertainty associated with an inference.

Suppose a client requires a narrower confidence interval without increasing α. Notice that the width of the confidence interval is reduced when n is increased due to division by the square root of n. Additionally, the value of t becomes smaller at a given confidence level as sample size increases. Therefore, narrower confidence intervals can be achieved at the expense of collecting a larger sample.

Sample Size

A requisite sample size can be estimated to accommodate a predetermined amount of sampling error (e). The equation for sample size is

$$n = \frac{Z^2 \sigma^2}{e^2}$$

Z is used in this calculation because the value of t cannot be determined until a sample size has been selected. Hence, this calculation yields an *ap-*

---

8. The confidence level is $1 - \alpha$.

proximate sample size. Furthermore, it is not unusual for some proportion of collected data to be unusable due to missing variables or "nonresponse." Therefore, it is good practice to attempt to collect a sample that is somewhat larger than indicated by the sample size calculation. As calculated here, sample size is an estimate of the number of usable observations needed to control the size of sampling error at a given level of confidence.

The sampling error for the 95% confidence interval on true lot price is $2,310 [($89,299 − $84,679) ÷ 2]. Assume, however, that the needs of a client dictate that a sampling error no larger than $1,500 is acceptable at a 95% confidence level. In order to calculate a revised sample size, Z is derived from the standard normal distribution and is equal to 1.96 at a 95% confidence level. σ is unknown but can be estimated as $6,828 based on the previous calculation of S.[9] On this basis, the sample size would have to be increased to at least 80 observations, computed as follows

$$n = \frac{1.96^2 \times 6,828^2}{1,500^2} = 79.6$$

Sample size is always rounded up. Furthermore, since t_{79} is 1.9905, the sample size could be increased to 83 based on

$$80 \times \frac{1.9905^2}{1.96^2} = 82.5$$

As this example demonstrates, increased accuracy can add to data collection expense. Here a 35% reduction in sampling error from $2,310 to $1,500 results in a need to increase sample size by 230% from 36 to 83.[10]

Regression Analysis

Regression analysis is a statistical technique whereby a mathematical equation can be derived to quantify the relationship between a dependent (outcome) variable and one or more independent (input) variables. In appraisal the dependent variable is usually price or rent. The independent variables are usually broadly derived from the four forces that affect value (social, economic, governmental, and environmental) plus the physical characteristics of the site and improvements. Often, data collection controls for the four forces affecting value by focusing on property sales or rents that are subject to common social, economic, governmental, and environmental influences. In some instances it is necessary to include a date of sale variable (or variable set) to account for economic change over time. In addition, it is not uncommon to include an environmental variable or variables when investigating the effects of an external environmental factor such as traffic noise or factory odor.

---

9. The population standard deviation is usually unknown and must be estimated based on prior research, a pilot sample, or other bases used to support an assumption.

10. Obviously, mean price could be known with certainty by analyzing all 1,500 lot prices. In many cases, however, it is simply not possible or is too costly to collect data on each item in a population.

Regression models have been used by property tax assessors for many years within the broad context of *mass appraisal modeling* because regression modeling is more resource-efficient than doing a traditional appraisal for each property in a large assessment district. Although regression modeling is not perfect, it is often viewed by assessors as the logical choice when the alternative is to appraise each property individually and resource constraints prohibit doing so as often as necessary to ensure equitable taxation.

Regression models (along with expert systems and neural networks) also form the basis for many AVMs, of which mass appraisal models are a subset. AVMs became important in the 1990s as lenders began to concentrate on shortening loan approval turnaround time and to compete more intensely on transaction fees. Employment of information technology, the Internet, and automated word processing by appraisers has mitigated the threat of AVMs to residential appraisal practice to some degree by shortening turnaround time and improving efficiency. Nevertheless, AVMs remain an important loan underwriting tool, and they continue to pose a perceived threat to the day-to-day practice of appraisal–especially residential appraisal in data-rich, fairly homogeneous markets.

Simple Linear Regression

In its simplest form linear regression captures a linear relationship between a single dependent variable and a single independent, or predictor, variable. This relationship is usually written as follows:

$$Y_i = \alpha + \beta x_i + \varepsilon$$

which reflects an underlying linear deterministic relationship of the form $Y = a + bx$ plus a stochastic (random) component (ε). The slope of the regression line is b and the intercept is a. In real estate appraisal, Y could be modeled as market price whereas x could be lot size, for example. The random component reflects sampling error plus the imperfection of real estate markets in terms of the influence of factors such as information advantages and the negotiating strengths of the parties to a sale or lease transaction. The model yields an estimate of the equation above of the following form:

$$\hat{Y}_i = a + bx_i + e$$

where a is an estimator of α, b is an estimator of β, and e is an estimator of ε. The outcome variable ($\hat{Y}_i$) is the expected market price (model's estimate of market value) of property i conditional on the value of x.

The presence of the random error term is an indication that regression models are inferential (stochastic). They provide estimates of the outcome variables that should be accompanied with a statement about the degree of uncertainty associated with the estimate. In addition, they provide estimates of the coefficient(s) on the independent variable(s), b in this context, which also incorporate a degree of uncertainty.

The prior lot sales data are augmented by adding lot area as a means of demonstrating a simple linear regression model. The additional data are presented in Table 22.3.

Table 22.3	Additional Sample Data	
Price	**Lot Area (Sq. Ft.)**	**Price/Sq. Ft.**
$72,000	15,030	$4.79
74,600	14,030	5.32
76,000	13,121	5.79
77,200	15,120	5.11
78,000	13,940	5.60
79,000	15,350	5.15
79,800	16,400	4.87
79,800	16,810	4.75
82,000	15,150	5.41
82,000	17,320	4.73
84,000	14,750	5.69
85,600	14,790	5.79
85,800	14,570	5.89
86,000	17,770	4.84
87,000	17,030	5.11
87,200	16,970	5.14
87,400	14,720	5.94
87,800	15,350	5.72
87,800	19,390	4.53
87,800	19,400	4.53
88,000	13,720	6.41
89,800	17,060	5.26
90,000	16,130	5.58
90,000	19,390	4.64
90,000	19,390	4.64
90,000	19,390	4.64
90,600	17,090	5.30
91,000	15,770	5.77
91,000	16,600	5.48
93,800	17,090	5.49
93,800	17,200	5.45
96,600	19,390	4.98
97,000	20,650	4.70
97,200	17,490	5.56
97,200	17,710	5.49
98,800	20,140	4.91
Median	$87,800	16,890	$5.28
Mean	$86,989	16,701	$5.25
S	$6,828	1,999	$0.47
Minimum	$72,000	13,121	$4.53
Maximum	$98,800	20,650	$6.41

Note that the range in price per square foot is $1.88 ($6.41 − $4.53), an indication that lot size probably is not the sole factor determining lot price. A simple linear regression model will uncover the extent to which lot price is explained by the lot size variable. The model can be run on a number of statistics packages. The following output was derived using SPSS:

Regression Equation:	Price = $49,355 + $2.25 × Lot Size
t-statistic on Lot Size:	5.12
Model F-statistic:	26.23
R^2:	.435
Adjusted R^2:	.419

This output says that the best fitting linear relationship between lot size and price is a line with intercept $49,355 and a slope of $2.25 per square foot of lot size variation. The model F-statistic is highly significant, meaning the model predicts lot price better than merely relying on the mean lot price. The t-statistic on lot size is also highly significant, meaning that lot size is an important factor for price estimation. R^2 (coefficient of determination) can vary from 0 to 1, with 0 indicating no explanatory power whatsoever and 1 indicating perfect explanatory power (a deterministic model). The R^2 of .435 indicates that 43.5% of the variation in price is accounted for by variation in lot size. Adjusted R^2 is useful for comparing multiple competing models having differing sets of independent variables because it accounts for the number of explanatory variables in relation to sample size. The model with the highest adjusted R^2 is usually the preferred model. In this instance, there is no competing model.

Obtaining an understanding of the intercept and slope is referred to as *structural modeling* because it uncovers the structure of the relationship between the dependent variable and the independent variable(s). In a simple linear model it facilitates development of a "best fit" line in two-space, which can be overlaid on a scatter plot of the data to demonstrate unexplained variation in the dependent variable. An example of such a plot is shown in Figure 22.2.

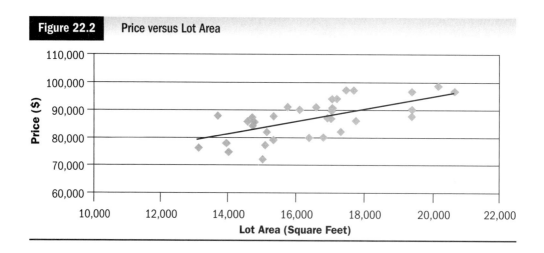

Figure 22.2   Price versus Lot Area

The scatter plot shows that price generally rises with lot size and the regression line is the best-fitting line, which minimizes the squares of the errors between the data and the line's fit to the data. Differences between actual prices and the regression line can be attributed to one of two causes—randomness in pricing (the stochastic element of price) or other unaccounted-for variables that are also important in determining price. Such elements might include amenities such as a good view or negative influences such as a location abutting a noisy street or topographic features that impair construction of a residence and inflate construction costs. Simple linear regression becomes *multiple linear regression* when more than one independent variable is included in a model.

simple linear regression analysis. A technique that captures a linear relationship between a single dependent variable and a single independent, or predictor, variable.

multiple linear regression analysis. A technique that captures a linear relationship between a single dependent variable and more than one independent, or predictor, variable.

Regression models are used to predict price and to understand the structure of a relationship among variables. Two forms of predictive models are generally employed. One form is used to predict the mean outcome, and the other form predicts a single, specific outcome. The primary difference is that the confidence interval for a prediction of the mean outcome is narrower than the confidence interval for prediction of a single, specific outcome. Furthermore, regression models should never be employed to predict outcomes using inputs that are outside of the ranges of the independent variables.

For example, assume an appraiser is interested in predicting price using the illustrative sample data for a lot area of 17,030 square feet. The predicted mean price for lots of this size and the predicted price for a single, specific 17,030-sq.-ft. lot are the same, $87,673.[11] However the confidence interval widths vary considerably, as follows:

95% Confidence interval on mean lot price (17,030-sq.-ft. lot): $85,944 to $89,519
95% Confidence interval on a single lot (17,030-sq.-ft. lot): $77,003 to $98,460

Note that the confidence interval on a specific lot is nearly as wide as the sample price range.

SPSS and Minitab are capable of calculating and reporting prediction confidence intervals for the mean and for a single outcome. They are charted in Figure 22.3 for these data, along with the regression line for lot price. Note that the prediction confidence intervals are narrowest near the mean lot size and grow wider as one departs from the mean. For this reason, they must be calculated separately for any given value of the independent variable (or values of the independent variables). This is a time-consuming process, which is best accomplished in SPSS or Minitab by inclusion of the predictor values for the independent variables in the regression model, omitting the value of the dependent variable when the model is run.

---

11. The SPSS program predicts $87,731, which differs from $87,673, when applying the text's equation due to rounding in the text material.

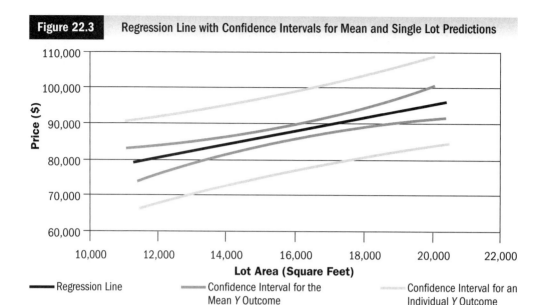

| Figure 22.3 | Regression Line with Confidence Intervals for Mean and Single Lot Predictions |

The equations for calculating prediction confidence intervals for simple linear regression are as follows:

Prediction Confidence Interval for the Mean Y Outcome

$$\text{Confidence Interval} = \hat{Y}_i \pm t_{n-2} \, S_{YX} \sqrt{\frac{1}{n} + \frac{(x_i - \bar{x})^2}{\sum_{i=1}^{n}(x_i - \bar{x})^2}}$$

Prediction Confidence Interval for an Individual Y Outcome

$$\text{Confidence Interval} = \hat{Y}_i \pm t_{n-2} \, S_{YX} \sqrt{1 + \frac{1}{n} + \frac{(x_i - \bar{x})^2}{\sum_{i=1}^{n}(x_i - \bar{x})^2}}$$

The value symbolized as S_{YX} in these equations is reported as the "Standard Error of the Estimate" in SPSS, "S" in Minitab, and "Standard Error" in Excel. The summation $\sum (x_i - \bar{x})^2$ is often referred to as SSX (sum of squares for the x variable) and is calculated as $S_{YX} \div S_b$. S_b is reported as "standard error" for the independent x variable coefficient in both SPSS and Excel and as "standard deviation" for the independent x variable coefficient in Minitab. Given this information it is possible to calculate confidence intervals by hand for a simple linear regression if the need arises. The confidence interval calculations become more complex with multiple linear regression and are best calculated using statistical software.

standard error of the estimate. An estimate of the variation likely to be encountered in making predictions from a regression equation; expressed as the standard deviation of the observed values about the regression line.

Multiple Linear Regression

In order to demonstrate a multiple linear regression model, assume that further investigation of the lot price data reveals that some lots have a picturesque creek view and also that several lots are affected by noise from a busy street. Characteristics such as these can be modeled numerically by creation of indicator (dummy) variables. To create a creek view variable, lots having the creek view are coded 1 and lots not having a creek view are coded 0. Likewise, lots subject to street noise are coded 1 and those unaffected by street noise are coded 0. The revised sample data are shown in Table 22.4.

Table 22.4	Revised Sample Data			
Price	**Lot Area (Sq. Ft.)**	**Price/Sq. Ft.**	**View**	**Street Noise**
$72,000	15,030	$4.79	0	0
74,600	14,030	5.32	0	0
76,000	13,121	5.79	1	0
77,200	15,120	5.11	0	0
78,000	13,940	5.60	1	0
79,000	15,350	5.15	0	0
79,800	16,400	4.87	0	0
79,800	16,810	4.75	0	0
82,000	15,150	5.41	0	0
82,000	17,320	4.73	0	0
84,000	14,750	5.69	0	0
85,600	14,790	5.79	0	0
85,800	14,570	5.89	1	0
86,000	17,770	4.84	0	0
87,000	17,030	5.11	0	0
87,200	16,970	5.14	0	0
87,400	14,720	5.94	1	0
87,800	15,350	5.72	0	0
87,800	19,390	4.53	0	1
87,800	19,400	4.53	0	1
88,000	13,720	6.41	1	0
89,800	17,060	5.26	0	0
90,000	16,130	5.58	0	0
90,000	19,390	4.64	0	1
90,000	19,390	4.64	0	1
90,000	19,390	4.64	0	1
90,600	17,090	5.30	0	0
91,000	15,770	5.77	0	0
91,000	16,600	5.48	0	0
93,800	17,090	5.49	0	0
93,800	17,200	5.45	0	0
96,600	19,390	4.98	0	1
97,000	20,650	4.70	0	1
97,200	17,490	5.56	0	0
97,200	17,710	5.49	0	0
98,800	20,140	4.91	0	1

A multiple regression model in SPSS yields the following price equation:

$$\text{Lot Price} = \$16{,}671 + \$4.26 \times \text{Lot Size} + \$6{,}605 \times \text{Creek View} - \$8{,}187 \times \text{Street Noise Influence}$$

t-statistics:	Lot Size = 4.80
	Creek View = 2.11
	Street Noise = -2.27
Model F-statistic	12.17
R^2	.533
Adjusted R^2	.489

This result indicates that lot size, creek view, and street noise are all significant in the determination of lot price (all t-statistics are significant at $\alpha \le .05$). The model's F-statistic is also highly significant. This model is preferred to the simple linear regression model because adjusted R^2 has gone up from .419 to .489 despite the loss in degrees of freedom resulting from adding more variables while keeping sample size constant. The expanded multiple linear regression model accounts for 53.3% of the variation in lot price, which is an improvement over the 43.5% coefficient of determination for the simple linear regression model.

If the appraiser needed to predict mean price and a specific lot price for a 17,030-sq.-ft. creek-view lot unaffected by street noise, the calculation would be

$$\text{Lot Price} = \$16{,}671 + \$4.26 \times 17{,}030 + \$6{,}605 \times 1 - \$8{,}187 \times 0 = \$95{,}823$$

(The actual SPSS estimate is $95,900, which is unaffected by rounding the coefficients to the nearest dollar.) The associated 95% confidence intervals are

95% confidence interval on mean lot price (17,030-sq.-ft. lot w/view):	$88,861 to $102,941
95% confidence interval on a single lot (17,030-sq.-ft. lot w/view):	$83,720 to $108,082

Model Specification

Model specification issues fall into two broad categories for valuation purposes–the functional form of the relationship between the dependent variable and the independent variables and the choice of variables to include in the model.

Functional Form

Functional form issues arise because of the regression model's presumed linear relationship between dependent and independent variables, even though many of these relationships are likely to be curvilinear.[12] For example, many characteristics of homes are thought to be subject to increasing or diminishing marginal utility. Consider bathroom counts.

---

12. Curvilinear relationships are characterized by curved lines instead of straight lines. Examples include logarithmic curves, exponential curves, inverse curves, and polynomial curves.

Keeping floor area and bedroom count constant, adding bathrooms could initially result in increasing marginal utility. However, as more bathrooms are added above some optimum level, the contribution to value begins to diminish (imagine a 3-bedroom home with 7 baths and the contribution to value for baths 5, 6, and 7). Other independent variables that may have a curvilinear relationship to price include property age, floor area, lot area, garage stall count, bedroom count, and proximity (e.g., distance) measures. Furthermore, the nature of the functional relationship between these variables and price or rent can vary by market area whether that area is defined geographically (i.e., region of the country) or economically (i.e., neighborhood norms).

Since the underlying functional form of the relationship between an independent variable set and a price or rent outcome variable is unknown, regression model builders must search for the functional form that best fits the data being analyzed. This involves variable transformations such as logarithms, exponents, polynomials, reciprocals, and square roots. In some cases a transformation applies to an entire equation. In others, transformations apply only to certain variables.

Two examples of entire equation transformations include a hypothesized multiplicative model and a hypothesized exponential model. Transformations are done in these cases to convert the underlying relationships from a nonlinear to a linear form amenable to regression analysis. These transformations are illustrated below.

Underlying Multiplicative Price (P) Model

$$P = \alpha \, x_1^{\beta_1} x_2^{\beta_2} \, \varepsilon$$

Log Transformation to Linear Form

$$\ln(P) = \ln \alpha + \beta_1 \ln x_1 + \beta_2 \ln x_2 + \ln \varepsilon$$

The transformed model is linear in the relationship between the logs of the independent and dependent variables, and the exponents of these variables are transformed into the linear regression coefficient estimates. The estimated coefficients can either be placed into the underlying model to directly estimate price (or value), or the linear model can be used to estimate the log of price, which can then be converted to price. This sort of multiplicative model accommodates a variety of variable relationship shapes depending on the value of the exponents (the βs). Models of this type are used extensively in property tax assessment mass appraisal.

Underlying Exponential Price (P) Model

$$P = e^{(\alpha + \beta_1 x_1 + \beta_1 x_1 + \varepsilon)}$$

Log Transformation to Linear Form

$$\ln(P) = \alpha + \beta_1 x_1 + \beta_2 x_2 + \varepsilon$$

Transformations into this log-linear form and the prior log-log transformation are often useful for controlling heteroscedasticity, which is explained later in this chapter.

It is also possible, and often appropriate, to include other variable transformations. For example, one variable may be curvilinear while others are linear in relation to the dependent variable. The curvilinear variable could be modeled as a quadratic (e.g., floor area) while the others are modeled in linear form. An estimation model of this sort would be similar to the following:

$$P = \alpha + \beta_1 x_1 + \beta_2 x_2 + \beta_3 x_2^2 + \varepsilon$$

In this case x_2 is entered in a quadratic form. If x_2 were to represent floor area, a positive coefficient on x_2 along with a negative coefficient on x_2-*squared* could indicate price increasing with floor area but at a decreasing rate as the negative x_2-*squared* variable diminishes the positive contribution of the x_2 variable. The decision to include a quadratic term should be based on whether its inclusion significantly improves the model, which would be evidenced by a significant t-statistic on the squared variable coefficient, improvement in adjusted R^2, or both.

Indicator variables are another form of variable transformation (e.g., the dummy variables for creek view and street noise). Indicator variables transform categorical variables into numerical variables in order to be able to include their effects in a regression model. Dummy variables are the simplest single-category form of indicator variables, coded 1 if the observation is included in the category and 0 if it is not. Sometimes more than one category is required to completely exhaust categorical variable possibilities. For example, assume that a data set spans 4 years (say, 2003 to 2006), and the year of sale is being entered as an indicator variable set. Dummy variables would be created for 2004, 2005, and 2006, each coded 1 or 0 depending on the year of sale for each observation. The year 2003 is accounted for in the model when 2004 = 0, 2005 = 0, and 2006 = 0, hence no variable is created for 2003. The general rules are

1. Create one less dummy variable than the number of categories.
2. All of the dummy variables from an indicator variable set must be included in the model even though some of them may not be significant. That is, the decision to include or exclude a categorical variable implies that all of the dummy variables related to the category must either be included or excluded.

Variable Inclusion

Variable inclusion decisions determine whether or not a model is under-specified or over-specified. Two problems arise here. First, if relevant variables are excluded from the model, its ability to account for change in the independent variable is diminished. Second, misspecification leads to biased estimates of population parameters (the coefficients on the independent variables). This happens because correlation among independent variables causes the model to adjust coefficient estimates when the model is under- or over-specified. Coefficients on included variables are altered within the regression model to account for their correlations with relevant excluded variables. Conversely, coefficients on relevant included variables are altered to account for correlations with irrelevant included variables.

The lot price data illustration demonstrates both of these effects. The model was initially estimated with only one independent variable–lot area. However, two other variables were found to be significant–creek view and proximity to street noise. These additional variables are correlated with lot size (the lots near to street noise are generally larger and the creek view lots are generally smaller). The correlation matrix shown below quantifies these relationships.[13]

Lot Price Data Variable Correlations

	Price	Lot Size	Creek View	Street Noise
Price	1			
Lot Size	.660	1		
Creek View	-.236	-.547	1	
Street Noise	.418	.798	-.215	1

All three variables are significantly correlated with price, indicating that inclusion of creek view and street noise should add explanatory power. Furthermore, creek view and street noise are highly and significantly correlated with lot size, an indication that omission of these variables from the model would bias the coefficient on lot size. Both of these occurred. When creek view and street noise were excluded, the model accounted for 43.5% of lot price variability and the coefficient on lot size was $2.25. After inclusion of these two additional variables, the model accounted for 53.3% of lot price variability and the coefficient on lot price was $4.26. The second model provides a better estimate of lot price and a less-biased estimate of the contributory value of additional lot size unclouded by an attempt to account for street noise and creek view due to correlation with them.

Model Validation

Statistics reference books offer several suggestions for regression model validation, including collecting new data and assessing the model's predictive ability on the new data, comparison of results with theory and with previously published empirical studies, and data splitting.

Collection of new data is generally not a practical option in applied valuation settings. Nevertheless, it is possible and recommended to assess the signs of the variables in the regression equation and compare them with theoretical and intuitive expectations. Also, the need to stay current regarding relevant published studies seems evident. However, data splitting provides the most practical sample-specific and model-specific means of model validation.

---

13. Correlation, symbolized as r, can range from -1 to +1. Perfect negative correlation is -1, whereas perfect positive correlation is +1. When $r = 0$, two variables are uncorrelated (i.e., independent or orthogonal).

Data splitting, or cross-validation, requires that the data be divided into two subsets—a model-building set and a validation set (usually referred to as a *holdout sample*). The holdout sample should be randomly chosen from the full data set, and it can be a small proportion of the full data set (i.e., 10% to 20%).

Two validation routines are possible and recommended. The first routine is to compare the coefficients and significance levels derived from the model-building set with the coefficients and significance levels derived from a regression model employing all of the data. The results should be consistent, otherwise a small number of influential observations may be overly affecting the model. The second routine is to use the regression model derived from the model building set to predict the dependent variable values for the holdout sample (validation set). One measure of how well the model predicts is to compute the correlation between the actual values in the holdout sample and the predicted values. When the model is valid, the correlation should be high (i.e., greater than .90).[14]

When the results from these two routines are satisfactory, the model is likely to be valid. A final regression model employing all of the data would therefore be appropriate for valuation purposes.[15]

Underlying Regression Model Assumptions

Regression modeling is theoretically supported by several important factors, in addition to linearity of the relationship, generally referred to as the *assumptions of regression*. The assumptions are that

- Errors are normally distributed.
- Variance is homoscedastic.
- Errors are independent.
- The explanatory variables are not highly interrelated.

The *normality assumption* means that the errors around the regression line are normally distributed for each independent variable value. Regression models are fairly resistant to violations of the normality assumption as long as error distributions are not dramatically different from normal.[16] This assumption is important because it is the basis for the validity of the F-tests and t-tests of model and variable significance. The detrimental effects of non-normality are diminished as sample size increases.

---

14. If the data set is too small to accommodate data splitting into a model-building sample and a holdout sample, then an alternative, but time-consuming, data-splitting procedure may be employed. The alternative procedure is to remove one observation from the data set, run the regression model with the remaining $n - 1$ observations, use the model to predict the value for the omitted observation, and repeat the procedure by sequentially omitting each observation in turn and re-estimating the model and predicting the value for each omitted observation. This procedure will generate n holdout samples of size = 1. The predicted value for each holdout observation should correlate highly with the actual observed values. A subroutine in SAS can automate this procedure. Unfortunately, the procedure cannot be automated in SPSS, Minitab, or Excel.

15. See Neter, Wasserman, and Kutner, *Applied Linear Statistical Models*, 3rd ed. (Homewood, Ill.: Irwin, 1990), 465–470, for a more complete discussion of model validation.

16. Levine, et al., 436.

Homoscedasticity refers to variation around the regression line being equal for all values of the independent variable. When this assumption is violated (i.e., when the data is *heteroscedastic*) significant variable coefficients are apt to appear to be insignificant. Visual examination of a plot of residuals versus the independent variables or the fitted values of the dependent variable is a simple means of examining for violation of the homoscedasticity assumption. The data are not heteroscedastic when the distribution of residuals is similar across the range of each independent variable or the fitted values of the dependent variable. However, a plot showing systematic narrowing or widening of the range of residual values as the values of an independent variable or fitted values of the independent variable change is an indication of violation of this assumption.

Suggested corrections for violation of this assumption include replacing the values of the independent variable with the natural logarithm of the dependent variable (i.e., log transformation) or replacing the values of the dependent variable with the square root of the dependent variable (square root transformation). These two transformations replace the dependent variable with less variable functional forms. However, the replacement variables are undefined for negative numbers. If the size of the residual is correlated with the values of one of the independent variables, then the values of the correlated independent variable can assist in stabilizing the variance by dividing the regression equation by the correlated independent variable (known as *weighted least squares*). For example, consider the simple regression equation $price = \alpha + \beta(size)$, where size is measured in square feet. If a plot shows residual variance increasing as size increases, then division of the model by size should correct the heteroscedasity problem. The resulting regression model would be

$$\frac{price}{size} = \alpha\left(\frac{1}{size}\right) + \beta$$

In the new size-weighted equation, α becomes the regression coefficient on the reciprocal of size and β becomes the constant term. The resulting regression model would estimate price per square foot as a function of the reciprocal of size, which can be easily transformed into a price estimate.

Violation of the assumption of error independence most often occurs with time-series data. Residuals in sequential time periods may be correlated as a result of occurrences in a prior time period influencing subsequent time periods. This phenomenon is referred to as *serial correlation* or *autocorrelation.* Variable coefficient estimates remain unbiased under conditions of autocorrelation. However, the standard

autocorrelation. A condition in which residual error terms from observations of the same variable at different times are related.

multicollinearity. A condition in which the independent variables in a regression analysis are highly interrelated.

errors of the coefficients are biased, which affects the validity of *t*-statistics produced by a regression model.[17]

High interrelation among independent variables is referred to as *multicollinearity*. When this occurs the independent variables share explanatory power, and the coefficients on the correlated independent variables are consequently biased. Multicollinearity is often difficult to correct. When possible, gathering more data (increasing n) may help. Also, data reduction methods such as factor analysis and use of proxy variables can be employed to gather correlated variables together into a single representative construct. Historically, ridge regression has been suggested as a means of dealing with multicollinearity.[18]

Importantly, multicollinearity has no effect on a model's predictive ability. It does, however, seriously affect structural interpretation of a model's coefficients. Investigation of the existence of multicollinearity includes analysis of an independent variable correlation matrix and an examination of regression model multicollinearity diagnostics including variance inflation factors (VIFs), which most statistical packages will generate (though they are not available in Excel). The general rule of thumb is that no VIF should be greater than 10 and mean VIF should not be considerably larger than 1.[19] Note that a VIF of 10 equates to multiple correlation of .95, which may be excessive in many instances. Use of a maximum VIF = 5 criterion for multicollinearity implies multiple correlation below .90, and is suggested by some authors.[20]

Data Sufficiency

Data sufficiency refers to a decision regarding how many data observations are necessary for application of a regression model. This issue differs from the sample size calculation presented earlier for inferences about a mean. Instead, it is based on degrees of freedom, the relationship between the number of observations (n) and the number of independent variables in the model (k). When the ratio of n to k is too low, the model is "overfitted" and the regression outcome is in danger of being data-specific and not representative of the underlying population. For example, consider a ratio of n to k of 2. It is always possible

---

17. The Durbin-Watson test is one well-known means of testing for first-order autocorrelation (correlation between a residual and the next residual in a time sequence). An easy-to-read, understandable text on regression modeling with an entire chapter on the identification of and correction for violations of underlying regression model assumptions is Terry Dielman, *Applied Regression Analysis*, 3rd ed. (Pacific Grove, Calif.: Duxbury, 2001).

18. Graeme J. Newell, "The Application of Ridge Regression to Real Estate Appraisal," *The Appraisal Journal* (January 1982): 116–119; Alan K. Reichert, James S. Moore, and Chien-Ching Cho, "Stabilizing Statistical Appraisal Models Using Ridge Regression," *The Real Estate Appraiser and Analyst* (Fall 1985): 17–22; Doug Sweetland, "Ridge Regression: A Word of Caution," *The Appraisal Journal* (April 1986): 294–300; Jonathon Mark, "Multiple Regression Analysis: A Review of the Issues," *The Appraisal Journal* (January 1988): 89–109.

19. Neter, Wasserman, and Kutner, 409–410.

20. Hair, Anderson, Tatham, and Black, *Multivariate Data Analysis with Readings*, 3rd ed. (New York: Macmillan, 1992), 48.

to connect two points with a straight line. In this case R^2 would always be equal to 1 in a simple linear regression model, but the model may not actually explain anything. Since R^2 and the ability to generalize from a sample to a population are affected by the ratio of n to k, many researchers suggest that the minimum ratio be in the range of 10 to 15 observations per independent variable,[21] with a ratio of 4 to 6 being an absolute minimum.[22] One indication of an overfit model due to too low a ratio of n to k is an increase in adjusted R^2 as the least significant variables are removed from the model.

Statistical Applications

The advent of personal computers, spreadsheet programs, and statistical software allows appraisers to easily and accurately incorporate statistics into their analyses and appraisal reports. In the early years of personal computing, statistical analysis was generally limited to descriptive statistics and accompanying charts, tables, and graphs. As graphical user interfaces became more prevalent in operating systems, statistical programs such as SPSS, Minitab, and SAS became more user-friendly, mostly because the user no longer had to write programming code.

Also, as computer users became more sophisticated, spreadsheet programs added statistical tools to accommodate the needs of customers. Currently, Microsoft Excel includes a statistical tool pack that will generate statistical output such as correlation matrices, F-tests of variances, t-tests of means, and linear regression models. However, Excel provides very little in the way of diagnostics to accompany its inferential tools. Excel's statistical strength continues to be in its charting capabilities.

Automated Valuation Models

Tax assessment mass appraisal techniques existed long before the advent of so-called automated valuation models (AVMs), and they are now considered to be a subset of the AVM universe. Mass appraisal models were developed by property tax assessors to improve productivity and equity in urban and suburban locations where the manpower available was insufficient to carry out the assessed value estimation function. Moreover, in the early mass appraisal years, tax assessors were in a unique position to take advantage of large amounts of data that had been converted into a computer-readable format. Assessors continue to use AVMs as a means of automating assessment and make use of the large amounts of digitally coded data they possess. In addition, Internet access to more

> **automated valuation models (AVMs).** Computer software programs that analyze property data using an automated process and produce a value or range of values that may be used in property assessment or appraisal.

---

21. Hair, et al., 46.

22. Hair, et al., caution readers that a ratio of 4 is an absolute minimum, whereas Neter, et al., refer to a ratio of 6 to 10 as a minimum.

reliable data from taxing authorities and third-party data sources has enabled most appraisers to access the large data resources required for statistical analyses.

Initial research on AVMs pitted neural networks and expert systems against regression-based models. *Neural networks* "learn" the relationships among variables to develop and continually update an internal and unknowable price-estimation algorithm. Neural networks are essentially "atheoretical" in terms of their algorithms and can only be tested by comparing estimation results to a known standard. Because of their "black box" decision model, they have not had much of a practical following. *Expert systems* develop decision models based on attempts to mimic expert (e.g., appraiser) behavior. They essentially attempt to automate the human problem-solving process. For example, some AVMs employ an expert systems layer for such tasks as selecting comparable sales.

Regression-based AVMs apply multiple regression models at some level within the valuation product to produce a value-estimation equation, a value estimate, adjustment coefficients for automatically selected comparable sales, or some combination of these outputs. Many AVMs now include other features that enable appraisers, reviewers, and underwriters to produce and review descriptive statistics by user-defined property characteristics, market area, subdivision, zip code, city, or county. These features provide scales of reasonableness against which human appraiser contentions, assumptions, and conclusions are measured. In addition to the quality control function, AVMs also enhance a lender's ability to pre-qualify borrowers, conduct audits, mitigate loss, assess portfolios of loans, provide home equity loans, and engage in numerous other functions.

A variety of AVM products are offered nationally. A current estimate indicates that there are at least eight commercially available AVM systems offered in the United States, with new products emerging constantly. As the lending industry is working through issues and problems related to data reporting, data transfer, data accuracy, and modeling, AVM standards are continually being refined by industry organizations such as the Joint Industry Task Force on Automated Valuation Models, the Real Estate Information Providers Association, the Mortgage Bankers Association, the Mortgage Industry Standards Maintenance Organization, and others.

Although AVMs were initially perceived as a means of replacing human appraisers with machines, they have developed more recently into underwriting devices and tools designed to assist human appraisers and review appraisers. Today, practicing real estate appraisers are struggling to gain an understanding of AVM technology and the shifting markets for appraisal services and to determine how to take advantage of new business opportunities resulting from AVMs.

Custom Valuation Models

Custom valuation models represent another opportunity for appraisers to apply statistics. Given access to adequate amounts of data, which are more available in residential appraisal settings than in commercial appraisal settings, appraisers with adequate statistical modeling skill and appropriate software can apply statistical models to customized, unique valuation questions. Applications vary widely and include property tax assessment and equity studies, price or rent trend analysis, augmentation of traditional valuation approaches, impact studies addressing the effects of nuisances or environmental hazards, and preparation of value estimates for litigation.

Some custom applications are straightforward and easily modeled, while others are complex and difficult to model. Because production of a credible work product is of paramount importance, appraisers should not attempt to build a statistical model that is beyond the limits of their education and experience. As with any appraisal specialty, the ability to address complex statistical problems grows with experience. Experience and knowledge are best gained through collaboration with a qualified statistical analyst and through education. Statistical applications to complex appraisal problems, perhaps more than most appraisal specialties, require knowledge beyond what is currently available in the tightly focused world of appraisal education. With this in mind, appraisers should consider a community college course or an introductory undergraduate course in business statistics coupled with an upper division (junior or senior level) course in regression analysis and specialized appraisal courses dealing with statistics as the best means of preparing themselves to provide custom applications of statistical valuation modeling.

Misuse of Statistical Methods

Statistical methods are powerful tools for summarizing and describing data. They are also useful for making inferences about population parameters and for the construction of predictive models. Unfortunately, they are also easily and frequently abused. Abuse usually falls into two categories–overt attempts to mislead or ignorance. Manipulation of scale in charts, the provision of insufficient categories in frequency distributions and related histograms, and intentional omission of variables in regression models are examples of the former. Unknowingly violating the underlying assumptions of regression, too low a ratio of n to k, and failure to recognize limitations on sample representativeness could be examples of the abuse of statistics due to ignorance.

Sample representativeness can be a problem in appraisal, and this issue is rarely discussed. The problem stems from the fact that sales data are generally not randomly selected from the population of real property they are purported to represent. In some instances, sales data are representative even though they have not been randomly selected, and inferences are appropriate. However, in other instances some underlying factor may have had a temporary or location-specific influence on the decision to offer properties for sale, and the data thus affected may not be representative of the market as a whole. In these situations inferences derived from sales data may not provide a true picture of the overall market.

It is incumbent upon professional appraisers to present charts, tables, and graphs that accurately reflect the data being portrayed. In addition, appraisers who employ inferential statistical methods should be competent—educated in inferential methods and have experience with the software being used. The burden of proof of competence and lack of bias ultimately lies with the appraiser.

Frequently encountered problems of statistical misuse include failure to fully understand the ramifications of violating the assumptions underlying regression models, omission of testing and assessing the validity of a regression model and its underlying assumptions, and failure to correct regression models when necessary in order to adequately comply with the underlying assumptions. Three particularly problematic areas are multicollinearity, heteroscedasticity, and autocorrelation, which were discussed earlier in this chapter.

Other frequently encountered problems fall under the label of misspecification of regression models. They include "overfitting" where the ratio of n to k is too low, inclusion of irrelevant variables, and omission of important variables. The effects of these issues have been discussed previously. Note, however, that inclusion of any variable, relevant or not, will result in an increase in R^2. Adjusted R^2 provides a test of whether inclusion of an additional variable adds sufficient explanatory power. When adjusted R^2 does not increase with addition of another variable, then the additional variable is most likely irrelevant.[23]

In conclusion, credible regression modeling includes an assessment of data sufficiency, a residual analysis, an assessment of which variables should be included in a model, and model validation. Regarding data sufficiency, often an analyst has too few observations to facilitate inclusion of all of the variables known or thought to be important due to the ratio of n to k. Credibility requires an assessment of the need for and availability of additional data, or exploration of means of variable reduction such as factor analysis or proxy variables. In addition, an appraiser's workfile should include an analysis of residuals regarding the assumptions underlying any model employed and an assessment of functional form and support for variable inclusion decisions.

As a final cautionary statement, be aware that the ease of use of modern statistical software can contribute to production of a less-than-credible work product when the steps to credible model building are overlooked.

---

23. The additional variable should probably be included, however, if there is strong theoretical support for its importance to the relationship being studied.

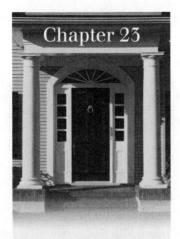

Chapter 23

Residential Appraisal Specialties

Traditionally, the most common appraisal assignment has been developing an opinion of the market value of a house for mortgage underwriting purposes. As the real estate and financial markets have matured and the appraisal profession has grown more competitive and more sophisticated, savvy, experienced residential appraisers have diversified their businesses. Many have moved into the appraisal of non-residential properties and others have expanded their expertise in specialized areas of residential appraisal. The residential niche markets can include specialized appraisal assignments involving a partial ownership interest in a typical residential property, appraisals of specialized residential property types, and value-related appraisal consulting services.

In a typical appraisal assignment, residential appraisers are most often asked for the market value of the fee simple estate (i.e., the complete bundle of rights of ownership), but they also encounter different types of ownership interests that require special considerations in the valuation process. Common ownership interests include

- Condominiums
- Cooperatives
- Timeshare properties
- Residences on leased land
- Planned unit developments (PUDs)

The sales comparison approach is generally the most applicable approach to value, although truly comparable sales can be difficult to find when a less-than-full bundle of rights is transferred. (Various forms of ownership were defined and described in Chapter 2.)

The special characteristics of certain categories of single-family residences set them apart from more typical houses.[1] These special-purpose residences often present problems for appraisers. Examples of residences with special physical, legal, and economic characteristics include

- Resort and vacation homes
- Senior housing
- Residential property in rural areas
- Manufactured housing
- Affordable housing
- Historic houses
- Solar, underground, and other experimental houses

In addition to market value appraisals of specialized ownership interests and residential property types, appraisers may provide appraisal-related services such as appraisal review and litigation support as well as other assignments outside the scope of work of an appraisal performed for underwriting purposes. Review appraisers must be proficient and experienced enough to judge the credibility of another appraiser's work, and they must be cognizant of the professional standards that relate specifically to appraisal review. Litigation support, which is often required in divorce proceedings, eminent domain cases, assessment appeals, and other situations, can be a lucrative niche for appraisers with the ability—and confidence—to deliver value opinions in court.

Many local and national real estate education providers offer continuing education that focuses on specialized property types and assignments. (A list of books, articles, and online resources related to the specialties covered can be found at www.appraisalinstitute.org/publications/books/resources/residential/.)

> **Competency**
>
> According to the Uniform Standards of Professional Practice, "Competency applies to factors such as, but not limited to, an appraiser's familiarity with a specific type of property, a market, a geographic area, or an analytical method." Specialized residential property types and appraisal problems often require specific knowledge and experience on the part of the appraiser to develop credible conclusions. The Competency Rule of USPAP requires appraisers to disclose the lack of relevant knowledge and experience before accepting the assignment and to take steps to acquire the necessary skills.

Condominiums

Individual condominium units are typically appraised using the sales comparison approach. A value indication derived from sales comparison may be supported by application of the income capitalization approach if rental data on units comparable to the subject unit are available. Resales of similar units in the same or similar condominium projects make the best comparables. Because it is difficult to make ac-

---

1. For a useful guide to appraising complex residential properties, see Frank E. Harrison, *Appraising the Tough Ones: Creative Ways to Value Complex Residential Properties* (Chicago: Appraisal Institute, 1996).

curate adjustments for differences in common charges, recreational facilities, size, design, and location, comparables must be selected from very similar complexes. The form of condominium ownership–i.e., fee simple or leasehold–is especially important in comparing properties. Adjustments for market conditions are also difficult to make because the market for condominiums is very volatile. Although the price of new, similar units should be considered, the resale prices of condominium units in some projects are substantially lower than the prices of comparable new units.

Many lenders require an analysis of the entire project when the value of an individual unit is estimated. The appraiser should examine the common charges and the expected rate of increase in these charges carefully because similar units in different projects may be subject to dissimilar charges.

Cooperatives

The most persuasive indication of the value of a cooperative apartment is obtained by analyzing the sale of ownership shares to comparable units in the same building or similar buildings. However, there may be some confusion about what constitutes the sale price of a cooperative apartment. For example, a share entitling an owner to exclusive occupancy of a three-bedroom apartment may be offered for $100,000. This price appears to be very low, but this amount is not the total price. If the entire building is subject to a $4.8 million mortgage and the shareholder's portion of this mortgage is $240,000, the real price of the unit is approximately $340,000. Therefore, in addition to normal operating expenses, the owner will have to make payments on a $240,000 share of the mortgage debt.

When sales of comparable units in the same cooperative corporation are available for analysis, no adjustment is needed to reflect the mortgage. However, the prices of similar units in different cooperative corporations may differ because the two corporations have dissimilar mortgage obligations.

Some cooperative corporations allow individual units to be rented to tenants, while others restrict the use of cooperative units to actual shareholders. If rentals are permitted in a given building, the appraiser can establish a correlation between rent and value and apply the income capitalization approach.

Timeshare Properties

To value a timeshare property, an appraiser first identifies the rights to be valued. These rights pertain to both the ownership and use of the property. The ownership of the shared property may be fee simple, tenancy in common, joint tenancy, condominium, cooperative, limited partnership, or real estate investment trust. The part of the property that is allocated for use by the shareholder must also be established.

The personal property included is an important consideration because many timeshare properties are sold furnished and equipped with appliances and utensils.

Resales of the timeshare property being appraised or of similar properties may provide reliable value indications. Resales are better evidence than new sales because new sales may be motivated by a developer's aggressive promotional campaign. If some of the units are rented during part of the year, the income capitalization approach may be applicable. Market research can help the appraiser establish the relationship between the rent a timeshare unit can command and its resale value.[2] If new timeshare units are being sold in the area and vacant land is available for construction of additional units, the cost approach may also be applied.

Residences on Leased Land

To value a residence on leased land, an appraiser uses the same techniques applied to residences subject to other forms of ownership. The value of the leasehold interest may be estimated by capitalizing the ground rent. An adjustment is usually required to reflect differences between the ground rents and lease terms of the subject property and the comparable properties. Depending on the appraisal problem, it may be necessary to estimate the value of both the leased fee interest and the leasehold interest.[3]

Planned Unit Developments (PUDs)

The problems encountered and the methods applied in appraising PUD residences are similar to those associated with the appraisal of condominiums and fee simple properties.

Resort and Vacation Homes

There are millions of resort and vacation homes and investment units in the United States. Most "second" homes are occupied by their owners on a seasonal basis. Some resort homes are mansions in resort areas for the wealthy, but the majority are modest homes located near a body of water or other recreational area.

Many developers are very active in the resort home market, subdividing large tracts of land and building extensively. Although there was some discussion about prohibiting the deduction of mortgage interest and real estate taxes on investment homes for income tax purposes, the Tax Reform Act of 1986 did not eliminate these deductions. The low interest rates of the late 1990s and early 2000s provided many homeowners with an opportunity to purchase investment property.

---

2. Weekly rental rates for similar timeshare units are compared with the rent of the subject unit and adjusted for the location, recreational amenities, and construction quality of the overall property and for the size, layout, and furnishings of the rental unit. See Kathleen Conroy, *Valuing the Timeshare Property* (Chicago: American Institute of Real Estate Appraisers, 1981), 35.

3. Edith J. Friedman, ed., *Encyclopedia of Real Estate Appraising* (Englewood Cliffs, N.J.: Prentice-Hall, Inc., 1978), 291–295.

In the mid-2000s, the Baby Boom generation dominated the resort homebuying market, and more than half of resort homebuyers had two or more properties in addition to their primary residence.

Appraisal Techniques

The resort home market can be volatile. Resales are persuasive indicators of the value of these residences. Initial sales, which are often the result of developer promotions, tend to be less reliable. When data on rents for seasonal residences are available, the income capitalization approach is applicable. When land is available for development and new homes are still being built, the cost approach may also be used.

Some homeowners have a timeshare interest in a resort home rather than the fee simple interest, which complicates the valuation process. The property rights conveyed is the most significant element of comparison in this case. (See the discussion of timeshare interests above.)

Senior Housing

Senior housing once referred to either age-restricted communities of single- and multi-unit housing or traditional nursing homes. Today, this property category encompasses a wide range of facilities providing an equally wide range of services, from independent living communities and congregate senior housing for seniors needing little assistance to assisted-living facilities (ALFs), continuing-care retirement centers (CCRCs), and skilled nursing facilities (SNFs) for seniors with greater needs.

The services provided in a senior housing facility fit into three general categories:

1. Hotel
2. Social work
3. Hospital/health services[4]

A benchmark measure of the level of social work and health care services required by the residents of a senior housing facility is the number of activities of daily living (ADLs) that each resident can perform. The developers of senior housing facilities increasingly design the improvements with the flexibility to provide services across the *continuum of care*, i.e., for both high-acuity and low-acuity patients, so that residents can "age in place" as their reliance on others for assistance with ADLs increases. Care providers see the aging-in-place concept as a strategy to diversify services, manage risk and operating costs, eliminate inefficiencies, and improve the quality and consistency of care.

When a new senior housing facility opens, it is likely to serve lower acuity residents; as the acuity levels rise over time, the facility can add direct care and nursing staff to accommodate the changing clientele.

---

4. Arthur E. Gimmy with Susan B. Brecht and Clifford J. Dowd, *Senior Housing: Looking Toward the Third Millennium* (Chicago: Appraisal Institute, 1998), 24. The licensing and regulation of nursing facilities varies by state. The American Seniors Housing Association publishes the *Seniors Housing State Regulatory Handbook* annually, which identifies key licensure and regulatory requirements for assisted living residences and continuing care retirement communities by state.

In the 1990s the number of assisted-living facilities serving low-acuity, private-pay patients grew significantly, as developers of senior housing facilities saw opportunities for growth in the underserved middle of the continuum of care. At the same time, longer life expectancies increased the number of residents in facilities serving residents needing more intensive care. With the first wave of the baby boom generation approaching retirement age in 2010, the demand for senior housing is expected to continue to rise across the continuum of care.

Traditionally, the senior market has been divided into two age groups:

- 50 to 64 years of age
- 65 and over

The first segment is composed of preretirement individuals or empty nesters. Many are still employed but find that their changing lifestyles warrant a different type of housing. Homebuyers in the senior housing market tend to prefer scaled-down single-family homes and townhouses in affluent neighborhoods or condominiums and cooperative apartments that require little maintenance. The second segment of the senior housing market can generally be broken down into three subgroups:

- Those 65 to 74 years of age who are enjoying their leisure time and may live in retirement communities
- Those 75 to 84 years of age who require some care but wish to preserve their independence and privacy
- Those age 85 and over who are frail or disabled

Appraisal Techniques

The appraisal of senior housing facilities at the lower end of the continuum of care–independent living units and congregate senior housing–is similar to the appraisal of resort homes and other limited-market residential properties. The appraiser may need to search a wide geographic area for comparable sales and rental units. Resales within a senior community tend to be the most persuasive evidence of market value, but initial sales of units in a community may not be as reliable if promotional discounts were offered for presales. In this case an adjustment for conditions of sale would likely be necessary in the application of the sales comparison approach. If an independent living unit has special construction and design features, locating comparables becomes even more problematic.

Special equipment and safety features such as fire-resistant construction add to the cost of congregate senior housing. Living units generally have less square footage than conventional housing and individual units may not have kitchens if residents take their meals in a central dining area. Also, rooms may be arranged for convenient access to facilities and public areas.

At the higher end of the continuum of care are ALFs, CCRCs, and SNFs, which may have more in common with health care facilities than with apartment buildings or other forms of multifamily housing. These differences have a significant effect on the appraisal techniques used to value these subcategories and the complexity of such assignments. The application of the income capitalization approach to nursing facilities must take into account factors such as the fee structure of the facility and the ability of patients to pay for services through personal finances or public means, e.g., Social Security, Medicare, and the prospective payment system (PPS). Comparable sales can be extremely difficult to find because the business operations of a nursing facility are often included in the sale along with the real property.

The appraisal of a senior housing facility that is sold with an operating business is often considered a classic example of business enterprise value appraisal.[5] Business enterprise value is different from the market value of the real property alone in that the value of the going concern (i.e., the business) must be accounted for. Analysis of business enterprise value is a sophisticated valuation assignment more often undertaken by appraisers specializing in non-residential property.

Residential Property in Rural Areas

Many factors distinguish the appraisal of residential property in rural areas from the appraisal of homes in urban and suburban market areas. The most obvious distinction is the distance between the subject property and population centers (commuting radius) and between the subject and comparable properties. The availability of data or at least the conformity of data is typically limited for rural market areas.

The lack of homogeneity among residential improvements in rural market areas is one of an appraiser's biggest challenges in the selection of comparable data. In urban areas, an appraiser typically selects comparables from a pool of properties with a similar building style, whereas residential properties in rural areas often include improvements with a mixture of building styles, ages, and uses. Typically, houses in rural areas have excess land. The presence of outbuildings (special-purpose, non-residential structures like stables and indoor arenas) is also typical of existing rural residential properties or proposed construction and requires an understanding of market recognition and lending practices.

The rural housing industry is supported by a network of mortgage lending organizations. Traditionally, rural residential properties have been financed through the Farm Credit System, Farmers Home Administration (FmHA), commercial banks, credit unions, and savings and loan associations. Other government-assisted loan programs are offered through the Department of Housing and Urban Development (HUD/FHA) and the Department of Veteran Affairs (VA). Secondary market lenders include Fannie Mae, Freddie Mac, and Farmer Mac.

Lenders may have specific property requirements that appraisers must consider in an appraisal for underwriting purposes. For example,

---

5. David C. Lennhoff, *A Business Enterprise Value Anthology* (Chicago: Appraisal Institute, 2001).

an urban-oriented lender may not recognize the impact of excess land, outbuildings, the distance from support communities, or the absence or limitations of public services and utilities. The appraiser may also need to consider additional instructions when the appraisal client is an attorney, relocation company, government agency such as the county government, Internal Revenue Service (IRS), or local, state and federal court, property owner, or potential purchaser.

Appraisal Techniques

Assignments to appraise residential property in rural areas generally require broader analysis of the market area, neighborhood, competitive supply and demand, and highest and best use than most appraisals in urban and suburban areas. The determination of highest and best use for an urban or suburban residential property is typically not a difficult process unless the property is in a transitional location. The highest and best use of rural residential property is often more complex and requires critical analysis of location and other value influences.

In general, location is the primary physical factor influencing value. With rural residential property, location factors include

- Adequacy and quality of access roads
- Convenience to support communities, schools, and main highways
- The availability of utilities such as electricity, natural gas, water, sanitary sewers, and septic systems
- The availability of schools, fire protection, police, shopping, and recreation

Economic factors to be studied include trend analysis of employment opportunities and rates, price ranges, and the direction of the local economy. Public and government influences that must be considered include utilities (or their absence), zoning (or the lack thereof), flood zones, wetlands, nuisance potential, scenic or conservation easements, the type and stability of local rules and the granting or application of zoning laws, real estate tax rate trends, and assessment procedures relating to excess land, recreational land, cropland, and other common uses of rural land. Social factors include population trends, the types and quality of rural homes, the appearance of the neighborhood, and price ranges.

Most appraisers working predominately in urban and suburban areas are trained to rely almost entirely on the local multiple listing service (MLS). Rural residential properties may be included within the local metropolitan MLS data, but as the distance from the population center increases, the amount of residential data to be found often decreases. Thus, rural residential appraisers must learn how to collect, verify, and analyze data from other sources. Professional real estate agents can provide primary data concerning the competitive listing and sale histories of comparable properties, especially in non-disclosure states. Other sources of general data include local newspapers, the

Chamber of Commerce, other appraisers and real estate firms, local and county assessors, and the client or owner. For specific data, common data sources include a search of public records, interviews with real estate agents, market participants (buyer and/or seller), attorneys, title companies, neighbors of the property being appraised, the builder (if applicable), the client, and the owner of the subject property.

Appraisals of residential rural properties most commonly involve parcels partitioned from farms and ranches, but assignments may also involve residential property on private land, government land, or Native American reservations. Rural appraisal assignments may also involve vacant rural land or land and improvements, various property rights and limitations on land use (such as utility and conservation easements, subsurface mineral rights, and water rights), and a variety of other improvements to land such as crops (timber, vineyards, and orchards) and natural resources. Specialized property rights or improvements complicate the appraisal of rural residential property further because comparable market data will be even more scarce.

Manufactured Housing

In 2005 manufactured homes made up approximately 6.4% of the United States single-family residential housing stock.[6] The appraisal of manufactured homes requires specialized appraisal knowledge to complete the assignment competently, and the demand for manufactured home appraisals is expected to expand, especially in rural areas where this property type represents an even larger percentage of the housing market.

Identification of a dwelling unit as a manufactured home is based on a specific definition. According to the Manufactured Housing Institute (MHI), a manufactured home is

> [A] single-family house constructed entirely in a controlled factory environment, built to the federal Manufactured Home Construction and Safety Standards (better known as the HUD Code).[7]

Other types of dwellings frequently grouped in the broader industrialized housing category, such as modular homes and mobile homes, are also assembled in a controlled factory environment, but they are typically not engineered and constructed to meet the performance standards established under the HUD code.

Again, according to the MHI

> [T]he Federal Manufactured Home Construction and Safety Standards (commonly known as the HUD Code) went into effect June 15, 1976. Manufactured homes may be single- or multi-section and are transported to the site and installed. The federal standards regulate manufactured housing design and construction,

---

6. U.S. Census Bureau, "Current Housing Reports, Series H150/05," *American Housing Survey for the United States: 2005* (Washington, D.C.: U.S. Government Printing Office, printed in 2006), Table 2-1. Available online at <www.census.gov/hhes/www/housing/ahs/ahs.html>.

7. Cited at <www.manufacturedhousing.org/lib/showtemp_detail.asp?id=446&cat=5> on Nov. 1, 2006.

strength and durability, transportability, fire resistance, energy efficiency and quality. The HUD code also sets performance standards for the heating, plumbing, air-conditioning, thermal and electrical systems. It is the only federally-regulated national building code. On-site additions, such as garages, decks and porches, often add to the attractiveness of manufactured homes and must be built to local, state or regional building codes.

A HUD label similar to that shown in Figure 23.1 should be mounted on every section of a manufactured home. In addition, each manufactured home will have a HUD data plate on the interior. It contains important manufacturing, identification, and design information. Many times, the HUD label(s) or the HUD data plate(s) have been removed from their original locations. The HUD labels are also often concealed by replacement siding, deck construction, or landscaping.

| Figure 23.1 | The HUD Label |

HUD Manufactured Housing Label
Aluminium 2" × 4" with white or silver writing

RAD1067875

THE MANUFACTURER CERTIFIES TO THE BEST OF THE MANUFACTURER'S KNOWLEDGE AND BELIEF THAT THIS MANUFACTURED HOME HAS BEEN INSPECTED IN ACCORD-ANCE WITH THE REQUIREMENTS OF THE DEPARTMENT OF HOUSING AND URBAN DEVELOPMENT AND IS CONSTRUCTED IN CONFORMANCE WITH THE FEDERAL MANUFACTURED HOME CONSTRUCTION AND SAFETY STANDARDS IN EFFECT ON THE DATE OF MANUFACTURE. SEE DATA PLATE.

Most manufactured homes are designed for single-family residential occupancy, and they can be an attractive housing option due primarily to their lower purchase costs. This savings is achieved through economies of scale for

- Administration, design, and engineering
- Labor
- Materials
- Equipment

In addition, factors such as weather, materials handling, security, lighting, and insurance are much easier to manage effectively in a controlled environment like a large assembly plant, rather than at a construction site. Also, scattered site construction of individual homes does not offer the same magnitude of vertical integration. Placement of the manufactured home on the site can be accomplished much faster than typical site-built construction. As a result, demand for housing, both for individuals and entire market areas, can be satisfied soon after the demand arises.

Although manufactured housing production in the United States has declined significantly from its high of 372,843 units in 1998 to about 131,000 in 2003 and 2004, there is a substantial supply of existing units that regularly cycle through the market for resale. Although production started to rebound in 2005, the nearly two-thirds decline in manufacturing from the peak years is attributed to

- Historically low interest rates, which made site-built housing more affordable than it had been for many years
- Tighter credit standards instituted by Fannie Mae and Freddie Mac in response to abuses during the manufactured home growth years of the late 1990s
- Excess production, stagnant inventory, and slow absorption

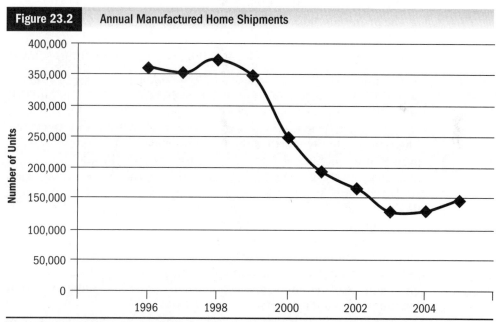

Figure 23.2   Annual Manufactured Home Shipments

Source: Manufactured Housing Institute, "Monthly Manufactured Housing Shipments," <www.manufacturedhousing.org/admin/template/subbrochures/387temp.pdf>

Appraisal Techniques

Valuations for secondary market mortgage financing, or government insured or guaranteed loans, likely comprise the bulk of manufactured home appraisal assignments. Thus, it is critical for the appraiser to be aware of the specific requirements that Fannie Mae, Freddie Mac, FHA, and VA have for appraisals of manufactured homes and to understand how the requirements influence the marketability and value of the manufactured home property being appraised. Because Fannie Mae and Freddie Mac are government-sponsored enterprises and FHA and VA are government agencies, their specific requirements are actually Supplemental Standards under USPAP.

Generally, the specific requirements focus on assuring that the manufactured home has been properly placed on the site, and that it has not been modified so that the home no longer meets the required minimum performance standards of the HUD code. Another important factor is the ability to determine if the manufactured home has been, or is able to be, classified as real property.

When constructed in the factory, manufactured homes are typically issued a vehicle title and are personal property until they are made into real property. This process requires that

1. The manufactured home be placed on a permanent foundation
2. The manufactured home have all transportation mechanisms such as axles, wheels, and hitches removed
3. The owner has the vehicle title voided by following the steps required in the specific jurisdiction
4. The property be assessed for taxation as a real estate improvement

As of January 1, 2006, Fannie Mae, Freddie Mac, FHA, and VA all required that appraisals of manufactured home properties completed under their Supplemental Standards be reported using the 2005 revision of the Uniform Residential Appraisal Report (URAR) Form 1004C/70C. The report actually clarifies the minimum scope of work that the appraiser must complete for manufactured homes. In addition to the normal property observation practices, the appraiser must investigate HUD code tags, which are mounted on the exterior of each section of the home, and the HUD data plate on the interior of the home.

The appraiser should always use great care in the property observation process to clearly identify the HUD code label and HUD data plate identification numbers, along with other important information such as the name and location of the manufacturer, the date of manufacture, and features of regional importance such as thermal efficiency, roof loading, and wind capacity.

The sales comparison approach is the preferred valuation technique for manufactured homes. Many intended users require development of the cost approach, even when the subject manufactured home is older and does not compete with new or recently constructed manufactured homes. In this case, the scope of work for Fannie Mae Form 1004C/Freddie Mac Form 70C requires the appraiser to develop the cost approach in such a manner that it can be replicated by others, such as appraisal reviewers or loan underwriters.

In general, appraisals of manufactured home properties require additional study and expertise that the appraiser may gain through continuing education, such as the Appraising Manufactured Housing seminar offered by the Appraisal Institute, or through association with appraisal professionals who are qualified in this property type.

Affordable Housing

The residential property submarket known as *affordable housing* or *low and moderate income housing* can been defined as "a hybrid between private market rate housing and a host of (largely non-economic) public purpose objectives."[8] The principal purpose of affordable housing programs is to provide housing for families who would not otherwise be able to secure adequate shelter because of their limited income. The affordable housing programs that have evolved over the years are very diverse and take many forms. Developments that qualify as affordable housing include owned and rented units, single-family and multifamily units, new and rehabilitated units, urban and rural dwellings as well as housing with programs targeted for people with special needs. However, there are certain characteristics and principles that all affordable housing units share, and these can form the basis for an appraisal or market study.

Affordable housing programs are based on a public and private recognition that housing markets are frequently out of balance, with costs of occupancy exceeding the income capabilities of low-income residents. There is a "societal good" in people living in adequate housing. Housing programs to serve low income populations have been in existence for 100 years and became significant programs in the 1930s.

Affordable housing developments are based on the following principles:

- Occupancy is targeted towards families with *below-market incomes.* Incomes are pegged to local median incomes published by the U.S. Department of Housing and Urban Development (HUD) and are updated annually. The levels established are typically no greater than 50% of median income for "low income" and no greater than 0% of median income for "moderate income" developments.
- There is typically a *time limit* attached to the restrictions on the units. The time restriction can vary from a relatively brief period such as five years to income restrictions in perpetuity.

---

8. Millennial Housing Commission, "Subsidized Rental Housing," background paper (July 26, 2001).

- Various types and combinations of subsidies are used to make the unit affordable. The subsidies fall into two general categories:
  1. *Capital subsidies* can be used to bring down the cost of building and operating the unit. These include direct grants, land grants, below-market interest rates, reduced property tax assessments, below-market utility charges, and other incentives.
  2. *Income subsidies* can provide residents with payments that bridge the gap between what they are able to afford and a market rent that is sufficient to pay for adequate housing. The Section 8 rent program is the most familiar program of this type.

Programs promoting affordable housing have evolved over time. The first programs were developed with Public Housing Authorities (PHAs) in the 1930s and are owned by local housing authorities. PHAs were particularly active in the 1970s. In recent years, there has not been significant new public housing development, but many of these developments have been reconfigured with a combination of demolition and replacement housing.

Later housing development programs used low-interest loans with mortgage insurance. (Within the industry, the programs were referred to by the relevant sections of the housing act, such as "221d3" and "221d4.") More recent housing developments were frequently linked with Section 8 subsidies and were structured to encourage investment though tax benefits. This type of development brought a significant number of "for profit" developers as well as non-profit institutions into the affordable housing field. The current affordable housing program is known as the *Low Income Housing Tax Credit Program* (LIHTC) or *Section 42 Housing.* This program began in 1987 as a means to promote private investment in affordable housing.

While the tax credit program is a federal housing program, the dominant federal agency is no longer HUD but the Internal Revenue Service (IRS). The principal benefit of investing in a qualified LIHTC property is to take advantage of federal tax credits that allow a direct deduction from the tax obligations of the investor under the terms of the program. Tax credits are sold to investors and the proceeds are used to write down the costs of development. Investors enter into a limited partnership that owns the development. The government supports the project by foregoing tax revenues and the threat of recapture of the tax credits helps ensure that the rules of the program are enforced.

A variety of developers participate in LIHTC projects–public agencies, non-profits, and profit-oriented developers. The principal investors are corporations seeking to "do well by doing good." Property owners may see additional value in depreciation, cash flow, and residual benefits at the end of the holding period.

Appraisal Techniques
A key part of any appraisal is the market analysis of the project's feasibility. A market analysis must include consideration of the market

area boundaries, demographics, the need and demand for the units, and income limitation requirements as well as comparable rental analysis (for both market-rate and affordable units), comparable expense analysis, and an understanding of any other special requirements such as special needs or age restrictions. While a property participating in an affordable housing program should have an economic advantage in the marketplace, there is no guarantee that the project will be feasible or will meet the needs of its intended market.

All of the conventional appraisal approaches to value can be appropriate in the right setting. The cost approach is useful in establishing insurable value and the cost basis of new projects. The sales comparison approach can be used in valuing "for sale" or "low-income homeowner" units. The sales comparison approach is also useful in establishing a value for rental projects when comparable income-restricted units have sold or the restrictions are ending within a reasonable time period.

Applying the sales comparison approach can be challenging because arm's-length sales of low-income housing developments, including tax credit projects, have been rare and must be substantially adjusted for financing terms, property rights conveyed, and condition of sales.

Appraisers generally give the greatest weight to the income capitalization approach in the valuation of low-income rental housing. Appraisers should consider the distinction between "tangible real estate" and "intangible values," such as tax credits and special financing. Operating costs should also be evaluated because they may be different from the costs experienced by market-rate rental operations. Capitalization rates are derived from a risk analysis of the property and by applying adjustments to the capitalization rates for comparable conventional apartments.

Appraisers valuing affordable housing must take care to meet basic competency standards because the programs and regulations are complex and can change. A careful review of legal and regulatory requirements is essential to ensure that the analysis conforms to evolving program issues and standards.

Historic Houses

Historic houses comprise a special category of residential appraisal. This property category is distinguished by the age, architectural character, and rarity of the houses and their ancillary structures.

A historic house is generally at least 50 years old and either associated with an event or an individual significant to national or local history or is an important example of an architectural style, a period, or an esteemed architect's work. To be a worthy historic property, a house should retain its basic architectural character, i.e., it should not have lost its significant characteristics through changes, additions, or eliminations. A relocated house has lost some of its historical integrity and hence its historic value, although it may have been necessary to move the improvements to preserve them. In addition, the new location may be superior for reasons other than historic context. A historic house may be one that contributes (i.e., is integral or complementary) to a historic district or other, more general historic locale, or it may have an individual designation conferred by the National Register of Historic Places or a state or local register.

Historic houses appeal to a segment of the residential market for several reasons:

- They are perceived to have more style and elegance than newer or more common houses.
- They are located in older neighborhoods with well-established amenities such as sidewalks, trees, parks, restaurants, shops, and public transportation.
- They are the work of a notable architect or an important part of national or local history.
- They present an opportunity to gain financial subsidies such as grants and tax credits for restoration or rehabilitation work. Designated historic properties are eligible for donations of preservation easements to non-profit organizations. In return, the donating owner receives deductions from taxable income.

In addition to their intellectual and artistic appeal to buyers, historic houses must incorporate adequate functional utility and comfort.

Historic houses may be eligible for certain financial benefits such as income tax credits, grants, or the income tax benefit from the donation of a preservation easement. Single-family dwellings are not eligible for federal income tax credits, but approximately half of the states have rehabilitation tax credits for houses. Each state has criteria establishing what buildings qualify for the credits as well as standards for the rehabilitation work. A state tax credit has value only to the extent that the owner carrying out the rehabilitation has sufficient state tax liability to make the tax credits worthwhile. In this regard, some states permit owners earning tax credits to sell them to another taxpayer who can use them.

To be eligible for tax credits for rehabilitating historic houses, houses must be listed on a historic register or contribute to historic districts that are listed on historic registers. The rehabilitation work must conform to a set of standards, most commonly the *Secretary of the Interior's Standards for Rehabilitation,* as interpreted by state historic preservation officers. Most state tax credits range from 20% to 30% of eligible rehabilitation costs. Their availability has made it possible for more owners to rehabilitate historic houses. Widespread rehabilitation has a cumulative effect: the more historic houses are rehabilitated, the more they become attractive to buyers.

Grants for the rehabilitation of historic houses are available on a state or local basis and differ widely throughout the country. The rehabilitations must meet the standards established by the grantors and, as is the case for tax credits, the objective is always to protect the architectural and historic qualities of the properties being rehabilitated.

Owners of houses that have historic designations or are certified as contributory to designated historic districts can donate preservation easements that prohibit or limit changes to the property. These easements must be binding in perpetuity, and consequently they diminish the market value of the properties so encumbered. A deduction from taxable income commensurate with the diminution in the market value of the property is available to the donor.

Appraisal Techniques

The sales comparison approach is usually the most applicable approach in valuing historic properties used as single-family homes. The income capitalization approach may also be applicable in valuing historic houses used as museums, conference centers, or bed and breakfast inns.

Historic house properties are subject to the same market value-influencing factors as non-historic homes. These factors include location, size, physical condition, functional utility, quality of building materials and construction, and landscaping. In addition, the appraisal of historic house properties requires analysis of factors such as the rarity of the historical associations, the relative importance of the architect involved and of the appraised property within the context of the architect's work, the popularity of the architectural style, the compatibility of the house with its surroundings, and the appropriateness of any rehabilitation work performed or contemplated with respect to the historic integrity of the house.

Applying the sales comparison approach to historic house properties can be a relatively simple process or a very difficult one. A historic house located within a historic district or neighborhood of similar houses can readily be compared with similar houses that have sold within the district or the neighborhood. If a historic house is atypical for its neighborhood, however, the search for comparables sales can be extended to a broader area. Very significant houses may be comparable only to houses of similar significance in other regions. Because location is the greatest variable in the market value of houses, any adjustment for a difference in location would have to be carefully derived.

The market for the greatest historic house properties may be national in scope and the prices paid well above the prices for more typical houses. At the other end of the range are small historic houses of various types. For instance, Lustron houses are now considered historic. In 1948 the Lustron Corporation began producing prefabricated enameled steel houses that could be washed with a garden hose and never needed painting. Approximately 2,500 Lustron houses were constructed before the company went out of business in 1950. Lustron houses have recently achieved public recognition for their design and history and a sufficient number of them are still standing to form a basis for market comparison.

Solar, Underground, and Experimental Houses

Investment in sustainable architecture tends to go hand in hand with energy conservation concerns. In 2005 the Energy Tax Incentives Act provided incentives to homeowners and developers for the purchase and construction of energy-efficient properties and improvements, including experimental building materials and techniques like solar hot water, photovoltaic and wind-turbine power-generating equipment, and fuel cell technology.

Passive solar heat is an alternative to heating systems that depend on fossil fuels. Because solar houses are built with special materials and designed for a particular orientation on their lots, they usually are more expensive to build. However, owners anticipate that long-term energy savings will offset the additional cost.

Houses built underground benefit from the fact that temperatures below grade are moderate year round. Because the heating and cooling equipment in these houses operates with less power, energy costs are significantly reduced. Earth-covered dwellings of poured concrete and concrete block are usually located on grade and bermed—i.e., set into a site that is partly or completely excavated.

Experimental houses are often built of unconventional materials such as plastic, fiberglass, and foams. These homes may be the work of nationally known architects and may incorporate unusual design features.

Appraisal Techniques

Application of the sales comparison approach to solar homes is difficult because these houses are scarce. Paired data analysis may be used if developers have built solar and nonsolar homes together. Solar houses are experimental, so part or all of the excess costs involved in their construction may add to the property's value. Some buyers will pay a premium for a solar home because they believe that the status associated with living in solar housing increases its value. On the other hand, the market may impose a value penalty on a solar home for its nonconformity. In some areas a solar home may represent an overimprovement. In each case the appraiser must carefully determine whether the value to be estimated is the actual market value or the use value to a specific owner.

Fannie Mae and Freddie Mac do not have restrictions against private power, water, or other utilities, but lenders with little experience with experimental houses may not accept a house with a private power source—rather than public utilities—as collateral if comparable sales with similar private utilities are not available.

In the United States, most underground housing is found in the Central Plains states where storm protection and reduced energy costs are important concerns. The sales comparison approach is generally applied to value these properties. Again, the availability of comparable sales may be limited.

The sales comparison approach is the best method for appraising experimental houses. Location is important, of course, and the status and amenity value associated with living in an experimental house may add to the property's value. However, the property's lack of conformity with neighborhood structures may affect market value adversely. As in the appraisal of solar houses, the appraiser should determine whether the value being sought is market value or use value to a specific owner.

Appraisal Review

The appraiser's work product often comes under the scrutiny of clients, other appraisers, and other users of appraisal services. The formal process of appraisal review is a quality control or auditing function with separate standards of professional practice that differ from those applicable to the development of an opinion of value. Review appraisers do not normally form an opinion of the value of the subject property but rather assess the adequacy and appropriateness of the opinions and evidence within the appraisal report being reviewed. If the review appraiser must form an opinion of value as part of the appraisal review assignment, then the professional standards relating to the development of an opinion of value do apply.

Residential lenders often keep review appraisers on staff to ensure that the appraisal reports submitted for underwriting purposes are credible support for the bank officer's loan decision. Likewise, mortgage insurers, federal agencies, and non-governmental enterprises often require appraisal reviews, and these entities may have specific appraisal requirements that will affect the scope of the appraisal review assignment. For example, an appraisal for a loan likely to be sold in the secondary market would need to meet all the requirements of the potential purchaser. The appraisal report forms used by Fannie Mae and Freddie Mac allow review appraisers to examine reports quickly and verify that all the relevant information is present.

Other common third-party appraisal review assignments include the review of appraisal reports related to condemnation proceedings, the acquisition of rights of way, and other government takings. Review appraisers also serve the corporate and private sectors by facilitating investment decisions as well as decisions relating to the management of properties as fixed assets. Courts also order appraisal reviews when the reported value opinions of appraisers on opposing sides of a legal issue cannot be reconciled.

The scope of work of an appraisal review is tied to the type of review required by the client (see Figure 23.3). For example, a lender making a low-risk home loan may only need a compliance review of the appraisal, i.e., due diligence that the appraisal report is complete. On the other hand, a contested value opinion in a court proceeding is more likely to require a thorough technical review of the appraisal report and perhaps even independent research by the review appraiser. Simple factual verification of the information within an appraisal report may not qualify as an appraisal review assignment as defined in USPAP if the information being reviewed does not relate to an opinion of value. An administrative review of an appraiser's work–i.e., a review performed by a non-appraiser–does not need to conform to professional standards of practice, but it should not be represented as an appraiser's review of another appraiser's work.

Figure 23.3	Types of Appraisal Reviews
administrative review	An appraisal review performed by a non-appraiser.
compliance review	A preliminary review of an appraisal to check the calculations and determine whether the appraisal report complies with basic content specifications. The compliance reviewer notes any discrepancies or omissions of items specified in the appraisal contract. A compliance review is generally performed by a client or user of appraisal services to exercise due diligence in making a business decision (e.g., underwriting, purchase, sale); it may be performed by an appraiser to assist a client with these functions.
technical review	An appraisal review performed by an appraiser in accordance with Standard 3 of the Uniform Standards of Professional Appraisal Practice to form an opinion as to whether the analyses, opinions, and conclusions of the report under review are appropriate and reasonable.
desk review	An appraisal review that is limited to the data presented in the report, which may or may not be independently confirmed. A desk review is generally performed using a customized checklist of items. The reviewer checks the accuracy of the calculations, the reasonableness of the data and the appropriateness of the methodology as well as compliance with client guidelines, regulatory requirements, and professional standards.
field review	An appraisal review that includes inspection of the exterior and sometimes the interior of the subject property and possibly inspection of the comparable properties to confirm the data provided in the report. A field review is generally performed using a customized checklist that covers the items examined in a desk review and may also include confirmation of market data, research to gather additional data, and verification of the software used in preparing the report.

In general, a review appraiser identifies and judges the reasoning and logic that underlie another appraiser's work but does not substitute his or her own judgment for the judgment of that appraiser. The reviewer appraiser's task is to analyze the total work product of the appraiser in an impartial and objective manner. Review appraisers violate rules of fairness and objectivity when they level undue criticism against an appraisal report. An appraisal review containing factual errors or substituting the review appraiser's judgment for that of the appraiser may constitute a breach of ethics. Also, the review appraiser must keep the opinion of value and the judgment of the appraiser confidential.

Litigation Support

Litigation work is often considered a subcategory of appraisal consulting, which encompasses a variety of professional services in which a value opinion is developed but a formal appraisal report is not necessarily submitted to the client. In our increasingly litigious environment, expert witnesses are in demand, and appraisers are often called as witnesses when the value of real property is at issue in a legal proceeding. Other matters in which appraisers can serve the courts and their clients include condemnation appraisals, easement disputes, estimates of property damages, insurance claims, fraud, property tax assessment appeals, estate taxes, and appraisal review for litigation support.

Appraisers who do litigation work must be highly skilled and confident of their abilities because of the adversarial nature of these assignments. Typically each party will hire an appraiser, and the value opinion and appraisal methodologies used to arrive at that opinion are likely to be challenged by the attorneys on each side. Appraisers may encounter conflict not only in the courtroom but also in dealing with client pressure to provide a predetermined opinion of value. Attorneys are advocates for their clients and are often paid on a contingency basis, which may put them at odds with appraisers, whose credibility is based on their objectivity and independence. Appraisers must clearly define the scope of work required by assignments for litigation purposes to avoid confusion as to whether an attorney is explaining a point of law or expressing an opinion regarding a value premise.

Testimony in court usually qualifies as an oral report, although a written appraisal report may be required, depending on the nature of the assignment and scope of work. While an appraiser's professional responsibility in a typical assignment usually ends when the appraisal report is delivered to the client, in litigation work the appraiser's responsibility continues until the case has been settled.

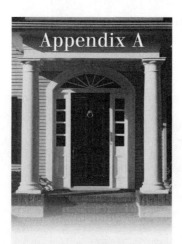

Building Components and Floor Plans

Professional appraisers must know residential construction details and local building codes. This appendix illustrates the construction components of a sample residence as well as floor plans and diagrams of the building's dimensions.

Residential construction details vary greatly in different sections of the country. For example, in much of Louisiana basements are not built because of the high water table. In Florida, it is unnecessary to build a deep foundation wall because there is no long period of freezing weather. In many parts of the Midwest, wide overhangs are used to get added protection from the hot sun.

Building codes often are different in adjoining municipalities within the same county. Therefore, what might be considered good construction in one area, could be below acceptable standards just five miles away. Obviously, the local building code takes precedence.

Adapted from "Anatomy of the House" by Joseph H. Polley

Section of Basement Wall with Brick Exterior

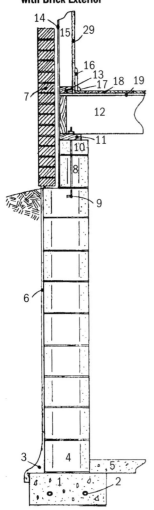

Poured Concrete Foundation

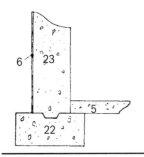

Foundation

1. *Concrete footing*—Usually 8" high and 4" wider (on each side) than the foundation wall.

2. *Reinforcing rods*—⅜" or ½" in diameter and used to strengthen the concrete footing, especially where the soil is porous or not firm.

3. *Cement cove*—Part of the cement parging on the exterior of the basement wall.

4. *Foundation wall*—Good construction requires 12" concrete block—sometimes 10" poured concrete is used. In small basements, 8" block is used to reduce cost. Cinder block should not be used below grade because it will deteriorate in certain soils.

5. *Concrete basement floor*—Usually 3" thick. Sometimes a plastic vapor barrier is installed under the slab.

6. *Cement parging and waterproofing*—Applied to the exterior to keep the basement dry.

7. *Brick veneer*—Standard size brick, used on the exterior to give the effect of a masonry dwelling. Often only part of the front wall is done this way.

8. When brick veneer is used, the tenth course of basement block is an 8" block to allow the 4" brick to bear on the outer edge of the 12" block.

9. *Anchor bolt*—½" in. diameter—16" or 18" long—Used to secure frame construction to masonry foundation.

10. The top course of block is a solid block which provides better bearing for the frame section of the building and also acts as a termite repellent since there are no openings through which termites could travel. Note the grading is held at least 12" below the nearest frame member.

11. *Sill plate*—A 2 × 6 or a 2 × 8 which is the first wood member installed in a building.

12. *Floor joists*—Depending on the span, 2 × 8, 2 × 10, or larger joists are used to support the floor load. Variances in type of lumber, grade of lumber, and size all have a bearing on the maximum permissible span.

13. *Sole plate*—The bottom member of frame wall section, 2 × 4 in a bearing wall and 2 x 3 in a nonbearing wall. Bearing walls support joists and rafters.

14. *Wall sheathing*—Usually asphalt impregnated celotex or gypsum. Sometimes ⅜" sheathing plywood or 1 × 8 sheathing boards are used.

15. *Wall stud*—2 × 4 in bearing walls and 2 × 3 in non-bearing walls. They are placed directly over floor joists for strength and are spaced 16" on centers since most building materials come in four-foot increments.

16. *Baseboard*—Usually 1 × 4 white pine trim lumber.

17. *Quarter round*—Usually ¾ × ¾—used to finish joint of baseboard and flooring. It is not installed when wall-to-wall carpeting is used.

18. *Finish flooring*—⁵⁄₁₆" strip hardwood, top-nailed. ²⁵⁄₃₂" tongue and groove hardwood in better floors and nails are concealed.

19. *Subflooring*—Usually ½" sheathing plywood. Better floors use 1 × 5 tongue-and-groove subfloors for extra strength and rigidity.

Scale: ¾" = 1'

20. A masonry exterior wall above the basement level is about 9" thick. It consists of 4" face brick, a 1" air space, and a 4" back-up cinderblock. Wood stripping is nailed to the blockwood on the inside so that lath can be installed.

21. Every seventh course of brick is installed so as to bond the brickwork and blockwork together. Sometimes corrugated metal strips called wall ties are used in the mortar instead of bonding with brick.

22. Poured concrete foundations are usually 4" wider (on each side) than the foundation wall. Note the keyway built into the footing so that the wall will lock into the footing.

23. A poured concrete foundation is usually 10" wide in residential construction. Plywood forms are erected to joist level. The forms are removed after the concrete has hardened and used again on another job.

24. Wood siding is applied over sheathing on frame exterior walls. Asbestos and aluminum siding are installed the same way.

Center Wall

25. The concrete footing under a Lally column is usually 24" × 24" × 10" high. The extra size is used to distribute the weight over a greater area and to prevent settling of the column.

26. A Lally column is a steel post, usually 4" in diameter and filled with concrete. It supports the steel center beam above it. Flanges are used as end caps to distribute the load.

27. Steel center beams vary in size according to the weight above. Typically, this beam is an 8" wide flange weighing 17 lbs. per linear foot of length.

28. A rowlock of brick, laid on edge beneath window sills.

29. *Drywall or plaster*—Drywall is usually ½" on walls and ⅜" on ceilings. Plaster is ⅜" rocklath plus two coats of wet plaster or a total thickness of ¾". A good plaster wall is three coats and ⅞" thick.

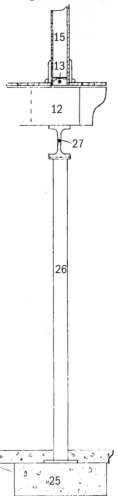

Center Beam with Bearing and Partion Above

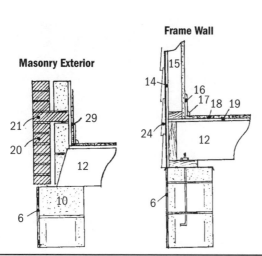

Masonry Exterior

Frame Wall

First Floor Section with Brick Veneer Below Window and Frame Construction Above

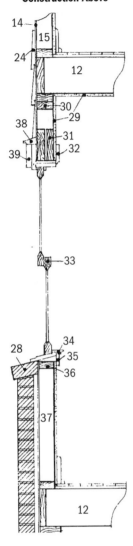

First Floor Wall

30. *Double top plate*—Two 2 × 4 members used to tie framing together at the ceiling line of all frame construction.

31. *Window header*—Double 2 × 6 over standard window rough opening to support load above windows. Wide windows require heavier headers.

32. White pine trim lumber around window on the inside.

33. Lower sash of double hung window.

34. *Stool*—Part of window assembly.

35. *Apron*—Part of window assembly.

36. *Rough header*—Part of opening prepared to receive window assembly.

37. Short stud called cripple stud.

38. Wood drip cap, which sheds rainwater.

39. *Wood casing*—Part of exterior window frame.

Roof Framing

40. *Rain gutter*—Various shapes—4" or 5". Attached to fascia.
41. *Fascia board*—1 × 8 white pine trim lumber.
42. *Soffit*—¼" plywood with vents inserted to relieve summer heat in attic space.
43. *Quarter round*—Used to seal joint between shingles and soffit.
44. *Outlooker*—2 × 3 or 2 × 2 on 16" centers to support soffit.
45. *Ceiling joist*—2 × 6 or heavier. Size depends on attic floor load above it.
46. *Insulation*—Loose spun glass or batts of glass wool.
47. *Roof rafter*—2 × 6 on 16" centers placed over studs which are directly over joists for maximum support.
48. *Roof shingles*—Wood, asbestos, or asphalt. Usually asphalt weighing 235# per square (10' x 10' or 100 sq. ft.).
49. *Felt paper*—15# roofing paper.
50. *Roof sheathing*—½" sheathing plywood or 1 × 8 roofing boards.
51. Diagram that indicates pitch of roof. This roof rises 5" for every 12" of run (horizontal).
52. *Collar beam*—2 × 8 used on alternate roof rafters to strengthen roof framing in order to support snow loads.
53. *Ridge rafter*—2 × 8 center beam— ties roof rafters together.
54. *Sidewall insulation*—Usually 2" batts.

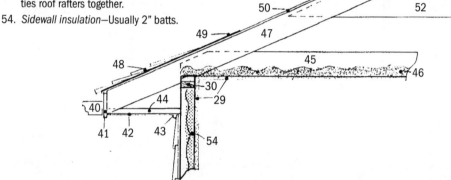

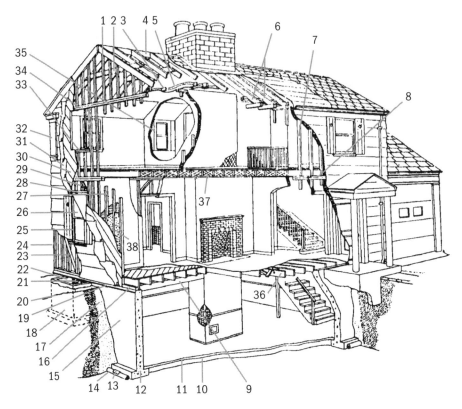

1. Gable stud	14. Drain tile	27. Wall studs
2. Collar beam	15. Foundation wall	28. Header
3. Ceiling joist	16. Sill	29. Window cripple
4. Ridge board	17. Backfill	30. Wall sheathing*
5. Insulation	18. Areaway wall	31. Building paper
6. Rafters	19. Termite shield	32. Pilaster
7. Stud	20. Grade line	33. Rough header
8. Double plate	21. Basement sash	34. Window stud
9. Girder	22. Areaway	35. Window casing
10. Gravel fill	23. Corner brace	36. Floor joists
11. Concrete floor	24. Corner stud	37. Bridging
12. Foundation footing	25. Window frame	38. Insulation
13. Paper strip	26. Window light	

*   These items are found only in older homes.

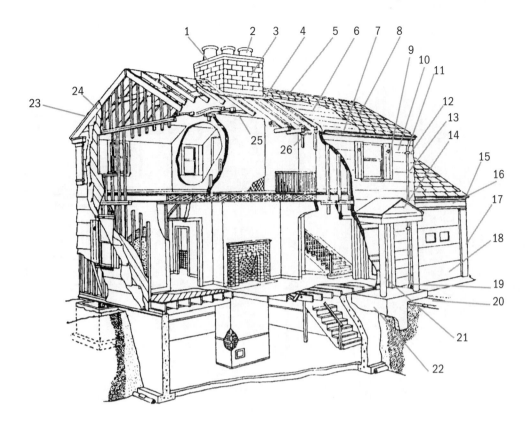

1. Chimney cap
2. Chimney pots
3. Chimney
4. Chimney flashing
5. Ridge
6. Roof boards
7. Eave gutter
8. Roofing
9. Blind or shutter
10. Bevel siding
11. Downspout gooseneck
12. Downspout strap
13. Downspout leader
14. Entrance canopy
15. Garage cornice
16. Frieze
17. Door jamb
18. Garage door
19. Downspout shoe
20. Sidewalk
21. Entrance post
22. Entrance platform
23. Cornice molding
24. Frieze board
25. Attic space
26. Lookout

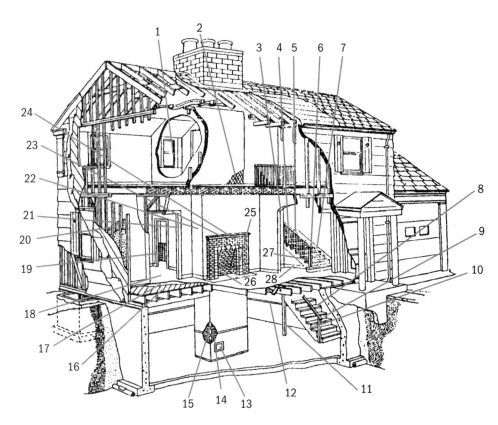

1. Window sash
2. Metal lath
3. Plaster arch
4. Balusters
5. Stair rail
6. Newel cap
7. Finish stringer
8. Stair tread
9. Stair riser
10. Stair stringer

11. Girder post
12. Chair rail*
13. Cleanout door
14. Furring strips
15. Corner stud
16. Diagonal subfloor*
17. Building paper
18. Finish floor
19. Wainscoting

20. Lath
21. Door trim
22. Chimney breast
23. Mantel
24. Fire brick
25. Fireplace hearth
26. Ash dump
27. Newel
28. Baseboard

* These items are found only in older homes.

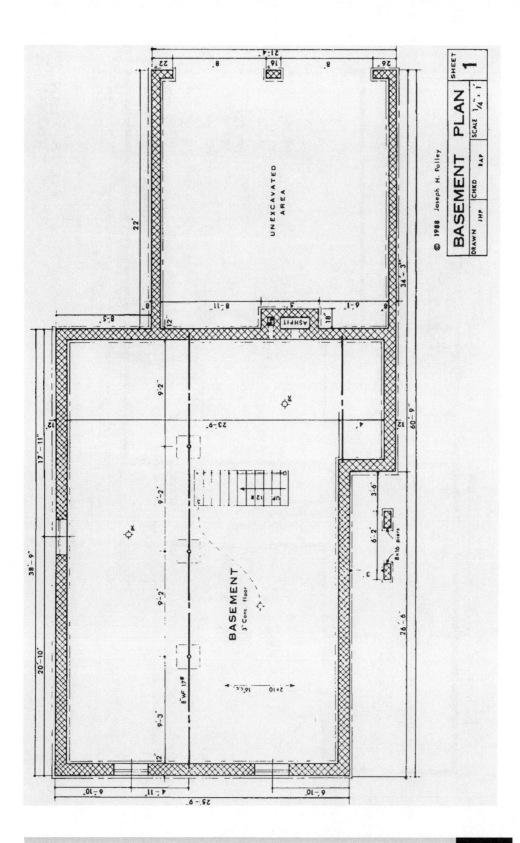

BASEMENT PLAN

© 1988 Joseph H. Folley

SHEET 1

| DRAWN JHP | CHKD RAP | SCALE ¼″: 1′ |

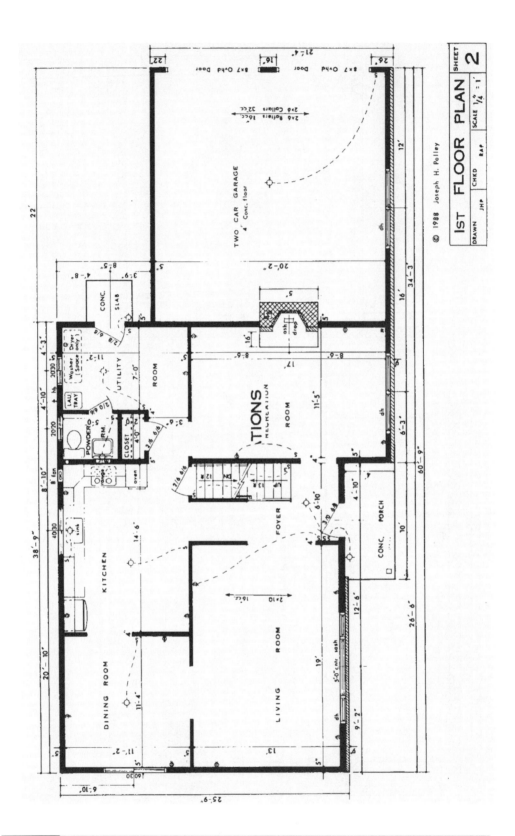

© 1988 Joseph H. Polley

1ST FLOOR PLAN

SHEET 2

SCALE ¼" = 1'

| DRAWN | JHP | CHKD | RAP |

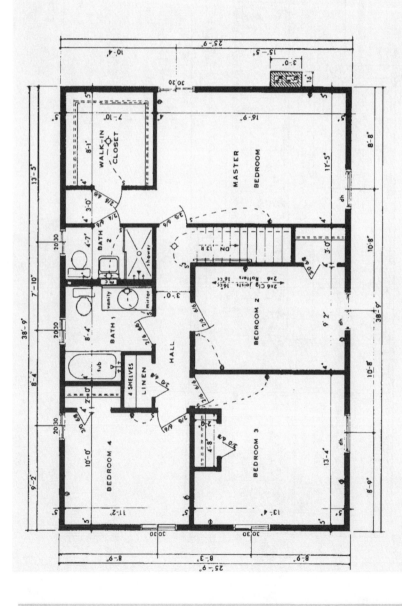

2ND FLOOR PLAN | SHEET 3

DRAWN	CHKD	SCALE
JHP	RAP	1/4" = 1'

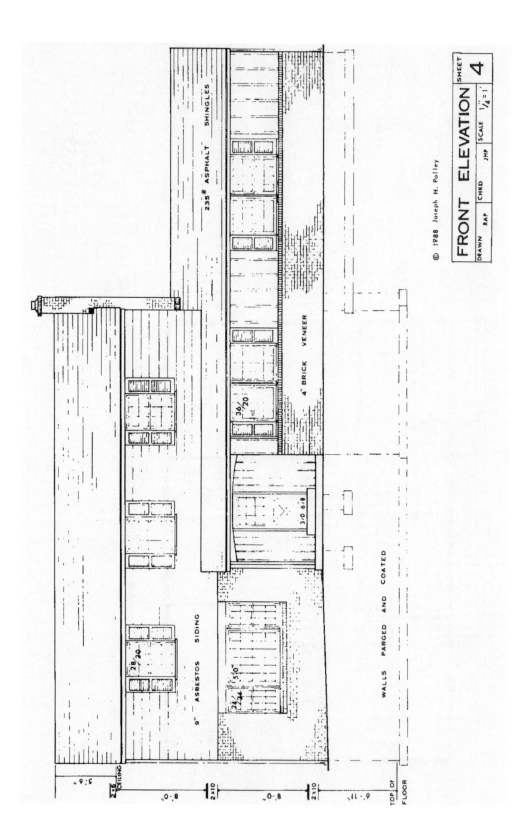

FRONT ELEVATION

SHEET 4

SCALE 1/4" = 1'

DRAWN RAP CHKD JHP JHP

© 1988 Joseph H. Polley

235# ASPHALT SHINGLES

4' BRICK VENEER

9" ASBESTOS SIDING

WALLS PARGED AND COATED

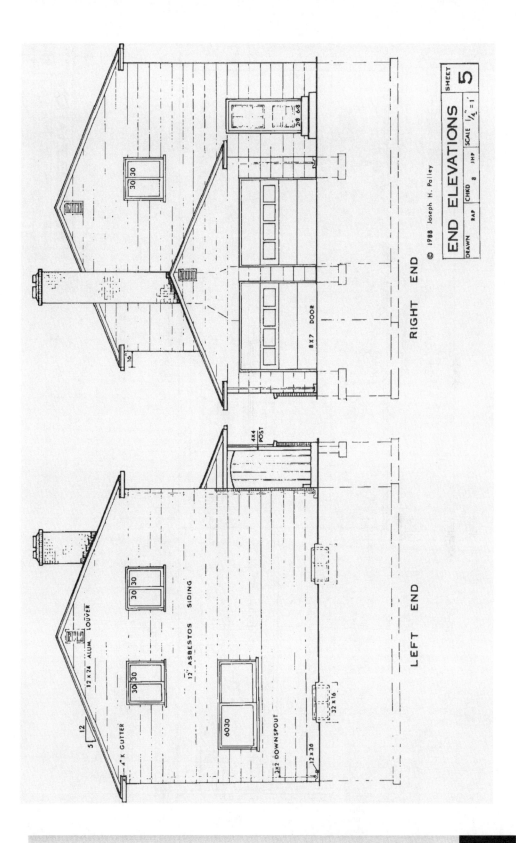

END ELEVATIONS

© 1988 Joseph H. Polley

DRAWN	CHKD	SHEET
RAP	8 JHP	5
	SCALE 1/4" = 1'	

RIGHT END

LEFT END

2/8 6•8

8 X 7 DOOR

30 30

4X4 POST

30 30

12 × 24 ALUM. LOUVER

12" ASBESTOS SIDING

30 30

6030

12

5

4" K GUTTER

32 × 16

2X2 DOWNSPOUT

12 × 36

16

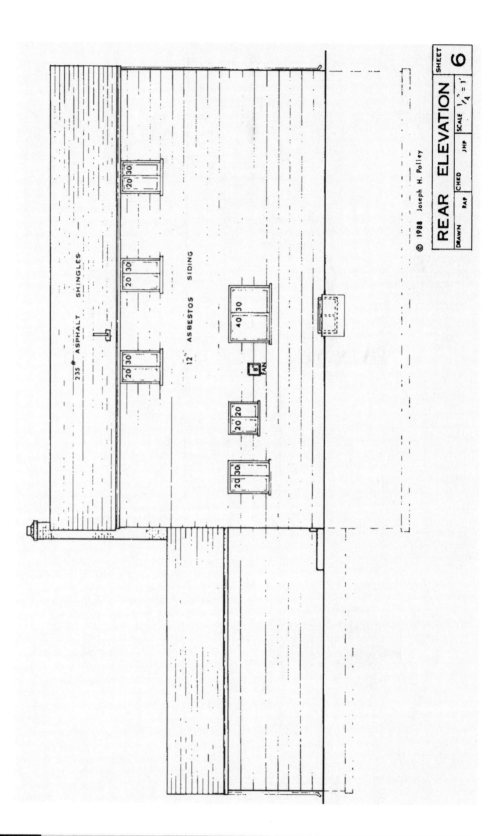

235 # ASPHALT SHINGLES

12' ASBESTOS SIDING

20	30
20	30
20	30

| 40 | 30 |

FAN

| 20 | 20 |

| 20 | 30 |

REAR ELEVATION

© 1988 Joseph H. Polley

DRAWN	CHKD	SCALE	SHEET
RAF	JHP	1/4" = 1'	6

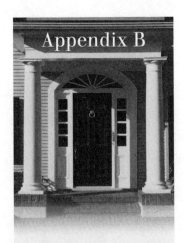

Square Footage–Method for Calculating:
ANSI Z765-2003

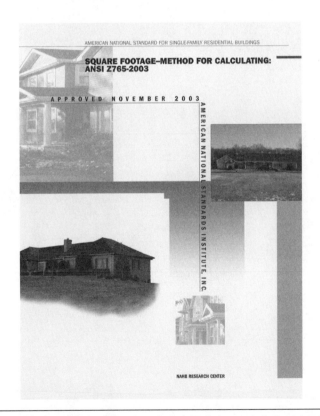

Published by
NAHB Research Center
400 Prince George's Boulevard
Upper Marlboro, Maryland
20774-8731
800-638-8556 phone
301-430-6180 fax

Printed in the United States
of America.

An American National Standard is developed through a consensus process that involves those organizations and individuals directly and materially affected by the existence of a standard. A standard itself is a voluntary guide for producers and consumers. The American National Standards Institute is the central body responsible for identifying a single, consistent set of voluntary standards and verifying that the principles of openness and due process are heeded. All American National Standards are subject to periodic review and revision.

A standard allows individuals and organizations that use different terminologies based on different points of view to communicate, cooperate, and calculate quantities on a common basis. This standard promotes these goals in the hope that square footage calculation can become an item of agreement rather than a point of contention between groups with different interests and concerns.

This standard for the calculation and reporting of above-grade square footage and below-grade square footage in single-family houses is offered for voluntary application. The standard must be applied as a whole. The standard is not meant to replace or supersede any legal or otherwise required existing area measurement method. It may be used in proposed, new, or existing single-family houses of any style or construction but is not applicable to apartment/multifamily buildings. It does not cover room dimensions.

Before the adoption of the standard in 1996, no nationwide standard existed in the United States for measuring square footage in single-family houses. By contrast, a standard applicable to commercial buildings has been in effect for 80 years. In 1915, the Building Owners and Managers Association International (BOMA) developed a standard method for measuring floor area in office buildings. The BOMA standard was revised in 1952, 1955, 1971, 1980, 1989, and 1996 and now bears the title Standard Method for Measuring Floor Area in Office Buildings, ANSI/BOMA Z65.1-1996.

The Ontario New Home Warranty Program issued Builder Bulletin No. 22—Floor Area Calculations on November 15, 1989. The bulletin's set of requirements for uniform floor area calculation applies to single-family houses and condominiums that enroll in the program and only when a numeric value for floor area is used in advertising and sales materials, in an agreement of purchase and sale, in a construction contract, or whenever the size of the house is stated in printed materials. Over the years, other groups have developed their own conventions for square footage calculation within their organizations.

In April 1994, the National Association of Home Builders (NAHB)—at the request of the Home Builders Association of Greater New Orleans and other builder members—commissioned the NAHB Research Center (a wholly owned subsidiary of NAHB) to act as secretariat for an ANSI Accredited Standards Committee and to assemble a group of organization representatives and individuals materially and directly affected by the development of an ANSI Standard for the measurement of square footage in detached and attached single-family houses. The committee held its first meeting on November 22, 1994.

ANSI procedures require periodic review to ensure that standards are current and relevant. In 2001 a standard committee was formed to consider changes to the 1996 edition of ANSI Z765. The committee accepted changes to Section 4 of the standard and to its Annex. The changes to Section 4 consisted of an editorial reorganization of its provisions and the addition of a subsection specifying reporting requirements for calculation results produced using other measurement methods. The changes to the Annex consisted of (1) the addition of a description of decorative finishes for concrete floors, along with recognition of this type of concrete floor as a type of floor finish; and (2) the addition of text acknowledging that the standard does not address differences between calculations made by multiple parties for the same property.

The standard embodies one informative Annex that is intended to comment on and illustrate the standard; however, the Annex is not considered part of the standard.

Suggestions for improvement of the standard are welcome and should be forwarded to the secretariat:

NAHB Research Center
400 Prince George's Boulevard
Upper Marlboro, Maryland 20774-8731
301-249-4000 phone
301-430-6180 fax
http://www.nahbrc.org

This standard was processed and approved for submittal to ANSI by the Accredited Standards Committee on Residential Square Footage, Z765. Committee approval of the standard does not necessarily imply that all committee members voted for its approval. At the time it approved this standard, the Z765 Committee consisted of the following members listed in the right column.

Wayne M. Foley, Chair
Thomas Kenney, Secretariat–NAHB Research Center

NAME OF REPRESENTATIVE AND ORGANIZATION REPRESENTED

Paul Armstrong
International Code Council

Craig Auberger
American Association of Certified Appraisers

John Battles
International Code Council

Ron Burton
BOMA International

Mark Chambers
Godfrey-Chambers Homes, Inc.

Gerald Davis
International Centre for Facilities

Wayne Foley
W. M. Foley Construction Group

Swayn Hamlet
National Association of Realtors

Charles Hardie
Fran-Hardy Homes, Inc.

James Hill
National Institute of Standards and Technology

Jane Kneessi
U.S. Department of Commerce, Bureau of the Census

A.J. Tony Martinez
Yavapai County Assessor

James Nanni
Consumers Union

Tracy Riggan
MCL Companies

ii

SQUARE FOOTAGE–METHOD FOR CALCULATING: ANSI Z765-2003

1. SCOPE AND PURPOSE

Scope

This standard describes the procedures to be followed in measuring and calculating the square footage of detached and attached single-family houses.

Purpose

It is the purpose of this standard to describe a method of measurement that will make it possible to obtain accurate and reproducible measurements of square footage in single-family houses.

2. DEFINITIONS

Attached Single-Family House

A house that has its own roof and foundation, is separated from other houses by dividing walls that extend from roof to foundation, and does not share utility services with adjoining houses; may be known as a townhouse, rowhouse, or duplex, for example.

Detached Single-Family House

A house that has open space on all its sides.

Finished Area

An enclosed area in a house that is suitable for year-round use, embodying walls, floors, and ceilings that are similar to the rest of the house.

Garage

A structure intended for the storage of automobiles and other vehicles.

Grade

The ground level at the perimeter of the exterior finished surface of a house.

Level

Areas of the house that are vertically within 2 feet of the same horizontal plane.

Square Footage

An area of a house that is measured and calculated in accordance with the standard. When employing Metric or Standard International (SI) measurement units, the term floor area is used in place of square footage.

Unfinished Area

Sections of a house that do not meet the criteria of finished area.

3. CALCULATION OF SQUARE FOOTAGE

To claim adherence to this standard, the following methods of measurement and calculation must be employed when quantifying square footage in single-family houses. When using English measurement units, the house is measured to the nearest inch or tenth of a foot; the final square footage is reported to the nearest whole square foot. When using Metric or Standard International (SI) measurement units, the house is measured to the nearest 0.01 meter; the final floor area is reported to the nearest 0.1 square meter.

Calculation Methods

Calculation of square footage made by using exterior dimensions but without an inspection of the interior spaces is allowed but must be stated as such when reporting the result of the calculation. Calculation of square footage for a proposed house made by using plans must be stated as such when reporting the result of the calculation.

Circumstances can exist when direct measurement of a structure is not possible. Access to the interior may not be available and the nature of the terrain, structure, or other obstacles may preclude direct physical measurement of the exterior in the time available. Building dimensions developed through some means other than direct measurement or plans can be susceptible to inaccuracy, as is the calculated area. Calculation of square footage developed under such circumstances must be identified as such when reporting the result of the calculation.

Detached Single-Family Finished Square Footage

For detached single-family houses, the finished square footage of each level is the sum of finished areas on that level measured at floor level to the exterior finished surface of the outside walls.

Attached Single-Family Finished Square Footage

For attached single-family houses, the finished square footage of each level is the sum of the finished areas on that level measured at floor level to the exterior finished surface of the outside wall or from the centerlines between houses, where appropriate.

Finished Areas Adjacent to Unfinished Areas

Where finished and unfinished areas are adjacent on the same level, the finished square footage is calculated by measuring to the exterior edge or unfinished surface of any interior partition between the areas.

Openings to the Floor Below

Openings to the floor below cannot be included in the square footage calculation. However, the area of both stair treads and landings proceeding to the floor below is included in the finished area of the floor from which the stairs descend, not to exceed the area of the opening in the floor.

Above- and Below-Grade Finished Areas

The above-grade finished square footage of a house is the sum of finished areas on levels that are entirely above grade. The below-grade finished square footage of a house is the sum of finished areas on levels that are wholly or partly below grade.

Ceiling Height Requirements

To be included in finished square footage calculations, finished areas must have a ceiling height of at least 7 feet (2.13 meters) except under beams, ducts, and other obstructions where the height may be 6 feet 4 inches (1.93 meters); under stairs where there is no specified height requirement; or where the ceiling is sloped. If a room's ceiling is sloped, at least one-half of the finished square footage in that room must have a vertical ceiling height of at least 7 feet (2.13 meters); no portion of the finished area that has a height of less than 5 feet (1.52 meters) may be included in finished square footage.

Finished Areas Connected to the House

Finished areas that are connected to the main body of the house by other finished areas such as hallways or stairways are included in the finished square footage of the floor that is at the same level. Finished areas that are not connected to the house in such a manner cannot be included in the finished square footage of any level.

Garages, Unfinished Areas, and Protrusions

Garages and unfinished areas cannot be included in the calculation of finished square footage. Chimneys, windows, and other finished areas that protrude beyond the exterior finished surface of the outside walls and do not have a floor on the same level cannot be included in the calculation of square footage.

4. STATEMENT OF FINISHED SQUARE FOOTAGE

Failure to provide the declarations listed below–where applicable–voids any claim of adherence to this standard.

Rounding

The finished square footage of a house is to be reported to the nearest whole square foot for above-grade finished square footage and for below-grade finished square footage. When using SI units, floor area is reported to the nearest 0.1 square meter.

Reporting of Above- and Below-Grade Areas

No statement of a house's finished square footage can be made without the clear and separate distinction of above-grade areas and below-grade areas.

Areas Not Considered Finished

Finished areas that are not connected to the house, unfinished areas, and other areas that do not fulfill the requirements of finished square footage prescribed above cannot be included in the Statement of Finished Square Footage but may be listed separately if calculated by the methods described in this standard. Any calculation and statement of unfinished square footage must distinguish between above-grade areas and below-grade areas.

Interior Spaces Not Inspected Method

If the calculation of finished square footage is made without an inspection of interior spaces to confirm finished areas, unfinished areas, or openings in the floor, the Statement of Finished Square Footage must include a declaration similar to the following:

DECLARATION 1

"Finished square footage calculations for this house were made based on measured dimensions only and may include unfinished areas, openings in floors not associated with stairs, or openings in floors exceeding the area of associated stairs."

Plans-Based Method

If the calculation of finished square footage is made from the plans of a proposed house, the Statement of Finished Square Footage must include a declaration similar to the following:

DECLARATION 2

"Finished square footage calculations for this house were made based on plan dimensions only and may vary from the finished square footage of the house as built."

Other Methods

Circumstances can exist when direct measurement of a structure is not possible. Access to the interior may not be available and the nature of the terrain, structure, or other obstacles may preclude direct physical measurement of the exterior in the time available. Building dimensions developed through some means other than direct measurement or plans can be susceptible to inaccuracy, as is the calculated area. Calculations developed under such circumstance must include a declaration similar to the following:

DECLARATION 3

"Finished square footage calculations for this house were made based on estimated dimensions only and may include unfinished areas, or openings in floors not associated with stairs, or openings in floors exceeding the area of associated stairs."

COMMENTARY ON ANSI Z765

This standard is not designed for and cannot be applied to the measurement of apartment/multifamily buildings, but it may be employed to measure all detached and attached single-family houses, including townhouses, rowhouses, and other side-by-side houses.

Practitioners of the standard are cautioned to confirm the appropriate legal definition of ownership of the house if applied to detached single-family or attached single-family condominium units to avoid violation of state law. Differences between the method for calculating finished square footage as set out in the standard and methods prescribed by state law to calculate the area of a condominium unit must be resolved on an individual basis. Legal definitions of condominium ownership can be obtained from the state body charged with archiving state law.

The committee chose to use the term square footage (instead of floor area) because of its common use by producers and consumers of housing.

The methods of measurement and calculation put forth in this standard are not intended or designed to cover the dimensions of rooms within single-family houses. Room dimensions are typically measured between interior finished surfaces rather than between exterior finished surfaces as described in this standard.

The term habitable space is often used by established building codes to describe a room or space that has as one of its requirements a specified amount of natural or mechanical light and ventilation sources. The definition of finished area—as employed in this standard—does not imply that finished spaces conform to any requirement for light and ventilation.

This standard makes a clear delineation between above-grade square footage and below-grade square footage; no statement of a house's square footage can be made without that clear and separate distinction. Given the above-grade and below-grade distinction and the definition of grade, the committee acknowledges that this may result in houses that—depending on topography, design, or grade line—have no calculated above-grade finished square footage derived from the method of measurement employed by this standard. This possible consequence arises from the committee's intent to quantify a house's area while minimizing the likelihood of misinterpretation or misapplication. Houses that are alternatively described as at grade or on grade are typically considered above-grade houses.

Wall and ceiling finishes include but are not limited to painted gypsum wall board, wallpaper-covered plaster board, and wood paneling. Floor finishes include but are not limited to carpeting, vinyl sheeting, hardwood flooring, and concrete floors with decorative finishes but do not include bare or painted concrete.

Decorative finishes are long-lasting or permanent components of the slab produced by such methods as chemical staining, integral coloration of the concrete, scoring, or stamping that modify the texture or appearance of the slab.

For a room to be included in the square footage calculation, the floor located under sloping ceilings must have a clearance of at least 5 feet (1.52 meters); further, at least one-half of the square footage in the room must have ceilings of at least 7 feet (2.13 meters) in height. For example, a one-and-one-half-story, 28 by 42 foot Cape Cod-style house has a first level with a ceiling height of 8 feet. On the second level, the ceiling has a maximum height of 9 feet but a minimum height of 4 feet at the walls as the ceiling slopes to match the pitch of the roof. All areas are finished. While the first level has 1,176 above-grade finished square feet, only that portion of the second level meeting the ceiling height requirements described above is included in the square footage calculation.

Where finished and unfinished areas are adjacent on the same level, finished square footage is calculated by measuring to the exterior edge or unfinished surface of any interior partition between the areas. For partitions between a finished area and a garage (usually a fire-rated wall), the measurement is made to the surface of the gypsum wall board on the garage side of the partition. For a partition that separates a finished area from an unfinished area (often not a fire-rated wall), the measurement is made to the portion of the partition closest to the unfinished area—usually a wood stud or other framing member.

Porches, balconies, decks, and similar areas that are not enclosed or not suitable for year-round occupancy cannot be included in the Statement of Finished Square Footage but may be listed separately, measured from the exterior finished surface of the house to the outer edge of the floor surface area or exterior surface, and calculated by using the method referenced in the standard.

The treatment of garage area in the standard allows practitioners to apply local customs. While garages can never be included in finished square footage, the standard does allow the area to be included in unfinished square footage. In the diagrams that accompany this standard, Figure 1 largely shows the garage (and the adjoining laundry) as a structure attached to the main body of the house. As such, the garage is not typically treated as an unfinished area of the house but rather as a separate area simply referred to as "garage." However, if the garage is located beneath the main body of the house, some localities treat the area as part of the house and contributing to unfinished square footage. Practitioners are urged to heed common local convention with regard to garages.

Finished areas above garages are included in the finished square footage that is at the same level in the main body of the house, but only if they are connected to the house by continuous finished areas such as hallways or staircases.

Exterior finishes include but are not limited to masonry or masonry veneer; wood, aluminum, or vinyl siding; or gypsum wall board when used on the exterior wall common to an attached garage.

Protruding areas beyond the exterior finished surface of the outside walls–such as chimneys and windows–cannot be included in finished square footage unless the protrusions have a floor on the same level and meet ceiling height requirements. For example, a hearth that is within the exterior finished surface is included, as is a window that extends from floor to ceiling. Further, if the hearth is on the first level and the chimney extends through the interior of the second level without a hearth on the second level, no deduction is made from the finished square footage of the second level. However, if the hearth or chimney is located beyond the exterior finished surface or the window does not have a floor, the area cannot be included in the finished square footage.

A common construction practice is to provide a floor opening for stairs that is the same size as the stairs themselves. Therefore, the area of stairs included in finished square footage is typically equal to the area of the opening in the floor. For example, a two-story, 28 by 42 foot house embodies 1,176 finished square feet on the first level and 1,176 finished square feet on the second level, provided that all areas are finished and the opening in the floor of the second level does not exceed the area of the stair treads. Further, stairs that descend to an unfinished basement are included in the finished square footage of the first level regardless of the degree of finish of the stairs or the degree of finish of the area around the stairs. In addition, areas beneath stairs are included in the finished square footage regardless of the distance between the stairs and the floor below or of the degree of finish of that area.

The standard makes no statement concerning differences between square footage calculations made by multiple parties for the same property. The method for calculating square footage requires measurements to be taken to the nearest inch or tenth of a foot using English measurement units or to the nearest hundredth of a meter using the Metric system. The final floor area must be reported to either the nearest square foot or tenth of a meter, as appropriate.

Examples

An example of a Statement of Finished Square Footage of a detached single-family house with basement follows:

DECLARATION 1

"A 28.2 by 42.5 foot two-story detached single-family house with 2,201 above-grade finished square feet and 807 below-grade finished square feet, plus 96 above-grade unfinished square feet in a utility room and 392 below-grade unfinished square feet in a basement. The first level has a 100-square-foot two-story space. In addition, the property includes a 240-square-foot enclosed porch and a two-car garage."

An example of the square footage description of a two-story attached single-family house follows:

DECLARATION 2

"A 22.1 by 30.9 foot two-story attached single-family carriage townhouse with 1,366 above-grade finished square feet and 176 above-grade unfinished square feet in a utility/storage room. In addition, the property includes a 120-square-foot deck and a one-car garage."

SQUARE FOOTAGE—METHOD FOR CALCULATING: ANSI Z765-2003

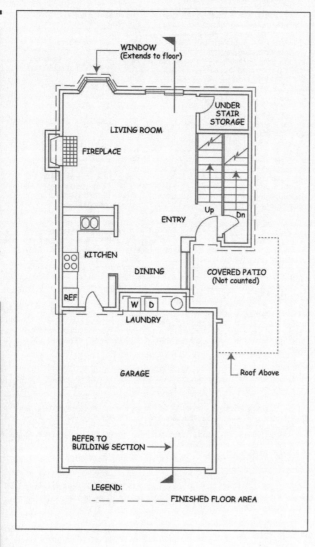

FIGURE 1.

Entry-Level Plan
(above grade)

Figures 1 through 4 depict a two-story single-family house with basement. The entry and upper levels are entirely above grade and the basement is entirely below grade. The dashed line encircles the finished floor area that is counted as above-grade finished square footage and below-grade finished square footage. As shown, the upper-level plan has an open foyer and a protruding window that does not extend to the floor; neither area contributes to the square footage of the upper level. The calculated finished square footage of the entry level does not include the protruding fireplace, covered patio, garage, or unfinished laundry. The finished area of the basement is counted toward the below-grade finished square footage in its entirety, including the area under the stairs that descend from the entry level. The area of the unfinished utility room is calculated by using the method prescribed in the standard but is not included in the below-grade finished square footage.

FIGURE 2.
Upper-Level Plan
(above grade)

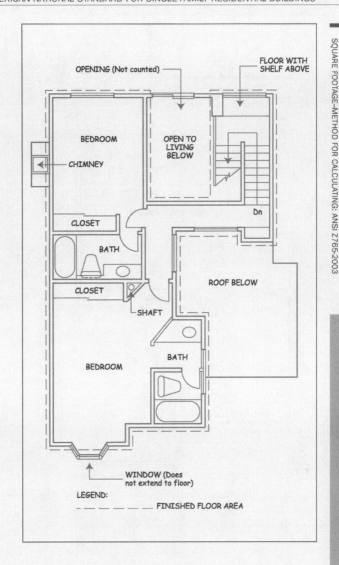

OPENING (Not counted)

FLOOR WITH
SHELF ABOVE

BEDROOM

OPEN TO
LIVING
BELOW

CHIMNEY

Dn

CLOSET

BATH

CLOSET

ROOF BELOW

SHAFT

BEDROOM

BATH

WINDOW (Does
not extend to floor)

LEGEND:

— — — — — FINISHED FLOOR AREA

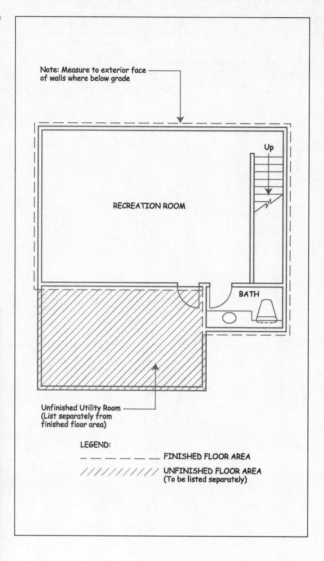

FIGURE 3.
Basement Plan
(below grade)

Note: Measure to exterior face of walls where below grade

Up

RECREATION ROOM

BATH

Unfinished Utility Room
(List separately from finished floor area)

LEGEND:

_ _ _ _ _ _ _ FINISHED FLOOR AREA

/ / / / / / / / / / / UNFINISHED FLOOR AREA
(To be listed separately)

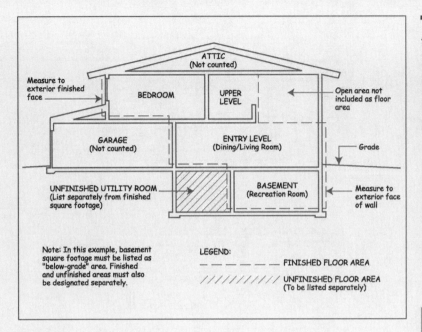

FIGURE 4.
Building Section

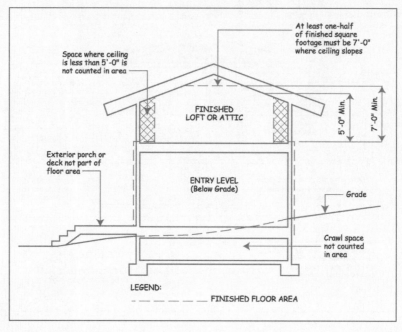

At least one-half
of finished square
footage must be 7'-0"
where ceiling slopes

Space where ceiling
is less than 5'-0" is
not counted in area

FINISHED
LOFT OR ATTIC

5'-0" Min.

7'-0" Min.

Exterior porch or
deck not part of
floor area

ENTRY LEVEL
(Below Grade)

Grade

Crawl space
not counted
in area

LEGEND:
——————— FINISHED FLOOR AREA

FIGURE 5.
Building Section

Figure 5 presents the building section of a one-and-one-half-story house with a partially below-grade entry level. The area in the finished loft/attic counting toward the finished square footage of that level has a ceiling height of at least 5 feet (1.52 meters), and at least one-half of the finished square footage has a ceiling height of at least 7 feet (2.13 meters). The entire area of the entry level is considered below-grade finished square footage.

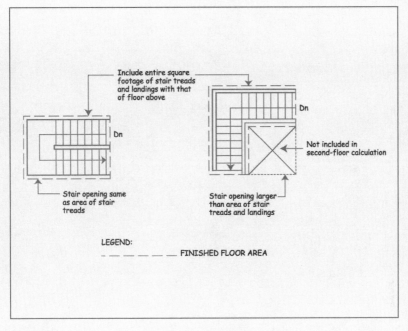

LEGEND:
_ _ _ _ _ FINISHED FLOOR AREA

FIGURE 6.
Stairs

Figure 6 demonstrates two typical stair configurations. Viewed from above, the stair treads and the landing in the drawing on the left fill the entire opening through which they descend. By definition, the area of the stairs and landing (or, by interpretation, the area of the opening) is included in the square footage of the level above. In the drawing on the right, the stair treads and landing merely skirt the opening. Here, the area of the treads and landing must be calculated to be included in the upper-level square footage; the remaining area of the opening is not included.

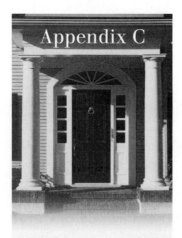

Appendix C

Financial Calculator Basics

The financial calculator has freed mortgage brokers, appraisers, and other real estate professionals from dependence on the printed tables of compound interest rates and sinking fund factors. Previously, calculating the present value of an investment or the growth of compound interest involved relatively simple algebraic calculations, assuming the appropriate interest rate or factor could be found in the financial tables. A typical collection of compound interest rate tables, however, would only include quarter-point increments, so calculating the future value of a loan made at an 8.55% annual rate forced the analyst to make an educated guess based on data in the 8½% and 8¾% tables or to use the financial formula $S^n = (1 + i)^n$. In contrast, the analyst who uses a financial calculator can choose any rate or holding period in calculations related to the six functions of $1, a significant advance in flexibility and accuracy.

Hewlett Packard's HP-12C financial calculator, in particular, is notable for its simplicity and staying power. It has remained relatively unchanged in form and function since its introduction in the early 1980s. The newer HP-12C Platinum calculator includes the ability to toggle between algebraic and Reverse Polish Notation systems and has more memory spaces, but otherwise the more recent version performs the same mathematical and statistical functions.

Reverse Polish Notation (RPN) refers to a mathematical order of operations developed to facilitate chain calculations. In short, numerals are entered before mathematical operators. For example, the sequence of keystrokes used to perform the arithmetic function $5 + 2$ on a typical calculator and the output display at each step would be

Keystrokes	Display
5	5
+	5 +
2	2
=	7

On an RPN calculator, the sequence of keystrokes and output would be

Keystrokes	Display
5	5
ENTER	5.00
2	2
+	7.00

Compare two sample sequences of keystrokes for a more complex series of calculations, say, for the arithmetic expression $(5 + 2) \times (12 - 4)$:

Algebraic Keystrokes	RPN Keystrokes
5	5
+	ENTER
2	2
=	+
STO	12
12	ENTER
−	4
4	−
=	X
X	
RCL	
=	

Using the algebraic keystrokes, the interim result of the first parenthetical expression must be stored in the calculator's memory or jotted down on a piece of scrap paper and reentered at the appropriate point in the chain of calculations. An HP-12C, however, automatically stores the displayed figures in continuous storage areas known as *stack registers*. (The function and operation of the storage registers in a financial calculator are explained in detail in the owner's manual.) Note that the route to the answer has no effect on the answer itself.

Performing simple mathematical calculations using Reverse Polish Notation can take some getting used to, but the benefits gained in performing financial analysis on a financial calculator are well worth it. Not only does the calculation using RPN require fewer keystrokes in the example above but, for experienced real estate professionals, the keystrokes become more intuitive than similar calculations would be on a calculator using a different operating system.

Common uses of a financial calculator by real estate professionals include computing mortgage payments (i.e., amortization calculations), discounting cash flows, and, of particular importance to residential appraisers, making cash equivalency adjustments for comparable sales with atypical financing or concessions.

Most of the variables related to the time value of money can be calculated with a few keystrokes. These variables have a prominent place across the top of the HP-12C keypad:

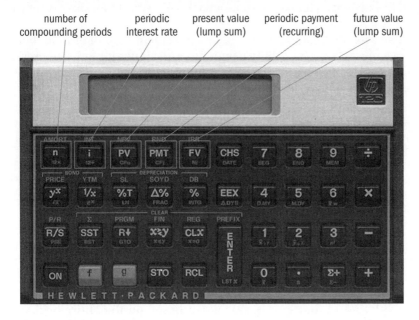

As an example, consider a fully amortized $150,000 mortgage loan with a 30-year term at a fixed rate of 6.35%. Calculating the monthly payment is straightforward using the HP-12C. The known mortgage terms are input, and the calculator then solves for the variable requested:

Calculation	Keystrokes	Display
Enter the term of the loan (and convert to number of months)	30 g n	360.00
Enter the annual interest rate (and convert to the effective monthly interest rate)	6.35 g i	0.53
Enter the loan amount	150,000 PV	150,000.00
Calculate the monthly payment	PMT	-933.35
Change the sign of the result	CHS	933.35

An analyst can then compare the result, $933.35, to market rent for a comparable property in the market area and answer the client's question of whether to buy or rent. A sophisticated user can extend the chain of calculations to determine the equity build-up at any point in the term of the loan, change the interest rate at a certain point in the loan term to model refinancing, and make other changes to address many other situations.

Note that other sequences of keystrokes could be used to solve the same problem with the HP-12C. For example, in the sequence of keystrokes above, the annual interest rate could be entered before the term of the loan without affecting the results generated in solving for the payment. Also, some appraisers enter the loan amount as a negative number, changing the sign between the loan amount (150,000) and [PV] keystrokes, which generates a positive result when solving for the periodic payment.

The financial calculator facilitates the calculation of annual, biannual, quarterly, or even daily payments, and allows for quick comparisons of various loan terms. As an example, consider the same loan with annual, end-of-year payments:

Calculation	Keystrokes	Display
Clear the registers	[f] [CLx]	0.00
Enter the term of the loan (in years)	30 [n]	30.00
Enter the annual interest rate	6.35 [i]	6.35
Enter the loan amount	150,000 [PV]	150,000.00
Calculate the monthly payment	[PMT]	-11,308.53
Change the sign of the result	[CHS]	11,308.53

The annual payment, $11,308.53, works out to be a larger amount than the total of a dozen monthly payments ($12 \times \$933.35 = \$11,200.20$) in the same year even though the same nominal interest rate, 6.35%, is used in both calculations. When annual payments are made, the principal is only reduced at the end of each year, so the amount of interest paid in that year is calculated based on the entire principal balance at the beginning of the year. In contrast, the principal balance (from which the portion of the monthly payment attributable to interest is calculated) drops incrementally in a monthly amortization schedule.[1] As a result, over the course of the year the portion of the $933.35 monthly payment attributable to the lender's return on the investment (i.e., the interest paid on the loan) becomes smaller. The difference between one annual payment and the total of 12 monthly payments on a loan reflects the time value of money. The cash flows received throughout the year have a higher future value than the income the lender receives at the end of the year because those funds can be reinvested and continue to grow.

More sophisticated analyses with a financial calculator include calculating the payment schedule, yield, and price or present value of balloon mortgages, graduated payment mortgages, wrap-around loans, construction loans, and other types of loans. In addition to mortgage analysis, a financial calculator can be used in the application of the income capitalization approach to calculate lease payments, the future value of an investment, discount rates, or other information needed for discounted cash flow analyses.

---

1. As an illustration of the decrease in interest paid as a portion of the constant monthly payment, consult typical amortization schedules readily available online from lenders, mortgage brokers, and others.

Resources

Appraisal Institute, *Financial Calculator Practice Exercises* (http://www.appraisalinstitute.org/education/downloads/fcale.pdf)

Appraisal Institute, *Using Your HP-12C Financial Calculator* online seminar (http://onlineed.appraisalinstitute.org/ai/onlineed/default.asp)

Elbert B. Greynolds, Jr., and Julius S. Aronofsky, *Practical Real Estate Financial Analysis: Using the HP-12C Calculator: A Step-by-Step Approach* (Chicago: Real Estate Education Co., 1983).

Hewlett-Packard, *HP-12C Owner's Handbook and Problem-Solving Guide*

Bibliography

Books

American Society of Farm Managers and Rural Appraisers and Appraisal Institute. *The Appraisal of Rural Property.* 2nd ed. Denver and Chicago: ASFMRA and Appraisal Institute, 2000.

Appraisal Institute. *The Appraisal of Real Estate.* 12th ed. Chicago: Appraisal Institute, 2001.

___. *The Dictionary of Real Estate Appraisal.* 4th ed. Chicago: Appraisal Institute, 2002.

Betts, Richard M., and Silas J. Ely. *Basic Real Estate Appraisal.* 4th ed. Englewood Cliffs, N.J.: Prentice-Hall, Inc., 1998.

Blankenship, Alan. *The Appraisal Writing Handbook.* Chicago: Appraisal Institute, 1997.

Bloom, George F., and Henry S. Harrison. *Appraising the Single Family Residence.* Chicago: American Institute of Real Estate Appraisers, 1980.

Boyce, Byrl N., and William N. Kinnard, Jr. *Appraising Real Property.* Lexington, Mass.: D.C. Heath and Company, 1984.

Brand, Stewart. *How Buildings Learn: What Happens After They're Built.* New York: Viking Penguin, 1994.

Castle, Gilbert H., III, et al. *GIS in Real Estate: Integrating, Analyzing, and Presenting Locational Information.* Chicago: Appraisal Institute, 1998.

Ching, Francis D.K. *Building Construction Illustrated.* 3rd ed. New York: John Wiley & Sons, Inc., 2001.

Coleman, Stephanie. *Scope of Work.* Chicago: Appraisal Institute, 2006.

Conroy, Kathleen. *Valuing the Timeshare Property.* Chicago: American Institute of Real Estate Appraisers, 1981.

Davis, Andrew N., and Paul E. Schaffman. *The Home Environmental Sourcebook: 50 Environmental Hazards to Avoid When Buying, Selling, or Maintaining a Home.* New York: Henry Holt and Company/ Owl Books, 1996.

Dombal, Robert W. *Appraising Condominiums: Suggested Data Analysis Techniques.* Chicago: American Institute of Real Estate Appraisers, 1981.

___. *Residential Condominiums: A Guide to Analysis and Appraisal.* Chicago: American Institute of Real Estate Appraisers, 1976.

Fanning, Stephen F. *Market Analysis for Real Estate: Concepts and Applications in Valuation and Highest and Best Use.* Chicago: Appraisal Institute, 2005.

Fisher, Clifford E., Jr. *Mathematics for Real Estate Appraisers.* Chicago: Appraisal Institute, 1996.

___. *Rates and Ratios Used in the Income Capitalization Approach.* Chicago: Appraisal Institute, 1995.

Fisher, Jeffrey D., and Dennis S. Tosh. *Questions and Answers To Help You Pass the Real Estate Appraisal Exams.* 4th ed. Chicago: Dearborn Real Estate Education, 2004.

Friedman, Edith J., ed. *Encyclopedia of Real Estate Appraising.* Englewood Cliffs, N.J.: Prentice-Hall, Inc., 1978.

Gimmy, Arthur E., with Susan B. Brecht and Clifford J. Dowd. *Senior Housing: Looking Toward the Third Millennium.* Chicago: Appraisal Institute, 1998.

Guy, Rebecca F., and Louis G. Pol. *Statistics for Real Estate Professionals.* New York: Quorum Books, 1989.

Harrison, Frank E. *Appraising the Tough Ones: Creative Ways to Value Complex Residential Properties.* Chicago: Appraisal Institute, 1996.

Harrison, Henry S. *Houses: The Illustrated Guide to Construction, Design, and Systems.* 3rd ed. Chicago: © 1998 by the Residential Sales Council of the Realtors National Marketing Institute, an affiliate of the National Association of Realtors. Published by Real Estate Education Company, a division of Dearborn Financial Publishing Inc.

Hines, Mary Alice. *Real Estate Appraisal.* New York: Macmillan Publishing Co., Inc., 1981.

The Illustrated Home. Chicago: © 2003 by Carson Dunlap & Associates Limited. Published by Dearborn Real Estate Education.

Jackson, Kenneth T. *Crabgrass Frontier: The Suburbanization of the United States.* New York: Oxford University Press, 1985.

Jacobs, Jane. *The Death and Life of Great American Cities.* New York: Random House, 1961.

Kane, M. Steven, Mark R. Linné, and Jeffrey A. Johnson. *Practical Applications in Appraisal Valuation Modeling: Statistical Methods for Real Estate Practitioners.* Chicago: Appraisal Institute, 2003.

Kostof, Spiro. *America by Design.* New York: Oxford University Press, 1987.

Lovell, Douglas D., and Robert S. Martin. *Subdivision Analysis.* Chicago: Appraisal Institute, 1993.

McMorrough, Julia. *Materials, Structures, and Standards.* Gloucester, Mass.: Rockport Publishers, Inc., 2006.

R.S. Means, Inc. *Means Illustrated Construction Dictionary,* 3rd ed. Kingston, Mass.: R.S. Means, Inc., 2000.

Miller, George H., and Kenneth W. Gilbeau. *Residential Real Estate Appraisal, An Introduction to Real Estate Appraising.* 3rd ed. Englewood Cliffs, N.J.: Prentice-Hall, Inc., 1998.

Mills, Arlen C., and Anthony Reynolds. *The Valuation of Apartment Properties.* Chicago: Appraisal Institute, 1999.

Minnerly, W. Lee. *Electronic Data Interchange (EDI) and the Appraisal Office.* Chicago: Appraisal Institute, 1996.

Nahorney, Dan J., and Vicki Lankarge. *How to Get Started in the Real Estate Appraisal Business.* New York: McGraw-Hill Companies, 2006.

Polton, Richard E., with Julia LaVigne. *Valuation and Market Studies for Affordable Housing.* Chicago: Appraisal Institute, 2005.

Rattermann, Mark. *Residential Sales Comparison Approach: Deriving, Documenting, and Defending your Value Opinion.* Chicago: Appraisal Institute, 2000.

___. *Using the Individual Condominium Unit Appraisal Report: Fannie Mae Form 1073 and Exterior-only Form 1075.* Chicago: Appraisal Institute, 2006.

___. *Using the Residential Appraisal Report Forms: URAR 2005 (Form 1004) and Exterior Inspection (Form 2005).* Chicago: Appraisal Institute, 2005.

___. *Using the Small Residential Income Property Appraisal Report: Fannie Mae Form 1025/Freddie Mac Form 72.* Chicago: Appraisal Institute, 2006.

Rayburn, William B., and Dennis S. Tosh. *Fair Lending and the Appraiser.* Chicago: Appraisal Institute, 1996.

Reynolds, Judith. *Historic Properties: Preservation and the Valuation Process.* 3rd ed. Chicago: Appraisal Institute, 2006.

Rybczynski, Witold. *Home: The History of an Idea.* New York: Viking Penguin, 1986.

___. *The Most Beautiful House in the World.* New York: Viking Penguin, 1989.

Shenkel, William M. *Modern Real Estate Appraisal.* New York: McGraw-Hill, 1978.

Simpson, John A. *Property Inspection: An Appraiser's Guide.* Chicago: Appraisal Institute, 1997.

Sorenson, Richard C. *Appraising the Appraisal: The Art of Appraisal Review.* Chicago: Appraisal Institute, 1998.

Stern, Robert. *Pride of Place: Building the American Dream.* Boston: Houghton Mifflin, 1986.

Werner, Raymond J., and Robert Kratovil. *Real Estate Law.* 10th ed. Englewood Cliffs, N.J.: Prentice-Hall, Inc., 1993.

Building Cost Data

Building Construction Cost Data. Duxbury, Mass.: R.S. Means Co.
   Lists average unit prices on many building construction items for use in engineering estimates. Components arranged according to uniform system adopted by the American Institute of Architects, Associated General Contractors, and Construction Specifications Institute.
   www.rsmeans.com

Marshall Valuation Service. Los Angeles: Marshall and Swift Publication Co.
   Cost data for determining replacement costs of buildings and other improvements in the United States and Canada. Includes current cost multipliers and local modifiers.
   www.marshallswift.com

Residential Cost Handbook. Los Angeles: Marshall and Swift Publication Co.
   Presents square-foot method and segregated-cost method. Local modifiers and cost-trend modifiers included.
   www.marshallswift.com

Periodicals

American Housing Survey. Bureau of the Census for the Department of Housing and Urban Development, Washington, D.C.
   Biannual updates. Data on U.S. housing markets in 47 selected metropolitan areas, including information on apartments, single-family homes, mobile homes, and owner demographics.
   www.census.gov/hhes/www/housing/ahs/ahs.html

The Appraisal Journal. Appraisal Institute, Chicago.
   Quarterly. Oldest periodical in the appraisal field. Includes technical articles on all phases of real property appraisal and regular feature on legal decisions.
   www.appraisalinstitute.org/publications/periodicals/taj

Appraiser News Online. Appraisal Institute, Chicago.
   Twice monthly. News bulletin covering current events and trends in appraisal practice.
   www.appraisalinstitute.org/publications/periodicals/ano

Buildings. Stamats Communications, Inc., Cedar Rapids, Iowa.
> Monthly. Journal of building construction and management.
> *www.buildings.com/buildingsmag*

The Canadian Appraiser. Appraisal Institute of Canada, Winnipeg, Manitoba.
> Quarterly. General and technical articles on appraisal and expropriation in Canada. Includes information on institute programs, news, etc.
> *www.aicanada.ca*

Journal of Property Management. Institute of Real Estate Management, Chicago.
> Bimonthly. Covers a broad range of property investment and management issues.
> *www.irem.org*

Journal of Property Tax Assessment & Administration. International Association of Assessing Officers, Chicago.
> Bimonthly. Includes articles on property taxation and assessment administration. Formerly *Assessment Journal.*
> *www.iaao.org*

Journal of Real Estate Research. American Real Estate Society, Cleveland, Ohio.
> Quarterly. Publishes the results of applied research on real estate development, finance, investment, management, market analysis, marketing, and valuation.
> *www.aresnet.org*

Journal of the American Society of Farm Managers and Rural Appraisers. Denver.
> Annual. Includes appraisal articles focussing on rural areas.
> *www.asfmra.org/fjournals.htm*

Land Economics. University of Wisconsin, Madison.
> Quarterly. Devoted to the study of economics and social institutions. Includes reports on university research and trends in land use. Frequently publishes articles on developments in other countries.
> *www.wisc.edu/wisconsinpress/journals/journals/le.html*

Land Lines. Lincoln Institute of Land Policy, Cambridge, Massachusetts.
> Quarterly. Publishes articles focusing on research and scholarly studies of land policy and land-related taxation.
> *www.lincolninst.edu/pubs/landlines.asp*

Real Estate Economics. American Real Estate and Urban Economics Association, Richmond, Virginia.
> Quarterly. Focuses on research and scholarly studies of current and emerging real estate issues. Formerly *Journal of the American Real Estate and Urban Economics Association.*
> *www.areuea.org/publications/ree*

Real Estate Issues. American Society of Real Estate Counselors, Chicago. Quarterly. Focuses on practical applications and applied theory for a cross section of real estate practitioners and related professionals. *www.cre.org/publications/rei.cfm*

Real Estate Law Journal. Warren, Gorham and Lamont, Inc., Boston. Quarterly. Publishes articles on legal issues and reviews current litigation of concern to real estate professionals.

Right of Way. American Right of Way Association, Los Angeles. Bimonthly. Publishes articles on all phases of right-of-way activity--e.g., condemnation, negotiation, pipelines, electric power transmission lines, highways. Includes association news. *www.irwaonline.org*

Survey of Current Business. U.S. Bureau of Economic Analysis, U.S. Department of Commerce, Washington, D.C. Monthly. Includes statistical and price data. Biennial supplement, *Business Statistics.* *www.bea.gov/bea/pubs.htm*

Valuation. American Society of Appraisers, Washington, D.C. Annual. Articles on real property valuation and the appraisal of personal and intangible property. Includes society news. Previously published as *Technical Valuation.* *www.appraisers.org/pubs/valuation*

Valuation Insights & Perspectives. Appraisal Institute, Chicago. Quarterly. Provides timely, practical information and ideas to assist real estate appraisers in conducting their businesses effectively. *www.appraisalinstitute.org/publications/periodicals/vip*

Wharton Real Estate Review. Samuel Zell and Robert Lurie Real Estate Center, University of Pennsylvania, Philadelphia. Semi-annual. Provides a forum for scholars, real estate practitioners, and public officials to introduce new ideas, present research and analytical findings, and promote widespread discussion of topical issues. *realestate.wharton.upenn.edu/review.php*

Index

block clubs, 203
blueprints, 94
boundaries of neighborhood, 35–37
bracketing, 348
breakdown method of estimating depreciation, 301–307
  applicability, 307
  examples of, 302–303, 305–307
  limitations, 307
  steps in, 301–305
breezeways, 189
building codes, 97, 118
  and highest and best use, 227
  and neighborhood stability, 208–209
  as public limitations on property rights, 118
  See also zoning
building construction, 163–195
  attachments, 188–190
  building materials, 173–178
    exterior, 173–177
    interior, 178
    substructure, 167–170
    superstructure, 170–173
  garages, 188–190
  insulation, 178–179
  interior covering and trim, 123
  mechanical systems, 182–188
    air-conditioning system, 187–188
    electrical system, 188
    heating system fuels, 184, 187
    heating systems, 184–187
    hot water system, 182
    miscellaneous systems and equipment, 164
    plumbing system, 182–183
    ventilation system, 187–188
  outbuildings, 189
  outline of building components, 163–164
  overall condition of the residence, 192–194
  special features, 190–192
  ventilation, 178–179
building line, width at the, 123
building size, 139–141
bulk regulations, 226
bungalow, 144
buydown plan, 63

cabinets, 190–191
calculator, 95
  keystrokes for discounting, 332
  See also Appendix C
California ranch architectural style, 144

Cape Ann architecture, 174
Cape Cod architecture, 144
capital, 47, 50
capitalization, 83–84, 357–359
  defined, 83
  of rent loss, 253–254
cash consideration, 106, 325, 328
cash equivalency, 327
  adjusting for considerations other than cash, 328
  adjusting for seller-paid points, 327–328
  adjustment techniques, 327
  comparison of sales transactions, 327
  determining effect of financing considerations on price, 325–327
  discounting cash flows, 328–332
CC&Rs (conditions, covenants, and restrictions), 20
ceilings, 178
central tendency, measures of, 335–336
certification
  and licensing, 8
  of value, statements in appraisal reports, 384
chimneys, 192
chronological age of building, 288
circulation areas of a house, 152–153
climate, 133
closing of property survey, 133
CMOs. *See* collateralized mortgage obligations
collateralized mortgage obligations (CMOs), 50–51
Colonial architectural style, 144
column footings, 169
commercial district, 36
community associations, 203
comparability, concept of, 102–103
comparable properties, 314–322
  analysis of sales, 316–324
    paired data analysis, 339–343
    reconciliation of indications in, 349–351
    units of comparison, 334–335
  collection of descriptive data on, 314–316
  as competitive properties, 313–314
  data sources for, 103–109, 314–315
  data verification, 110, 316
  identifying, 102–109, 314–315
  subject property and, 102
  See also sales comparison approach
comparative-unit method of estimating costs, 274–277
  applicability, 276–277
  example of, 275–276
compatibility, 138

data analysis, accuracy and adequacy in final reconciliation, 371–372
data sources, for comparable data, 103–110
    regarding property rights and restrictions, 118–120
    for tax and zoning information, 118, 121–122
data standards, 108–109
date of value opinion, 70
decay, 180–181
decks, 189
decline, in neighborhood life cycle, 42
deed restrictions, 119–120
    and neighborhood stability, 209
    See also property rights
deeds
    defined, 18
    elements of, 18
    types of, 18
deeds of trust, 62
deferred maintenance, 192, 284
deficiency, 97–98, 284–285
    requiring additions, 284–285
        estimating curable functional obsolescence for, 304–305
    requiring substitution or modernization, 284–285
Department of Treasury. *See* Treasury, U.S. Department of
depreciation, 283–309
    age and life of residences, 287
    age-life method of estimating, 290–291, 295–301
        applicability, 297–301
        example of, 296
    breakdown method of estimating, 291, 301–307
        applicability, 307
        examples of, 302–305
        steps in, 301–302
    combined methods of estimating, 307–309
    in cost approach, 283–286
    market extraction method of estimating, 289–290, 292–295
        applicability, 295
        example of, 293–294
        used to test results of breakdown method, 295
    reproduction and replacement cost bases, 291–292
    straight-line assumption, 295
    types of, 283–286
    variations of the age-life method of estimating, 288–300
        applicability, 299–301

examples, 298–300
description of improvements, 137–195
    architectural compatibility, 138, 141–142
    architectural styles, trends in, 141, 143–145
    describing and rating the improvements, 96–98
    design problems, 153
    house zones, 152–154
    inspection tools, 94–95, 138
    materials, 142
    orientation on site, 138
    photographs in appraisal report, 138, 141
    popular design features, 154
    rooms in residential properties, 154–162
    size, 139–141
    sketch of the house, 141
    steps in, 137–141
    See also house
desire, as an economic factor, 32
development, and neighborhood values, 206
dictation equipment, 95
digital cameras, 94–95
dining areas, 159
direct costs, in cost approach, 263–266
discount factor, 328–332
discount rate, 329–332
    defined, 57
discounting cash flows, 328–332
disintermediation, 48
disposable income, 204
district(s), 35–36
    See also neighborhoods; market areas
dollar adjustments, in sales comparison approach, 336
doors
    exterior, 175–176
    interior, 175–176
dormers, 189
drainage, 126–128
drain systems, 164
drain tile, 168–169
driveways, as site improvements, 191
due-on-sale clauses, 63

earthquakes, 132
easements, 14–15
    appurtenant, 15
    estates subject to, 14–15
    See also property rights
economic base analysis, 44–45
economic conditions, impact of, on value, 38
economic factors, 32

housing supply, 206
HUD. *See* Housing and Urban Development, Department of.
hypothetical conditions, 73–74

improvement(s)
description of, 137–141
defined, 92
ideal, 222–223
orientation and placement of, 138
See also house(s); residence(s); site improvements
income capitalization approach, 83–84, 357–368
applicability, 84, 357–359
data collection, 358–361, 367–368
defined, 84
gross rent multiplier (*GRM*), 359–363
defined, 84
derivation of, from market data, 84, 359–361
expense characteristics, 360–361
lease provisions, 361
reconciling, 362
identifying comparables for, 84, 358–361
monthly market rent estimate, 84, 363–364
elements of comparison, 364–367
example of, 364
lease provisions, 366
market conditions, 366
operating expenses, 367
property characteristics, 366–367
and principle of anticipation, 357
and principle of substitution, 33–34
rent survey, 367–368
steps in, 358
use of sales comparison in, 362
income tax
benefits of home ownership, 1
and special assessments, 122
incurable functional obsolescence, 284–285, 290–291
in breakdown method, 301–305
incurable physical deterioration, 284, 291
in breakdown method, 301–303
indirect costs
in comparative-unit method, 274
in cost approach, 263–266
Individual Condominium Unit Appraisal Report, 387
Individual Cooperative Interest Appraisal Report, 387
inflation, 40, 54

insect damage, 180–181
inspection
appraiser's inspection versus home inspection, 93–94
liability in, 98–102
of neighborhood, 217–219
preparation for, 94–96
of site, 92
See also site inspection; building description
installment sale contract, 63–64
insulation, 178–180
insurable value, 27
interest rates, 326
See also federal discount rate
interim uses, and highest and best use, 209, 232
interior covering and trim, 178
baseboards, 178
cabinets, 190–191
ceilings, 178
doors, 178
fireplaces, 191–192
floor covering, 176
molding, 178
painting and decorating, 164
stairs, 164
walls, 178
interior doors, 175–176
interior wall covering, 178
Internet, as data source, 106
investment value, 22
island kitchen, 157

joists, 166, 171, 173
junior mortgage, 62
jurisdictional exceptions, 73–74
just compensation, 19

kitchens, 155–158
common problems, 158
corridor, 156–157
galley, 156–157
new trends in, 158
typical designs of, 157
work triangle, 155

land, 237–238
in appraisal, 237
defined, 11–12, 237
distinction between site and, 237
leased, 253–254
as source of value, 237–238
utility of, 238

and highest and best use, 198

influence of, on mortgage market, 205

planning analysis and collecting data, 215

    collection tools, 217

    essential data needs, 215–216

  reporting conclusions of, 218–219

  steps in, 215

market conditions

  analysis of, in sales comparison, 320

market data, derivation of gross rent multiplier from, 359–361

market data grid, in sales comparison approach, 338–348

market exposure, analysis of, in sales comparison, 319

market extraction method, of estimating depreciation, in cost approach, 292–295

market forces, influence of, on land value, 238–239

marketing time, 319

market rent, 363–364

market segmentation, 35

market study, 7, 197

market value 22–25

  defined, 2–3, 24

  opinion, requirements under USPAP, 2

  relation of, to assessed value, 22

  See also Neighborhood value influences

Marshall & Swift, 96

masonry walls, 173

master bedroom, 159

maximum productivity, and highest and best use, 230

measuring equipment, 95

measuring a house, 139–141

  See also Appendix B

mechanical systems. *See* equipment and mechanical systems

meridians, 115

metes and bounds system,71, 113–114

mill rate, 122

MISMO, 109

Mission architectural style, 144

mobile homes. *See* manufactured housing

mold, 181

molding, 178

monthly market rent, 363–367

  application of gross rent multiplier to, 368

mortgage(s)

  assumption of, 63, 330–331

  average life of, 61

  at below-market rate, 329

  conventional, 61

estates encumbered by, 14

and foreclosures, 62

guaranteed or insured, 61

loan-to-value ratios, 61–62

sources of money for, 48–51

subordinate, 62

See also financing plans

mortgage-backed securities program. *See* Ginnie Mae.

mortgage constant (R_M), 329

mortgage fraud, 47, 59

  property flipping, 59

mortgage funds, sources of, 48–51

  primary sources, 48

  secondary sources, 48–51

mortgage market

  impact on real estate activities, 54–55

  influences on, 51–54

  loan risk and points, 57

  secondary mortgage market, 48–51

multiple listing service (MLS), 38, 103–105

natural gas, 187

neighborhood(s)

  and area analysis, 197

  boundaries, 35

  characteristics of, 35

  defined, 35–36, 199

  inspection, 217–218

  life cycles, 35, 41

    decline, 42

    growth, 41

    revitalization, 43–44

    stability, 42

  and redlining, 42

  signs of change in, 41–44

  in transition, and highest and best use, 234–236

  See also market area

neighborhood analysis. *See* market area analysis.

neighborhood associations, 203

neighborhood inspection, 217–218

neighborhood value influences, 200–215

  economic influences, 204–210

    development, construction, conversions and vacant land, 206

    economic profile of residents, 204–205

    extent of occupant ownership, 207

    property price and rent levels, 205–206

    types and terms of financing, 205

  environmental influences, 210–214

    adequacy and quality of utilities, 214

real estate economics, 29–45
changes in local and regional markets, 40–44
characteristics of real estate markets, 37–38
forces in the local residential market, 39–40
forces that influence value, 38–39
general economic theory, 29–30
principles of, 29
real estate investment trusts (REITs), 51, 205
real estate markets
characteristics of, 35, 37
comparison to efficient markets, 37
real estate taxes
and assessed value, 121–122
and income tax deduction,
and neighborhood value, 207–208
and property rights, 121–122
and special assessments, 122
real estate values, affect of seasonal cycles on, 40–41
real property, 11
defined, 13
See also estate; property; property rights
real property rights conveyed, analysis of, in sales comparison, 318
Realtors, as source of data, 106
reconciliation, 369–378
in sales comparison approach, 349–351
See also final reconciliation
reconciliation criteria, in final reconciliation of value, 374–377
recreational areas, as site improvements, 191
recreational facilities, and neighborhood analysis, 213
recreation room, 160–161
rectangular survey system, 71, 113, 115–117
redlining, 42
reflective insulation, 178
regression analysis, 401–415
modeling, 408–415
multiple linear regression, 407–408
simple linear regression, 402–406
relative comparison analysis, 346–348
See also adjustment techniques
remaining economic life, 288
remaining useful life, 288
rent. *See* contract rent; market rent
rent controls, 359
rent levels, and neighborhood analysis, 205–206
rent survey, 367–368
replacement cost
basis, in estimating depreciation, 291–292

in cost approach, 262–267
versus reproduction cost, 262–263, 291–292
reproduction cost
basis, in estimating depreciation, 291–292
in cost approach, 262–267
versus replacement cost, 262–263, 291–292
reserve requirements, 53–54
See also Federal Reserve System
residence(s)
age and life of, and depreciation, 287–289
on leased land, 14, 253–254, 422
operating expenses of,
overall condition of, 192–194, 287, 302, 315
items requiring immediate repair, 192–193, 302
long-lived items, 194, 287
short-lived items, 193–194, 287
in rural areas, 425–427
See also house(s); improvement(s)
residential appraisals. *See* appraisal(s)
residential appraiser. *See* appraiser
residential construction, components of, 164
See also Appendix A
residential financing. *See* financing plans
residents, economic profile of, and neighborhood analysis, 204–205
resort homes, 422–423
restricted use report, 7, 85–86, 382–383
retrospective value, 70
reverse annuity mortgage (RAM). *See* reverse mortgages
reverse mortgages, 64–65
review, of appraisal reports, 370–374
revitalization, in neighborhood life cycle, 43–44
right of way, 15, 20
riparian rights, 120, 191
rollover mortgages, 54–55
roof(s)
attachments, 189
construction, 173
covering, 173, 175
types of, 173–174
rounding, of value indications, 378
See also point estimate; value opinion
row house architectural style, 144
R value, of insulation, 178–179

sale prices
adjusting, to reflect differences in comparable properties, 333–346
of land, 240–242
reduced to unit prices, 241–242
verification, 110, 316

surface soil, 128
surplus land, 124, 126, 234
swimming pools, as site improvements, 191

taxation, as public limitation on property use, 19
tax(es)
    and appraisals, 4
    assessors, 4
    benefits of home ownership, 1
    burden, 121–122
    rate, 121–122
    records, 106
    rolls, 121
    special assessments, 122
    status, and property rights, 19–20
    See also income tax; real estate taxes
terrazzo flooring, 176
time adjustment, 320
timeshare properties, 16
    appraisal techniques, 421–422
    ownership interests, 16
time value of money, 329
title insurance companies, as source of data, 104
title reports, 104
    property rights in, 121
topography, 213
    of neighborhood, 213
    of site, 126–128
township, 115
township lines, 115–116
transfer records, 104
transfer tax stamp, 110
transitional neighborhood
    in highest and best use, 234
    in neighborhood analysis, 209
transportation
    effect on site value, 212
    systems and linkages, and neighborhood values, 211
Treasury, U.S. Department of, 51
trend analysis, 243–244
    defined, 40, 243
trusses, 173
Tudor architectural style, 144
two-story house, 146, 148–149

underground homes, 436–437
underimprovement, 97
Uniform Residential Appraisal Report (URAR), 72, 78, 217, 385–387

Uniform Standards of Professional Appraisal Practice (USPAP), 1, 8, 70, 74, 379–380
unit costs, 271–273
unit-in-place method of estimating costs, 278–279
    applicability, 278–279
    example of, 278–279
unit price, 317
units of comparison, in sales comparison, 241–242
urea-formaldehyde foam insulation (UFFI), 180
useful life, 287–288
    remaining useful life, 288
use value, 25–26
USPAP. *See* Uniform Standards of Professional Appraisal Practice
utilities
    adequacy and quality of, and neighborhood values, 214
    onsite and offsite, 135–136
utility, as an economic factor, 32

VA. *See* Veterans Affairs, U.S. Department of
vacancy rates,
    and neighborhood values, 204
vacant land, and neighborhood analysis, 206
vacation homes, 422–423
valuation process, 67–85
    cost approach, 77, 82, 257–269
    date of value opinion, 70
    defined, 67–68
    definition of appraisal problem, 67–68
    definition of value, 70
    description of scope of appraisal, 71–72
    extraordinary assumptions, 73
    highest and best use analysis, 78–80
    hypothetical conditions, 73
    identification of property rights to be valued, 71, 88
    identification of real estate, 88
    illustrated, 68
    income capitalization approach, 77, 83–84, 357–368
    jurisdictional exceptions, 73–74
    limiting conditions and assumptions, 72
    preliminary analysis, data selection, and collection, 75–78
    reconciliation of value indications and final value opinion, 84–85, 369–378
    report of defined value, 85–86
    sales comparison approach, 77, 82–83, 311–355